Praise for

JFK and the Unspeakable

"Jim Douglass has unraveled the story of President Kennedy's astonishing and little-known turn toward peace, and the reasons why members of his own government felt he must be eliminated. This disturbing, enlightening, and ultimately inspiring book should be read by all Americans. It has the power to change our lives and to set us free."   **—Martin Sheen**

"*JFK and the Unspeakable* is an exceptional achievement. Douglass has made the strongest case so far in the JFK assassination literature as to the Who and the Why of Dallas. The conjunction of unrestrained elements in Cold War America—defense industry elites, Pentagon planners, and the heads of the intelligence community—were the forces that led inexorably to Dallas and the assassination of President John F. Kennedy."   **—Gerald McKnight**, author, *Breach of Trust: How the Warren Commission Failed the Nation and Why*

"With penetrating insight and unswerving integrity, Douglass probes the fundamental truths about JFK's assassination. If, he contends, humanity permits those truths to slip into history ignored and undefined it does so at its own peril. By far the most important book yet written on the subject."

—Gaeton Fonzi, former Staff Investigator, U.S. House Select Committee on Assassinations

"Douglass presents, brilliantly, an unfamiliar yet thoroughly convincing account of a series of creditable decisions of John F. Kennedy—at odds with his initial Cold War stance—that earned him the secret distrust and hatred of hard-liners among the Joint Chiefs of Staff and the CIA. Did this suspicion and rage lead directly to his murder by agents of these institutions, as Douglass concludes? Many readers who are not yet convinced of this 'beyond reasonable doubt' by Douglass's prosecutorial indictment will find themselves, perhaps—like myself—for the first time, compelled to call for an authoritative criminal investigation. Recent events give all the more urgency to learning what such an inquiry can teach us about how, by whom, and in whose interests this country is run."

—Daniel Ellsberg, author, *Secrets: A Memoir of Vietnam and the Pentagon Papers*

"A remarkable book: devastating in its documented indictment of the dark forces that have long deformed the public life of this country, while also illuminating JFK's final vision of world peace and documenting beyond reasonable doubt the unspeakable assassination of our last partially admirable president. This book should be required reading for every American citizen."

—Richard Falk, Milbank Professor of International Law Emeritus, Princeton University

"For forty years Jim Douglass has been our leading North American Catholic theologian of peace. But this monumental work on the witness of JFK is something deeper still. Douglass is trying to get us to connect the dots between our

'citizen denial,' the government's 'plausible deniability,' and the Unspeakable. This book has the potential to change our narrative about our country, and our lives as citizens and disciples."   —**Ched Myers**, author,
Binding the Strong Man: A Political Reading of Mark's Story of Jesus

"Jim Douglass's spiritual and eloquent telling of President John F. Kennedy's martyrdom for peace is a peerless and extraordinary historical contribution."
—**Vincent J. Salandria**, author,
False Mystery: Essays on the Assassination of JFK

"This book's story of JFK and the 'unspeakable' is a stunning mix of political thriller and meticulous scholarship. . . . Douglass's book offers a goldmine of information and is indispensable for building prophetic spirit and hope."
—**Mark Lewis Taylor**, Princeton Theological Seminary

"This is the most thoroughly researched and documented book ever written about President Kennedy's determination to prevent a nuclear war—and how his success in that struggle cost him his life. And yet, Douglass leads us well beyond the 'whodunit' dimensions of the story. He leads us straight into the urgent implications for the present, into what Thomas Merton called the 'unspeakable.' In the shadows of our own time we begin to become better prepared to break free of the violence that threatens all of us today."
—**Don Mosley**, co-founder, Jubilee Partners

"A remarkable achievement, outstanding even in an overcrowded field. It is profoundly conceived, researched, considered, argued, and written. . . . Not all will agree with his detailed speculation as to what happened in Dallas. But Douglass's large picture of America's political agony is, I believe, incontrovertible and certain to last."   —**Peter Dale Scott**, author, *Deep Politics and the Death of JFK*

"Douglass writes with moral force, clarity, and the careful attention to detail that will make *JFK and the Unspeakable* a sourcebook for many years to come, for it provides us with the stubborn facts needed to rebuild a constitutional democracy within the United States."   —**Marcus Raskin**, co-founder,
Institute for Policy Studies

"Jim Douglass never ceases to surprise us, taking us where we do not expect or often wish to go. In this fascinating work he links politics and spirituality. In reforming the past he reshapes the future, with hope, thank God."
—**Bill J. Leonard**, Dean and Professor of Church History,
Wake Forest University Divinity School

"Jim Douglass is a courageous and single-minded Christian whose convictions are reflected in his life and witness. In this provocative new book, he brings together history and spirituality at the intersection of one of the most pivotal—and yet still mystifying—events of the past century. A myth-exploding story and compelling read."   —**Timothy George**, Dean,
Beeson Divinity School of Samford University

Also by James W. Douglass

The Nonviolent Cross
Resistance and Contemplation
Lightning East to West
The Nonviolent Coming of God

JFK and the UNSPEAKABLE

Why He Died and Why It Matters

James W. Douglass

A Touchstone Book
Published by Simon & Schuster
New York London Toronto Sydney

Touchstone
A Division of Simon & Schuster, Inc.
1230 Avenue of the Americas
New York, NY 10020

First Touchstone trade paperback edition October 2010

TOUCHSTONE and colophon are registered trademarks of Simon & Schuster, Inc.
Published by arrangement with Orbis Books.

For information about special discounts for bulk purchases,
please contact Simon & Schuster Special Sales at 1-866-506-1949
or business@simonandschuster.com.

The Simon & Schuster Speakers Bureau can bring authors to your live event.
For more information or to book an event contact the Simon & Schuster Speakers
Bureau at 866-248-3049 or visit our website at www.simonspeakers.com.

Manufactured in the United States of America

30 29 28

Library of Congress Cataloging-in-Publication Data

Douglass, James W.
  JFK and the unspeakable : why he died and why it matters / by James W. Douglass.
    p. cm.
  Originally published: Maryknoll, N.Y. : Orbis Books, 2008.
  Includes bibliographical references and index.
  1. Kennedy, John F. (John Fitzgerald), 1917–1963—Assassination. 2. Presidents—
United States—Biography. I. Title.
  E842.9.D68 2010
  973.922092—dc22

                                                              2010024799

ISBN 978-1-4391-9388-4
ISBN 978-1-4391-9642-7 (ebook)

To Vince Salandria and Marty Schotz

teachers and friends

"You believe in redemption, don't you?"

John F. Kennedy
May 1, 1962

Contents

Preface

We can know the essential truth of President John F. Kennedy's assassination. That truth can set us free.

Thanks to the pioneer investigators into President Kennedy's murder, the truth-telling of many witnesses, and a recent flood of documents through the JFK Records Act, the truth is available. Not only can the conspiracy that most Americans have thought was likely now be seen in detail. Not only can we know what happened in Dallas. More important than filling in the crime scene, we can know the larger historical context of the assassination—why President Kennedy was murdered. We can know the liberating truth. The story of why JFK was gunned down is the subject of this book.

I have told the story thematically and chronologically, point by point through a sea of witnesses. In brief that story is:

On our behalf, at the height of the Cold War, John F. Kennedy risked committing the greatest crime in history, starting a nuclear war.

Before we knew it, he turned toward peace with the enemy who almost committed that crime with him.

For turning to peace with his enemy (and ours), Kennedy was murdered by a power we cannot easily describe. Its unspeakable reality can be traced, suggested, recognized, and pondered. That is one purpose of this book. The other is to describe Kennedy's turning.

I hope that, by following the story of JFK's encounter with the unspeakable, we will be willing to encounter it, too.

John Kennedy's story is our story, although a titanic effort has been made to keep it from us. That story, like the struggle it embodies, is as current today as it was in 1963. The theology of redemptive violence still reigns. The Cold War has been followed by its twin, the War on Terror. We are engaged in another apocalyptic struggle against an enemy seen as absolute evil. Terrorism has replaced Communism as the enemy. We are told we can be safe only through the threat of escalating violence. Once again, anything goes in a fight against evil: preemptive attacks, torture, undermining governments, assassinations, whatever it takes to gain the end of victory over an enemy portrayed as irredeemably evil. Yet the redemptive means John Kennedy turned to, in a similar struggle, was dialogue with the enemy. When the enemy is seen as human, everything changes.

That reconciling method of dialogue—where mutual respect overcomes fear, and thus war—is again regarded as heretical in our dominant political theology. As a result, seeking truth in our opponents instead of victory over them can lead, as it did in the case of Kennedy, to one's isolation and death as a traitor. That ultimate crown is, as Dietrich Bonhoeffer said, "the cost of discipleship." There is no better reason for it than loving one's enemies—not a sentimental love but, first of all, respect. Respect means recognizing and acknowledging our enemies' part of the truth, whether or not that makes life more difficult for us. Recognizing his enemies' truths made life much more difficult, and finally impossible, for Kennedy—leaving us with the responsibility of recognizing the painfully obvious truth of Kennedy's death.

As recent polls indicate, three out of four Americans believe Kennedy was killed by a conspiracy. The evidence has long pointed toward our own government. Yet with recurrent defenses of the Warren Commission, conjectures of Mob plots, and attacks on Kennedy's character, we in this media-drenched society drink the waters of uncertainty. We believe we cannot know . . . a truth whose basic evidence has been present since the work of the Warren Commission's earliest critics. Could there be a deeper reason for our reluctance to know the truth?

Is our wariness of the truth of JFK's assassination rooted in our fear of truth's consequences, to him and to us? For President Kennedy, a deepening commitment to dialogue with our enemies proved fatal. If we are unwilling as citizens to deal with that critical precedent, what twenty-first-century president will have the courage on our behalf to resist the powers that be and choose dialogue instead of war in response to our current enemies?

The reader may wonder why the perspective of a contemplative monk, Thomas Merton, figures so prominently in a book about the JFK assassination. Why is the Trappist monk Thomas Merton my Virgil on this pilgrimage?

Although this book is filled with history and biographical reconstruction, its ultimate purpose is to see more deeply into history than we are accustomed. If, for example, war is an unalterable reality of history, then we humans have a very short future left. Einstein said, "The unleashed power of the atom has changed everything save our modes of thinking, and we thus drift toward unparalleled catastrophes." Unless we turn our thinking (and acting) away from war, we humans have had our day. Thomas Merton said it again and again at the height of the Cold War, as did Martin Luther King—and John F. Kennedy. What the contemplative Thomas Merton brought to that fundamental truth of our nuclear age was an ontology of nonviolence, a Gandhian vision of reality that can transform the world as we know it. Reality is bigger than we think. The contemplative knows this transforming truth from experience.

Thomas Merton has been my guide through a story of deepening dialogue, assassination, and a hoped-for resurrection. While Kennedy is the subject of this story, Merton is its first witness and chorus from his unique perspective in a monastery in the hills of Kentucky. In terms of where this narrative began and how it has been guided, it is contemplative history. Thanks to Merton's questions and insights, grounded on a detachment few other observers seemed to have, we can return to the history of JFK, the Cold War, and Dallas on a mind-bending pilgrimage of truth. Reality may indeed be bigger than we think.

What is the reality underlying the possibility of nonviolent change? I believe the story of JFK and the unspeakable, a story of turning, is a hopeful way into that question.

Jim Douglass
July 29, 2007

Introduction

When John F. Kennedy was president, I was a graduate student struggling with the theological dimensions of the same question he grappled with more concretely in the White House: How could we survive our weapons of war, given the Cold War attitudes behind them? At the time I wrote articles seeking a way out of an apocalyptic war, without realizing that Kennedy—at great risk—was as president seeking a genuine way out for us all.

At that critical moment in history, Thomas Merton was the greatest spiritual writer of his generation. His autobiography, *The Seven Storey Mountain*, was seen as the post–World War II equivalent of *The Confessions of Saint Augustine*. Merton had gone on to write a series of classic works on prayer. However, when he turned his discerning writer's eye in the early sixties to such issues as nuclear war and racism, his readers were shocked—and in some cases, energized.

I first wrote Thomas Merton in 1961, at his monastery, the Abbey of Gethsemani in Kentucky, after reading a poem he had published in the *Catholic Worker*. Merton's poem was really an anti-poem, spoken by the commandant of a Nazi death camp. It was titled: "Chant to Be Used in Processions around a Site with Furnaces." Merton's "Chant" proceeded matter-of-factly through the speaker's daily routine of genocide to these concluding lines: "Do not think yourself better because you burn up friends and enemies with long-range missiles without ever seeing what you have done." [1]

When I read those words, I was living in the spiritual silence that in 1961 surrounded the threat of a nuclear holocaust. The reality underlying Cold War rhetoric was unspeakable. Merton's "Chant" broke the silence. The Unspeakable had been spoken—by the greatest spiritual writer of our time. I wrote him immediately.

He answered my letter quickly. We corresponded on nonviolence and the nuclear threat. The next year Merton sent me a copy of a manuscript he had written, *Peace in the Post-Christian Era*. Because his superiors had forbidden him to publish a book on war and peace that they felt "falsifies the monastic message," Merton mimeographed the text and mailed it to friends. *Peace in the Post-Christian Era* was a prophetic work responding to the spiritual climate that was pushing the United States government toward nuclear war. One of its recurring themes was Merton's fear that the United States would launch a preemptive strike on the Soviet Union. He wrote, "There can be no question that at the time of writing what seems to be the most serious and crucial development in the policy of the United States is this indefinite but growing assumption of the necessity of a first strike." [2]

Thomas Merton was acutely aware that the president who might take such a fateful step was his fellow Catholic, John F. Kennedy. Among Merton's many correspondents at the time and another recipient of *Peace in the Post-Christian Era* was the president's sister-in-law, Ethel Kennedy. Merton shared his fear of war with Ethel Kennedy and his hope that John Kennedy would have the vision and courage to turn the country in a peaceful direction. In the months leading up to the Cuban Missile Crisis, Merton agonized, prayed, and felt impotent, as he continued to write passionate antiwar letters to scores of other friends.

During the thirteen fearful days of October 16–28, 1962, President John F. Kennedy did, as Thomas Merton feared, take the world to the brink of nuclear war, with the collaboration of Soviet premier Nikita Khrushchev. Through the grace of God, however, Kennedy resisted the pressures for preemptive war. He instead negotiated a resolution of the missile crisis with his communist enemy by their making mutual concessions, some without the knowledge of JFK's national security advisers. Kennedy thereby turned away from a terrible evil and began a thirteen-month spiritual journey toward world peace. That journey, marked by contradictions, would result in his assassination by what Thomas Merton would identify later, in a broader context, as the Unspeakable.

In 1962–64, I was living in Rome, studying theology and lobbying Catholic bishops at the Second Vatican Council for a statement condemning total war and supporting conscientious objection. I knew little of John Kennedy's halting spiritual journey toward peace. I did feel there was a harmony between him and Pope John XXIII, as would be confirmed later by journalist Norman Cousins. When I met Cousins in Rome, I learned of his shuttle diplomacy as a secret messenger between the president, the pope, and the premier. I had no sense in those years that there may have been forces lining up to murder Kennedy. Thomas Merton did, as shown by a strange prophecy he made.

In a letter written to his friend W. H. Ferry in January 1962, Merton assessed Kennedy's character at that point in a negative, insightful way: "I have little confidence in Kennedy, I think he cannot fully measure up to the magnitude of his task, and lacks creative imagination and the deeper kind of sensitivity that is needed. Too much the *Time* and *Life* mentality, than which I can imagine nothing further, in reality, from, say, Lincoln. What is needed is really not shrewdness or craft, but what the politicians don't have: depth, humanity and a certain totality of self-forgetfulness and compassion, not just for individuals but for man as a whole: a deeper kind of dedication. Maybe Kennedy will break through into that some day by miracle. But such people are before long marked out for assassination." [3]

Merton's skeptical view of Kennedy allowed for a grain of hope and a contingent prophecy. As the United States moved closer to nuclear war, the monk undoubtedly prayed for the president's unlikely but necessary (for us all) conversion to a deeper, wider humanity—which, if it happened, would before long mark him out for assassination. As measured by the world, it was a dead-end prayer. But in terms of faith, such a sequence and consequence could be seen as cause for celebration.

In the next twenty-two months, did Kennedy break through by miracle to a deeper humanity?

Was he then marked out for assassination?

John F. Kennedy was no saint. Nor was he any apostle of nonviolence. However, as we are all called to do, he was turning. *Teshuvah*, "turning," the rabbinic word for repentance, is the explanation for Kennedy's short-lived, contradictory journey toward peace. He was turning from what would have been the worst violence in history toward a new, more peaceful possibility in his and our lives.

He was therefore in deadly conflict with the Unspeakable.

"The Unspeakable" is a term Thomas Merton coined at the heart of the sixties after JFK's assassination—in the midst of the escalating Vietnam War, the nuclear arms race, and the further assassinations of Malcolm X, Martin Luther King, and Robert Kennedy. In each of those soul-shaking events Merton sensed an evil whose depth and deceit seemed to go beyond the capacity of words to describe.

"One of the awful facts of our age," Merton wrote in 1965, "is the evidence that [the world] is stricken indeed, stricken to the very core of its being by the presence of the Unspeakable." The Vietnam War, the race to a global war, and the interlocking murders of John Kennedy, Malcolm X, Martin Luther King, and Robert Kennedy were all signs of the Unspeakable. It remains deeply present in our world. As Merton warned, "Those who are at present so eager to be reconciled with the world at any price must take care not to be reconciled with it under this particular aspect: *as the nest of the Unspeakable*. This is what too few are willing to see." [4]

When we become more deeply human, as Merton understood the process, the wellspring of our compassion moves us to confront the Unspeakable. Merton was pointing to a kind of systemic evil that defies speech. For Merton, the Unspeakable was, at bottom, a void: "It is the void that contradicts everything that is spoken even before the words are said; the void that gets into the language of public and official declarations at the very moment when they are pronounced, and makes them ring dead with the hollowness of the abyss. It is the void out of which Eichmann drew the punctilious exactitude of his obedience . . ." [5]

In our Cold War history, the Unspeakable was the void in our government's covert-action doctrine of "plausible deniability," sanctioned by the June 18, 1948, National Security Council directive NSC 10/2.[6] Under the direction of Allen Dulles, the CIA interpreted "plausible deniability" as a green light to assassinate national leaders, overthrow governments, and lie to cover up any trace of accountability—all for the sake of promoting U.S. interests and maintaining our nuclear-backed dominance over the Soviet Union and other nations.[7]

I was slow to see the Unspeakable in the assassination of John Kennedy. After JFK was killed, for more than three decades I saw no connection between his assassination and the theology of peace I was pursuing. Although I treasured Merton's insight into the Unspeakable, I did not explore its implications in the national security state whose nuclear policies I rejected. I knew nothing of "plausible deniability," the unspeakable void of responsibility in our own national security state. That void of accountability for the CIA and our other security agencies, seen as necessary for covert crimes to protect our nuclear weapons primacy, made possible the JFK assassination and cover-up. While I wrote and acted in resistance to nuclear weapons that could kill millions, I remained oblivious of the fact that their existence at the heart of our national security state underlay the assassination of a president turning toward disarmament.

By overlooking the deep changes in Kennedy's life and the forces behind his death, I contributed to a national climate of denial. Our collective denial of the obvious, in the setting up of Oswald and his transparent silencing by Ruby, made possible the Dallas cover-up. The success of the cover-up was the indispensable foundation for the subsequent murders of Malcolm X, Martin Luther King, and Robert Kennedy by the same forces at work in our government—and in ourselves. Hope for change in the world was targeted and killed four times over. The cover-up of all four murders, each leading into the next, was based, first of all, on denial—not the government's but our own. The unspeakable is not far away.

Martin Luther King's assassination awakened me. When King was murdered, I was a thirty-year-old professor of religion at the University of Hawaii. I had a seminar entitled "The Theology of Peace" with a dozen students. At our first class after Dr. King was killed, several of the students failed to show up on time. When they came in, they made an announcement to the class. They said that in response to the assassination of King, who had given his life for peace and justice, they had held an impromptu rally on campus. They had burned their draft cards, thereby becoming liable to years in prison. They said they were now forming the Hawaii Resistance. They asked if I would like to join their group. It was a friendly invitation, but it bore the implication: "Put up or shut up, Mr. Professor of Nonviolence." A month later, we sat in front of a convoy of trucks taking the members of the Hawaii National Guard to Oahu's Jungle Warfare Training Center, on their way to the jungles of Vietnam. I went to jail for two weeks—the beginning of the end of my academic career. Members of the Hawaii Resistance served from six months to two years in prison for their draft resistance or wound up going into exile in Sweden or Canada.

Thirty-one years later I learned much more about King's murder. I attended the only trial ever held for it. The trial took place in Memphis, only a few blocks from the Lorraine Motel where King was killed. In a wrongful death lawsuit initiated by the King family, seventy witnesses testified over a six-week period. They described a sophisticated government plot that involved the FBI, the CIA, the Memphis Police, Mafia intermediaries, and an Army Special Forces sniper team. The twelve jurors, six black and six white, returned after two and one-half hours of deliberation with a verdict that King had been assassinated by a conspiracy that included agencies of his own government.[8]

In the course of my journey into Martin Luther King's martyrdom, my eyes were opened to parallel questions in the murders of John F. Kennedy, Malcolm X, and Robert F. Kennedy. I went to Dallas, Chicago, New York, and other sites to interview witnesses. I studied critical government documents in each of their cases. Eventually I came to see all four of them together as four versions of the same story. JFK, Malcolm, Martin, and RFK were four proponents of change who were murdered by shadowy intelligence agencies using intermediaries and scapegoats under the cover of "plausible deniability." Beneath their assassinations lay the evil void of responsibility that Merton identified as the unspeakable.

The Unspeakable is not far away. It is not somewhere out there, identical with a government that became foreign to us. The emptiness of the void, the vacuum of responsibility and compassion, is in ourselves. Our citizen denial provides the ground for the government's doctrine of "plausible deniability." John F. Kennedy's assassination is rooted in our denial of our nation's crimes in World War II that began the Cold War and the nuclear arms race. As a growing precedent to JFK's assassination by his own national security state, we U.S. citizens supported our government when it destroyed whole cities (Hamburg, Dresden, Tokyo, Hiroshima, Nagasaki), when it protected our Cold War security by world-destructive weapons, and when it carried out the covert murders of foreign leaders with "plausible deniability" in a way that was obvious to critical observers. By avoiding our responsibility for the escalating crimes of state done for our security, we who failed to confront the Unspeakable opened the door to JFK's assassination and its cover-up. The Unspeakable is not far away.

It was Thomas Merton's compassion as a human being that drew him into his own encounter with the Unspeakable. I love what Merton wrote about compassion in *The Sign of Jonas*: "It is in the desert of compassion that the thirsty land turns into springs of water, that the poor possess all things."[9]

Compassion is our source of nonviolent social transformation. A profoundly human compassion was Merton's wellspring for his encounter with the Unspeakable in the Holocaust, the Vietnam War, and nuclear annihilation. Merton's understanding and encouragement sustained many of us through those years, especially in our resistance to the Vietnam War. As Merton's own opposition deepened to the evil of that war, he went on a pilgrimage to the East for a more profound encounter. He was electrocuted by a fan at a conference center in Bangkok on December 10, 1968, the conclusion of his journey into a deeper, more compassionate humanity.

"The human being" was Jesus' name for himself, literally "the son of the man," in Greek *ho huios tou anthrōpou*.[10] Jesus' self-identification signified a new, compassionate humanity willing to love our enemies and walk the way of the cross. Jesus told his disciples again and again about "the human being," meaning a personal and collective humanity that he identified with himself. Against his followers' protests, he told them repeatedly that the human being must suffer. The human being must be rejected by the ruling powers, must be killed, and will rise again.[11] This is the glory of humanity. As he put it in John's Gospel, "The hour has come for the human being to be glorified. Truly, truly, I say to you, unless a grain of wheat falls into the earth and dies, it remains alone; but if it dies, it bears much fruit" (John 12:24).

What Jesus was all about, what we as human beings are all about in our deepest nature, is giving our lives for one another. By bearing that witness of martyrdom, he taught, we will come to know what humanity really is in its glory, on earth as it is in heaven. A martyr is therefore a living witness to our new humanity.

Was John F. Kennedy a martyr, one who in spite of contradictions gave his life as witness to a new, more peaceful humanity?

That question never occurred to me when Kennedy died. Nor did it arise in my mind until more than three decades later. Now that I know more about JFK's journey, the question is there: Did a president of the United States, while in command of total nuclear war, detach himself enough from its power to give his life for peace?

From researching JFK's story, I know much more today than I did during his life about his struggle to find a more hopeful way than the Cold War policies that were about to incinerate the United States, the Soviet Union, and much of the world. I know now why he became so dangerous to those who believed in and profited from those policies.

But how much of his future was John Kennedy willing to risk?

Kennedy was not naïve. He knew the forces he was up against. Is it even conceivable that a man with such power in his hands could have laid it down and turned toward an end to the Cold War, in the knowledge he would then be, in Merton's phrase, marked out for assassination?

Let the reader decide.

I will tell the story as truthfully as I can. I have come to see it as a transforming story, one that can help move our own collective story in the twenty-first century from a spiral of violence to a way of peace. My methodology is from Gandhi. This is an experiment in truth. Its particular truth is a journey into darkness. If we go as far as we can into the darkness, regardless of the consequences, I believe a midnight truth will free us from our bondage to violence and bring us to the light of peace.

Whether or not JFK was a martyr, his story could never have been told without the testimony of risk-taking witnesses to the truth. Even if their lives were not taken—and some were—they were all martyrs in the root meaning of the word, witnesses to the truth.

The belief behind this book is that truth is the most powerful force on earth, what Gandhi called *satyagraha*, "truth-force" or "soul-force." By his experiments in truth Gandhi turned theology on its head, saying "truth is God." We all see a part of the truth and can seek it more deeply. Its other side is compassion, our response to suffering.

The story of JFK and the Unspeakable is drawn from the suffering and compassion of many witnesses who saw the truth and spoke it. In living out the truth, we are liberated from the Unspeakable.

Chronology 1961–1963

January 17, 1961: President Dwight D. Eisenhower delivers his Farewell Address, warning U.S. citizens of the rise in power of "the military-industrial complex," the "conjunction of an immense military establishment and a large arms industry [that] is new in the American experience . . . We must never let the weight of this combination endanger our liberties or democratic processes."

Congo leader Patrice Lumumba is assassinated by the Belgian government with the complicity of the CIA in the Congo's secessionist province of Katanga, three days before the presidential inauguration of John F. Kennedy, known for his support of African nationalism.

January 19, 1961: During his last day in the White House, President Eisenhower gives President-elect Kennedy a transitional briefing. When Kennedy raises the possibility of the United States supporting a coalition government in Laos that would include Communists, Eisenhower says it would be far better to intervene militarily with U.S. troops.

January 20, 1961: President Kennedy delivers his Inaugural Address, balancing Cold War statements with the hope "that both sides begin anew the quest for peace, before the dark powers of destruction unleashed by science engulf all humanity in planned or accidental self-destruction."

March 23, 1961: Over the opposition of the Joint Chiefs of Staff and the CIA, President Kennedy changes policy on Laos by ending U.S. support of anti-communist ruler General Phoumi Nosavan, whose government was installed by CIA-Pentagon forces under Eisenhower. At a news conference Kennedy says the United States "strongly and unreservedly" supports "the goal of a neutral and independent Laos" and wants to join in an international conference on Laos.

April 15–19, 1961: A Cuban exile brigade, trained and commanded by the CIA, invades Cuba at the Bay of Pigs. As the Cuban army led by Premier

Fidel Castro surrounds the invading force, President Kennedy refuses to send in U.S. combat forces. The exile brigade surrenders, and more than one thousand of its members are taken prisoner. President Kennedy realizes he has been drawn into a CIA trap designed to force him to escalate the battle by ordering a full-scale invasion of Cuba by U.S. troops. Kennedy says he wants "to splinter the CIA in a thousand pieces and scatter it to the winds."

June 3–4, 1961: At a summit meeting in Vienna, John Kennedy and Nikita Khrushchev agree to support a neutral and independent Laos—the only issue they can agree upon. Khrushchev's apparent indifference to the deepening threat of nuclear war shocks Kennedy.

July 20, 1961: At a National Security Council Meeting, the Joint Chiefs of Staff and CIA director Allen Dulles present a plan for a preemptive nuclear attack on the Soviet Union "in late 1963, preceded by a period of heightened tensions." President Kennedy walks out of the meeting, saying to Secretary of State Dean Rusk, "And we call ourselves the human race."

August 30, 1961: The Soviet Union resumes atmospheric testing of thermonuclear weapons, exploding a 150-kiloton hydrogen bomb over Siberia.

September 5, 1961: After the Soviet testing of two more hydrogen bombs, President Kennedy announces he has ordered the resumption of U.S. nuclear tests.

September 25, 1961: President Kennedy delivers a speech on disarmament at the United Nations in which he states: "The weapons of war must be abolished before they abolish us . . . It is therefore our intention to challenge the Soviet Union, not to an arms race, but to a peace race—to advance together step by step, stage by stage, until general and complete disarmament has been achieved."

September 29, 1961: Nikita Khrushchev writes a first confidential letter to John Kennedy. He smuggles it to the president in a newspaper brought by a Soviet intelligence agent to Kennedy's press secretary Pierre Salinger. In the letter Khrushchev compares their common concern for peace in the nuclear age "with Noah's Ark where both the 'clean' and the 'unclean' found sanctuary. But regardless of who lists himself with the 'clean' and who is considered to be 'unclean,' they are all equally interested in one thing and that is that the Ark should successfully continue its cruise."

October 16, 1961: Kennedy responds privately to Khrushchev, writing: "I like very much your analogy of Noah's Ark, with both the 'clean' and the 'unclean' determined that it stay afloat. Whatever our differences, our collaboration to keep the peace is as urgent—if not more urgent—than our collaboration to win the last world war."

October 27–28, 1961: After a summer of U.S.–Soviet tensions over Berlin culminating in Khrushchev's August order to erect a wall between East and West Berlin, General Lucius Clay, President Kennedy's personal representative in West Berlin, provokes a sixteen-hour confrontation between U.S. and Soviet tanks at the Berlin Wall. Kennedy sends an urgent, back-channel appeal to Khrushchev, who then initiates their mutual withdrawal of the tanks, prefiguring the resolution of the Cuban Missile Crisis one year later.

November 22, 1961: While refusing the Joint Chiefs' recommendation that U.S. combat troops be deployed to defeat an insurgency in Vietnam, President Kennedy orders the sending of military advisers and support units—the beginning of a steady military buildup in Vietnam during his presidency.

November 30, 1961: President Kennedy authorizes "Operation Mongoose," a covert-action program "to help Cuba overthrow the communist regime." He appoints counterinsurgency specialist General Edward Lansdale as its Chief of Operations.

April 13, 1962: President Kennedy, backed by overwhelming public support, forces the leaders of the steel industry to rescind a price increase that violates a Kennedy-brokered agreement to combat inflation. Kennedy's anti-business statements and beginning cancellation of the steel companies' defense contracts make him notorious among the power brokers of the military-industrial complex.

April 25, 1962: As authorized by President Kennedy, the United States sets off the first of a series of twenty-four nuclear tests in the South Pacific.

May 8, 1962: Following President Kennedy's instructions, Defense Secretary Robert McNamara orders General Paul Harkins at a Saigon conference "to devise a plan for turning full responsibility [for the war in Vietnam] over to South Vietnam and reducing the size of our military command, and to submit this plan at the next conference."

June 13, 1962: With his Russian wife, Marina, and infant daughter, June, Lee Harvey Oswald returns to the United States with a loan from the State Department, after his highly publicized October 1959 defection to the Soviet Union and two and one-half years living as an expatriate in Minsk.

As the Oswalds settle in Fort Worth, Texas, Lee Oswald begins to be shepherded by intelligence asset George de Mohrenschildt, at the instigation of Dallas CIA agent J. Walton Moore.

July 23, 1962: The United States joins thirteen other nations at Geneva in signing the "Declaration on the Neutrality of Laos." CIA and Pentagon opponents regard Kennedy's negotiation of the Laotian agreement as surrender to the Communists. They undermine it by supporting General Phoumi's violations of the cease-fire.

In another conference on the war in Vietnam, at Camp Smith, Hawaii, Secretary McNamara discovers that his May 8 order to General Harkins has been ignored. He repeats President Kennedy's order for a program to phase out U.S. military involvement in Vietnam.

October 16, 1962: President Kennedy is informed that photographs from a U-2 reconnaissance flight show Soviet medium-range ballistic missiles in Cuba. Kennedy calls a top-secret meeting of his key advisers, who become the Executive Committee (ExComm) of the National Security Council. At their first meeting, they debate ways of destroying the Soviet missiles by preemptive attacks on Cuba, prompting Robert Kennedy to write a note to the president saying: "I now know how Tojo felt when he was planning Pearl Harbor."

October 19, 1962: As President Kennedy resolves to blockade further Soviet missile shipments rather than bomb and invade Cuba, he meets with his Joint Chiefs of Staff. They push for an immediate attack on the missile sites. General Curtis LeMay tells him, "This [blockade and political action] is almost as bad as the appeasement [of Hitler] at Munich."

October 22, 1962: President Kennedy delivers a televised speech to the nation, announcing the U.S. discovery of Soviet missile sites in Cuba. He declares "a strict quarantine on all offensive military equipment under shipment to Cuba" and calls for "the prompt dismantling and withdrawal of all offensive weapons in Cuba."

October 27, 1962: A Soviet surface-to-air missile shoots down a U-2 reconnaissance plane over Cuba, killing the Air Force pilot. The Joint Chiefs and ExComm urge a quick retaliatory attack. Kennedy sends a letter accepting Khrushchev's proposal to withdraw the Soviet missiles in return for JFK's pledge not to invade Cuba, while ignoring Khrushchev's later demand that the United States remove its analogous missiles from Turkey beside the Soviet border. JFK sends Robert Kennedy to meet with Soviet ambassador Anatoly Dobrynin. RFK gives Dobrynin a secret promise that the missiles in Turkey will also be withdrawn as part of the agreement. He appeals for a quick response by Khrushchev, saying many generals are pushing for war and the president may lose control. Upon receipt of this message from Dobrynin, Khrushchev announces publicly he is taking the Soviet missiles out of Cuba in exchange for Kennedy's no-invasion pledge.

The Joint Chiefs of Staff are outraged by Kennedy's refusal to attack Cuba and his concessions to Khrushchev.

December 18, 1962: After visiting Vietnam at President Kennedy's request, Senator Mike Mansfield issues a report cautioning Kennedy against being drawn "inexorably into some variation of the unenviable position in Vietnam which was formerly occupied by the French."

March 19, 1963: At a Washington news conference, the CIA-sponsored Cuban exile group Alpha 66 announces its having raided a Soviet "fortress" and ship in Cuba, causing a dozen casualties. The secret purpose of the attack in Cuban waters, according to Alpha 66's incognito CIA adviser, David Atlee Phillips, is "to publicly embarrass Kennedy and force him to move against Castro."

March 31, 1963: President Kennedy orders a crackdown on Cuban refugee gunboats being run by the CIA out of Miami. Robert Kennedy's Justice Department confines the movement of anti-Castro commando leaders to the Miami area, while the Coast Guard seizes their boats and arrests the crews.

April 11, 1963: Pope John XXIII issues his encyclical letter, **Pacem in Terris** ("Peace on Earth"). Norman Cousins presents an advance copy in Russian to Nikita Khrushchev. The papal encyclical's principles of mutual trust and cooperation with an ideological opponent provide a foundation for the Kennedy–Khrushchev dialogue and Kennedy's American University address in June.

President Kennedy writes secretly to Premier Khrushchev that he is "aware of the tensions unduly created by recent private attacks on your ships in Cuban waters; and we are taking action to halt those attacks which are in violation of our laws."

Also in early April, James Donovan, U.S. negotiator, returns to Cuba to confer with Premier Fidel Castro for the further release of Bay of Pigs prisoners. The CIA attempts through an unwitting Donovan to foist a CIA-contaminated diving suit on Castro, as a gift by the Kennedy-appointed negotiator, in a failed effort to simultaneously assassinate Castro, scapegoat Kennedy, and sabotage a beginning Cuban–American dialogue.

April 18, 1963: Dr. Jose Miro Cardona, head of the Cuban Revolutionary Council in Miami, subsidized by the CIA, resigns in protest against Kennedy's shift in Cuban policy. Cardona concludes from Kennedy's actions: "the struggle for Cuba is in the process of being liquidated by the [U.S.] Government."

May 6, 1963: In another conference on Vietnam chaired by Secretary McNamara at Camp Smith, Hawaii, the Pacific Command finally presents President Kennedy's long-sought plan for withdrawal from Vietnam. However, McNamara has to reject the military's overextended time line. He orders that concrete plans be drawn up for withdrawing one thousand U.S. military personnel from South Vietnam by the end of 1963.

President Kennedy issues National Security Action Memorandum 239, ordering his principal national security advisers to pursue both a nuclear test ban treaty and a policy of general and complete disarmament.

May 8, 1963: At a protest in Hue, South Vietnam, by Buddhists claiming religious repression by the Diem government, two explosions attributed to government security forces kill eight people, wounding fifteen others. The government accuses the Viet Cong of setting off the explosions. A later, independent investigation identifies the bomber as a U.S. military officer, using CIA-supplied plastic bombs. The Buddhist Crisis touched off by the Hue explosions threatens to topple Ngo Dinh Diem's government, destroying the possibility of a Diem–Kennedy agreement for a U.S. military withdrawal from Vietnam.

June 10, 1963: President Kennedy delivers his Commencement Address at American University in Washington proposing, in effect, an end to the Cold War. Rejecting the goal of "a Pax Americana enforced on the world by American weapons of war," Kennedy asks Americans to reexamine their attitudes toward war, especially in relation to the people of the Soviet Union, who suffered incomparable losses in World War II. Now nuclear war would be far worse: "All we have built, all we have worked for, would be destroyed in the first 24 hours." He announces his unilateral suspension of further nuclear tests in the atmosphere, so as to promote "our primary long-range interest," "general and complete disarmament."

June 25, 1963: Lee Harvey Oswald is issued a United States passport in New Orleans, twenty-four hours after his application and one year after his return from defecting to the Soviet Union. On his passport application, he identifies his destination as the Soviet Union.

July 25, 1963: In Moscow, on behalf of President Kennedy, U.S. negotiator Averell Harriman agrees with Soviet negotiators to the Limited Test Ban Treaty, outlawing nuclear tests "in the atmosphere, beyond its limits, including outer space, or under water, including territorial waters or high seas."

July 26, 1963: President Kennedy makes a television appeal to the nation for support of the test ban treaty, quoting Nikita Khrushchev on a nuclear war they both hope to avoid: "The survivors would envy the dead."

August 9–10, 1963: Lee Harvey Oswald is arrested in New Orleans while passing out Fair Play for Cuba leaflets. He and three anti-Castro Cuban exiles, who confront him and tear up his leaflets, are charged with disturbing the peace. After Oswald spends the night in jail, he meets privately with New Orleans FBI agent John Quigley. Oswald's street theater discredits the Fair Play for Cuba Committee and prepares the ground for his portrayal in November as a pro-Castro assassin of President Kennedy.

August 24, 1963: Presidential advisers Roger Hilsman, Averell Harriman, and Michael Forrestal draft a telegram to newly appointed Saigon ambassador Henry Cabot Lodge that conditionally authorizes U.S. support of a coup by rebel South Vietnamese generals. President Kennedy, who is in Hyannis Port, endorses the telegram. He soon regrets the hasty policy decision that puts the U.S. government on record in support of a coup.

September 12, 1963: At a National Security Council meeting, the Joint Chiefs of Staff again present a report evaluating a projected nuclear first strike against the Soviet Union, in a time scheme of 1964 through 1968. President Kennedy turns the discussion to his conclusion: "Preemption is not possible for us." He passes over without comment the report's implication that the remaining months of 1963 are still the most advantageous time for the United States to launch a preemptive strike.

September 20, 1963: In an address to the United Nations, President Kennedy expresses the hope that the Limited Test Ban Treaty can serve as a lever for a just and lasting peace. In a meeting with UN ambassador Adlai Stevenson, he approves U.S. diplomat William Attwood contacting Dr. Carlos Lechuga, Cuba's UN ambassador, to open a secret dialogue with Premier Castro.

In El Paso, Texas, U.S. counterintelligence agent Richard Case Nagell, who has met with Kennedy assassination planners, walks into a bank and fires two pistol shots into a plaster wall just below the ceiling. He waits outside to be arrested and tells the FBI, "I would rather be arrested than commit murder and treason."

September 23, 1963: At a party arranged as a cover by television newscaster Lisa Howard, William Attwood meets Carlos Lechuga. Attwood tells Lechuga he is about to travel to the White House to request authorization from the president to meet secretly with Premier Castro. The meeting's purpose would be to discuss the feasibility of a rapprochement between Havana and Washington. Lechuga expresses great interest.

September 24, 1963: In Washington, William Attwood meets with Robert Kennedy, who tells Attwood to continue pursuing with Lechuga a secret meeting with Castro but to seek a less risky location than Cuba.

The Senate approves the Limited Test Ban Treaty by a vote of 80 to 19.

September 27, 1963: Attwood meets Lechuga at the UN Delegates' Lounge, saying he is authorized to meet with Castro at a site other than Cuba. Lechuga says he will so inform Havana.

In Mexico City, a man identifying himself as Lee Harvey Oswald visits the Cuban and Soviet consulates, displaying leftist credentials and applying for immediate visas to both Communist countries. When suspicious employees put him off and escort him outside, he flies into a rage, creating memorable scenes.

September 28, 1963: The man identifying himself as Oswald returns to the Mexico City Soviet Embassy, renewing his request for a quick visa to the Soviet Union. When Soviet officials offer him forms to fill out, he becomes even more agitated than on the previous day. He places a revolver on the table, saying it is necessary for his protection. He is again escorted to the door.

This visit to the Soviet Embassy becomes a repeated reference during incriminating phone calls by "Oswald," wiretapped and transcribed by the CIA, in which the speaker associates himself with a Soviet assassination expert working at the embassy. When it is pointed out that the phone caller speaks broken Russian, whereas Oswald is fluent in the language, the CIA claims the audiotapes are no longer available for voice comparisons because they were routinely erased.

September 30, 1963: President Kennedy reopens a secret channel of communication between himself and Nikita Khrushchev, via Press Secretary Pierre Salinger and a Washington-based Soviet Secret Police agent. He thereby circumvents a State Department he can no longer trust for his communications with the Soviet leader.

October 11, 1963: President Kennedy issues National Security Action Memorandum 263, making official government policy the withdrawal from Vietnam of "1,000 U.S. military personnel by the end of 1963" and "by the end of 1965 . . . the bulk of U.S. personnel."

October 16, 1963: After a successful job referral by Ruth Paine, Lee Harvey Oswald begins work at the Texas School Book Depository in Dallas.

October 24, 1963: French journalist Jean Daniel interviews President Kennedy, before Daniel's trip to Cuba to interview Premier Castro. Kennedy speaks warmly of the Cuban revolution led by Castro, but asks Daniel if Castro realizes that "through his fault the world was on the verge of nuclear war in October 1962." Kennedy asks Daniel to tell him what Castro says in reply, when Daniel returns from Cuba at the end of November.

October 31, 1963: Fidel Castro's aide Rene Vallejo speaks by phone with Lisa Howard. Through Vallejo, Castro offers to expedite the process of meeting with William Attwood by sending a plane to pick up Attwood in Mexico. Attwood would be flown to a private airport in Cuba, where he would talk confidentially with Castro, then be flown back immediately. Howard conveys this to Attwood, who alerts the White House.

November 1, 1963: Rebel South Vietnamese army units, supported by the CIA, encircle and bombard President Diem's presidential palace in Saigon. Diem and his brother Nhu flee from the palace in darkness. They take refuge in the Saigon suburb of Cholon.

In Chicago, the Secret Service arrests two members of a four-man sniper team suspected of planning to assassinate President Kennedy during his visit to Chicago the following day. The other two snipers escape. Thomas Arthur Vallee, a mentally damaged ex-Marine working in a building over Kennedy's motorcade route, is monitored by the Chicago Police.

November 2, 1963: From his refuge in Cholon, Diem phones Ambassador Lodge and the coup generals. He surrenders, requesting for Nhu and himself only safe conduct to the airport and departure from Vietnam. Rebel general Minh sends a team of five men to pick up the two men. The armored personnel carrier into which Diem and Nhu descend delivers their dead, bullet-sprayed bodies to the generals' headquarters.

At the White House, President Kennedy is handed a telegram from Lodge informing him that Diem and Nhu are dead and that the coup leaders claim their deaths are suicides. Kennedy rushes from the room with a look of shock and dismay on his face.

Forty minutes later, White House press secretary Pierre Salinger announces President Kennedy's trip to Chicago has been cancelled. While the two suspected snipers are questioned at Chicago Secret Service headquarters, potential assassination scapegoat Thomas Arthur Vallee is arrested. The other two alleged snipers remain at large in Chicago. Only Vallee is ever identified publicly.

November 5, 1963: William Attwood briefs President Kennedy's National Security Adviser McGeorge Bundy on Premier Castro's concrete offer to expedite a meeting with Attwood as Kennedy's representative. Bundy then updates Kennedy on Castro's proposal. Kennedy says Attwood should sever his formal relation with the government as a precaution, so as to meet with Castro under the cover of his former work as a journalist.

November 18, 1963: Rene Vallejo talks by phone with William Attwood, while Fidel Castro listens. Attwood says a preliminary meeting is essential to identify what he and Castro will discuss. Vallejo says they will send instructions to Cuban ambassador Carlos Lechuga to set an agenda with Attwood for his meeting with Castro.

In a speech in Miami, President Kennedy issues a challenge and a promise to Premier Castro, saying that if Cuba ceases being "a weapon in an effort dictated by external powers to subvert the other American Republics," "everything is possible."

In Washington, the Soviet Embassy receives a crudely typed, badly spelled letter dated nine days earlier and signed by "Lee H. Oswald" of Dallas. The letter seems to implicate the Soviet Union in conspiring with Oswald in the assassination of President Kennedy that will occur four days later. Soviet authorities recognize the letter as a forgery or provocation and decide to return it to the U.S. government, whose FBI agents had already opened and copied the letter on its way into the embassy.

November 19–20, 1963: Fidel Castro meets for six hours with Jean Daniel at his Havana hotel to learn more about a dialogue with Kennedy. After Daniel recounts Kennedy's endorsement of the Cuban revolution and his accusation that Castro almost caused a nuclear war, Castro explains the reasoning for the introduction of Soviet missiles in Cuba—to deter the imminent U.S. invasion that he feared. Reassessing Kennedy, he expresses the hope that Kennedy will win reelection and become the United States' greatest president—by recognizing there can be coexistence between capitalists and socialists, even in the Americas.

November 20, 1963: At Red Bird Air Field in Dallas, a young man and woman try to charter a plane for Friday afternoon, November 22, from Wayne January, owner of a private airline. From their questions, January suspects they may hijack the plane to Cuba. He rejects their offer. The man he sees waiting for the couple in their car he recognizes two days later from media pictures as Lee Harvey Oswald.

In Eunice, Louisiana, heroin addict Rose Cheramie tells Louisiana State Police lieutenant Francis Fruge that the two men with whom she stopped at the Silver Slipper Lounge that night, on a drive from Miami to Dallas, plan to kill President Kennedy when he comes to Dallas.

November 21, 1963: Before leaving on his trip to Texas, President Kennedy, after being given a list of the most recent casualties in Vietnam, says to Assistant Press Secretary Malcolm Kilduff: "After I come back from Texas, that's going to change. Vietnam is not worth another American life."

November 22, 1963: At 12:30 P.M., with security having been withdrawn from the surrounding area and the presidential limousine, President Kennedy is driven around a dogleg turn to a virtual stop in Dealey Plaza, Dallas, where sniper teams assassinate him by crossfire.

While Fidel Castro and Jean Daniel are having lunch together in Varadero Beach, Cuba, they receive the news of Kennedy's death in Dallas. Castro says, "Everything is changed. Everything is going to change."

When the president's body is brought to Parkland Hospital, Dallas, twenty-one witnesses see a massive head wound in the right rear of his skull, evidence of a fatal head shot from the front. At a press conference, Dr. Malcolm Perry repeatedly describes an entrance wound in the front of the throat, further evidence of shooting from the front.

Lee Harvey Oswald is arrested in the Texas Theater at 1:50 P.M., following the murder of Dallas Police officer J. D. Tippit at 1:15 by a man whom witnesses identify as Oswald. At 1:53 P.M., a man resembling Oswald is also arrested in the Texas Theater and taken out a different door. At 3:30 P.M., an Oswald double is flown out of Dallas on a CIA C-54 cargo plane.

During the president's autopsy held at Bethesda Naval Hospital, Bethesda, Maryland, Admiral Calvin Galloway, hospital commander, orders the doctors not to probe the throat wound. X-rays taken that night show an intact rear skull, where a large occipital fragment of the president's skull, which will be found the next day in Dealey Plaza, was blown out—proving the X-rays are fraudulent, created to disguise a massive exit wound in the rear.

At 11:55 P.M. on the third floor of Dallas Police headquarters, CIA-connected nightclub owner Jack Ruby, whom a witness saw deliver a gunman to the grassy knoll that morning, is given access to the doorway where prisoner Lee Harvey Oswald is about to be brought by police to a midnight press conference. Ruby (with a revolver in his pocket) fails to shoot Oswald.

November 24, 1963: At 11:21 A.M., an armed Jack Ruby is again given access to the prisoner Lee Harvey Oswald, this time as Oswald is brought from the basement to the garage of Dallas Police headquarters while being transferred to the Dallas County Jail. Ruby shoots Oswald to death at point blank range, as seen on television by millions.

In mid-afternoon in Washington, President Lyndon Johnson meets with Ambassador Henry Cabot Lodge, back from Vietnam. Johnson tells Lodge, "I am not going to lose Vietnam. I am not going to be the President who saw Southeast Asia go the way China went."

CHAPTER ONE

A Cold Warrior Turns

As Albert Einstein said, with the unleashing of the power of the atom, humanity reached a new age. The atomic bombing of Hiroshima marked a crossroads: either we would end war or war would end us. In her reflections on Hiroshima in the September 1945 issue of the *Catholic Worker*, Dorothy Day wrote: "Mr. Truman was jubilant. President Truman. True man; what a strange name, come to think of it. We refer to Jesus Christ as true God and true Man. Truman is a true man of his time in that he was jubilant."[1]

President Truman was aboard the cruiser *Augusta*, returning from the Potsdam conference, when he was informed of the United States' incineration of Hiroshima by the atomic bomb. Truman was exultant. He declared, "This is the greatest thing in history!" He went from person to person on the ship, officers and crew alike, telling them the great news like a town crier.

Dorothy Day observed: " 'Jubilant' the newspapers said. *Jubilate Deo*. We have killed 318,000 Japanese."

Seventeen years later, during the Cuban Missile Crisis, another president, John F. Kennedy, under enormous pressure, almost committed the United States to a nuclear holocaust that would have multiplied the explosive power of the Hiroshima bomb thousands of times. Kennedy's saving grace was that unlike Truman he recognized the evil of nuclear weapons. Kennedy resisted the Joint Chiefs of Staff and most of his civilian advisers, who pressured him for a preemptive attack on Soviet missile sites in Cuba. Thanks to the sheer grace of God, to Kennedy's resistance to his advisers, and to Nikita Khrushchev's willingness to retreat, humanity survived the crisis.

Kennedy, however, survived it for only a little more than a year. As we shall see, because of his continuing turn from nuclear war toward a vision of peace in the thirteen months remaining to him, he was executed by the powers that be.

1

Two critical questions converge at Kennedy's assassination. The first is: Why did his assassins risk exposure and a shameful downfall by covertly murdering a beloved president? The second is: Why was John Kennedy prepared to give his life for peace, when he saw death coming?

The second question may be key to the first, because there is nothing so threatening to systemic evil as those willing to stand against it regardless of the consequences. So we will try to see this story initially through the life of John Kennedy, to understand why he became so threatening to the most powerful military-economic coalition in history that its wielders of power were willing to risk everything they had in order to kill him.

In assessing the formation of John Kennedy's character, biographers have zeroed in on his upbringing as a rich young man in a dysfunctional marriage. Seen through that lens, Kennedy was a reckless playboy from youth to death, under the abiding influence of a domineering, womanizing father and an emotionally distant, strictly Catholic mother. These half-truths miss the mark. They do not explain the later fact of President Kennedy's steely resistance to the pressures of a military-intelligence elite focused on waging war.

Kennedy's life was formed, first of all, by death—the hovering angel of death reaching down for his life. He suffered long periods of illness. He saw death approach repeatedly—from scarlet fever when he was two and three years old, from a succession of childhood and teen illnesses, from a chronic blood condition in boarding school, from what doctors thought was a combination of colitis and ulcers, from intestinal ailments during his years at Harvard, from osteoporosis and crippling back problems intensified by war injuries that plagued him the rest of his life, from the adrenal insufficiency of Addison's disease[2] . . . To family and friends, Jack Kennedy always seemed to be sick and dying.

Yet he exuded an ironic joy in life. Both the weaknesses and strengths of his character drew on his deeply held belief that death would come soon. "The point is," he told a friend during a long talk on death, "that you've got to live every day like it's your last day on earth. That's what I'm doing."[3] From that perspective, he could indeed be reckless, as he was in sexual escapades that after his death would become a media focus on his life. He could also be courageous to the point of heroism. Death was not to be feared. As president, he often joked about his death's approach. The angel of death was his companion. By smiling at his own death, he was free to resist others' deaths.

John Kennedy's World War II experience was characterized by a willingness to give his life for his friends. Two years before the Hiroshima bombing, Kennedy was a *PT* boat commander in the South Pacific. On the night of August 1–2, 1943, he was at the wheel of his *PT 109*, patrolling Blackett Strait in the Solomon Islands, a corridor of water used by Japanese destroyers. It was a moonless night. A ship suddenly broke through the black, headed for the *109*. As a man forward shouted, "Ship at two o'clock!" Kennedy spun the wheel. The Japanese destroyer smashed into the *109* and cut a giant strip off its starboard side. "This is how it feels to be killed," Kennedy thought, while being thrown through the cockpit. There was a terrific roar, as the gasoline aboard went up in flames.

The section of the boat Kennedy was on stayed afloat. He discovered four of his twelve crewmembers still on it. Two others were never seen or heard from again. Six more were scattered in the water but alive. Kennedy, who had been on the Harvard swimming team, swam through the dark to shouts, finding his badly burned engineer, McMahon. He coaxed and cajoled others not to give up, then towed McMahon a hundred yards back to the floating hulk identified by a crew member's blinking light. All the survivors in the water reached the tilted deck and collapsed on it. They wondered how long it would take for them to be rescued by *PT*s from their base on Rendova Island, forty miles away.

When daylight and noon came with no rescue, the group abandoned the sinking hulk. They swam to a small, deserted island, in the midst of larger islands with Japanese soldiers. Nine of the crew held onto a two-by-six timber and kicked and paddled their way to the island. Kennedy again towed McMahon, holding a strap from McMahon's life preserver in his teeth.

Kennedy would swim in ten-minute spurts, then pause to rest and check on McMahon. A chronicler of this episode described it from McMahon's point of view:

"Being a sensitive person, McMahon would have found the swim unbearable if he had realized that Kennedy was hauling him through three miles or so of water with a bad back. He was miserable enough without knowing it. Floating on his back with his burned hands trailing at his sides, McMahon could see little but the sky and the flattened cone of [the volcanic island] Kolombangara. He could not see the other men, though while all of them were still together, he could hear them puffing and splashing. He could not see Kennedy but he could feel the tugs forward with each stretch of Kennedy's shoulder muscles and could hear his labored breathing.

"McMahon tried kicking now and then but he was extremely weary. The swim seemed endless, and he doubted that it would lead to salvation. He was hungry and thirsty and fearful that they would be attacked by sharks. The awareness that he could do nothing to save himself from the currents, the sharks or the enemy oppressed him. His fate, he well knew, was at the end of a strap in Kennedy's teeth."[4]

With Kennedy and McMahon leading the way, it took the eleven men four hours to reach the little island. They staggered up the beach and ducked under trees, barely avoiding a Japanese barge that chugged by and failed to see them.

When early evening came with no sign of help, Kennedy told the crew he would swim from the island out into Ferguson Passage, a mile and a half away, where the *PT* boats usually patrolled after dark. He took the *109*'s lantern, wrapped in a life jacket, to signal the boats. Kennedy swam for half an hour, forded a reef, then swam for another hour, reaching his intended point of interception. He treaded water, waiting in the darkness. After a while, he saw the flares of an action beyond the island of Gizo, ten miles away. The *PT* boats had taken a different route.

Kennedy tried to swim back to his men. He was very tired. The swift current carried him past the island, toward open water.

New Yorker writer John Hersey interviewed *PT 109* crewmembers and wrote their story of survival. He described Kennedy's hours of drifting toward almost certain death: "He thought he had never known such deep trouble, but something he did shows that unconsciously he had not given up hope. He dropped his shoes, but he held onto the heavy lantern, his symbol of contact with his fellows. He stopped trying to swim. He seemed to stop caring. His body drifted through the wet hours, and he was very cold. His mind was a jumble. A few hours before he had wanted desperately to get to the base at Rendova. Now he only wanted to get back to the little island he had left that night, but he didn't try to get there; he just wanted to. His mind seemed to float away from his body. Darkness and time took the place of a mind in his skull. For a long time he slept, or was crazy, or floated in a chill trance.

"The currents of the Solomon Islands are queer. The tide shoves and sucks through the islands and makes the currents curl in odd patterns. It was a fateful pattern into which Jack Kennedy drifted. He drifted in it all night. His mind was blank, but his fist was tightly clenched on the kapok around the lantern. The current moved in a huge circle—west past Gizo, then north and east past Kolombangara, then south into Ferguson Passage. Early in the morning the sky turned from black to gray, and so did Kennedy's mind. Light came to both at about six. Kennedy looked around and saw that he was exactly where he had been the night before when he saw the flares beyond Gizo."[5]

Kennedy swam back to the island, stumbled up on the beach, and collapsed in the arms of his crew. He said later of the experience, "I never prayed so much in my life."[6]

As is well known from the story of *PT 109*, eventually Melanesian natives came to the aid of the eleven Americans. The natives carried Kennedy's SOS message, scratched on a coconut shell, to an Australian Navy coastwatcher, Reg Evans, who was working behind enemy lines. Evans radioed the U.S. Navy for assistance.

In the meantime, Kennedy and fellow officer Barney Ross, not realizing the nearness of their rescue, almost died in another failed effort to signal *PT*s at night in Ferguson Passage. They found a dugout canoe, and paddled it into high waves in the darkness. The canoe was swamped. The waves threw the two men against a reef, but they again survived.

Kennedy's crew never forgot his commitment to their lives. They reunited with him periodically after the war. What Kennedy took first from his war experience was a heightened sense of the precious value of his friends' lives. Among the wartime deaths he mourned besides the *PT* boat casualties were those of his brother Joe Kennedy, Jr., and brother-in-law Billy Hartington. He knew many others who died. He reflected, too, on the repeated nearness of his own death. As we have seen, since childhood chronically poor health had brought him near death many times. Illness, pain, and the process of almost dying came as a lifelong discipline.

After JFK's assassination, Robert Kennedy wrote of his brother: "At least one half of the days that he spent on this earth were days of intense physical pain. He had scarlet fever when he was very young, and serious back trouble when he was older. In between he had almost every other conceivable ailment. When we were growing up together we used to laugh about the great risk a mosquito took in biting Jack Kennedy—with some of his blood the mosquito was almost sure to die. He was in Chelsea Naval Hospital for an extended period of time after the war, had a major and painful operation on his back in 1955, campaigned on crutches in 1958. In 1951 on a trip we took around the world he became ill. We flew to the military hospital in Okinawa and he had a temperature of over 106 degrees. They didn't think he would live.

"But during all this time, I never heard him complain. I never heard him say anything that would indicate that he felt God had dealt with him unjustly. Those who knew him well would know he was suffering only because his face was a little whiter, the lines around his eyes were a little deeper, his words a little sharper. Those who did not know him well detected nothing."[7]

After the *PT 109* crew's rescue, Kennedy wondered at the purpose of a life that had been spared again, this time through the circular pattern of deep-running currents and the compassion of Melanesian natives.[8]

Preventing another war became John Kennedy's main motivation for entering politics after the Second World War. When he announced his candidacy for Congress on April 22, 1946, in Boston, Kennedy sounded more like he was running for president on a peace ticket than for a first term as a Democratic member of Congress from Massachusetts: "What we do now will shape the history of civilization for many years to come. We have a weary world trying to bind the wounds of a fierce struggle. That is dire enough. What is infinitely far worse is that we have a world which has unleashed the terrible powers of atomic energy. We have a world capable of destroying itself. The days which lie ahead are most difficult ones. Above all, day and night, with every ounce of ingenuity and industry we possess, we must work for peace. We must not have another war."[9]

Where had this twenty-eight-year-old candidate for Congress forged such a vision of peace in the nuclear age?

After his bad back and colitis had forced his discharge from the Navy, Kennedy had attended the San Francisco conference that founded the United Nations in April-May 1945, as a journalist for the Hearst press. He later told friends it was his experience at the UN meeting and at the Potsdam conference in July that made him realize that the political arena, "whether you really liked it or not, was the place where you personally could do the most to prevent another war." [10]

However, what he witnessed in San Francisco, even before the war was over, was an intense conflict between wartime allies. On April 30 he warned his readers that "this week at San Francisco" would be "the real test of whether the Russians and the Americans can get along." [11]

The power struggle he saw at the UN moved Kennedy to write to a PT boat friend: "When I think of how much this war has cost us, of the deaths of Cy and Peter and Orv and Gil and Demi and Joe and Billy and all of those thousands and millions who have died with them—when I think of all those gallant acts that I have seen or anyone has seen who has been to the war—it would be a very easy thing to feel disappointed and somewhat betrayed . . . You have seen battlefields where sacrifice was the order of the day and to compare that sacrifice to the timidity and selfishness of the nations gathered at San Francisco must inevitably be disillusioning." [12]

In a notebook, Kennedy identified an ultimate solution to the problem of war and the difficulty in realizing it: "Admittedly world organization with common obedience to law would be solution. Not that easy. If there is not the feeling that war is the ultimate evil, a feeling strong enough to drive them together, then you can't work out this internationalist plan." [13]

"Things cannot be forced from the top," the future president wrote his PT boat friend. He then expressed a prophetic, long-range view: "The international relinquishing of sovereignty would have to spring from the people—it would have to be so strong that the elected delegates would be turned out of office if they failed to do it . . . War will exist until that distant day when the conscientious objector enjoys the same reputation and prestige that the warrior does today." [14]

Kennedy had reason to refer again to that distant day of the conscientious objector while he was traveling through postwar Europe in the summer of 1945. On July 1 in London, he had dinner with William Douglas-Home, a former captain in the British army who had been sentenced to a year in jail for refusing an order to fire on civilians. Douglas-Home became his lifelong friend. Kennedy observed in his diary, "prowess in war is still deeply respected. The day of the conscientious objector is not yet at hand." [15]

In the same diary, he anticipated the impact of world-destructive weapons. In the entry dated July 10, 1945, six days before the first atomic test in Alamogordo, New Mexico, Kennedy envisioned such a terrible weapon and speculated on its meaning in relation to Russia: "The clash [with Russia] may be finally and indefinitely postponed by the eventual discovery of a weapon so horrible that it will truthfully mean the abolishment of all the nations employing it." [16]

During his legislative career in the House and Senate, John Kennedy's aspirations to be a post–World War II peacemaker were submerged beneath the seas of the Cold War. His more bellicose views in the fifties reflected the book he had written in 1940, *Why England Slept*, an expansion of his

Harvard senior thesis. Kennedy's book found Britain too slow in rearming to resist Nazi Germany. He applied the lesson uncritically to United States–Soviet policies. As a freshman senator in June 1954, he led a Democratic effort to add $350 million to the defense budget to restore two Army divisions that President Eisenhower had cut and thus guarantee "a clear margin of victory over our enemies." [17] Kennedy was challenging Secretary of State John Foster Dulles in his reliance on the massive threat of nuclear weapons. Kennedy's amendment failed, but his commitment to a "flexible" Cold War strategy emphasizing conventional forces and "smaller" nuclear weapons would be carried over into his presidency. It was an illusory policy supported by Democrats that could easily have led to the same global destruction threatened by the Dulles doctrine.

In 1958, Senator John Kennedy delivered a major speech attacking the Eisenhower administration for allowing a "missile gap" to open up between allegedly superior Soviet forces and those of the United States. Kennedy repeated the charge of a missile gap in his successful 1960 presidential campaign, developing it into an argument for increased military spending. When he became president, his science adviser, Jerome Wiesner, informed him in February 1961 that "the missile gap was a fiction"—to which Kennedy replied with a single expletive, "delivered," Wiesner said, "more in anger than in relief." [18] The United States in fact held an overwhelming strategic advantage over the Soviets' missile force.[19] Whether or not Kennedy already suspected the truth, he had taken a Cold War myth, had campaigned on it, and now partly on its basis, was engaged in a dangerous military buildup as president. Marcus Raskin, an early Kennedy administration analyst who left his access to power to become its critic, summarized the ominous direction in which the new president was headed: "The United States intended under Kennedy to develop a war-fighting capability on all levels of violence from thermonuclear war to counterinsurgency." [20]

Yet, as we shall see, Raskin also observed a significant change in Kennedy after the Cuban Missile Crisis, a development of more positive instincts in the president that were already in evidence. Even in his years espousing Cold War principles of defense, Senator Kennedy had occasionally broken ranks with the West on its colonial wars, particularly in Indochina and Algeria. Speaking in the Senate on April 6, 1954, Kennedy critiqued predictions of a U.S.-sponsored French victory in Vietnam over Ho Chi Minh's revolutionary forces. "No amount of American military assistance in Indochina," Kennedy warned in words he would be forced to recall as president, "can conquer an enemy which is everywhere and at the same time nowhere, 'an enemy of the people' which has the sympathy and covert support of the people." [21] In an exchange with Senator Everett Dirksen, Kennedy said he envisioned two peace treaties for Vietnam, "one granting the Vietnamese people complete independence," the other "a tie binding them to the French Union on the basis of full equality." [22]

In 1957 Kennedy came out in support of Algerian independence. That spring he talked with Algerians who were seeking a hearing at the United

Nations for their national liberation movement. In July 1957, he gave a major Senate speech in their support, saying, "No amount of mutual politeness, wishful thinking, nostalgia, or regret should blind either France or the United States to the fact that, if France and the West at large are to have a continuing influence in North Africa . . . the essential first step is the independence of Algeria." [23] The speech created a furor. Kennedy was widely attacked for imperiling the unity of NATO. His biographer, Arthur M. Schlesinger, Jr., wrote of the episode, "Even Democrats drew back. Dean Acheson attacked him scornfully. Adlai Stevenson thought he had gone too far. For the next year or two, respectable people cited Kennedy's Algerian speech as evidence of his irresponsibility in foreign affairs." [24] However, in Europe the speech provoked positive attention, and in Africa excitement.

When Kennedy then became chair of the African Subcommittee, he told the Senate in 1959: "Call it nationalism, call it anti-colonialism, call it what you will, Africa is going through a revolution . . . The word is out—and spreading like wildfire in nearly a thousand languages and dialects—that it is no longer necessary to remain forever poor or in bondage." He there-fore advocated "sympathy with the independence movement, programs of economic and educational assistance and, as the goal of American policy, 'a strong Africa.'" [25] Historians have scarcely noticed JFK's continuing support for a free Africa during his 1960 presidential campaign and in the presi-dency itself, documented in Richard D. Mahoney's comprehensive study *JFK: Ordeal in Africa*.[26]

Equally overlooked, and in tension with his campaign claim of a missile gap, was Kennedy's renewal of his purpose in entering politics: the attain-ment of peace in the nuclear age. As the 1960 primaries increased his presi-dential prospects, Kennedy told a journalist visiting his Senate office that the most valuable resource he could bring to the presidency, based on personal experience, was his horror of war. Kennedy said he "had read the books of great military strategists—Carl Von Clausewitz, Alfred Thayer Mahan, and Basil Henry Liddell Hart—and he wondered if their theories of total vio-lence made sense in the nuclear age. He expressed his contempt for the old military minds, exempting the U.S.'s big three, George Marshall, Douglas MacArthur, and Dwight Eisenhower . . . War with all of its modern horror would be his biggest concern if he got to the White House, Kennedy said." [27]

The journalist who had listened to Senator Kennedy's 1960 reflections on war, Hugh Sidey, wrote thirty-five years later in a retrospective essay: "If I had to single out one element in Kennedy's life that more than anything else influenced his later leadership it would be a horror of war, a total revulsion over the terrible toll that modern war had taken on individuals, nations, and societies, and the even worse prospects in the nuclear age as noted earlier. It ran even deeper than his considerable public rhetoric on the issue." [28]

In his inaugural address on January 20, 1961, John Kennedy's Cold War convictions were interlaced with statements of hope for people around the world who were unaccustomed to having a U.S. president address their concerns. He both inspired and warned them. For example, emerging non-aligned leaders, some of whom received Kennedy's support in the Senate, heard this pledge:

"To those new states whom we welcome to the ranks of the free, we pledge our word that one form of colonial control shall not have passed away merely to be replaced by a far more iron tyranny. We shall not always expect to find them supporting our view. But we shall always hope to find them strongly supporting their own freedom—and to remember that, in the past, those who foolishly sought power by riding the back of the tiger ended up inside." [29]

The new president's tiger parable could cut in opposite directions. What to an American audience was a cunning communist tiger was to nonaligned listeners at least as likely to have capitalist as communist stripes. That would prove to be the case in Kennedy's presidency by his support of U.S. counter-insurgent warfare in South Vietnam, where a client government would then wind up inside the U.S. tiger it had been riding.

One of Kennedy's worst decisions as president would be to develop the role of counterinsurgent warfare by enlarging the U.S. Army's Special Forces, then re-baptizing them as the Green Berets. Kennedy promoted the Green Berets as a response to communist guerrillas, failing to recognize that counterinsurgent warfare would turn into a form of terrorism. The idea that the United States could deploy Green Beret forces in client states "to win the hearts and minds of the people" was a contradiction that would become a negative part of Kennedy's legacy.

In his inaugural address, the new president recognized no such conflict. He combined his pledge to the world's poor with a disclaimer of Cold War motives: "To those peoples in the huts and villages of half the globe strug-gling to break the bonds of mass misery, we pledge our best efforts to help them help themselves, for whatever period is required—not because the com-munists may be doing it, not because we seek their votes, but because it is right."

At the heart of his inaugural, Kennedy turned to the enemy and his own deepest preoccupation, peace: "Finally, to those nations who would make themselves our adversary, we offer not a pledge but a request: that both sides begin anew the quest for peace, before the dark powers of destruc-tion unleashed by science engulf all humanity in planned or accidental self-destruction."

Again there was the warning: "We dare not tempt them with weakness. For only when our arms are sufficient beyond doubt can we be certain beyond doubt that they will never be employed."

And the hope: "Let both sides explore what problems unite us instead of belaboring those problems which divide us . . .

"Let both sides unite to heed in all corners of the earth the command of Isaiah—to 'undo the heavy burdens . . . (and) let the oppressed go free.'"

What is noteworthy about John F. Kennedy's Inaugural Address is that it reflects accurately the profound tensions of his political philosophy. In the nuclear age, how were his experience of the horror of war and his commitment to peacemaking to be reconciled with his passionate resistance to a totalitarian enemy? From the lives he had seen lost in World War II, Kennedy had envisioned in 1945 "the day of the conscientious objector," with an international relinquishing of sovereignty and the abolition of war by popular demand. However, as he took his oath of office, no such day was at hand. Moreover, John Kennedy remained a Cold Warrior in his understanding of the means needed to resist tyranny—armaments that had now gone beyond all measure of destruction. For the sake of both peace and freedom, he therefore had no way out except to negotiate a just peace with the enemy, within the context of the most dangerous political conflict in world history. He would learn just how dangerous it was, from his own side of that conflict, to push through such negotiations.

As the reader knows from the introduction to this book, my perspective on the assassination of President Kennedy comes from the writings of the Trappist monk Thomas Merton, perhaps an unlikely source. The two men's personal histories were worlds apart. While John Kennedy in 1943 was being carried by the movements of a Pacific current, Thomas Merton was a novice monk at the Abbey of Gethsemani in the hills of Kentucky. Yet one can discern a providential hand saving each of their lives for a further purpose. As readers of Merton's autobiography, *The Seven Storey Mountain,* know, the ex-Cambridge and Columbia University man-about-campus came to Gethsemani on currents as unpredictably merciful as those that brought John Kennedy around to his dawn awakening in Blackett Strait and through a series of life-threatening illnesses. What Kennedy half-dreamed that night in the Pacific in relation to the little island his men were on could be said also of Merton's spiritual journey to Gethsemani. He didn't try to get there. He just wanted to, in a heartfelt prayer that had no fixed attachment to its goal. Merton arriving at Gethsemani was like Kennedy stumbling up on the beach and collapsing in the arms of his crew.

In the early sixties, Thomas Merton began responding to the imminent threat of an inconceivable evil, total nuclear war. His writings on the nuclear crisis, which drew him into what he called "the Unspeakable," are an illuminating context in which to view the presidential struggles and Cold War murder of John F. Kennedy. As Merton wrote impassioned articles protesting the nuclear buildup, he became a controversial figure. His alarmed monastic superiors ordered him to stop publishing on peace. Merton was obedient, yet deeply determined to keep articulating a gospel truth, if not in a forbidden format. Even before he experienced the inevitable crackdown on his published work, he had already found another way to follow his conscience—by writing a voluminous series of letters on peace.

For a year at the center of the Kennedy presidency, from October 1961 (shortly after the Berlin crisis) to October 1962 (just after the Cuban Missile Crisis), Merton wrote letters on war and peace to a wide circle of correspondents. They included psychologists Erich Fromm and Karl Stern, poet Lawrence Ferlinghetti, Archbishop Thomas Roberts, Ethel Kennedy, Dorothy Day, Clare Boothe Luce, nuclear physicist Leo Szilard, novelist Henry Miller, Shinzo Hamai, the mayor of Hiroshima, and Evora Arca de Sardinia, the wife of a Cuban exile leader in the CIA-sponsored Bay of Pigs invasion. Merton collected over a hundred of these letters, had them mimeographed and bound, and sent them out to friends in January 1963. He called this informal volume of reflections "The Cold War Letters."

In his preface to the letters, Merton identified the forces in the United States that threatened a nuclear holocaust: "In actual fact it would seem that during the Cold War, if not during World War II, this country has become frankly a warfare state built on affluence, a power structure in which the interests of big business, the obsessions of the military, and the phobias of political extremists both dominate and dictate our national policy. It also seems that the people of the country are by and large reduced to passivity, confusion, resentment, frustration, thoughtlessness and ignorance, so that they blindly follow any line that is unraveled for them by the mass media." [30]

Merton wrote that the protest in his letters was not only against the danger or horror of war. It was "not merely against physical destruction, still less against physical danger, but against a suicidal moral evil and a total lack of ethics and rationality with which international policies tend to be conducted. True," he added, "President Kennedy is a shrewd and sometimes adventurous leader. He means well and has the highest motives, and he is, without doubt, in a position sometimes so impossible as to be absurd." [31]

As we follow "a shrewd and sometimes adventurous leader" on his journey into a deeper darkness than he ever faced in the Pacific, the letters of an observer in a Kentucky monastery will serve as a commentary on a time that placed John Kennedy "in a position sometimes so impossible as to be absurd."

Merton did not always feel such sympathy for President Kennedy. In a critical, prophetic letter a year earlier to his friend W. H. Ferry, he wrote: "I have little confidence in Kennedy, I think he cannot fully measure up to the magnitude of his task, and lacks creative imagination and the deeper kind of sensitivity that is needed. Too much the *Time* and *Life* mentality, than which I can imagine nothing further, in reality, from, say, Lincoln. What is needed is really not shrewdness or craft, but what the politicians don't have: depth, humanity and a certain totality of self forgetfulness and compassion, not just for individuals but for man as a whole: a deeper kind of dedication. Maybe," Merton speculates in an inspired insight, "Kennedy will break through into that someday by miracle. But such people are before long marked out for assassination." [32]

Thomas Merton's sense of what Kennedy needed to break through to, and the likely consequences if he did so, call to mind a scene early in Kennedy's presidency. He had just met with Soviet premier Nikita Khrushchev in Vienna. Late at night on the June 5, 1961, flight back to Washington, the weary president asked his secretary Evelyn Lincoln if she would please file the documents he had been working on. As she started to clear the table, Lincoln noticed a little slip of paper that had fallen on the floor. On it were two lines in Kennedy's handwriting, a favorite saying of his from Abraham Lincoln:

"I know there is a God—and I see a storm coming;

If he has a place for me, I believe that I am ready." [33]

The summit meeting with Khrushchev had deeply disturbed Kennedy. The revelation of a storm coming had occurred at the end of the meeting, as the two men faced each other across a table. Kennedy's gift to Khrushchev, a model of the USS *Constitution*, lay between them. Kennedy pointed out that the ship's cannons had been able to fire half a mile and kill a few people. But if he and Khrushchev failed to negotiate peace, the two of them could kill seventy million people in the opening exchange of a nuclear war. Kennedy looked at Khrushchev. Khrushchev gave him a blank stare, as if to say, "So what?" Kennedy was shocked at what he felt was his counterpart's lack of response. "There was no area of accommodation with him," he said later. [34] Khrushchev may have felt the same way about Kennedy. The result of their unsuccessful meeting would be an ever more threatening conflict. As Evelyn Lincoln thought when she read what the president had written, " 'I see a storm coming' was no idle phrase." [35]

While reflecting that night on such a storm, John Kennedy echoing Lincoln had written first to himself, "I know there is a God." Thomas Merton in his initial sense of Kennedy had doubted if JFK, by falling short of Lincoln's character, was capable of weathering a storm. Kennedy, continuing Lincoln's saying, prayed and hoped that he was: "If [God] has a place for me, I believe that I am ready."

Merton saw that if Kennedy became what he needed to be, he would be "marked out for assassination." How clearly did Kennedy see the dangers to himself of meeting the coming storm as faithfully as he hoped to?

The president's friend Paul Fay, Jr., told of an incident that showed JFK was keenly conscious of the peril of a military coup d'état. One summer weekend in 1962 while out sailing with friends, Kennedy was asked what he thought of *Seven Days in May*, a best-selling novel that described a military takeover in the United States. JFK said he would read the book. He did so that night. The next day Kennedy discussed with his friends the possibility of their seeing such a coup in the United States. Consider that he said these words after the failed Bay of Pigs invasion and before the Cuban Missile Crisis:

"It's possible. It could happen in this country, but the conditions would have to be just right. If, for example, the country had a young President, and he had a Bay of Pigs, there would be a certain uneasiness. Maybe the military would do a little criticizing behind his back, but this would be written off as the usual military dissatisfaction with civilian control. Then if there were another Bay of Pigs, the reaction of the country would be, 'Is he too young and inexperienced?' The military would almost feel that it was their patriotic obligation to stand ready to preserve the integrity of the nation, and only God knows just what segment of democracy they would be defending if they overthrew the elected establishment."

Pausing a moment, he went on, "Then, if there were a third Bay of Pigs, it could happen." Waiting again until his listeners absorbed his meaning, he concluded with an old Navy phrase, "But it won't happen on my watch." [36]

On another occasion Kennedy said of the novel's plot about a few military commanders taking over the country, "I know a couple who might wish they could." [37] The statement is cited by biographer Theodore Sorensen as a joke. However, John Kennedy used humor in pointed ways, and Sorensen's preceding sentence is not a joke: "Communications between the Chiefs of Staff and their Commander in Chief remained unsatisfactory for a large part of his term." [38]

Director John Frankenheimer was encouraged by President Kennedy to film *Seven Days in May* "as a warning to the republic." [39] Frankenheimer said, "The Pentagon didn't want it done. Kennedy said that when we wanted to shoot at the White House he would conveniently go to Hyannis Port that weekend." [40]

As we know, the young president John Kennedy did have a Bay of Pigs. It was a covert project initiated by his predecessor, President Dwight D. Eisenhower.[41] By late summer 1960, when Kennedy became the Democratic nominee for president, the CIA had already begun training fifteen hundred Cuban exile troops at a secret base in Guatemala for an invasion of Cuba.[42] As the new president in March 1961, Kennedy rejected the CIA's current Trinidad Plan for "an amphibious/airborne assault" on Cuba, favoring a quiet landing at night in which there would be "no basis for American military intervention." [43] When a skeptical Kennedy finally approved the CIA's revised plan for the Bay of Pigs landing in April, he reemphasized that he would not intervene by introducing U.S. troops, even if the exile brigade faced defeat on the beachhead. The CIA's covert-action chief, Richard Bissell, reassured him there would be only a minimum need for air strikes and that Cubans on the island would join the brigade in a successful revolt against Castro.[44]

At dawn on April 15, 1961, eight B-26 bombers of the Cuban Expeditionary Force carried out air strikes to destroy the Cuban Air Force on the ground, achieving only partial success. Premier Castro then ordered his pilots "to sleep under the wings of the planes," ready to take off immediately.[45] The next night, as the exile brigade prepared for its overnight landing at the Bay of Pigs, Kennedy's National Security Adviser, McGeorge

Bundy, phoned CIA deputy director General Charles P. Cabell to say that "the dawn air strikes the following morning should not be launched until planes can conduct them from a strip within the beachhead." [46] Since no such opportunity came, this order in effect canceled the air strikes. Castro's army surrounded the invading force in the following days. The exile brigade surrendered on April 19, 1961. More than one thousand members were taken prisoner.[47]

The new president had bitterly disappointed the CIA and the military by his decision to accept defeat at the Bay of Pigs rather than escalate the battle. Kennedy realized after the fact that he had been drawn into a CIA scenario that was a trap. Its authors assumed he would be forced by circumstances to drop his advance restrictions against the use of U.S. combat forces.

How else, he asked his friends Dave Powers and Ken O'Donnell, could the Joint Chiefs have approved such a plan? "They were sure I'd give in to them and send the go-ahead order to the [Navy's aircraft carrier] *Essex*," he said. "They couldn't believe that a new President like me wouldn't panic and try to save his own face. Well, they had me figured all wrong." [48]

The major players in deceiving Kennedy were his CIA advisers, especially Director Allen Dulles. As Arthur M. Schlesinger, Jr., observed, "the Joint Chiefs of Staff had only approved the Bay of Pigs. The CIA had invented it." [49]

At his death Allen Dulles left the unpublished drafts of an article that scholar Lucien S. Vandenbroucke has titled "The 'Confessions' of Allen Dulles." In these handwritten, coffee-stained notes, Dulles explained how CIA advisers who knew better drew John Kennedy into a plan whose prerequisites for success contradicted the president's own rules for engagement that precluded any combat action by U.S. military forces. Although Dulles and his associates knew this condition conflicted with the plan they were foisting on Kennedy, they discreetly kept silent in the belief, Dulles wrote, that "the realities of the situation" would force the president to carry through to the end they wished:

"[We] did not want to raise these issues—in an [undecipherable word] discussion—which might only harden the decision against the type of action we required. We felt that when the chips were down—when the crisis arose in reality, any action required for success would be authorized rather than permit the enterprise to fail." [50] But again, as Kennedy said, "They had me figured all wrong."

Four decades after the Bay of Pigs, we have learned that the CIA scenario to trap Kennedy was more concrete than Dulles admitted in his handwritten notes. A conference on the Bay of Pigs was held in Cuba March 23–25, 2001, which included "ex-CIA operatives, retired military commanders, scholars, and journalists." [51] News analyst Daniel Schorr reported on National Public Radio that "from the many hours of talk and the heaps of declassified secret documents" he had gained one new perception of the Bay of Pigs:

"It was that the CIA overlords of the invasion, director Allen Dulles and deputy Richard Bissell, had their own plan of how to bring the United States into the conflict. It appears that they never really expected an uprising against Castro when the liberators landed as described in their memos to the White House. What they did expect was that the invaders would establish and secure a beachhead, announce the creation of a counterrevolutionary government and appeal for aid from the United States and the Organization of American States. The assumption was that President Kennedy, who had emphatically banned direct American involvement, would be forced by public opinion to come to the aid of the returning patriots. American forces, probably Marines, would come in to expand the beachhead.

"In effect, President Kennedy was the target of a CIA covert operation that collapsed when the invasion collapsed." [52]

Even if President Kennedy had said no at the eleventh hour to the whole Bay of Pigs idea (as he was contemplating doing), the CIA, as it turned out, had a plan to supersede his decision. When the four anti-Castro brigade leaders told their story to writer Haynes Johnson, they revealed how the Agency was prepared to circumvent a presidential veto. The Cubans' chief CIA military adviser, whom they knew only as "Frank," told them what to do if he secretly informed them that the entire project had been blocked by the administration: "If this happens you come here and make some kind of show, as if you were putting us, the advisers, in prison, and you go ahead with the program as we have talked about it, and we will give you the whole plan, even if we are your prisoners." [53]

The brigade leaders said "Frank" was quite specific in his instructions to them for "capturing" their CIA advisers if the administration should attempt to stop the plan: "they were to place an armed Brigade soldier at each American's door, cut communications with the outside, and continue the training until he told them when, and how, to leave for Trampoline base [their assembly point in Nicaragua]." [54] When Robert Kennedy learned of this contingency plan to override the president, he called it "virtually treason." [55]

John Kennedy reacted to the CIA's plotting with a vehemence that went unreported until after his death and has been little noted since then. In a 1966 *New York Times* feature article on the CIA, this statement by JFK appeared without further comment: "President Kennedy, as the enormity of the Bay of Pigs disaster came home to him, said to one of the highest officials of his Administration that he wanted 'to splinter the C.I.A. in a thousand pieces and scatter it to the winds.'" [56]

Presidential adviser Arthur M. Schlesinger, Jr., said the president told him, while the Bay of Pigs battle was still going on, "It's a hell of a way to learn things, but I have learned one thing from this business—that is, that we will have to deal with CIA . . . no one has dealt with CIA." [57]

In his short presidency, Kennedy began to take steps to deal with the CIA. He tried to redefine the CIA's mandate and to reduce its power in his National Security Action Memoranda (NSAMs) 55 and 57, which took military-type operations out of the hands of the CIA. Kennedy's NSAM 55 informed the Joint Chiefs of Staff that it was they (not the CIA) who were his principal military advisers in peacetime as well as wartime. Air Force Colonel L. Fletcher Prouty, who at the time was in charge of providing military support for the CIA's clandestine operations, described the impact of NSAM 55 addressed to General Lyman Lemnitzer, Chairman of the Joint Chiefs:

"I can't overemphasize the shock—not simply the words—that procedure caused in Washington: to the Secretary of State, to the Secretary of Defense, and particularly to the Director of Central Intelligence. Because Allen Dulles, who was still the Director, had just lived through the shambles of the Bay of Pigs and now he finds out that what Kennedy does as a result of all this is to say that, 'you, General Lemnitzer, are to be my Advisor'. In other words, I'm not going to depend on Allen Dulles and the CIA. Historians have glossed over that or don't know about it." [58]

President Kennedy then asked the three principal CIA planners for the Bay of Pigs to resign: Director Allen Dulles, Deputy Director Richard Bissell, Jr., and Deputy Director General Charles Cabell. JFK also "moved quietly," as Schlesinger put it, "to cut the CIA budget in 1962 and again in 1963, aiming at a 20 per cent reduction by 1966." [59] He never managed to splinter the CIA in a thousand pieces and scatter it to the winds. But Kennedy's firing of Dulles, Bissell, and Cabell, his reduction of the CIA budget, and his clear determination to deal with the Agency placed him in direct conflict with a Cold War institution that had come to hold itself accountable to no one.

After John Kennedy's assassination, Allen Dulles returned to prominence in a curious way. Foreign observers, many more familiar than Americans with Dulles's history in assassination plots and the overthrow of governments, wondered at the former CIA director's possible involvement in the murder of the man who had fired him and then tried to rein in the CIA. However, far from being considered a suspect, one week after the assassination Dulles was appointed by the new president Lyndon Johnson to serve on the Warren Commission. He thus directed an investigation that pointed toward himself. [60]

Allen Dulles's own closely guarded feelings toward John Kennedy were revealed years later in a remark to a prospective ghostwriter. *Harper's* young assistant editor Willie Morris had gone to Dulles's Georgetown mansion in Washington to collaborate with him on a piece in defense of the CIA's role in the Bay of Pigs—a never-to-be-published article whose most revealing, handwritten notes would one day be cited in "The 'Confessions' of Allen Dulles." In one discussion they had about President Kennedy, Dulles stunned Morris with an abrupt comment. "That little Kennedy," Dulles said, ". . . he thought he was a god." "Even now," Morris wrote over a quarter of a century later, "those words leap out at me, the only strident ones I would hear from my unlikely collaborator." [61]

The Bay of Pigs awakened President Kennedy to internal forces he feared he might never control. Supreme Court Justice William O. Douglas recalled

Kennedy saying what the Bay of Pigs taught him about the CIA and the Pentagon: "This episode seared him. He had experienced the extreme power that these groups had, these various insidious influences of the CIA and the Pentagon on civilian policy, and I think it raised in his own mind the specter: Can Jack Kennedy, President of the United States, ever be strong enough to really rule these two powerful agencies?" [62]

It was while John Kennedy was being steered into combat by the CIA and the Pentagon at the Bay of Pigs that Thomas Merton was being blocked from publishing his thoughts on nuclear war by his monastic superiors. Merton, like Kennedy, decided to find another way. The words pouring out of Merton's typewriter were spilling over from unpublished manuscripts into his Cold War letters. As he wrote in one such letter to antinuclear archbishop Thomas Roberts, "At present my feeling is that the most urgent thing is to say what has to be said and say it in any possible way. If it cannot be printed, then let it be mimeographed. If it cannot be mimeographed, then let it be written on the backs of envelopes, as long as it gets said." [63]

Thomas Merton saw the Bay of Pigs incident especially through the eyes of one of his Cold War correspondents, Evora Arca de Sardinia in Miami. She wrote to Merton saying that her husband, a leader of the anti-Castro forces in the invasion, had been taken prisoner in Cuba. Merton replied to her on the day he received her letter, May 15, 1961, expressing his "deep compassion and concern in this moment of anguish." [64]

In their subsequent correspondence, Thomas Merton gave spiritual direction to Evora Arca de Sardinia as she became concerned at the divisions and spirit of revenge in the Cuban exile movement. In January 1962 he wrote to her: "The great error of the aggressive Catholics who want to preserve their power and social status at all costs is that they believe this can be done by force, and thus they prepare the way to lose everything they want to save." [65]

While President Kennedy and his brother Attorney General Robert Kennedy were working to raise a ransom to free the Bay of Pigs prisoners, Merton was warning Evora Arca de Sardinia about the militant context in which she was living, which questioned the process of such a ransom. In the Miami Cuba colony, as she had written to Merton, paying a ransom to an evil force (the communist Fidel Castro), even to free their loved ones, was considered a breach of ethics and loyalty.

Merton wrote back: "One thing I have always felt increases the trouble and the sorrow which rack you is the fact that living and working among the Cuban émigrés in Miami, and surrounded by the noise of hate and propaganda, you are naturally under a great stress and in a sense you are 'forced' against your will to take an aggressive and belligerent attitude which your conscience, in its depth, tells you is wrong." [66]

As Merton knew, his concern about a surrounding stress applied not only to his friend in the midst of Cuban émigrés in Miami but to everyone living in Cold War America, a nation whose anti-communism and commitment to nuclear supremacy had placed, for example, its newly elected president "in a position sometimes so impossible as to be absurd."

On December 31, 1961, Merton wrote a letter anticipating the Cuban Missile Crisis ten months later. It was addressed to Clare Boothe Luce, the wife of *Time-Life-Fortune* owner Henry Luce, a Cold War media baron whose editorial policies demonized the communist enemy. Clare Boothe Luce, celebrated speaker, writer, and diplomat, shared Henry Luce's Cold War theology. In 1975 Clare Boothe Luce would lead investigators into the JFK assassination, working for the House Select Committee on Assassinations (HSCA), on a time-consuming wild goose chase based on disinformation. HSCA analyst Gaeton Fonzi discovered that Luce at the time was on the board of directors of the CIA-sponsored Association of Former Intelligence Officers.[67] Even in the early sixties, Merton with his extraordinary sensitivity may have suspected Luce's intelligence connections. In any case he knew her as one of the wealthiest, most influential women in the world, with a decidedly anti-communist mind-set. He welcomed her, as he did one and all, into his circle of correspondents.

In his New Year's Eve letter to Clare Boothe Luce, Merton said he thought the next year would be momentous. "Though 'all manner of things shall be well,'" he wrote, "we cannot help but be aware, on the threshold of 1962, that we have enormous responsibilities and tasks of which we are perhaps no longer capable. Our sudden, unbalanced, top-heavy rush into technological mastery," Merton saw, had now made us servants of our own weapons of war. "Our weapons dictate what we are to do. They force us into awful corners. They give us our living, they sustain our economy, they bolster up our politicians, they sell our mass media, in short we live by them. But if they continue to rule us we will also most surely die by them."[68]

Merton was a cloistered monk who watched no television and saw only an occasional newspaper. However, he had far-flung correspondents and spiritual antennae that were always on the alert. He could thus identify in his letter to Clare Boothe Luce the strategic nuclear issue that would bring humanity to the brink in October 1962: "For [our weapons] have now made it plain that they are the friends of the 'preemptive strike'. They are most advantageous to those who use them first. And consequently nobody wants to be too late in using them second. Hence the weapons keep us in a state of fury and desperation, with our fingers poised over the button and our eyes glued on the radar screen. You know what happens when you keep your eye fixed on something. You begin to see things that aren't there. It is very possible that in 1962 the weapons will tell someone that there has been long enough waiting, and he will obey, and we will all have had it."[69]

"We have to be articulate and sane," Merton concluded, "and speak wisely on every occasion where we can speak, and to those who are willing to listen. That is why for one I speak to you," he said hopefully to Luce. "We have to try to some extent to preserve the sanity of this nation, and keep it from going berserk which will be its destruction, and ours, and perhaps also the destruction of Christendom." [70]

As Merton challenged the Cold War dogmas of Clare Boothe Luce, he was raising similar questions of conscience to another powerfully situated woman, Ethel Kennedy. This was the period in which Merton still had little confidence in John Kennedy. He was nevertheless beginning to catch glimpses of a man who, like himself, was deeply troubled by the prevailing Cold War atmosphere. He began a December 1961 letter to Ethel Kennedy by noting a parallel between JFK's and his own thinking: "I liked very much the President's speech at Seattle which encouraged me a bit as I had just written something along those same lines." [71] Merton was referring to John Kennedy's rejection, like his own, of the false alternatives "Red or dead" in a speech the president gave at the University of Washington in November 1961. Kennedy had said of this false dilemma and those who chose either side of it: "It is a curious fact that each of these extreme opposites resembles the other. Each believes that we have only two choices: appeasement or war, suicide or surrender, humiliation or holocaust, to be either Red or dead." [72]

Merton made an extended analysis of the same Cold War cliché, "Red or dead," in the book his monastic superiors blocked from publication, *Peace in the Post-Christian Era*. There he observed: "We strive to soothe our madness by intoning more and more vacuous cliches. And at such times, far from being as innocuous as they are absurd, empty slogans take on a dreadful power." [73]

The slogan he and Kennedy saw exemplifying such emptiness had begun in Germany in the form, "Better Red than dead." "It was deftly fielded on the first bounce by the Americans," Merton said, "and came back in reverse, thus acquiring an air of challenge and defiance. 'Better dead than Red' was a reply to effete and decadent cynicism. It was a condemnation of 'appeasement'. (Anything short of a nuclear attack on Russia rates as 'appeasement'.)"

What the heroic emptiness of "Better dead than Red" ignored was "the real bravery of patient, humble, persevering labor to effect, step by step, through honest negotiation, a gradual understanding that can eventually relieve tensions and bring about some agreement upon which serious disarmament measures can be based" [74]—precisely what he hoped Ethel Kennedy's brother-in-law would do from the White House. In his letter to her, Merton therefore went on to praise John Kennedy, yet did so while encouraging him to break through Cold War propaganda and speak the truth: "I think that the fact that the President works overtime at trying to get people to face the situation as it really is may be the greatest thing he is doing. Certainly our basic need is for truth, and not for 'images' and slogans that 'engineer consent.' We are living in a dream world. We do not know ourselves or our adversaries. We are myths to ourselves and they are myths to us. And we are secretly persuaded that we can shoot it out like the sheriffs on TV. This is not reality and the President can do a tremendous amount to get people to see the facts, more than any single person." [75]

With inclusive language that did not single out JFK, but again with heavy implications for the president, Merton continued: "We cannot go on indefinitely relying on the kind of provisional framework of a balance of terror. If as Christians we were more certain of our duty, it might put us in a very tight spot politically but it would also merit for us special graces from God, and these we need badly." [76]

Merton was praying that Christians in particular—and a particular Christian, John Kennedy—would become more certain of their duty to take a stand against nuclear terror, which would place JFK especially "in a very tight spot politically." Besides praying, Merton was doing more than writing words of protest on the backs of envelopes. He was appealing to the president, through Ethel Kennedy, for a courageous stand in conscience. Whether or not JFK ever read Merton's graceful letter to his sister-in-law, he would soon have to respond, in October 1962, to "special graces from God" if humanity were to survive.

In the terminology of his own reflection on a military coup, John Kennedy did have a second "Bay of Pigs." The president alienated the CIA and the military a second time by his decisions during the Cuban Missile Crisis.

The Cuban Missile Crisis may have been the most dangerous moment in human history. In the thirteen days from October 16 to 28, 1962, as the Soviet Union installed nuclear-armed missiles in Cuba, President Kennedy demanded publicly that Soviet Premier Nikita Khrushchev dismantle and withdraw the missiles immediately. Kennedy also set up a naval "quarantine" that blockaded Soviet ships proceeding to the island. Ignoring the parallel of the already existing deployment of U.S. missiles in Turkey alongside the Soviet Union, Kennedy declared that the deployment of Soviet missiles in Cuba was "a deliberately provocative and unjustified change in the status quo which cannot be accepted by this country." [77] In spite of Kennedy's militant stand, his and Khrushchev's eventual resolution of the crisis by mutual concessions was not viewed favorably by Cold War hard-liners.

The missile crisis arose because, as Nikita Khrushchev wrote in his memoirs, "we were quite certain that the [Bay of Pigs] invasion was only the beginning and that the Americans would not let Cuba alone." [78] To defend Cuba from the threat of another U.S. invasion, Khrushchev said he "had the idea of installing missiles with nuclear warheads in Cuba without letting the United States find out they were there until it was too late to do anything about them." [79] His strategy was twofold: "The main thing was that the installation of our missiles in Cuba would, I thought, restrain the United States from precipitous military action against Castro's government. In addition to protecting Cuba, our missiles would have equalized what the West likes to call 'the balance of power.' The Americans had surrounded our country with military bases and threatened us with nuclear weapons, and now they would learn just what it feels like to have enemy missiles pointing at you." [80]

Khrushchev's logic overlooked the frenzied mind of Cold War America. As Merton put it in a March 1962 letter, "the first and greatest of all commandments is that America shall not and must not be beaten in the Cold War, and the second is like unto this, that if a hot war is necessary to prevent defeat in the Cold War, then a hot war must be fought even if civilization is to be destroyed." [81] In that context, the discovery of Soviet missiles in Cuba placed President Kennedy in what Merton described as "a position so impossible as to be absurd." In a struggle between good and evil involving world-destructive weapons, the installation of Soviet missiles ninety miles from Florida brought home to Washington the temptation to strike first. Merton's warning to Clare Boothe Luce about a preemptive strike that year was coming true. As the construction of Soviet missile sites in Cuba accelerated, the pressures on President Kennedy for a preemptive U.S. strike became overwhelming. However, Kennedy resisted his advisers' push toward a nuclear war that he told them would obviously be "the final failure." [82]

He secretly taped the White House meetings during the crisis. The tapes were declassified, transcribed, and published in the late 1990s.[83] The transcripts reveal how isolated the president was in choosing to blockade further Soviet missile shipments rather than bomb and invade Cuba. Nowhere does he stand more alone against the pressures for a sudden, massive air strike than in his October 19, 1962, meeting with the Joint Chiefs of Staff. In this encounter the Chiefs' disdain for their young commander-in-chief is embodied by Air Force Chief of Staff General Curtis LeMay, who challenges the president:

> LeMay: "This [blockade and political action] is almost as bad as the appeasement at Munich [a 1938 conference in Munich at which Britain, trying to avoid war with Nazi Germany, compelled Czechoslovakia to cede territory to Hitler] . . . I just don't see any other solution except direct military intervention *right now*."

A historian who has studied the missile crisis tapes for over twenty years, Sheldon Stern, has noted a pause in the conversation at this point, during which the Joint Chiefs "must have held their collective breath waiting for a reaction from the President. The general had gone well beyond merely giving advice or even disagreeing with his commander-in-chief. He had taken their generation's ultimate metaphor for shortsightedness and cowardice, the 1938 appeasement of Hitler at Munich, and flung it in the President's face."

"President Kennedy," Stern says, "in a remarkable display of *sang froid* refused to take the bait; he said absolutely nothing." [84]

Ending the awkward silence, the Navy, Army, and Marine Corps Chiefs of Staff argue for the prompt military action of bombing and invading Cuba. General LeMay breaks in, reminding Kennedy of his strong statements about responding to offensive weapons in Cuba. He almost taunts the president:

LEMAY: "I think that a blockade and political talk would be considered by a lot of our friends and neutrals as bein' a pretty weak response to this. And I'm sure a lot of our own citizens would feel that way, too.

"In other words, you're in a pretty bad fix at the present time."

KENNEDY: "What'd you say?"

LEMAY: "I say, you're in a pretty bad fix."

KENNEDY: [laughing] "You're in with me, personally." [85]

The discussion continues, with Kennedy probing the Chiefs for further information and LeMay pushing the president to authorize a massive attack on Soviet missiles, Cuban air defenses, and all communications systems. As the meeting draws to a close, Kennedy rejects the arguments for a quick, massive attack and thanks his military commanders.

KENNEDY: "I appreciate your views. As I said, I'm sure we all understand how rather unsatisfactory our alternatives are." [86]

A few minutes later, the president leaves the room, but the tape keeps on recording. General LeMay, Army Chief of Staff General Earle Wheeler, and Marine Corps Commandant General David Shoup remain. Shoup, who is usually the most supportive of the Joint Chiefs toward Kennedy, praises LeMay's attack on the president:

SHOUP: "You were a . . . You pulled the rug right out from under him."

LEMAY: "Jesus Christ. What the hell do you mean?"

SHOUP: ". . . He's finally getting around to the word 'escalation.' . . . When *he* says 'escalation,' that's it. If somebody could keep 'em from doing the *goddamn thing* piecemeal, *that's* our problem . . ."

LEMAY: "That's right."

SHOUP: "You're screwed, screwed, screwed. He could say, 'either do the son of a bitch and do it right and quit friggin' around.'"

LEMAY: "That was my contention." [87]

The White House tapes show Kennedy questioning and resisting the mounting pressure to bomb Cuba coming from both the Joint Chiefs and the Executive Committee (ExComm) of the National Security Council. One statement by Robert Kennedy that may have strengthened the president's resolve against a preemptive strike is unheard on the tapes. In his memoir of the missile crisis, *Thirteen Days,* RFK wrote that, while listening to the proposals for attack, he passed a note to the president: "I now know how Tojo felt when he was planning Pearl Harbor." [88]

How John and Robert Kennedy felt together is best conveyed by Robert's description of his brother at one of the most terrible moments of the crisis. On Wednesday, October 24, a report came in that a Soviet submarine was about to be intercepted by U.S. helicopters with depth charges, unless by some miracle the two Soviet ships it was accompanying turned back from the U.S. "quarantine" line. The president feared he had lost all control of the situation and that nuclear war was imminent. Robert looked at his brother:

"His hand went up to his face and covered his mouth. He opened and closed his fist. His face seemed drawn, his eyes pained, almost gray. We stared at each other across the table. For a few fleeting seconds, it was almost as though no one else was there and he was no longer the president.

"Inexplicably, I thought of when he was ill and almost died; when he lost his child; when we learned that our oldest brother had been killed; of personal times of strain and hurt. The voices droned on . . ." [89]

The miracle occurred—through the enemy, Nikita Khrushchev. Khrushchev ordered the Soviet ships to stop dead in the water rather than challenge the U.S. quarantine. At that moment he saved John Kennedy and everyone else.

What moved Khrushchev to his decision? The incident goes unmentioned in his memoirs, as does another, hidden chapter of events that may help to explain it—Nikita Khrushchev's secret correspondence with John Kennedy.

In July 1993, the U.S. State Department, in response to a Freedom of Information Act request by a Canadian newspaper, declassified twenty-one secret letters between John F. Kennedy and Nikita Khrushchev.[90] These private, confidential letters between the Cold War leaders, begun in September 1961 and continued for two years, will be examined here for the bright light they shed on a relationship critical to the world's preservation.

Khrushchev had sent his first private letter to Kennedy on September 29, 1961, during the Berlin crisis. Wrapped in a newspaper, it was brought to Kennedy's press secretary Pierre Salinger at a New York hotel room by a Soviet "magazine editor" and KGB agent, Georgi Bolshakov, whom Khrushchev trusted to maintain silence. The secrecy was at least as much to avoid Soviet attention as American. As presidential aide Theodore Sorensen said three decades later, Khrushchev was "taking his risks, assuming that these letters were, as we believe, being kept secret from the (Soviet) military, from the foreign service, from the top people in the Kremlin. He was taking some risk that if discovered, they would be very unhappy with him." [91]

Khrushchev's first letter was written from a retreat beside the Black Sea. While the Berlin crisis was still not over, the Soviet premier began the correspondence with his enemy by meditating on the beauty of the sea and the threat of war. "Dear Mr. President," he wrote, "At present I am on the shore of the Black Sea . . . This is indeed a wonderful place. As a former Naval officer you would surely appreciate the merits of these surroundings, the beauty of the sea and the grandeur of the Caucasian mountains. Under this bright southern sun it is even somehow hard to believe that there still exist problems in the world which, due to lack of solutions, cast a sinister shadow on peaceful life, on the future of millions of people." [92]

Kennedy had been stunned in Vienna by what he felt was Khrushchev's hardness of heart toward a nuclear war and his unwillingness to compromise. Now as the threat of war over Berlin continued, Khrushchev expressed a regret about Vienna. He said he had "given much thought of late to the development of international events since our meeting in Vienna, and I have decided to approach you with this letter. The whole world hopefully expected that our meeting and a frank exchange of views would have a soothing effect, would turn relations between our countries into the correct channel and promote the adoption of decisions which would give the peoples confidence that at last peace on earth will be secured. To my regret—and, I believe, to yours—this did not happen." [93]

However, Kennedy's abiding hopes for peace, beneath the bellicose rhetoric that he and Khrushchev exchanged publicly, had somehow gotten through to his counterpart. Khrushchev continued with deepening respect:

"I listened with great interest to the account which our journalists Adjubei and Kharlamov gave of the meeting they had with you in Washington. They gave me many interesting details and I questioned them most thoroughly. You prepossessed them by your informality, modesty and frankness which are not to be found very often in men who occupy such a high position."

Again Khrushchev mentioned Vienna, this time as a backdrop to his decision to write such a letter:

"My thoughts have more than once returned to our meetings in Vienna. I remember you emphasized that you did not want to proceed towards war and favored living in peace with our country while competing in the peaceful domain. And though subsequent events did not proceed in the way that could be desired, I thought it might be useful in a purely informal and personal way to approach you and share some of my ideas. If you do not agree with me you can consider that this letter did not exist while naturally I, for my part, will not use this correspondence in my public statements. After all only in confidential correspondence can you say what you think without a backward glance at the press, at the journalists."

"As you see," he added apologetically, "I started out by describing the delights of the Black Sea coast, but then I nevertheless turned to politics. But that cannot be helped. They say that you sometimes cast politics out through the door but it climbs back through the window, particularly when the windows are open." [94]

Khrushchev's first private letter to Kennedy was twenty-six pages long. It did deal passionately with politics, in particular Berlin (where the two leaders backed away from war but never reached agreement) and the civil war in Laos (where they agreed to recognize a neutral government). Even though in the process Khrushchev forgot his Black Sea calm and argued his points with a vengeance, he was as insistent on the fundamental need for peace as Kennedy had been in Vienna. The communist emphasized their common ground with a biblical analogy. Khrushchev liked, he said, the comparison of their situation "with Noah's Ark where both the 'clean' and the 'unclean' found sanctuary. But regardless of who lists himself with the 'clean' and who is considered to be 'unclean,' they are all equally interested in one thing and that is that the Ark should successfully continue its cruise. And we have no other alternative: either we should live in peace and cooperation so that the Ark maintains its buoyancy, or else it sinks." [95]

Kennedy responded privately to Khrushchev on October 16, 1961, from his own place of retreat beside the ocean, Hyannis Port. He began in a similar vein:

"My family has had a home here overlooking the Atlantic for many years. My father and brothers own homes near my own, and my children always have a large group öf cousins for company. So this is an ideal place for me to spend my weekends during the summer and fall, to relax, to think, to devote my time to major tasks instead of constant appointments, telephone calls and details. Thus, I know how you must feel about the spot on the Black Sea from which your letter was written, for I value my own opportunities to get a clearer and quieter perspective away from the din of Washington."

He thanked Khrushchev for initiating the correspondence and agreed to keep it quiet: "Certainly you are correct in emphasizing that this correspondence must be kept wholly private, not to be hinted at in public statements, much less disclosed to the press." Their private letters should supplement public statements "and give us each a chance to address the other in frank, realistic and fundamental terms. Neither of us is going to convert the other to a new social, economic or political point of view. Neither of us will be induced by a letter to desert or subvert his own cause. So these letters can be free from the polemics of the 'cold war' debate."

Kennedy agreed wholeheartedly with Khrushchev's biblical image: "I like very much your analogy of Noah's Ark, with both the 'clean' and the 'unclean' determined that it stay afloat. Whatever our differences, our collaboration to keep the peace is as urgent—if not more urgent—than our collaboration to win the last world war." [96]

After a year of private letters that included more than a little "cold war debate," Kennedy and Khrushchev had by October 1962 not resolved their most dangerous differences. The missile crisis was proof of that. Their mutual respect had given way to mistrust, counter-challenges, and steps toward the war they both abhorred. In the weeks leading up to the crisis, Khrushchev felt betrayed by Kennedy's contingency plans for another Cuba invasion, whereas Kennedy thought Khrushchev was betraying him by sneaking nuclear missiles into Cuba. Both were again acting out Cold War beliefs that threatened everyone on earth. Nevertheless, as they faced each other and issued potentially world-destructive orders, it was still thanks to the Vienna meeting and their secret letters that each knew the other as a human being he could respect. They also knew they had once agreed warmly that the world was a Noah's Ark, where both the "clean" and the "unclean" had to keep it afloat. It was in just such a world, where "clean" and "unclean" were together under a nuclear threat, that Khrushchev stopped his ships dead in the water and the Ark remained afloat.

However, the crisis was not over. Work on the missile sites was in fact speeding up. Pentagon and ExComm advisers increased their pressures on the president for a preventive strike.

On Friday night, October 26, Kennedy received a hopeful letter from Khrushchev in which the Soviet premier agreed to withdraw his missiles. In exchange, Kennedy would pledge not to invade Cuba. However, on Saturday morning, Kennedy received a second, more problematic letter from Khrushchev adding to those terms the demand for a U.S. commitment to remove its analogous missiles from Turkey. In exchange, Khrushchev would pledge not to invade Turkey. Tit for tat.

Kennedy was perplexed. Khrushchev's second proposal was reasonable in its symmetry. However, Kennedy felt he could not suddenly surrender a NATO ally's defenses under a threat, failing to recognize for the moment that he was demanding Khrushchev do the equivalent with his ally Castro.

While the Joint Chiefs pressed their demands on the president for an air strike on Monday, an urgent message arrived heightening those pressures. Early that Saturday morning, a Soviet surface-to-air missile (SAM) had shot down a U-2 reconnaissance plane over Cuba, killing the Air Force pilot, Major Rudolf Anderson, Jr. The Joint Chiefs and ExComm had already recommended immediate retaliation in such a case. They now urged an attack early the next morning to destroy the SAM sites. "There was the feeling," said Robert Kennedy, "that the noose was tightening on all of us, on Americans, on mankind, and that the bridges to escape were crumbling." [97] "But again," he adds, "the President pulled everyone back." [98] JFK called off the Air Force reprisal for the U-2's downing. He continued the search for a peaceful resolution. The Joint Chiefs were dismayed. Robert Kennedy and Theodore Sorensen then drafted a letter accepting Khrushchev's first proposal, while ignoring the later demand that the United States withdraw its missiles from Turkey.

As the war currents swirled around the White House, John and Robert Kennedy met in the Oval Office. Robert described later the thoughts his brother shared with him.

He talked first about Major Anderson and how the brave died while politicians sat home pontificating about great issues. He talked about miscalculations leading to war, a war Russians didn't want any more than Americans did. He wanted to make sure he had done everything conceivable to prevent a terrible outcome, especially by giving the Russians every opportunity for a peaceful settlement that would neither diminish their security nor humiliate them. But "the thought that disturbed him the most," Robert said, "and that made the prospect of war much more fearful than it would otherwise have been, was the specter of the death of the children of this country and all the world—the young people who had no role, who had no say, who knew nothing even of the confrontation, but whose lives would be snuffed out like everyone else's. They would never have a chance to make a decision, to vote in an election, to run for office, to lead a revolution, to determine their own destinies."

"It was this," wrote Robert in a work published after his own assassination, "that troubled him most, that gave him such pain. And it was then that he and Secretary Rusk decided that I should visit with Ambassador Dobrynin and personally convey the President's great concern."[99]

Robert Kennedy's climactic meeting with Soviet Ambassador Anatoly Dobrynin became the moving force for Khrushchev's dramatic announcement that he was withdrawing the missiles. Khrushchev wrote in his memoirs what he thought Robert Kennedy told Dobrynin, who had relayed it to Khrushchev:

"'The President is in a grave situation,' Robert Kennedy said, 'and he does not know how to get out of it. We are under very severe stress. In fact we are under pressure from our military to use force against Cuba . . . We want to ask you, Mr. Dobrynin, to pass President Kennedy's message to Chairman Khrushchev through unofficial channels . . . Even though the President himself is very much against starting a war over Cuba, an irreversible chain of events could occur against his will. That is why the President is appealing directly to Chairman Khrushchev for his help in liquidating this conflict. If the situation continues much longer, the President is not sure that the military will not overthrow him and seize power.'"[100]

After the fall of the Soviet Union, the Russian Foreign Ministry declassified Ambassador Anatoly Dobrynin's October 27, 1962, cable describing his critical one-on-one meeting with Robert Kennedy. Dobrynin's report offers a less dramatic version than Khrushchev's memoirs of Robert Kennedy's words concerning the military pressures on President Kennedy: "taking time to find a way out [of the situation] is very risky. (Here R. Kennedy mentioned as if in passing that there are many unreasonable heads among the generals, and not only among the generals, who 'are itching for a fight.') The situation might get out of control, with irreversible consequences."[101]

In Robert Kennedy's own account of the meeting in *Thirteen Days*, he does not mention telling Dobrynin of the military pressures on the president. However, his friend and biographer Arthur Schlesinger says, whatever the Attorney General said to Dobrynin, RFK was himself of the opinion there were many generals eager for a fight. Robert thought the situation could get totally out of control.[102]

In any case, Khrushchev felt the urgency of the pressures on the president. He responded by withdrawing his missiles.

Is there any evidence U.S. military leaders took advantage of the missile crisis, not to overthrow President Kennedy but to bypass him? Were they trying to trigger a war they felt they could win?

According to political scientist Scott Sagan in his book *The Limits of Safety*, the U.S. Air Force launched an intercontinental ballistic missile from Vandenberg Air Force Base on October 26, 1962, the day before the U-2 was shot down. The ICBM was unarmed, a test missile destined for Kwajalein in the Marshall Islands. The Soviet Union could easily have thought otherwise. Three days before, a test missile at Vandenberg had received a nuclear warhead, changing it to full alert status for the crisis. By October 30, nine Vandenberg "test" missiles were armed for use against the Soviets.[103] At the height of the missile crisis, the Air Force's October 26th launch of its missile could have been seen by the Soviets as the beginning of an attack. It was a dangerous provocation. Had the Soviets been suckered into giving any sign of a launch of their own, the entire array of U.S. missiles and bombers were poised to preempt them. They were already at the top rung of their nuclear war status, DefCon (Defense Condition)-2, totally prepared for a massive strike.

Also at the height of the crisis, as writer Richard Rhodes learned from a retired Air Force commander, "SAC [Strategic Air Command] airborne-alert bombers deliberately flew past their customary turnaround points toward the Soviet Union—an unambiguous threat that Soviet radar operators would certainly have recognized and reported."[104] With their far superior number of missiles and bombers, U.S. forces were prepared for a preemptive attack at the slightest sign of a Soviet response to their provocation. Fortunately the Soviets didn't bite.

President Kennedy had reason to feel he was being circumvented by the military so they could win a nuclear showdown. Kennedy may also have recalled that Khrushchev, in his second secret letter to the president, on November 9, 1961, regarding Berlin, had hinted that belligerent pressures in Moscow made compromise difficult from his own side. "You have to understand," he implored Kennedy, "I have no ground to retreat further, there is a precipice behind."[105] Kennedy had not pushed him. Now there was a precipice behind Kennedy, and Khrushchev understood.

Khrushchev recalled the conclusion of Dobrynin's report as Robert Kennedy's words, "I don't know how much longer we can hold out against our generals."[106] Since Khrushchev had also just received an urgent message from Castro that a U.S. attack on Cuba was "almost imminent,"[107] he hastened to respond: "We could see that we had to reorient our position swiftly ... We sent the Americans a note saying that we agreed to remove our missiles and bombers on the condition that the President give us his assurance that there would be no invasion of Cuba by the forces of the United States or anybody else."[108]

Kennedy agreed, and Khrushchev began removing the Soviet missiles. The crisis was over.[109] Neither side revealed that, as part of the agreement, on the analogous issue of U.S. missiles in Turkey Robert Kennedy had in fact promised Anatoly Dobrynin that they, too, would be withdrawn but not immediately.[110] It could not be done unilaterally at a moment's notice. The promise was fulfilled. Six months later the United States took its missiles out of Turkey.

Twenty-five years after the missile crisis, Secretary of State Dean Rusk would reveal that President Kennedy was prepared to make a further concession to Khrushchev in order to avoid war. Rusk said that on October 27, after Robert Kennedy left to meet Dobrynin, the president "instructed me to telephone the late Andrew Cordier, then [president] at Columbia University, and dictate to him a statement which would be made by U Thant, the Secretary General of the United Nations [and a friend of Cordier], proposing the removal of the Jupiters [in Turkey] and the missiles in Cuba. Mr. Cordier was to put that statement in the hands of U Thant only after further signal from us."[111] Rusk phoned the statement to Cordier. However, when Khrushchev accepted Robert Kennedy's promise to Dobrynin that the Jupiter missiles would be removed, Kennedy's further readiness for a public trade mediated by U Thant became unnecessary. The president's willingness to go that extra mile with Khrushchev, at a heavy political cost to himself, shocked the former ExComm members to whom Rusk revealed it for the first time at the Hawk's Cay (Florida) Conference on March 7, 1987.

The extent to which Kennedy's willingness to trade away missiles with Khrushchev was beyond political orthodoxy at the time can be illustrated by my own experience. In May 1963 I wrote an article on Pope John XXIII's encyclical *Pacem in Terris*. It was published by Dorothy Day in her radically pacifist *Catholic Worker* newspaper. The article said that, in harmony with Pope John's theme of increasing mutual trust as the basis for peace, the United States should have resolved the Cuban Missile Crisis by negotiating a mutual withdrawal of missile bases with the Soviet Union. Unknown to Dorothy Day and myself, our politically unacceptable view was what President Kennedy had committed himself to doing in the midst of that crisis, at whatever political cost, and had in fact carried through secretly with Nikita Khrushchev.[112]

How close did the United States and the Soviet Union come to a nuclear holocaust?

From the Joint Chiefs' standpoint, not close enough. The only real danger, they thought, came from the President's lack of will in not attacking the Russians in Cuba.

At the October 19 meeting between the president and the Chiefs, when General LeMay argued for a surprise attack on the Russian missiles as soon as possible, President Kennedy had asked him skeptically, "What do you think their reprisal would be?"

LeMay said there would be no reprisal so long as Kennedy warned Khrushchev that he was ready to fight also in Berlin.

After Admiral George Anderson made the same point, Kennedy said sharply, "They can't let us just take out, after all their statements, take out their missiles, kill a lot of Russians, and not do . . . not do anything."[113]

After the meeting, the President recounted the conversation to his aide Dave Powers and said, "Can you imagine LeMay saying a thing like that? These brass hats have one great advantage in their favor. If we listen to them, and do what they want us to do, none of us will be alive later to tell them that they were wrong."[114]

In a conversation that fall with his friend John Kenneth Galbraith, Kennedy again spoke angrily of the reckless pressures his advisers, both military and civilian, had put on him to bomb the Cuban missile sites. "I never had the slightest intention of doing so," said the president.[115]

Thirty years after the crisis, Kennedy's Defense Secretary Robert McNamara was surprised to learn the contents of a November 1992 article in the Russian press. The article revealed that at the height of the crisis Soviet forces in Cuba had possessed a total of 162 nuclear warheads. The more critical strategic fact, unknown to the United States at the time, was that these weapons were ready to be fired. On October 26, 1962, the day before the U-2 was shot down, the nuclear warheads in Cuba had been prepared for launching. Enlightened by this knowledge, McNamara wrote in his memoirs:

"Clearly, there was a high risk that, in the face of a U.S. attack—which, as I have said, many in the U.S. government, military and civilian alike, were prepared to recommend to President Kennedy—the Soviet forces in Cuba would have decided to use their nuclear weapons rather than lose them.

"We need not speculate about what would have happened in that event. We can predict the results with certainty . . . And where would it have ended? In utter disaster." [116]

In the climactic moments of the Cold War, John Kennedy's resistance to pressures for a first strike, combined with Nikita Khrushchev's quick understanding and retreat, saved the lives of millions of people, perhaps the life of the planet.

In those days, however, when compromise was regarded as treason, U.S. military leaders were not pleased by the Kennedy-Khrushchev resolution of the crisis. The Joint Chiefs of Staff were outraged at Kennedy's refusal to attack Cuba and even his known concessions to Khrushchev. McNamara recalled how strongly the Chiefs expressed their feelings to the president. "After Khrushchev had agreed to remove the missiles, President Kennedy invited the Chiefs to the White House so that he could thank them for their support during the crisis, and there was one hell of a scene. LeMay came out saying, 'We lost! We ought to just go in there today and knock 'em off!' " [117]

Robert Kennedy was also struck by the Chiefs' anger at the president. "Admiral [George] Anderson's reaction to the news," he said, "was 'We have been had.' " [118]

"The military are mad," President Kennedy told Arthur Schlesinger, "They wanted to do this." [119] Yet as angry as the Chiefs were at Kennedy's handling of the missile crisis, their anger would deepen in the following year. They would witness a Cold War president not only refusing their first-strike mandate but also turning decisively toward peace with the enemy.

On Sunday morning, October 28, after Kennedy and Khrushchev had agreed mutually to withdraw their most threatening missiles, JFK went to Mass in Washington to pray in thanksgiving. As he and Dave Powers were about to get into the White House car, Kennedy looked at Powers and said, "Dave, this morning we have an extra reason to pray." [120]

At the Abbey of Gethsemani, Thomas Merton's response to the Cuban Missile Crisis was also a prayer of thanksgiving. He wrote Daniel Berrigan:

"As for Cuba, well thank God we escaped the results of our own folly this time. We excel in getting ourselves into positions where we 'have to' press the button, or the next thing to it. I realize more and more that this whole war question is nine-tenths our own fabricated illusion . . . I think Kennedy has enough sense to avoid the worst injustices, he acts as if he knew the score. But few others seem to." [121]

Regarding the president's handling of the crisis, Merton wrote Etta Gullick in England: "Of course things being what they were, Kennedy hardly had any alternative. My objection is to things being as they are, through the stupidity and shortsightedness of politicians who have no politics." [122]

To Ethel Kennedy he said further: "The Cuba business was a close call, but in the circumstances I think JFK handled it very well. I say in the circumstances, because only a short-term look at it makes one very happy. It was a crisis and something had to be done and there was only a choice of various evils. He chose the best evil, and it worked. The whole thing continues to be nasty." [123]

On Sunday afternoon, October 28, with the crisis over, Robert Kennedy returned to the White House and talked with the president for a long time. When Robert got ready to leave, John said, in reference to the death of Abraham Lincoln, "This is the night I should go to the theater." His brother replied, "If you go, I want to go with you." [124] They would both go soon.

John Kennedy's third Bay of Pigs was his Commencement Address at American University in Washington. *Saturday Review* editor Norman Cousins summed up the significance of this remarkable speech: "At American University on June 10, 1963, President Kennedy proposed an end to the Cold War." [125]

The Cold Warrior John F. Kennedy was turning, in the root biblical sense of the word "turning"—*teshuvah* in the Hebrew Scriptures, *metanoia* in the Greek, "repentance" in English. In the Cuban Missile Crisis John Kennedy as president of the United States had begun to turn away from, to repent from, his own complicity with the worst of U.S. imperialism—its willingness to destroy the world in order to "save it" from Communism. Nevertheless, in the process of turning from the brink, Kennedy seemed unable to begin walking in a new direction.

In the aftermath of the missile crisis, he was alternately hopeful and frustrated. The imminence of holocaust had pushed him and Khrushchev toward a new commitment to negotiations. Yet in the months following the crisis, the Cold War opponents seemed unable to seize the moment.

They agreed that a ban on nuclear testing was a critical next step away from the brink. Yet both men had a history of conducting nuclear tests that contaminated the atmosphere and heightened the tensions between them. In response to the Soviet Union's nuclear tests in the summer of 1961, Kennedy had resumed U.S. atmospheric tests on April 25, 1962. The United States then carried out a series of twenty-four nuclear blasts in the South Pacific from April to November of 1962.[126]

In the context of their precarious resolution of the missile crisis and their tit-for-tat nuclear testing, Kennedy and Khrushchev struggled to agree on a test ban. Khrushchev said the United States was using its condition of on-site inspections as a strategy for spying on the U.S.S.R. For the sake of peace, he had already agreed to the U.S. position of three annual inspections, only to see the Americans suddenly demand more. Kennedy said Khrushchev had mistaken the original U.S. position. Khrushchev replied pointedly through an intermediary:

"You can tell the President I accept his explanation of an honest misunderstanding and suggest that we get moving. But the next move is up to him."[127]

Kennedy accepted Khrushchev's challenge. His American University address broke the deadlock by transforming the context. By the empathy he expressed toward the Russian perspective, Kennedy created a bridge to Khrushchev. They would then have five and a half months left to make peace before JFK's murder. At the same time as Kennedy's speech reached out to Khrushchev, it opened a still wider chasm between the president and his own military and intelligence advisers. To the Pentagon and CIA, the president's words of peace at American University seemed to put him on the enemy's side.

Their resistance to Kennedy's stand can be understood from the standpoint of the independent power base they had developed during the Cold War. We have already seen how President Truman exulted at the bombing of Hiroshima. From a failure to internalize the suffering beneath the mushroom clouds at Hiroshima and Nagasaki, the Truman administration began an era of atomic diplomacy based on hubris. Truman, supremely confident because he had unilateral possession of the atomic bomb, tried to dictate postwar terms in Eastern Europe to the Soviet Union. A month after Hiroshima, the Soviets rejected U.S. demands backed by the bomb at the London Council of Foreign Ministers. John Foster Dulles, who attended the London meeting, regarded it as the beginning of the Cold War.[128] President Truman then announced in September 1945 that he was not interested in seeking international control over nuclear weapons. If other nations wanted to "catch up" with the United States, he said, "they [would] have to do it on their own hook, just as we did." Truman agreed with a friend's comment on the implications of this policy: "Then Mister President, what it amounts to is this. That the armaments race is on."[129]

Truman continued to use the bomb as a threat to force Soviet concessions. He felt he did so successfully in Iran just seven months after Hiroshima and Nagasaki. The Russian army was prolonging a wartime occupation in northern Iran, seeking Soviet oil leases like those of the British in the south. Truman later told Senator Henry Jackson that he had summoned Soviet Ambassador Andrei Gromyko to the White House. The president demanded that the Russian troops evacuate Iran within forty-eight hours or the United States would use the atomic weapon that only it possessed. "We're going to drop it on you," he told Gromyko. The troops moved in twenty-four hours.[130]

On a wider front, the United States enforced a Cold War strategy of containing the Soviet Union. The containment policy was formulated by State Department diplomat George Kennan, writing as "X" in the July 1947 *Foreign Affairs*. Although Kennan said the purpose of containment was more diplomatic and political than military, the Pentagon carried it out by encircling the U.S.S.R. with U.S. bases and patrolling forces.

To match the efficiency of a totalitarian enemy, U.S. military leaders urged legislation that would mobilize the nation to a state of constant readiness for war. Thus the National Security Act of 1947 laid the foundations of a national security state: the National Security Council (NSC), the National Security Resources Board (NSRB), the Munitions Board, the Research and Development Board, the Office of the Secretary of Defense, the Joint Chiefs of Staff, and the Central Intelligence Agency (CIA).[131] Before the act was passed, Secretary of State George Marshall warned President Truman that it granted the new intelligence agency in particular powers that were "almost unlimited,"[132] a criticism of the CIA that Truman would echo much too late—soon after the assassination of John Kennedy.

On June 18, 1948, Truman's National Security Council took a further step into a CIA quicksand and approved top-secret directive NSC 10/2, which sanctioned U.S. intelligence to carry out a broad range of covert operations: "propaganda, economic warfare, preventive direct action including sabotage, anti-sabotage, demolition and evacuation measures; subversion against hostile states including assistance to underground resistance movements, guerrillas, and refugee liberation groups."[133] The CIA was now empowered to be a paramilitary organization. George Kennan, who sponsored NSC 10/2, said later in the light of history that it was "the greatest mistake I ever made."[134]

Since NSC 10/2 authorized violations of international law, it also established official lying as their indispensable cover. All such activities had to be "so planned and executed that any US government responsibility for them is not evident to unauthorized persons, and that if uncovered the US government can plausibly deny any responsibility for them."[135] The national security doctrine of "plausible deniability" combined lying with hypocrisy. It marked the creation of a Frankenstein monster.

Plausible deniability encouraged the autonomy of the CIA and other covert-action ("intelligence") agencies from the government that created them. In order to protect the visible authorities of the government from protest and censure, the CIA was authorized not only to violate international law but to do so with as little consultation as possible. CIA autonomy went hand in glove with plausible deniability. The less explicit an order from the president, the better it was for "plausible deniability." And the less consultation there was, the more creative CIA authorities could become in interpreting the mind of the president, especially the mind of a president so uncooperative that he wanted to splinter the CIA in a thousand pieces and scatter it to the winds.

At the 1975 Senate hearings on U.S. intelligence operations chaired by Senator Frank Church, CIA officials testified reluctantly on their efforts to kill Fidel Castro. In late 1960, without the knowledge of President Dwight Eisenhower, the CIA had contacted underworld figures John Rosselli, Sam Giancana, and Santos Trafficante, offering them $150,000 for Castro's assassination.[136] The gangsters were happy to be hired by the U.S. government to murder the man who had shut down their gambling casinos in Cuba. If they were successful, they hoped a U.S.-sponsored successor to Castro would allow them to reopen the casinos.

In the spring of 1961, without the knowledge of the new president John Kennedy, the CIA's Technical Services Division prepared a batch of poison pills for Castro. The pills were sent to Cuba through John Rosselli. The murder plot failed because the CIA's Cuban assets were unable to get close enough to Castro to poison him.[137] The CIA's purpose was to kill Castro just before the Bay of Pigs invasion. As Bay of Pigs planner Richard Bissell said later, "Assassination was intended to reinforce the [invasion] plan. There was the thought that Castro would be dead before the landing. Very few, however, knew of this aspect of the plan." [138]

After President Kennedy fired Bissell from the CIA for his role in the Bay of Pigs, Richard Helms, his successor as Deputy Director of Plans, took up where Bissell had left off in conspiring to kill Castro. Helms testified to the Church Committee that he never informed either the president or his newly appointed CIA director John McCone of the assassination plots. Nor did he inform any other officials in the Kennedy administration. Helms said he sought no approval for the murder attempts because assassination was not a subject that should be aired with higher authority.[139] When he was asked if President Kennedy had been informed, Helms said that "nobody wants to embarrass a President of the United States by discussing the assassination of foreign leaders in his presence." [140] He also didn't seek the approval of the Special Group Augmented that oversaw the anti-Castro program because, he said, "I didn't see how one would have expected that a thing like killing or murdering or assassination would become a part of a large group of people sitting around a table in the United States Government." [141]

John McCone and the other surviving members of the Kennedy Administration testified that "assassination was outside the parameters of the Administration's anti-Castro program." [142] Yet Richard Helms and other CIA insiders kept running assassination plots in conflict with the president's wishes.

In November 1961, seven months after the Bay of Pigs invasion, John Kennedy asked journalist Tad Szulc in a private conversation in the Oval Office, "What would you think if I ordered Castro to be assassinated?" The startled

Szulc said he was against political assassination in principle and in any case doubted if it would solve the Cuban problem. The president leaned back in his rocking chair, smiled, and said he had been testing Szulc and agreed with his answer. Kennedy said "he was under great pressure from advisors in the Intelligence Community (whom he did not name) to have Castro killed, but that he himself violently opposed it on the grounds that for moral reasons the United States should never be party to political assassinations."

"I'm glad you feel the same way," Kennedy told Szulc.[143]

Richard Helms, however, did not feel the same way. Helms was known as "the man who kept the secrets," the title of his biography.[144] He was a master of the possibilities beneath plausible deniability, exemplified by his command and control of the CIA's plots to kill Castro. As Helms demonstrated in his Church Committee testimony, he and other CIA Cold War veterans thought they knew the president's mind better than the president did himself. This assumed responsibility became a problem for the CIA and its Pentagon allies when President Kennedy acted with a mind of his own and decided to end the Cold War.

In the weeks leading up to his American University address, Kennedy prepared the ground carefully for the leap of peace he planned to take. He first joined British Prime Minister Harold MacMillan in proposing to Khrushchev new high-level talks on a test ban treaty. They suggested that Moscow be the site for the talks, itself an act of trust. Khrushchev accepted.

To reinforce the seriousness of the negotiations, Kennedy decided to suspend U.S. tests in the atmosphere unilaterally. Surrounded by Cold War advisers, he reached his decision independently—without their recommendations or consultation. He knew few would support him as he went out on that limb; others might cut it down before he could get there. He announced his unilateral initiative at American University, as a way of jump-starting the test-ban negotiations.

In both speech and action, Kennedy was trying to reverse eighteen years of U.S.–Soviet polarization. He had seen U.S. belligerence toward the Russians build to the point of Pentagon pressures for preemptive strikes on the Cuban missile sites. In his decision in the spring of 1963 to turn from a demonizing Cold War theology, Kennedy knew he had few allies within his own ruling circles.

He outlined his thoughts for what he called "the peace speech" to adviser and speechwriter Sorensen, and told him to go to work. Only a handful of advisers knew anything about the project. Arthur Schlesinger, who was one of them, said, "We were asked to send our best thoughts to Ted Sorensen and to say nothing about this to anybody."[145] On the eve of the speech, Soviet officials and White House correspondents were alerted in general terms. The speech, they were informed, would be of major importance.[146]

On June 10, 1963, President Kennedy introduced his subject to the graduating class at American University as "the most important topic on earth: world peace."

"What kind of peace do I mean?" he asked, "What kind of peace do we seek?"

"Not a Pax Americana enforced on the world by American weapons of war. Not the peace of the grave or the security of the slave. I am talking about genuine peace, the kind of peace that makes life on earth worth living, the kind that enables men and nations to grow and to hope and to build a better life for their children—not merely peace for Americans but peace for all men and women—not merely peace in our time but peace for all time." [147]

Kennedy's rejection of "a Pax Americana enforced on the world by American weapons of war" was an act of resistance to what President Eisenhower had identified in his Farewell Address as the military-industrial complex. "This conjunction of an immense military establishment and a large arms industry," Eisenhower had warned three days before Kennedy's inauguration, "is new in the American experience. The total influence—economic, political, even spiritual—is felt in every city, every State house, every office of the Federal government . . ."

"In the councils of government, we must guard against the acquisition of unwarranted influence, whether sought or unsought, by the military-industrial complex. The potential for the disastrous rise of misplaced power exists and will persist." [148]

What Eisenhower in the final hours of his presidency revealed as the greatest threat to our democracy Kennedy in the midst of his presidency chose to resist. The military-industrial complex was totally dependent on "a Pax Americana enforced on the world by American weapons of war." That Pax Americana policed by the Pentagon was considered the system's indispensable, hugely profitable means of containing and defeating Communism. At great risk Kennedy was rejecting the foundation of the Cold War system.

In his introduction at American University, President Kennedy noted the standard objection to the view he was opening up: What about the Russians?

"Some say that it is useless to speak of world peace or world law or world government—and that it will be useless until the leaders of the Soviet Union adopt a more enlightened attitude. I hope they do. I believe we can help them do it."

He then countered our own prejudice with what Schlesinger called "a sentence capable of revolutionizing the whole American view of the cold war": "But I also believe that we must reexamine our own attitude—as individuals and as a Nation—for our attitude is as essential as theirs."

Kennedy's turn here corresponds to the Gospel insight: "Why do you see the speck in your neighbor's eye, but do not notice the log in your own eye?" (Luke 6:41).

The nonviolent theme of the American University Address is that self-examination is the beginning of peace. Kennedy was proposing to the American University graduates (and the national audience behind them) that they unite this inner journey of peace with an outer journey that could transform the Cold War landscape.

"Every graduate of this school, every thoughtful citizen who despairs of war and wishes to bring peace, should begin by looking inward—by examining his own attitude toward the possibilities of peace, toward the Soviet Union, toward the course of the cold war and toward freedom and peace here at home."

Thus ended Kennedy's groundbreaking preamble, an exhortation to personal and national self-examination as the spiritually liberating way to overcome Cold War divisions and achieve "not merely peace in our time but peace for all time." In his American University address, John Kennedy was proclaiming a way out of the Cold War and into a new human possibility.

One pawn in the Cold War who needed a way out before it was too late was a young ex-Marine, Lee Harvey Oswald.

In following Kennedy's path through a series of critical conflicts, we have been moving more deeply into the question: Why was John F. Kennedy murdered? Now as we begin to trace Oswald's path, which will converge with Kennedy's, we can see the emergence of a strangely complementary question: Why was Lee Harvey Oswald so tolerated and supported by the government he betrayed?

On October 31, 1959, Lee Harvey Oswald, who had been discharged two months earlier from the U.S. Marine Corps in California, presented himself at the American Embassy in Moscow to Consul Richard E. Snyder. Oswald said his purpose in coming was to renounce his U.S. citizenship. He handed Snyder a note he had written, in which he requested that his citizenship be revoked and affirmed that "my allegiance is to the Union of Soviet Socialist Republics." [149] According to the Warren Report, "Oswald stated to Snyder that he had voluntarily told Soviet officials that he would make known to them all information concerning the Marine Corps and his specialty therein, radar operation, as he possessed." [150] To the Soviet officials who received his offer, Oswald said he "intimated that he might know something of special interest." [151]

The Soviets had reason to think Oswald knew "something of special interest." From September 1957 to November 1958 Oswald had been a Marine Corps radar operator at Atsugi Air Force Base in Japan. Atsugi, located about thirty-five miles southwest of Tokyo, served as the CIA's main operational base in the Far East. It was one of two bases from which the CIA's top-secret U-2 spy planes took off on their flights over the Soviet Union and China. The U-2 was the creation of the CIA's Richard Bissell, also the main author of the Bay of Pigs scenario. Bissell worked closely on the U-2's Soviet overflights with CIA director Allen Dulles. Radar operator Oswald was a small cog in the machine, but he was learning how it worked. From his radar control room at Atsugi, where he had a "crypto" clearance (higher than "top secret"), Oswald listened regularly to the U-2's radio communications. [152]

After Atsugi, Oswald was reassigned as a radar operator to Marine Air

Control Squadron No. 9 in Santa Ana, California, which was attached to the larger Marine Air Station in El Toro. Oswald continued to have access to secret information that would have been of interest to a Cold War enemy. Former Marine Corps Lieutenant John E. Donovan, who was Oswald's officer in the Santa Ana radar unit, testified to the Warren Commission that Oswald "had the access to the location of all bases in the west coast area, all radio frequencies for all squadrons, all tactical call signs, and the relative strength of all squadrons, number and type of aircraft in a squadron, who was the commanding officer, the authentication code of entering and exiting the ADIZ, which stands for Air Defense Identification Zone. He knew the range of our radar. He knew the range of our radio. And he knew the range of the surrounding units' radio and radar."[153]

However, Donovan's knowledge of Oswald's connection to the top-secret U-2 was clearly off limits for his Warren Commission questioners. Their avoidance of the U-2 puzzled Donovan. Wasn't Oswald's possible access to top-secret U-2 information a critical issue to probe in relation to his defection? Donovan told author John Newman years later that, at the end of his testimony, he asked a Warren Commission lawyer, "Don't you want to know anything about the U-2?" The lawyer said, "We asked you exactly what we wanted to know from you and we asked you everything we wanted for now and that is all. And if there is anything else we want to ask you, we will." Donovan asked a fellow witness who also knew Oswald's U-2 connection, "Did they ask you about the U-2?" He said, "No, not a thing."[154]

On May 1, 1960, six months after Oswald defected to the Soviet Union, a U-2 was shot down by the Soviets for the first time. The downing of the U-2, piloted by Francis Gary Powers, wrecked the Paris summit meeting between President Eisenhower and Premier Khrushchev. Gary Powers later raised the question whether his plane may not have been shot down as a result of information Oswald handed over to the Soviets.[155] Powers's question was at least reasonable. It reinforces the case that Oswald's volunteering all the information he had as a Marine radar specialist to the Soviets was an apparently criminal act.

Yet when Oswald returned to the U.S. Embassy in Moscow after working for over a year at a Soviet factory in Minsk, he was welcomed back by American officials with open arms. Not only did the United States make no move to prosecute him, but the embassy gave him a loan to return to the country he had betrayed.[156] The toleration of Oswald's apparent treason extended to his later obtaining a new passport overnight. On June 25, 1963, Oswald was miraculously issued a passport in New Orleans twenty-four hours after his application.[157] He identified his destination as the Soviet Union.[158]

After analyzing this strange history in her classic work on the Warren Commission, *Accessories after the Fact*, Sylvia Meagher concluded: "Decision after decision, the [State] Department removed every obstacle before Oswald—a defector and would-be expatriate, self-declared enemy of his native country, self-proclaimed discloser of classified military information, and later self-appointed propagandist for Fidel Castro—on his path from Minsk to Dallas."[159]

The process would, of course, be reversed in Dallas. There Oswald would be arrested and killed quickly, before he could say what he knew of the president's murder. In Dallas whatever light Oswald might cast on the assassination would be switched at once into darkness.

The Warren Commission dealt with the U.S. government's odd toleration of the apparently treasonous Oswald, first of all, by a selective reading of his history. When the authors of the *Warren Report* mentioned Oswald's work in the Marine Corps as a radar operator, they neglected to point out that the future defector had a "Crypto" clearance, which was higher than "Top Secret," and that his work immersed him in information about the CIA's super-secret U-2 flights.[160] By omitting such facts, the government's story was able to sidestep questions arising from Oswald's offer of U-2 information to the Soviet Union, his defection to that Cold War enemy, and his wondrous acceptance back into the good graces of the U.S. government.

According to the *Warren Report*, Lee Harvey Oswald had been a lone assassin in the making for years, "moved by an overriding hostility to his environment."[161] In the government's story, Oswald became a defector to Russia, a Fair Play For Cuba Committee demonstrator in New Orleans, and a presidential assassin for psychological reasons: "He does not appear to have been able to establish meaningful relationships with other people. He was perpetually disconnected with the world around him. Long before the assassination he expressed his hatred for American society and acted in protest against it."[162] The *Warren Report* portrayed Oswald as a young man alienated from society who then became an angry Marxist, abandoned his country, and killed its president. In the *Report*'s conclusion on Oswald's motivation, the commission attributed his assassin's impulse to a megalomania tinged with Marxism: "He sought for himself a place in history—a role as the 'great man' who would be recognized as having been in advance of his times. His commitment to Marxism and communism appears to have been another important factor in his motivation."[163]

If we turn from *Warren Report* psychology to Cold War history, why was the ex-Marine Lee Harvey Oswald not arrested and charged a year and a half before the assassination when he came back to the United States from the Soviet Union, where he had announced at the American Embassy in Moscow that he would hand over military secrets (about U-2 flights) to the Soviets? Whereas in Dallas Oswald would be arrested and murdered before we knew it, on his preceding odyssey as a traitor in and out of Russia and back to the United States he overcame government barriers with an almost supernatural ease. What was the secret of Oswald's immunity to prosecution for having criminally betrayed the United States at the height of the Cold War? How did this unrepentant enemy of his country merit treatment as a prodigal son, embraced by his government with financial help and preferential passport rulings while he continued to proclaim allegiance to the USSR and Cuba?

A solution to the mystery was suggested by former CIA agent Victor Marchetti, who resigned from the Agency in disillusionment after being executive assistant to the Deputy Director. The CIA fought a legal battle to suppress Marchetti's book *The CIA and the Cult of Intelligence*. In regard to Oswald, Marchetti told author Anthony Summers of a CIA-connected Naval intelligence program in 1959, the same year Oswald defected to the USSR: "At the time, in 1959, the United States was having real difficulty in acquiring information out of the Soviet Union; the technical systems had, of course, not developed to the point that they are at today, and we were resorting to all sorts of activities. One of these activities was an ONI [Office of Naval Intelligence] program which involved three dozen, maybe forty, young men who were made to appear disenchanted, poor American youths who had become turned off and wanted to see what communism was all about. Some of these people lasted only a few weeks. They were sent into the Soviet Union, or into eastern Europe, with the specific intention the Soviets would pick them up and 'double' them if they suspected them of being U.S. agents, or recruit them as KGB agents. They were trained at various naval installations both here and abroad, but the operation was being run out of Nag's Head, North Carolina." [164]

The counterintelligence program described by Marchetti dovetails with the Oswald story. It provides an explanation for the U.S. government's indulgence of his behavior. That Oswald was in fact a participant in such a program was the belief of James Botelho, his former roommate in Santa Ana. Botelho, who later became a California judge, stated in an interview with Mark Lane that Oswald's Communism was a pose. Botelho said: "I'm very conservative now [in 1978] and I was at least as conservative at that time. Oswald was not a Communist or a Marxist. If he was I would have taken violent action against him and so would many of the other Marines in the unit." [165]

Judge Botelho said Oswald's "defection" was nothing but a U.S. intelligence ploy: "I knew Oswald was not a Communist and was, in fact, anti-Soviet. Then, when no real investigation occurred at the base [after Oswald's presence in the Soviet Union was made public], I was sure that Oswald was on an intelligence assignment in Russia . . . Two civilians dropped in [at Santa Ana], asked a few questions, took no written statements, and recorded no interviews with witnesses. It was the most casual of investigations. It was a cover-investigation so that it could be said there had been an investigation . . . Oswald, it was said, was the only Marine ever to defect from his country to another country, a Communist country, during peacetime. That was a major event. When the Marine Corps and American intelligence decided not to probe the reasons for the 'defection,' I knew then what I know now: Oswald was on an assignment in Russia for American intelligence." [166]

As we continue to reflect on John Kennedy's vision at American University, which sought a way of peace, we can foresee the falling stars of lives that would be brought down with the death of that vision. Among them would be Lee Harvey Oswald, a young man on assignment in Russia for American intelligence. Oswald's trajectory, which would end up meeting Kennedy's in Dallas, was guided not by the heavens or fate or even, as the *Warren Report* would have it, by a disturbed psyche. Oswald was guided by intelligence handlers. Lee Harvey Oswald was a pawn in the game. He was a minor piece in the deadly game Kennedy wanted to end. Oswald was being moved square by square across a giant board stretching from Atsugi to Moscow to Minsk to Dallas. For the sake of victory in the Cold War, the hands moving Oswald were prepared to sacrifice him and any other piece on the board. However, there was one player, John Kennedy, who no longer believed in the game and was threatening to turn over the board.

Self-examination, Kennedy said at American University, was the foundation of peace. In that speech he asked Americans to examine four basic attitudes in ourselves that were critical obstacles to peace.

"First: Let us examine our attitude toward peace itself. Too many of us think it is impossible. Too many think it unreal. But that is a dangerous, defeatist belief. It leads to the conclusion that war is inevitable—that mankind is doomed—that we are gripped by forces we cannot control."

I remember well the United States' warring spirit when President Kennedy said those words. Our deeply rooted prejudice, cultivated by years of propaganda, was that peace with Communists was impossible. The dogmas in our Cold War catechism ruled out peace with the enemy: You can't trust the Russians. Communism could undermine the very nature of freedom. One had to fight fire with fire against such an enemy. In the nuclear age, that meant being prepared to destroy the world to save it from Communism. Sophisticated analysts called it "the nuclear dilemma."

With the acceptance of such attitudes, despair of peace was a given. Thomas Merton wrote of this Cold War mentality: "The great danger is that under the pressures of anxiety and fear, the alternation of crisis and relaxation and new crisis, the people of the world will come to accept gradually the idea of war, the idea of submission to total power, and the abdication of reason, spirit and individual conscience. The great peril of the cold war is the progressive deadening of conscience." [167] As Kennedy observed, in such an atmosphere peace seemed impossible, as in fact it was, unless underlying attitudes changed. But how to change them?

Kennedy suggested a step-by-step way out of our despair. It corresponded in the world of diplomacy to what Gandhi had called "experiments in truth." Kennedy said we could overcome despair by focusing "on a series of concrete actions and effective agreements which are in the interest of all concerned." In spite of our warring ideologies, peace could become visible again by our acting in response to particular, concrete problems that stood in its way.

As JFK was learning himself from his intense dialogue with Khrushchev,

the practice of seeking peace through definable goals drew one irresistibly deeper. Violent ideologies then fell away in the process of realizing
peace.

"Peace need not be impracticable, and war need not be inevitable," he
said in reference to his own experience. "By defining our goal more clearly,
by making it seem more manageable and less remote, we can help all peoples
to see it, to draw hope from it, and to move irresistibly toward it."

The second point in Kennedy's theme was that self-examination was
needed with respect to our opponent: "Let us examine our attitude toward
the Soviet Union." We needed to examine the root cause of our despair,
namely, our attitude toward our enemy.

Kennedy cited anti-American propaganda from a Soviet military text and
observed, "It is sad to read these Soviet statements—to realize the extent of
the gulf between us."

Then with his listeners' defenses down, he brought the theme of self-
examination home again: "But it is also a warning—a warning to the American people not to fall into the same trap as the Soviets, not to see only a
distorted and desperate view of the other side, not to see conflict as inevitable, accommodation as impossible, and communication as nothing more
than an exchange of threats."

It was a summary of our own Cold War perspective. The key question
was not: What about the Russians? It was rather: What about our own attitude that can't get beyond "What about the Russians"? The point was again
not the speck in our neighbor's eye but the log in our own.

Kennedy's next sentence was a nonviolent distinction between a system
and its people: "No government or social system is so evil that its people
must be considered as lacking in virtue." With these words President John
Kennedy was echoing a theme of Pope John XXIII's papal encyclical *Pacem
in Terris* ("Peace on Earth"), published two months earlier on April 11,
1963.

In response to the threat of nuclear war, Pope John had issued his hopeful letter to the world just before he took leave of it. He died of cancer one
week before Kennedy's speech. In *Pacem in Terris* Pope John drew a careful distinction between "false philosophical teachings regarding the nature,
origin and destiny of the universe and of humanity" and "historical movements that have economic, social, cultural or political ends, . . . even when
these movements have originated from those teachings and have drawn and
still draw inspiration therefrom." Pope John said that while such teachings
remained the same, the movements arising from them underwent changes
"of a profound nature." [168]

The pope then struck down what seemed at the time to be insurmount-
able barriers to dialogue and collaboration with a militantly atheist opponent: "Who can deny that those movements, insofar as they conform to the
dictates of right reason and are interpreters of the lawful aspirations of the
human person, contain elements that are positive and deserving of approval?

"It can happen, then, that meetings for the attainment of some practical end, which formerly were deemed inopportune or unproductive, might now or in the future be considered opportune and useful." [169]

The pope's actions were ahead of his words. He was already in friendly communication with Nikita Khrushchev, sending him appeals for peace and religious freedom. His unofficial emissary to the Soviet premier, Norman Cousins, had delivered a Russian translation of *Pacem in Terris* personally to Khrushchev, even before the encyclical was issued to the rest of the world.[170] Khrushchev displayed proudly to Communist Party co-workers the papal medallion that Pope John had sent him.[171]

John Kennedy took heart from the elder John's faith that peace was made possible through such trust and communication with an enemy. Kennedy knew from Cousins the details of his meetings with Khrushchev on behalf of Pope John. Kennedy sent along with Cousins backdoor messages of his own to the Soviet premier, as Cousins describes in his book *The Improbable Triumvirate: John F. Kennedy, Pope John, Nikita Khrushchev*. Something was going on here behind the scenes of Christian–Communist conflict that was breathtaking in the then-dominant context of Armageddon theologies.

So it was natural for John Kennedy to speak at American University with empathy about the suffering of the Soviet Union. "No nation in the history of battle ever suffered more than the Soviet Union suffered in the course of the Second World War," he said. "At least 20 million lost their lives. Countless millions of homes and farms were burned or sacked. A third of the nation's territory, including nearly two thirds of its industrial base, was turned into a wasteland—a loss equivalent to the devastation of this country east of Chicago."

The suffering that the Russian people had already experienced was Kennedy's backdrop for addressing the evil of nuclear war, as it would affect simultaneously the U.S., the U.S.S.R., and the rest of the world: "All we have built, all we have worked for, would be destroyed in the first 24 hours."

"In short," he said, "both the United States and its allies, and the Soviet Union and its allies, have a mutually deep interest in a just and genuine peace and in halting the arms race." He added, in an ironic play on Woodrow Wilson's slogan for entering World War I: "If we cannot end now our differences, at least we can help make the world safe for diversity."

John Kennedy, portrayed by unsympathetic writers as a man with few feelings, had broken through to the feelings of our Cold War enemy, not only the ruler Nikita Khrushchev but an entire people decimated in World War II. What *about* the Russians? Kennedy's answer was that when we felt the enemy's pain, peace was not only possible. It was necessary. It was as necessary as the life of one's own family, seen truly for the first time. The vision that John F. Kennedy had been given was radically simple: Our side and their side were the same side.

"For, in the final analysis," Kennedy said, summing up his vision of interdependence, "our most basic common link is that we all inhabit this small planet. We all breathe the same air. We all cherish our children's future. And we are all mortal."

If we could accept such compassion for the enemy, Kennedy's third, most crucial appeal for self-examination could become more possible for his American audience. "Third: Let us reexamine our attitude toward the cold war, remembering that we are not engaged in a debate, seeking to pile up debating points."

When the missile crisis was resolved, the president stringently avoided, and ordered his staff to avoid, any talk of victory or defeat concerning Khrushchev. The only victory was avoiding war. Yet for Khrushchev's critics in the Communist world who could tolerate no retreat from the capitalist enemy, the Soviet premier had suffered a humiliating defeat. For that reason alone, Kennedy believed, there must never be another missile crisis, for it would only repeat pressures for terrible choices that had very nearly resulted in total war.

"Above all, while defending our own vital interests, nuclear powers must avert those confrontations which bring an adversary to a choice of either a humiliating retreat or a nuclear war. To adopt that kind of course in the nuclear age would be evidence only of the bankruptcy of our policy—or of a collective death-wish for the world."

Kennedy moved on to concrete steps, already in progress, toward realizing his vision of world peace. He announced first the decision made by Macmillan, Khrushchev, and himself to hold discussions in Moscow on a test ban treaty. He then proclaimed his unilateral initiative, a suspension of atmospheric tests, with the explicit hope that it would foster trust with the enemy:

"To make clear our good faith and solemn convictions on the matter [of a comprehensive test ban treaty], I now declare that the United States does not propose to conduct nuclear tests in the atmosphere so long as other states do not do so. We will not be the first to resume."

For those who knew the strength of will behind Kennedy's vision, there was something either inspiring or threatening in his next statement of "our primary long-range interest": "general and complete disarmament—designed to take place by stages, permitting parallel political developments to build the new institutions of peace which would take the place of arms." As we shall see, Kennedy meant what he said, and U.S. intelligence agencies knew it. So did the corporate power brokers who had clashed with him the year before in the steel crisis, an overlooked chapter in the Kennedy presidency that we will explore. The military-industrial complex did not receive his swords-into-plowshares vision as good news.

In the fourth and final section of his plea for self-examination, JFK appealed to his American audience to examine the quality of life within our own borders: "Let us examine our attitude toward peace and freedom here at home . . . In too many of our cities today, the peace is not secure because freedom is incomplete."

He would say more on this subject the following night in his ground-breaking civil rights speech. On the day after President Kennedy spoke at American University, Alabama governor George Wallace let the president's will prevail and backed away from blocking a door at the University of Alabama, allowing two black students to register. That night in a televised address to the nation, Kennedy described the suffering of black Americans under racism with a strength of feeling that recalled his compassion the day before for the Russian people in World War II:

"The Negro baby born in America today, regardless of the section of the Nation in which he is born, has about one-half as much chance of completing a high school as a white baby born in the same place on the same day, one-third as much chance of completing college, one-third as much chance of becoming a professional man, twice as much chance of becoming unemployed, about one-seventh as much chance of earning $10,000 a year, a life expectance which is 7 years shorter, and the prospects of earning only half as much.

"We are confronted primarily with a moral issue. It is as old as the scriptures and is as clear as the American Constitution." [172]

In his American University address, after Kennedy identified "peace and freedom here at home" as a critical dimension of world peace, he went on to identify peace itself as a fundamental human right: "And is not peace, in the last analysis, basically a matter of human rights—the right to live out our lives without fear of devastation—the right to breathe air as nature provided it—the right of future generations to a healthy existence?"

Kennedy concluded his "peace speech" with a promise whose beginning fulfillment in the next five months would confirm his own death sentence: "Confident and unafraid, we labor on—not toward a strategy of annihilation but toward a strategy of peace."

John Kennedy's greatest statement of his turn toward peace was his American University address. In an ironic turn of events, the Soviet Union became its principal venue. JFK's identification with the Russian people's suffering penetrated their government's defenses far more effectively than any missile could have. Sorensen described the speech's impact on the other side of the Cold War:

"The full text of the speech was published in the Soviet press. Still more striking was the fact that it was heard as well as read throughout the U.S.S.R. After fifteen years of almost uninterrupted jamming of Western broadcasts, by means of a network of over three thousand transmitters and at an annual cost of several hundred million dollars, the Soviets jammed only one paragraph of the speech when relayed by the Voice of America in Russian (that dealing with their 'baseless' claims of U.S. aims)—then did not jam any of it upon rebroadcast—and then suddenly stopped jamming all Western broadcasts, including even Russian-language newscasts on foreign affairs. Equally suddenly they agreed in Vienna to the principle of inspection by the International Atomic Energy Agency to make certain that Agency's reactors were used for peaceful purposes. And equally suddenly the outlook for some kind of test-ban agreement turned from hopeless to hopeful." [173]

Nikita Khrushchev was deeply moved. He told test-ban negotiator Averell

Harriman that Kennedy had given "the greatest speech by any American President since Roosevelt."[174] Khrushchev responded by proposing to Kennedy that they now consider a limited test ban encompassing the atmosphere, outer space, and water, so that the disputed question of inspections would no longer arise. He also suggested a nonaggression pact between NATO and the Warsaw Pact to create a "fresh international climate."[175]

Kennedy's speech was received less favorably in his own country. The *New York Times* reported his government's skepticism: "Generally there was not much optimism in official Washington that the President's conciliation address at American University would produce agreement on a test ban treaty or anything else."[176] In contrast to the Soviet media, which were electrified by the speech, the U.S. media ignored or downplayed it. For the first time Americans had less opportunity to read and hear their president's words than did the Russian people. A turnabout was occurring in the world on different levels. Whereas nuclear disarmament had suddenly become feasible, Kennedy's position in his own government had become precarious. Kennedy was turning faster than was safe for a Cold War leader.

After the American University address, John Kennedy and Nikita Khrushchev began to act like competitors in peace. They were both turning. However, Kennedy's rejection of Cold War politics was considered treasonous by forces in his own government. In that context, which Kennedy knew well, the American University address was a profile in courage with lethal consequences. President Kennedy's June 10, 1963, call for an end to the Cold War, five and one-half months before his assassination, anticipates Dr. King's courage in his April 4, 1967, Riverside Church address calling for an end to the Vietnam War, exactly one year before his assassination. Each of those transforming speeches was a prophetic statement provoking the reward a prophet traditionally receives. John Kennedy's American University address was to his death in Dallas as Martin Luther King's Riverside Church address was to his death in Memphis.

On June 13, 1962, Lee Harvey Oswald returned to the United States after his defection to the Soviet Union. He was not met by arrest and prosecution. Nor was he confronted in any way by the government he had betrayed. Instead Oswald was welcomed by order of the U.S. government, as he and his Russian wife Marina disembarked with their infant daughter June from the ocean liner *Maasdam* in Hoboken, New Jersey. The *Warren Report* tells us that, on the recommendation of the State Department, the Oswalds were greeted at the dock by Spas T. Raikin, a representative of the Traveler's Aid Society.[177] The *Warren Report* does not mention, however, that Raikin was at the same time secretary-general of the American Friends of the Anti-Bolshevik Nations, an anti-communist organization with extensive intelligence connections[178]—like the American government, an unlikely source of support for a traitor. The *Warren Report* does say that, with Spas

T. Raikin's help, the Oswald family passed smoothly through immigration and customs.

In the summer of 1962 the Oswalds settled in Fort Worth, Texas. They were welcomed by a local White Russian community characterized by its pronounced anti-communist view of the world. Lee was befriended by George de Mohrenschildt, the son of a czarist official. "The Baron," as he liked to be called, traveled around the world as a geologist, consulting for Texas oil companies and doubling as an intelligence asset. In 1957 the CIA's Richard Helms wrote a memo saying that de Mohrenschildt, after making a trip as a consultant in Yugoslavia, provided the CIA with "foreign intelligence which was promptly disseminated to other federal agencies in 10 separate reports." [179] De Mohrenschildt would admit in a 1977 interview that he had been given a go-ahead to meet Oswald by J. Walton Moore, the Dallas CIA Domestic Contacts Service chief.[180]

In that March 29, 1977, interview, the last he would ever give, George de Mohrenschildt told author Edward Jay Epstein he had "on occasion done favors" since the early 1950s for government officials connected with the CIA. It was a mutually beneficial relationship. The CIA contacts then helped de Mohrenschildt arrange profitable business connections overseas.

De Mohrenschildt said that in late 1961 he had met in Dallas with the CIA's J. Walton Moore, who began to tell him about "an ex-American Marine who had worked in an electronics factory in Minsk for the past year and in whom there was 'interest.'" [181] The Baron had grown up in Minsk, as Moore seemed to know before being told. The ex-Marine, Moore said, would be returning to the Dallas area. De Mohrenschildt felt he was being primed.

In the summer of 1962, de Mohrenschildt said, he was handed Lee Harvey Oswald's address in Fort Worth by "one of Moore's associates," who suggested that de Mohrenschildt meet Oswald. De Mohrenschildt then phoned Moore to confirm such a mission and set up another mutually beneficial relationship. He told Moore he would appreciate help from the U.S. embassy in Haiti in arranging approval by Haitian dictator "Papa Doc" Duvalier for an oil exploration deal. Moore then gave de Mohrenschildt the go-ahead to befriend the Oswalds, which de Mohrenschildt promptly did—with the firm understanding that he was carrying out the CIA's wishes. "I would never have contacted Oswald in a million years if Moore had not sanctioned it," de Mohrenschildt said in his final interview. "Too much was at stake." [182]

On October 7, 1962, nine days before the Cuban Missile Crisis began, de Mohrenschildt urged his new friend Lee Harvey Oswald to move to Dallas, where more of the Russian immigrants lived. Oswald took him so seriously that the next day he quit his job at a Fort Worth welding company and made the move.[183] De Mohrenschildt then became Oswald's mentor in Dallas. The Baron's wife and daughter said it was he who organized Oswald's securing a new job, four days after his move, with a Dallas graphic arts company, Jaggars-Chiles-Stovall.[184] The official record is that Louise Latham of the

Texas Employment Commission sent Oswald to the firm. Author Henry Hurt interviewed Ms. Latham, who denied that de Mohrenschildt got the job for Oswald.[185]

Whoever was responsible for Oswald's immediate hiring, it was a remarkable achievement. Jaggars-Chiles-Stovall, described by the Warren Commission simply as "a commercial advertising photography firm," [186] had contracts with the U.S. Army Map Service. Its classified work connected with Oswald's history as an apparent traitor. From interviews with Jaggars-Chiles-Stovall employees, Hurt concluded, "Part of the work appears to have been related to the top secret U-2 missions, some of which were then making flights over Cuba." [187] Four days before President Kennedy was shown U-2 photos that confirmed Soviet missiles in Cuba, Lee Harvey Oswald reported to work at a defense contractor that was apparently involved in logistics support for the U-2 mission. According to Oswald's co-workers, some of them were setting type for Cuban place names to go on maps[188]—probably for the same spy planes whose radar secrets the ex-Marine had already offered to the Soviet Union. Oswald was once again, through the intervention of undercover angels, defying the normal laws of government security barriers.

As it turned out, in mid-March 1963 George de Mohrenschildt did receive a Haitian government contract for $285,000.[189] In April he left Dallas, and in May he met in Washington, D.C., with CIA and U.S. Army intelligence contacts to further his Haitian connections.[190] De Mohrenschildt then departed for Haiti. He never saw Oswald again.

None of George de Mohrenschildt's extensive U.S. intelligence connections are mentioned in the *Warren Report*, which describes him vaguely as "a highly individualistic person of varied interests" who befriended Oswald.[191] Relying on U.S. intelligence for its questions and answers, the *Report* concludes concerning George and his wife, Jeanne de Mohrenschildt: "Neither the FBI, CIA, nor any witness contacted by the Commission has provided any information linking the de Mohrenschildts to subversive or extremist organizations." [192]

New Orleans district attorney Jim Garrison in his investigation of the Kennedy assassination asked a different kind of question about George de Mohrenschildt. Garrison identified de Mohrenschildt as one of Oswald's CIA "baby-sitters," "assigned to protect or otherwise see to the general welfare of a particular individual." [193] Garrison concluded from his conversations with George and Jeanne de Mohrenschildt that the Baron was in some sense an unwitting baby-sitter, without foreknowledge of what was in store for the "baby" in his custody. Both de Mohrenschildts, Garrison said, were vigorous in their insistence to him that Oswald had been the assassination scapegoat.[194]

On March 29, 1977, three hours after his revelation of the CIA's sanctioning his contact with Oswald, George de Mohrenschildt was found shot to death in the house where he was staying in Manalapan, Florida. His death also occurred on the day Gaeton Fonzi, an investigator for the House

Select Committee on Assassinations, left his card with de Mohrenschildt's daughter and told her he would be calling her father that evening for an appointment to question him. Soon after de Mohrenschildt took the card and put it in his pocket, he went upstairs, then apparently put the barrel of a .20-gauge shotgun in his mouth and pulled the trigger.[195]

Though he had been Oswald's CIA-approved shepherd in Dallas, George de Mohrenschildt had no "need to know," and thus probably no understanding in advance of the scapegoat role that lay ahead for his young friend. In the years after John Kennedy and Lee Oswald were gunned down, the de Mohrenschildts seemed to grow in remorse for the evil in which they had become enmeshed. Jim Garrison said, "I was particularly affected by the depth of their unhappiness at what had been done not only to John Kennedy but to Lee Oswald as well."[196] George de Mohrenschildt was another casualty of Dallas. Like Oswald, he, too, was a pawn in the game.

President Kennedy's fourth Bay of Pigs toward the coup d'état he saw as possible was the Partial Nuclear Test Ban Treaty that he and Nikita Khrushchev signed.

In the months before his American University address, Kennedy had become increasingly pessimistic about achieving a test ban. Domestic opposition was rising. Liberal Republican governor Nelson Rockefeller of New York denounced the idea of a test ban. Senate Republican leader Everett Dirksen said of Kennedy's efforts to gain one, "This has become an exercise not in negotiation but in give-away." The Joint Chiefs of Staff declared themselves "opposed to a comprehensive ban under almost any terms."[197]

In Geneva the U.S.–Soviet negotiations were at a deadlock over the question of on-site inspections. Meanwhile, the Atomic Energy Commission was pushing Kennedy to schedule another series of atmospheric tests. The U.S. Congress had similar views. Kennedy supporter Senator John O. Pastore of Rhode Island, chairman of the Joint Committee on Atomic Energy, wrote the president that even if the current U.S. test ban proposal were accepted by the Soviets, "on the basis of informal discussions with other Senate leaders I am afraid that ratification of such a treaty could only be obtained with the greatest difficulty." Moreover, Pastore added, "I personally have reservations as to whether such a treaty would be in the best interests of the United States at this time."[198]

At his March 21, 1963, news conference, the president was asked if he still had hopes of arriving at a test-ban agreement. He replied doggedly, "Well, my hopes are dimmed, but nevertheless, I still hope."[199] Only three weeks before the American University address, he answered another test-ban question with even less optimism, "No, I'm not hopeful, I'm not hopeful . . . We have tried to get an agreement [with the Soviets] on all the rest of it and then come to the question of the number of inspections, but we were unable to get that. So I would say I am not hopeful at all."[200]

He felt, nevertheless, the time to push for a treaty was right then: "I have said from the beginning that [it] seemed to me that the pace of events was such in the world that unless we could get an agreement now, I would think the chance of getting it would be comparatively slight. We are therefore going to continue to push very hard in May and June in every forum to see if we can get an agreement." [201]

So while not hopeful, Kennedy was more determined than ever to turn the corner on a test ban treaty. It was then, on June 10, that he launched the peace initiative of his American University address, which broke through Soviet defenses. In response, Khrushchev made preparations to welcome the U.S. test-ban negotiators to Moscow. Kennedy saw the moment was ripe for at least a partial test ban, bypassing the negotiators' impasse on inspections. At this point Glenn T. Seaborg, chairman of the Atomic Energy Commission, noted in his journal that whereas JFK had been dedicated to a test ban since the beginning of his presidency, "Now, he decided to *really go for it!*" [202]

He did so at a personal cost. As we have seen, the response to the American University address was much warmer on the Soviet side than the American. The Joint Chiefs and CIA were adamantly opposed to Kennedy's turn toward peace. Cold War influences so dominated the U.S. Congress that the president felt getting Senate ratification of a test ban agreement would be "almost in the nature of a miracle," as he described the task to advisers. [203] That process, miraculous or not, was engineered humanly by a president committed at all costs to seeing it accomplished.

Kennedy named Averell Harriman, former ambassador to the U.S.S.R., his top negotiator in the Moscow talks. Known as a tough bargainer, Harriman was liked and respected by the Russians. They saw his appointment as a sign of the president's seriousness in wanting a test-ban agreement.

Kennedy personally prepared the negotiators. He emphasized the importance of their mission—perhaps a last chance to stop the spread of testing and radioactive fallout. If they were successful, it would mean a concrete step toward mutual trust with the Russians. In both literal and symbolic senses, they stood to achieve a more peaceful atmosphere in the world. [204] Their head negotiator would be, in effect, not Harriman but the president himself. He would stay in regular communication with them from Washington. He underlined confidentiality. No one outside a tight circle of officials personally approved by him was to know any of the details. [205]

During the negotiations, Kennedy spent hours in the cramped White House Situation Room, editing the U.S. position as if he were at the Moscow table himself. Soviet ambassador Anatoli Dobrynin was astounded at the president's command of every stage of the process. "Harriman would just get on the phone with Kennedy," he said, "and things would be decided. It was amazing." [206]

On July 25, 1963, when the final text was ready, Harriman phoned Kennedy and read it to him twice. The president said, "Okay, great!" Harriman returned to the conference room and initialed the Limited Test Ban Treaty, outlawing nuclear tests "in the atmosphere, beyond its limits, including outer space, or under water, including territorial waters or high seas."[207]

The next night President Kennedy made a television appeal to the nation for support of the test ban treaty. Against the advice of Secretary of State Dean Rusk, Kennedy had decided to take the issue of ratification immediately to the people. He wanted to do everything he could to turn public opinion around as quickly as possible. "We've got to hit the country while the country's hot," he told Rusk, "That's the only thing that makes any impression to these god-damned Senators . . . They'll move as the country moves."[208]

In his speech Kennedy said, "This treaty is not the millennium . . . But it is an important first step—a step toward peace—a step toward reason—a step away from war."[209]

As in the American University address, he opened up a vision beyond the Cold War, that of an era of mutual peacemaking. "Nuclear test ban negotiations have long been a symbol of East-West disagreement." Perhaps "this treaty can also be a symbol—if it can symbolize the end of one era and the beginning of another—if both sides can by this treaty gain confidence and experience in peaceful collaboration."

He reiterated the consequences of a nuclear war: "A full-scale nuclear exchange, lasting less than 60 minutes, with the weapons now in existence, could wipe out more than 300 million Americans, Europeans, and Russians, as well as untold numbers elsewhere." He quoted Chairman Khrushchev: "The survivors would envy the dead."

Besides helping to prevent war, he said, the test ban treaty "can be a step towards freeing the world from the fears and dangers of radioactive fallout." He called to mind "the number of children and grandchildren with cancer in their bones, with leukemia in their blood, or with poison in their lungs . . . this is not a natural health hazard—and it is not a statistical issue. The loss of even one human life, or the malformation of even one baby—who may be born long after we are gone—should be of concern to us all. Our children and grandchildren are not merely statistics toward which we can be indifferent."

Kennedy's sense of the vulnerability of children was again the force behind some of his most deeply felt words: "[This treaty] is particularly for our children and our grandchildren, and they have no lobby here in Washington."

After reminding his listeners of "the familiar places of danger and conflict"—Cuba, Southeast Asia, Berlin, and all around the globe—he concluded with the expression of a deep hope, less than four months before his assassination:

"But now, for the first time in many years, the path of peace may be open. No one can be certain what the future will bring. No one can say whether the time has come for an easing of the struggle. But history and our own conscience will judge us harsher if we do not now make every effort to test our hopes by action, and this is the place to begin. According to the ancient Chinese proverb, 'A journey of a thousand miles must begin with a single step.'

"My fellow Americans, let us take that first step. Let us, if we can, step back from the shadows of war and seek out the way of peace. And if that journey is a thousand miles, or even more, let history record that we, in this land, at this time, took the first step."

Kennedy was fiercely determined but not optimistic that the test ban treaty would be ratified by the defense-conscious Senate. It was on August 7, 1963, that he made his comment to advisers that a near-miracle was needed. He said that if a Senate vote were held right then it would fall far short of the necessary two-thirds.[210] Larry O'Brien, his liaison aide with the Congress, confirmed the accuracy of the president's estimate. Congressional mail was running about fifteen to one against a test ban.[211]

Kennedy initiated a whirlwind public education campaign on the treaty, coordinated by Norman Cousins. The president told an August 7 meeting of key organizers that they were taking on a very tough job and had his total support. Led by Cousins and calling themselves the Citizens Committee, the group mounted a national campaign for Senate ratification. The National Committee for a Sane Nuclear Policy, which had been formed in 1958 to dramatize the dangers of nuclear testing, played a key role in the campaign. Kennedy and Cousins also successfully sought help from the National Council of Churches, the Union of American Hebrew Congregations, Catholic Bishop John Wright of Pittsburgh and Cardinal Richard Cushing of Boston, union leaders, sympathetic business executives, leading scientists and academics, Nobel Laureates, and, at a special meeting with the president, the editors of the nation's leading women's magazines, who gave their enthusiastic support. As the campaign grew, public opinion began to shift. By the end of August, the tide of congressional mail had gone from fifteen to one against a test ban to three to two against. The president and his committee of activists hoped that in a month public opinion would be on their side.

In the meantime, they were bucking the military-industrial complex, which had become alarmed at the president's sudden turn toward peace and his alliance with peace activists in support of the test ban. The August 5, 1963, *U.S. News and World Report* carried a major article headlined, "Is U.S. Giving up in the Arms Race?" The article cited "many authorities in the military establishment, who now are silenced," as thinking that the Kennedy administration's "new strategy adds up to a type of intentional and one-sided disarmament."[212]

The alarm was sounded even more loudly in the August 12 *U.S. News* with an article headlined, "If Peace Does Come—What Happens to Business?" The article began:

"This question once again is being raised: If peace does come, what happens to business? Will the bottom drop out if defense spending is cut?

"There is a lull in the cold war. Before the U.S. Senate is a treaty calling for an end to testing of nuclear weapons in the air or under water. A nonaggression agreement is being proposed by Russia's Khrushchev.

"Talk of peace is catching on. Before shouting, however, it is important to bear some other things in mind."

U.S. News went on to reassure its readers that defense spending would be sustained by such Cold War factors as Cuba remaining "a Russian base, occupied by Russian troops" and "the guerrilla war in South Vietnam" where "the Red Chinese, in an ugly mood, are capable of starting a big war in Asia at any time." [213]

However, an insider could have asked, what would it mean to defense contractors if Kennedy extended his peacemaking to Cuba and Vietnam?

The president's peacemaking had moved beyond any effective military control or even monitoring. In the test-ban talks, the military weren't in the loop. Kennedy had made a quick end run around them to negotiate the treaty. As JFK biographer Richard Reeves observed, "By moving so swiftly on the Moscow negotiations, Kennedy politically outflanked his own military on the most important military question of the time." [214]

Kennedy pointed out to Cousins that he and Khrushchev had come to have more in common with each other than either had with his own military establishment: "One of the ironic things about this entire situation is that Mr. Khrushchev and I occupy approximately the same political positions inside our governments. He would like to prevent a nuclear war but is under severe pressure from his hard-line crowd, which interprets every move in that direction as appeasement. I've got similar problems." [215]

Almost four decades later, Nikita Khrushchev's son Sergei would provide a wistful footnote to John Kennedy's political empathy with his father. On February 4, 2001, Sergei Khrushchev, by then a senior fellow in international studies at Brown University, in the course of commenting on the film *Thirteen Days* (a dramatization of the Cuban Missile Crisis), wrote in *The New York Times*:

"A great deal changed after the [missile] crisis: A direct communication link between Moscow and Washington was established, nuclear testing (except for underground tests) was banned, and the confrontation over Berlin was ended.

"But there was much that President Kennedy and my father did not succeed in seeing through to the end. I am convinced that if history had allowed them another six years, they would have brought the cold war to a close before the end of the 1960's. I say this with good reason, because in 1963 my father made an official announcement to a session of the U.S.S.R. Defense Council that he intended to sharply reduce Soviet armed forces from 2.5 million men to half a million and to stop the production of tanks and other offensive weapons.

"He thought that 200 to 300 intercontinental nuclear missiles made an attack on the Soviet Union impossible, while the money freed up by reducing the size of the army would be put to better use in agriculture and housing construction.

"But fate decreed otherwise, and the window of opportunity, barely cracked open, closed at once. In 1963 President Kennedy was killed, and a year later, in October 1964, my father was removed from power. The cold war continued for another quarter of a century . . ."[216]

Kennedy finally obtained the support of the Joint Chiefs for the test ban treaty, although Air Force chief LeMay said he would have opposed it had it not already been signed.[217] Strategic Air Command general Thomas Power denounced the treaty.[218] Other military leaders testified against the test ban. Admiral Lewis Strauss said, "I am not sure that the reduction of tensions is necessarily a good thing." Admiral Arthur Radford, former chairman of the Joint Chiefs, said, "I join with many of my former colleagues in expressing deep concern for our future security . . . The decision of the Senate of the United States in connection with this treaty will change the course of world history."[219]

The Citizens Committee continued its campaign in support of the test ban. In September public opinion polls showed a turnaround—80 percent in favor of the treaty. The Senate vote on ratification was held on September 24, 1963. The Senate approved the test ban treaty by a vote of 80 to 19—14 more than the required two-thirds. Sorensen noted that no other single accomplishment in the White House gave the president greater satisfaction.[220]

Before he initiated his all-out campaign for approval of the test ban, Kennedy told his staff that the treaty was the most serious congressional issue he had faced. He was, he said, determined to win if it cost him the 1964 election.[221] He did win. But did it cost him his life?

CHAPTER TWO

Kennedy, Castro, and the CIA

In his final Cold War Letter, written to Rabbi Everett Gendler in October 1962, Thomas Merton searched for an effective way out of a Cold War politics that seemed destined to end in nuclear war. In that month of the Cuban Missile Crisis, Merton expressed a deep pessimism as well as a hope that no politics of war could suppress. He said that while he supported wholeheartedly the efforts of the peace movement to communicate new ideas against a tidal wave of propaganda, "at the same time I am impressed with the fact that all these things are little more than symbols. Thank God they are at least symbols, and valid ones. But where are we going to turn for some really effective political action? As soon as one gets involved in the machinery of politics one gets involved in its demonic futilities and in the great current that sweeps everything toward no one knows what."

Yet with a Gandhian faith in the power of truth, Merton continued to hope: "Every slightest effort at opening up new areas of thought, every attempt to perceive new aspects of truth, or just a little truth, is of inestimable value in preparing the way for the light we cannot see." [1]

When Merton wrote those words, nothing was more opposed to the great current of American Cold War politics sweeping everyone to oblivion than was a dialogue with Fidel Castro. Anti-communism had become a dogmatic theology that paralyzed even the thought of such a conversation. For Americans, the unthinkable was not the act of waging nuclear war but the act of talking with the Communist devil who ruled the island nation ninety miles from Florida, who was in fact key to stopping a nuclear holocaust. We can recall the reluctance of Merton's Miami correspondent, Evora Arca de Sardinia, and her Cuban exile community to consider the idea of paying a ransom to Castro, even to free family members who were his prisoners from the Bay of Pigs. To the anti-Castro émigrés in Miami, that would have meant compromising with the satanic incarnation of an evil, Communism, in a way that would violate their theology, ethics, and loyalty. At the level of national politics, America's Cold War theology was enforced by excommunication. One couldn't talk with the devil in Havana and remain in communion with the gods of Washington.

No one in the United States knew this political fact of life better than President John F. Kennedy. To be seen as open in any way to the thinking of Fidel Castro was, as Kennedy knew well, a death sentence in U.S. politics, especially for a president. Yet that was precisely the "little truth of inestimable value for the light we cannot see," envisioned by Merton in his last Cold War Letter, that Kennedy cultivated during the final months of his life.

For John Kennedy's fifth Bay of Pigs was in essence a return to the Bay of Pigs. His fifth alienation from his CIA and military advisers came from his risk-filled turn toward dialogue with an even more irreconcilable enemy than Nikita Khrushchev: Fidel Castro.

Based on recently declassified Kennedy administration documents, National Security Archive analyst Peter Kornbluh has concluded in a little-noted article that "in 1963 John Kennedy began pursuing an alternative script on Cuba: a secret dialogue toward an actual rapprochement with Castro." [2] The documents Kornbluh discovered have confirmed and filled in a story that Cuban and American diplomats have been telling for decades.

In the fall of 1962, New York lawyer James Donovan secretly represented John and Robert Kennedy in negotiations with Fidel Castro for the release of the Bay of Pigs prisoners, so they could return to their families in Miami and elsewhere. In that process, which proved successful, a human encounter overcame politics. Donovan and Castro became friends. On Donovan's January 1963 follow-up trip to Cuba, Rene Vallejo, Castro's aide and physician, raised a new possibility that Donovan reported to U.S. intelligence officials. As Donovan was about to board his plane to return to the United States, Vallejo "broached the subject of re-establishing diplomatic relations with the U.S." and invited Donovan to return for talks "about the future of Cuba and international relations in general." [3]

In March 1963, John Kennedy took careful note of this development and tried to smooth the way for further dialogue with Fidel Castro. On the eve of another Donovan trip to Havana, the president overruled a State Department recommendation for Donovan's talks with Castro that would have raised a major obstacle in a new Cuban–American relationship. In a March 4, 1963, Top Secret/Eyes Only memorandum, Gordon Chase, deputy to the National Security Adviser, stated Kennedy's more open position toward Castro: "The President does not agree that we should make the breaking of Sino/Soviet ties a non-negotiable point. We don't want to present Castro with a condition that he obviously cannot fulfill. We should start thinking along more flexible lines."

The memorandum went on to emphasize both secrecy and Kennedy's keen attention to what was opening up with Cuba: "The above must be kept close to the vest. The President, himself, is very interested in this one."[4]

JFK was ahead of RFK on Cuba. In a March 14 memorandum, Robert Kennedy unsuccessfully urged the president to move against Castro: "I would not like it said a year from now that we could have had this internal breakup in Cuba but we just did not set the stage for it."[5] Robert apparently received no response from his brother, as he wrote him again on March 26 in frustration: "Do you think there was any merit to my last memo? . . . In any case, is there anything further on this matter?"[6]

While John Kennedy was responding to his brother's anti-Castro schemes with silence, he was himself turning toward a new approach to Fidel. Although he would not forsake all U.S. efforts to subvert Cuba, before the month was over President Kennedy made a policy decision that in effect signaled his own opening toward Castro. It pitted him against the CIA once again. He was provoked into it by the Agency.

On March 19, the CIA-sponsored Cuban exile group Alpha 66 announced at a Washington press conference that it had raided a Soviet "fortress" and ship in Cuba, causing a dozen casualties and serious damage.[7] Alpha 66 was one of the commando teams maintained by the giant CIA station in Miami, "JM/WAVE," for its attacks on Cuba. Alpha 66 exile leader Antonio Veciana would admit years later to Gaeton Fonzi, a federal investigator for the House Select Committee on Assassinations (HSCA), that the purpose of the CIA-initiated attack on the Soviet vessel in Cuban waters was "to publicly embarrass Kennedy and force him to move against Castro."[8] Veciana's CIA adviser was a man who used the cover name "Maurice Bishop." Veciana revealed that "[Bishop] kept saying Kennedy would have to be forced to make a decision, and the only way was to put him up against the wall."[9] So Bishop targeted Soviet ships to create another Soviet–American crisis. As Fonzi showed by his HSCA investigation, "Maurice Bishop" was in fact David Atlee Phillips, who would become a key player in John Kennedy's assassination and would subsequently be promoted to chief of the CIA's Western Hemisphere Division.[10]

"Maurice Bishop"/David Phillips carefully kept his distance from the Washington press conference that he had set up to publicize the Alpha 66 attack. However, he arranged for high-ranking officials in the Departments of Health and Agriculture to attend it, thus giving the event legitimacy and prominent coverage in the next day's New York Times.[11]

The Alpha 66 raid was only the beginning. It was followed up eight days later by another Cuban exile attack that damaged a Soviet freighter in a Cuban port.[12] The JM/WAVE chief of operations coordinating these efforts to force Kennedy's hand against Castro was the CIA's David Sanchez Morales, a longtime co-worker of David Atlee Phillips. Morales would also participate in JFK's murder, as he would admit to friends in the 1970s.[13]

The Cuban exile attacks prompted a Soviet protest to Washington. Khrushchev naturally held Kennedy responsible for refugee gunboats that the CIA was running out of Miami. Soviet ambassador Anatoly Dobrynin met with Robert Kennedy, and RFK reported Dobrynin's complaint to JFK: "It isn't possible [for him] to believe that if we really wanted to stop these raids that we could not do so." [14] The CIA's tactic was forcing the president to choose between the militant Cold War politics of a Miami exile community manipulated by the CIA and the almost indefinable politics that JFK was developing with Nikita Khrushchev. He chose the latter.

As in the CIA's Bay of Pigs plot to trap Kennedy, its Alpha 66 ploy backfired. Instead of backing Alpha 66, President Kennedy ordered a government crackdown on all Miami exile raids into Cuba. In doing so, he enlisted the help of his brother.

On March 31, Robert Kennedy's Justice Department took its first step in implementing a policy of preventing Cuban refugees from using U.S. territory to organize or launch raids against Cuba. The Justice Department ordered eighteen Cubans in the Miami area, who were already involved in raids, to confine their movements to Dade County (or in some cases, the U.S.), under the threat of arrest or deportation. One of them was Alpha 66 leader Antonio Veciana.[15] Within a week, the Coast Guard in Florida, working in concert with British officials in the Bahamas, seized a series of Cuban rebel boats and arrested their commando groups before they could attack Soviet ships near Cuba.

The initial arrests and boat confiscations resulted in confusing news reports that mirrored the internal government conflict between Kennedy and the CIA. The owner of one of the confiscated boats, Alexander I. Rorke, Jr., told the *New York Times* that "the United States Government, through the Central Intelligence Agency, had had advance knowledge of the trips" of his boat, the *Violin III*, into Cuban waters.[16] Rorke also said that "the C.I.A. had financed trips of the Violin III." He added that his boat, if released, "would be used in future Cuban operations." [17]

In response to the exiles' determination to continue the attacks, the president increased his efforts to stop them. Under an April 6 headline, "U.S. Strengthens Check on Raiders," the *Times* reported:

"The United States is throwing more planes, ships, and men into its effort to police the straits of Florida against anti-Castro raiders operating from this country.

"Coast Guard headquarters announced today that it had ordered six more planes and 12 more boats into the Seventh District to reinforce the patrols already assigned to the Florida-Puerto Rico area.

". . . The action followed the Government's announcement last weekend that it intended to 'take every step necessary' to halt commando raids from United States territory against Cuba and Soviet ships bound for Cuba." [18]

By enforcing President Kennedy's new policy, the Justice Department and the Coast Guard were restraining a covert arm of the CIA from drawing the United States into a war with Cuba. Premier Fidel Castro responded with evident surprise by saying that Kennedy's curtailment of the hit-and-run raids was "a step forward toward reduction of the dangers of crisis and war."[19] However, as the *Times* reported on April 10, the Florida refugee groups subsidized by the CIA exploded with bitterness, charging the Kennedy administration with engaging in "coexistence" with the Castro regime.[20]

While U.S. and British forces continued to round up anti-Castro rebels and boats, Dr. Jose Miro Cardona, head of the Cuban Revolutionary Council (CRC) in Miami, resigned in protest to the shift in U.S. policy. The Cuban Revolutionary Council had been created by the U.S. government prior to the Bay of Pigs as a provisional Cuban government to seize power when Castro was overthrown. It also served as an umbrella organization for the variety of Miami exile groups. The CRC's budget and funding came from the CIA. In the wake of Cardona's resignation, a spokesperson for the Cuban Revolutionary Council stated that the organization received "only" $972,000 a year (rather than $2,000,000 as previously reported) "and this sum is not even distributed by the council but by the Central Intelligence Agency with the help of a public accounting firm."[21]

In his April 18 resignation statement, which the *New York Times* headlined as an "Attack on Kennedy,"[22] Miro Cardona said, "American Government policy has shifted suddenly, violently, and unexpectedly—as dangerously and without warning as on that other sad occasion [the Bay of Pigs], with no more reasonable explanation than Russia's note protesting the breaking of an agreement [Kennedy's agreement with Khrushchev, in exchange for the Soviet missiles' removal, that the U.S. would not invade Cuba]." Cardona concluded from the confinement of Cuban exile raiders and the immobilization of their boats that "the struggle for Cuba was in the process of being liquidated by the Government. This conclusion," he felt, "appears to be confirmed, strongly confirmed, with the announcement that every refugee has received his last allotment this month, forcing them to relocate."[23]

With rebel raiders under arrest and government funding for the exile army suddenly drying up, forcing them to disperse, Cardona saw the handwriting on the wall and the initials beneath it: JFK. The Florida exile community united behind Cardona and against JFK, whom they now saw as an ally of Castro. They mourned the president's turnaround as a virtual death to their political vision. As the Associated Press reported on April 18 from Miami, "The dispute between the Cuban exile leaders and the Kennedy administration was symbolized here today by black crepe hung from the doors of exiles' homes."[24]

Kennedy wrote Khrushchev secretly on April 11, 1963, explaining to his Cold War counterpart a policy chosen partly on Khrushchev's behalf that was already beginning to cost Kennedy dearly. The U.S. president said he was "aware of the tensions unduly created by recent private attacks on your ships in Caribbean waters; and we are taking action to halt those attacks which are in violation of our laws, and obtaining the support of the British

Government in preventing the use of their Caribbean islands for this purpose. The efforts of this Government to reduce tensions have, as you know, aroused much criticism from certain quarters in this country. But neither such criticism nor the opposition of any sector of our society will be allowed to determine the policies of this Government. In particular, I have neither the intention nor the desire to invade Cuba . . ."[25]

In early April, James Donovan returned to Cuba to negotiate the release of more prisoners. In the meantime, the CIA had been at work on a plan to assassinate Castro, through his negotiating friend, Donovan. The top secret 1967 Inspector General's *Report on Plots to Assassinate Fidel Castro* described the scheme: "At about the time of the Donovan-Castro negotiations for the release of the Bay of Pigs prisoners a plan was devised to have Donovan present a contaminated skin diving suit to Castro as a gift . . . According to Sidney Gottlieb [head of the CIA's Technical Services Division], this scheme progressed to the point of actually buying a diving suit and readying it for delivery. The technique involved dusting the inside of the suit with a fungus that would produce a disabling and chronic skin disease (Madura foot) and contaminating the breathing apparatus with tubercle bacilli."[26]

CIA executive Sam Halpern, who was in on the scheme, later recalled, "The plan was abandoned because it was overtaken by events: Donovan had already given Castro a skin diving suit on his own initiative."[27] By trying to use negotiator Donovan as an unwitting instrument for Castro's murder, the CIA knew it was also setting up the authority Donovan represented, President Kennedy, who would have been blamed for the Cuban premier's easily traceable death. Thus the intended demise of three targets: Castro's life, Kennedy's credibility, and the hope of a Cuban–American dialogue. The aborted scenario was an odd foreshadowing of the scapegoating process in JFK's murder, in which a CIA-created trail would lead visibly from the victim, through Oswald, toward Castro, effectively destroying through Dallas any possible Cuban–American rapprochement. Nor was the CIA's Donovan-Castro plot without high-level authority. The Inspector General's report noted explicitly that among "those who were involved in the plot or who were identified to us by the participants as being witting" was Richard Helms, then covert-action chief.[28] By 1967 when the report was written on the CIA's plots to kill Castro, Helms had become the director of Central Intelligence.

Thanks to Donovan's own fortuitous gift to Castro of a harmless diving suit, his dialogue partner survived the plot and their April conversations transpired hopefully. Castro raised with Donovan the issue of future U.S. policy. Donovan noted Kennedy's recent steps in restricting exile groups. Castro in turn said pointedly that his "ideal government was not to be Soviet oriented," and asked how diplomatic ties with the United States might be resumed. Donovan asked Castro, "Do you know how porcupines make love?" Castro said, "No." "The answer," Donovan said, "is 'very carefully.'"[29]

In late April at Donovan's recommendation, Castro granted ABC reporter Lisa Howard an interview.[30] On her return from Cuba, Howard innocently briefed the CIA in detail on Castro's surprising openness toward Kennedy. She reported that when she asked Castro how a rapprochement between the United States and Cuba could be achieved, Castro said that "steps were already being taken." Pressed further, he said, nodding toward Kennedy's initiative, that he considered "the U.S. limitation on exile raids to be a proper step toward accommodation." Howard concluded from the ten-hour interview that Castro was "looking for a way to reach a rapprochement with the United States Government." She said Castro also indicated, however, "that if a rapprochement was wanted President John F. Kennedy would have to make the first move."[31]

Each of these Castro overtures for a new U.S.–Cuban relationship was noted word for word in a secret CIA memorandum written on May 1, 1963, by the Deputy Director of Plans (head of covert action) Richard Helms, that was not declassified until 1996. It was addressed to CIA Director John McCone. A scribbled "P saw" on the upper right-hand side of the document indicates it was read also by the president.[32] Thus we have become witnesses to Kennedy watching the CIA watching Castro approaching Kennedy, in response to Kennedy's crackdown on the CIA's covert-action anti-Castro groups. As the increasingly interested porcupines edged toward each other very carefully, the CIA's chief of covert action was, as the president knew, monitoring very carefully their prickly courtship.

The CIA tried to block the door that could be seen opening through Howard's interview. CIA Director John McCone argued that Howard's approach to Cuba "would leak and compromise a number of CIA operations against Castro."[33] In a May 2, 1963, memorandum to National Security Adviser McGeorge Bundy, McCone urged that the "Lisa Howard report be handled in the most limited and sensitive manner" and "that no active steps be taken on the rapprochement matter at this time."[34]

As would become apparent years later from research into the background of Lee Harvey Oswald, the CIA was then also setting in motion a covert operation in New Orleans to ensure there would never be a Kennedy–Castro rapprochement.

In April 1963, when John Kennedy responded to CIA duplicity by turning toward his enemy Fidel Castro, Lee Harvey Oswald was going through a transition of his own—a move from Dallas to New Orleans. Unlike Kennedy, Oswald chose not to turn in an independent direction, but in the course of his move to New Orleans to continue to be directed by others for their own purposes.

Oswald quickly found work in New Orleans at the Reily Coffee Company. It was owned by William B. Reily, a wealthy supporter of the CIA-sponsored Cuban Revolutionary Council.[35] As researcher William Davy has shown by a recently declassified government document, Reily's Coffee Company seems to have long been part of the CIA's New Orleans network. According to a CIA memorandum dated January 31, 1964, "this firm [Reily's] was of interest as of April 1949." [36] In a 1968 interview with the New Orleans District Attorney's Office, CIA contract employee Gerry Patrick Hemming "confirmed that William Reily had worked for the CIA for years." [37] As Lee Harvey Oswald went to work in New Orleans, he was in the company of the Company.

The Reily Coffee Company was located at the center of the U.S. intelligence community in New Orleans, close by the offices of the CIA, FBI, Secret Service, and Office of Naval Intelligence (ONI). [38] Directly across the street from Naval Intelligence and the Secret Service was another office that Oswald worked in, the detective agency of former FBI agent Guy Banister. [39]

Guy Banister Associates functioned more as a covert-action center for U.S. intelligence agencies than it did as a detective agency. Banister's office helped supply munitions for CIA operations ranging from the Bay of Pigs to the Cuban exile attacks designed to ensnare Kennedy. Guns and ammunition littered the office. [40] CIA paramilitaries checked in with Banister on their way to and from nearby anti-Castro training camps. Daniel Campbell was an ex-Marine hired by Banister to assist in small arms training for the Cuban exiles and to inform on radical students at New Orleans colleges. Campbell later told researcher Jim DiEugenio, "Banister was a bagman for the CIA and was running guns to Alpha 66 in Miami." [41]

Banister's secretary and confidante Delphine Roberts said Lee Harvey Oswald came to Banister's office sometime in 1963, ostensibly to fill out an application form to become one of Banister's agents. Roberts told author Anthony Summers, "During the course of the conversation I gained the impression that he and Guy Banister already knew each other." [42] Oswald and Banister then met behind closed doors for a long conversation. "I presumed then, and now am certain," Roberts said, "that the reason for Oswald being there was that he was required to act undercover." [43] Oswald was given the use of an office on the second floor, "above the main office where we worked," Roberts said. "I was not greatly surprised when I learned he was going up and down, back and forth." [44] Roberts noticed that Oswald had pro-Castro leaflets upstairs, and she later saw him passing them out on the street. When she complained to Banister about Oswald's pro-Castro demonstrating, Banister said not to worry about him, "He's with us, he's associated with the office." [45]

Banister's office became the base for a political theater that Oswald acted out on the streets of New Orleans during the summer of 1963, whose final meaning would not become apparent until November 22. Oswald had written in May to the New York headquarters of the Fair Play for Cuba Committee (FPCC), saying he planned to establish his own New Orleans branch of the pro-Castro organization. He was warned explicitly, by a letter from the FPCC national director, V. T. Lee, against provoking "unnecessary incidents which frighten away prospective supporters" in an atmosphere as politically hostile to their efforts as was that of New Orleans.[46] Oswald then pushed ahead and tempted fate on June 16 by passing out pro-Castro leaflets to the unlikely audience of sailors disembarking from an aircraft carrier, the USS *Wasp,* on the dock at the port of New Orleans. Oswald may have been smiling to himself at his efforts to stir up a *Wasp*'s nest for the FPCC. However, before he could provoke precisely the kind of incident he had been warned against, a patrolman in the harbor police ordered him to leave, and he did so.[47]

In August, Oswald tried harder to make such an impact and, with the assistance of others, succeeded. He managed to dramatize his support for Fidel Castro to the entire city of New Orleans, in such a way as to highlight Oswald's own public history as an expatriate Marine recently returned from his defection to the Soviet Union.

He began on August 5 by visiting Carlos Bringuier, a leader in the anti-Castro exile community. Bringuier was the New Orleans delegate of the Directorio Revolucionario Estudiantil (DRE), a group that a 1967 CIA memorandum described as "conceived, created, and funded by CIA."[48] A House Select Committee on Assassinations report said "the DRE was, of all the anti-Castro groups, one of the most bitter toward President Kennedy for his [Cuban Missile Crisis] 'deal' with the Russians."[49] Former CIA agent E. Howard Hunt testified before the House Committee that the DRE was "run" for the CIA by David Phillips,[50] the same CIA man behind the scenes who as "Maurice Bishop" had directed the Alpha 66 raids designed to push President Kennedy into war with Cuba. Carlos Bringuier's specific duties in New Orleans for the CIA-run DRE were, as he told both Lee Harvey Oswald and the Warren Commission, "propaganda and information."[51] In the summer of 1963, Oswald was a transparent collaborator in fulfilling Bringuier's propaganda mission.

The story that Carlos Bringuier told the Warren Commission about his interactions with Oswald gave no hint of the CIA background the two men had in common—the key to interpreting the drama Bringuier narrated. He began his account by describing Oswald as a suspicious, unannounced visitor on August 5 to the New Orleans clothing store Bringuier managed. He said Oswald told him he was against Communism, had been in the Marine Corps, and "was willing to train Cubans to fight against Castro."[52] Bringuier continued his story by saying he turned down Oswald, who he felt might be an infiltrator. Undeterred, Oswald returned the next day, and in Bringuier's absence left Oswald's Marine Corps training manual as a personal gift for the fight against Castro.

Oswald's and Bringuier's street theater occurred three days later. Bringuier said he was in his store when he was told about a demonstrator on Canal Street carrying a sign saying "Viva Fidel." He and two Cuban friends rushed out and confronted the Fidel activist, who to Bringuier's anger turned out to be the same man who had been offering to help him fight Castro, Lee

Harvey Oswald. Then, as Bringuier described the scene to Warren Commission assistant counsel Wesley J. Liebeler, "many people start to gather around us to see what was going on over there. I start to explain to the people what Oswald did to me, because I wanted to move the American people against him, not to take the fight for myself as a Cuban but to move the American people to fight him, and I told them that that was a Castro agent, that he was a pro-Communist, and that he was trying to do to them exactly what he did to us in Cuba, kill them and send their children to the execution wall . . .

"The people in the street became angry and they started to shout to him, 'Traitor! Communist! Go to Cuba! Kill him!' and some other phrases that I do not know if I could tell in the record."

One of Bringuier's friends snatched Oswald's leaflets, tore them up, and threw them in the air.

"And I was more angry," Bringuier continued, "I took my glasses off and I went near to him to hit him, but when he sensed my intention, he put his arm down as an X."

Bringuier paused in his narrative to demonstrate to Liebeler the X Oswald had made by crossing his arms in front of him. Then Bringuier resumed: "[Oswald] put his face [up to mine] and told me, 'O.K. Carlos, if you want to hit me, hit me."

Ignoring in his story the almost friendly way in which Oswald had provoked him, Bringuier told Liebeler that he realized Oswald "was trying to appear as a martyr if I will hit him, and I decide not to hit him." [53]

A few seconds later two police cars pulled up. The street scene between the coolly controlled "pro-Castro demonstrator" and his three "opponents," all players in a script they had not written, was suddenly over. The police officers arrested Oswald, Bringuier, and his two Cuban friends, and took all four to a police station, where they were charged with disturbing the peace. Bringuier and his friends were released on bond, and Oswald spent the night in jail. The three Cubans eventually had their charges dismissed. Oswald pled guilty and was fined $10.00. [54]

From jail Oswald asked through the police to speak with an FBI agent. It was a strange request for an anti-government demonstrator. He then met with New Orleans Special Agent John Quigley for an hour and a half. Why? Quigley told the Warren Commission vaguely the following spring that he felt Oswald "was probably making a self-serving statement in attempting to explain to me why he was distributing this literature, and for no other reason." [55]

The Warren Commission was well aware, by the time of Quigley's testimony, of another possible reason why Oswald might have wanted to meet with an FBI agent—that Oswald was on the same payroll, "employed by the F.B.I. at $200 per month from September of 1962 up to the time of the assassination," [56] as stated by the commission's general counsel J. Lee Rankin, at their closed-door meeting on January 27, 1964. The transcript of this remarkable session was classified "top secret" for a decade until researcher Harold Weisberg gained access to it through a legal battle and published all of it as his *Whitewash IV* in 1974. The purpose of the Warren Commissioners' entire January 27 meeting was to deal with the disturbing information Rankin had received from Texas attorney general Waggoner Carr that "Oswald was an undercover agent for the F.B.I." [57] Rankin called Carr's report, with its specific payroll information, "a dirty rumor that is very bad for the Commission," and said "it must be wiped out insofar as it is possible to do so by this Commission." [58] The Commission did so by simply asking officials of the FBI, and the CIA as well (for whom Oswald was also said to have been an agent), to testify on whether Oswald had in fact been working for them. They said he had not.[59] Former CIA director Allen Dulles put their denials in a national security perspective at the January 27 meeting by saying frankly that the CIA employers of an agent "ought not tell it under oath." [60] Dulles said that the same code of denial (or perjury, a word he didn't use) applied to the FBI.[61] The January 27 meeting's transcript is a revelation of how Allen Dulles, one of the master plotters of the Cold War and by logic a prime suspect in JFK's murder, kept a bemused composure while guiding the circle of distinguished elders through the cover-up.

Oswald seems to have been working with both the CIA and the FBI. For the CIA, he was acting as a provocateur, subverting the public image of the Fair Play for Cuba Committee. As we shall see, Oswald was also being drawn into the plot to kill the president, in which his activities as a pro-Castro demonstrator were preparing the ground for his role as the assassination scapegoat. At the same time, Oswald was apparently an FBI informant. As we learn more about Lee Harvey Oswald, we will have to consider the possibility that the information he was giving the FBI may have actually been an attempt to stop the killing of the president.

Six days after his release from jail, Oswald was back on the streets passing out more pro-Castro leaflets. This time he succeeded in gaining wider media attention, to the increasing detriment of the Fair Play for Cuba Committee. His leafleting was carried on the TV news, and he was interviewed by local radio commentator William Stuckey, who probed into his personal background. Oswald presented a Marine Corps past in which he "served honorably," omitting his later betrayal to the Soviet Union and his undesirable discharge—thereby setting himself up to be exposed as a turncoat. He accepted Stuckey's invitation to take part in a radio debate against his presumed antagonist, Carlos Bringuier, and Bringuier's ally Ed Butler, a CIA asset who was head of the stridently anti-communist Information Council of the Americas (INCA). According to a CIA memorandum that is now in the National Archives, "Butler, Staff Director of INCA, is a contact of our New Orleans Office and the source of numerous reports." [62]

The radio debate on August 21 quickly became an expose of Oswald's history with Soviet Communism. William Stuckey had been primed earlier that day, he said to the Warren Commission, both by an unidentified "news source" and by Ed Butler, about Oswald's past in Russia.[63] Stuckey said he conferred with Butler, and "we agreed together to produce this information on the program that night."[64] As the debate began, Stuckey therefore introduced Oswald by citing newspaper clippings showing he had tried to renounce his American citizenship to become a Soviet citizen in 1959 and had remained in the Soviet Union for three years.[65] Bringuier and Butler then peppered Oswald with questions about the FPCC as a communist front and Cuba as a Soviet satellite. Oswald responded to the coordinated ambush with as cool a response as he had given Bringuier on the street. He calmly acknowledged his expatriate history in the U.S.S.R., then added his own touch to the discrediting of the FPCC by repeatedly bringing up its investigations by the federal government, protesting perhaps too much that nothing incriminating had been found.[66]

The "debate" succeeded in thoroughly identifying Oswald's FPCC chapter with his treasonous past. With this public relations disaster, his whirlwind New Orleans campaign had ended. He had not only succeeded in thoroughly discrediting the FPCC in New Orleans. After John Kennedy's assassination, Oswald's public association with the national Fair Play for Cuba Committee would demolish what little there was left of it.[67]

More important, Oswald's pro-Castro masquerade in New Orleans would be used later to introduce Fidel Castro into the background of John Kennedy's murder. Through Oswald, whose Cuban connection would be further dramatized in the days ahead, Castro could become the larger assassination scapegoat, thereby justifying an invasion of Cuba in retaliation for its apparent murder of a president who had pledged personally not to invade Cuba.

John Kennedy's turn toward peace was not without reversals and compromises. On June 19, 1963, President Kennedy succumbed to Cold War pressures and stepped backward. He approved a CIA program of sabotage and harassment against targets in Cuba that included electric power, transportation, oil, and manufacturing facilities.[68] Kennedy was responding both to mounting demands in his own administration for increasing pressure on Castro and to the appearance of a more aggressive Cuban government policy of exporting revolution to other Latin American countries. While adhering to his promise to Khrushchev not to launch a U.S. invasion of Cuba, Kennedy nevertheless agreed to a modified version of the covert-action campaign against Cuba that he had endorsed as Operation Mongoose in November 1961. Only nine days after his American University address, Kennedy had ratified a CIA program contradicting it.

Kennedy's regression can be understood in the political context of the time. He was, after all, an American politician, and the Cold War was far from over. For the remaining five months of his life, John Kennedy continued a policy of sabotage against Cuba that he may have seen as a bone thrown to his barking CIA and military advisers but was in any case a crime against international law. It was also a violation of the international trust that he and Nikita Khrushchev had envisioned and increasingly fostered since the missile crisis. Right up to his death, Kennedy remained in some ways a Cold Warrior, in conflict with his own soaring vision in the American University address. What is remarkable, however, is not that Kennedy compromised that vision and continued to support the subversion of the Cuban government in 1963, but that beneath that given political reality of his day he secretly explored a different possibility with Fidel Castro. He did so with an increasingly open Castro through the mediation, unknown to him, of his other enemy, Nikita Khrushchev.

When Khrushchev had agreed with Kennedy to withdraw Soviet missiles from Cuba in exchange for a promise of no invasion, Castro had been almost as angry with Khrushchev as he was with Kennedy. He had reason to be upset. As Cuba's former UN ambassador Carlos Lechuga put it in his book on the missile crisis, "[Castro] had been neither consulted nor even informed of the decision made in the Kremlin. The withdrawal of the missiles and the way that decision was made was a painful blow to both the Cuban government and people. Even though, looking back on events, it may be considered that war was averted, the problem had not been solved in a way that would remove the threat to Cuba." [69]

All Cuba gained from the superpowers' agreement was the promise by an imperialist president that the United States would not invade its tiny neighbor. Yet there were no guarantees that Kennedy or his successors would fulfill that pledge. Nor did the vow of no invasion mean an end to U.S. subversion of Cuba, as subsequent events proved. Castro was furious that his Soviet ally had suddenly withdrawn without consultation a nuclear deterrent to U.S. aggression. After the missile crisis, for days Castro was so angry that he refused even to meet with the Soviet ambassador in Havana. [70] In his view Nikita Khrushchev had become a traitor.

Khrushchev responded to his repudiation by Castro by writing him what the Cuban premier described three decades later as "really a wonderful letter . . . a beautiful, elegant, very friendly letter." [71] In that January 31, 1963, letter to his estranged comrade, Khrushchev began, as he had in his first secret letter to Kennedy, with a description of the beauty surrounding him, in this case as he rode in a train returning to Moscow from a conference in Berlin:

"Our train is crossing the fields and forests of Soviet Byelorussia and it occurs to me how wonderful it would be if you could see, on a sunny day like this, the ground covered with snow and the forests silvery with frost.

"Perhaps you, a southern man, have seen this only in paintings. It must surely be fairly difficult for you to imagine the ground carpeted with snow and the forests covered with white frost. It would be good if you could visit our country each season of the year; every one of them, spring, summer, fall, and winter, has its delights." [72]

Khrushchev said the principal theme of his letter was "the strong desire my comrades and I feel to see you and to talk, to talk with our hearts open."[73] He acknowledged the current strain "in the relations between our states—Cuba and the Soviet Union—and in our own personal relationship. Speaking frankly, these relations are not what they were before the crisis. I will not conceal the fact that this troubles and worries us. And it seems to me that the development of our relations will depend, in large part, on our meeting."[74]

He then reviewed the Caribbean crisis, in which "our viewpoints did not always coincide," appealing to Castro to recognize finally: "There are, in spite of everything, commitments that the United States of North America has undertaken through the statement of their president. Obviously, one cannot trust them and take it as an absolute guarantee, but neither is it reasonable to ignore them totally."[75]

Khrushchev was, ever so gently, urging Castro to risk trusting Kennedy, as Khrushchev himself was beginning to do, in tandem with Kennedy's beginning to trust him, sometimes to one or the other's regret but with their mutually discovered commitment to peace as the foundation to which they could always return.

Castro accepted Khrushchev's invitation to visit him that spring. He toured almost the entire Soviet Union in May and early June 1963, spending at least half the time with the leader he had rejected and shunned in November. According to Nikita Khrushchev's son Sergei, it was then that "Father and Fidel developed a teacher-student relationship."[76] Castro's own description of his time with Khrushchev has confirmed both its tutorial dimension and its focus on the missile crisis: "for hours [Khrushchev] read many messages to me, messages from President Kennedy, messages sometimes delivered through Robert Kennedy . . . There was a translator, and Khrushchev read and read the letters sent back and forth."[77]

Khrushchev was trying to pass on to his Cuban comrade the paradoxical enlightenment for peace that he and Kennedy had received together from the brink of total war. While trying not to sound overly positive about a capitalist leader, Khrushchev also couldn't help but reveal the extraordinary hope he felt because of what he and Kennedy had managed to resolve. As Sergei Khrushchev put it, "Father tried to persuade Castro that the U.S. president would keep his word and that Cuba was guaranteed six years of peaceful development, which was how long Father thought Kennedy would be in the White House. Six years! Almost an eternity!"[78]

In the course of reading aloud his correspondence with Kennedy, Khrushchev also inadvertently revealed to Castro that he and Kennedy had exchanged the withdrawal of missiles in Cuba for the withdrawal of missiles in Turkey and Italy. It showed that Khrushchev had other strategic considerations in mind besides the defense of Cuba. Castro recalled: "When this was read, I looked at him and said: 'Nikita, would you please read that part again about the missiles in Turkey and Italy?' He laughed that mischievous laugh of his. He laughed, but that was it. I was sure that they were not going to repeat it again because it was like that old phrase about bringing up the issue of the noose in the home of the man who was hung." [79]

As we know, even before Castro visited the Soviet Union, he had already begun to turn toward Kennedy through his friendly exchanges with the president's negotiator for the Bay of Pigs prisoners, James Donovan, and in response to Kennedy's April crackdown on Cuban exile attacks. Further encouraged by Khrushchev's tutorial, Castro returned to Havana confirmed in his resolve to negotiate with his enemy, John Kennedy. The CIA continued to monitor every step of this process. In a secret June 5, 1963, memorandum, Richard Helms wrote that the CIA had just received a report that, "at the request of Khrushchev, Castro was returning to Cuba with the intention of adopting a conciliatory policy toward the Kennedy administration 'for the time being.'" [80]

The CIA cut short this development by its sabotage program (that Kennedy approved on June 19) and by its own attempt once again to assassinate Castro. Toward the end of the summer of 1963, CIA case officers met with an undercover CIA agent code-named AM/LASH, who lived in Cuba. AM/LASH was close to Fidel Castro. At the meeting he discussed with his CIA case officers an "inside job" against Castro. He said he was "awaiting a U.S. plan of action." [81] This was reported to CIA Headquarters on September 7. We will learn more about that Castro assassination plan, as the CIA shapes and directs it to converge with John Kennedy's assassination.

Early the next morning, Premier Fidel Castro was interviewed at the Brazilian Embassy in Havana following a reception. In a September 9 article in U.S. papers, Associated Press reporter Daniel Harker said Castro had delivered "a rambling, informal post-midnight dissertation," in the course of which he warned "U.S. leaders" if they aided any attempt to eliminate Cuban leaders: "We are prepared to fight them and answer in kind. U.S. leaders should think that if they are aiding terrorist plans to eliminate Cuban leaders, they themselves will not be safe." [82]

When Castro was questioned about this statement by the HSCA in 1978, he said, "I don't remember literally what I said, but I remember my intention in saying what I said and it was to warn the government that we know about the (attempted) plots against our lives . . . So, I said something like those plots start to set a very bad precedent, a very serious one—that that could become a boomerang against the authors of those actions . . . but I did not mean to threaten by that . . . I did not mean by that that we were going to take measures—similar measures—like a retaliation for that." [83]

With Kennedy and Castro expressing mutual hostility and backing away from any dialogue during the summer, it was not until late September that the two porcupines began to resume their prickly courtship. Their renewed interest in a dialogue came about through the mediation of Lisa Howard, the ABC newswoman who had interviewed Castro in April, and William Attwood, a U.S. diplomat attached to its United Nations mission.

After her return from Cuba, Lisa Howard had written an article in the journal *War/Peace Report* on "Castro's Overture," based on her interview with the Cuban premier. She wrote that in their private conversations Castro had been "even more emphatic about his desire for negotiations with the United States . . . In our conversations he made it quite clear that he was ready to discuss: the Soviet personnel and military hardware on Cuban soil; compensation for expropriated American lands and investments; the question of Cuba as a base for Communist subversion throughout the Hemisphere." [84]

It was Howard who envisioned the next step. Her article urged the Kennedy administration to "send an American government official on a quiet mission to Havana to hear what Castro has to say." [85] This was the risk-filled secret mission that William Attwood actually began to undertake on behalf of President John Kennedy in September 1963.

More than a decade after JFK's assassination, on January 10, 1975, William Attwood testified at a top-secret executive session of Senator Frank Church's Committee on Intelligence Activities. There the question was posed to Attwood: "Were you asked by President Kennedy to explore the possibility of a rapprochement with Fidel Castro and Cuba?"

Attwood answered: "Yes . . . yes, approaches were made and contact was established and this was done with the knowledge, approval, and encouragement of the White House." [86]

William Attwood was well qualified for such a role. As a distinguished journalist, Attwood had interviewed Fidel Castro in 1959 soon after the Cuban revolution for two articles in *Look* magazine. In a September 18, 1963, memorandum to the White House, Attwood wrote of his journalistic relationship with Castro: "Although Castro did not like my final article in 1959, we got along well and I believe he remembers me as someone he could talk to frankly." [87] Attwood had also been a speechwriter for both Adlai Stevenson and John Kennedy. President Kennedy appointed him ambassador to Guinea. Attwood had known Kennedy since their school days. In the fall of 1963, William Attwood was between diplomatic assignments by JFK, serving then for a few months at the United Nations as an African affairs adviser to UN ambassador Adlai Stevenson. Attwood was in a perfect position to be JFK's point man in a secret dialogue with Castro. As he put it in his September 18 memorandum briefing Stevenson and Kennedy, "I have enough rank to satisfy Castro that this would be a serious conversation. At the same time I am not so well-known that my departure, arrival or return [to and from Cuba] would be noticed." [88]

On September 20 President Kennedy went to New York to address the UN General Assembly. He met with Ambassador Stevenson and gave his approval for William Attwood "to make discreet contact" with Dr. Carlos Lechuga, Cuba's UN ambassador, in order to explore a possible dialogue with Castro. [89] At this point Adlai Stevenson said prophetically why he thought such a Kennedy–Castro dialogue would never be allowed to happen. "Unfortunately," he told Attwood, "the CIA is still in charge of Cuba." [90] Nevertheless, President Kennedy, while knowing the danger of his once again heading upstream against the CIA, had decided the time was right to begin talking with Castro.

In collaboration with Attwood, Lisa Howard organized a party at her New York apartment on September 23 to serve as the pretext and social cover for a first conversation between Attwood and Lechuga. When she invited Carlos Lechuga to the party, she made sure he would come by saying, in Lechuga's recollection years later, "that Ambassador William Attwood of the U.S. delegation wanted to talk with me and that it was urgent, as he was going to Washington the next day." [91]

Both Lechuga and Attwood later wrote memoirs that included complementary descriptions of their seminal conversation at Lisa Howard's party, Lechuga's *In the Eye of the Storm* and Attwood's *The Twilight Struggle*. According to Lechuga's more detailed account, Attwood was introduced to him "in the midst of cocktails, sandwiches, diplomats, and journalists," and "lost no time in saying why he had wanted to meet me. He said that Stevenson had authorized him to do so and that he would be flying to Washington in a few hours to request authorization from the president to go to Cuba to meet with Fidel Castro and ask about the feasibility of a rapprochement between Havana and Washington." Lechuga was astounded by Attwood's overture. He sensed rightly that not only Stevenson but also the president had already approved their initial contact. He told Attwood that, in view of the conflicts between their countries, "what he was telling me came as a surprise and that I would listen to him with great interest." [92]

Attwood asked if Lechuga felt the chances of the Cuban government allowing him to go to Havana for such a purpose were fifty-fifty. Lechuga said, "That may be a good guess." [93] The two men agreed that current U.S. policies, with Kennedy's American University address and test ban treaty presenting one aspect, and the CIA's saboteurs in Cuba and spy flights overhead presenting another, had created "an absurd situation." Attwood told Lechuga "that Kennedy had often confessed in private conversations that he didn't know how he was going to change U.S. policy on Cuba, and that neither the United States nor Cuba could change it overnight because of the prestige involved. However, Kennedy said something had to be done about it and a start had to be made." [94]

William Attwood's account of the same conversation adds a few details. Lechuga "said Castro had hoped to establish some sort of contact with Kennedy after he became president in 1961, but the Bay of Pigs ended any chance of that, at least for the time being. But Castro had read Kennedy's American University speech in June and had liked its tone. I mentioned my Havana visit in 1959 and Fidel's 'Let us be friends' remark in our conversation. Lechuga said another such conversation in Havana could be useful and might be arranged. He expressed irritation at the continuing exile raids and our freezing $33 million in Cuban assets in U.S. banks in July. We agreed the present situation was abnormal [Lechuga thought they had agreed the situation was "absurd"] and we should keep in touch." [95]

On September 24 Attwood met Robert Kennedy in Washington and reported on his meeting with Lechuga the night before. RFK thought Attwood's going to Cuba was too risky—"it was bound to leak," provoking accusations of appeasement.[96] He wondered if Castro would agree to meet somewhere outside Cuba, perhaps at the United Nations. He said Attwood should continue pursuing the matter with Lechuga.[97]

Three days later Attwood met Lechuga at the UN Delegates Lounge, "always a good place for discreet encounters," Attwood noted, "because of its noise and confusion."[98] He told Lechuga it would be difficult for him as a government official to go to Cuba. However, "if Castro or a personal emissary had something to tell us, we were prepared to meet him and listen wherever else would be convenient."[99] Lechuga said he would pass on the information to Havana.

Lechuga then warned his secret dialogue partner that he'd be "making a tough anti-American speech on October 7, but not to take it too seriously."[100] When Adlai Stevenson replied to Lechuga on October 7 with his own anti-Cuban speech, it had been written by Attwood—and was in turn taken with a grain of salt by Lechuga, in view of his knowledge of John Kennedy's turn toward a dialogue with Fidel Castro.[101] U.S.–Cuban polemics at the UN now served as a cover for a beginning Kennedy–Castro dialogue.

After three weeks without a reply from Havana, with Attwood's approval Lisa Howard began phoning Rene Vallejo, Castro's aide and confidant, who favored a U.S.–Cuban dialogue. Howard doubted the message from Lechuga had ever gotten past the Cuban Foreign Office. She wanted to make sure through Vallejo that Castro himself knew there was a U.S. official ready to talk with him. For another week she and Vallejo left phone messages for each other.[102]

On October 28, Attwood was finally told by Lechuga in the UN Delegates' Lounge that Havana did not think "sending someone to the United Nations for talks" would be "useful at this time."[103] Like Howard, Attwood felt that Lechuga's message had never even reached Castro through an unsympathetic Foreign Office.[104]

In the meantime, an impatient John Kennedy had decided to create his own back channel to communicate with Fidel Castro, just as he had done with Nikita Khrushchev through Norman Cousins and other intermediaries. On Thursday, October 24, the president was interviewed at the White House by French journalist Jean Daniel, editor of the socialist newsweekly *L'Observateur*. Daniel was an old friend of William Attwood, who knew he was on his way to Cuba to interview Castro. Attwood had urged Daniel to see Kennedy first. Kennedy granted the interview as a perfect way for him to communicate informally with Castro, through pointed remarks that Daniel would inevitably share with his next interview subject. Daniel realized that Kennedy, who asked to see him again right after he saw Castro, wanted to know Castro's response. The president was making Daniel his unofficial envoy to the Cuban prime minister.

In the *New Republic* article he wrote on his historic interviews with Kennedy and Castro, Daniel stressed the emphasis with which Kennedy spoke about the Cuban revolution: "John Kennedy then mustered all his persuasive force. He punctuated each sentence with that brief, mechanical gesture which had become famous." [105]

"From the beginning," Kennedy said, "I personally followed the development of these events [in Cuba] with mounting concern. There are few subjects to which I have devoted more painstaking attention . . . Here is what I believe." Then came the words that could have become the seeds for a just peace between the United States and Cuba. Just as Kennedy's American University paragraphs on Russian suffering had profoundly impressed his Russian enemy Nikita Khrushchev, so would the president's next words to Jean Daniel on Cuban suffering, repeated to Fidel Castro, break through the ideological resistance of his Cuban enemy:

"I believe that there is no country in the world, including all the African regions, including any and all the countries under colonial domination, where economic colonization, humiliation and exploitation were worse than in Cuba, in part owing to my country's policies during the Batista regime . . . I approved the proclamation which Fidel Castro made in the Sierra Maestra, when he justifiably called for justice and especially yearned to rid Cuba of corruption. I will go even further: to some extent it is as though Batista was the incarnation of a number of sins on the part of the United States. Now we shall have to pay for those sins. In the matter of the Batista regime, I am in agreement with the first Cuban revolutionaries. That is perfectly clear." [106]

Kennedy looked at Daniel in silence. He noticed his surprise and heightened interest. Then the president went on to define in Cold War terms what he saw as the essence of his conflict with Castro:

"But it is also clear that the problem has ceased to be a Cuban one, and has become international—that is, it has become a Soviet problem . . . I know that through [Castro's] fault—either his 'will to independence' [Kennedy had just spoken with Daniel on General Charles de Gaulle's 'will to independence' for France, a psycho-political strategy requiring a constant tension with the United States], his madness or Communism—the world was on the verge of nuclear war in October, 1962. The Russians understood this very well, at least after our reaction; but so far as Fidel Castro is concerned, I must say I don't know whether he realizes this, or even if he cares about it."

Kennedy smiled, then added: "You can tell me whether he does when you come back." [107]

After his ringing endorsement of the Cuban revolution, Kennedy's argument with Castro rested on Cold War assumptions that Kennedy himself was beginning to doubt but had not yet discarded. Even after his American University address, he was still unable to see that it had been the ongoing threat of a U.S. invasion of Cuba (provoking the Soviet-Cuban decision to deter that invasion by nuclear missiles) that had caused the Cuban Missile Crisis, not Castro's " 'will to independence,' madness, or Communism." Yet at the same time Daniel could see Kennedy was distinctly uncomfortable with the dead end where his assumptions led for the revolution he had just endorsed. His last comment to Daniel was: "The continuation of the block-ade [against Cuba] depends on the continuation of subversive activities." [108] He meant Castro's subversive activities, not his own, but as Daniel said to his readers, "I could see plainly that John Kennedy had doubts, and was seeking a way out." [109] However, he had less than a month left to find that way out.

In the fall of 1963, as John Kennedy and Fidel Castro sought secretly a way of rapprochement, the CIA took its own secret steps in an opposite direction, toward setting up Lee Harvey Oswald as an identifiable Soviet-and-Cuban-directed assassin of the president. "Sheepdipping," the process whereby sheep are plunged into a liquid to destroy parasites, had been applied in its intelligence sense to Oswald in New Orleans. There Oswald's potentially incriminating associations in Fort Worth and Dallas with George de Mohrenschildt and the White Russian community were expunged in the pool of Oswald's Fair Play for Cuba dramatics. Oswald would now be moved back to Dallas, but with his visible, CIA-connected mentor de Mohrenschildt having been safely removed to Haiti. Into de Mohrenschildt's place stepped a less visible figure. However, thanks to the dedicated probing of an investigator for the House Select Committee on Assassinations, we have been given a glimpse of the man in the shadows.

In early September, Oswald met CIA agent David Atlee Phillips in the busy lobby of a downtown office building in Dallas. Alpha 66 leader Antonio Veci-ana, who worked for years under Phillips and knew him by his pseudonym "Maurice Bishop," witnessed the Dallas scene. He described it in 1975 to the HSCA investigator he had learned to trust, Gaeton Fonzi, who included it in his book *The Last Investigation*: "as soon as he walked in, [Veciana] saw Bishop standing in a corner of the lobby talking with a pale, slight and soft-featured young man. Veciana does not recall if Bishop introduced him by name, but Bishop ended his conversation with the young man shortly after Veciana arrived. Together, they walked out of the lobby onto the busy side-walk. Bishop and the young man stopped behind Veciana for a moment, had a few additional words, then the young man gestured farewell and walked away. Bishop immediately turned to Veciana and began a discussion of the current activities of Alpha 66 as they walked to a nearby coffee shop. He never spoke to Veciana about the young man and Veciana didn't ask." [110]

On November 22, Veciana would immediately recognize the newspaper and television pictures of Lee Harvey Oswald as being of the young man he had seen in Dallas with his own CIA handler "Maurice Bishop." However, in his subsequent meetings with Bishop, Veciana would be careful never to allude to the Oswald meeting both men knew he had observed, which if known further could serve as a critical evidentiary link between the CIA and the accused assassin of the president. [111] Sixteen years later, after Veciana did finally describe the Oswald meeting to the House Committee and came to the very edge of identifying David Atlee Phillips as "Maurice Bishop," he was shot in the head by an unidentified gunman in Miami. Veciana recovered from the assassination attempt. He never admitted publicly that Phillips was Bishop, though he acknowledged as much privately to Fonzi.[112]

When I interviewed Antonio Veciana, he added details about the attempt to assassinate him. He said the FBI had warned him three times that he was about to be killed. Yet after he was shot, the FBI did nothing to investigate the incident. They said it was the responsibility of the Miami police, who in turn did no investigation.[113] By avoiding any investigation, the FBI and the police seemed to be deferring to a higher authority.

We have already seen how David Phillips, as Antonio Veciana's CIA sponsor, guided Alpha 66's efforts to draw President Kennedy into an all-out war with Fidel Castro. Phillips was Chief of Covert Action at the CIA's Mexico City Station. Two months before JFK's murder, Phillips became Mexico City's Chief of Cuban Operations.[114] Phillips was, from the beginning to the end of his CIA career, a team player. Following the Kennedy assassination, he rose to the rank of chief of the CIA's Western Hemisphere Division. Shortly before his retirement in 1975, he was awarded the Distinguished Intelligence Medal, the CIA's highest honor.[115] In the fall of 1963, David Atlee Phillips was working under Richard Helms, the CIA's Deputy Director of Plans and mastermind of covert action.

According to the *Warren Report*, Lee Harvey Oswald was in Mexico City from September 27 to October 2, 1963, and visited both the Cuban and Soviet Consulates.[116] This is the point at which the person Lee Harvey Oswald begins to disappear down a black hole. As a Cold War actor who took on assigned roles, the person Oswald was never easy to see. In Mexico City the real Oswald almost drops out of sight, but with his absence covered by impersonators and the CIA's smoke and mirrors.

The CIA's Mexico City Station kept a close watch on activities at the Cuban and Soviet Consulates. Agents had set up hidden observation posts across the street that took pictures of visitors to the two sites.[117] The Agency had also wiretapped the phones at both the Cuban and Soviet facilities.[118] Thus, the CIA had front-row surveillance seats for what transpired there.

The Agency's reports on what were supposedly Lee Harvey Oswald's visits and phone calls to the two consulates inadvertently revealed more about the CIA than they ever did about Oswald. The Mexico City story being created about Oswald in carefully preserved documents was written with such dexterity in some places, and with such clumsiness in others, that it eventually drew more attention to itself and its authors than it did to its fictionalized subject. As a result, what Oswald himself really did in Mexico City is in fact less certain today than what the CIA did in his name. The documents containing this self-revelation have finally been declassified and made available to the American public during the past decade as a result of the JFK Records Act passed by Congress in 1992. However, only a few dedicated researchers of the Kennedy assassination have studied these materials and have understood their implications.[119]

On October 9, 1963, CIA headquarters received a cable from its Mexico City Station about an October 1 phone call to the Soviet Consulate that had been wiretapped, taped, transcribed, and translated from Russian into English. The call came from "an American male who spoke broken Russian" and who "said his name [was] Lee Oswald."[120] The man who said he was Oswald stated that he had been at the Soviet Embassy on September 28, when he spoke with a consul he believed was Valery Vladimirovich Kostikov. He asked "if there [was] anything new re telegram to Washington." The Soviet guard who answered the phone said nothing had been received yet, but the request had been sent. He then hung up.

The CIA's October 9 cable from Mexico City is noteworthy in two respects. The first is the connection between Oswald and Valery Vladimirovich Kostikov. Kostikov was well known to the CIA and FBI as the KGB (Soviet Committee for State Security) agent in Mexico City who directed Division 13, the KGB department for terrorism, sabotage, and assassination. Former FBI director Clarence M. Kelley stressed in his autobiography: "The importance of Kostikov cannot be overstated. As [Dallas FBI agent] Jim Hosty wrote later: 'Kostikov was the officer-in-charge for Western Hemisphere terrorist activities—including and especially assassination. In military ranking he would have been a one-star general. As the Russians would say, he was their Line V man—the most dangerous KGB terrorist assigned to this hemisphere!'"[121]

Equally noteworthy in the October 9 cable is the evidence it provides that the "Lee Oswald" who made the October 1 phone call was an impostor. The caller, it said, "spoke broken Russian." The real Oswald was fluent in Russian.[122] The cable went on to say that the Mexico City Station had surveillance photos of a man who appeared to be an American entering and leaving the Soviet Embassy on October 1. He was described as "apparent age 35, athletic build, circa 6 feet, receding hairline, balding top."[123] In a CIA cable back to Mexico City on October 10, the Lee Oswald who defected to the U.S.S.R. in October 1959 was described as not quite 24, "five feet ten inches, one hundred sixty five pounds, light brown wavy hair, blue eyes."[124]

What one is confronted with in the October 9 cable is an apparently damning connection between Oswald and a KGB assassination expert, but a connection made by a man impersonating Oswald. It is the beginning of a two-tracks Mexico City story. On one track is the CIA's attempt to document Oswald's complicity with the Soviet Union and Cuba in the assassination of John F. Kennedy. On the other track is the recurring evidence within the same documents of a fraudulent Oswald at work.

Given the notoriety of Valery Kostikov in U.S. intelligence circles, it is remarkable that when CIA headquarters cabled the State Department, the FBI, and the Navy on October 10 to relay the wiretapped information it had received on Oswald the day before, the cable made no reference to his specific connection with Kostikov.[125] Kostikov was not even mentioned. This would be like a 2001 intelligence report on a suspected terrorist neglecting to mention that he had just met with Osama bin Laden. CIA headquarters was keeping its knowledge of the Oswald–Kostikov connection close to its vest. The CIA's silence regarding Kostikov was maintained just long enough for Oswald to be moved quietly (without being placed on the FBI's Security Index) into a position overlooking Dealey Plaza on November 22. After the assassination, the CIA used its dormant Mexico City documents to link the accused assassin Oswald with the KGB's Kostikov.

On November 25, 1963, Richard Helms sent a memorandum to J. Edgar Hoover that marshaled the CIA's phone-tapped evidence suggesting that Oswald had received not only Soviet but also Cuban government support in assassinating Kennedy.[126] Attached to the Helms memorandum were transcripts for the audiotapes of seven calls to the Soviet Mexico City embassy attributed to Oswald. Two of them stood out. One was the October 1 call in which "Oswald" identified Kostikov as the Soviet consul he had met with on September 28. In the other outstanding call, reportedly made on September 28, the same man, speaking from the Cuban Consulate, made reference to his having just been at the Soviet Embassy. To understand this revealing call, we need to put it in the context of what may or may not have been the real Oswald's shuttles between the Cuban and Soviet Consulates during his first two days in Mexico City, September 27 and 28.

Given Lee Harvey Oswald's willingness to take on intelligence roles, the primary question concerning his visits to the Cuban and Soviet Consulates is not: Was it really he?[127] Whether it was Oswald or someone using his name, the "he" was still an actor following a script. If the actor was himself, from his limited standpoint his role's purpose would have been, as in New Orleans, to discredit the Fair Play for Cuba Committee in a minor Cold War battle. According to an FBI memorandum dated September 18, 1963, discovered by the Church Committee,[128] the CIA advised the FBI two days earlier that the "Agency is giving some consideration to countering the activities of [the FPCC] in foreign countries."[129] Nine days later in Mexico City, "Oswald" visited the Cuban and Soviet Consulates displaying his FPCC credentials and seeking visas to both those Communist countries. Whether it was Oswald or not who was playing out another FPCC-discrediting role in his name, the more basic question is: What was the Mexico City scenario's purpose in the larger script written for the president's murder? It is this question of ultimate purpose that the CIA's Mexico City surveillance tapes will assist us in answering, after we first consider the September 27–28 visits to the consulates that were acted out in the name of Oswald.

According to Silvia Duran, the Cuban Consulate's Mexican employee who spoke with Oswald, he (or an impostor) visited their consulate three times on Friday, September 27. At his 11:00 A.M. visit, Oswald applied for a Cuban transit visa for a trip to the Soviet Union. Duran was a little suspicious of Oswald. She felt the American was too eager in displaying his leftist credentials: membership cards in the Fair Play for Cuba Committee and the American Communist Party, old Soviet documents, a newspaper clipping on his arrest in New Orleans, a photo of Oswald being escorted by a policeman on each arm that Duran thought looked phony.[130] Duran also knew that belonging to the Communist Party was illegal in Mexico in 1963. For that reason, a Communist would normally travel in the country with only a passport. Yet here was Oswald documented in a way that invited his arrest.[131]

Duran told Oswald he lacked the photographs he needed for his visa application. She also said he would first need permission to visit the Soviet Union before he could be issued a transit visa for Cuba. Visibly upset, Oswald departed, but returned to the consulate an hour later with his visa photos.

In the late afternoon, Oswald returned again to the Cuban Consulate, insisting this time to Silvia Duran that he be granted a Cuban visa at once. He claimed that the Soviet Consulate had just assured him he would be given a Soviet visa. Duran checked by phone with the Soviets and learned otherwise. She told Oswald, who then flew into a rage. He ranted at Duran, then at the Cuban consul, Eusebio Azcue, who had stepped out of his office into the commotion. Oswald raged in response to Azcue's explanation of the visa procedure. Azcue yelled back at him.[132] Oswald called Azcue and Duran mere "bureaucrats."[133] Then, as Silvia Duran recalled in 1978 to the House Select Committee on Assassinations (HSCA), Azcue went to the door, opened it, and asked Oswald to leave.[134] The extraordinary episode had, perhaps as intended, left an indelible impression on Duran and Azcue.

Oswald's two visits to the Soviet Embassy have been described by the KGB officer who served as its vice consul, Col. Oleg Maximovich Nechiporenko, in his 1993 memoir *Passport to Assassination*. At his first visit on Friday afternoon, September 27, Oswald did indeed speak briefly with Valery Vladimirovich Kostikov. Nechiporenko refers to Kostikov casually as "one of the consulate employees who on that particular day was receiving visitors from eleven in the morning until one in the afternoon."[135] Oswald said he was seeking a visa to the Soviet Union. Kostikov handed him over to Nechiporenko, who listened to Oswald's urgent request for an immediate visa. Nechiporenko explained that their Washington, D.C., embassy handled all matters regarding travel to the Soviet Union. He could make an exception for Oswald and send his papers on to Moscow, "but the answer would still be sent to his permanent residence, and it would take, at the very least, four months."[136]

Oswald listened with growing exasperation. "When I had finished speaking," Nechiporenko recalled, "he slowly leaned forward and, barely able to restrain himself, practically shouted in my face, 'This won't do for me! This is not my case! For me, it's all going to end in tragedy!'"[137] Nechiporenko showed the unruly American out of the compound.

Oswald returned to the Soviet Embassy the next morning. He renewed his request for a quick visa to the U.S.S.R., this time to Valery Kostikov (this being their September 28 meeting) and Soviet consul Pavel Yatskov. Oswald became even more agitated than he had been the day before, referring to

FBI surveillance and persecution. He took a revolver from his jacket pocket, placed it on a table, and said, "See? This is what I must now carry to protect my life." [138] The Soviet officials carefully took the gun and removed its bullets. They told Oswald once again they could not give him a quick visa. They offered him instead the necessary forms to be filled out. Oswald didn't take them. Oleg Nechiporenko joined the three men as their conversation was ending. For the second day in a row, he accompanied a depressed Oswald to the gate of the embassy, this time with Oswald's returned revolver and its loose bullets stuck back in his jacket pocket. Nechiporenko says that he, Kostikov, and Yatskov then immediately prepared a report on Oswald's two embassy visits that they cabled to Moscow Center. [139]

Oswald's three visits to the Cuban Consulate on September 27, and his two visits to the Soviet Embassy on September 27–28, comprise the background to the September 28 phone transcript sent by Richard Helms to J. Edgar Hoover. The CIA's transcript states that the Saturday, September 28, call came from the Cuban Consulate. The first speaker is identified as Silvia Duran. However, Silvia Duran has insisted repeatedly over the years, first, that the Cuban Embassy was closed to the public on Saturdays, and second, that she never took part in such a call. [140]

"Duran" is said to be phoning the Soviet Consulate. Oleg Nechiporenko denies in turn that this call occurred. He says it was impossible because the Soviet switchboard was closed. [141]

The "Duran" speaker in the transcript says that an American in her consulate, who had been in the Soviet Embassy, wants to talk to them. She passes the phone to a North American man. The American insists that he and the Soviet representative speak Russian. They engage in a conversation, with the American speaking what the translator describes as "terrible hardly recognizable Russian." This once again argues against the speaker being Oswald, given his fluent Russian. The CIA transcript of this unlikely conversation then reads:

> NORTH AMERICAN: "I was just now at your embassy and they took my address."
> SOVIET: "I know that."
> NORTH AMERICAN: "I did not know it then. I went to the Cuban Embassy to ask them for my address because they have it."
> SOVIET: "Why don't you come again and leave your address with us. It is not far from the Cuban Embassy."
> NORTH AMERICAN: "Well, I'll be there right away." [142]

What is the purpose behind this strange, counterfeit dialogue?

Richard Helms, in his accompanying letter to J. Edgar Hoover, states that the "North American" in the Saturday, September 28, call is the same man who identified himself as Lee Oswald in the October 1 call (which confirmed and documented Oswald's Saturday meeting with Kostikov). In that connection the bogus Saturday call has "Oswald" saying he was "just now" at the Soviet Embassy (with KGB assassination expert Kostikov) and that his correct address is known only by the Cuban Embassy, not himself. He will bring it to the Soviets. Thus, in the CIA's interpretation of events, documented by fraudulent phone calls, the Cuban authorities and Soviet assassin Kostikov were working together in their control of Oswald's address and movements, two months before Kennedy's assassination. As researcher John Newman said in a presentation on these documents, "It looks like the Cubans and the Russians are working in tandem. It looks like [Oswald] is going to meet with Kostikov at a place designated by the Cubans . . . Oswald expected to be at some location fixed by the Cuban Embassy and wanted the Russians to be able to reach him there." [143]

In addition, Oswald (or an impostor) was applying for Cuban and Soviet visas, which could be used as evidence of his attempting to gain asylum in Communist countries. The Mexico City scenario had laid the foundation for blaming the president's upcoming murder on Cuba and the U.S.S.R., thereby providing the rationale in its aftermath for an invasion of Cuba and a possible nuclear attack on Russia.

The alarming implications of the CIA's Mexico City case against Oswald had to be faced on the morning after the assassination by the new president, Lyndon Baines Johnson. As a result of the public disclosure under the JFK Act of LBJ's taped conversations, we now know how Johnson was informed of the CIA setup. Michael Beschloss, editor of the Johnson tapes, tells us that at 9:20 A.M. on November 23, 1963, Johnson was briefed by CIA director John McCone about "information on foreign connections to the alleged assassin, Lee Harvey Oswald, which suggested to LBJ that Kennedy may have been murdered by an international conspiracy." [144] Then at 10:01 A.M. Johnson received a phone briefing on Oswald from FBI director J. Edgar Hoover. It included the following exchange:

> LBJ: "Have you established any more about the visit to the Soviet embassy in Mexico in September?"
> HOOVER: "No, that's one angle that's very confusing, for this reason— we have up here the tape and the photograph of the man who was at the Soviet embassy, using Oswald's name. That picture and the tape do not correspond to this man's voice, nor to his appearance. In other words, it appears that there is a second person who was at the Soviet embassy down there. We do have a copy of a letter which was written by Oswald to the Soviet embassy here in Washington [a November 9, 1963, letter that Oswald began by referring to 'my meetings with comrade Kostin in the Embassy of the Soviet Union, Mexico City, Mexico,' which was interpreted to mean Kostikov][145] . . . Now if we can identify this man who was at the . . . Soviet embassy in Mexico City . . ." [146]

Having just been briefed on Oswald by CIA director McCone, Johnson was anxious to get to the bottom of "the visit to the Soviet embassy in Mexico in September." Hoover's briefing adds to Johnson's anxiety. Hoover confronts Johnson with strong evidence of an Oswald impostor at the Soviet Embassy: "The tape and the photograph of the man who was at the Soviet embassy" do not correspond to "this man's [Oswald's] voice, nor to his appearance." Hoover says he has the proof: "We have up here the tape and the photograph of the man who was at the Soviet embassy, using Oswald's name." Hoover knows very well that the falsified evidence of a Cuban-Soviet plot to kill Kennedy (which Johnson has just been given by McCone) came from the CIA. Hoover simply gives Johnson the raw fact of an Oswald impostor in Mexico City, then lets Johnson chew on its implications. Hoover's own reaction to the CIA's Mexico City subterfuge was recorded seven weeks later, when he scribbled at the bottom of an FBI memorandum about keeping up with CIA operations in the United States: "O.K., but I hope you are not being taken in. I can't forget the CIA withholding the French espionage activities in the USA nor *the false story re Oswald's trip to Mexico*, only to mention two instances of their double-dealing." [147]

Lyndon Johnson's CIA and FBI briefings left him with two unpalatable interpretations of Mexico City. According to the CIA, Oswald was part of a Cuban-Soviet assassination plot that was revealed by the audio-visual materials garnered by its surveillance techniques. According to Hoover, Oswald had been impersonated in Mexico City, as shown by a more critical examination of the same CIA materials. Hoover left it to Johnson to draw his own conclusions as to who was responsible for that impersonation.

The CIA's case scapegoated Cuba and the U.S.S.R. through Oswald for the president's assassination and steered the United States toward an invasion of Cuba and a nuclear attack on the U.S.S.R. However, LBJ did not want to begin and end his presidency with a global war.

Hoover's view suggested CIA complicity in the assassination. Even assuming for the moment that Johnson himself was innocent of any foreknowledge or involvement in the plot, nevertheless for the new president to confront the CIA over Kennedy's murder, in a war within the U.S. government, would have been at least as frightening for him as an international crisis.

One must give the CIA (and the assassination sponsors that were even further in the shadows) their due for having devised and executed a brilliant setup. They had played out a scenario to Kennedy's death in Dallas that pressured other government authorities to choose among three major options: a war of vengeance against Cuba and the Soviet Union based on the CIA's false Mexico City documentation of a Communist assassination plot; a domestic political war based on the same documents seen truly, but a war the CIA would fight with every covert weapon at its command; or a complete cover-up of any conspiracy evidence and a silent coup d'état that would reverse Kennedy's efforts to end the Cold War. Lyndon Johnson, for his part, took little time to choose the only option he felt would leave him with a country to govern. He chose to cover up everything and surrender to Cold War prerogatives. However, he was not about to attack Cuba and the U.S.S.R. His quick personal acceptance of what had to be would only emerge more gradually in public. Rather than end it all quickly and hero-ically against Castro and Khrushchev, he would ride gently, through the 1964 election, into the full fury of Vietnam.

Once the CIA realized its Mexico City scenario was being questioned and could implicate not the Communists but the CIA itself in the assassina-tion, the Mexico City Station back-pedaled to cover up the false evidence. It began to say that its audiotapes of the "Oswald" phone calls to the Soviet Embassy had been routinely destroyed, and therefore no voice compari-sons were possible to determine if the speaker really was Oswald.[148] (This bogus CIA claim was being made at the same time that Hoover and the FBI were listening to their own copies of the tapes, then making voice com-parisons, and reporting their provocative conclusions to President Lyndon Johnson.) Thus, on November 23, Mexico City CIA employee Ann Good-pasture, an assistant to David Phillips, sent a cable to CIA headquarters in which she reported the Saturday, September 28, call, then stated: "Sta-tion unable compare voice as first tape erased prior receipt second call." [149] On the next day, Mexico City cabled headquarters that it was now unable to locate any tapes at all for comparisons with Oswald's voice: "Regret complete recheck shows tapes for this period already erased." [150] After an extensive analysis, the House Select Committee's *Lopez Report* concluded that these and other CIA statements about tapes having been erased before voice comparisons could be made conflicted with sworn testimony, the information on other cables, and the station's own wiretapping proce-dure.[151] Although FBI director Hoover was angry at not having been let in initially by the CIA on "the false story re Oswald's trip to Mexico," from this point on the FBI cooperated in revising its story, too, to cover the CIA's tracks.

Unknown to ordinary citizens watching President Kennedy's funeral on their television sets, the agencies of a national security state had quickly formed a united front behind the official mourning scenes to cover up every aspect of JFK's assassination. National security policies toward enemies beyond the state (with whom the slain president had been negotiating a truce) made necessary the denial of every trace of conspiracy within the state. As a saddled, riderless horse followed the coffin through the capital's streets, plausible deniability had come home to haunt the nation.

On November 25, 1963, Deputy Attorney General Nicholas deB. Kat-zenbach sent a memorandum to Bill Moyers, President Johnson's press sec-retary, urging a premature identification of Oswald as the lone assassin lest speculation of either a Communist or a right-wing conspiracy get out of hand:

"1. The public must be satisfied that Oswald was the assassin; that he did not have confederates who are still at large; and that the evidence was such that he would have been convicted at trial.

"2. Speculation about Oswald's motivation ought to be cut off, and we should have some basis for rebutting thought that this was a Communist conspiracy or (as the Iron Curtain press is saying) a right-wing conspiracy to blame it on the Communists. Unfortunately the facts on Oswald seem about too pat—too obvious (Marxist, Cuba, Russian wife, etc.)." [152]

To rebut any thought of either kind of conspiracy, Katzenbach's memorandum recommended "the appointment of a Presidential Commission of unimpeachable personnel to review and examine the evidence and announce its conclusions." [153]

Before Lyndon Johnson jettisoned the CIA's Mexico City case against Cuba and the Soviet Union, he used it (without Hoover's reference to an impostor) as a lever to help put together just such a presidential commission of respected Cold War leaders. He ensured the commission's public acceptance by convincing Supreme Court Chief Justice Earl Warren to chair it. Warren at first refused to become Johnson's pawn. However, in a taped phone conversation on Friday, November 29, LBJ described to Senator Richard Russell how he had co-opted Warren's conscience, by an argument that accepted at face value the CIA's Mexico City evidence. Johnson then manipulated Russell onto the commission, using the same Mexico City argument with which he had coerced Warren:

LBJ: "Warren told me he wouldn't do it under any circumstances. Didn't think a Supreme Court Justice ought to go on . . .

"He came down here and told me *no*—twice. And I just pulled out what Hoover told me about a little incident in Mexico City and I said, 'Now I don't want Mr. Khrushchev to be told tomorrow—and be testifying before a camera that he killed this fellow and that Castro killed him and all I want you to do is look at the facts and bring in any other facts you want in here and determine who killed the President.'" [154]

Russell told LBJ that he couldn't work with Warren, but to no avail:

RUSSELL: "Now, Mr. President, I don't have to tell you of my devotion to you, but I just can't serve on that commission. I'm highly honored you'd think about me in connection with it. But I couldn't serve on it with Chief Justice Warren. I don't like that man . . ."

LBJ: "Dick, it has already been announced. And you can serve with anybody for the good of America. And this is a question that has a good many more ramifications than on the surface. And we've got to take this out of the arena where they're testifying that Khrushchev and Castro did this and did that and kicking us into a war that can kill forty million Americans in an hour . . .

". . . The Secretary of State came over here this afternoon. He's deeply concerned, Dick, about the idea that they're spreading throughout the Communist world that Khrushchev killed Kennedy. Now he didn't. He didn't have a damned thing to do with it."

RUSSELL: "I don't think he did directly. I know Khrushchev didn't because he thought he'd get along better with Kennedy." [155]

Russell's final remark shows his own sense of the differences between Kennedy and Johnson and of the foreign policy changes that began at Dallas. As tapes editor Michael Beschloss notes, "Russell means [Khrushchev thought he'd get along] better with Kennedy than Johnson."

In November 1963, it could also be said of Fidel Castro that he, too, thought he'd get along better with Kennedy. Castro's openness toward Kennedy was confirmed in November by JFK's unofficial envoy to Castro, French correspondent Jean Daniel.

After his meeting with President Kennedy, Jean Daniel spent the first three weeks of November touring Cuba and interviewing people from every sector of the society, but without ever gaining access to Fidel Castro. He was told Castro was snowed under with work and had no desire to receive any more Western journalists. Daniel almost gave up hope of seeing him. Then on November 19, the eve of Daniel's scheduled departure from Havana, Castro suddenly showed up at his hotel. Fidel had heard of Daniel's interview with Kennedy. He was eager to learn the details of their conversation. Castro knew from the secret Attwood-Lechuga meetings that Kennedy was reaching out to him. In fact even as Daniel was trying to see Castro, Castro had been trying to firm up negotiations with Kennedy through Lisa Howard and William Attwood. We will fill in that part of the story before taking up the extraordinary conversation between Castro and Daniel that went right up to and through the hour of JFK's assassination.

On October 29, after a week of leaving phone messages for Lisa Howard, Castro's aide Rene Vallejo finally reached Howard at her home. He assured her that Castro was as eager as he had been during her visit in April to improve relations with the United States. However, it was impossible for Castro to leave Cuba at that time to go to the UN or elsewhere for talks with a Kennedy representative. Howard told Vallejo there was now a U.S. official authorized to listen to Castro. Vallejo said he would relay that message to Castro and call her back soon.[156]

On October 31, Vallejo phoned Howard again, saying "Castro would very much like to talk to the U.S. official anytime and appreciated the importance of discretion to all concerned."[157] The phrase "to all concerned" was significant. At this point Castro, like Kennedy and Khrushchev, was circumventing his own more bellicose government in order to talk with the enemy. Castro, too, was struggling to transcend his Cold War ideology for the sake of peace. Like Kennedy and Khrushchev, he had to walk softly. He was now prepared to negotiate with a peacemaking U.S. president just as secretly as he had plotted guerrilla warfare against Batista. Thus, Vallejo said Castro was "willing to send a plane to Mexico to pick up the official and fly him to a private airport near Varadero, where Castro would talk to him alone. The plane would fly him back immediately after the talk. In this way there would be no risk of identification at the Havana airport."[158] Howard told

Vallejo she doubted if a U.S. official could come to Cuba. Could Vallejo, as Castro's personal spokesman, come to meet the U.S. official at the UN or in Mexico? Vallejo replied that "Castro wanted to do the talking himself," but wouldn't rule out that possibility if there were no other way to engage in a dialogue with Kennedy.[159]

Howard reported the Vallejo calls to Attwood, who in turn relayed the information to the White House. On November 5, Attwood met with Kennedy's National Security Adviser, McGeorge Bundy, and Gordon Chase of the National Security Council staff. He filled them in on Castro's eagerness to facilitate a dialogue with Kennedy. On November 8, at Chase's request, Attwood put all this in a memorandum.[160] There were now two weeks left before Kennedy would be in Dallas.

On November 11, Rene Vallejo phoned Lisa Howard again on behalf of Castro to reiterate their "appreciation of the need for security."[161] He said Castro would go along with any arrangements Kennedy's representatives might want to make. He was again willing to provide a plane, if that would be helpful. As Attwood reported to the White House, Castro through Vallejo "specifically suggested that a Cuban plane could come to Key West and pick up the emissary; alternatively they would agree to have him come in a U.S. plane which could land at one of several 'secret airfields' near Havana. [Vallejo] emphasized that only Castro and himself would be present at the talks and that no one else—he specifically mentioned Guevara—would be involved."[162] As both sides of the prospective negotiations knew, Che Guevara, like many of Castro's associates, was opposed to a rapprochement with Kennedy. Castro was reassuring Kennedy of his independence from the opposition in his own government.

On November 12, after hearing Attwood's report, McGeorge Bundy said that before a meeting with Castro himself there should be a preliminary talk with Vallejo at the United Nations to find out specifically what Castro wanted to talk about.[163]

On November 14, Lisa Howard relayed this information to Rene Vallejo, who said he would discuss it with Castro.[164]

On November 18, Howard called Vallejo again. This time she passed the phone to Attwood. At the other end of the line Fidel Castro was listening in on the Vallejo-Attwood conversation, as he would tell Attwood many years later.[165] Attwood asked Vallejo if he could come to New York for a preliminary meeting. Vallejo said he could not come at that time but that "we" would send instructions to Lechuga to propose and discuss with Attwood "an agenda" for a later meeting with Castro. Attwood said he would await Lechuga's call.

Thus the stage was being set, four days before Dallas, for the beginning of a Kennedy–Castro dialogue on U.S.–Cuban relations. Both Kennedy and Castro, with the encouragement and support of Nikita Khrushchev, were listening to the high notes of a song of peace their governments were still unable to hear. As carefully as porcupines making love, they were preparing to engage in a dialogue on the strange proposition that the United States and Cuba might actually be able to live together in peace.

Unaware of these behind-the-scenes developments, Jean Daniel was shocked by the sudden appearance of Fidel Castro at his Havana hotel the night of November 19. Castro wanted to hear about Kennedy. He met with Daniel in his room for six straight hours, 10:00 P.M. to 4:00 A.M. The interviewer became the interviewee. Castro turned the interview around, so that he could absorb every meaning and nuance from Daniel's recitation of his conversation with Kennedy. Daniel described later Castro's reaction to the explicit and subliminal messages he was receiving from the president, through the medium of his "unofficial envoy," two and a half days before Kennedy's death:

"Fidel listened with devouring and passionate interest: He pulled at his beard, yanked his parachutist's beret down over his eyes, adjusted his maqui tunic, all the while making me the target of a thousand malicious sparks cast by his deep-sunk, lively eyes. At one point I felt as though I were play- ing the role of that partner with whom he had as strong a desire to confer as to do battle; as though I myself were in a small way that intimate enemy in the White House whom Khrushchev described to Fidel as someone with whom 'it is possible to talk.' Three times he had me repeat certain remarks, particularly those in which Kennedy expressed his criticism of the Batista regime, those in which Kennedy showed his impatience with the comments attributed to General de Gaulle, and lastly those in which Kennedy accused Fidel of having almost caused a war fatal to all humanity." [166]

When Daniel finished speaking, he waited, expecting an explosion. Instead Castro was silent for a long while. He knew Daniel was returning to Washington, so the U.S. president could hear of the Cuban premier's response to his overture. In essence their dialogue had already begun, even before Castro's meeting with Kennedy's representative Attwood—a meeting that would soon be struck down, with a world of other possibilities, in Dal- las. Finally Castro spoke, weighing his words.

"I believe Kennedy is sincere," he began. "I also believe that today the expression of this sincerity could have political significance. I'll explain what I mean," he said, then gave a sharp critique of Kennedy that at the same time revealed his unique understanding of the president's situation:

"I haven't forgotten that Kennedy centered his electoral campaign against Nixon on the theme of firmness toward Cuba. I have not forgotten the Machiavellian tactics and the equivocation, the attempts at invasion, the pressures, the blackmail, the organization of a counter-revolution, the block- ade and, above everything, all the retaliatory measures which were imposed before, long before there was the pretext and alibi of Communism. But I feel that he inherited a difficult situation; I don't think a President of the United States is ever really free, and I believe Kennedy is at present feeling the impact of this lack of freedom. I also believe he now understands the extent to which he has been misled, especially, for example, on Cuban reaction at the time of the attempted Bay of Pigs invasion." [167]

Castro was stung by Kennedy's charge that he bore the primary responsibility for having brought humanity to the brink of nuclear war in the missile crisis. He responded with his own reading of that history, in a way that would have deeply challenged Kennedy in turn, had he lived to hear it from Daniel:

"Six months before these missiles were installed in Cuba, we had received an accumulation of information warning us that a new invasion of the island was being prepared under sponsorship of the Central Intelligence Agency, whose administrators were humiliated by the Bay of Pigs disaster and by the spectacle of being ridiculed in the eyes of the world and berated in US government circles. [Castro had put his finger on a critical period in U.S. history, when the CIA's leaders from the Bay of Pigs hated Kennedy with a passion that only Castro, the other target of their hatred, could intuit.] We also knew that the Pentagon was vesting the CIA preparations with the mantle of its authority, but we had doubts as to the attitude of the President. There were those among our informants who even thought it would suffice to alert the President and give him cause for concern in order to arrest these preparations. [If Castro had then, like Khrushchev, taken the risk of initiating a secret correspondence with Kennedy, what might he and JFK have seen together?] Then one day Khrushchev's son-in-law, Adzhubei, came to pay us a visit before going on to Washington at the invitation of Kennedy's associates. Immediately upon arriving in Washington, Adzhubei had been received by the American Chief Executive, and their talk centered particularly on Cuba. A week after this interview, we received in Havana a copy of Adzhubei's report to Khrushchev. It was this report which triggered the whole situation.

"What did Kennedy say to Adzhubei? Now listen to this carefully," Castro urged Daniel, "for it is very important: he had said that the new situation in Cuba was intolerable for the United States, that the American government *had decided it would not tolerate it any longer*; he had said that peaceful coexistence was seriously compromised by the fact that 'Soviet influences' in Cuba altered the balance of strength, was destroying the equilibrium agreed upon and [at this point Castro emphasized his statement to Daniel by pronouncing each syllable separately] *Kennedy reminded the Russians that the United States had not intervened in Hungary*, which was obviously a way of demanding Russian non-intervention in the event of a possible invasion. To be sure, the actual word 'invasion' was not mentioned and Adzhubei, at the time, lacking any background information, could not draw the same conclusion as we did. But when we communicated to Khrushchev all our previous information, the Russians too began to interpret the Kennedy-Adzhubei conversation as we saw it and they went to the source of our information. By the end of a month, the Russian and Cuban governments had reached the *definite conviction* that an invasion might take place from one moment to the next. This is the truth."

At this point Castro was speaking to Daniel as if he were Kennedy himself.

"What was to be done? How could we prevent the invasion? We found that Khrushchev was concerned about the same things that were worrying us. He asked us what we wanted. We replied: *do whatever is needed to convince the United States that any attack on Cuba is the same as an attack on the Soviet Union.* And how to realize this objective? All our thinking and discussions revolved around this point. We thought of a proclamation, an alliance, conventional military aid. The Russians explained to us that their concern was twofold: first, they wanted to save the Cuban revolution (in other words, their socialist honor in the eyes of the world), and at the same time they wished to avoid a world conflict. They reasoned that if conventional military aid was the extent of their assistance, the United States might not hesitate to instigate an invasion, in which case Russia would retaliate and this would inevitably touch off a world war . . .

". . . Soviet Russia was confronted by two alternatives: an absolutely inevitable war (because of their commitments and their position in the socialist world), if the Cuban revolution was attacked; or the risk of a war if the United States, refusing to retreat before the missiles, would not give up the attempt to destroy Cuba. They chose socialist solidarity and the risk of war.

". . . In a word, then we agreed to the emplacement of the missiles. And I might add here that for us Cubans it didn't really make so much difference whether we died by conventional bombing or a hydrogen bomb. Nevertheless, we were not gambling with the peace of the world. The United States was the one to jeopardize the peace of mankind by using the threat of war to stifle revolutions." [168]

In the midst of the Cuban Missile Crisis itself, Kennedy had had sufficient detachment to understand Khrushchev's position so as not to back his adversary into a corner. Would he have also been able to understand Castro's counter-challenge to his understanding of the cause of that crisis?

Castro went on to discuss Kennedy's Alliance for Progress in Latin America with surprising sympathy. "In a way," he said, "it was a good idea, it marked progress of a sort. Even if it can be said that it was overdue, timid, conceived on the spur of the moment, under constraint . . . despite all that, I am willing to agree that the idea in itself constituted an effort to adapt to the extraordinarily rapid course of events in Latin America." [169]

Castro added, however, his political assessment that "Kennedy's good ideas aren't going to yield any results. It is very easy to understand and at this point he surely is aware of this because, as I told you, he is a realist. For years and years American policy—not the government, but the trusts and the Pentagon—has supported the Latin American oligarchies. All the prestige, the dollars, and the power was held by a class which Kennedy himself has described in speaking of Batista."

Kennedy's statement that "Batista was the incarnation of a number of sins on the part of the United States" that "now we shall have to pay for" inspired Castro to an understanding of how dangerous life was becoming for Kennedy. "Suddenly a President arrives on the scene," he said, "who tries to support the interests of another class (which has no access to any of the levers of power) to give the various Latin American countries the impression that the United States no longer stands behind the dictators, and so there is no more need to start Castro-type revolutions. What happens then? The trusts see that their interests are being a little compromised (just barely, but still compromised); the Pentagon thinks the strategic bases are in danger; the powerful oligarchies in all the Latin American countries alert their American friends; they sabotage the new policy; and in short, Kennedy has everyone against him." [170]

Fidel Castro saw the isolation in which John Kennedy had been placed by even the moderate reforms of his Alliance for Progress. And he understood the much deeper waters Kennedy was negotiating by his beginning détente with Nikita Khrushchev, and by his now initiating a dialogue with Castro himself. Kennedy's courage gave him hope. As the hand of the clock in Daniel's hotel room neared 4:00 A.M. on November 20, Castro expressed his hope for Kennedy:

"I cannot help hoping that a leader will come to the fore in North America (why not Kennedy, there are things in his favor!), who will be willing to brave unpopularity, fight the trusts, tell the truth and, most important, let the various nations act as they see fit. Kennedy could still be this man. He still has the possibility of becoming, in the eyes of history, the greatest President of the United States, the leader who may at last understand that there can be coexistence between capitalists and socialists, even in the Americas. He would then be an even greater President than Lincoln." [171]

Castro's view of Kennedy was changing. He had been influenced especially by his pro-Kennedy tutorial in the Soviet Union with Nikita Khrushchev. "I know," Castro told Daniel, "that for Khrushchev, Kennedy is a man you can talk with. I have gotten this impression from all my conversations with Khrushchev." [172]

Like Khrushchev, Castro hoped to work with the U.S. president during his second four-year term to fulfill a vision of coexistence. He joked with Daniel that maybe he could help Kennedy's campaign for reelection. He said with a broad, boyish grin, "If you see him again, you can tell him that I'm willing to declare Goldwater my friend if that will guarantee Kennedy's re-election!" [173]

On the afternoon of November 22, Jean Daniel was having lunch with Fidel Castro in the living room of his summer home on Varadero Beach. It was 1:30 P.M. in the time zone Havana shared with Washington. While Daniel questioned Castro again about the missile crisis, the phone rang. A secretary in a guerrilla uniform said Mr. Dorticos, President of the Cuban Republic, had an urgent message for the prime minister. Castro took the phone. Daniel heard him say, *"Como? Un atentado?"* ("What's that? An attempted assassination?"). He turned to tell Daniel and the secretary that Kennedy had been struck down in Dallas. Castro returned to the phone. He exclaimed loudly, *"Herido? Muy gravemente?"* ("Wounded? Very seriously?").[174]

When Castro had hung up the phone, he repeated three times, *"Es una mala noticia.*" ("This is bad news"). He remained silent, waiting for another call with more news. As he began to speculate on who might have targeted Kennedy, a second call came in: The hope was that the president was still alive and could be saved. Castro said with evident satisfaction, "If they can, he is already re-elected." [175]

Just before 2:00 P.M., Castro and Daniel waited by a radio for more news. Rene Vallejo, Castro's liaison for the Kennedy negotiations, stood by. He translated the NBC reports coming in from Miami. Finally the words came through: President Kennedy was dead.

Castro stood up, looked at Daniel, and said, "Everything is changed. Everything is going to change." [176]

After the death of JFK, Lyndon Johnson put on permanent hold any dialogue between the White House and Fidel Castro, who kept seeking it. On December 4, William Attwood was told by Carlos Lechuga at the United Nations that "he now had a letter from Fidel himself, instructing him to talk with me about a specific agenda." [177] Attwood asked the White House for its response to Castro. Gordon Chase said all policies were in the course of being reviewed by the new administration and advised patience. [178] Attwood did not know that, with the lightning change of presidents, former rapprochement proponent Chase had felt a corresponding change in the political climate and was now among those who were already turning Kennedy's policy around. On November 25 Chase had written a memorandum to National Security Adviser McGeorge Bundy that stated: "Basically, the events of November 22 would appear to make accommodation with Castro an even more doubtful issue than it was. While I think that President Kennedy could have accommodated with Castro and gotten away with it with a minimum of domestic heat, I'm not sure about President Johnson." [179]

Chase also recognized that the pro-Castro image of Oswald was not helpful: "In addition, the fact that Lee Oswald has been heralded as a pro-Castro type may make rapprochement with Cuba more difficult—although it is hard to say how much more difficult." [180]

Therefore, Kennedy's former dialogue advocate wrote, "If one concludes that the prospects for accommodation with Castro are much dimmer than they were before November 22, then Bill Attwood's present effort loses much of its meaning." [181]

After being put off by Chase for two weeks, Attwood finally had a chance to hear from President Johnson himself, when Johnson visited the U.S. delegation to the United Nations in New York on December 17. Attwood was simply told by Johnson at lunch that "he'd read my chronological account of our Cuban initiative 'with interest.'" [182]

"And that was it," Attwood wrote two decades later in describing the end of "the Cuban connection." [183] It had in fact died on November 22, 1963, with John Kennedy. It would not be revived by any other U.S. president in the twentieth century.

Against increasing odds, the Cuban side of the connection had still not given up. Inspired by his progress with Kennedy, Castro continued to seek a dialogue with the United States, in spite of President Johnson's silence in response to his overtures. In February 1964, Lisa Howard returned from another news assignment in Cuba carrying an unusual memorandum, a "verbal message" addressed to Lyndon Johnson from Fidel Castro. In his message Castro went to extraordinary lengths to encourage Johnson to emulate Kennedy's courage in attempting a dialogue with their number one enemy, himself. That enemy had been won over to the dialogue, first, by the counsel of Kennedy's other enemy Khrushchev, then by the courage of Kennedy himself. Now Castro was using the example of Kennedy to encourage Johnson simply to talk with the enemy. He was also speaking much less like an enemy than a potentially helpful friend. It was as if Kennedy, in crossing a divide, had taken Castro with him. Castro said to Howard:

"Tell the President that I understand quite well how much political courage it took for President Kennedy to instruct you [Lisa Howard] and Ambassador Attwood to phone my aide in Havana for the purpose of commencing a dialogue toward a settlement of our differences . . . I hope that we can soon continue where Ambassador Attwood's phone conversation to Havana left off . . . though I'm aware that pre-electoral political considerations may delay this approach until after November.

"Tell the President (and I cannot stress this too strongly) that I seriously hope that Cuba and the United States can eventually sit down in an atmosphere of good will and of mutual respect and negotiate our differences. I believe that there are *no* areas of contention between us that cannot be discussed and settled in a climate of mutual understanding. But first, of course, it is necessary to *discuss* our differences. I now believe that this hostility between Cuba and the United States is both unnatural and unnecessary—and it can be eliminated . . .

"Tell the President I realize fully the need for absolute secrecy, if he should decide to continue the Kennedy approach. I revealed nothing at that time . . . I have revealed nothing since . . . I would reveal nothing now." [184]

Just how far Castro was willing to go to promote a dialogue with Kennedy's successor was shown by his willingness to help Johnson's presidential campaign, even by calling off Cuban retaliation to a hostile U.S. action:

"If the President feels it necessary during the campaign to make bellicose statements about Cuba or even to take some hostile action—if he will inform me, unofficially, that a specific action is required because of domestic political considerations, I shall understand and not take any serious retaliatory action." [185]

Although Johnson as usual made no reply to this message, Castro kept trying to communicate with him through Lisa Howard and UN ambassador Adlai Stevenson. (William Attwood was no longer in the loop, having been appointed U.S. ambassador to Kenya in January 1964.) On June 26, 1964, Stevenson wrote a "Secret and Personal" memo to Johnson saying Castro felt that "all of our crises could be avoided if there was some way to communicate; that for want of anything better, he assumed that he could call [Howard] and she call me and I would advise you."[186] Again Johnson gave no response.

Castro even enlisted the help of Cuban Minister of Industry Ernesto "Che" Guevara, previously an opponent to dialogue, in what had become a Cuban diplomatic offensive for negotiations with the United States. During Guevara's December 1964 visit to the United Nations, he tried to arrange a secret meeting with a White House or State Department representative but was unsuccessful. Finally Guevara met with Senator Eugene McCarthy at Lisa Howard's apartment. The next day McCarthy reported to Under Secretary of State George Ball that Guevara's purpose was "to express Cuban interest in trade with the U.S. and U.S. recognition of the Castro regime."[187] Ball rewarded McCarthy by admonishing him for even meeting with Guevara, because there was "suspicion throughout Latin America that the U.S. might make a deal with Cuba behind the backs of the other American states."[188] Ball told McCarthy to say nothing publicly about the meeting. When Lyndon Johnson ignored this Cuban initiative as well, Castro gave up on him. He realized that John Kennedy's successor as president had no interest whatsoever in speaking with Fidel Castro, no matter what he had to say.

In the 1970s, Fidel Castro reflected on a peculiar fact of Cold War history that related closely to the story of John Kennedy. Thanks to the decisions made by Khrushchev and Kennedy, "in the final balance Cuba was not invaded and there was no world war. We did not, therefore, have to suffer a war like Vietnam—because many Americans could ask themselves, why a war in Vietnam, thousands of miles away, why millions of tons of bombs dropped on Vietnam and not in Cuba? It was much more logical for the United States to do this to Cuba than to do it ten thousand kilometers away."[189]

Castro's comparison between Cuba and Vietnam provokes further questions about John Kennedy. If JFK had the courage to resist the CIA and the Pentagon on Cuba, as Castro recognized, how could he have allowed himself to be sucked into the war in Vietnam? Or did he finally turn around on Vietnam in a way that paralleled his changes toward the Soviet Union and Cuba? Did John Kennedy ultimately make a decision for peace in Vietnam that would become the final nail in his coffin?

CHAPTER THREE

JFK and Vietnam

Ten years before he became president, John F. Kennedy learned that it would be impossible to win a colonial war in Vietnam.

In 1951, when he was a young member of Congress, Kennedy visited Vietnam with his twenty-two-year-old brother, Robert. At the time France was trying to reassert control over its pre–World War II colony of Indochina. Although the French army's commander in Saigon insisted to the Kennedys that his 250,000 troops couldn't possibly lose to the Viet Minh guerrillas, JFK knew better. He was convinced by the more skeptical view of Edmund Gullion, an official at the U.S. Consulate. Kennedy knew and trusted Gullion, who had helped him earlier as a speechwriter on foreign policy.[1]

At an evening meeting on top of a Saigon hotel, in a conversation punctuated by distant blasts from the Viet Minh's artillery, Gullion told Kennedy: "In twenty years there will be no more colonies. We're going nowhere out here. The French have lost. If we come in here and do the same thing, we will lose, too, for the same reason. There's no will or support for this kind of war back in Paris. The homefront is lost. The same thing would happen to us."[2]

After becoming president, Kennedy would cite Edmund Gullion's far-sighted analysis to his military advisers, as they pushed hard for the combat troops that JFK would never send to Vietnam. Instead, on October 11, 1963, six weeks before he was assassinated, President Kennedy issued his secret order for a U.S. withdrawal from Vietnam in National Security Action Memorandum (NSAM) 263.[3] It was an order that would never be obeyed because of his murder.

Kennedy had decided to pull out one thousand members of the U.S. military by the end of 1963, and all of them by the end of 1965. In the month and a half before his death, this welcome decision received front page headlines in both the military and civilian press: in the Armed Forces' *Pacific*

Stars and Stripes, "White House Report: U.S. Troops Seen Out of Viet[nam] by '65";[4] in the *New York Times*, "1,000 U.S. Troops to Leave Vietnam."[5]

However, because of the president's assassination, even the first phase of his withdrawal plan was quietly gutted. *The Pentagon Papers*, a revealing Defense Department history of the Vietnam War that was made public by defense analyst Daniel Ellsberg, points out: "Plans for phased withdrawal of 1,000 U.S. advisers by end-1963 went through the motions by concentrating rotations home in December and letting strength rebound in the subsequent two months."[6]

JFK's decision to withdraw from Vietnam was part of the larger strategy for peace that he and Nikita Khrushchev had become mutually committed to, which in Kennedy's case would result in his death. Thomas Merton had seen it all coming. He had said prophetically in a Cold War letter that if President Kennedy broke through to a deeper, more universal humanity, he would before long be "marked out for assassination."[7] Kennedy agreed. As we have seen, he even described the logic of a coming coup d'etat in his comments on the novel *Seven Days in May*.[8] JFK felt that his own demise was increasingly likely if he continued to buck his military advisers. He then proceeded to do exactly that. After vetoing the introduction of U.S. troops at the Bay of Pigs, he resisted the Joint Chiefs' even more intense pressures to bomb and invade Cuba in the October 1962 missile crisis. Then he simply ignored his military and CIA advisers by turning sharply toward peace in his American University address, his Partial Test Ban Treaty with Nikita Khrushchev, and his quest for a dialogue with Fidel Castro. His October 1963 decision to withdraw from Vietnam once again broke the Cold War rule of his national security state. As Merton had hoped, Kennedy was breaking through to a deeper humanity—and to its fatal consequences.

Yet for those who could see beyond the East–West conflict, Kennedy's high-risk steps for peace made political sense. Four decades after these events, we have lost their historical context. It was a time of hope. JFK, like many, was inspired by the yearning for peace spanning the world like a rainbow after the barely averted storm of the Cuban Missile Crisis. John Kennedy, Nikita Khrushchev, and even Khrushchev's Caribbean partner Fidel Castro were, in the relief of those months, all beginning to break free from their respective military establishments and ideologies. As 1963 began, political commentators sensed a new morning after the long night of the Cold War.

For example, Drew Pearson in his *Washington Merry-Go-Round* column datelined January 23, 1963, headlined the presidential challenge of the year ahead, "Kennedy Has Chance to End the Cold War." Pearson stressed the need for the president to seize the time for peace:

"President Kennedy today faces his greatest opportunity to negotiate a permanent peace, but because of division inside his own Administration he may miss the boat.

"That is the consensus of friendly diplomats long trained in watching the ebb and flow of world events.

"They add that Europe is moving so fast that it may take the leadership away from Mr. Kennedy and patch up its own peace with Soviet Premier Khrushchev."[9]

The diplomats Pearson was drawing upon could already discern a massive shifting of political fault lines beneath the Kennedy-Khrushchev settlement of the missile crisis. At the same time they had identified the primary obstacle to an end of the Cold War—powerful forces in the U.S. government who did not believe in such a change, and who were throwing their weight against it.

Pearson noted that, in spite of this deep opposition within the government, the president was nevertheless "sitting on top of the diplomatic world" in settling the problems of the Cold War. He cited Kennedy's decision to remove U.S. missiles from Turkey and Italy without fanfare:

"This should decrease tension between the U.S.A. and USSR, but the United States has neither taken credit for it nor used it as Khrushchev used his removal of missiles from Cuba."

Pearson was unaware that Kennedy was already collaborating with Khrushchev, and that the president's withdrawal of missiles was actually a quiet fulfillment of his October pledge to his Soviet counterpart.

The columnist had interviewed Khrushchev at his villa on the shores of the Black Sea over a year before. He believed the Soviet leader sincerely wanted peace. Khrushchev's retreat from Cuba and his subsequent statements for peace reinforced that conclusion. "The latest," Pearson wrote in his January 1963 column, "is his amazing speech in East Berlin last week in which he renounced war as an instrument of Communist policy."

As a result of these swirling currents of change, the United States and the Soviet Union were on the "brink of peace," especially on nuclear testing and Berlin. However, Pearson emphasized, if the sharply divided Kennedy administration kept "gazing passively at this rapidly changing picture," other Western leaders such as President de Gaulle would jump ahead of Kennedy and make their own peace with Khrushchev. The moment was ripe for change. Would the President seize it? In the hopeful summer of 1963, Kennedy responded to that question with his American University address, the Test Ban Treaty, and his deepening détente with Khrushchev. Then, showing that anything was becoming possible, Kennedy sought out a dialogue with his greatest nemesis, Fidel Castro. JFK's October decision to withdraw from Vietnam was the next logical step in the increasingly hopeful process that he and Khrushchev had become engaged in.

These now forgotten winds of change in which John Kennedy had set sail in 1963 put him in the position of becoming a peacemaker while still commanding a military force with the capacity to destroy the world many times over. He was trapped in a contradiction between the mandate of peace in his American University address and the continuing Cold War dogmas of his national security state. Kennedy heightened the conflict himself by getting caught up in Cold War rhetoric, as when he spoke dramatically to a vast crowd in front of West Berlin's city hall on June 26, 1963. After seeing the barbarity of the Berlin Wall, the U.S. president said exuberantly, to his later chagrin, "there are some who say in Europe and elsewhere we can work with the Communists [as he himself had said and was doing]. Let them come to Berlin." [10]

Yet despite his own inner conflicts and the deeper tensions between himself and his advisers, Kennedy had rejected the dominant mythology of his time, according to which a victory over Communism was the supreme value. Kennedy had chosen an alternative to victory—an end to the Cold War. He was breaking free from the contradiction of his Cold War presidency. To advisers like the Joint Chiefs of Staff, that presidential turn from a reliance on war seemed like a surrender to the enemy. Whatever the president might say or do, the military knew they had their own mandate to follow—victory over the enemy.

What is unrecognized about JFK's presidency, which then makes his assassination a false mystery, is that he was locked in a struggle with his national security state. That state had higher values than obedience to the orders of a president who wanted peace. The defeat of Communism was number one. As JFK sought an alternative to victory or defeat in a world of nuclear weapons, he became increasingly isolated in his own government. He had been freed from the demonizing theology of the Cold War by the grace of his deepening relationship to his enemy Khrushchev. At the same time he was forced to realize that, in his own administration, he was becoming more and more isolated. His isolation grew as he rejected his military advisers' most creatively destructive proposals on how to win the Cold War.

On March 13, 1962, the chairman of the Joint Chiefs of Staff, whom Kennedy inherited from Eisenhower, General Lyman L. Lemnitzer, proposed such a secret victory plan to Defense Secretary Robert McNamara. It was called "Operation Northwoods." Its purpose was to justify a U.S. invasion of Cuba. Reading this clandestine Cold War proposal today gives one a sense of the mentality of Kennedy's military advisers and the victory schemes he was being urged to adopt. In "Operation Northwoods," General Lemnitzer recommended the following steps to pave the way for a U.S. invasion of Cuba:

"1. . . . Harassment plus deceptive actions to convince the Cubans of imminent invasion would be emphasized. Our military posture throughout execution of the plan will allow a rapid change from exercise to intervention if Cuban response justifies.

"2. A series of well coordinated incidents will be planned to take place in and around [the U.S. Marine base at] Guantanamo to give genuine appearance of being done by hostile Cuban forces.

Incidents to establish a credible attack (not in chronological order):

    (1) Start rumors (many). Use clandestine radio.
    (2) Land friendly Cubans in uniform 'over-the-fence' to stage attack
        on base.

(3) Capture Cuban (friendly) saboteurs inside the base.

(4) Start riots near the base main gate (friendly Cubans).

(5) Blow up ammunition inside the base; start fires.

(6) Burn aircraft on air base (sabotage).

(7) Lob mortar shells from outside of base into base. Some damage to installations.

(8) Capture assault teams approaching from the sea or vicinity of Guantanamo City.

(9) Capture militia group which storms the base.

(10) Sabotage ship in harbor; large fires—napthalene.

(11) Sink ship near harbor entrance. Conduct funerals for mock-victims (may be lieu of (10)).

b. United States would respond by executing offensive operations to secure water and power supplies, destroying artillery and mortar emplacements which threaten the base.

c. Commence large scale United States military operations.

"3. A 'Remember the Maine' incident could be arranged in several forms: We could blow up a US ship in Guantanamo Bay and blame Cuba. We could blow up a drone (unmanned) vessel anywhere in the Cuban waters. We could arrange to cause such incident in the vicinity of Havana or Santiago as a spectacular result of Cuban attack from the air or sea, or both. The presence of Cuban planes or ships merely investigating the intent of the vessel could be fairly compelling evidence that the ship was taken under attack. The nearness to Havana or Santiago would add credibility especially to those people that might have heard the blast or have seen the fire. The US could follow up with an air/sea rescue operation covered by US fighters to 'evacuate' remaining members of the non-existent crew. Casualty lists in US newspapers would cause a helpful wave of national indignation." [11]

General Lemnitzer's next recommendation in "Operation Northwoods" went even more deeply into deception and internal subversion. He urged the Secretary of Defense to support a campaign of terrorism within the United States as a necessary evil in overcoming Communist Cuba:

"4. We could develop a Communist Cuban terror campaign in the Miami area, in other Florida cities and even in Washington. The terror campaign could be pointed at Cuban refugees seeking haven in the United States. We could sink a boatload of Cubans enroute to Florida (real or simulated). We could foster attempts on lives of Cuban refugees in the United States even to the extent of wounding in instances to be widely publicized. Exploding a few plastic bombs in carefully chosen spots, the arrest of Cuban agents and the release of prepared documents substantiating Cuban involvement also would be helpful in projecting the idea of an irresponsible government." [12]

General Lemnitzer said he and the Joint Chiefs of Staff wanted to direct this terrorist campaign that would be blamed on Cuba. He wrote Secretary McNamara that he assumed "a single agency will be given the primary responsibility for developing military and para-military aspects of the basic plan." He recommended "that this responsibility for both overt and covert military operations be assigned the Joint Chiefs of Staff."[13]

Lemnitzer submitted his "Operation Northwoods" proposal to McNamara at a meeting on March 13, 1962. There is no record of McNamara's response.[14] However, according to the record of a March 16 White House meeting, President Kennedy told Lemnitzer and other key advisers that he could not foresee any circumstances "that would justify and make desirable the use of American forces for overt military action" in Cuba.[15]

Although "Operation Northwoods" had been blocked by the president, General Lemnitzer kept pushing on behalf of the Joint Chiefs for a preemptive invasion of Cuba. In an April 10, 1962, memorandum to McNamara, he stated: "The Joint Chiefs of Staff believe that the Cuban problem must be solved in the near future. . . . they believe that military intervention by the United States will be required to overthrow the present communist regime. . . . They also believe that the intervention can be accomplished rapidly enough to minimize communist opportunities for solicitation of UN action."[16]

Kennedy had finally had enough of Lemnitzer. In September 1962 he replaced him as chairman of the Joint Chiefs of Staff. However, Lemnitzer was not alone in his beliefs. He claimed that his terrorist "Operation Northwoods" had been backed by the entire Joint Chiefs. Kennedy's problem was not so much Lemnitzer per se as it was the Cold War mind-set of his government. He had to deal with a block of military and CIA leaders who justified any means whatever of defeating what they saw as the absolute evil of Communism. On the other hand, these men saw President Kennedy's agreement with Khrushchev not to invade Cuba, his withdrawal of missiles from Turkey and Italy, his American University address, the Test Ban Treaty, and his beginning dialogue with Castro, as the initial stages of a Communist victory. They held a dogmatic belief that they thought John Kennedy had forgotten, that there was no alternative to military might when it came to defeating Communism. They thought it was Kennedy, not themselves, who had gone off the deep end. The future of the country was in their hands. For the CIA and the Joint Chiefs, the question was: How could Kennedy's surrender to the Communists be stopped in time to save America? In their world of victory or defeat, JFK's decision to withdraw from Vietnam was the last straw.

On the eve of his inauguration, Kennedy had shown his doubts about war in Southeast Asia. When he was given a transitional briefing by President Eisenhower on January 19, 1961, the president-elect asked an unexpected question. It pertained to the rising conflict with Communist forces in Laos, Vietnam's western neighbor. Which option would Eisenhower prefer, Kennedy asked, a "coalition with the Communists to form a government in Laos or intervening [militarily] through SEATO [the Southeast Asia Treaty Organization, to which the U.S. belonged]?"[17] Eisenhower was taken aback by his successor's gall in raising the possibility of a coalition with Communists. He said it would be "far better" to intervene militarily. As his Secretary of State, Christian Herter had already said, any coalition with the Communists would end up with the Communists in control. Even unilateral intervention by U.S. troops was preferable to that. It would be "a last desperate effort to save Laos." [18]

Kennedy listened skeptically. He thought he was hearing a prescription for disaster, from a man who in a few hours would no longer have to bear any responsibility for it.

"There he sat," he told friends later, "telling me to get ready to put ground forces into Asia, the thing he himself had been carefully avoiding for the last eight years." [19]

Kennedy knew, on the other hand, that by pursuing the question of a coalition with Communists he was initiating a policy struggle on Southeast Asia in his own administration. The CIA and the Joint Chiefs of Staff, with Eisenhower's support, had already assumed the burden of somehow "saving" Laos and Vietnam. These same men would now become Kennedy's advisers. Though a Cold Warrior himself, Kennedy was still too critical a thinker not to go ahead and question their consensus, by considering seriously what they felt was a dangerous accommodation with the enemy as preferable to a hopeless war in Asia.

As *The Pentagon Papers* note, Vietnam was of relatively minor importance in 1961, compared to Laos: "Vietnam in 1961 was a peripheral crisis. Even within Southeast Asia it received far less of the Administration's and the world's attention than did Laos." [20] For example, *The New York Times Index for 1961* lists twenty-six columns of items on Laos, but only eight on Vietnam.[21] For Kennedy, Laos was a crisis from the beginning, whose settlement would raise the question of Vietnam.

On February 3, 1961, two weeks after he became president, Kennedy met alone with the U.S. ambassador to Laos, Winthrop Brown. The diplomat had a hard time believing his new president's desire to hear only the truth about Laos. As Brown was explaining the official policy, Kennedy stopped him. He said, "That's not what I asked you. I said, 'What do you think,' you, the Ambassador?" [22] Brown opened up. With the president concentrating intently on his words, Brown critiqued the CIA's and the Pentagon's endorsement of the anti-communist ruler General Phoumi Nosavan. The autocratic general had risen to power through the CIA's formation, under the Eisenhower administration, of a Laotian "patriotic organization," the Committee for the Defense of the National Interest (CDNI).[23] Brown told Kennedy frankly that Laos could be united only under the neutralist Souvanna Phouma, whose government had been deposed by CIA-Pentagon forces under Eisenhower. JFK questioned Brown extensively about the possibility of a neutral government under Souvanna that Britain, France, and the Soviet Union could all support, if the United States were to change policy.[24] Years later, Brown recalled his hour-long conversation with the president on a neutralist Laos as "a very, very moving experience." [25]

As Kennedy began to turn toward a neutral Laos, the Joint Chiefs of Staff stepped up their pressure for military intervention in support of General Phoumi. Their point was that the Communist Pathet Lao army, supported by the Soviet Union, China, and North Vietnam, would achieve complete control over Laos unless the United States intervened quickly. Pushed by Cold War dynamics and Pathet Lao advances, Kennedy was tempted yet skeptical.

In a March 9 meeting at the White House, he peppered his National Security Council with questions that exposed contradictions in U.S. policy and pointed the way toward a neutralist Laos. His questioning uncovered the uncomfortable truth that the United States had sent in much more military equipment in the past three months to aid Phoumi Nosavan than the Soviets had in support of the Communist Pathet Lao forces.[26] The president then pointed out that it was "a basic problem to us that all the countries who are supposedly our allies favor the same person (Souvanna), as the Communists do."[27] JFK was about to join them. The next day, Kennedy's Soviet ambassador Llewellyn Thompson told Nikita Khrushchev in Moscow that the United States was now seeking a "neutralization of Laos accomplished by a commission of neutral neighbors."[28] Khrushchev was surprised at Kennedy's turnaround. He said the new American position differed agreeably from the old one.[29]

At a March 23 news conference on Laos, Kennedy made his policy change public by stating that the United States "strongly and unreservedly" supported "the goal of a neutral and independent Laos, tied to no outside power or group of powers, threatening no one, and free from any domination."[30] He endorsed the British appeal for a cease-fire between General Phoumi's army and the neutralist-communist forces arrayed against them. He also joined the British in calling for an international conference on Laos.[31]

The Russians agreed. Kennedy's new direction enabled the Russians to come together with the British, the Americans, and eleven other countries in Geneva on May 11 in an effort to resolve the question of Laos.

In the meantime, however, Kennedy was being led to the brink of war. The Communist forces continued to advance in Laos. They seemed to be on their way to total victory before the Geneva Conference even convened. The president was determined not to let them overrun the country. At the same time, as his special counsel Ted Sorensen pointed out, he was unwilling "to provide whatever military backing was necessary to enable the pro-Western forces [of General Phoumi] to prevail. This was in effect the policy he had inherited—and he had also inherited most of the military and intelligence advisers who had formed it."[32] These men kept pressing him to turn back from the neutralist coalition he was pursuing, which they saw as a foolish concession to the Communists. In spite of the president's turn toward neutralism at his March 23 press conference, on March 30 General Lemnitzer told reporters that the neutralist leader Souvanna Phouma was not to be trusted. While Souvanna might not be a Communist, Lemnitzer said, "he couldn't be any worse if he were a communist."[33]

Lemnitzer and the Joint Chiefs were resisting the president's new direction. They urged him instead to support Phoumi with U.S. combat troops to halt the Communist offensive before it was too late. Otherwise there would be nothing left to negotiate in Geneva, even in the direction of neutralism. As the crisis deepened in March and April, Kennedy agreed to preparations for a military buildup. However, he emphasized to everyone around him that he had not given a final go-ahead to intervene in Laos.[34] Then a series of events convinced him in time that he was being drawn into a trap.

The first was the Bay of Pigs. As we have seen, Kennedy realized that the CIA and the Joint Chiefs had set him up at the Bay of Pigs for a full-scale invasion of Cuba, by a scenario designed to fail unless he agreed under over-whelming pressure to send in the troops. When he refused to go along and accepted the defeat, he refocused his attention more critically on Laos. The same CIA and military advisers who had deceived him on Cuba were urging him to intervene in Laos. Moreover, the Joint Chiefs kept revising upward the number of troops they wanted him to deploy there: asking initially for 40,000; raising the number to 60,000 by the end of March; hiking it to 140,000 by the end of April.[35] Kennedy began to balk at their scenarios. General Lemnitzer then cabled the president more cautiously from a trip to Laos, recommending a "more limited commitment" there. A suspicious JFK backed away from the entire idea of troops in Laos. As he told Schlesinger at the time, "If it hadn't been for Cuba, we might be about to intervene in Laos." Waving Lemnitzer's cables, he said, "I might have taken this advice seriously."[36]

Instead he questioned more sharply his military chiefs, exposing the holes in their thinking. At an April 28 meeting, Admiral Burke said to the president, "Each time you give ground [as he thought JFK was doing in Laos], it is harder to stand next time." Burke said the U.S. had to be prepared somewhere in Southeast Asia to "throw enough in to win—the works."[37] Army general George H. Decker seconded Burke, saying, "If we go in, we should go in to win, and that means bombing Hanoi, China, and maybe even using nuclear weapons."[38] With his customary insolence toward the president, Air Force general Curtis LeMay told JFK the next day before a room full of national security advisers that he did not know *what* U.S. policy was on Laos. He underlined his disdain by adding that he knew what the president had said, but "the military had been unable to back up the President's statements."[39] At another meeting, General Lemnitzer provoked deeper questions in Kennedy about the Joint Chiefs by outlining a strategy of unlimited escalation in Southeast Asia, concluding, "If we are given the right to use nuclear weapons, we can guarantee victory."[40] The president looked at him, said nothing, and dismissed the meeting. Later he commented, "Since he couldn't think of any further escalation, he would have to promise us victory."[41]

In light of the Bay of Pigs and the chiefs' push for war in Laos, Kennedy told columnist Arthur Krock he had simply "lost confidence" in the Joint Chiefs of Staff.[42]

A military authority who reinforced Kennedy's resistance to the Joint

Chiefs was retired general Douglas MacArthur, who visited him in late April. MacArthur told the president, "Anyone wanting to commit American ground forces to the mainland of Asia should have his head examined."[43] Kennedy cited MacArthur's judgment to his own generals for the duration of his presidency. To put U.S. combat troops into Laos or Vietnam was a line he adamantly refused to cross for the rest of his life. General Maxwell Taylor said MacArthur's statement made "a hell of an impression on the President. . . . so that whenever he'd get this military advice from the Joint Chiefs or from me or anyone else, he'd say, 'Well, now, you gentlemen, you go back and convince General MacArthur, then I'll be convinced.' "[44]

MacArthur made another statement, about the political situation Kennedy had inherited in Indochina, that struck the president so much that he dictated it in an oral memorandum of their conversation: "He said that 'the chickens are coming home to roost' from Eisenhower's years and I live in the chicken coop."[45] Malcolm X would become notorious for the same barnyard saying after JFK was killed in the chicken coop.

A s John Kennedy began to take a stand against sending troops to Southeast Asia that would become one more reason for his assassination, he met a man who would take equally strong stands on his behalf, Secret Service agent Abraham Bolden.

In the Cold War years when JFK had been a congressman and a senator, Abe Bolden was a black kid growing up in East St. Louis, Illinois. By determination and discipline, Bolden survived the inner-city war zone of East St. Louis. He then worked his way through Lincoln University in Jefferson City, Missouri. From the beginning to the end of his college days, Bolden walked to the beat of his own drummer. While other freshmen obeyed the hazing commands of upperclassmen, Bolden defied them, saying he would do nothing that was not included in the school manual.[46] He outraged campus opinion by writing a letter to the school paper challenging the granting of scholarships to star athletes who were poor students. Bolden graduated *cum laude* from Lincoln. A classmate said Abraham Bolden could be described "as foolish or as a man of courage, depending upon one's views,"[47] a characterization that would be borne out by his journey into the life and death of John F. Kennedy.

After serving as an Illinois state trooper for four years with an outstanding record, Bolden joined the U.S. Secret Service in 1960. He became an agent in its Chicago office. Thus it was that on the night of April 28, 1961, when President Kennedy came to speak at Chicago's McCormick Exposition Center, Abraham Bolden was standing outside a men's restroom to which he'd been assigned as security. Just as he was thinking that he'd probably never see Kennedy, he suddenly saw the president coming down the steps toward him, together with Mayor Richard Daley and other dignitaries.

Kennedy stopped in front of Bolden. He said, "Who are you?"

"I'm Abraham Bolden, Mr. President."

"Are you a member of the Secret Service?"

"Yes, sir."

"Mr. Bolden, has there ever been a Negro member of the White House Detail of the Secret Service?"

"No, sir, there has not."

"Would you like to be the first?"

"Yes, sir."

"I'll see you in Washington." [48]

Abraham Bolden joined the White House Secret Service detail in June 1961. He experienced personally John Kennedy's concern for people. Kennedy never passed Bolden without speaking to him. He asked about him and his family, in such a way that Bolden knew he meant it. He engaged him in small talk about Chicago and its baseball teams. The president often introduced Bolden to his White House visitors. Bolden could also see in Kennedy's eyes a worry, a feeling that something was wrong around him. [49]

Abraham Bolden saw increasing evidence of the president's isolation and danger from the standpoint of security. Most of the Secret Service agents seemed to hate John Kennedy. They joked among themselves that if someone shot at him, they'd get out of the way. The agents' drunken after-hours behavior carried over into lax security for the president. Bolden refused to drink or play cards with them. The other agents made remarks about "niggers" in his presence. [50]

As he had before in his life, Abraham Bolden spoke up. He complained to his superiors about the president's poor security. They did nothing. After forty days as a member of the White House detail, Bolden refused to take part any longer in a charade. He returned voluntarily to the Chicago office. He had demoted himself on principle from the highest position an African American had ever held in the Secret Service. However, in a deeper scheme of things, the White House detail had been one more apprenticeship for Bolden. He had grown in love and respect for the president, while speaking up for his life. From East St. Louis to the White House, Abraham Bolden was being primed to be a witness to the unspeakable.

At the June 3–4, 1961, summit meeting in Vienna, John Kennedy succeeded in negotiating with Nikita Khrushchev for their mutual support of a neutral and independent Laos under a government to be chosen by the Laotians themselves. [51] It was the only issue they could agree upon. Khrushchev's apparent indifference toward the deepening Cold War threat of nuclear war had shocked Kennedy. It inspired his midnight reflection echoing Lincoln written on the flight back to Washington:

"I know there is a God—and I see a storm coming;
If he has a place for me, I believe that I am ready." [52]

Kennedy had had to push Khrushchev at Vienna to get him to agree on Laos. At first Khrushchev taunted his American counterpart with Cold War history, saying Kennedy "knew very well that it had been the US government [under Eisenhower] which had overthrown Souvanna Phouma." [53] JFK conceded the point. He said, "Speaking frankly, US policy in that region has not always been wise." [54] Nevertheless, he went on, the United States now wanted a Laos that would be as neutral and independent as Cambodia and Burma were. Khrushchev said that was his view as well. [55]

He then became as amused by the U.S. policy about-face on Laos as Kennedy's military and CIA advisers were upset by it. He said wryly to Kennedy, "You seem to have stated the Soviet policy and called it your own." [56] Kennedy's Cold War critics grimly agreed. For his part, JFK was relieved to have found at least one place in the world, Indochina, where he and Khrushchev seemed ready to pursue peace together.

Kennedy immediately ordered his representative at the Geneva Conference, Averell Harriman, to seize the time and resolve the Laos crisis peacefully. He phoned Harriman in Geneva and said bluntly, "Did you understand? I want a negotiated settlement in Laos. I don't want to put troops in." [57]

Nevertheless, putting troops in continued to be the Joint Chiefs' demand to the president, for not only Laos but also for the former French colony on its eastern border, Vietnam. What now gave Vietnam added significance in the Kennedy administration was the stand that the president had taken on Laos. Before Kennedy reached his first half-year in office, in Cold War terms he was already thought to have "lost Laos" by joining the Soviet Union in supporting a coalition government that would include Communists. He therefore came under increasing pressure to "save South Vietnam" by introducing there the U.S. combat troops he refused to send to Laos. However, the anti-communist South Vietnamese government Kennedy was being asked to save was itself highly problematic.

On November 11, 1960, three days after JFK was elected U.S. president, South Vietnam's president Ngo Dinh Diem was almost turned out of office by a military coup with a populist base of support. The November 1960 attempted coup foreshadowed the November 1963 successful coup that would kill Diem and his brother, Ngo Dinh Nhu. Holed up in both cases with a handful of presidential guards, the wily, despotic ruler negotiated just long enough in November 1960 with the rebel forces surrounding his palace to enable a loyalist armored battalion to reach him in the nick of time. The tank commanders then turned their guns on the rebels, routing them. [58] When he would try to follow a similar delaying strategy in 1963, Diem would be dealing with more seasoned coup leaders who were resolved not to repeat the mistakes of three years ago. But in 1960 Diem survived the coup and reasserted his control over South Vietnam. Claiming initially that he had reformed his ways, he continued his autocratic rule, relying on U.S. support to defeat both democratic opponents and a Communist-led guerrilla movement.

The *Pentagon Papers* have described the special American commitment to Vietnam that existed when Kennedy became president. Unlike any of the other countries in Southeast Asia, Vietnam was "essentially the creation of the United States,"[59] as was the leadership of Ngo Dinh Diem:

"Without U.S. support Diem almost certainly could not have consolidated his hold on the South during 1955 and 1956. [Senator John F. Kennedy, because of his Cold War politics and his first impression of Diem as a sincere Vietnamese nationalist, had been among the U.S. supporters of Diem's government.]

"Without the threat of U.S. intervention, South Vietnam could not have refused to even discuss the elections called for in 1956 under the Geneva settlement without being immediately overrun by the Viet Minh armies.

"Without U.S. aid in the years following, the Diem regime certainly, and an independent South Vietnam almost as certainly, could not have survived."[60]

In the context of the U.S. creation of South Vietnam as a bulwark against Communism (with John F. Kennedy's participation), President Kennedy's decision in the spring of 1961 to neutralize neighboring Laos was a shock to Diem. He regarded Kennedy's new policy in Laos as a threat to the survival of his own government. JFK tried to reassure Diem by sending Vice President Lyndon Johnson in May 1961 to visit him along with other anti-Communist Asian allies who were dismayed by Kennedy's turn toward neutralism. Johnson's written report back to the president was a rebuke of his policy. Johnson described what he thought was the disastrous impact of the decision to neutralize Laos:

"Country to country, the degree differs but Laos has created doubt and concern about intentions of the United States throughout Southeast Asia. No amount of success at Geneva can, of itself, erase this. The independent Asians do not wish to have their own status resolved in like manner in Geneva.

"Leaders such as Diem, Chiang [Kai-Shek of Taiwan], Sarit [of Thailand], and Ayub [Khan of Pakistan] more or less accept that we are making 'the best of a bad bargain' at Geneva. Their charity extends no farther. . . .

"Our [Johnson's] mission arrested the decline of confidence in the United States. It did not—in my judgment—restore any confidence already lost. The leaders were as explicit, as courteous and courtly as men could be in making it clear that deeds must follow words—soon.

"We didn't buy time—we were given it.

"If these men I saw at your request were bankers, I would know—without bothering to ask—that there would be no further extensions on my note."[61]

Johnson then summed up for Kennedy a belligerent Cold War challenge to his policy that came not only from the anti-Communist allies whom LBJ had just visited but also from the Pentagon and from the vice president himself:

"The fundamental decision required of the United States—and time is of the greatest importance—is whether we are to attempt to meet the challenge of Communist expansion now in Southeast Asia by a major effort in support of the forces of freedom in the area or throw in the towel." [62]

Kennedy's response to this reproach from his vice president was not "to throw in the towel" to Communist expansion in Southeast Asia, but neither was it to approve the combat troops that the Joint Chiefs now wanted for Vietnam. Kennedy drew the same line in South Vietnam that he had drawn in Laos and Cuba. He would not authorize the sending of U.S. combat troops.

On May 10, and again on May 18, the Joint Chiefs had recommended that combat troops be sent to Vietnam.[63] Diem then sent Kennedy a June 9 letter with a more modest request, for "selected elements of the American Armed Forces to establish training centers for the Vietnamese Armed Forces." [64] As the *Pentagon Papers* point out in this connection, "the crucial issue, of course, was whether Americans would be sent to Vietnam in the form of organized combat units, capable of, if not explicitly intended for conducting combat operations." [65] Kennedy would agree to send military support to Diem, such as U.S. advisers and helicopters. However, no matter what pressures were put upon him, he would always refuse to send "American units capable of independent combat against the guerrillas." [66]

The author of this section of the *Pentagon Papers*, Daniel Ellsberg, puzzled over why Kennedy took such a stand. Why wouldn't John F. Kennedy send combat units to Vietnam? The focus of Ellsberg's question in his *Pentagon Papers* analysis was the fall of 1961, when Kennedy had advisers on all sides urging him to send U.S. troops before it was too late to stop a Viet Cong victory.

The pressure on the president began to build in late summer. "The situation [in South Vietnam] gets worse almost week by week," journalist Theodore White reported to the White House in August. "The guerrillas now control almost all the southern delta—so much so that I could find no American who would drive me outside Saigon in his car even by day without military convoy." [67]

In September the number of guerrilla attacks in South Vietnam almost tripled from the previous months' totals. Saigon was shocked when Phuoc Thanh, a provincial capital nearby, was seized and Diem's province chief was beheaded before the insurgents retreated.[68]

As the pressures increased for U.S. troops, Kennedy stalled by sending a fact-finding mission to Saigon in October. General Maxwell Taylor was its head. He was no help. Taylor wired Kennedy from Saigon that the United States should take quick advantage of a severe flood in South Vietnam by introducing six thousand to eight thousand U.S. troops under the guise of "flood relief," including combat units that would then "give a much needed shot in the arm to national morale." [69] In a follow-up wire from the Philippines, Taylor acknowledged that those first eight thousand troops could well be just the beginning: "If the ultimate result sought is the closing of the frontiers and the clean-up of the insurgents within SVN, there is no limit to our possible commitment (unless we attack the source in Hanoi)." [70] On the other hand, regardless of the number of troops needed, Taylor thought "there can be no action so convincing of U.S. seriousness of purpose and hence so reassuring to the people and Government of SVN and to our other friends and allies in [Southeast Asia] as the introduction of U.S. forces into SVN." [71] Taylor's enthusiasm for troops was seconded in a cable by Ambassador Frederick Nolting, who cited "conversations over past ten days with Vietnamese in various walks of life" showing a "virtually unanimous desire for introduction of U.S. forces into Viet-Nam."

The case for troops was becoming formidable. On November 8, Defense Secretary Robert McNamara, his deputy Roswell Gilpatric, and the Joint Chiefs of Staff all recommended to Kennedy in a memorandum that "we do commit the U.S. to the clear objective of preventing the fall of South Vietnam to Communism and that we support this commitment by the necessary military actions," including Taylor's proposed "U.S. force of the magnitude of an initial 8,000 men in a flood relief context" and expanding to as many as six divisions of ground forces, "or about 205,000 men." [72]

Kennedy rejected the virtually unanimous recommendation of his advisers in the fall of 1961 to send combat troops to Vietnam. Taylor reflected later on the uniqueness of JFK's position: "I don't recall anyone who was strongly against [sending ground troops], except one man and that was the President. The President just didn't want to be convinced that this was the right thing to do. . . . It was really the President's personal conviction that U.S. ground troops shouldn't go in." [73]

Kennedy was so resistant to the military's demand for troops that he took a step he knew would further alienate them. He subverted his military leaders' recommendations by planting a story that they were against sending combat units.

In mid-October the *New York Times* reported erroneously: "Military leaders at the Pentagon, no less than General Taylor himself, are understood to be reluctant to send organized U.S. combat units into Southeast Asia." [74] The opposite was the truth. As we have seen, the Pentagon leaders and General Taylor were in fact beating their war drums as loudly as they could in the president's ears. They wanted combat troops. Kennedy fought back with a public lie. As the *Pentagon Papers* noted, "It is just about inconceivable that this story could have been given out except at the direction of the president, or by him personally." [75] The president was undermining his military leaders by dispensing the false information that they were against the very step they most wanted him to take. The ploy worked. As the *Pentagon Papers* observed, "The *Times* story had the apparently desired effect. Speculation about combat troops almost disappeared from news stories. . . ." However, besides misleading the public, Kennedy was playing a dangerous game with the Pentagon's leaders. His misrepresentation of their push for combat troops would prove to be one more piece of evidence in their mounting case against the president.

But Kennedy would do anything he could to keep from sending combat troops to Vietnam. He told Arthur Schlesinger, "They want a force of American troops. They say it's necessary in order to restore confidence and maintain morale. But it will be just like Berlin. The troops will march in; the bands will play; the crowds will cheer; and in four days everyone will have forgotten. Then we will be told we have to send in more troops. It's like taking a drink. The effect wears off, and you have to take another." [76]

Nevertheless, although he refused to send combat troops, Kennedy did agree in November 1961 to increase the U.S. commitment to South Vietnam. What he chose to send instead of combat troops were advisers and support units. According to the advice he was being given, Kennedy's military support program for South Vietnam would almost certainly fall far short of anything that could stop the Viet Cong. This was what puzzled Daniel Ellsberg so deeply when he analyzed JFK's decision in the *Pentagon Papers*, as he has written more recently in his memoir, *Secrets*:

"Kennedy had chosen to increase U.S. involvement and investment of prestige in Vietnam and to reaffirm our rhetorical commitment—not as much as his subordinates asked him to, but significantly while rejecting an element, ground forces, that nearly all his own officials described as essential to success. In fact, at the same time he had rejected another element that all his advisers, including [Secretary of State Dean] Rusk, had likewise described as essential: an explicit full commitment to defeating the Communists in South Vietnam. Why?" [77]

While Ellsberg was trying to figure out JFK's odd stand, he had the opportunity to raise the question in a conversation with Robert Kennedy. As a U.S. senator in 1967, Kennedy had invited Ellsberg, a Pentagon analyst, to talk with him in his office about a mutual concern, the escalating war in Vietnam. Ellsberg had boldly seized the chance to question RFK about JFK's decision making in 1961. Why, Ellsberg asked him, had President Kennedy rejected both ground troops and a formal commitment to victory in Vietnam, thereby "rejecting the urgent advice of every one of his top military and civilian officials"? [78]

Robert Kennedy answered that his brother was absolutely determined never to send ground combat units to Vietnam, because if he did, the U.S. would be in the same spot as the French—whites against Asians, in a war against nationalism and self-determination.

Ellsberg pressed the question: Was JFK willing to accept defeat rather than send troops?

RFK said that if the president reached the point where the only alternatives to defeat were sending ground troops or withdrawing, he intended to withdraw. "We would have handled it like Laos," his brother said. [79]

Ellsberg was even more intrigued. It was obvious to him that none of President Kennedy's senior advisers had any such conviction about Indochina. Ellsberg kept pushing for more of an explanation for Kennedy's stand.

"What made him so smart?" he asked John Kennedy's brother.

Writing more than thirty years after this conversation, Ellsberg could still feel the shock he had experienced from RFK's response:

"*Whap!* His hand slapped down on the desk. I jumped in my chair. 'Because *we were there!*' He slammed the desktop again. His face contorted in anger and pain. 'We were there, in 1951. We saw what was happening to the French. *We saw it.* My brother was determined, determined never to let that happen to us.'"[80]

John Kennedy had been there. He had seen it with Robert, when the French troops were doing it. A friend on the spot, Edmund Gullion, had underlined the futility of American combat troops replacing the French. Ellsberg wrote that he believed what Robert Kennedy said, "that his brother was strongly convinced that he should never send ground troops to Indochina and that he was prepared to accept a 'Laotian solution' if necessary to avoid that."[81]

JFK was not primarily concerned with Vietnam, or even Laos, in the middle of 1961. The focus of the president's attention was on Germany. In the summer and fall following the Bay of Pigs, John Kennedy's struggle with Nikita Khrushchev over the divided city of Berlin was the context in which Kennedy was also discerning what to do in Laos—and in relation to Laos, Vietnam.

His military advisers continued to ride hard toward the apocalypse. Kennedy was appalled by Generals Lemnitzer's and LeMay's insistence at two summer meetings that they wanted his authorization to use nuclear weapons in both Berlin and Southeast Asia. His response was to walk out of the meetings.[82]

After one such walkout, he threw his hands in the air, glanced back at the generals and admirals left in the Cabinet Room, and said, "These people are crazy."[83] The Joint Chiefs wondered in turn why their commander-in-chief was reluctant to authorize their use of the means they considered essential to victory. Was he crazy?

In October 1961, the president's newly appointed personal representative in West Berlin, retired general Lucius Clay, tried to escalate the Berlin crisis to a point where the president would be forced to choose victory. In August, Khrushchev had ordered the building of the Berlin Wall, thereby ending a mass exodus of East Germans to the capitalist side of the city. In September, General Clay began secret preparations to tear down the wall. He ordered Major General Albert Watson, the U.S. military commandant in West Berlin, to have army engineers build a duplicate section of the Berlin Wall in a forest. U.S. tanks with bulldozer attachments then experimented with assaults on the substitute wall. General Bruce Clarke, who commanded U.S. forces in Europe, learned of Clay's exercise and put a stop to it.[84] When he told Clay to end the wall-bashing rehearsals, Clarke looked at Clay's red telephone to the White House and said, "If you don't like that, call the President and see what he says."[85] Clay chose not to. Nor did either man ever inform the president of what had gone on at the secret wall in the forest.

While Kennedy remained unaware of Clay's provocative planning,

Khrushchev was much better informed. Soviet spies had watched the forest maneuvers, had taken pictures of them, and had relayed their reports and pictures to Moscow. Khrushchev then assembled a group of close advisers to plot out step by step their counterscenario to a U.S. assault on the Berlin Wall.[86] However, Nikita Khrushchev doubted that John Kennedy had authorized any such attack. He and the president had already begun their secret communications and had in fact even made private progress in the previous month on the question of Berlin. Khrushchev strongly suspected that Kennedy was being undermined.[87]

Khrushchev's son, Sergei, in his memoir, *Nikita Khrushchev and the Creation of a Superpower*, has described from the Soviet standpoint how the two Cold War leaders had begun to conspire toward coexistence. His account has been corroborated at key points by Kennedy's press secretary, Pierre Salinger.

At their Vienna meeting in June, Kennedy had proposed to Khrushchev that they establish "a private and unofficial channel of communications that would bypass all formalities."[88] Khrushchev agreed. In September the Soviet premier made a first use of the back channel.

After a summer of increasing tensions over Berlin, JFK was about to give his first speech at the United Nations. On the weekend before his UN appearance, as the Berlin crisis was continuing, the president and Pierre Salinger were staying overnight at a Manhattan hotel. Salinger agreed to an urgent phone request from Georgi Bolshakov, Soviet embassy press attaché, that he meet in private with Soviet press chief Mikhail Kharlamov.

When Salinger opened his hotel room door to his Russian visitor, Kharlamov was smiling. "The storm in Berlin is over," he said.[89] A puzzled Salinger replied, on the contrary, the situation couldn't have been much worse.

Kharlamov kept smiling. "Just wait, my friend," he said.

When Kharlamov was inside the room, his words came tumbling out. His urgent message to John Kennedy from Nikita Khrushchev was that Khrushchev "was now willing, for the first time, to consider American proposals for a rapprochement on Berlin."[90] The Soviet premier hoped he and Kennedy could arrange a summit meeting as soon as possible. Kharlamov said Khrushchev was feeling intense pressure from the communist bloc to keep pushing Kennedy on the German question. However, the Soviet leader felt himself that it was time for a settlement on Berlin. He was afraid that a major military incident there could spark terrible consequences.

Kharlamov ended Khrushchev's message to Kennedy with an appeal: "He hopes your President's speech to the UN won't be another warlike ultimatum like the one on July 25 [when Kennedy had said the U.S. was willing to wage war to stop the Soviets in Germany]. He didn't like that at all."[91] It was obvious that Khrushchev wanted Kennedy to know his more conciliatory attitude on Germany before the president made his UN speech.

Salinger conveyed Khrushchev's message personally to the president at 1:00 A.M. Kennedy had been sitting up reading in his hotel bed. He asked his press secretary to repeat the key points carefully. Then he got up, went to a window, and stood for a long time in his white pajamas gazing at the lights of the Manhattan skyline.

Finally he said, "There's only one way you can read it. If Khrushchev is ready to listen to our views on Germany, he's not going to recognize the [Walter] Ulbricht [East German] regime—not this year, at least—and that's good news." [92]

He dictated a message to Khrushchev, for Salinger to give verbally to Kharlamov, that he was "cautiously receptive to Khrushchev's proposal for an early summit on Berlin. But first there should be a demonstration of Soviet good faith in Laos," according to the agreement they had reached in Vienna. [93] Berlin and Laos were linked. The Communist Pathet Lao army needed to back off and allow the neutralist Souvanna Phouma to form a coalition government, just as he and Khrushchev had agreed in Vienna. He would return to this theme repeatedly in his messages to Khrushchev.

The president's more substantive response to the premier's secretly conveyed "good news" was the speech he gave on September 25 to the United Nations. The speech had been written before he received Khrushchev's message, but he reviewed it in his hotel room in that light. Like his opponent, Kennedy had already felt the need to back away from the brink in Berlin. He saw that he didn't have to revise the speech's text.

His central theme, in contrast to his speech of July 25, was disarmament. He told the United Nations that disarmament was not an option but an absolute imperative:

"Today, every inhabitant of this planet must contemplate the day when this planet may no longer be habitable. Every man, woman and child lives under a nuclear sword of Damocles, hanging by the slenderest of threads, capable of being cut at any moment by accident or miscalculation or by madness. The weapons of war must be abolished before they abolish us.

". . . It is therefore our intention to challenge the Soviet Union, not to an arms race, but to a peace race—to advance together step by step, stage by stage, until general and complete disarmament has been achieved." [94]

How much did he mean it? Nikita Khrushchev wasn't sure and wouldn't be until the American University address two years later. But he already knew enough about Kennedy by October 1961 to doubt if it was he who was behind the reported plans to demolish the Berlin Wall. That had to be the work of other minds and hands. As Sergei Khrushchev commented, "It seemed to Father that other forces, bypassing the president, were interfering." [95]

The irony was that Kennedy had appointed the man, retired general Lucius Clay, who was now suddenly leading those forces into darkness. However, Lucius Clay, like Kennedy's Pentagon generals, had a mind of his own when it came to a young president's naïve belief that he could win a struggle with evil without going to war. As an old World War II general, Clay knew better. When an October controversy arose at the Berlin Wall over the showing of allied credentials, General Clay seized the opportunity as a personal mandate.

On October 27, ten American M-48 tanks, with bulldozers mounted on the lead tanks, ground their way up to Checkpoint Charlie at the center of the Berlin Wall. They were confronted by ten Soviet tanks, which had been waiting for them quietly on the side streets of East Berlin. A well-briefed Nikita Khrushchev and his advisers had set their counterplan in motion. Twenty more Soviet tanks arrived soon after as reinforcements, and twenty more U.S. tanks moved up from the allied side. The American and Russian tanks faced off, with their long-nosed guns trained on one another, ready to fire. Throughout the night and for a total of sixteen hours, the confrontation continued.

Soviet foreign affairs adviser Valentin Falin was beside Khrushchev throughout the crisis. Falin said later that if the U.S. tanks and bulldozers had advanced farther, the Soviet tanks would have fired on them, bringing the U.S. and the U.S.S.R. "closer to the third world war than ever. . . . Had the tank duel started then in Berlin—and everything was running toward it—the events most probably would have gone beyond any possibility of control." [96]

An alarmed President Kennedy phoned Lucius Clay. Although Kennedy left no record of the conversation, Clay claims the president said, "I know you people over there haven't lost your nerve." Clay said his bold reply was: "Mr. President, we're not worried about our nerves. We're worrying about those of you people in Washington." [97]

At that point the president sent an urgent message to Khrushchev via the back channel. Robert Kennedy contacted Soviet press attaché Georgi Bolshakov. RFK said that if Khrushchev would withdraw his tanks within twenty-four hours, JFK would do the same within thirty minutes later. [98] The president then ordered Lucius Clay to be ready to carry out the U.S. side of such a withdrawal.

The next morning the Soviet tanks backed away, and the U.S. tanks followed suit in thirty minutes. The Checkpoint Charlie crisis was over. Its resolution prefigured that of the Cuban Missile Crisis one year later. In both cases Kennedy asked Khrushchev to take the first step. The Soviet leader did so, in gracious recognition that Kennedy was under even more intense pressure than he was. In both cases a back-channel communication via Robert Kennedy was critical. And in both cases Khrushchev, in withdrawing his tanks and later his missiles, achieved his own objectives in exchange from Kennedy: the removal of U.S. threats to bulldoze the Wall and to invade Cuba, and the withdrawal of U.S. missiles from Turkey and Italy.

However, both the mini-crisis at the Berlin Wall and the huge one over Cuban missiles revealed the shakiness of Kennedy's position in relation to his own military. In the crisis at the wall, Khrushchev knew more about the U.S. plans for attack than Kennedy did. Fortunately Khrushchev was sensitive to the forces subverting JFK, beginning at the wall with General Lucius Clay. Although Clay was technically a civilian and theoretically the president's representative, he acted like a free-wheeling Cold War general. His attitude toward the president's order that he withdraw U.S. tanks from the wall anticipated the Joint Chiefs' anger a year later at their commander-in-chief's pledge not to invade Cuba. Two and a half weeks after the tanks confrontation that threatened a nuclear holocaust, its instigator, Lucius Clay, sent a telegram to Secretary of State Dean Rusk in which he stated:

"Today, we have the nuclear strength to assure victory at awful cost. It no longer suffices to consider our strength as a deterrent only and to plan to use it only in retaliation. No ground probes on the highway which would use force should or could be undertaken unless we are prepared instantly to follow them with a nuclear strike. It is certain that within two or more years retaliatory power will be useless as whoever strikes first will strike last." [99]

To Lucius Clay's regret, the president had not been prepared instantly to follow Clay's assault on the Berlin Wall with a nuclear first strike. Like his cohorts in the Pentagon at the height of the missile crisis, Clay wanted to seize the moment, so the United States could "win" the Cold War by striking first. His analysis, like theirs, was that time was running out. In the meantime, the military conscience was coming to see the president's conscience as a threat to the nation's survival. Moreover, his deepening collusion with Khrushchev seemed treasonous.

As a committed Cold Warrior, John Kennedy from the first moments of his presidency had wanted to "let every nation know, whether it wishes us well or ill, that we shall pay any price, bear any burden, meet any hardship, support any friend, oppose any foe to assure the survival and the success of liberty." [100] Kennedy was a true believer in his inaugural's collective adaptation of Patrick Henry's "Give me liberty or give me death." He was articulating a vision of political freedom, however one-sided its implications, that not only most Americans but hundreds of millions of allies believed in fervently at the time. It was set against a countervision of economic freedom believed by hundreds of millions of Communist opponents. Thus arose the thousand-day-long series of crises between those two opposite believers, John Kennedy and Nikita Khrushchev, who almost unwillingly then became co-creators of a new, more peaceful vision. Both the crises, which were beginning to fade away, and the new vision that was taking their place ended with Kennedy's assassination.

From Kennedy's side of their dogmatic battle, the saving factor was what few commentators have remembered from his inaugural address but what he believed in just as profoundly as he did freedom—peace in the nuclear age, through negotiation with the enemy:

"Finally, to those nations who would make themselves our adversary, we offer not a pledge but a request: that both sides begin anew the quest for peace, before the dark powers of destruction unleashed by science engulf all humanity in planned or accidental self-destruction." [101]

How to square the circle, or negotiate his way out of a circular conflict, was not evident to Kennedy at the beginning. His conflicting commitments to freedom (backed by world-ending weapons) and to peace (backed by an openness to dialogue) were not easily reconciled. In the context of his own struggle to resolve those beliefs, we can understand his more visible struggle with Nikita Khrushchev, particularly on Laos and Vietnam.

Kennedy thought he and Khrushchev had in effect settled the issue of Laos at their Vienna meeting. He said so repeatedly in their secret communications. In his October 16, 1961, letter to Khrushchev, Kennedy said, as he had in his verbal message through Salinger and Kharlamov three weeks before, that any second summit meeting should be preceded by a peaceful resolution of Laos: "Indeed I do not see how we can expect to reach a settlement on so bitter and complex an issue as Berlin, where both of us have vital interests at stake, if we cannot come to a final agreement on Laos, which we have previously agreed should be neutral and independent after the fashion of Burma and Cambodia." [102]

In Khrushchev's first private letter to Kennedy, on September 29, 1961, the Soviet premier had written: "I note with gratification that you and I are of the same opinion as to the need for the withdrawal of foreign troops from the territory of Laos." [103]

In Kennedy's October 16 response, he underlined their agreement on foreign troop withdrawals and stressed the need to verify such withdrawals through the work of the International Control Commission (ICC):

"As you note, the withdrawal of foreign troops from the territory of Laos is an essential condition to preserving that nation's independence and neutrality. There are other, similar conditions, and we must be certain that the ICC has the power and the flexibility to verify the existence of these conditions to the satisfaction of everyone concerned." [104]

At this juncture, Kennedy identified the specific Laos–Vietnam connection that would prove critical to an expanding war in Vietnam: "In addition to so instructing your spokesmen at Geneva [to support the ICC's verification of troop withdrawals], I hope you will increasingly exercise your influence in this direction on all of your "corresponding quarters" [meaning especially the North Vietnamese]; for the acceleration of attacks on South Viet-Nam, many of them from within Laotian territory, are a very grave threat to peace in that area and to the entire kind of world-wide accommodation you and I recognize to be necessary." [105]

The strategic location of Laos, just to the west of Vietnam, made its eastern highlands an ideal conduit for North Vietnamese troops moving covertly into South Vietnam, as would happen increasingly over the remaining two years of Kennedy's presidency. That continuing military buildup via the "Ho Chi Minh Trail" in Laos would make inevitable a Communist victory in Vietnam, while disrupting the "neutral and independent Laos" Kennedy and Khrushchev had already agreed to. However, Khrushchev was powerless to stop it even if he wanted to. Just as Kennedy would discover he had no control over Ngo Dinh Diem in South Vietnam, neither was Khrushchev able to control Ho Chi Minh in North Vietnam. Diem and Ho had minds and policies of their own.

In Khrushchev's November 10, 1961, letter to Kennedy, he dismissed the infiltration of North Vietnamese troops through Laos and emphasized the weakest link in U.S. policy in Southeast Asia, namely Ngo Dinh Diem: "I think that looking at facts soberly you cannot but agree that the present struggle of the population of South Vietnam against Ngo Dinh Diem cannot be explained by some kind of interference or incitement from outside. The events that are taking place there are of internal nature and are connected with the general indignation of the population at the bankrupt policy of Ngo Dinh Diem and those who surround him. This and only this is the core of the matter." [106]

Kennedy, in his November 16 reply, shrewdly bypassed Khrushchev's critique of Diem to reemphasize the "external interference" of North Vietnam: "I do not wish to argue with you concerning the government structure and policies of President Ngo Dinh Diem, but I would like to cite for your consideration the evidence of external interference or incitement which you dismiss in a phrase." [107]

After drawing on a South Vietnamese government letter to the ICC, Kennedy concluded that "Southern Vietnam is now undergoing a determined attempt from without to overthrow the existing government using for this purpose infiltration, supply of arms, propaganda, terrorization, and all the customary instrumentalities of communist activities in such circumstances, all mounted and developed from North Vietnam." [108]

Kennedy and Khrushchev each had a piece of the truth. North Vietnam was in fact sending its troops and arms through "a neutral and independent" Laos into South Vietnam. But this infiltration was part of a nationalist Communist movement that would have been ruling all of Vietnam had not Diem, backed by the Eisenhower administration, blocked an election called for by the Geneva settlement. As Kennedy argued, North Vietnam was indeed violating the neutrality of Laotian territory. But as Khrushchev insisted, Ngo Dinh Diem's government, illegitimate from the start, was suppressing its own people. The overarching truth plaguing Kennedy's and Khrushchev's agreement on a neutral and independent Laos was that peace in Laos and Vietnam was interdependent.

John Kennedy contradicted his commitment to a peaceful settlement of the Laos crisis by his decision to deploy CIA and military advisers there and to arm covertly the members of the Hmong tribe (known by the Americans as the "Meos"). On August 29, 1961, following the recommendations of his CIA, military, and State Department advisers, Kennedy agreed to raise the total of U.S. advisers in Laos to five hundred and to go ahead with the equipping of two thousand more "Meos." That brought to eleven thousand the number of mountain men of Laos recruited into the CIA's covert army.[109] From Kennedy's standpoint, he was supporting an indigenous group of people who were profoundly opposed to their land's occupation by the Pathet Lao army. He was also trying to hold on to enough ground, through some effective resistance to the Pathet Lao's advance, to leave something for Averell Harriman to negotiate with in Geneva toward a neutralist government. But he was working within Cold War assumptions and playing into the hands of his own worst enemy, the CIA. The Agency was eager to manipulate his policy to benefit their favorite Laotian strongman, General Phoumi Nosavan. Aware of this danger, Kennedy went ahead in strengthening the CIA-"Meo" army, so as to stem a Communist takeover in Laos, while at the same time trying by other means to rein in the CIA.

Following the Bay of Pigs, Kennedy had tried to reassert control over the CIA by firing the primary architects of the Bay of Pigs invasion, Allen Dulles, Richard Bissell, and General Charles Cabell; by launching a critical inquiry into the Bay of Pigs under the watchful eye of Robert Kennedy; and by cutting the CIA's budget.[110] A further measure by which JFK tried to keep the CIA from making foreign policy on the ground was his May 29, 1961, letter to each American ambassador abroad. The president wrote: "You are in charge of the entire U.S. Diplomatic Mission, and I expect you to supervise all its operations. The Mission includes not only the personnel of the Department of State and the Foreign Service, but also representatives of all other United States agencies."[111] That included, of course, the CIA, which Schlesinger notes was the particular target of JFK's letter.[112]

The Agency didn't like it. Its people were therefore pleased whenever Kennedy made a concession to their covert agenda, as he did in Laos to counter the Pathet Lao. That particular concession gave them the opportunity not only to strengthen General Phoumi's hand but also to encourage Phoumi to undercut the president's neutralist policy. Phoumi was happy to oblige.

In early 1962 General Phoumi built up the garrison of Nam Tha, only fifteen miles from the Chinese border. Phoumi used his reinforced base to launch provocative probes into nearby Pathet Lao territory. For a time the Pathet Lao ignored Phoumi, aware that he was trying to create an international incident. Eventually they did engage in a series of firefights with Phoumi forces, but refrained from attacking Nam Tha. However, Phoumi's troops abandoned Nam Tha anyhow, claiming they were under attack, and fled across the Mekong River into Thailand.[113] Then they waited for the United States to intervene in the conflict they had choreographed.

As the *Times* of London reported, "CIA agents had deliberately opposed the official American objective of trying to establish a neutral government, had encouraged Phoumi in his reinforcement of Nam Tha, and had negatived the heavy financial pressure brought by the Kennedy administration upon Phoumi by subventions from its own budget."[114] Emboldened by his knowledge of his CIA backing, Phoumi was brazen in his defiance of President Kennedy's policy. The *Times* correspondent stated: "The General apparently was quite outspoken, and made it known that he could disregard the American embassy and the military advisory group because he was in communication with other American agencies." [115]

The CIA's Phoumi ploy failed, however, to create a crisis that would push Kennedy to intervene and kill the developing coalition in Laos. [116] Instead the president did nothing more than make a show of force, first to the Communists by deploying troops to neighboring Thailand, and second to his advisers by having contingency plans drawn up for a Laotian intervention that would never happen. But JFK also authorized Averell Harriman to transfer Jack Hazey, the CIA officer closest to Phoumi. [117] Hazey had been the Agency's counterpart in Laos of David Atlee Phillips in the Caribbean, who would deploy anti-Castro Cubans in raids designed to draw JFK into a war with Cuba. In neither case did the president bite.

A t the Geneva Conference, Averell Harriman was trying to carry out the president's order to negotiate a settlement for a neutral Laos. JFK had been explicit to him that the alternative was unacceptable: "I don't want to put troops in." [118] Harriman brought to the conference the asset of a mutual respect with the Russians. He had done business in the Soviet Union. The Russians regarded Harriman as a friendly capitalist. He and Nikita Khrushchev had visited each other for informal diplomatic exchanges, first at the Kremlin, then at Harriman's Manhattan home, during the year before Kennedy became president. JFK had recognized Khrushchev's confidence in Harriman and would use that relationship later to great effect when Harriman represented JFK in negotiating the test ban treaty with Khrushchev in Moscow. In Geneva, Harriman and his counterpart, Soviet negotiator Georgi M. Pushkin, were developing a wary friendship as they tried to find a way together through Laotian battlegrounds and Cold War intrigues. While representing opposite, contentious sides of the Cold War, Harriman and Pushkin respected each other and were inclined to conspire together for peace.

A turning point at Geneva came in October 1961, when leaders of the three Laotian factions agreed to neutralist Souvanna Phouma's becoming prime minister of a provisional coalition government. Then, as Rudy Abramson, Harriman's biographer, put it, the Soviets "agreed to take responsibility for all the Communist states' compliance with the neutrality declaration and accepted language declaring that Laotian territory would not be used in the affairs of neighboring states—meaning the North Vietnamese could not use the trails through Laos to support the insurgency in South Vietnam." [119] This largely unwritten understanding would become known in U.S. circles as the "Pushkin agreement."

A major obstacle arose, however, when the Soviets, the North Vietnamese, and the Pathet Lao insisted on the right of all three Laotian factions to approve any movements of the International Control Commission. The Pathet Lao would thereby be given a veto power over inspections to monitor violations of the accord.[120] The communists wouldn't budge on the issue. With the Pathet Lao controlling the battlefield, Harriman became convinced that the Geneva Conference would collapse unless the United States was willing to compromise. Although the State Department was adamantly opposed, Kennedy reluctantly decided with Harriman that the critical compromise with the Communists was necessary. The negotiations moved on. But from then on, a "neutral Laos" would take the form of a partitioned country under the guise of a coalition government. Georgi Pushkin would soon die. The agreement named after him would never be honored by Soviet leaders, who lacked the power to tell the Pathet Lao and the North Vietnamese what to do. The corridor running down the eastern border of Laos would become known as the "Ho Chi Minh Trail" for its infiltrating North Vietnamese soldiers on their way to South Vietnam—or as State Department critics would call the same route, the "Averell Harriman Highway."[121] Kennedy, struggling to avoid both war and Communist domination of Laos in the midst of the larger East–West conflicts over Cuba, Berlin, and the Congo, was happy to get the compromise Harriman had worked out with Pushkin.

The president's most bitter opponents to a Laotian settlement, in the Defense Department and the CIA, tried to destroy the agreement. They kept up their support of General Phoumi's provocations and violations of the cease-fire. Averell Harriman told Arthur Schlesinger in May 1962 that JFK's Laos policy was being "systematically sabotaged" from within the government by the military and the CIA. "They want to prove that a neutral solution is impossible," Harriman said, "and that the only course is to turn Laos into an American bastion."[122]

On April 4, 1962, John Kenneth Galbraith, the ambassador to India, raised a ruckus among JFK's advisers by proposing in a memorandum to the president that the United States explore with North Vietnam a disengagement and mutual withdrawal from the growing war in South Vietnam. Galbraith suggested that either Soviet or Indian diplomats "should be asked to ascertain whether Hanoi can or will call off the Viet Cong activity in return for phased American withdrawal, liberalization in the trade relations between the two parts of the country and general and non-specific agreement to talk about reunification after some period of tranquillity."[123]

If the United States instead increased its military support of Diem, Galbraith wrote Kennedy, "there is consequent danger we shall replace the French as the colonial force in the area and bleed as the French did."[124] Galbraith's warning echoed what John Kennedy remembered hearing as a congressman from his friend Edmund Gullion in Saigon in 1951.

Predictably, the Joint Chiefs were furious at Galbraith's proposal. To McNamara they argued that "any reversal of U.S. policy could have disastrous effects, not only on our relationship with South Vietnam, but with the rest of our Asian and other allies as well."[125] A Defense Department memorandum to the president dismissed Galbraith saying, "His proposal contains the essential elements sought by the Communists for their takeover. . . ." [126]

But the State Department also opposed Galbraith. Even Averell Harriman, JFK's advocate for a neutral Laos, was against a neutral solution in Vietnam, as he told the president. [127]

Kennedy, however, considered Galbraith's proposal feasible. He tried unsuccessfully to explore it. In a conversation with Harriman in the Oval Office on April 6, he asked his newly appointed Assistant Secretary of State to follow up Galbraith's memorandum. He told Harriman to send Galbraith instructions to pursue an Indian diplomatic approach to the North Vietnamese about exploring a mutual disengagement with the United States. Harriman resisted, saying they should wait a few days until they received an International Control Commission report on Vietnam. Kennedy agreed but insisted, according to a record of their conversation, "that instructions should nevertheless be sent to Galbraith, and that he would like to see such instructions." [128] Harriman said he would send the instructions the following week. [129]

In fact Averell Harriman sabotaged Kennedy's proposal for a mutual de-escalation with North Vietnam. In response to the president's order to wire such instructions to Galbraith, Harriman "struck the language on de-escalation from the message with a heavy pencil line," as scholar Gareth Porter discovered by examining Harriman's papers. Harriman dictated instructions to his colleague Edward Rice for a telegram to Galbraith that instead "changed the mutual de-escalation approach into a threat of U.S. escalation of the war if the North Vietnamese refused to accept U.S. terms," thereby subverting Kennedy's purpose. [130]

When Rice tried to re-introduce Kennedy's peaceful initiative into the telegram, Harriman intervened. He again crossed out the de-escalation proposal, then "simply killed the telegram altogether." [131] As a result of Harriman's obstruction, Galbraith never did receive JFK's mutual de-escalation proposal to North Vietnam. [132]

The president continued to remind his aides of the need to move in the direction Galbraith recommended. He told Harriman and the State Department's Michael Forrestal that, in Forrestal's words, "He wished us to be prepared to seize upon any favorable moment to reduce our involvement [in Vietnam], recognizing that the moment might yet be some time away." [133] JFK then made his own preparations, through his Secretary of Defense, to seize that favorable moment to reverse course in Vietnam.

In the spring of 1962, as Kennedy moved steadily toward a Laotian settlement, he instructed Robert McNamara to initiate a plan to withdraw the U.S. military from Vietnam. The first step was taken by McNamara at a Secretary of Defense (SECDEF) conference on the Vietnam War held in Saigon on May 8, 1962.

When the Saigon conference was almost over, McNamara said there would be a special briefing for a few of his top decision makers. Those he asked to remain in the room included Joint Chiefs chairman General Lyman Lemnitzer, Admiral Harry Felt, General Paul Harkins, Ambassador Frederick Nolting, and the Defense Intelligence Agency's top expert on Vietnam, civilian analyst George Allen. It was George Allen who would describe this closed-door meeting in an interview and an unpublished manuscript decades later.[134]

When the door had shut, McNamara began examining the men on how each thought the United States should respond to an imminent Communist victory in Laos. The question, not on the conference agenda, took them by surprise. Admiral Felt's response was typical of the group's big-bang attitude that John Kennedy knew all too well. Felt said they could "launch air strikes immediately, and in forty-eight hours, for example, we could wipe the town of Tchepone right off the face of the map."[135]

McNamara pointed out that such an assault could easily provoke nearby North Vietnamese and Chinese forces to counterattack. What then? Should U.S. forces strike the North Vietnamese and Chinese bases, too? And what next? The men remained silent.

By his quick examination the Secretary of Defense had demonstrated the president's position that the United States had nowhere to go militarily in Laos. The choice they had to make was between the negotiated compromise JFK was seeking (which the military regarded as a sellout to the Communists) and an absurd commitment to wage an ever-escalating war in Laos, North Vietnam, and China.

With the necessity of negotiating a neutral Laos as his preamble, McNamara introduced the military leaders to an even more unthinkable policy—withdrawal from Vietnam. He said, "It is not the job of the U.S. to assume responsibility for the war but to develop the South Vietnamese capability to do so."[136] He asked the men in the room when they thought the point would be reached when the South Vietnamese army could take over completely.

George Allen has described the response to this question by the general in charge of U.S. forces in Vietnam. He said, "Harkins' chin nearly hit the table."[137] General Harkins told McNamara they "had scarcely thought about that." They had been much too busy, he said, with plans to expand their military structure in South Vietnam "to think about how it might all be dismantled."[138]

But that is what McNamara told them they now had to do. They not only had to think about "how it might all be dismantled," but to prepare a concrete plan to do so. He ordered Harkins, as the commander of MACV [Military Assistance Command, Vietnam], "to devise a plan for turning full responsibility over to South Vietnam and reducing the size of our military command, and to submit this plan at the next conference."[139] The die was cast.

Thus began President John F. Kennedy's policy to withdraw U.S. military personnel from Vietnam. As of May 1962, Kennedy simply wanted his generals to draw up a plan for withdrawal. He had not yet reached the point of ordering a withdrawal. But he wanted that concrete option on the table in front of him. His military chiefs were shocked. They thought Kennedy had already surrendered to the Communists in Laos. For the United States to withdraw from Vietnam was unthinkable.

JFK knew the depth of their hostility. The previous fall he had told Galbraith, in reference to the Bay of Pigs and a neutral Laos, "You have to realize that I can only afford so many defeats in one year." [140] By McNamara's order to Harkins, Kennedy was telegraphing a punch to the stomach of his military—withdrawal from Vietnam. He was thereby provoking them to launch a preemptive punch at himself.

JFK tried to override what he knew would be the Pentagon's resistance to a plan for a Vietnam withdrawal by having his Secretary of Defense introduce the idea as a matter-of-fact order to a small circle of commanders at the Saigon conference. It was a strategy he had used before. Robert McNamara served as Kennedy's buffer to military heads whose rising anger toward the president gave way to insubordination. When Kennedy told Galbraith in August 1963 that after the election he might replace Rusk with McNamara as his Secretary of State, he said revealingly, "But then if I don't have McNamara at Defense to control the generals, I won't have a foreign policy." [141]

However, McNamara had at first agreed with the generals, not the president, on the critical issue of introducing combat troops into Vietnam. And when it came to enforcing the president's will over the Pentagon's, McNamara was not always that effective. His order to the generals to draw up a plan to withdraw from Vietnam would take more than a year to come back in a form the president could consider for approval.

On July 23, 1962, the day on which the United States joined thirteen other nations at Geneva in signing the "Declaration on the Neutrality of Laos," Robert McNamara convened another Secretary of Defense Conference on the Vietnam War, this one at Camp Smith, Hawaii. McNamara's May 8 order to General Harkins to submit a plan for withdrawal from Vietnam had been ignored. On July 23, the Defense Secretary repeated the order, directing Harkins once again to lay out a long-range program for the completion of training for the South Vietnamese army, so that U.S. advisers could be withdrawn. McNamara specified what he called a "conservative" three-year time line for the end of U.S. military assistance. He also indicated an early awareness in John Kennedy of what an antiwar movement would demand if the United States did not withdraw.

McNamara said, "We must line up our long range program [for withdrawal] as it may become difficult to retain public support for our operations in Vietnam. The political pressure will build up as U.S. losses continue to occur. In other words, we must assume the worst and make our plans accordingly." [142]

"Therefore," he concluded, "planning must be undertaken now and a program devised to phase out U.S. military involvement." [143]

The *Pentagon Papers* note that three days later, on July 26, 1962, the Joint Chiefs of Staff formally directed the commander in chief of the Pacific to develop such a Comprehensive Plan for South Vietnam (CPSVN). The plan's stated objective reads like an elephant trying to tiptoe through a mine field so as to avoid an explosion into the word "withdrawal." The Joint Chiefs said the plan's objective was to "develop a capability within military and para-military forces of the GVN [Government of Vietnam] by the end of Calendar Year 65 that will help the GVN to achieve the strength necessary to exercise permanent and continued sovereignty over that part of Vietnam which lies below the demarcation line [of the 1954 Geneva Agreement, which established no separate "South Vietnam"] without the need for continued U.S. special military assistance." [144] Although the Joint Chiefs refused to identify Kennedy's plan for withdrawal as what it was,[145] the plan had at least begun to move through military channels—like molasses.

In the meantime, Kennedy was making piecemeal concessions to the military on Vietnam. That fall marked one of the worst. On October 2, 1962, he authorized a "limited crop destruction operation" in Phu Yen Province by South Vietnamese helicopters spraying U.S.-furnished herbicides.[146] Dean Rusk had argued against the military's push for crop destruction, saying that even though "the most effective way to hurt the Viet Cong is to deprive them of food," nevertheless those doing it "will gain the enmity of people whose crops are destroyed and whose wives and children will either have to stay in place and suffer hunger or become homeless refugees living on the uncertain bounty of a not-too-efficient government." [147] While sensitive to Rusk's argument, Kennedy had yielded to the pressures of McNamara, Taylor, and the Joint Chiefs of Staff, and approved a criminal action.

By going along with the military on crop destruction, Kennedy was violating both his conscience and international law. In August he had already approved a separate herbicide operation whose purpose of defoliation, as recommended by McNamara, was to "deny concealed forward areas, attack positions, and ambush sites to the Viet Cong." [148] However, in his August approval, Kennedy had asked "that every effort be made to avoid accidental destruction of the food crops in the areas to be sprayed." [149]

In October, the actual purpose of the program he approved was crop destruction. Why did he do it? According to Michael Forrestal, "I believe his main train of thinking was that you cannot say no to your military advisors all the time." [150]

JFK had in fact said yes in 1961 to a policy of widening military support to South Vietnam. The consequences were adding up. By November 1963, there would be a total of 16,500 U.S. military personnel in Vietnam. Although they were identified as "advisers," many were fighting alongside the South Vietnamese troops they were advising. In spite of JFK's having ruled out U.S. combat units, he was being moved along step by step by his military command toward the brink of just such a commitment.

His order to McNamara, and from McNamara to the generals, to open up the opposite option of withdrawal, was going nowhere. General Harkins continued to drag his heels on a withdrawal plan. A report on McNamara's next SECDEF conference, held October 8, 1962, in Honolulu, states: "General Harkins did not have time to present his plan for phasing out US personnel in Viet-Nam within 3 years." [151] At this meeting McNamara did not push Harkins, probably because Kennedy did not push McNamara. At the time JFK was preoccupied with reports of Soviet missiles being sent secretly to Cuba, which when confirmed a week later would begin the October 16–28, 1962, Cuban Missile Crisis.

However, he did find time in the midst of the crisis to write an important letter to his friend Senator Mike Mansfield, who was becoming more and more critical of JFK's Vietnam policy. Kennedy asked Mansfield to visit Vietnam and report back to him on what he learned there. It would turn out to be more than the president wanted to hear.

Mike Mansfield was in a unique position to advise Kennedy on Vietnam. When Lyndon Johnson became Vice President, Mansfield succeeded him as Senate Majority Leader, thereby becoming one of the most influential people in Washington. Like John Kennedy, Mansfield had for years taken a special interest in Southeast Asia. He had visited Vietnam three times in the 1950s. He was known as the Senate's authority on Indochina. Moreover, he had been singularly responsible for convincing the Eisenhower administration to support the rise to power of Ngo Dinh Diem. Mansfield had endorsed Diem as a Vietnamese nationalist independent of both the French and the Viet Minh. The Senator's support proved so critical to the survival of Diem's government in the late fifties that Mansfield was known popularly as "Diem's godfather." [152] Nevertheless, by the fall of 1962, Mansfield had become opposed to the increasing U.S. commitment to a war in support of that same government. His reversal moved JFK to ask him to investigate the situation firsthand.

Mansfield's December 18, 1962, report was uncomfortable reading for the president. Mansfield wrote that Vietnam, outside its cities, was "run at least at night largely by the Vietcong. The government in Saigon is still seeking acceptance by the ordinary people in large areas of the countryside. Out of fear or indifference or hostility the peasants still withhold acquiescence, let alone approval of that government. In short, it would be well to face the fact that we are once again at the beginning of the beginning." [153] While continuing to praise Ngo Dinh Diem, Mansfield questioned the capacity of the Saigon government—under the increasing dominance of Diem's manipulative brother, Ngo Dinh Nhu—to gain any popular support.

Mansfield cautioned Kennedy against trying to win a war in support of an unpopular government by "a truly massive commitment of American military personnel and other resources—in short going to war fully ourselves against the guerrillas—and the establishment of some form of neocolonial rule in South Vietnam." [154] To continue the president's policy, Mansfield warned, may "draw us inexorably into some variation of the unenviable position in Vietnam which was formerly occupied by the French." [155]

Kennedy was stunned by his friend's critique. He was again confronted by his own first understanding of Vietnam, shared first by Edmund Gullion, repeated by John Kenneth Galbraith, and now punched back into his consciousness by Mike Mansfield. The Senate Majority Leader's comparison between the French rule and JFK's policy stung the president. But the more Kennedy thought about Mansfield's challenging words, the more they struck him as the truth—a truth he didn't want to accept but had to. He summed up his reaction to the Mansfield report by a razor-sharp comment on himself, made to aide Kenny O'Donnell: "I got angry with Mike for disagreeing with our policy so completely, and I got angry with myself because I found myself agreeing with him." [156]

By accepting the truth of Mansfield's critique of an increasingly disastrous policy, JFK turned a corner on Vietnam. Just as Ambassador Winthrop Brown's honest analysis had helped turn Kennedy toward a new policy in Laos, so did Mike Mansfield's critical report return him to an old truth on Vietnam. A little noted characteristic of John Kennedy, perhaps remarkable in a U.S. president, was his ability to listen and learn.

Isaiah Berlin, the British philosopher, once observed of Kennedy: "I've never known a man who listened to every single word that one uttered more attentively. And he replied always very relevantly. He didn't obviously have ideas in his own mind which he wanted to expound, or for which he simply used one's own talk as an occasion, as a sort of launching pad. He really listened to what one said and answered *that*." [157]

The way John Kenneth Galbraith put it was: "The President faced a speaker with his wide gray-blue eyes and total concentration. So also a paper or an article. And, so far as one could tell, once it was his it was his forever." [158]

Mike Mansfield said of Kennedy's response to his critique: "President Kennedy didn't waste words. He was pretty sparse with his language. But it was not unusual for him to shift position. There is no doubt that he had shifted definitely and unequivocally on Vietnam but he never had the chance to put the plan into effect." [159]

Kennedy was now on the alert to remove any obstacles from the way to a future withdrawal from Vietnam. On January 25, 1963, he phoned Roger Hilsman, the head of State Department intelligence, at his home to complain about a front-page box in the *New York Times* on a U.S. general visiting Vietnam. In what Hilsman remembered as "decidedly purple language," [160] Kennedy took him to task. He ordered Hilsman to stop military visits that seemed to increase the U.S. commitment in Vietnam.

Kennedy said, "That is exactly what I don't want to do. Remember Laos," he emphasized. "The United States must keep a low profile in Vietnam so we can negotiate its neutralization like we did in Laos." [161]

After listening to the angry president, Hilsman pointed out that he had no authority as a State Department officer to deny a Pentagon general permission to visit Vietnam.

"Oh," said Kennedy and slammed down the phone. That afternoon the president issued National Security Action Memorandum Number 217, forbidding "high ranking military and civilian personnel" from going to South Vietnam without being cleared by the State Department office where Hilsman worked.[162] This action by JFK, reining in the military's travel to Vietnam, for the sake of a neutralization policy, did not please the Pentagon.

Even as Kennedy turned toward a withdrawal from Vietnam, he continued to say publicly that he was opposed to just such a change in policy. At his March 6, 1963, press conference, a reporter asked him to comment on Mansfield's recommendation for a reduction in aid to the Far East.

The president responded: "I don't see how we are going to be able, unless we are going to pull out of Southeast Asia and turn it over to the Communists, how we are going to be able to reduce very much our economic programs and military programs in South Viet-Nam, in Cambodia, in Thailand. . . ."

As Mansfield knew, Kennedy was in fact changing his mind in favor of a complete military withdrawal from Vietnam. However, JFK thought such a policy would never be carried out by any of his possible opponents in the 1964 election, and that its announcement now would block his own reelection. Neither of the two most likely Republican presidential candidates, New York governor Nelson Rockefeller or Arizona senator Barry Goldwater, had any tolerance whatsoever for a possible withdrawal from Vietnam. In the context of 1963 presidential Cold War politics, a Vietnam withdrawal was the unthinkable. President John F. Kennedy was not only thinking the unthinkable. He was on the verge of doing it. But he wanted to be able to do it—by being reelected president. So he lied to the public about what he was thinking.

Kennedy made all this explicit in a conversation with Mike Mansfield. It happened in the spring of 1963 after Mansfield again criticized the president on Vietnam, this time at a White House breakfast attended by the leading members of Congress. Kennedy was annoyed by the criticism before colleagues, but invited Mansfield into his office to talk about Vietnam. Kenny O'Donnell, who sat in on part of their meeting, has described it:

"The President told Mansfield that he had been having serious second thoughts about Mansfield's argument and that he now agreed with the Senator's thinking on the need for a complete military withdrawal from Vietnam.

"'But I can't do it until 1965—after I'm reelected,' Kennedy told Mansfield.

"President Kennedy explained, and Mansfield agreed with him, that if he announced a withdrawal of American military personnel from Vietnam before the 1964 election, there would be a wild conservative outcry against returning him to the Presidency for a second term.

"After Mansfield left the office, the President said to me, 'In 1965, I'll become one of the most unpopular Presidents in history. I'll be damned everywhere as a Communist appeaser. But I don't care. If I tried to pull out completely now from Vietnam, we would have another Joe McCarthy red scare on our hands, but I can do it after I'm reelected. So we had better make damned sure that I *am* reelected.'" [163]

Nevertheless, to government insiders, Kennedy began to tip his hand. In preparation for a complete military withdrawal from Vietnam by 1965, the president wanted to initiate the decision-making process in 1963. Yet he still didn't even have the plan for withdrawal he had asked his military leaders, through McNamara, to draw up a year ago.

Finally, at the May 6, 1963, SECDEF Conference in Honolulu, the Pacific Command presented the president's long-sought plan. However, McNamara immediately had to reject its extended time line, which was so slow that U.S. numbers would not even reach a minimum level until fiscal year 1966.[164] The Defense Secretary said he wanted the pace revised "to speed up replacement of U.S. units by GVN units as fast as possible." [165]

The May 1963 meeting in Honolulu took place one month before Kennedy would give his American University address. It is in the context of that dawning light of peace in the spring of 1963, when Kennedy and Khrushchev were about to begin their rapprochement, that McNamara again shocked his military hierarchy on Vietnam. He ordered them to begin an actual U.S. withdrawal from Vietnam that fall. As the *Pentagon Papers* described this change of tide, McNamara "decided that 1,000 U.S. military personnel should be withdrawn from South Vietnam by the end of Calendar Year 63 and directed that concrete plans be so drawn up." [166]

McNamara's startling order would be met with more resistance by the Joint Chiefs. They saw where Kennedy was going, on Vietnam as on the Cold War in general. They were not going to go there with him.

The Diem government in South Vietnam was alarmed by the Mansfield report, as the U.S. government knew. Diem's brother, Ngo Dinh Nhu, whom Mansfield had singled out for criticism, understood precisely what the report meant. As a State Department memorandum noted, "The reaction [to the Mansfield report] within the GVN [Government of Vietnam], particularly at the higher levels, has been sharp. We are informed by Saigon that the GVN, and in particular Counselor Ngo Dinh Nhu, sees the report as a possible prelude to American withdrawal." [167]

Ngo Dinh Nhu told U.S. embassy official John Mecklin in Saigon on

March 5, 1963, that the Mansfield report was "treachery."[168] Nhu added that "it changes everything." When Mecklin objected that the report was not U.S. government policy, Nhu, he thought, doubted the explanation "on the assumption that [the report] could not have been released without the President's approval."[169]

President Ngo Dinh Diem and his brother-adviser, Ngo Dinh Nhu, were both deeply aware that Mike Mansfield had for years been Diem's greatest supporter in the U.S. Senate. For Mansfield, now as Senate Majority Leader, to give such a stinging report to his close friend, President John F. Kennedy, was for the Ngo brothers more than a hint of a change in U.S. policy. They surmised correctly that the president was deciding to withdraw from Vietnam. Diem and Nhu therefore began to make their own adjustments to a U.S. withdrawal.

On April 4, 1963, President Diem told U.S. ambassador Frederick Nolting that the U.S. government had too many Americans stationed in South Vietnam. Nolting reported to the State Department in a telegram the next day that Diem had become convinced that Americans, by their very number and zeal, were advising his government in too much detail on too many matters.[170] The Vietnamese people were thereby being given the impression that South Vietnam was "a U.S. protectorate." The remedy, Diem said, was to gradually cut back the number of U.S. advisers, thus restoring his government's control over the situation. To Nolting's dismay, Diem also said that he would no longer allow the United States to control any of the counterinsurgency funds that came from the South Vietnamese government.[171]

Nolting said in his State Department telegram that he was "gravely concerned and perplexed" by Diem's abrupt declaration of independence from the United States. The South Vietnamese president even seemed to have a sense of peace about taking a stand that could prove threatening to himself. Diem "gave the impression," Nolting wired, "of one who would rather be right, according to his lights, than President."[172]

Diem's brother, Nhu, sounded the same theme of independence when he met on April 12 with CIA station chief John Richardson. Nhu said the Americans should recall that Diem "had spent a great part of his life in reaction against and resistance to French domination."[173] Nhu was reminding the U.S. government of that trait in his brother's character and beliefs that had so impressed Senators John Kennedy and Mike Mansfield a decade earlier—Diem's stubborn nationalism, which had once kept him independent of both the French and the Viet Minh. It was therefore not surprising, Nhu pointed out, that Diem was now deciding to resist U.S. controls that implied a protectorate status.

Nhu, like Diem, wanted fewer Americans in Vietnam. He told the Saigon CIA chief "that it would be useful to reduce the numbers of Americans by anywhere from 500 to 3,000 or 4,000."[174]

Nhu was delivering this unwelcome message directly to a key representative of the institution most involved in trying to control the South Vietnamese government: the CIA. It was the CIA that, operating under its front organization, the Agency for International Development (AID), had already managed to put advisers in at least twenty of the government's forty-one provinces.[175] William Colby, Richardson's predecessor at the CIA's Saigon station, said that even by early 1962, "the station had contacts and influence throughout Vietnam, from the front and rear doors of the Palace, to the rural communities, among the civilian opponents of the regime and the commanders of all the key military units."[176] In April 1963, when the Ngo brothers declared their intent to reassert control over their own government, the CIA was pushing hard to have a controlling agent working alongside every province chief in South Vietnam. Just as the U.S. military wanted total control over the South Vietnamese army, so did the CIA want total control at every level of the civilian hierarchy. That was why Diem and Nhu used the all-inclusive term "Americans" for what they wanted many fewer of—fewer American advisers of every kind: CIA, military, whatever. Our Vietnamese were getting tired of being told by Americans what decisions they had to make to keep themselves free from domination by other Vietnamese.

As of mid-April 1963, Diem and Nhu were suddenly steering the South Vietnamese government in a more independent direction, asking that Americans of every stripe be withdrawn from Vietnam. The JFK Pentagon had already become aware of Diem's resistance to a widening of the U.S. military presence in Vietnam. Diem had been telling more and more people that he would never agree to the new air and naval bases the United States wanted to establish in his country. In July 1962, during an inspection of Cam Ranh Bay, he pointed to a mountain and said to his aides, "The Americans want a base there but I shall never accept that."[177] Diem also shared his rejection of U.S. military bases with the French ambassador. But by April 1963, Diem wasn't just resisting more bases. Now he wanted the U.S. to withdraw thousands of its people who were already in South Vietnam.

The military and the CIA were alarmed at the Ngo brothers' change of course. On the other hand, the Ngos' turn toward autonomy held the hope for JFK of facilitating his decision to withdraw from Vietnam, shared with Mike Mansfield and understood by the Ngos in response to the Mansfield report. A Kennedy withdrawal policy had now become more feasible, if done in conjunction with Diem's desire that Vietnam "not become a U.S. protectorate." Diem and Nhu had decided they wanted their government and army back, in sudden response to JFK's desire to give them back. It was a ripe and dangerous moment.

On May 6, Kennedy began to implement his withdrawal policy through the order McNamara gave the generals at the Honolulu conference that one thousand U.S. military personnel be pulled out of South Vietnam by the end of the year. For a few days, the time seemed hopeful for a convergence of interests between Kennedy and Diem leading toward a U.S. withdrawal. Then on May 8, 1963, mysterious explosions set off in the South Vietnamese city of Hue began a chain reaction of events that in the next six months would obliterate the hope of a Kennedy-Diem alliance for peace, overthrow the Diem government, and result in the November 2 assassinations of Diem and Nhu.

On May 8, the fateful Buddhist crisis of South Vietnam began to simmer in Hue, as thousands of Buddhists gathered to celebrate the 2507 birthday of Buddha. The South Vietnamese government had just revived a dormant regulation against flying any religious flags publicly. That public honor had been reserved by the Diem government exclusively for the national flag. It was a part of Diem's "uphill struggle to give some sense of nationhood to Vietnamese of all faiths,"[178] as the *New York Herald Tribune*'s Marguerite Higgins wrote. It was claimed later that the enforcement of Diem's nationalist order was provoked ironically by fellow Catholics who had flown the Vatican flag in Da Nang a few days earlier. In any case, the edict from the Catholic president of South Vietnam was proclaimed in Hue on the eve of the Buddha's birthday, when Buddhist flags were already flying. In response the next morning, the Buddhist monk Thich Tri Quang gave a spirited speech to a crowd at Hue's Tu Dam Pagoda protesting the order. Tri Quang accused the government of religious persecution. The crowd responded enthusiastically.[179]

What happened next, as described here, is based on Ellen J. Hammer's *A Death in November*, Marguerite Higgins's *Our Vietnam Nightmare*, and testimony received by the United Nations Fact-Finding Mission to South Viet-Nam in October 1963.[180]

On the evening of May 8, encouraged by Tri Quang and other Buddhist leaders, a crowd gathered outside the government radio station in Hue. At about 8:00 P.M., Tri Quang arrived carrying a tape recording of his morning speech. He and the people demanded that the tape be broadcast that night. When the station director refused, the crowd became insistent, pushing against the station's doors and windows. Firefighters used water hoses to drive them back. The station director put in a call for help to the province security chief, Major Dang Sy. As Dang Sy and his security officers were approaching the area in armored cars about fifty meters away, two powerful explosions blasted the people on the veranda of the station, killing seven on the spot and fatally wounding a child. At least fifteen others were injured.

Major Dang Sy claimed later that he thought the explosions were the beginning of a Viet Cong attack. He ordered his men to disperse the crowd with percussion grenades, crowd-control weapons that were described by a U.S. Army Field Manual as nonlethal. However, from the moment the armored cars drove up and the percussion grenades were thrown, Major Dang Sy and the South Vietnamese government were blamed for the night's casualties by Thich Tri Quang and the Buddhist movement. The Buddhists' interpretation of the event was adopted quickly by the U.S. media and government.

Dr. Le Khac Quyen, the hospital director at Hue, said after examining the victims' bodies that he had never seen such injuries. The bodies had been decapitated. He found no metal in the corpses, only holes. There were no wounds below the chest. In his official finding, Dr. Quyen ruled that "the death of the people was caused by an explosion which took place in mid-air," [181] blowing off their heads and mutilating their bodies.

Neither the Buddhists nor the government liked his verdict. Although Dr. Quyen was a disciple of Thich Tri Quang and a government opposition leader, his finding frustrated his Buddhist friends because it tended to exonerate Diem's security police. They were apparently incapable of inflicting the kinds of wounds he described. On the other hand, the government imprisoned Dr. Quyen for refusing to sign a medical certificate it had drawn up that claimed the victims' wounds came from a type of bomb made by the Viet Cong—something Quyen didn't know and wouldn't certify.[182]

The absence of any metal in the bodies or on the radio station's veranda pointed to powerful plastic bombs as the source of the explosions. However, the Saigon government's eagerness to identify plastic bombs with its enemy, the Viet Cong, was questionable. As Ellen Hammer pointed out in her investigation of the incident, "In later years, men who had served with the Viet Cong at that time denied they had any plastic that could have produced such destruction." [183]

Who did possess such powerful plastic bombs?

An answer is provided by Graham Greene's prophetic novel *The Quiet American*, based on historical events that occurred in Saigon eleven years before the bombing in Hue. Greene was in Saigon on January 9, 1952, when two bombs exploded in the city's center, killing ten and injuring many more. A picture of the scene, showing a man with his legs blown off, appeared in *Life* magazine as the "Picture of the Week." The *Life* caption said the Saigon bombs had been "planted by Viet Minh Communists" and "signaled general intensification of the Viet Minh violence." [184] In like manner, the *New York Times* headlined: "Reds' Time Bombs Rip Saigon Center." [185]

In Saigon, Graham Greene knew the bombs had been planted and claimed proudly not by the Viet Minh but by a warlord, General The, whom Greene knew. General The's bombing material, a U.S. plastic, had been supplied to him by his sponsor, the Central Intelligence Agency. Greene observed in his memoir, *Ways of Escape*, it was no coincidence that "the *Life* photographer at the moment of the explosion was so well placed that he was able to take an astonishing and horrifying photograph which showed the body of a trishaw driver still upright after his legs had been blown off." [186] The CIA had set the scene, alerting the *Life* photographer and *Times* reporter so they could convey the terrorist bombing as the work of "Viet Minh Communists" to a mass audience.[187]

Horrified and inspired by what he knew, Graham Greene wrote the truth in his novel, portraying a quiet American CIA agent as the primary source of the Saigon bombing. In *The Quiet American*, Greene used the CIA's plastic as a mysterious motif, specifically mentioned in ten passages,[188] whose deadly meaning was revealed finally in the Saigon explosions blamed falsely on the communists.

A decade later, plastic bombs were still a weapon valued in covert U.S. plots designed to scapegoat an unsuspecting target. In March 1962, as we have seen, General Lyman Lemnitzer, chairman of the Joint Chiefs of Staff, proposed "exploding a few plastic bombs in carefully chosen spots" in the United States, then arresting and blaming Cuban agents for the terrorist acts.[189]

In May 1963, Diem's younger brother, Ngo Dinh Can, who ruled Hue, thought from the beginning that the Viet Cong had nothing to do with the explosions at the radio station. According to an investigation carried out by the Catholic newspaper *Hoa Binh*, Ngo Dinh Can and his advisers were "convinced the explosions had to be the work of an American agent who wanted to make trouble for Diem."[190] In 1970 *Hoa Binh* located such a man, a Captain Scott, who in later years became a U.S. military adviser in the Mekong Delta. Scott had come to Hue from Da Nang on May 7, 1963. He admitted he was the American agent responsible for the bombing at the radio station the next day. He said he used "an explosive that was still secret and known only to certain people in the Central Intelligence Agency, a charge no larger than a matchbox with a timing device."[191]

Hue's Buddhists were incensed by a massacre they attributed to the Diem government. The U.S. Embassy in Saigon acted quickly in support of the Buddhists. Ambassador Frederick Nolting urged Diem to accept responsibility for the May 8 incident, as the Buddhists demanded. Diem agreed to compensate the victims' families, but said that he would never assume responsibility for a crime his government had not in fact committed.[192]

As the Buddhist crisis began to unfold, the Ngo brothers shocked the U.S. government by publicizing in Washington their wish for far fewer Americans in Vietnam. On Sunday, May 12, an article based on an interview with Ngo Dinh Nhu appeared on the front page of the *Washington Post* headlined: "Viet-Nam Wants 50% of GIs Out."[193] The article began: "South Viet-Nam would like to see half of the 12,000 to 13,000 American military personnel stationed here leave the country."[194]

Ngo Dinh Nhu told *Post* reporter Warren Unna that "at least 50 per cent of the U.S. troops in Viet-Nam are not absolutely necessary." Their unnecessary presence simply reinforced the Communists' claim that "it is not the people of Viet-Nam who are fighting this war,"[195] only a colonial power giving them orders.

Moreover, Nhu and Diem distrusted Americans working at local levels in Vietnam. Many of them, Nhu said pointedly, were nothing more than U.S. intelligence agents.[196]

"Five months ago I told the American authorities that it was possible to withdraw about one half of the Americans," [197] Nhu said, thus dating his earlier wish for fewer Americans to December 1962, when Mike Mansfield had made his report to the president urging a similar policy.

Putting a pro-Kennedy spin on his remarks, Nhu said that a large withdrawal of Americans from Vietnam "could do something spectacular to help show the success of the Kennedy Government's policy in Viet-Nam." [198]

The Ngo brothers had preempted Kennedy. They had succeeded, for the moment, in proclaiming their ardent wish for a U.S. withdrawal that JFK had already quietly decided upon.

Making the connection, the *Post* article noted that, although "no formal request to withdraw troops has ever been made" by South Vietnam, the meeting earlier that week in Honolulu of "top American military and civilian officials" presided over by McNamara "is known to have focused on the problem. A compromise reportedly was reached in which Viet-Nam will assume that about a thousand of the U.S. troops here will be withdrawn within a year." [199]

It was suddenly becoming evident in Washington, D.C., that a U.S. withdrawal was in the works, now in apparent response to the wishes of the South Vietnamese government. However, Ngo Dinh Nhu's remarks provoked quick rebuttals.

The *Washington Post* was outraged by his call for a U.S. withdrawal. A *Post* editorial tried to dismiss Nhu's desire for 50 percent fewer Americans in Vietnam by linking it with his government's failure to carry out the reforms necessary for a victory over the communists. The *Post* editors asked in dismay:

"How long must the United States help President Diem to lose his war and waste its money, to delay the reforms that alone might gather his regime the popular support that victory requires?" [200]

Kennedy's Cold War advisers were also alarmed. Secretary of State Dean Rusk cabled the U.S. Embassy in Saigon he was worried that Nhu's public call for a cut in U.S. forces was "likely [to] generate new and reinforce already existing US domestic pressures for complete withdrawal from SVN." [201] Roger Hilsman appealed to Ambassador Nolting to try to restrain Nhu in his public remarks lest there be "considerable domestic criticism and opposition to our Viet-Nam policy as direct result." [202]

The only person in the administration who seems to have welcomed Nhu's encouragement of a U.S. withdrawal was President Kennedy. Asked about it at his May 22 press conference, JFK said all the Ngo brothers had to do was make their request official, then the process of withdrawal would begin: "we would withdraw the troops, any number of troops, any time the Government of South Viet-Nam would suggest it. The day after it was suggested, we would have some troops on their way home. That is number one." [203]

Kennedy then took advantage of the opportunity to introduce the public gingerly to his own closely held withdrawal plan:

"Number two is: we are hopeful that the situation in South Viet-Nam would permit some withdrawal in any case by the end of the year, but we can't possibly make that judgment at the present time. . . . I couldn't say that today the situation is such that we could look for a brightening in the skies that would permit us to withdraw troops or begin to by the end of this year. But I would say, *if requested to, we will do it immediately.*" [204]

JFK and Diem were signaling their mutual hopes for a U.S. withdrawal. But Diem was too late in doing so to join forces with Kennedy. Any hope of his coming together with JFK in a withdrawal policy had already been effectively blocked by the opposite forces released in the Buddhist movement and Diem's government by the explosions in Hue on May 8.

The Buddhist crisis was gaining steam. On May 15, a delegation of Buddhist leaders met with Diem, demanding that discrimination against Buddhists cease and that his government accept responsibility for those killed at Hue. Diem agreed to investigate the charges of discrimination. But he said that the Buddhists were "damn fools" to be concerned about a right of religious freedom guaranteed by the constitution. "And I *am* the constitution," Diem added.[205]

In regard to May 8, he again promised aid to the victims' families, but refused to declare the government at fault for a crime he thought others had committed. Ambassador Nolting wired Washington that, on the contrary, the South Vietnamese government needed to accept "responsibility for actions [of] its authorities during Hue riot." [206]

The Buddhists were frustrated by their meeting with Diem. They organized marches, hunger strikes, and memorial services honoring the dead at Hue. Diem chose a hard line in response to the protests. Demonstrators were dispersed by government troops using tear gas.

Even as President Kennedy said eagerly of a U.S. withdrawal from Vietnam, "if requested to, we will do it immediately," the only government that could have made such a request was discrediting itself beyond any possibility of recovery. Diem's increasingly brutal response to a movement he didn't understand was turning his already unpopular government into an international pariah. As the Buddhist crisis deepened, Kennedy saw Diem's repression of the Buddhists as a confirmation of Mansfield's diagnosis that Diem was unable to gain popular support from the Vietnamese people. It strengthened JFK's decision to carry out in Vietnam the same kind of neutralization policy he had chosen for Laos. However, he would have to overcome the political obstacle of a South Vietnamese government that was becoming notorious.

On May 9, the day after the Hue explosions, Roger Hilsman had been confirmed by the Senate in his new State Department position as the primary officer responsible for Vietnam. During the next month, President Kennedy ordered Hilsman to prepare for the neutralization of Vietnam. Hilsman said later in an interview:

"[Kennedy] began to instruct me, as Assistant Secretary for Far Eastern

Affairs, to position ourselves to do in Vietnam what we had done in Laos, i.e., to negotiate the neutralization of Vietnam. He had made a decision on this. He did not make it public of course, but he had certainly communicated it to me as I say, in four-letter words, good earthy anglo-saxon four-letter words, and every time that I failed to do something [in a way] he felt endangered this position, he let me know in very clear language." [207]

As spring turned into the summer of 1963, President John F. Kennedy had decided to withdraw the U.S. military and neutralize Vietnam, just as he had done in Laos. When he said that one day to his aides Dave Powers and Kenny O'Donnell, they asked him bluntly: How could he do it? How could he carry out a military withdrawal from Vietnam without losing American prestige in Southeast Asia?

"Easy," the president said. "Put a government in there that will ask us to leave." [208]

It was a contradictory formula for peace. It was also easier said than done. By June 1963, Kennedy had been manipulated by forces more powerful than his presidency into the beginning stages of a process that was the opposite of his stated intention. He was succumbing to pressures to take out a government in Vietnam that had just shown itself on the verge of asking the U.S. to leave—precisely what Kennedy knew he most needed to facilitate a withdrawal. While aware of the irony, JFK was afraid that Diem was personally incapable of reversing the suicidal course he had chosen. Under his brother Nhu's dominant influence, Diem was trying to repress a popular Buddhist uprising, which was thereby bound to turn into a revolution. Diem, Kennedy concluded, was a hopeless case. JFK's now more extended hope was that, after the Diem government's inevitable fall, he would then be able to "put a government in there that will ask us to leave."

Besides the inherent contradiction of trying to impose peace on a client state, Kennedy also had the problem of time. He only had six months left to live. On June 10, 1963, at American University, he began those six months by turning toward an inspiring vision of peace. But how much of that vision could he realize, in Vietnam and elsewhere, before his assassins would strike?

CHAPTER FOUR

Marked Out for Assassination

John Kennedy was not afraid to die. Nor was he lacking in the practice of living while dying. By the time he reached the White House, he had gone through a series of near-death experiences from repeated illness. The physical pain Kennedy endured from childhood to death was excruciating. "At least one half of the days that he spent on this earth," Robert Kennedy said, "were days of intense physical pain."[1] He masked his pain by a deceptively sunny detachment. In a rare comment on the pain he felt regularly in his back, JFK told his wife and a couple of friends that "he thought he could stand any kind and any amount of pain, provided he knew that it would end."[2]

He knew the threat of death as pain's companion. He nearly died of scarlet fever as a child, of a blood condition as a teenager, from the ramming of his *PT 109* by a Japanese destroyer in the Solomon Islands, and from recurrences of malaria during and after the war. In the Solomons, he risked his life to the point of total exhaustion in efforts to save the lives of his crewmembers. In one such attempt, he lost consciousness in the middle of Ferguson Passage and drifted through a night of delirium to the edge of an open sea. Then the current moved him through a huge circle back to the start of his odyssey and new life. Kennedy knew death intimately. When he met death again in the gaze of his generals, he was not afraid.

In a new foreword to John Kennedy's *Profiles in Courage*, Robert Kennedy wrote shortly after his brother's death, "Courage is the virtue that President Kennedy most admired. He sought out those people who had demonstrated in some way, whether it was on a battlefield or a baseball diamond, in a speech or fighting for a cause, that they had courage, that they would stand up, that they could be counted on."[3] The issue on which his brother most valued courage, Robert said, was in preventing nuclear war and "the specter of the death of the children of this country and around the world."[4]

JFK had been inspired to write *Profiles in Courage* during another one of his bouts with death, in the course of a long hospitalization and convalescence from a spinal operation in 1954. The book's theme was "political courage in the face of constituent pressures." [5] Although Kennedy's stories of political courage were drawn mainly from the Senate, he gave one revealing example of a president who followed his conscience against "the pressures of constituent and special interests":

"President George Washington stood by the Jay Treaty with Great Britain to save our young nation from a war it could not survive, despite his knowledge that it would be immensely unpopular among a people ready to fight. Tom Paine told the President that he was 'treacherous in private friendship and a hypocrite in public . . . The world will be puzzled to decide whether you are an apostate or imposter; whether you have abandoned good principles, or whether you ever had any.' With bitter exasperation, Washington exclaimed: "I would rather be in my grave than in the Presidency'; and to Jefferson he wrote:

'I am accused of being the enemy of America, and subject to the influence of a foreign country . . . and every act of my administration is tortured, in such exaggerated and indecent terms as could scarcely be applied to Nero, to a notorious defaulter, or even to a common pickpocket.'"

Kennedy commented on Washington, "But he stood firm." [6] Washington had resisted the pressures for a war his newly born country could not have survived. Kennedy in his presidency had to keep on resisting the pressures for a war neither his country nor the world could have survived.

The pressures on President Kennedy came less from constituents than from the weapons-making corporations that thrived on the Cold War, and from the Pentagon and the CIA that were dedicated to "winning" that war, whatever that might mean. For JFK, who stood virtually alone in the Oval Office against these forces, the question of political courage became more intense than it was in any of the conflicts he described in *Profiles in Courage*.

The political context of Kennedy's assassination was described best by the president who preceded him.

On January 17, 1961, three days before JFK was inaugurated as president, Dwight D. Eisenhower in his farewell address warned of a new threat to freedom from within the United States. In response to a threat from without, Eisenhower said, "We have been compelled to create a permanent armaments industry of vast proportions. Added to this, three and a half million men and women are directly engaged in the defense establishment. We annually spend on military security more than the net income of all United States corporations.

"This conjunction of an immense military establishment and a large arms industry is new in the American experience. The total influence—economic, political, even spiritual—is felt in every city, every State house, every office of the Federal government. We recognize the imperative need for this development. Yet we must not fail to comprehend its grave implications. Our toil, resources and livelihood are all involved; so is the very structure of our society.

"In the councils of government, we must guard against the acquisition of unwarranted influence, whether sought or unsought, by the military-industrial complex. The potential for the disastrous rise of misplaced power exists and will persist.

"We must never let the weight of this combination endanger our liberties or democratic processes. We should take nothing for granted."[7]

Eisenhower himself never used the power of his presidency to challenge this new threat to democracy. He simply identified it in a memorable way when he was about to leave office. He thereby passed on the possibility of resisting it to his successor.

In Kennedy's short presidency, the military-industrial complex actually increased its profits and power. JFK's initial call to develop a military response to the Soviet Union and its allies that would be "more flexible" than the Eisenhower policy of mutual assured destruction expanded the Pentagon's contracts with U.S. corporations. Yet in the summer of 1963, the leaders of the military-industrial complex could see storm clouds on their horizon. After JFK's American University address and his quick signing of the Test Ban Treaty with Khrushchev, corporate power holders saw the distinct prospect in the not distant future of a settlement in the Cold War between the United States and the Soviet Union. Both Kennedy and Khrushchev were prepared to shift their war of conflicting ideologies to more peaceful fronts. Kennedy wanted a complete ban on the testing of nuclear weapons, then mutual steps in nuclear disarmament. He saw a willing partner in Khrushchev, who wanted to ease the huge burden of arms expenditures on the Soviet economy. In that direction of U.S.-Soviet disarmament lay the diminished power of a corporate military system that for years had controlled the United States government. In his turn toward peace, Kennedy was beginning to undermine the dominant power structure that Eisenhower had finally identified and warned against so strongly as he left the White House.

In 1962 Kennedy had already profoundly alienated key elements of the military-industrial complex in the steel crisis. The conflict arose from JFK's preoccupation with steel prices, whose rise he believed "quickly drove up the price of everything else."[8] The president therefore brokered a contract, signed on April 6, 1962, in which the United Steelworkers union accepted a modest settlement from the United States Steel Company, with the understanding that the company would help keep inflation down by not raising steel prices. Kennedy phoned identical statements of appreciation to union headquarters and the company managers, congratulating each for having reached an agreement that was "obviously non-inflationary."[9] When he finished the calls, he told adviser Ted Sorensen that the union members "cheered and applauded their own sacrifice," whereas the company representatives were "ice-cold" to him.[10] It was a foretaste of the future.

On April 10, 1962, Roger Blough, chairman of U.S. Steel, asked to meet with Kennedy. At 5:45 P.M., seated next to JFK, Blough said, "Perhaps the easiest way I can explain the purpose of my visit . . . ,"[11] and handed Kennedy four mimeographed pages. Blough knew the press release in the president's hands was being passed out simultaneously to the media by other U.S. Steel representatives. It stated that U.S. Steel, "effective at 12:01 A.M. tomorrow, will raise the price of the company's steel products by an average of about 3.5 percent . . ."[12]

Kennedy read the statement, recognizing immediately that he and the steelworkers had been double-crossed by U.S. Steel. He looked up at Blough and said, "You've made a terrible mistake."[13]

After Blough departed, Kennedy shared the bad news with a group of his advisers. They had never seen him so angry. He said, "My father always told me that all businessmen were sons-of-bitches, but I never believed it until now."[14] His explosive remark appeared in the *New York Times* on April 23, 1962.[15] The corporate world never forgot it.

He phoned steelworkers union president David McDonald and said, "Dave, you've been screwed and I've been screwed."[16]

The next morning U.S. Steel was joined in its price increase by Bethlehem Steel, the second largest company, and soon after by four others. In response Kennedy mustered every resource he could to force the steel companies to roll back their prices. He began at the Defense Department.

Defense contracts were critical to "Big Steel," an industry that embodied the intertwined influence with the Pentagon that Eisenhower had warned against. Defense Secretary McNamara told the president that the combined impact in defense costs from the raise in steel prices would be a billion dollars. Kennedy ordered him to start shifting steel purchases at once to the smaller companies that had not yet joined in the raise. McNamara announced that a steel-plate order previously divided between U.S. Steel and Lukens Steel, a tiny steel company that had not raised prices, would now go entirely to Lukens.[17] Walter Heller, who chaired the President's Council of Economic Advisers, "calculated that the government used so much steel that it could shift as much as 9 percent of the industry's total business away from the six companies that had announced price rises to six that were still holding back."[18] The president even ordered the Defense Department to take its steel business overseas, if that were necessary to keep defense contracts away from U.S. Steel and its cohorts.[19] Big Steel executives saw that Kennedy meant business, their business—and that substantial Cold War profits were already being drained away from them.

Attorney General Robert Kennedy moved quickly to convene a federal grand jury to investigate price fixing in Big Steel's corporate network. He looked into the steel companies' possible violation of anti-trust laws, an investigation his Anti-Trust Division had actually begun before the steel crisis. He now ordered the FBI to move on the steel executives with speed and thoroughness. As RFK said later in an interview, "We were going to go for broke: their expense accounts and where they'd been and what they were doing. I picked up all their records and I told the FBI to interview them all—march into their offices the next day. We weren't going to go slowly. I said to have them done all over the country. All of them were hit with meetings the next morning by agents. All of them were subpoenaed for their personal records. All of them were subpoenaed for their company records." [20]

Steel executives suddenly found themselves being treated as if they were enemies of the people. The president then stated that they were precisely that. He opened his April 11 press conference by saying:

"Simultaneous and identical actions of United States Steel and other leading steel corporations increasing steel prices by some $6 a ton constitute a wholly unjustifiable and irresponsible defiance of the public interest . . . the American people will find it hard, as I do, to accept a situation in which a tiny handful of steel executives whose pursuit of private power and profit exceeds their sense of public responsibility can show such utter contempt for the interests of 185 million Americans." [21]

Reporters gasped at the intensity of Kennedy's attack on Big Steel. After describing the ways in which steel executives had defied the public interest, JFK concluded with an ironic reference to his inaugural address:

"Some time ago I asked each American to consider what he would do for his country and I asked the steel companies. In the last 24 hours we had their answer." [22]

On April 12, Kennedy sent his lawyer, Clark Clifford, to serve as a mediator with U.S. Steel. The steel executives, feeling the heat from the White House, proposed a compromise. Clifford phoned the president to say, "Blough and his people want to know what you would say if they announce a partial rollback of the price increases, say 50 percent?"

"I wouldn't say a damn thing," Kennedy replied. "It's the whole way." [23]

Clifford was instructed to say that "if U.S. Steel persisted, the President would use every tool available to turn the decision around." [24] That included especially switching more defense contracts away from them to more affordable companies. There was to be no compromise.

Clifford reported back to the steel heads that "the President was already setting in motion to use the full power of the Presidency to divert contracts from U.S. Steel and the other companies," adding that "he still had several actions in reserve, including tax audits, antitrust investigations, and a thorough probe of market practices." [25] The president was prepared to wage a domestic war against Big Steel's price increase.

On April 13, 1962, Big Steel's executives surrendered. The first company to yield was Bethlehem Steel, another major defense contractor. The reason, reported back to the White House, was that "Bethlehem had gotten wind that it was to be excluded from bidding on the construction of three naval vessels the following week and decided to take quick action." [26] Bethlehem was followed soon by the giant, U.S. Steel. The president's offensive, backed by overwhelming public support, had been too much for them. All six steel companies rescinded the entire price raise that their point man, Roger Blough, had conveyed to JFK as an accomplished fact three days before.

As would be his attitude after the Cuban Missile Crisis, Kennedy, as Sorensen said, "permitted no gloating by any administration spokesman and no talk of retribution." [27] He was especially gracious toward Roger Blough, whom he subsequently invited often to the White House for consultations. [28] When asked by a reporter at a press conference about his "rather harsh statement about businessmen," JFK revised his infamous s.o.b. remark. He said that his father, a businessman himself, had meant only "the steel men" with whom he had been "involved when he was a member of the Roosevelt administration in the 1937 strike." [29]

This explanation would not win the hearts of business leaders. As they knew, JFK's father, Joseph P. Kennedy, Sr., while a businessman himself, had also been President Franklin D. Roosevelt's first chairman of the Securities and Exchange Commission (SEC). As a former Wall Street insider who knew the system, the senior Kennedy had cracked down on Wall Street profiteers. Some of the financial titans of the thirties regarded JFK's father as a class traitor, "the Judas of Wall Street," for his work on behalf of FDR. [30] It was in the light of Joseph Kennedy's fight to initiate government controls over Wall Street, and the opposition he encountered, that he made his all-businessmen-are-s.o.b.'s remark to JFK.

That opinion of his father, President Kennedy told the press, "I found appropriate that evening [when] we had not been treated altogether with frankness . . . But that's past, that's past. Now we're working together, I hope." [31]

It was a vain hope. John and Robert Kennedy had become notorious in the ranks of big business. JFK's strategy of withdrawing defense contracts and RFK's aggressive investigating tactics toward men of power were seen as unforgivable sins by the corporate world. As a result of the president's uncompromising stand against the steel industry—and implicitly any corporation that chose to defy his authority—a bitter gap opened up between Kennedy and big business, whose most powerful elements coincided with the military-industrial complex.

The depth of corporate hostility toward Kennedy after the steel crisis can be seen by an unsigned editorial in *Fortune*, media czar Henry Luce's magazine for the most fortunate. The editors of *Fortune* knew the decision to raise steel prices had been made by the executive committee of U.S. Steel's board of directors. It included top-level officers from other huge financial institutions, such as the Morgan Guaranty Trust Company, the First National City Bank of New York, the Prudential Insurance Company, the Ford Foundation, and AT&T. [32] When Roger Blough handed U.S. Steel's provocative press release to the president, he did so on behalf of not only U.S. Steel but also these other financial giants in the United States. The *For-*

tune editorial therefore posed an intriguing question: Why did the financial interests behind U.S. Steel announce the price increase in such a way as to deliberately "provoke the President of the U.S. into a vitriolic and demagogic assault?" [33]

With the authority of an insider's knowledge that it denied having, *Fortune* answered its own question: "There is a theory—unsupported by any direct evidence—that Blough was acting as a 'business statesman' rather than as a businessman judging his market." According to "this theory," Kennedy's prior appeal to steel executives not to raise prices, leading to the contract settlement between the company and the union, had "poised over the industry a threat of 'jawbone control' of prices. For the sake of his company, the industry, and the nation, Blough sought a way to break through the bland 'harmony' that has recently prevailed between government and business." [34]

In plainer language, the president was acting too much like a president, rather than just another officeholder beholden to the powers that be. U.S. Steel on behalf of still higher financial interests therefore taunted Kennedy so as to present him with a dilemma: he either had to accept the price hike and lose credibility, or react as he did with power to roll back the increase and thereby unite the business world against him. His unswerving activist response then served to confirm the worst fears of corporate America:

"That the threat of 'jawbone control' was no mere bugaboo was borne out by the tone of President Kennedy's reaction and the threats of general business harassment by government that followed the 'affront.'" [35]

Thus the steel crisis, in *Fortune*'s view, threatened to propel an activist, anti-business president toward a fate like that of Julius Caesar. As Shakespeare had it, Caesar was warned of his coming assassination by a soothsayer: "Beware the ides of March." *Fortune* gave Kennedy a deadly warning of its own by the title of its editorial: "Steel: The Ides of April."

Robert Kennedy's Justice Department continued its anti-trust investigation into the steel companies. U.S. Steel and seven other companies were eventually forced to pay maximum fines in 1965 for their price-fixing activities between 1955 and 1961.[36] The steel crisis defined John and Robert Kennedy as Wall Street enemies. The president was seen as a state dictator. As the *Wall Street Journal* put it in the week after Big Steel surrendered to the Kennedys, "The Government set the price. And it did this by the pressure of fear—by naked power, by threats, by agents of the state security police." [37] *U.S. News and World Report* gave prominence in its April 30, 1962, issue to an anti-Kennedy article on "Planned Economy" that suggested the president was acting like a Soviet commissar.[38]

Attorney General Robert Kennedy became a symbol of "ruthless power" to the business titans he treated so brusquely, whose corporations he then found in violation of the law. Media controlled by the same interests adopted the characterization of RFK as ruthless until his murder six years later.

As John Kennedy became persona non grata to the economic elite of the

United States, his popularity increased elsewhere. He said on May 8, 1962, to a warmly welcoming convention of the United Auto Workers:

"Last week, after speaking to the Chamber of Commerce and the presidents of the American Medical Association, I began to wonder how I got elected. And now I remember.

"I said last week to the Chamber that I thought I was the second choice for President of a majority of the Chamber; anyone else was first choice." [39]

John Kennedy, the son of a rich man who had fought Wall Street in the Roosevelt administration, was beginning to sound like a class heretic himself. He told the U.A.W.: "Harry Truman once said there are 14 or 15 million Americans who have the resources to have representatives in Washington to protect their interests, and that the interests of the great mass of other people, the hundred and fifty or sixty million, is the responsibility of the President of the United States. And I propose to fulfill it." [40]

After the steel crisis, President Kennedy felt so much hostility from the leaders of big business that he finally gave up trying to curry their support. He told advisers Sorensen, O'Donnell, and Schlesinger, "I understand better every day why Roosevelt, who started out such a mild fellow, ended up so ferociously anti-business. It is hard as hell to be friendly with people who keep trying to cut your legs off." [41] If *Fortune*'s editors were right in seeing a deliberate provocation of Kennedy, the instigators had succeeded in alienating the business elite from the president, and vice versa.

JFK joked about what his corporate enemies would do to him, if they only had the chance. A year after the steel crisis, he learned before giving a speech in New York that elsewhere in the same hotel "the steel industry was presenting Dwight D. Eisenhower with its annual public service award."

"I was their man of the year last year," said the president to his audience. "They wanted to come down to the White House to give me their award, but the Secret Service wouldn't let them do it." [42]

For the dark humor to work, Kennedy and his audience had to assume a Secret Service committed to shielding the president. However, as Secret Service agent Abraham Bolden had learned before he left the White House detail, the S.S. agents around Kennedy were joking in a more sinister direction—that they would step out of the way if an assassin aimed a shot at the president. [43] In Dallas the Secret Service would step out of the way not just individually but collectively.

In his deepening alienation from the CIA, the Pentagon, and big business, John Kennedy was moving consciously beyond the point of no return. Kennedy knew well the complicity that existed among the Cold War's corporate elite, Pentagon planners, and the heads of "intelligence agencies." He was no stranger to the way systemic power worked in and behind his national security state. But he still kept acting for "the interests of the great mass of other people"—and as his brother Robert put it, to prevent "the specter of the death of the children of this country and around the world." That put him more and more deeply in conflict with those who controlled the system.

We have no evidence as to who in the military-industrial complex may have given the order to assassinate President Kennedy. That the order was carried out by the Central Intelligence Agency is obvious. The CIA's fingerprints are all over the crime and the events leading up to it.

According to the *Warren Report*, Lee Harvey Oswald told the U.S. Embassy in Moscow on October 31, 1959, that his new allegiance was to the U.S.S.R. He said he had promised Soviet officials he "would make known to them all information concerning the Marine Corps and his specialty therein, radar operation, as he possessed."[44] However, the *Warren Report* did not mention that in the Marine Corps Oswald had been a radar operator specifically for the CIA's top-secret U-2 spy plane. By not admitting Oswald's U-2 or CIA connections, the Warren Commission avoided the implications of his offering to give "something of special interest" to the Soviets.[45] Oswald was either a blatant traitor or, as his further history reveals, a U.S. counterintelligence agent being dangled before the Russians as a Marine expatriate.

The head of the CIA's Counterintelligence Branch from 1954 to 1974 was James Jesus Angleton, known as the "Poet-Spy." As an undergraduate at Yale in the early forties, Angleton had founded a literary journal, *Furioso*, which published the poetry of Ezra Pound, e. e. cummings, and Archibald MacLeish. After he went on to Harvard Law School, Angleton was drafted into the U.S. Army. He became a member of the Counterintelligence Branch of the Office of Strategic Services (OSS), World War II predecessor to the CIA. The OSS and CIA suited Angleton perfectly. Counterintelligence became less a wartime mission than a lifelong obsession. For Angleton, the Cold War was an anti-communist crusade, with his CIA double agents engaged in a battle of light against darkness.

Investigative journalist Joseph Trento testified in a 1984 court deposition that, according to CIA sources, James Angleton was the supervisor of a CIA assassination unit in the 1950s. The "small assassination team" was headed by Army colonel Boris Pash.[46] At the end of World War II, Army Intelligence colonel Pash had rounded up Nazi scientists who could contribute their research skills to the development of U.S. nuclear and chemical weapons.[47] The CIA's E. Howard Hunt, while imprisoned for the Watergate break-in, told the *New York Times* that Pash's CIA assassination unit was designed especially for the killing of suspected double agents.[48] That placed Pash's terminators under the authority of counterintelligence chief Angleton. Joseph Trento testified that his sources confirmed, "Pash's assassination unit was assigned to Angleton."[49]

In the 1960s, Angleton retained his authority over assassinations. In November 1961, the CIA's Deputy Director of Plans, Richard Bissell, directed his longtime associate William Harvey to develop an assassination program known as "ZR/RIFLE" and to apply it to Cuba, as the Senate's

Church Committee later discovered.[50] Among the notes for ZR/RIFLE that Harvey then scribbled to himself were: "planning should include provisions for blaming Sovs or Czechs in case of blow. Should have phony 201 [a CIA file on any person "of active operational interest"][51] in RG [Central Registry] to backstop this, all documents therein forged and backdated."[52] In other words, in order to blame an assassination on the Communists, the patsy should be given Soviet or Czechoslovakian associations. (Oswald's would be Soviet and Cuban.) An appropriately fraudulent CIA 201 personnel file should be created for any future assassination scapegoat, with "all documents therein forged and updated." Harvey also reminded himself that the phony 201 "should look like a CE [counterespionage] file," and that he needed to talk with "Jim A."[53]

William Harvey headed Staff D, a top-secret CIA department that was responsible for communications intercepts received from the National Security Agency. Assassinations prepared by Harvey were therefore given the same ultimate degree of secrecy as the NSA's intercepts, under the higher jurisdiction of James Angleton. Any access to Staff D could be granted only by "Angleton's men," according to CIA agent Joseph B. Smith.[54]

As we shall see in the Oswald project under Angleton's supervision, the CIA's Counterintelligence head blended the powers of assassination and disinformation. Deception was Angleton's paradoxical way toward a victory of the light. In the war against Communism, Angleton thrived on deceiving enemies and friends alike in a milieu he liked to call "the wilderness of mirrors." His friend e. e. cummings suggested the contradictions in James Angleton in a letter he wrote to Angleton's wife: "What a miracle of momentous complexity is the Poet."[55]

In the mid 1970s, the Senate's Church Committee on intelligence and the House Select Committee on Assassinations (HSCA) opened the CIA's lid on Lee Harvey Oswald and discovered James Jesus Angleton. They found that Angleton's Special Investigations Group (SIG) in CIA Counterintelligence held a 201 file on Oswald in the three years prior to JFK's assassination. Considering what William Harvey wrote about creating phony 201 files for ZR/RIFLE scapegoats, an obvious first question is: How genuine is Oswald's file (or what little we have been given from it)? In any case, judging from the interview of a key witness about Oswald's file in Angleton's SIG office, its mere presence in that particular location was enough to give the game away.

It was Angleton's staff member, Ann Egerter, who opened Oswald's 201 SIG file on December 9, 1960.[56] Egerter was questioned by the House Select Committee. They knew they could not expect her, as a CIA employee, to answer truthfully, even under oath, the question whether Oswald was a CIA agent. Allen Dulles, Kennedy's fired CIA director, had said in the January 27, 1964, closed-door Warren Commission meeting that no CIA employee, even under oath, should ever say truthfully if Oswald (or anyone else) was in fact a CIA agent.[57] The House Select Committee therefore had to get the answer from Angleton's associate, Ann Egerter—by then retired and some-what obliging—by indirect questioning.

When Egerter was asked the purpose of Counterintelligence's Special Investigations Group (CI/SIG), she said, "We were charged with the *investigation of Agency personnel who were suspected one way or another.*" [58]

Egerter had thereby already made a crucial admission, whose implications would be drawn out step by step. Her HSCA interviewer then asked Egerter to confirm this specific purpose of SIG: "Please correct me if I am wrong. In light of the example that you have given and the statements that you have made it seems that the *purpose of CI/SIG* was very limited and that limited purpose was being [sic] to *investigate Agency employees who for some reason were under suspicion.*"

Egerter replied, "That is correct." [59]

She was then asked: "When a 201 file is opened does that mean that whoever opens the file has either an intelligence interest in the individual, or, if not an intelligence interest, he thinks that the individual may present a counterintelligence risk?"

> EGERTER: "Well, in general, I would say that would be correct."
> INTERVIEWER: "Would there be any other reason for opening up a file?"
> EGERTER: "No, I can't think of one." [60]

Researcher Lisa Pease concluded from Ann Egerter's testimony that Oswald's 201 file in CI/SIG "implies strongly that either Oswald was indeed a member of the CIA or was being used in an operation involving members of the CIA, which for my money is essentially the same thing." [61] In either case, Oswald was a CIA asset.

Egerter also indicated by her testimony that Oswald was a particular kind of CIA asset, an Agency employee who was suspected of being a security risk. That would have been the reason for opening a 201 file on him specifically in Angleton's Special Investigations Group of Counterintelligence. Egerter said SIG was known in the Agency as "the office that spied on spies," [62] and repeatedly identified the spies being spied upon as CIA employees. She again described the work of her SIG office as "investigations of Agency employees where there was an indication of espionage." [63]

Her interviewer in turn patiently sought reconfirmation of this stated purpose of her office that so strongly implied Oswald was a CIA employee under investigation by the Agency:

> INTERVIEWER: "I hope you understand my questions are directed toward trying to find out what the purpose of the CI/SIG Office was and under what circumstances was the opening up of the 201 file [on Oswald]. I am given the impression that the purpose of CI/SIG was very limited, primarily to investigate Agency employees who for one reason or

another might be under suspicion of getting espionage against the United States. Is that an accurate statement of the purpose of CI/SIG?"

EGERTER: "Well, it is employees and also penetration, which is the same thing, of the Agency."[64]

Ann Egerter's testimony points toward Oswald having been a CIA employee who by December 1960 had come under suspicion by the Agency. He was to be carefully watched. As a security risk, he was also the ideal kind of person for the CIA to offer up three years later as a scapegoat in the assassination of a president who some believed had become a much greater security risk.

Former CIA finance officer Jim Wilcott confirmed the implications of Egerter's deposition. In his own HSCA testimony, Wilcott said Oswald served the CIA specifically as a double agent in the Soviet Union who afterwards came under suspicion by the Agency.

Jim Wilcott's straightforward testimony on Oswald was made possible by his and his wife's courageous decision to divorce themselves from the CIA and speak the truth. After nine years working for the CIA as a husband-and-wife team, Jim and Elsie Wilcott resigned from the Agency in 1966. "My wife and I both left the CIA," Wilcott testified before the House Select Committee, "because we became convinced that what CIA was doing couldn't be reconciled to basic principles of democracy or basic principles of humanism."[65] In 1968 as participants in the anti–Vietnam War and civil rights movements, Jim and Elsie Wilcott became the first former CIA couple to go public with what they knew, in spite of the risks to themselves. They made the decision in conscience to speak out, they said, in order "to sleep better nights."[66] Thus their marriage became a CIA profile in courage.

Jim Wilcott worked in the finance branch of the Tokyo CIA Station from 1960 to 1964. During the same years, Elsie Wilcott was a secretary at the Tokyo station. When President Kennedy was assassinated, the station went on alert. Jim was assigned to twenty-four-hour security duty. He passed the time with agents whose tongues had been loosened by alcohol. They told him the CIA was involved in the assassination.[67]

"At first I thought 'These guys are nuts,'" he said, "but then a man I knew and had worked with before showed up to take a disbursement and told me Lee Harvey Oswald was a CIA employee. I didn't believe him until he told me the cryptonym under which Oswald had drawn funds when he returned from Russia to the U.S."[68]

The man at the disbursing cage window who revealed the Oswald connection was, Wilcott said, a case officer who supervised agents.[69] The case officer said Wilcott himself had issued an advance on funds for the CIA's Oswald project under the cryptonym. "It was a cryptonym," Wilcott told the House Committee, "that I was familiar with. It must have been at least two or three times that I had remembered it, and it did ring a bell."[70] In recognizing the cryptonym, Wilcott had to confront his own complicity in the CIA's Oswald counterintelligence project that was the background to the president's assassination.

In a 1978 interview with the *San Francisco Chronicle*, Jim Wilcott said, "It was common knowledge in the Tokyo CIA station that Oswald worked for the agency."

"That's true," Elsie Wilcott said. "Right after the President was killed, people in the Tokyo station were talking openly about Oswald having gone to Russia for the CIA. Everyone was wondering how the agency was going to be able to keep the lid on Oswald. But I guess they did," she said.[71]

In an article based on what he learned at the Tokyo Station, Jim Wilcott wrote: "[Oswald] had been trained [by the CIA] at Atsugi Naval Air Station, a plush super secret cover base for Tokyo Station special operations . . .

"Oswald was recruited from the military for the express purpose of becoming a double agent assignment to the USSR . . . More than once, I was told something like 'so-and-so was working on the Oswald project back in the late '50s.'

"One of the reasons given for the necessity to do away with Oswald was the difficulty they had with him when he returned. Apparently, he knew the Russians were on to him from the start, and this made him very angry."[72]

Oswald's anger, while he was trying to arrange his return to the United States in late 1960, would have been reason enough for James Jesus Angleton to order his Special Investigations Group to keep a security watch on the CIA's double agent. Thus, Ann Egerter opened his 201 SIG file on December 9, 1960.

Jim and Elsie Wilcott paid a price for speaking out against the CIA. In the early 1970s after Jim became finance analyst for the Utica, California, community renewal program, the Utica mayor was informed by the FBI that the Wilcotts were under surveillance pending a possible federal indictment. The mayor decided not to fire Jim but asked him to sign a resignation form which the mayor would date the day previous to the date that the federal indictment came down.[73] The Wilcotts received threatening phone calls. They had intimidating notes left under their car's windshield wipers. Their tires were slashed.[74] On October 5, 1986, Elsie Wilcott died of cancer.

In the decade following his HSCA testimony, Jim Wilcott joined Vietnam veteran Brian Willson and the Nuremberg Actions community outside the Concord Naval Weapons Station in nonviolent resistance to weapons shipments to the CIA-sponsored Contra war in Nicaragua. While sitting on the railroad tracks, Willson was run over by a weapons train, which severed both his legs. Undeterred, Jim Wilcott was arrested for blocking a later train.[75]

In the late 1980s, a reporter for a small Bay Area journal described Jim Wilcott in his faithful vigil by the tracks of the Concord weapons train: "a gentle, unprepossessing person of indeterminate middle age" who had spent nine years as a CIA accountant. "Now disabled by an obscure nerve disorder (whose rapid onset was accompanied by a small circle on his arm), he spent his time in humble supportive activities for Nuremberg Actions. It was his way of replying to what his old friends were fomenting south of the border."[76] The reporter observed that at the protest site beside the tracks, alongside wooden crosses inscribed with the names of Central American martyrs, were large blocks of stone with epitaphs to John F. Kennedy and Robert F. Kennedy. Jim Wilcott soon joined the witnesses he remembered in his vigil by the tracks, dying of cancer on February 10, 1994.[77]

Because Jim and Elsie Wilcott were unswerving witnesses to the truth behind John Kennedy's assassination, we can see through their eyes how the unspeakable became possible. By having unwittingly funded the Oswald double agent project, Jim Wilcott was an example of how CIA people were being used piecemeal in compartmentalized Cold War plots. Like Lee Harvey Oswald, they had no "need to know" anything beyond their assigned tasks. Through the need-to-know restriction in their national security state, the majority of CIA employees were kept ignorant before the fact of the much larger covert designs they helped embroider by their actions. Thus, even the assassination of a president could be funded unconsciously by American taxpayers and carried out unknowingly by government employees, while only a few such as CIA Deputy Director for Plans Richard Helms and Counterintelligence head James Angleton knew the intended result beforehand.

On June 3, 1963, ignoring evidence that implicated itself, the CIA reported in Washington "the weight of evidence indicating that government cannon-fire caused the deaths in Hue" on May 8 that had ignited the Buddhist crisis in South Vietnam.[78] Ngo Dinh Diem, on the other hand, insisted the deaths "were due to a Viet Cong terrorist grenade."[79] However, as we have seen, neither the Saigon government nor the Viet Cong possessed the kind of powerful plastic explosives that decapitated the victims at Hue on May 8. It was only the CIA that had such an explosive, as admitted later by Captain Scott, the U.S. military adviser responsible for the bombing.[80] Graham Greene had exposed earlier the CIA's preoccupation with plastic explosives. In The Quiet American, Greene dramatized the Agency's use of plastic bombs in Saigon in 1952 to scapegoat the Viet Minh as terrorists. The pattern was repeated in Hue, with Diem the propaganda target. The CIA's June 3 report blamed Diem for the Hue fatalities, which had in fact polarized him and the Buddhists, discredited his government, and derailed a possible Kennedy–Diem alliance for a negotiated U.S. withdrawal from Vietnam. Both Kennedy and Diem had been outmaneuvered by the CIA.

On June 11, 1963, a Buddhist monk, Thich Quang Duc, burned himself to death in Saigon in protest to Diem's repressive policies. Reporter Malcolm Browne's wire service photo of the bonze's self-immolation shocked the world. When John Kennedy opened his June 12 newspaper and saw the picture of the burning monk, he exclaimed, "Jesus Christ!" to his brother Robert on the phone.[81] Secretary of State Dean Rusk had already cabled the

U.S. Embassy in Saigon: "In our judgment the Buddhist situation is dangerously near the breaking point. Accordingly, you are authorized to tell Diem that in the United States view it is essential for the GVN [Government of Vietnam] promptly to take dramatic action to regain confidence of Buddhists and that the GVN must fully and unequivocally meet Buddhist demands . . .

"If Diem does not take prompt and effective steps to reestablish Buddhist confidence in him we will have to reexamine our entire relationship with his regime." [82]

Kennedy's advisers were running ahead of him. Rusk's instructions to the Saigon Embassy led Acting Ambassador William Trueheart to convey an ultimatum to Diem on June 12 that the president had not authorized. JFK found out by reading a CIA Intelligence Checklist on June 14. A White House memorandum that day emphasized: "The President noticed that Diem has been threatened with a formal statement of disassociation. He wants to be absolutely sure that no further threats are made and no formal statement is made without his own personal authorization." [83]

Vietnam was spiraling out of Kennedy's control. So was a crisis in Alabama. On June 11, Governor George Wallace placed himself in the doorway of the University of Alabama to keep two black students from registering. Working closely with his brother in the Attorney General's office, the president federalized the Alabama National Guard in the same hour to move Wallace aside and register the students. He decided to address the nation that night on the moral and civic crisis it was facing at home, as dramatized by Wallace.

At the same time, Kennedy had just turned a corner in his East–West struggle with Nikita Khrushchev. The day before, JFK had delivered his American University address, calling for an end to the Cold War, inspiring Khrushchev to hail his words as "the greatest speech by any American President since Roosevelt." [84] The Soviet leader agreed quickly with Kennedy to a test ban treaty, to the dismay of the military-industrial complex. *U.S. News and World Report* would ask in a major article, "Is U.S. Giving Up in the Arms Race?," citing military authorities' fears that Kennedy's new strategy added up to "a type of intentional and one-sided disarmament."

On the night of June 11, as Kennedy continued to ponder Vietnam and to absorb in particular the flaming image of Thich Quang Duc, he gave his televised speech to the American people on civil rights, saying it was "a moral issue," "as old as the scriptures and as clear as the American Constitution." [85] Four hours later, as if in response to his speech, a hidden assassin shot NAACP leader Medgar Evers in the back as he approached his home in Jackson, Mississippi, causing Evers to bleed to death in front of his wife and children. [86]

In two critical days, John Kennedy's words had inspired millions of people on opposite sides of the globe, some to act profoundly for peace and justice, others to hate and to kill. By those words and his decisions implementing them, he had become simultaneously a catalyst of hope and a target of hate.

JFK's friend John Kenneth Galbraith, his ambassador to India, said in a reflection published the day of the president's funeral that none of Kennedy's advisers could keep up with the man's own understanding:

"What Mr. Kennedy had come to know about the art and substance of American Government was prodigious . . . My Harvard colleague Professor Carl Kaysen, who has worked in the White House these last years, has said that when asked who is the most knowledgeable of the President's advisers he always felt obliged to remind his questioner that none was half so well-informed as the President himself.

"Departments and individuals, in approaching the President, invariably emphasized the matters which impress them most. Mr. Kennedy knew how to make the appropriate discounts without anyone quite realizing they were being made. He had a natural sense for all of the variables in a problem; he would not be carried away by anyone." [87]

Galbraith said, "No one knew the President well." [88]

That was especially true of his advisers. Their thinking on Vietnam ran counter to his own widening strategy for peace, as stated in his American University address. It was a relative outsider, Senator Mike Mansfield, who convinced him to withdraw from Vietnam, a decision consistent with JFK's unfolding vision of peace. Yet Kennedy was perplexed at how to manage a military withdrawal that was against the direction of his Cold War government. A prospective withdrawal now lay also in the context of the Buddhist crisis, which had prompted an international revulsion at the repressive rule of South Vietnamese President Diem.

It was at this point that Kennedy made a crucial mistake on Vietnam.

His ambassador to the Saigon government, Frederick Nolting, had asked to be relieved. Kennedy's first choice to become the new ambassador was his friend, Edmund Gullion,[89] who as a consul in Saigon in 1951 had told him it would be a disaster for the U.S. to follow the French example in Vietnam. Gullion had already served the president as his ambassador to the Congo, which for a while was the hottest spot in the Cold War.

In his book *JFK: Ordeal in Africa*, Richard Mahoney noted that Kennedy considered Gullion his most trusted third world ambassador. He sent Gullion into the Congo in 1961 because that African nation had become "a testing ground of the views shared by Kennedy and Gullion on the purpose of American power in the Third World. As Kennedy remarked over the phone one day, if the U.S. could support the process of change—'allow each country to find its own way'—it could prevent the spread of the Cold War and improve its own security." [90]

In the Congo, Gullion also represented Kennedy's support of a UN policy forged by the late Dag Hammarskjold. Kennedy and Gullion promoted Hammarskjold's vision of a united, independent Congo, to the dismay of multinational corporations working ceaselessly to carve up the country and control its rich resources.[91] After Kennedy's death, the corporations would succeed in controlling the Congo with the complicity of local kingpins.

While JFK was alive, a Kennedy-Hammarskjold-UN vision kept the Congo together and independent.

Seventeen years after JFK's death, Gullion said, "Kennedy, I think, risked a great deal in backing this operation [of UN forces in the Congo], backing this whole thing." [92] The risk came from within his own government. Kennedy rejected his State Department's and Joint Chiefs' proposals for "direct U.S. military intervention in the Congo in September 1961 and December 1962." [93] Kennedy had again feared he was being entrapped by his advisers, as in the Bay of Pigs, Laos, and Vietnam, in an ever-deepening U.S. military involvement. His Congo policy was also being subverted by the CIA, which had been arming the Congo's secessionist regime in Katanga in order to promote Belgian mining interests. "This [CIA] practice," wrote Richard Mahoney, "was expressly contrary to U.S. policy and in direct violation of the UN Security Council resolutions." [94] Kennedy's policy, carried out by Gullion, was to support the UN peacekeeping operation. The president often quoted the statement his UN ambassador Adlai Stevenson made to the Security Council, that the only way to keep the Cold War *out* of the Congo was to keep the UN *in* the Congo. [95] But the CIA *wanted* the Cold War in the Congo.

In the summer of 1963, Edmund Gullion's anticolonial diplomacy, as practiced already in the Congo, held the promise—or threat to some—of opening new doors to Kennedy in Vietnam. However, Secretary of State Dean Rusk told the president he was opposed to Gullion as the new Saigon ambassador. [96] In a decision JFK would live to regret, he then went along with Rusk's veto of Gullion and chose instead as ambassador his old Republican rival from Massachusetts, Henry Cabot Lodge. Kennedy wound up agreeing with Rusk's view that to choose a distinguished Republican as his ambassador would take the air out of the Republican right's demands for an escalated war. [97] But in forgoing Gullion, whose views were in harmony with his own, for the Republican Lodge, the president was not only giving up the appointment of a trusted colleague but also surrendering power to a political enemy.

In 1952 Kennedy had been elected to the Senate over the heavily favored incumbent senator, Henry Cabot Lodge. From 1953 to 1960, Lodge served the Eisenhower administration as UN ambassador, squashing UN opposition to CIA coups carried out in Iran and Guatemala under the direction of Allen Dulles. When JFK defeated Nixon for the presidency in 1960, Lodge as Nixon's vice-presidential candidate lost to Kennedy again. Lodge had then been hired by anti-Kennedy media magnate Henry Luce as his consultant on international affairs. [98] The struggle for power between the two dueling Massachusetts dynasties, the Fitzgerald Kennedys and the Cabot Lodges, continued. In 1962 Ted Kennedy, like JFK, began his Senate career by beating a Cabot Lodge. In that mid-term election of the Kennedy presidency, JFK's youngest brother defeated George Cabot Lodge, Henry Cabot Lodge's thirty-five-year-old son. [99]

For a decade, Henry Cabot Lodge (and his son) had been trying unsuccessfully to beat John Kennedy (and his brother) in an election. Lodge was no Kennedy man. Yet he had taken the curious step in 1963 of letting it be known in Washington that he would like to become the president's Saigon ambassador. Why did Lodge offer to become the ambassador of a man he so often opposed?

Henry Cabot Lodge was a major general in the U.S. Army Reserves. He had spent a month at the Pentagon in January 1963 being briefed on Vietnam and counterinsurgency. Author Anne Blair, who was given access to Lodge's private papers for her book *Lodge in Vietnam*, determined that it was probably during his Pentagon tour of duty "that Lodge began to float his name as a possibility for Vietnam." [100] Blair concluded from her reading of Lodge's confidential journal that he wanted to use a Vietnam appointment as the basis for a late run for the presidency in 1964. [101] Several of Lodge's close associates in South Vietnam, including his special assistant, John Michael Dunn, confirmed to Blair that Lodge "had accepted the South Vietnam post to increase his chances of gaining the Republican nomination." Henry Cabot Lodge wanted to represent his longtime opponent, John Kennedy, in Vietnam in such a way that he would be able to replace him in the White House.

Robert Kennedy warned his brother that he was making a mistake in appointing Lodge. He said Lodge would cause the president "a lot of difficulty in six months." [102] Even RFK was being too optimistic about Lodge. JFK's difficulties with his new ambassador would begin almost as soon as Lodge arrived in Vietnam.

With a sense of having just added one more shark to those already swimming around him, Kennedy joked to his aides Kenny O'Donnell and Dave Powers about his own motives for the appointment: "The idea of getting Lodge mixed up in such a hopeless mess as the one in Vietnam was irresistible." [103] Kennedy had in fact taken a magnanimous risk in appointing his political adversary to an influential post. Lodge would not return the favor by obeying the president's orders. Kennedy had made a mistake that would dog him that fall in Vietnam. By appointing Henry Cabot Lodge as his ambassador rather than holding out against Rusk for Edmund Gullion, Kennedy had lost a critical degree of power over Vietnam. Once Lodge took up residence in Saigon in August, it would not be Kennedy but his old political enemy, Lodge, who would be in control of the situation on the ground.

We saw earlier how Lee Harvey Oswald was continually impersonated in Mexico City in September 1963. Oswald disappeared down a black hole. His CIA-alleged visits and phone calls to the Cuban and Soviet consulates ended up revealing more about the CIA than they ever did about Oswald. In preparation for his patsy role in Dallas, Oswald was being given a false identity in Mexico City as a communist conspirator by an unknown impersonator. CIA transcripts of fraudulent Oswald phone calls to the Soviet Consulate "documented" the future scapegoat's supposed communications with a Soviet assassination expert. As William Harvey had written in his notes for the ZR/RIFLE assassination program, "planning should include provisions for blaming Sovs . . ." [104] The Mexico City scenario highlighted the CIA's plan to blame the Soviets and the Cubans for the president's murder.

However, the Soviets had discovered the plot to kill the president and knew the CIA planned to implicate them.

As we learned from the confrontation of U.S. and Soviet tanks at the Berlin Wall, Nikita Khrushchev and his advisers sometimes knew more about U.S. military operations than did their commander in chief in the White House, John Kennedy. The same was true in the case of the conspiracy to kill Kennedy, being carried out unknown to the president by his own Central Intelligence Agency—but not unknown to Soviet agents. JFK's opponents in the Kremlin were not only secretly monitoring the CIA's preparations to kill Kennedy. They were also trying to disrupt the plot, save the life of a president they knew they could work with, and keep from being scapegoated for his murder.

One of the most exhaustively researched books on President Kennedy's assassination, Dick Russell's *The Man Who Knew Too Much*, tells the story of a U.S. counterintelligence agent hired by the Soviets to kill Lee Harvey Oswald and thereby prevent JFK's assassination. The double agent's reluctance to become either Oswald's assassin for the KGB, or a part of JFK's assassination for the CIA, moved him to a desperate act.

Richard Case Nagell, "the man who knew too much," walked into a bank in El Paso, Texas, on September 20, 1963, and calmly fired two shots from a Colt .45 pistol into a plaster wall just below the bank's ceiling. He then went outside and waited in his car until a police officer came to arrest him. When questioned by the FBI, Nagell made only one statement: "I would rather be arrested than commit murder and treason." [105]

Richard Case Nagell had been a U.S. Army counterintelligence officer from 1955 to 1959. He was assigned to Field Operations Intelligence (FOI), which he later described as "a covert extension of CIA policy and activity designed to conceal the true nature of CIA objectives." [106] During his FOI orientation at Far East Headquarters in Japan, Nagell was familiarized, he said, with "simple and intricate weapons to be used in assassinations." He was also "advised that in the event I was apprehended, killed or compromised during the performance of my illegal FOI duties, the Department of the Army would publicly disclaim any knowledge of or connection with such duties, exercising its right of plausible denial." [107]

In the late fifties while stationed in Japan, Nagell began his Army/CIA role as a double agent in liaison with Soviet intelligence. In Tokyo, Nagell's path converged with that of counterintelligence agent Lee Harvey Oswald. Both men worked in a counterintelligence operation with the code name "Hidell," which Oswald later used as part of his alias, "Alek James Hidell." Nagell's biographer Dick Russell believes it was Nagell who actually assigned the "Hidell" alias to Oswald.[108]

As a continuing double agent in 1963, Nagell was working with Soviet intelligence in Mexico City. He was reporting back to the CIA, in an operation directed by the chief of the CIA's Cuban Task Force, Desmond Fitz-Gerald. Assigned by the KGB to monitor Lee Harvey Oswald in the United States after Oswald returned from Russia, Nagell became involved in New Orleans and Texas with Oswald and two Cuban exiles in what he saw was a "large" operation to kill JFK.[109] The Cubans were known by their "war names" of "Angel" and "Leopoldo." Nagell told Dick Russell that Angel and Leopoldo "were connected with a violence-prone faction of a CIA-financed group operating in Mexico City and elsewhere."[110] He identified Angel's and Leopoldo's CIA-financed group as Alpha 66.[111]

Alpha 66 was the group of Cuban exile paramilitaries we have already encountered who were directed by David Atlee Phillips, Chief of Covert Action at the CIA's Mexico City Station. In early 1963, Phillips deployed Alpha 66 in attacks on Russian ships in Cuban ports. The purpose of the provocative raids was to draw JFK into a war with Cuba. Kennedy responded by ordering a government crackdown on the CIA-sponsored raids, further antagonizing both the CIA and the exile community. Alpha 66 had ignited not a U.S. war with Cuba but a more lethal hatred of the president. This was the CIA-funded group Richard Case Nagell said Angel and Leopoldo belonged to, while they were meeting with Oswald.

In September 1963, Nagell was ordered by the KGB to convince Oswald that he was being set up by Angel and Leopoldo as the assassination patsy—or if that failed, to murder Oswald in Mexico City and then take up residence abroad. The Soviets wanted to save Kennedy by eliminating the scenario's patsy, and to keep from becoming scapegoats themselves. As Nagell told Dick Russell, "If anybody wanted to stop the assassination, it would be the KGB. But they didn't do enough."[112]

Nagell met with Oswald in New Orleans. He warned Oswald that Leopoldo and Angel were manipulating him. Oswald was evasive and unresponsive to Nagell's appeals that he quit the assassination plot.[113]

By that time Nagell had lost contact with his CIA case worker under Desmond FitzGerald. Rather than carry out the KGB's orders to kill Oswald, he sent the FBI's J. Edgar Hoover a registered letter on September 17 warning of the president's impending assassination, spelling out what Nagell knew of it. As he described the letter years later, "I informed the Director of the Federal Bureau of Investigation, *and others* [in his communications with the CIA], as early as September 17, 1963, that Lee Harvey Oswald and two of his Cuban associates were planning to assassinate the President of the United States."[114] Nagell also said that his letter to the FBI made explicit he "had received instructions 'to take care of' Lee Oswald, that is, to kill him, in September 1963."[115]

It is noteworthy that Nagell's letter to Hoover specified that the attempt to kill Kennedy would take place around the latter part of September, "probably on the 26th, 27th, 28th, or 29th," [116] and that the location would be in Washington, D.C.[117] From his mid-September knowledge of the assassination plot, Nagell thought Kennedy would be killed in Washington, at a time almost two months before his actual murder in Dallas.

Two weeks before Nagell's letter to Hoover, Oswald was already preparing to follow a similar time line and itinerary. On September 1, 1963, Oswald wrote to the Communist Party in New York City: "Please advise me as to how I can contact the Party in the Baltimore-Washington area, to which I shall relocate in October." [118]

Also on September 1, Oswald wrote to the Socialist Workers Party in New York: "Please advise me as to how I can get into direct contact with S.W.P. representatives in the Washington D.C.-Baltimore area. I and my family are moving to that area in October." [119]

Nagell's and Oswald's pre-assassination letters were focused on the same area, Washington, D.C., and had roughly the same time frame—"probably" September 26–29 in Nagell's assassination prediction, and "October" in Oswald's anticipated move to "the Washington D.C.-Baltimore area." But their letters were at cross purposes. Oswald, in his letter to the Communist and Socialist Workers parties, was obediently laying down a paper trail that could, if necessary, be used later to incriminate him as a Communist assassin of Kennedy in D.C. Nagell, in his letter to Hoover, was blowing a whistle on the same plot.

Having put his warning on record, Nagell then decided to remove himself from any possible role in the assassination plot. He therefore did his bank escapade in El Paso on September 20, 1963, to place himself in federal custody rather "than commit murder and treason." He was convicted of armed robbery and served four and one-half years in prison.

Nagell's shots in the El Paso bank gave his FBI letter a public exclamation point. Hoover knew that Nagell knew the CIA was planning to kill Kennedy in Washington around the end of the month (or in October—if, as likely, the FBI was also reading Oswald's correspondence to two closely monitored Communist offices). In a dramatic but oblique fashion, with his shots in El Paso, Nagell had made public his noncooperation with the plot to kill the president. Up to that point, Oswald had apparently been scheduled to be moved into position "in the Washington D.C.-Baltimore area" for the strike on JFK. Now Nagell, by his shots in the bank, had given the CIA and FBI public notice that, unlike Oswald, he refused to be a pawn in the plot. Although the whistle Nagell blew to Hoover did not save Kennedy's life, it may have been just loud enough with his bank caper to set back the plot two months.

After Nagell was arrested in El Paso, Oswald was redirected to Dallas. In late October, Oswald wrote from Dallas to Arnold Johnson, information director of the Communist Party in New York City: "In September I had written you saying I expected to move from New Orleans, La., to the Philadelphia-Baltimore area . . . Since then my personal plans have changed and I have settled in Dallas, Texas for the time." [120]

The sheep-dipping of Oswald continued. To Johnson, Oswald noted he had attended an ACLU meeting in Dallas. He asked the communist's advice on how he "could attempt to highten [sic] its progressive tendencies," thereby associating himself with both the Communist Party and the ACLU.

In 1967 as a federal prisoner in Springfield, Missouri, Richard Case Nagell contacted New Orleans District Attorney Jim Garrison. For Garrison's investigation of the Kennedy assassination, Nagell offered to turn over the tape recording he had made containing evidence of a conspiracy. Nagell said he had secretly taped a meeting he attended in late August 1963 with three other low-level participants in the plot to kill Kennedy. He identified the three voices on the tape beside his own as those of Oswald, Angel, and "Arcacha"—very likely Sergio Arcacha Smith, a Cuban exile leader who had worked closely with Guy Banister before moving from New Orleans to Texas in 1962.[121] Nagell withdrew the offer of the tape, however, when Garrison's staff member and intermediary, William R. Martin, told him he had been a CIA officer. Nagell suspected Martin's association with the CIA had not ended, as Garrison himself would later conclude.[122]

In the decades after his release from prison in 1968, Nagell allowed a few researchers such as Dick Russell and Bernard Fensterwald to interview him, without ever disclosing the most critical evidence he retained. Nagell was afraid of the consequences to his two children if he revealed anything more than he had already.[123] After talking with Nagell and investigating his story, Jim Garrison concluded: "Richard Case Nagell is the most important witness there is." [124]

How did Nagell manage to stay alive all these years?

In 1990 he acknowledged that, after surviving three attempts on his life in the late sixties,[125] he made a deal: "Stay silent and get your benefits from the military." [126] It would turn out to be a shaky deal. The dealers would recognize that Nagell's conscience was too active for him to remain silent.

As a U.S. double agent in the fall of 1963, Nagell was stuck in an impossible Cold War dilemma. As a CIA counterintelligence agent, Nagell was acting out a role with the KGB in the United States and Mexico. But in his KGB-assigned task of watching Oswald, Nagell in turn infiltrated a CIA plot to kill Kennedy, one in which he was unwittingly becoming a participant alongside the patsy, Oswald. At that critical point his CIA case agent cut him off, leaving Nagell out in the cold to "commit murder and treason" by continuing to take part in the assassination of the president. On the other hand, if Nagell followed his Soviet orders to kill CIA-pawn Oswald and block Kennedy's murder, he would also—this time from the CIA's in-house viewpoint—"commit murder and treason," against U.S. intelligence at the behest of the Soviet Union.[127] Nagell decided the safest place for him to ride out the dilemma was in jail. But before putting himself there, he tried to preempt the plot to kill Kennedy (and to put his effort on record) by sending his registered letter to J. Edgar Hoover exposing the plot. The FBI would always claim, however, in denying it had any foreknowledge of the assassination, that it knew nothing of Nagell's letter. Nagell was again left out in the cold—for the rest of his life.

On October 31, 1995, the Assassinations Records Review Board (ARRB) mailed Richard Case Nagell a letter seeking access to documents he claimed to have about a conspiracy to kill President Kennedy. The ARRB had also decided to get a sworn deposition from Nagell. Thus a moment of truth was at hand. Dick Russell knew from remarks Nagell had made that "if an official government body ever took him seriously," as was now finally the case, "*he would probably cooperate.*" [128] After three decades, the stage had at last been set for Nagell to tell his full story under oath, putting it on record before a government body authorized to review JFK evidence.

On November 1, 1995, the day after the ARRB's letter was mailed from Washington, D.C., Richard Case Nagell was found dead in the bathroom of his Los Angeles house.

The autopsy's conclusion was that he died from a heart attack. [129] However, Nagell had told Russell in their last phone conversation the year before that he was in great health. The person to whom he was closest, his niece, confirmed that his health had improved considerably of late. He had no history of heart problems. [130]

Yet something had happened to impair Nagell's health and equilibrium only a week and a half before his death. He had fallen badly and was hospitalized for a couple of days. Totally unlike himself, he phoned his niece to tell her about it, then began asking neighbors to check on him every day.

His niece said, "There were indications of his either losing confidence in his health and stability—or being suspicious of something. One or the other had to be the case." [131]

Then he was found dead—of an apparent heart attack.

Russell asked an investigator for the Los Angeles coroner, Gary Kellerman, if a heart attack could be induced. Kellerman said it was indeed possible to kill in such a way, while leaving no clues:

"I'm not sure what chemical you have to use, but I've heard of it. From what I understand, it's a chemical that gets into the system and then it's gone. You can't find it." [132]

Nagell had entrusted his niece with the knowledge of a purple trunk in which he had stored "what everybody is trying to get ahold of," as he put it—critical evidence, including his secretly recorded audiotape of his meeting with Oswald, Angel, and Arcacha. Robert Nagell, Richard's son, discovered in his father's house after his death the address of a Tucson, Arizona, storage unit. Robert drove immediately to the site, and retrieved the footlockers his father had stored there. They contained only family items. The purple trunk was missing. At the same time as Robert Nagell was racing to Tucson, his own house back in California was being broken into and ransacked. [133]

Even after his death, Richard Case Nagell's turn toward the truth seemed to threaten the security of the covert action agencies he had once served.

To his friend and biographer Dick Russell, Nagell had once reflected in an offhand, despondent way on his failure to prevent the murder of John Kennedy:

"I don't think much about it, to tell you the truth. Sometimes, though, I get thinking and I can't go to sleep. Thinking what I could have done, the mistakes that could have been handled differently . . . I was in a quandary in September '63. I didn't know what to do . . . What did I accomplish? Not a goddamned thing." [134]

As a CIA double agent working alongside Oswald, Nagell had been an active participant in the conspiracy to kill Kennedy. By his dramatic resistance to that evil, even though it persisted without him, Richard Case Nagell did accomplish something. He showed personally, in the depths of murder and deceit, that one can still turn toward the truth. And by his noncooperation with evil, he may have accomplished one more thing. He may have set back the plot to assassinate the president just enough to give John F. Kennedy another two months in which to live.

In the last week of September 1963, Silvia Odio, a twenty-six-year-old Cuban immigrant living in Dallas, was visited at her apartment door in the early evening by three strange men. Silvia's seventeen-year-old sister, Annie, who had come to babysit for Silvia's children, answered the door and spoke with the men first. They asked to see the oldest sister in the Odio family. Annie went to find Silvia, who was preparing to go out for the evening. Both Annie and Silvia had enduring impressions of the men, but Annie spoke with them for only a minute or two. Silvia talked with them for about twenty minutes.

Two of the men looked Latin and spoke rapidly in Spanish. They acted as if they were Cuban exiles. The taller, more vocal man gave his "war name," or Cuban underground alias, as "Leopoldo." Silvia recalled the name of the shorter, stockier man with glasses as "Angelo" or "Angel." [135] The third man, their "gringo American" friend, said little. To Silvia he seemed unable to follow the Spanish. Yet the third man's silent presence for a few minutes at her door would traumatize her future. He was introduced to her as "Leon Oswald." She would later identify him in her Warren Commission testimony as the man charged in Dallas with the murder of President Kennedy. [136] (She had no knowledge of Richard Case Nagell's recent involvement with Oswald and two Cubans using the same war names of Leopoldo and Angelo or Angel.)

Leopoldo and Angel told Silvia they were members of JURE (Junta Revolucionaria Cubana), the anti-Castro group in which her parents were well known. The men claimed they were very good friends of her father, Amador Odio, then being held in a Cuban prison. They said they also knew JURE's leader, Manolo Ray, with whom her father had worked closely. The strangers' show of familiarity with her imprisoned father made Silvia uneasy.

Amador Odio and his wife, Sarah, had been active in struggles against Cuban dictators since the thirties.[137] As the idealistic owner of Cuba's largest trucking company, Amador Odio was an important early ally of Fidel Castro in the fight against the military dictatorship of Fulgencio Batista. Odio transported most of the arms and medical supplies to Castro's rebel army in the Sierra Maestra mountains. After Castro's triumph over Batista, Amador and Sarah began to see Fidel as a dictator himself. As Amador put it, they thought "Fidel betrayed the Revolution."[138] The Odios then took part in gun-running operations against the Cuban government. In October 1961 they were arrested for storing arms on their land and harboring a man who tried to assassinate Castro.[139] They were imprisoned for eight years. The government confiscated their estate outside Havana, making it into a women's prison. Sarah became an inmate in her former home. Amador was jailed on the Isle of Pines. Friends spirited their ten children out of the country. As the oldest at twenty-four, Silvia stepped into the shoes of her parents.[140]

By the fall of 1963, with her parents in jail in Cuba, two brothers in a Dallas orphanage, and the rest of the family scattered, Silvia Odio, divorced and with four children of her own, was struggling to keep both her family and her life together. The pressures sometimes overcame her. For a year she had fainting spells, passing out for hours at a time, and had seen a Dallas psychiatrist for help.[141] Carrying on the tradition of her parents, she had also become a JURE activist. She was working with their friend, Manolo Ray, at raising funds for JURE. That made her not only an opponent of Castro but, in a more immediate context, an outsider in the Dallas exile community and a problem to the CIA. Most anti-Castro activists and their CIA sponsors regarded JURE, with its platform in support of economic justice and agrarian reform, as "Fidelism without Fidel." For anti-Castro organizers, JURE's democratic socialism had too much in common with the enemy.[142]

CIA organizers of the Bay of Pigs invasion even suspected that JURE founder, Manolo Ray, Castro's recently resigned Minister of Public Works, was a Cuban agent—or at least a fellow traveler of Castro—in their midst. Bay of Pigs tactician Howard Hunt said, "Ray was the only [Cuban exile] leader concerning whose loyalties CIA remained unsure. The sequestration device [putting the exile leaders under house arrest at a CIA base during the invasion] was directed primarily at Ray, to ensure his not informing the enemy."[143] Ray was a critic of the CIA's role in the invasion before it happened. The agency's later top-secret internal report on the Bay of Pigs commented acidly that Ray "who never favored an invasion said after the defeat 'I told you so' to all available newspapers."[144]

Perhaps Ray's greatest liability in the eyes of the CIA was his favored-Cuban-activist status with John and Robert Kennedy. Ray's leftist convictions, which alienated him from the exile community and the CIA, were what moved the Kennedys to overrule the agency and insist on Ray's inclusion in the coalition of exile leaders. For as John Kennedy told French journalist Jean Daniel (to convey to Castro), the president agreed with the basic vision of the Cuban revolution[145]—the same position held by Manolo Ray, the Odio family, and JURE.

The way Ray put it, in response to the charge of "Fidelism without Fidel," was: "I don't know what it means to be a leftist. If it means to be in favor of all the people and for the welfare of the masses, then I am."[146] Howard Hunt commented on this statement: "Fidel Castro could not have phrased it better."[147]

As cited in a CIA dispatch in July 1963, Ray's defensiveness among the exiles for his being a Kennedy ally only made matters worse. He told a presumably anti-Kennedy Cuban that he thought CIA agents "were more dangerous than the Kennedy administration." He waded into still deeper water by adding, "The Kennedy administration would end but CIA agents always stayed, and their memory was longer than the memory of elephants and they never forgot or forgave."[148] Further CIA cables noted that in September and October 1963, Ray was "conferring with Attorney General Kennedy about the Cuban situation,"[149] at exactly the same time as the CIA knew John and Robert Kennedy were exploring a possible rapprochement with Fidel Castro.

The CIA's tensions with Manolo Ray (suspected Castroite and confirmed Kennedy ally) and JURE ("Fidelism without Fidel") provided the backdrop to the visit to known JURE activist Silvia Odio by "JURE members" Leopoldo and Angel—and, most significantly, their friend Leon Oswald. The CIA saw Manolo Ray and JURE too closely related to a president who had become a national security risk. The encounter at Silvia Odio's door would link the man portrayed as Kennedy's assassin-to-be with a group the CIA wanted to contaminate.

As Leopoldo and Angel introduced themselves, speaking warmly of Amador Odio, Silvia listened suspiciously.

Leopoldo said, "We wanted you to meet this American. His name is Leon Oswald." In the course of the conversation, he repeated Oswald's name. He said Oswald was "very much interested in the Cuban cause."[150]

Silvia would remember the American vividly. He himself told her his name was Leon Oswald. As she would later recall the scene at her door, Oswald was standing between the two Cubans just inside the vestibule, less than three feet away from her.[151] While Leopoldo talked on quickly, Oswald just "kept smiling most of the time," with the bright overhead lights shining down on his face. "He had a special grin," she recalled, "a kind of funny smile."[152]

Leopoldo said they had just come directly from New Orleans.[153] The three men did appear "tired, unkempt and unshaven, as if they had just come from a long trip," Silvia recalled.[154] Leopoldo also said they were about to go on another trip. Silvia had the feeling she was being deliberately told about this unspecified trip.[155] The probable date of the men's visit at her door, September 25, was the eve of Lee Harvey Oswald's trip to Mexico

City, when he or an imposter would implicate him with the Cuban and Soviet consulates. The three men's "trip" fit that scenario.

Leopoldo said the purpose of their visiting Silvia was to ask her help in raising funds for JURE. Would she write for them some very nice letters in English as appeals to local businessmen? Silvia offered little comment, making no commitment.

As the strained conversation ended, Leopoldo gave her the impression he would contact her again. From her window Silvia watched the two Cubans and their American friend get in a car and drive away.

When Silvia got home from work a night or two later, she received a phone call from Leopoldo.

He asked her, "What do you think of the American?"

She said, "I don't think anything."

Leopoldo said, "You know, our idea is to introduce him to the underground in Cuba because he is great, he is kind of nuts. He told us we don't have any guts, 'you Cubans,' because President Kennedy should have been assassinated after the Bay of Pigs, and some Cubans should have done that, because he was the one that was holding the freedom of Cuba actually." [156]

Silvia was getting upset with the conversation, but Leopoldo continued telling her what the American, "Leon Oswald," supposedly said.

"And he said, 'It is so easy to do it.' He has told us." Leopoldo swore in Spanish, emphasizing Oswald's point about how easy it was to kill Kennedy. Leopoldo added that the American had been a Marine and was an expert shot. He was "kind of loco." [157]

Leopoldo repeated what he had said at Silvia's door—that he, Angel, and Oswald were leaving on a trip. They would very much like to see her again on their return to Dallas.[158] He hung up. Silvia never heard from him again.

Three days later Silvia wrote to her father in prison about the visit of the three strangers, saying two had called themselves friends of his. He wrote back that he knew none of the men, and that she should not get involved with any of them.[159]

In the early afternoon of November 22, 1963, in Dallas, Silvia Odio heard of President Kennedy's assassination on the radio on her way back to work from lunch. Although the radio made no mention yet of Oswald, Silvia thought immediately of the three men's visit to her apartment and what Leopoldo said on the phone about Leon's remarks on killing Kennedy. She felt a deep sense of fear. She began saying to herself, "Leon did it! Leon did it!" [160] While everyone was being sent home from Silvia's workplace, she became more terrified. As she was walking to her car, she fainted. She woke up in the hospital.

When Silvia's sister, Annie, first saw Oswald on television that afternoon, she thought, "My God, I know this guy from somewhere!" She kept asking herself where she'd seen him. Her sister Serita phoned: Silvia had fainted at work and was in the hospital. Annie went immediately to the hospital.

When Annie visited Silvia, she told her she knew she'd seen the guy on the

TV who'd shot President Kennedy, but she didn't know where. Silvia began to cry. She asked Annie if she remembered the three men's visit to the apartment. Then Annie realized she'd not only seen Oswald but had spoken with him at the door. Silvia told her of Leopoldo's follow-up phone call about Oswald's threats against the president. Annie, too, became deeply frightened. Silvia by now had also seen television pictures of the presumed assassin. She was certain Lee Harvey Oswald was identical to the "Leon Oswald" who had stood at her door under the light between the two Cubans.

Because of Silvia's and Annie's fears for themselves and their scattered family, the two sisters vowed to each other not to tell the authorities what they knew.[161] However, a friend who heard their story told the FBI. Silvia was interviewed by the FBI in December 1963, but was not called to testify before the Warren Commission until the end of July 1964. Her evidence of a conspiracy setting up Oswald was not something the Warren Commission wanted to hear. As the Commission's General Counsel, J. Lee Rankin, said to the author of a memorandum supporting Odio's story, "At this stage, we are supposed to be closing doors, not opening them."[162]

The *Warren Report* dismissed Silvia Odio's testimony by arguing Oswald had already left for Mexico City before the three men's visit to her door.[163] But whether it was Oswald or a look-alike at the door, Leopoldo's phone call made the purpose of the visit obvious. Oswald was being set up. The incident was proof of a conspiracy designed to make Oswald the patsy.[164]

An assassination scenario that included the Odio incident was still more comprehensive. In the case of the Odio family and Manolo Ray, the targets of guilt by association with Oswald included Kennedy allies in the Cuban exile community. They were also to be silenced by fear. That worked to some degree on Silvia Odio. But when it came to facing a question of conscience forced upon her, Silvia Odio was a witness to the truth.

In the fall of 1963, while Lee Harvey Oswald was being redirected to Dallas, John F. Kennedy was trying to begin his withdrawal from Vietnam. He was being obstructed by military officials—and by his own hasty support of a coup d'etat against the South Vietnamese government.

In the early summer, Kennedy had kept his military and CIA advisers out of his discussions on Vietnam. This significant fact was mentioned years later by his Assistant Secretary of Defense William P. Bundy in an unpublished manuscript. According to Bundy, during the early part of Kennedy's final summer in office, he consulted on Vietnam with just a few advisers in the State Department and White House, thereby leaving out representatives of the Defense Department, the Joint Chiefs of Staff, and the CIA.[165] But this is hardly surprising. The dysfunctional relationship between Kennedy and his Cold War hierarchy had already reached the point where he kept his thinking on controversial subjects to himself—and a tight circle of friends with whom he shared that thinking sporadically. By leaving the Pentagon and the CIA out of the Vietnam loop, he wasn't fooling them. They knew he planned to withdraw from Vietnam. They also knew they'd been left out of other key decisions. At precisely the same time, the early summer of 1963, besides sidestepping the Pentagon and the CIA on Vietnam, the president had also left them out of consultations for his American University address and the test ban treaty. The reason was simple. Kennedy knew the military-intelligence elite was opposed to all his efforts to end the Cold War. They wanted to win it.

At the Pentagon, the Joint Chiefs of Staff were dragging their heels on the Vietnam withdrawal plan. The chiefs used the Buddhist crisis as a rationale for bogging down McNamara's May order that a specific plan be prepared for the withdrawal of one thousand military personnel by the end of 1963. On August 20, the chiefs wrote to McNamara that "until the political and religious tensions now confronting the Government of Vietnam have eased," "no US units should be withdrawn from the Republic of Vietnam." [166] The chiefs argued, for the same reason, that "the final decision to implement the withdrawal plan should be withheld until late October"—one month before Kennedy would be assassinated. But Kennedy and McNamara sped up the process. The decision for withdrawal would in fact be made in early October.

Even the select few in the State Department whom Kennedy was consulting on Vietnam did not serve him well. In late August, Averell Harriman, who had returned triumphantly from the test ban negotiations in Moscow, and Roger Hilsman, now in charge of the Vietnam desk, precipitated a decision for U.S. support of a coup against Diem. On August 24, during a weekend when Kennedy was in Hyannis Port, Hilsman, working with Harriman and Kennedy's aide Michael Forrestal, drafted an urgent telegram to newly appointed Saigon ambassador Henry Cabot Lodge. The telegram authorized U.S. support of a looming coup by rebel South Vietnamese generals, if Diem refused to remove from power his brother Nhu and sister-in-law Madame Nhu.

Ngo Dinh Nhu seemed to be taking over the Saigon government. His ever more violent repression of the Buddhists, together with Madame Nhu's statements applauding Buddhist immolations, had outraged Vietnamese and American public opinion. In the face of the generals' imminent coup, the State Department telegram read in a crucially important sentence: "We wish give Diem reasonable opportunity to remove Nhus, but if he remains obdurate, then we are prepared to accept the obvious implication that we can no longer support Diem." [167]

When Kennedy was urged by Forrestal in Washington to endorse the telegram because all his advisers had done so (which proved not to be the case), the president said to go ahead and send it. Then the generals backed down from the coup. However, in a hasty policy decision that Kennedy soon regretted but never reversed, he had put the government on record as being in conditional support of a coup—after giving "Diem reasonable opportunity to remove Nhus."

At the Saigon Embassy, Henry Cabot Lodge interpreted this condition in terms of a diplomatic strategy he had worked out with someone other than the president. After his appointment by Kennedy and before his move to Vietnam, Lodge had consulted his old friend and employer Henry Luce at *Time* on how he should deal with Diem.

By his decision to look to Luce for guidance in Saigon, Lodge was already indicating where his real allegiance lay. It was not to the president who had just given him his appointment as ambassador. Lodge was meeting in the enemy's camp. Henry Luce was, first of all, a longtime CIA ally. As Graham Greene pointed out, it was Luce's *Life* magazine that worked with the CIA to scapegoat "Viet Minh Communists" for the CIA's terrorist bombings of Saigon in 1952. Besides being CIA-friendly, Henry Luce was an enemy to Kennedy. In the wake of the April 1962 steel crisis, Luce's *Fortune* magazine had implicitly warned the president, on behalf of America's business elite, to beware "the ides of April" for his dominant role in settling the crisis.[168] The *Fortune* editorial was a corporate declaration of war against the Kennedy administration and a veiled personal threat to the president. Henry Luce and his media empire epitomized the corporate, military, and intelligence forces that wanted to stop Kennedy. For Henry Cabot Lodge to consult Henry Luce on how Lodge should act as Kennedy's Vietnam ambassador was asking for trouble for the president. Luce was happy to oblige.

He recommended that Lodge read the *Time* articles on Vietnam by staff writer Charles Mohr. Lodge did. He was especially impressed by Mohr's argument that Lodge's predecessor, Ambassador Frederick Nolting, had been "too weak" in confronting Diem with demands for change. Mohr's graphic analogy was that the United States and Diem were like "two teenagers playing head-on collision chicken in souped-up hot rods . . . The trouble is, the U.S. chickens out before Diem does."[169]

Lodge became inspired by the thought of playing his own game of "chicken" with Diem. He knew Diem could not hope to win such a game with Washington. The United States had a crushing vehicle compared to its client ruler. All Lodge had to do was refuse to deal with Diem, threaten implicitly to run him over while U.S. political and economic pressures mounted, and not "chicken out." If Diem should be so proud as to refuse to "chicken out" himself, he would be run over by the United States with Lodge's foot on the throttle. When he moved into the ambassador's residence in Saigon, Lodge used an abstract of Mohr's "chicken" article as background for his own primer: "Talking Points for Conversation Between Ambassador Lodge and President Diem."[170]

Following the August 24 telegram, Lodge showed how unwilling he was to give Diem any "reasonable opportunity to remove Nhus." In response to those specific instructions, he cabled back the State Department:

"Believe that chances of Diem meeting our demands are virtually nil. At same time, by making them we give Nhu chance to forestall or block action by military. Risk, we believe, is not worth taking, with Nhu in control combat forces Saigon. Therefore, propose we go straight to Generals with our demands, without informing Diem." [171]

The State Department agreed at once to Lodge's downward revision of an already disastrous directive. In Hyannis Port, President Kennedy was informed after the fact by Michael Forrestal that Acting Secretary of State James Ball, Averell Harriman, and Roger Hilsman had approved Lodge's "modification" [172] that now gave Diem no opportunity at all to forestall a coup.

When Kennedy returned to Washington, he was furious at discovering how his decision making had been usurped and manipulated over the weekend. "This shit has got to stop!" he said. [173]

Michael Forrestal offered to resign for his role in the short-circuited process. Kennedy snapped, "You're not worth firing. You owe me something, so you stick around." [174]

Before the generals backed away from the coup, Lodge met with Diem on August 26. Diem said pointedly to the new American ambassador, "I hope there will be an end to reports of diverse activities interfering in Vietnamese affairs by United States agencies."

Lodge replied evasively, "I've just arrived. Naturally I can't know everything that's going on. But I'll look into it." [175]

In fact, from his arrival in Saigon, Lodge had been actively promoting a coup. Through longtime CIA operative in Vietnam Colonel Lucien Conein, Lodge maintained regular contact with the generals. Conein had known most of the coup generals for years, ever since he conducted the CIA's sabotage operations against the Viet Minh in the mid-fifties under the direction of Edward Lansdale. [176] Lodge was continually frustrated over the next two months that he could not, even through Conein's urging, get the generals to stage a coup sooner. Lodge saw no possibility that Diem could act any differently than he had. For Lodge, the sooner the coup, the better.

Kennedy, on the other hand, continued to hope Diem might still somehow back away from his repressive policies and remove the Nhus, who seemed to be the force behind them. Through Secretary of State Rusk, the president repeatedly urged Lodge to explore such alternatives with Diem.

On August 28, Rusk wired Lodge: "We have concurred until now in your belief that nothing should be said to Diem, but changing circumstances, including his probable knowledge that something is afoot, lead us to ask again if you see value in one last man-to-man effort to persuade him to govern himself and decisively to eliminate political influence of Nhus." [177]

Lodge rejected Rusk's suggestion: "I believe that such a step has no chance of getting the desired result and would have the very serious effect of being regarded by the Generals as a sign of American indecision and delay. I believe this is a risk which we should not run." [178]

Rusk tried again the next day, wiring Lodge: "Purpose of this message is to explore further question of possible attempt to separate Diem and the Nhus. In your telegram you appear to treat Diem and the Nhus as a single package . . ." Rusk said he would be glad to have Lodge's thoughts "on whether further talks with Diem are contemplated to continue your opening discussions with him." [179]

However, Lodge was in no mood to talk with the man he regarded as his diplomatic enemy in a game of "chicken." He was determined to carry out his Luce-induced strategy against Diem. In a rebuttal telegram to Rusk, Lodge lectured the Secretary of State (and through him the president) that removing the Nhus "surely cannot be done by working through Diem. In fact Diem will oppose it . . . The best chance of doing it is by the Generals taking over the government lock, stock and barrel." He concluded: "I am contemplating no further talks with Diem at this time." [180]

In another wire to Lodge on September 3, Rusk pressed the issue further: "In this situation feeling here is that it is essential that central negotiations should be conducted directly with Diem and that you should proceed to a first meeting as soon as in your judgment you think it is desirable . . . We should be inclined to press for earliest such meeting." [181]

Again Lodge deflected his orders from the president, replying to Rusk: "If I correctly understand instructions, they are based on a very different reading of the situation here and the possibilities than my own and my colleagues." [182] Lodge repeated that he would continue to put off a meeting with Diem.

Kennedy was becoming exasperated, at both Lodge's mulishness and at his own folly in not having heeded his brother Robert's warning against his appointing Lodge ambassador. Thanks to that appointment, he now had not only a stubborn South Vietnamese president to deal with but an equally stubborn American ambassador. Lodge was even resistant to the suggestion that he take the obvious diplomatic step of talking with Diem. JFK knew the chances of Diem's sidelining the Nhus or reforming his government were miniscule. But the president had another objective in mind in his eleventh-hour efforts to appeal to Diem, an objective he realized Henry Cabot Lodge was not going to facilitate. He wanted to save Diem's life.

To the Cold War establishment, Ngo Dinh Diem was becoming disposable. Washington's Cold War leaders had been divided for some time over the merits of retaining Diem as their client "democratic" head of state for the Vietnam War. However, as a result of Diem's disastrous repression of the Buddhists, the factions were moving toward consensus. It was becoming obvious that Diem, an incompetent despot, had to go. Kennedy was under mounting pressure from the more liberal side of his government, the State Department, to end Diem's flagrantly authoritarian rule by a coup. In that respect, State's leading coup advocates, Harriman and Hilsman, had put themselves in an unlikely alliance with the CIA's Deputy Director of Plans, Richard Helms.

When Helms was asked by Harriman to approve the August 24 telegram to Lodge since CIA Director John McCone (a Diem supporter) was out of town, the Deputy Director of Plans did so without hesitation. It was the CIA's career tactician Helms, not Kennedy's appointee McCone, who was running the Agency's covert operations—in this case beyond McCone's knowledge or control. McCone was a figurehead out of the CIA's covert-action loop. Helms felt no need to seek out, or defer to, McCone's judgment when it came to the CIA's endorsing (and facilitating) a coup in South Vietnam. "It's about time we bit this bullet," Helms told Harriman,[183] in direct conflict with what McCone would say to Kennedy on his return to Washington. But it was Helms who was literally calling the CIA's shots, not McCone.

Kennedy wanted to save Diem's life from the looming generals' coup that had picked up a steamrolling momentum not only in South Vietnam (with Lodge pushing it) but also from opposite sides of the U.S. government in Washington. As a senator, John Kennedy, like Mike Mansfield, had helped bring Diem to power in South Vietnam. Regardless of Diem's downward path since then, Kennedy did not want to see him killed in a coup, especially one he was condoning. Because he was surrounded by people he couldn't trust, Kennedy called in an old friend to help him try to save Diem's life.

Torby Macdonald had been Jack Kennedy's closest friend at Harvard. Like Kennedy, Macdonald was Irish Catholic, a second son, an athlete (Harvard football team captain), and an avid reader. Torby was at Jack's side through severe illnesses at Harvard. He also helped his physically less talented friend practice long hours catching passes on the Harvard football field and backstroking in the indoor swimming pool. Both men had sharp wits. They enjoyed each other's company immensely. In time they became political comrades in Washington. Torbert Macdonald was elected a Massachusetts member of the House of Representatives in 1954, with Senator John Kennedy's support. When Kennedy was elected president, Macdonald remained his closest friend in Congress.[184] It was to Torbert Macdonald, perhaps the man JFK trusted most after his brother Robert, that the president turned in the fall of 1963 to help him try to save the life of Diem.

Kennedy commissioned Macdonald to go to Saigon to appeal personally to Diem on behalf of the president. Macdonald was to bypass the CIA, the State Department, and Henry Cabot Lodge, in order to make an urgent personal appeal to the South Vietnamese president to take the steps necessary to save his life. Macdonald would fly in and out of Saigon on military, not civilian, planes to maintain as much secrecy as possible,[185] with the assistance of the one arm of Kennedy's government, the military, whose command still maintained a lingering (though lessening) support for Diem. Macdonald's preparations for his mission and the trip itself were carried out in total secrecy, with no known written records. Kennedy's biographer, Herbert S. Parmet, discovered the hidden story after Macdonald's death in 1976. It was revealed to Parmet by Macdonald's lover, Eleanore Carney, identified in Parmet's *JFK: The Presidency of John F. Kennedy* only as a confidential source.[186] Her report was confirmed by Torbert Macdonald, Jr., who said his father told him about the secret journey,[187] and by Macdonald's administrative assistant, Joe Croken.[188] Kennedy's aide Michael Forrestal provided further confirmation. He had briefed Macdonald for the trip.[189]

As JFK wished, Torbert Macdonald met with Diem. He presented Kennedy's personal plea that Diem remove the Nhus from power and that he himself take refuge in the American Embassy in Saigon.

Macdonald warned Diem: "They're going to kill you. You've got to get out of here temporarily to seek sanctuary in the American Embassy and you must get rid of your sister-in-law and your brother." [190]

Diem would not budge.

"He just won't do it," Macdonald reported back to the President. "He's too stubborn; just refuses to." [191]

As Kennedy was trying to save Diem's life while going along with a coup that would take it, Lee Harvey Oswald was gaining employment at the Texas School Book Depository in Dallas. He got the job that would place him strategically right over the president's parade route through the intercession of Marina Oswald's friend Ruth Paine, a housewife with connections.

It was through CIA asset George de Mohrenschildt that Ruth Paine had met Lee and Marina Oswald. When Warren Commission lawyer Wesley Liebeler asked Ruth Paine if Marina Oswald had ever mentioned George de Mohrenschildt to her, Paine answered, "Well, that's how I met her." She said her meeting with Marina occurred at a February 1963 party in Dallas. [192] De Mohrenschildt had helped arrange the party, which took place at the home of a friend. [193] Ruth Paine attended it especially to meet Marina. As a student of the Russian language, Ruth wanted to meet somebody with whom she could practice. [194] George de Mohrenschildt brought the Oswalds to the party. [195] Ruth Paine then spent part of the evening conversing in Russian with Marina. [196] De Mohrenschildt told the Warren Commission, "I noticed immediately that there was another nice relationship developed there between Mrs. Paine and Marina." [197] Ruth followed up her introduction to the Oswalds by letters, phone calls, and visits to Marina in particular.

In late April, Ruth convinced Marina to move into Ruth's house in Irving, a suburb of Dallas, for two weeks, while Lee went ahead "to look for work" in New Orleans—the context where he would be sheep-dipped by U.S. intelligence that summer as a follower of Fidel Castro. Marina's living with Ruth Paine would become a more permanent arrangement in the fall. It was supported from the beginning by Ruth's husband, Michael Paine, then separated from Ruth and their two young children and living in his own apartment. When Lee Oswald said he was settled in New Orleans, Ruth with her children drove Marina and her fourteen-month-old daughter June down to New Orleans, again with the encouragement and financial support of Michael Paine.

By the time George de Mohrenschildt dropped out of the Oswalds' lives in April 1963, Ruth and her husband, Michael Paine, had taken de Mohrenschildt's place as Marina's and Lee's Dallas sponsors. De Mohrenschildt's sponsorship was sanctioned by the CIA. Three hours before his death in 1977 in Florida by an apparently self-inflicted shotgun blast, George de Mohrenschildt revealed in an interview that he befriended Lee Harvey Oswald at the encouragement of Dallas CIA agent J. Walton Moore, with whom he had been meeting regularly for years.[198] In return for his shepherding of Oswald, de Mohrenschildt asked for and received a discreetly facilitated $285,000 contract with dictator "Papa Doc" Duvalier to do a geological survey in Haiti.[199] De Mohrenschildt did no geological survey in Haiti, but still deposited over $200,000 in his bank account.[200] When de Mohrenschildt left Dallas in April for Haiti (stopping off in Washington, D.C., for a meeting with CIA and Army intelligence officials),[201] Ruth and Michael Paine stepped into his place as the Oswalds' Dallas benefactors.

It was as if de Mohrenschildt had handed off the Oswalds to the Paines like a football in a reverse end run. When the Dallas play-action began, the Oswalds were being carried by a prominent White Russian anti-communist. As de Mohrenschildt with CIA assistance left the Dallas action for Haiti, the Oswalds were suddenly in the hands of a Quaker-Unitarian couple who belonged to the ACLU. If it was in fact a handoff, one trick play in a larger game plan, its sleight of hand was so successful that when the game was over, hardly anyone even remembered this one critical play.

FBI director J. Edgar Hoover apparently did notice, however, that there was a de Mohrenschildt-Paine parallel of a classified nature whose public revelation could threaten the credibility of the Warren Commission. Hoover wrote a letter to head Warren Commission counsel J. Lee Rankin on October 23, 1964, urging him not to release certain FBI "reports and memoranda dealing with Michael and Ruth Paine and George and Jeanne de Mohrenschildt." Hoover warned Rankin: "Making the contents of such documents available to the public could cause serious repercussions to the Commission."[202]

Who, then, were Michael and Ruth Paine?

When the Oswalds came under the protective wings of the Paines, Michael Paine was working as a research engineer with a defense contractor, Bell Helicopter, in Fort Worth, Texas.[203] Paine acknowledged in his testimony to the Warren Commission that his job had a security clearance but claimed, "I don't happen to know what the classification is."[204] However, Michael Paine was no ordinary Bell Helicopter engineer. His stepfather, Arthur Young, with whom he worked previously, was the inventor of the Bell Helicopter—a fact discovered by researchers thirty years after the Kennedy assassination.[205] By heritage Michael Paine was well connected in the military-industrial complex.

Michael Paine's mother, Ruth Forbes Paine Young, was connected to Allen Dulles. Descended from the blueblood Forbes family of Boston, Ruth Forbes Paine Young was a lifelong friend of Mary Bancroft, who worked side by side with Allen Dulles as a World War II spy in Switzerland and became his mistress.[206] Mary Bancroft said in an oral history interview that she "knew the mother of Michael Paine where Oswald stayed. She was Ruth Forbes, a very good friend of mine." [207]

When Michael Paine testified before the Warren Commission, Allen Dulles asked one question that veered perilously close to relevance. He said to Michael Paine, "Is this Mr. Young your stepfather?" Paine said, "That is right." [208] Dulles retreated quickly into silence, allowing a commission lawyer to continue the questioning. Allen Dulles had ample reason not to ask follow-up questions about Arthur Young. Such queries might have surfaced Michael's stepfather's fame in the military-industrial complex as the inventor of the Bell Helicopter. Michael Paine's mother was even more dangerous territory for Dulles. He asked nothing at all about her. Least of all did Allen Dulles want it to emerge that the mother of the Oswald sponsor they were questioning lightly was a very good friend of his wartime mistress, with whom he maintained close contact. [209]

Ruth Hyde Paine, Michael's wife and Marina Oswald's caregiver, was the daughter of William Avery Hyde. To the Warren Commission Ruth Paine described her father's occupation in modest terms: "He is an insurance underwriter; he composes the fine print." [210] William Avery Hyde was at the time an insurance executive destined for an influential government post.

In October 1964, right after the publication of the *Warren Report* featuring his daughter Ruth as the government's key witness (other than Marina Oswald) to the guilt of Lee Harvey Oswald in murdering John Kennedy, William Avery Hyde received a three-year government contract from AID (Agency for International Development). From October 1964 to August 1967, William Avery Hyde was AID's Regional Insurance Adviser for all of Latin America. [211] Hyde's job description was to provide technical assistance from the U.S. State Department to insurance cooperatives being launched throughout the region. At the same time, the reports Hyde filed from his time in Peru, Bolivia, Ecuador, and Panama can be seen in the context of what a later AID director, former Ohio governor John Gilligan, admitted frankly was AID's collateral CIA function:

"At one time, many AID field offices [under the auspices of the State Department] were infiltrated from top to bottom with CIA people. It was pretty well known in the agency who they were and what they were up to . . . The idea was to plant operatives in every kind of activity we had overseas, government, volunteer, religious, every kind." [212]

If William Avery Hyde was acting as a CIA "executive agent," [213] then his expertise in helping to provide lower-cost insurance in Latin American countries was his cover for gathering information on people the CIA was watching carefully in the ferment of the sixties. While it was to the State Department's AID office that William Avery Hyde made his August 8, 1967, end-of-tour report from Lima, Peru, still as noted explicitly on its cover page, Hyde's report went to the CIA as well. [214]

Ruth Hyde Paine was also the younger sister of Sylvia Hyde Hoke, who in 1963 was living in Falls Church, Virginia. Thirty years after John Kennedy's assassination, a CIA Security File Memorandum on Sylvia Hyde Hoke was declassified at the National Archives. The CIA memorandum noted that Sylvia Hoke was identified as a CIA employee in the 1961 issue of the Falls Church, Virginia, City Directory. The memorandum warned: "Since it is known that opposition intelligence services have in the past checked similar publications, it should be presumed that the indicated employment of Subject by CIA is known to other intelligence organizations."[215]

However, Sylvia's CIA employment—in its eighth year in 1963[216]—was not known to her sister Ruth, at least according to Ruth's later testimony.

Ruth stayed with Sylvia at her Falls Church home near CIA headquarters in September 1963.[217] After her visit at Sylvia and John Hoke's CIA-related household (as his father-in-law would soon, John worked for the agency's front, AID),[218] Ruth drove to New Orleans to meet the Oswalds. Ruth then drove Marina back to Dallas, so Marina could settle more permanently into the Paines' home while awaiting the birth of her second child. In October, Ruth arranged Lee Oswald's employment at the Texas School Book Depository overlooking Dealey Plaza.

With this sequence of events as the background, New Orleans District Attorney Jim Garrison questioned Ruth Paine before a grand jury in 1968. Garrison asked Paine if her sister Sylvia did any work in connection with the U.S. government in 1963.

PAINE: "She has worked . . . she did something with G9, what is this . . . well, it would be a government job."

GARRISON: "What did she do with the government?"

PAINE: "She majored in psychology, one of the things I recall is making testing angles, how to test a Bedouin to know whether he can be a good oil drill operator, this kind of thing."

GARRISON: "Do you know what government agency she has worked for?"

PAINE: "No, just worked for the government."[219]

Without access to government documents identifying Ruth Paine's sister as a CIA employee, Garrison asked Paine: "Do you know why the investigative file on Sylvia Hyde Hoke is still classified in the archives as secret?"

PAINE: "No, is it?"

GARRISON: ". . . Yes, most of the file's still classified. Do you have any idea why they would do that? It seems there is no reason."

PAINE: "No."[220]

The *Warren Report* states that on October 14, 1963, "at the suggestion of a neighbor, Mrs. Paine phoned the Texas School Book Depository and was told that there was a job opening. She informed Oswald who was interviewed the following day at the Depository and started to work there on October 16, 1963."[221]

However, the Warren Commission also knew that on October 15, the day before Oswald began work at the Texas School Book Depository, Robert Adams of the Texas Employment Commission phoned the Paine residence with a much better job prospect for Oswald. Adams spoke with someone at the Paines' number about his being prepared to give Oswald a referral for permanent employment as a baggage or cargo handler at Trans Texas Airways, for a salary $100 per month higher than that offered by the Book Depository's only temporary job. Adams told the Warren Commission, "I learned from the person who answered the phone that Oswald was not there. I left a message with that person that Oswald should contact me at the Commission." [222]

Adams tried phoning the Paine residence about the higher-paying job again the next morning. He said he "learned from the person who answered that Oswald was not there and that he had in the meantime obtained employment and was working." [223] Adams accordingly cancelled Oswald as a referral for the more lucrative job. [224]

Ruth Paine was questioned by a sympathetic Warren Commission lawyer, Albert Jenner, about this more promising job possibility. She first denied knowing anything about it, then recalled it vaguely, and finally said she knew about it from Lee himself:

JENNER: "Did you ever hear anything by way of discussion or otherwise by Marina or Lee of the possibility of his having been tendered or at least suggested to him a job at Trans-Texas, as a cargo handler at $310 per month?"

PAINE: "No; in Dallas?"

JENNER: "Yes."

PAINE: "I do not recall that. $310 a month?"

JENNER: "Yes. This was right at the time that he obtained employment at the Texas School Book Depository."

PAINE: "And he was definitely offered such a job?"

JENNER: "Well, I won't say it was offered—that he might have been able to secure a job through the Texas Employment Commission as a cargo handler at $310 per month."

PAINE: "I do recall some reference of that sort, which fell through—that there was not that possibility."

JENNER: "Tell us what you know about that. Did you hear of it at the time?"

PAINE: "Yes."

JENNER: "Now, would you please relate that to me?"

PAINE: "I recall some reference to—"

JENNER: "How did it come about?"

PAINE: "From Lee, as I recall."

JENNER: "And was it at the time, or just right—"

PAINE: "It was at the time, while he was yet unemployed."

JENNER: "And about the time he obtained employment at the Texas School Book Depository?"

PAINE: "It seemed to me he went into town with some hopes raised by the employment agency—whether a public or private employment agency I don't know—but then reported that the job had been filled and not available to him."

JENNER: "But that was—"

PAINE: "That is my best recollection."

JENNER: "Of his report to you and Marina?"

PAINE: "Yes."

JENNER: "But you do recall his discussing it?"

PAINE: "I recall something of that nature. I do not recall the job itself." [225]

Robert Adams concluded from his own efforts to notify Oswald of the Trans Texas job by phoning the Paine residence: "I do not know whether he was ever advised of this referral, but under the circumstances I do not see how he could have been." [226]

The same New Orleans grand jury that heard Ruth Paine's testimony about the Oswalds also heard Marina Oswald's testimony about Ruth Paine. A juror asked Marina if she still saw Ruth in 1968.

Marina answered, "No, I like her and appreciate what she did. I was advised by Secret Service not to be connected with her." Marina said the reason she was advised by the Secret Service to stay away from Ruth was "she was sympathizing with the CIA."

Could she elaborate, she was asked, on what the Secret Service told her about Ruth Paine and the CIA?

MARINA: "Seems like she had friends over there and it would be bad for me if people find out connection between me and Ruth and CIA."

QUESTION: "In other words, you were left with the distinct impression that she was in some way connected with the CIA?"

MARINA: "Yes." [227]

As a consequence of both Lee Harvey Oswald's successful referral by Ruth Paine to the Texas School Book Depository and his missed opportunity for a better job at Trans Texas Airways, Oswald began work on October 16, 1963, at the Book Depository. The scapegoat was now in place at an ideal ambush site. It was five weeks before President Kennedy's motorcade would pass through Dealey Plaza.

CHAPTER FIVE

Saigon and Chicago

At the height of the Cuban Missile Crisis, Nikita Khrushchev said something totally unexpected to his Foreign Minister, Andrei Gromyko. He said, "We have to let Kennedy know that we want to help him." [1]

As Khrushchev's son, Sergei, describes that surprising moment, his father hesitated to use the word "help" in response to John Kennedy's plea for precisely that. When Khrushchev did say the word aloud, it forced him to ask himself: Did he really want to *help* his enemy Kennedy?

Yet Khrushchev knew from his secret correspondence with the U.S. president that the two men agreed on Noah's Ark as a crucial symbol of their common predicament in the nuclear age. The precarious boat in which they and all of humanity were living on a sea of conflict had to stay afloat.

After a short silence inspired by the sense of his word, "help," Khrushchev repeated it to a wondering Gromyko:

"Yes, help. We now have a common cause, to save the world from those pushing us toward war." [2]

In that grace-filled moment, Nikita Khrushchev, his new partner John Kennedy, and the world with them, went from darkness to dawn.

What especially moved Khrushchev to help Kennedy by withdrawing the Soviet missiles from Cuba was Ambassador Anatoly Dobrynin's description of his meeting with Robert Kennedy. The president's brother was exhausted. Dobrynin could see from Robert Kennedy's eyes that he hadn't slept for days. RFK told him the president "didn't know how to resolve the situation. The military is putting great pressure on him, insisting on military actions against Cuba and the President is in a very difficult position . . . Even if he doesn't want or desire a war, something irreversible could occur against his will. That is why the President is asking for help to solve this problem." [3]

In his memoirs, Khrushchev reported a further, chilling sentence from Robert Kennedy's appeal to Dobrynin: "If the situation continues much longer, the President is not sure that the military will not overthrow him and seize power." [4]

Sergei has described his father's thoughts when he read Dobrynin's report relaying the Kennedys' plea: "The president was calling for help: that was how father interpreted Robert Kennedy's talk with our ambassador. The tone of the conversation was evidence of the fact that to delay could be fatal. The temperature in the Washington boiler had apparently reached a dangerous point and was about to explode." [5]

Half a world apart, in radical ideological conflict, both Kennedy in his call for help and Khrushchev in his response had recognized their interdependence with each other and the world. They suddenly joined hands. After threatening to destroy the world, the two enemies turned to each other in desperation and grace. Instead of annihilation, they chose, in Khrushchev's words, "a common cause, to save the world from those pushing us toward war."

Khrushchev's decision to help Kennedy in the Missile Crisis was reciprocated by Kennedy's helping Khrushchev by the American University address, which led in turn to their signing the Nuclear Test Ban Treaty. Both men were ready for more cooperation. Neither wanted the Cold War to continue.

The deepening Kennedy–Khrushchev détente was the larger context of the unfolding plot to assassinate Kennedy. It had become clear to America's power brokers that the president of their national security state was struggling with his Communist opponent not so much over who would win the Cold War as on how to end it. From a national security standpoint, the president had become a traitor.

In the fall of 1963, Kennedy, like Khrushchev, had been given new eyes. JFK saw everything in relation to the threat of annihilation he and the Soviet premier had retreated from the previous fall and the hope of peace they had discovered. The Cold War was receding. The moment was ripe with hope. Now was the time to make politics obedient to that hope.

On September 20, 1963, two months and two days before his death, Kennedy spoke to the United Nations. He took the opportunity to return to a theme of his American University address—pursuing a strategy of peace through a step-by-step process.

"Peace," he said, "is a daily, a weekly, a monthly process, gradually changing opinions, slowly eroding old barriers, quietly building new structures. And however undramatic the pursuit of peace, that pursuit must go on." [6]

In the wake of the test-ban agreement, he identified the time as one of huge responsibility:

"Today we may have reached a pause in the cold war—but that is not a lasting peace. A test ban treaty is a milestone—but it is not the millennium. We have not been released from our obligations—we have been given an opportunity. And if we fail to make the most of this moment and this momentum—if we convert our new-found hopes and understandings into new walls and weapons of hostility—if this pause in the cold war merely leads to its renewal and not to its end—then the indictment of posterity will rightly point its finger at us all. But if we can stretch this pause into a period of cooperation—if both sides can now gain new confidence and experience in concrete collaborations for peace—if we can now be as bold and farsighted in the control of deadly weapons as we have been in their creation—then surely this first small step can be the start of a long and fruitful journey." [7]

Kennedy challenged the Soviet Union to join the United States in developing a new means of security:

"I would say to the leaders of the Soviet Union, and to their people, that if either of our countries is to be fully secure, we need a much better weapon than the H-bomb—a weapon better than ballistic missiles or nuclear submarines—and that better weapon is peaceful cooperation." [8]

As a concrete step in peaceful cooperation, he suggested a joint expedition to the moon, a project that could involve not only the U.S. and the U.S.S.R. "but the representatives of all our countries." [9] However, neither American nor Soviet military leaders, jealous of their rocket secrets, would look on his idea with enthusiasm. Kennedy was pushing the generals and scientists on both sides of the East–West struggle. He knew that merging their missile technologies in a peaceful project would help to defuse the Cold War. It was part of his day-by-day strategy of peace.

More broadly, he proposed that their rival nations transform the Cold War into its moral equivalent: "a desire not to 'bury' one's adversary, but to compete in a host of peaceful arenas, in ideas, in production, and ultimately in service to all mankind . . . And in the contest for a better life all the world can be a winner." [10]

In his American University address, Kennedy had appealed to Americans and Russians alike to recognize, for the sake of all, what they had in common: "if we cannot end now our differences, at least we can help make the world safe for diversity. For, in the final analysis, our most basic common link is that we all inhabit this small planet. We all breathe the same air. We all cherish our children's future. And we are all mortal." [11]

Now speaking to the representatives of all nations, he again envisioned the hope of a peaceful, transformed planet over against the threat of extermination:

"Never before has man had such capacity to control his own environment, to end thirst and hunger, to conquer poverty and disease, to banish illiteracy and massive human misery. We have the power to make this the best generation of mankind in the history of the world—or to make it the last." [12]

He concluded by suggesting that the members of the United Nations engage together in an experiment in peace:

"Two years ago I told this body that the United States had proposed, and was willing to sign, a limited test ban treaty. Today that treaty has been signed. It will not put an end to war. It will not remove basic conflicts. It will not secure freedom for all. But it can be a lever, and Archimedes, in explaining the principles of the lever, was said to have declared to his friends: 'Give me a place where I can stand—and I shall move the world.'

"My fellow inhabitants of this planet: Let us take our stand here in this Assembly of nations. And let us see if we, in our own time, can move the world to a just and lasting peace." [13]

When he said these words, John Kennedy was secretly initiating his own risky experiment in peace. That same day at the United Nations, Kennedy told UN ambassador Adlai Stevenson that his assistant, William Attwood, should go ahead "to make discreet contact" with Cuba's UN ambassador Carlos Lechuga. [14] Was Fidel Castro interested in a dialogue with John Kennedy? A strongly affirmative answer would come back from Castro, who had been urged by Khrushchev to begin trusting Kennedy. Although Kennedy specified that the CIA not be told of his Cuban initiative, Attwood later wrote, "the CIA must have had an inkling of what was happening from phone taps and surveillance of Lechuga." [15] Attwood also said, "There is no doubt in my mind. If there had been no assassination we probably would have moved into negotiations leading to a normalization of relations with Cuba." [16] In September 1963, eleven months after the Cuban Missile Crisis, JFK had turned in a new direction. He was now following up the test ban treaty with Nikita Khrushchev by reaching out to his other enemy, Fidel Castro, in spite of the obvious dangers involved.

Kennedy and Khrushchev, in almost choosing total darkness, had been moved to see the light. They had then reached an agreement whereby they could lead by example, in the presence of all nations, in seeking the moral equivalent of war—using the test ban as a lever to move the world to a just and lasting peace. Thanks to John Kennedy's and Nikita Khrushchev's mutual turning away from nuclear war, they now had the power to make peace. But with determined Cold Warriors surrounding them, neither man would long retain that power. Their time for making peace would soon pass.

On October 9, 1963, one week before Lee Harvey Oswald began his job at a site overlooking the president's future parade route, an FBI official in Washington, D.C., disconnected Oswald from a federal alarm system that was about to identify him as a threat to national security. The FBI man's name was Marvin Gheesling. He was a supervisor in the Soviet espionage section at FBI headquarters. [17] His timing was remarkable. As author John Newman remarked in an analysis of this phenomenon, Gheesling "turned off the alarm switch on Oswald literally an instant before it would have gone off." [18]

Four years earlier, in November 1959 shortly after Oswald told the U.S. Embassy in Moscow he would give military secrets to the Soviet Union, the FBI issued a FLASH on Oswald. A "Wanted Notice Card" was sent throughout the Bureau stating that anyone who received information or an inquiry on Oswald should notify the Espionage Section, Division 5.[19] By its FLASH the FBI had put a security watch on Oswald that covered all its offices. That watch was abolished on October 9, 1963, for no apparent reason, only hours before the FBI received critical information on Oswald. When Marvin Gheesling canceled Oswald's FLASH,[20] he effectively silenced the national security alarm that was just about to sound from an incoming CIA report on Oswald's (or an impostor's) activities in Mexico.

From the perspective of the plot to kill Kennedy, the cancellation of the FBI's FLASH came in the nick of time. Oswald was to play the indispensable role of scapegoat in the scenario, requiring that he be quietly manipulated right up through the assassination. Had the FBI alarm sounded, Oswald would have been placed on the Security Index, drawing critical law enforcement attention to him prior to Kennedy's visit to Dallas. That much pre-Dallas focus on the patsy would have made it impossible to play out the assassination scenario. The FBI watch on Oswald had to be revoked immediately. It was.

What would have sounded the alarm on Oswald was the CIA's October 10, 1963, message to the FBI about Oswald contacting the Soviet Embassy in Mexico City.[21] Because Oswald's security watch had just been lifted, the CIA's October 10 message managed to document his latest Soviet connection in a way that would become explosive *after* the assassination, while at the same time avoiding a security alert on Oswald *before* the assassination. It was a brilliant tactic in manipulating the FBI that demonstrated just how sophisticated the plotters' knowledge and control was of their national security bureaucracy. John Kennedy was killed by people who knew their national security state inside out and could direct it according to their will.

Even FBI director J. Edgar Hoover was subservient to this kind of power.

When Hoover learned after the assassination that supervisor Marvin Gheesling in the FBI's Soviet Espionage section had canceled the security watch on Oswald, he imposed censure and probation on Gheesling.[22] We have no evidence that Hoover himself had given any order to cancel the FLASH on Oswald. On the contrary, he seems to have been quite upset by Gheesling's action. He wrote angrily on the document censuring Gheesling: "Yes, send this guy to Siberia!"[23] ("Siberia" in Hoover's geography turned out to be the Detroit FBI office.)[24]

Hoover's comments suggest he was not a total master of his own house. A higher authority in the national security complex was bypassing him. We have already seen how Hoover scrawled another revealing comment on an FBI memo whose subject was that of keeping track of CIA operations in the United States. In that case Hoover was skeptical that the FBI could avoid being manipulated by the CIA. He wrote doubtfully: "O.K., but I hope you are not being taken in. I can't forget the CIA withholding the French espionage activities in the USA nor *the false story re Oswald's trip to Mexico*, only to mention two instances of *their double-dealing.*"[25]

By "false story," Hoover meant false to the FBI—not the CIA's staged duplicity to the public whereby Oswald posed as a pro-Castro activist, but rather the CIA's behind-the-scenes lies to its co-intelligence agency, the FBI, by a deeper cover story. What was the CIA story on Oswald's trip to Mexico that was false to the FBI?

An important clue has been provided by a Senate committee's 1976 investigation of U.S. intelligence agencies. The Church Committee discovered that on September 16, 1963, the CIA informed the FBI in a memorandum that the "Agency is giving some consideration to countering the activities of [the Fair Play for Cuba Committee] in foreign countries . . . CIA is also giving some thought to planting deceptive information which might embarrass the Committee in areas where it does have some support." [26]

The obvious "foreign country" for the CIA's planting of such "deceptive information" was Mexico, near New Orleans, where Lee Harvey Oswald had already just embarrassed the FPCC by his summer antics in its name. As we know, Oswald or someone acting in his name was just about to make his famous trip to Mexico. But as the FBI would learn, "Oswald's" trip would have a much deeper purpose than to counter and embarrass the Fair Play for Cuba Committee.

On the day after the CIA's deceptive advisory memo to the FBI, Oswald (or an impersonator) stood in line to get his tourist card from the Mexican Consulate in New Orleans. Immediately ahead of him was CIA agent William Gaudet, who had worked secretly for the Agency for more than twenty years. Gaudet then went to Mexico at the same time as Oswald. [27] Oswald, or his stand-in, was again being shepherded by the CIA. As we have seen, the CIA then proceeded to record "Oswald's" communications with the Cuban and Soviet consulates. The evident purpose was not so much to discredit the Fair Play for Cuba Committee (the CIA's false story to the FBI) as to identify Oswald with Cuba and the Soviet Union, in order to scapegoat all three together in the president's upcoming murder.

The FBI's Marvin Gheesling may then have canceled Oswald's FLASH because of the CIA's false advisory, or from a similar memorandum that has not been declassified. From the CIA story, Gheesling could easily have been misled into thinking Oswald was only working under cover in Mexico to counter the Fair Play for Cuba Committee. As a CIA operative, Oswald did not belong on the Security Index. Thus his security watch was lifted. His staged Soviet connection could then be documented for scapegoating purposes after Dallas, but without sounding a national security alarm that would have put a spotlight on Oswald and prevented Dallas from happening.

In spite of Hoover's recognition of the CIA's "double-dealing," the FBI went along with it by covering up the Oswald-Gaudet-CIA connection. Oswald's Mexican tourist card was No. 824085. The FBI claimed after the assassination that it could find no record of the holder of preceding card No. 824084. In 1975 the name that corresponded to 824084 was mistakenly declassified. It was the CIA's William Gaudet. [28]

Even within his own FBI domain, the notoriously autocratic J. Edgar Hoover gave way to a greater authority when it came to the forward progress of the plot to kill the president, as well as its cover-up afterwards. A more powerful agency was in control of key mechanisms throughout the entire U.S. government. Hoover told an associate, "People think I'm so powerful, but when it comes to the CIA, there's nothing I can do." [29]

In early August 1963, what has been recognized as the first organized protest against the Vietnam War took place.[30] In New York, Tom Cornell and Chris Kearns of the Catholic Worker vigiled by themselves for nine days in front of the Manhattan residence of South Vietnam's observer to the United Nations. Their signs read: "We Demand an End to U.S. Military Support of Diem's Government." On the tenth day, Cornell and Kearns were joined by 250 more demonstrators from the Catholic Worker and other peace groups. They were filmed by ABC News.[31] The antiwar movement had begun—three months after John Kennedy told Mike Mansfield he was preparing for a complete U.S. military withdrawal from Vietnam.

This is not to say that the president was ahead of the peace movement. He had merely told Mansfield that he intended to end the U.S. military involvement. Nevertheless, his first step in actually withdrawing troops was not far behind the first antiwar demonstration. It was only two months later, on October 11, 1963, that he signed his presidential order for an initial withdrawal of one thousand U.S. troops from Vietnam by the end of the year, anticipating in that same order a complete troop withdrawal by the end of 1965.[32]

But how does a president of the United States try to end a war, when virtually his entire Cold War bureaucracy wants to continue it? That was the problem John Kennedy was trying to work through in the fall of 1963, like a coach trying to guide a team that is determined to do the wrong thing on the playing field no matter what. Kennedy's team was only half-listening to him on war and peace, when they listened to him at all.

The president's increasing isolation from his bureaucracy was evident in the resistance and outright manipulation he was beginning to experience from even his inner circle. Even the more liberal members of that circle could not agree with the glimpses they were getting of his heretical thinking on Vietnam. As John Kenneth Galbraith recognized, John Kennedy was constantly thinking ahead of everyone on his staff. Nevertheless, those around him were catching on to the benumbing truth that their president, who kept his cards extremely close to the vest, *did* want to withdraw from Vietnam and *did not* want the Saigon coup that several of them had pushed and that he had reluctantly authorized. The coup they thought necessary before they could defeat the Communists on the battlefield was a step he feared would only make matters worse in a disastrous cause. To their dismay, it seemed that Kennedy thought the Southeast Asian battlefield they were warming up to with anti-communist gusto was already a complete loss.

Averell Harriman, for example, who had been the president's trusted test-ban negotiator in Moscow, was now doing everything he could with Hilsman and Forrestal (and the CIA's Helms behind the scenes) to push through with Lodge the Saigon coup they had manipulated Kennedy into supporting in the first place. They were soon joined by National Security Adviser McGeorge Bundy, who on September 11 supported a cable from Lodge calling for the overthrow of Diem.[33] At this point they all thought, with mutual affirmation, that they knew better than their chief what had to be done to win the war, beginning with a coup to remove Diem as soon as possible. They hoped the president, with their help, would come to his senses. None of Kennedy's advisers was considering the unthinkable option of a U.S. withdrawal, except McNamara behind closed doors with the president, and Robert Kennedy in questions he began to raise in key meetings. But the president not only thought the unthinkable. He chose it. He was now trying to bring his advisers around to it.

When Kennedy managed to escape the suffocating thinking of the circles around him in Washington, he confided bluntly in people he thought he could trust his decision to withdraw from Vietnam.

The previous May on a visit to Canada, he had asked Canadian prime minister Lester Pearson for his advice on Vietnam. Pearson said the United States should "get out." Pearson was struck by Kennedy's undiplomatic reply.

"That's a stupid answer. Everybody knows that," said JFK, ignoring all the anti-withdrawal sentiment in Washington. "The question is: How do we get out?"[34]

As we saw, he had already developed a withdrawal scenario with McNamara to begin gradually taking out troops that fall, finishing the process in 1965. How he would justify such a move politically, he didn't know yet. Pearson had been no help on a political strategy, saying only what Kennedy thought obvious.

After the president told Mike Mansfield his plan to pull out completely after the 1964 election, he made the same point with brutal honesty to his old friend, Washington correspondent and columnist Charles Bartlett. Kennedy said to Bartlett:

"We don't have a prayer of staying in Vietnam. We don't have a prayer of prevailing there. Those people hate us. They are going to throw our tails out of there at almost any point. But I can't give up a piece of territory like that to the Communists and then get the American people to reelect me."[35]

Pearson, Mansfield, and Bartlett were not the last to hear Kennedy's statements on withdrawing from a war he was convinced couldn't be won. Democratic House Leader Tip O'Neill was another.

After JFK's death, O'Neill liked to tell friends again and again the story of how the president had summoned him to the Oval Office "on an autumn day in 1963." There the two men "had talked about the situation in Congress, and the upcoming trip to Dallas, and how Kennedy had vowed that he was pulling the American troops out of Vietnam once the 1964 election was over." [36]

The president also aired his decision to withdraw from Vietnam with an old friend in Hyannis Port. On October 20, 1963, during his last visit to Hyannis Port, Kennedy said to his next-door neighbor, Larry Newman:

"This war in Vietnam—it's never off my mind, it haunts me day and night.

"The first thing I do when I'm re-elected, I'm going to get the Americans out of Vietnam."

He again acknowledged his puzzlement at a political strategy for what he had already decided to do: "Exactly how I'm going to do it, right now, I don't know, but that is my number one priority—get out of Southeast Asia. I should have listened to MacArthur. I should have listened to De Gaulle.

"We are not going to have men ground up in this fashion, this far away from home. I'm going to get those guys out because we're not going to find ourselves in a war it's impossible to win." [37]

He said the same thing to General David M. Shoup, commander of the Marines and the member of the Joint Chiefs of Staff whom Kennedy most trusted. Shoup strengthened Kennedy's conviction that Vietnam was a total trap. JFK had asked his Marine commandant "to look over the ground in Southeast Asia and counsel him." Shoup did so and advised the president that "unless we were prepared to use a million men in a major drive, we should pull out before the war expanded beyond control." [38]

On the morning of November 11, the president and General Shoup met at the White House and walked over together to the Tomb of the Unknown Soldier for a wreath-laying ceremony. Moved by their remembrance of the American war dead and further convinced by Shoup's dramatic one-million men assessment, Kennedy told the general that he was withdrawing U.S. forces from Vietnam. As General David Shoup's widow, Zola D. Shoup, told me in an interview, "Dave came home saying, 'I know Kennedy's getting out of Vietnam.' Then two weeks later, Dave was walking behind the body in Arlington." [39]

The day after Kennedy told Shoup of his withdrawal plans, Senator Wayne Morse came to the White House to see the president about his education bills. Kennedy wanted to talk instead about Vietnam—to his most vehement war critic. Morse had been making two to five speeches a week in the Senate against Kennedy on Vietnam. JFK took Morse out into the White House Rose Garden to avoid being overheard or bugged by the CIA. [40]

The president then startled Morse by saying: "Wayne, I want you to know you're absolutely right in your criticism of my Vietnam policy. Keep this in mind. I'm in the midst of an intensive study which substantiates your position on Vietnam. When I'm finished, I want you to give me half a day and come over and analyze it point by point."

Taken aback, Morse asked the president if he understood his objections.

Kennedy said, "If I don't understand your objections by now, I never will." [41]

JFK made sure Morse understood what he was saying. He added: "Wayne, I've decided to get out. Definitely!"[42]

Yet a mind needs hands to carry out its intentions. A president's hands are his staff and extended government bureaucracy. As Kennedy knew, when it came down to the nitty-gritty of carrying out his decision to end the Vietnam War, his administrative hands were resistant to doing what he wanted them to do, especially his Pentagon hands. He also knew that to withdraw from Vietnam "after I win the election" in the fall of 1964, he now had to inspire his aides to continue moving the machinery for withdrawal that he activated on October 11 with National Security Action Memorandum 263.

That was why, on the day before he left for Dallas, he took aside one of his reluctant aides on Vietnam, Michael Forrestal. Kennedy first gave Forrestal "odds of a hundred-to-one that the U.S. could not win" in Vietnam.[43] He then told Forrestal to prepare to do what Kennedy had said more frankly, in his conversation with Wayne Morse, he himself was already doing as a basis for his decision to withdraw from Vietnam:

"I want to start a complete and very profound review of how we got into this country, what we thought we were doing, and what we now think we can do. I even want to think about whether or not we should be there."[44]

Kennedy was trying to bring aboard not only Michael Forrestal but his entire reluctant government by a "complete and very profound review" designed for a Vietnam withdrawal. The president's mind had to coax his government hands gently and circumspectly to get them to function as he wished, in response to his new thinking on not only the U.S.S.R. and Cuba, but most urgently in his own mind, Vietnam.

Not the least of Kennedy's obstacles on Vietnam from September on continued to be the noncooperation of his coup-pushing ambassador, Henry Cabot Lodge. After Kennedy's and Rusk's persistent appeals, Lodge had finally met with Diem on September 9 to appeal to him to send his brother Nhu away and thereby lift the worst government repression. The meeting had gone poorly, and Lodge's patrician attitude toward Diem had not helped. The ambassador's report back to the State Department dismissed Diem for "his medieval view of life."[45] Following the failed meeting, Lodge reverted to his strategy of "chicken" with Washington's client ruler, refusing to communicate with Diem. Thus, the South Vietnamese ruler had to surrender to U.S. demands or he would be run over by the coup Lodge wanted and thought inevitable.

Kennedy urged a different course. On September 17, the president sent a personal telegram to his ambassador that, first of all, put a brake on the coup that Lodge and his Washington collaborators were trying to accelerate:

"We see no good opportunity for action to remove present government in immediate future. Therefore, as your most recent messages suggest, we must for the present apply such pressures as are available to secure whatever modest improvements on the scene may be possible. We think it likely that such improvements can make a difference, at least in the short run."[46]

Kennedy then appealed once again to his ambassador to act more like a diplomat than a coup leader, asking that Lodge engage in a serious dialogue with Diem:

"We note your reluctance to continue dialogue with Diem until you have more to say but we continue to believe that discussions with him are at a minimum an important source of intelligence and may conceivably be a means of exerting some persuasive effect even in his present state of mind . . . We ourselves can see much virtue in effort to reason even with an unreasonable man when he is on a collision course."

The president added on this critical matter that he was nevertheless not issuing a command: "We repeat, however, that this is a matter for your judgment." [47]

Kennedy was, in essence, appealing to Lodge's resistant mind in the same way he hoped Lodge would appeal to Diem's resistant mind. Without knowing Lodge's "chicken" game paradigm for his refusal to talk with Diem, Kennedy had discerned the problem and its solution: "We ourselves can see much virtue in effort to reason even with an unreasonable man when he is on a collision course"—an insight that applied just as much to Lodge as it did to Diem. Both were on a collision course, just as Lodge wished. But a strategy of dialogue (no matter what) that had worked well for Kennedy with his enemy Khrushchev got him nowhere with his own Saigon ambassador, nor as a consequence, with Diem.

In a personal reply to the president, Lodge immediately rejected his appeal for a dialogue with Diem, insisting instead on his own "policy of silence": "I have been observing a policy of silence which we have reason to believe is causing a certain amount of apprehension and may just be getting the family into the mood to make a few concessions." [48]

What most upset Lodge, however, in the president's telegram was that Kennedy had announced that he was about to send Defense Secretary Robert McNamara and General Maxwell Taylor, chairman of the Joint Chiefs of Staff, to Vietnam. The ambassador protested that Kennedy would thereby nullify Lodge's ploy of distancing himself from Diem.

"The effect of this [policy of silence toward Diem]," Lodge rebuked the president, "will obviously be lost if we make such a dramatic demonstration as that of having the Secretary of Defense and General Taylor come out here," given the diplomatic necessity of their then meeting with Diem. [49]

Kennedy's main State Department advisers on Vietnam, Averell Harriman and Roger Hilsman, and his White House aide, Michael Forrestal, were all just as dismayed as Lodge was by the president's decision to send McNamara and Taylor to Vietnam. When Harriman learned about it, he phoned Forrestal to say he and Hilsman thought the president's proposal was "a disaster" because it meant "sending two men opposed to our policy" of promoting a coup. Forrestal glumly agreed. [50]

But Kennedy had made his decision. The coup that his closest State Department advisers on Vietnam and his Saigon ambassador regarded as *their* policy, and that they had manipulated the president into endorsing, was not in fact *his* policy. Nor for that matter was *his* policy the troop escalation to full-scale U.S. intervention that his Joint Chiefs Chairman Maxwell Taylor had pushed from the beginning, and that his Defense Secretary, McNamara, had backed until Kennedy made clear his resistance to it. As would eventually become clear, in sending McNamara and Taylor to Vietnam under a mandate for withdrawal, Kennedy was steering a course that went between and beyond both the coup-makers on his left and the war-makers on his right, with the CIA's Richard Helms in both camps. They all had their own policies on Vietnam and regarded the president's as a disaster.

Kennedy responded by return cable to Lodge's objections to the McNamara-Taylor visit. He said McNamara and Taylor would definitely be coming, in order to carry out a critical mission he had given them. "My need for this visit is very great indeed," he said firmly.[51]

The McNamara-Taylor mission was designed by Kennedy to meet his "very great need indeed" of not only forestalling the coup that Henry Cabot Lodge, Richard Helms, and even the president's more liberal State Department advisers sought. It was also meant to lay the foundation for the beginning withdrawal of U.S. troops from Vietnam that fall, which only John Kennedy sought.

We have already seen how deeply entwined the CIA had become in the infrastructure of the South Vietnamese government. As former Saigon station chief William Colby said, by early 1962, "the station had contacts and influence throughout Vietnam, from the front and rear doors of the Palace, to the rural communities, among the civilian opponents of the regime and the commanders of all the key military units."[52] Through its front, the Agency for International Development (AID), the CIA had placed advisers in at least twenty of the government's forty-one provinces.[53] By the fall of 1963, when John Kennedy was trying to extricate the United States from the Vietnam War, the CIA had become heavily invested in continuing the war under its own control.

Even the Pentagon found itself in a supporting role to the CIA's covert rule over South Vietnam. The agency's dominance reached back to its installation of Diem as Saigon's ruler in 1954. By funding and advising the Saigon government's security forces, the CIA was the ultimate power behind the throne. The CIA also had operatives in key positions in the U.S. and South Vietnamese military.[54] In addition, it was advising tens of thousands of armed "Meo" (actually Hmong) tribal members. By its further infiltration of the South Vietnamese government, the CIA was virtually running the show in 1963—as Diem and his brother Nhu were aware and deeply resented. Their alternating dependence on and resistance to the CIA was the undercurrent to their sinking ship of state.

American journalists had begun to break the silence on the CIA's covert control of South Vietnam. *New York Times* columnist Arthur Krock commented on the CIA's growing notoriety in Saigon. Krock began his October 3, 1963, column by observing: "The Central Intelligence Agency is getting a very bad press in dispatches from Vietnam to American newspapers and in articles originating in Washington." [55]

Krock noted that the CIA in Vietnam was coming under fire "almost every day now in dispatches from reporters—in close touch with intra-Administration critics of the CIA—with excellent reputations for reliability." [56] His prime example was Richard Starnes of the Scripps-Howard newspapers, whose dispatch on the CIA the same day had shocked readers of the *Washington Daily News*. Starnes's provocative theme was how the CIA's "unrestrained thirst for power" in Vietnam had become a threat to its own government back in Washington. [57]

Ambassador Henry Cabot Lodge's response to the CIA's ominous seizure of power in Vietnam was to harness that power to his own ambition to overthrow Diem.

On September 13, 1963, Lodge sent a letter to Secretary of State Dean Rusk asking him to send longtime CIA operative Edward Lansdale to Saigon "at once to take charge, under my supervision, of all U.S. relationships with a change of government here." [58] Lodge wanted Lansdale's expertise in "changing governments" so as to facilitate, "under my supervision," the stalled coup. For Lansdale to be effective, Lodge wrote, he "must have a staff and I therefore ask that he be put in charge of the CAS ["Controlled American Source," meaning the CIA] station in the Embassy, relieving the present incumbent, Mr. John Richardson." [59]

Although CIA director McCone denied Lodge's request for Lansdale, Richardson, whom Lodge thought too close to Diem, was recalled to Washington, just as Lodge wished. The ambassador then became in effect his own CIA station chief in Saigon. He could now supervise directly Lucien Conein, the CIA's intermediary to the South Vietnamese generals plotting against Diem. [60]

Lodge's commitment to engineering a coup against Diem was no problem to the CIA's chief of covert operations, Richard Helms, who had the same goal. When Helms allied the CIA to the State Department circle pressuring Kennedy for a coup, he told Harriman, "It's about time we bit this bullet." [61] Helms could only welcome Lodge's and the State Department's enthusiasm for a coup as additional cover for company business. Whether knowingly or not, Henry Cabot Lodge, in his push to carry out a Saigon coup that was facilitated by the CIA, was helping to provide the impetus for a Washington coup as well.

Kennedy had continued to puzzle over the question: How could he begin withdrawing U.S. troops from Vietnam when practically his entire military command and circle of advisers wanted to expand the war?

The president knew his key ally in the Pentagon was his loyal civilian bureaucrat Secretary of Defense Robert McNamara. However, McNamara's power on his behalf was hedged in by the noncooperation of the top brass. McNamara had been stalled by his generals for a full year from getting the Vietnam withdrawal plan JFK wanted drawn up. When the Pacific Command did finally come up with a plan in May 1963, McNamara had to reject its time line as at least a year too slow.[62] After the Defense Secretary ordered an expedited plan, the Joint Chiefs balked again. They wrote McNamara on August 20 that "until the political and religious tensions now confronting the Government of Vietnam have eased," "no US units should be withdrawn from the Republic of Vietnam."[63] They now wanted any decision on a withdrawal put on hold until late October.[64]

Pushed by his recognition of the war's futility and its rising death toll, John Kennedy had waited long enough to begin withdrawing from Vietnam. Although pressured by the Pentagon for a bigger war and by the State Department for a CIA-aided coup, the president decided to authorize a troop withdrawal, while continuing to hold off a coup. He did so through his stratagem of the McNamara-Taylor mission to Vietnam.

When Robert McNamara and Maxwell Taylor returned from their trip to Vietnam on October 2, President Kennedy already knew the recommendations of the report they delivered to him. They had originally come from the president himself.

While McNamara and Taylor were gathering information in Vietnam, they cabled their data back to General Victor Krulak's Pentagon office. Krulak's editorial and stenographic team worked twenty-four hours a day to put together the fact-finding trip's report. As one of the report's authors, Colonel Fletcher Prouty, later revealed, Krulak went regularly to the White House to confer confidentially with John and Robert Kennedy.[65] There the president and his brother dictated to Krulak the recommendations of the "McNamara-Taylor Report." When the secretaries finished typing up the report in Krulak's office, it was then bound in a leather cover, flown to Hawaii, and placed in the hands of McNamara and Taylor on their way back from Vietnam. They read the report on their flight to Washington, and presented it to Kennedy at the White House on the morning of October 2.[66] JFK accepted its recommendations, most significantly one for the withdrawal of one thousand military personnel from Vietnam by the end of that year. That 1963 withdrawal, together with Kennedy's plan "to withdraw the bulk of U.S. personnel by the end of 1965," became official government policy on October 11, 1963, in the president's National Security Action Memorandum (NSAM) Number 263.[67]

However, the process wasn't easy. Kennedy convened a National Security Council (NSC) meeting the evening of October 2 to discuss the McNamara-Taylor Report. What ensued was, as McNamara said, "heated debate about our recommendation that the Defense Department announce plans to withdraw U.S. military forces by the end of 1965, starting with the withdrawal of 1,000 men by the end of the year . . . once discussion began, we battled over the recommendation."[68]

Not surprisingly, the majority of the NSC members were opposed to the withdrawal.[69] The president himself hesitated over the critical phrase "by the end of this year" as a preface to the sentence, "The U.S. program for training Vietnamese should have progressed to the point where 1,000 U.S. military personnel can be withdrawn." He wavered, saying, "If we are not able to take this action by the end of the year, we will be accused of being overoptimistic."[70]

McNamara argued in favor of the time commitment, saying, "It will meet the view of Senator Fulbright and others that we are bogged down forever in Vietnam. It reveals that we have a withdrawal plan."[71] Kennedy agreed, so long as the time limits were presented as a part of the report rather than his own predictions. He then bypassed the National Security Council majority and endorsed the report's withdrawal recommendations that had come from himself. He also agreed with McNamara that the withdrawal plan should be announced publicly after the meeting to "set it in concrete."[72] As McNamara was leaving the room to give the news of the withdrawal to White House reporters, Kennedy called out to him, "And tell them that means all of the helicopter pilots, too."[73]

Nine days later he signed NSAM 263, thus making official government policy the McNamara-Taylor recommendations for the withdrawal of "1,000 U.S. military personnel by the end of 1963" and "by the end of 1965 . . . the bulk of U.S. personnel."[74]

Nevertheless, Kennedy still hesitated as to how he was going to justify the withdrawal in political terms. Although CIA and military intelligence reports from Vietnam continued to be optimistic, the president had seen through to the truth, thanks especially to MacArthur, Galbraith, and Mansfield. As he told Charles Bartlett, "We don't have a prayer of staying in Vietnam. We don't have a prayer of prevailing there."[75]

While he knew the optimistic intelligence reports being used to justify the war were wrong, he now used the momentum of those same reports, like a judo expert, to justify a withdrawal.[76] Kennedy was no fool when presented with disinformation by his intelligence agencies. He had learned from the Bay of Pigs. He sensed the intelligence reports from Vietnam might suddenly turn sour, now that he had reversed their intention and was using them to justify a withdrawal. If they in turn became more realistic, threatening defeat, the president needed to turn them around again, using the basis of a new argument for escalation as a reason instead for withdrawal. Thus we can understand the tension between his agreement with McNamara, that it was good to set the withdrawal policy in concrete by a public announcement, and his repeated hesitation to do so, because the policy's political justification might have to change according to shifting reports from the battlefield.

In NSAM 263, he therefore "directed that no formal announcement be made of the implementation of plans to withdraw 1,000 U.S. military personnel by the end of 1963."[77] Yet as he agreed, the White House had already made an announcement on the withdrawal after the meeting on October

2, generating front-page headlines in the *New York Times* and the Armed Forces newspaper, *Pacific Stars and Stripes*.[78] Moreover, by signing NSAM 263, Kennedy had officially ordered the implementation of the withdrawal plans. But he sensed that the CIA and the military would now try to cut the political ground out from under his withdrawal plans by changing their reports from good to bad. Hence his continuing caution on saying what he had done, and why, as an election year approached.

He also needed to finesse his way around his publicly stated opposition to a withdrawal he had already been planning.

On September 2, he had been interviewed by television anchorman Walter Cronkite, who said, "Mr. President, the only hot war we've got running at the moment is of course the one in Vietnam, and we have our difficulties there quite obviously."

The first part of Kennedy's reply was consistent with his Vietnam policy from the beginning. He said: "I don't think that unless a greater effort is made by the government to win popular support that the war can be won out there. In the final analysis, it is their war. They are the ones who have to win it or lose it. We can help them, we can give them equipment, we can send our men out there as advisers, but they have to win it, the people of Vietnam, against the Communists."[79]

Here was Kennedy's basic assumption all along, that this was the non-Communist Vietnamese's war to win or to lose, not the United States'. "In the final analysis, it is their war." In October he would use that assumption consistently in the logic of NSAM 263 as the basis for a U.S. withdrawal.

He also said that the war could not be won without important changes being made by the Saigon government to win popular support. Neither Diem nor his authoritarian successors would allow those changes to be made. That political fact could also serve as a reason for withdrawal.

However, Kennedy did not tell Walter Cronkite what he would tell his Hyannis Port neighbor Larry Newman on October 20, nine days after signing NSAM 263 for his Vietnam withdrawal: "I'm going to get those guys out because we're not going to find ourselves in a war that it's impossible to win."

In fact on September 2, while repeating his constant theme that it was their war, not ours, Kennedy told Cronkite defensively that he was opposed to a withdrawal: "in the final analysis it is the people and the government itself who have to win or lose this struggle. All we can do is help, and we are making it very clear, but I don't agree with those who say we should withdraw. That would be a great mistake."[80]

He went on to distinguish himself from people whom he characterized in terms that, if the truth were known, applied, first of all, to himself: "I know people don't like Americans to be engaged in this kind of an effort. Forty-seven Americans have been killed in combat with the enemy, but this is a very important struggle even though it is far away."[81]

Kennedy was carrying in his conscience the number of Americans he thought had been killed in combat in Vietnam, forty-seven. (The actual number was about 170.) [82] It was those American war dead who were the moving force behind his decision to withdraw from an increasingly futile war.

Yet in his interview with Walter Cronkite, he tried to distance himself from people who "don't like Americans to be engaged in this kind of an effort." He knew he was among them. "This kind of an effort," he had come to realize, was an unwinnable war in Southeast Asia with mounting casualties. His claim that he didn't agree with a withdrawal, and that it would be a great mistake, was defensive and deceptive, if not an outright lie. Since the previous spring, he had been telling friends that he not only agreed with a withdrawal but was planning one. When he spoke with Cronkite, Kennedy knew he was headed in that contentious direction, but he was not prepared to admit it in advance on national television.

One week later, in an interview with two other television anchors, Chet Huntley and David Brinkley, he again denied the withdrawal policy he was plotting: "I think we should stay [in Vietnam]. We should use our influence in as effective a way as we can, but we should not withdraw." [83]

By making defensive public statements that contradicted his beliefs and his intentions, Kennedy was digging himself into a hole concerning the withdrawal he was about to authorize. Once he did make it official by his national security memorandum, his withdrawal order would then fall into a deeper darkness after his assassination—compromised in execution, covered up by the government, and obscured by the record of his own public denials. When NSAM 263 was finally declassified three decades later, skeptics could question its authenticity by citing JFK's public statements opposing a withdrawal, made only one month before he signed one into national security policy.

Even when he had implemented a withdrawal policy by NSAM 263, he still hesitated as to how to justify it politically during the final weeks of his life. He was wary lest the withdrawal order be taken, in the context of the Buddhist crisis, as only a form of pressure against Diem. He continued to assess the uncertain direction of battlefield reports, whether positive or negative. For short-range political reasons, he delayed identifying himself publicly—until it was too late to do so—with the historic order he had signed withdrawing U.S. soldiers from Vietnam.

Kennedy's mistaken judgment in appointing Lodge his ambassador began his downward path toward a Saigon coup. Once the president was manipulated by his advisers into approving the August 24 telegram, he never succeeded in reversing a policy that favored a coup, reinforced by an ambassador determined to have one. Lodge was methodical in pursuing his goal.

On September 14, Lodge invited his old friend, influential journalist Joseph Alsop, to dinner in Saigon. Lodge then became the unacknowledged source for Alsop's sensational column, "Very Ugly Stuff," which appeared in the September 18 *Washington Post* and other newspapers. [84] Alsop's thesis was that Ngo Dinh Nhu was being seriously tempted by North Vietnamese representatives "to open negotiations [for a ceasefire] behind the backs of the Americans," as Nhu himself put it in an interview with Alsop. Nhu was quick to add, "That was out of the question." [85] However, Alsop's column left the impression that a Saigon–Hanoi truce was a distinct possibility, on the condition that the Ngo brothers would first expel the United States from South Vietnam.

Alsop's column had a germ of truth in it, as revealed years later by Mieczyslaw Maneli, a Polish diplomat who served as an intermediary between the North and South governments. The contacts between Saigon and Hanoi were only tentative and indirect.[86] Nhu deliberately spread rumors about them in order to threaten the U.S. government. His tactic backfired when Alsop, at Lodge's encouragement, used the Nhu-inspired rumors to write "Very Ugly Stuff." As Lodge knew, Alsop's column was certain to build up the pressure in Washington for a coup against Diem and Nhu. In the context of the Cold War, it was indeed considered "very ugly stuff" that our anti-communist rulers, put in power by the United States, now seemed willing to become traitors to the cause.

The CIA knew the conspiring South Vietnamese generals were already being pushed toward a coup by their suspicions of a Saigon–Hanoi connection. General Tran Thien Khiem told the CIA in Saigon that "the Generals would under no condition go along with Nhu should he make any step toward the North or even toward neutralization a la Laos." [87] The generals and the CIA knew that "neutralization a la Laos" had been accomplished in Laos itself by President John F. Kennedy. The generals were reassuring their CIA allies that Nhu's moves, toward the kind of peace Kennedy had already made with the Communists in Laos, would prompt a coup in South Vietnam.

On September 19, Lodge sent a telegram to Kennedy rejecting once again the president's suggestion that the ambassador "resume dialogue" with Diem and Nhu[88] (a dialogue never really begun). Lodge told Kennedy that such a dialogue was hopeless: "Frankly, I see no opportunity at all for substantive changes." He continued to think his silence was better than dialogue: "There are signs that Diem-Nhu are somewhat bothered by my silence." [89]

By this time, Kennedy had realized that he could not rely on his newly appointed ambassador to carry out his wishes. Thus he chose to send McNamara and Taylor, two coup opponents, to Vietnam to assess the situation and meet with Diem. The McNamara-Taylor mission stalled the forward progress of Lodge's coup-making with the CIA and the generals. However, the president's purpose was being undermined at the same time by a letter sent surreptitiously to Lodge by Roger Hilsman, principal author of the August 24 telegram. Hilsman's letter of September 23 was delivered to Lodge in Saigon by a member of the McNamara-Taylor mission, Michael Forrestal, who was Kennedy's aide but Hilsman's ally.

Noting that he was "taking advantage of Mike Forrestal's safe hands" to deliver his letter, Hilsman wrote Lodge: "I have the feeling that more and more of the town is coming around to our view [for a coup against Diem] and that if you in Saigon and we in the [State] Department stick to our guns the rest will also come around. As Mike will tell you, a determined group here will back you all the way." [90]

Hilsman's secret message spurring on Lodge subverted Kennedy's purpose. The back-channel letter demonstrated just how isolated Kennedy had become. Even his aide for the Far East, Forrestal, and his point man on Vietnam, Hilsman, were encouraging Lodge behind the president's back to launch a coup against Diem.

Kennedy was losing control of his government. In early September, he discovered that another key decision related to a coup had been made without his knowledge.

A White House meeting with the president was discussing whether or not to cut off the Commodity Import Program that propped up South Vietnam's economy. It was a far-reaching decision. For the United States to withdraw the AID program could prompt a coup against Diem.

David Bell, head of AID, made a casual comment that stopped the discussion. He said, "There's no point in talking about cutting off commodity aid. I've already cut it off."

"You've done what?" said John Kennedy.

"Cut off commodity aid," said Bell.

"Who the hell told you to do that?" asked the president.

"No one," said Bell. "It's an automatic policy. We do it whenever we have differences with a client government."

Kennedy shook his head in dismay.

"My God, do you know what you've done?" said the president. [91]

He was staring at David Bell, but seeing a deeper reality. Kennedy knew Bell's agency, AID, functioned as a CIA front. AID administrator David Bell would not have carried out his "automatic" cutoff without CIA approval. "We do it whenever we have differences with a client government" could serve as a statement of CIA policy. By cutting South Vietnam's purse strings, the CIA was sending a message to its upstart client ruler, Diem, as well as to the plotting generals waiting in the wings for such a signal. Most of all, the message was meant for the man staring at David Bell in disbelief. He was being told who was in control. It was not the president.

By having AID cut off the Commodity Import Program, the CIA had made it almost impossible for Kennedy to avoid a coup in South Vietnam. The aid cutoff was a designated signal for a coup. In late August, the CIA had agreed with the plotting South Vietnamese generals that just such a cut in economic aid would be the U.S. government's green light to the generals for a coup.

The critical meeting is described in Ellen Hammer's book on the coup, *A Death in November*. On August 29 at a top-secret meeting in Vietnam approved by Lodge, the CIA's Lucien Conein had asked coup leader General Duong Van Minh point-blank, "What would you consider a sign that the American government does indeed intend to support you generals in a coup?"

Minh answered, "Let the United States suspend economic aid to the Diem government." [92]

It was twelve days later when David Bell told Kennedy at the White House that he had in fact already cut off commodity aid to Diem. The CIA had thereby sent a signal to the generals to prepare a coup. The aid cutoff was the official confirmation that the U.S. government supported the generals' plot.

The generals certainly understood it that way. "At least six of the generals who masterminded the revolt," journalist Marguerite Higgins wrote, "told me and others that the reduction in U.S. assistance was the decisive event that persuaded them to proceed with plans to overthrow the Diem regime." [93]

General Minh said, "The aid cuts erased all our doubts." [94]

General Tran Thien Khiem, the army chief of staff, said, "We looked on this U.S. decision on aid as a signal from Washington that the Vietnamese military had to choose between the Americans and Diem." [95]

Given the accomplished fact of the aid cutoff, Kennedy was left with the choice of either relieving that economic pressure on Diem, which would be taken as Kennedy's consent to Diem's repression of the Buddhists, or allowing the suspension of aid to take its gradual toll on the South Vietnamese economy and government—thus proceeding step by step toward a coup.

Through the McNamara-Taylor Report, Kennedy tried to find a way out of the coup box in which he'd been placed. He approved McNamara's and Taylor's recommendation of a middle way between an unconditional reconciliation with an unchanged Diem, on the one hand, and the active promotion of a coup, on the other. The theoretical middle way, endorsed by Kennedy, was to apply only selective pressures, with "the resumption of the full program of economic and military aid" to be "tied to the actions of the Diem government." [96] However, the more moderate policy the president was trying to choose had been largely superseded by the CIA's suspension of the Commodity Import Program, as a signal to the generals, and by Lodge's own active promotion of a coup.

JFK's slender hope was that the gradual impact of the aid cutoff, combined with a genuine effort at dialogue with Diem, could still persuade Diem to lift his repression of the Buddhists in time to avoid a coup. The moment even seemed ripe for a change in Diem, who surprised his critics by deciding to invite a United Nations fact-finding mission to South Vietnam to investigate the Buddhist crisis.

At an October 5 White House meeting, Kennedy emphasized the openness with which he wanted Ambassador Lodge to negotiate with Diem:

"We should not consider the political recommendations [to Diem] to be in the nature of a hard and fast list of demands, and that this point should be made more clear in the draft instructions [to Lodge]. The most likely and desirable result of any U.S. pressures would be to bring Diem to talk seriously to Lodge about the whole range of issues between us." [97]

Kennedy then directed Lodge in a cable the same day to "maintain sufficient flexibility to permit US to resume full support of Diem regime at any time US government deems it appropriate." [98] The president added the stipulation: "we do not now wish to prejudge question of balance or quantity of actions which may justify resumption of full cooperation with [the Government of Vietnam]." [99] Kennedy would make that judgment himself. He did not want Lodge to confront the South Vietnamese ruler with "a hard and fast list of demands," as the ambassador was prone to do.

Recognizing that Lodge was as much of a challenge as Diem, Kennedy conceded to his stubborn ambassador the unbudging position of silence he had staked out but expressed the hope Lodge would be ready to communicate with Diem when necessary:

"Your policy toward the [Government of Vietnam] of cool correctness in order to make Diem come to you is correct. You should continue it. However, we realize it may not work and that at some later time you may have to go to Diem to ensure he understands over-all US policy." [100]

Kennedy's instructions to Lodge, wired through Secretary of State Dean Rusk, recognized that Diem's brother and sister-in-law were the primary obstacles to reform in the South Vietnamese government. Any specific reforms were "apt to have little impact without dramatic symbolic move which convinces Vietnamese that reforms are real. As practical matter this can only be achieved by some feasible reduction in influence of Nhus, who are—justifiably or not—a symbol of authoritarianism."

Lodge responded to the president's instructions with objections. He wired back to Rusk that "'restriction on role of Nhus' seems unrealistic . . . we cannot remove the Nhus by nonviolent means against their will." [101]

The ambassador saw absolutely no hope of negotiating a resolution of the political crisis with Diem: "the only thing which the U.S. really wants—the removal of or restriction on the Nhus—is out of the question." [102]

However, there was in fact something more fundamental that most of the U.S. government, and Lodge in particular, wanted from Diem. Lodge devoted the bulk of his October 7 telegram to documenting the most basic reason why he thought Diem and his dominant brother had in any case to be removed from power. It was not the Buddhist crisis but something more worrisome: "Nhu says in effect that he can and would like to get along without the Americans. He only wants some helicopter units and some money. But he definitely does not want American military personnel who, he says, are absolutely incapable of fighting a guerrilla war." [103]

The bottom line for Lodge was that Diem and Nhu were dangerously close to doing what they had been threatening to do for months—asking the U.S. government to withdraw its forces from Vietnam.

Lodge concluded his rebuttal to Kennedy by making an ominous connection between a withdrawal request and a coup: "we should consider a request to withdraw as a growing possibility. The beginning of withdrawal might trigger off a coup." [104]

Lodge had Kennedy in a corner. At the very moment when Kennedy was quietly ordering the beginning of his own U.S. withdrawal from Vietnam, Lodge was warning him that the request for a withdrawal by Diem and Nhu could trigger a coup in Saigon that Lodge was facilitating.

Only five days before Lodge's telegram, *Washington Daily News* reporter Richard Starnes's alarming article on the CIA's "unrestrained thirst for power" in Vietnam had appeared. Starnes had cited a "very high American official" in Saigon who "likened the CIA's growth to a malignancy, and added he was not sure even the White House could control it any longer." [105] President Kennedy had read Starnes's article closely. He was so disturbed by it that he brought it up in the October 2 meeting of the National Security Council, asking the NSC members, "What should we say [in a public statement] about the news story attacking CIA which appeared in today's *Washington Daily News*?" [106] Kennedy decided to say nothing about the article,[107] but it had shaken him. Starnes had also cited an unnamed U.S. official who spoke of a possible CIA coup in Washington. The official had said prophetically, the month before John Kennedy's assassination, "If the United States ever experiences a *Seven Days in May* [the novel envisioning a military takeover of the U.S. government], it will come from the CIA, and not the Pentagon." [108] In the light of Lodge's telegram five days later, the president may have wondered if Starnes's unnamed U.S. official in Saigon who gave that warning was Henry Cabot Lodge.

Did Lodge's cable warning Kennedy that the beginning of a U.S. withdrawal might trigger a Saigon coup carry overtones of a Washington coup as well?

In his efforts to gain control of his own government on a Vietnam policy, Kennedy found himself in another struggle with the Central Intelligence Agency. When he was checkmated by a CIA front, AID, Kennedy was experiencing one effect of the way in which the CIA had established its invisible control over Vietnam. In that particular case, Kennedy could see what was going on. He knew AID was a CIA front.

However, there were other, less-visible CIA fronts. Richard Starnes had revealed further examples of the CIA's takeover in Vietnam in the article JFK had read. From the president's raising the article to the National Security Council, we know how seriously he took Starnes's following description of the CIA in Vietnam:

"CIA 'spooks' (a universal term for secret agents here) have penetrated every branch of the American community in Saigon, until non-spook Americans here almost seem to be suffering a CIA psychosis.

"An American field officer with a distinguished combat career speaks angrily about 'that man at headquarters in Saigon wearing a colonel's uniform.' He means the man is a CIA agent, and he can't understand what he is doing at U.S. military headquarters here, unless it is spying on other Americans . . .

"Few people other than [Saigon station chief John] Richardson and his close aides know the actual CIA strength here, but a widely used figure is 600. Many are clandestine agents known only to a few of their fellow spooks . . .

" 'There are spooks in the U.S. Information Service, in the U.S. Operations mission, in every aspect of American official and commercial life here,' one official—presumably a non-spook—said.

" 'They represent a tremendous power and total unaccountability to anyone,' he added." [109]

How had the CIA managed to place undercover agents in every branch of the American government in Saigon by the fall of 1963?

The answer opens a door to understanding the murder of John F. Kennedy, because the process whereby the CIA took over Vietnam was part of a broader problem JFK faced in Washington. While the president struggled to push his newly found politics of peace past the anti-communist priorities of the CIA, that creature from the depths of the Cold War kept sprouting new arms to stop him. As in Vietnam, the CIA had agents operating in other branches of the government. Those extended arms of the agency acted to forward its policies and frustrate Kennedy's, as in the case of AID's suspension of the Commodity Import Program, thereby setting up a coup. J. Edgar Hoover knew the CIA had infiltrated the FBI's decision making as well, making it possible for the CIA to cancel the FBI's FLASH on Oswald at a critical moment in October, setting up the assassination of Kennedy. How had the CIA's covert arms been grafted onto these other parts of the government?

One man in a position to watch the arms of the CIA proliferate was Colonel Fletcher Prouty. He ran the office that did the proliferating. In 1955, Air Force Headquarters ordered Colonel L. Fletcher Prouty, a career Army and Air Force officer since World War II, to set up a Pentagon office to provide military support for the clandestine operations of the CIA. Thus Prouty became director of the Pentagon's "Focal Point Office for the CIA." [110]

CIA Director Allen Dulles was its actual creator. In the fifties, Dulles needed military support for his covert campaigns to undermine opposing nations in the Cold War. Moreover, Dulles wanted subterranean secrecy and autonomy for his projects, even from the members of his own government. Prouty's job was to provide Pentagon support and deep cover for the CIA beneath the different branches of Washington's bureaucracy. Dulles dictated the method Prouty was to follow.

"I want a focal point," Dulles said. "I want an office that's cleared to do what we have to have done; an office that knows us very, very well and then an office that has access to a system in the Pentagon. But the system will not be aware of what initiated the request—they'll think it came from the Secretary of Defense. They won't realize it came from the Director of Central Intelligence." [111]

Dulles got Prouty to create a network of subordinate focal point offices in the armed services, then throughout the entire U.S. government. Each office that Prouty set up was put under a "cleared" CIA employee. That person took orders directly from the CIA but functioned under the cover of his particular office and branch of government. Such "breeding," Prouty said decades later in an interview, resulted in a web of covert CIA representatives "in the State Department, in the FAA, in the Customs Service, in the Treasury, in the FBI and all around through the government—up in the White House . . . Then we began to assign people there who, those agencies thought, were from the Defense Department. But they actually were people that we put there from the CIA." [112]

The consequence in the early 1960s, when Kennedy became president, was that the CIA had placed a secret team of its own employees through the entire U.S. government. It was accountable to no one except the CIA, headed by Allen Dulles. After Dulles was fired by Kennedy, the CIA's Deputy Director of Plans Richard Helms became this invisible government's immediate commander. No one except a tight inner circle of the CIA even knew of the existence of this top-secret intelligence network, much less the identity of its deep-cover bureaucrats. These CIA "focal points," as Dulles called them, constituted a powerful, unseen government within the government. Its Dulles-appointed members would act quickly, with total obedience, when called on by the CIA to assist its covert operations.

As the son of an ambassador to Britain and from his many years in the House and Senate, John Kennedy had come to understand the kind of power he would face as a changing president, trying to march to the beat of a different drummer. However, in his struggles with the CIA, Kennedy had no one to tell him just how extensive the agency's Cold War power had become beneath the surface of the U.S. government, including almost certainly members of his own White House staff. In his final months, JFK knew he was being blocked by an enemy within. However, he was surrounded by more representatives of that enemy than he could have known.

On October 24, coup plotter General Tran Van Don informed Lucien Conein that the Saigon coup was imminent. It would take place no later than November 2. [113] Conein and the CIA passed the word to Lodge, and Lodge to the State Department.

On the same day, the United Nations Fact-Finding Mission to South Vietnam was welcomed to Saigon by President Ngo Dinh Diem for its investigation into the Buddhist crisis. [114] The UN Mission would still be in Vietnam collecting information at the time of Diem's assassination the following week. [115]

Also on October 24, President Diem invited Ambassador Lodge to spend the day with him three days later. Apparently Diem wanted to talk. Lodge accepted the invitation.[116]

The State Department in a telegram encouraged Lodge in his upcoming dialogue with Diem: "Diem's invitation to you may mean that he has finally decided to come to you . . . As you know, we wish to miss no opportunity to test prospect of constructive changes by Diem."[117]

Lodge's October 27 talk with Diem turned into another confrontation. Lodge reported back to Dean Rusk what he had told the South Vietnamese president on behalf of the United States: "We do not wish to be put in the extremely embarrassing position of condoning totalitarian acts which are against our traditions and ideals."[118]

"Repeatedly," Lodge reported, "I asked him, 'What do you propose to do for us?' His reply several times was either a blank stare or change of subject or the statement: 'je ne vais pas servir' which makes no sense. He must have meant to say 'ceder' rather than 'servir', meaning: 'I will not give in.' He warned that the Vietnamese people were strange people and could do odd things if they were resentful."[119]

Lodge was fluent in French. Diem's repeated statement, "Je ne vais pas servir," "I will not serve," made no sense to Lodge not because he didn't understand the language but because he didn't understand Diem. From Diem's point of view, he was refusing in principle to *serve* American interests—what he thought the patrician American statesman, Henry Cabot Lodge, was ordering him to do. To Lodge's incessant question, "What do you propose to do for us?" Diem's very genuine response was: "I will not serve." He was not going to bow and scrape in front of the Americans.

Lodge was convinced that Diem was "simply unbelievably stubborn," as he told Rusk earlier in his report. Lodge was like a Southern landowner dismissing a nonconforming black sharecropper as "stubborn." So Lodge thought Diem must have meant to say, "I will not give in," rather than "I will not serve." Stubbornness, not principle, was what Lodge was prepared to deal with in terms of the "chicken" metaphor, or head-on crash scenario, that he was following in his strategy toward Diem. He thought the United States' client ruler was being "simply, unbelievably stubborn" in not backing down from "totalitarian acts which are against our traditions and ideals."

Yet Diem was in fact preparing to back away from just such acts, as shown by his government's surprising reception of the UN Fact-Finding Mission. Nevertheless, he refused to serve unconditionally the imperial interests of the government Lodge represented. He might even kick it out of Vietnam, as Lodge feared. Diem was refusing to be a Vietnamese servant obedient to Lodge's wishes. That is why he told Lodge that the Vietnamese people could do odd things if they were resentful (an attitude Diem had increasingly in common with Ho Chi Minh)—which Lodge again failed to understand. He thought Diem could only have meant all along that he would not give in, not that there was something deeper at stake.

Even in Lodge's own description of their conversation, it was Diem who spoke more to the point. Diem said bluntly, "The CIA is intriguing against the Government of Vietnam."

Lodge, who was directing the CIA's communications with the generals plotting against Diem, said in response (presumably with a straight face): "Give me proof of improper action by any employee of the U.S. Government and I will see that he leaves Vietnam." [120]

Lodge concluded, in his report to Rusk, that the conversation with Diem, taken by itself, "does not offer much hope that [his viewpoint] is going to change." [121]

Nor, more momentously, did the conversation offer much hope that Lodge was going to change his viewpoint on Diem. That would have required a radical change of heart for Lodge. For the coup he had striven to bring into being was now about to begin.

On Wednesday, October 30, the four generals who were plotting together, Minh, Don, Dinh, and Khiem, met secretly at a private club in Cholon, Saigon's Chinese quarter. The generals then made their final decision to go ahead with the coup against Diem that would begin two days later.[122]

Also on October 30, Ambassador Henry Cabot Lodge wired the State Department that, contrary to what President Kennedy was saying, Lodge did "not think we have the power to delay or discourage a coup. [General] Don has made it clear many times that this is a Vietnamese affair. It is theoretically possible for us to turn over the information which has been given to us in confidence to Diem and this would undoubtedly stop the coup and would make traitors out of us." [123] For Lodge to imagine his becoming "a traitor" only to the coup leaders, and not Diem, he apparently had become already in his mind an ambassador to the generals.

Lodge was explicitly rejecting Kennedy's statement at a White House meeting the day before: "We can discourage a coup in ways other than telling Diem of the rebel Generals' plans. What we say to the coup Generals can be crucial short of revealing their plans to Diem." [124] Bundy wired Kennedy's position to Lodge.[125] Kennedy was insisting on his prerogative to block a coup by intervening with the generals. Lodge, as the man who would have to do the intervening, was claiming it would be futile to try. Yet only two days before, Lodge reported that General Don had sought him out at the Saigon airport to get confirmation that the CIA's Lucien Conein "was authorized to speak for me [and the U.S. government]." [126] The nervous generals needed last-minute reassurance that the United States would not thwart them—as Kennedy was telling Lodge he still might do, in spite of Lodge's counterarguments that it couldn't be done.

The generals were also acutely aware that Kennedy had already committed himself to a total withdrawal from Vietnam by the end of 1965. They were even using JFK's withdrawal order as a reason for their coup. Lodge reported that General Don "stated flatly [at the airport] the only way to win before the Americans leave in 1965 was to change the present regime." [127]

On a more practical note, Lodge told the State Department: "As to requests from the Generals, they may well have need of funds at the last moment with which to buy off potential opposition. To the extent that these funds can be passed discreetly, I believe we should furnish them . . ." [128]

At the same time as the generals were confirming their plot in Saigon, the FBI was discovering a plot to assassinate President Kennedy in Chicago three days later—within hours of the time Diem would be assassinated.

On Wednesday, October 30, the agents at the Chicago Secret Service office were told of the Chicago plot by Special Agent in Charge Maurice Martineau. Abraham Bolden was one of the agents present. Bolden had left the White House detail voluntarily two years before in protest against the poor security being given the president. Bolden would now suffer for bearing witness to the Chicago plot against Kennedy.

I know former Secret Service agent Abraham Bolden. Between 1998 and 2004, I interviewed him on seven distinct visits to his South Side Chicago home. [129] I hope my brief narration can do justice to the story of Abraham Bolden—and of his wife, Barbara Louise Bolden, who at the age of seventy died at home from an asthma attack on December 27, 2005. [130] With the help of their faith, the love of their family and friends, and the writings of a few supportive researchers, Abraham and Barbara Bolden survived truthfully for decades the retaliation of a systemic evil that goes beyond the imagination of most Americans. [131]

Special Agent in Charge Martineau's startling announcement to his Chicago Secret Service agents about a plot against Kennedy came in the context of their preparations for the president's arrival at O'Hare Airport three days later on Saturday, November 2, at 11:40 A.M. [132] On Saturday afternoon, JFK was scheduled to attend the Army–Air Force football game at Soldier Field. At 9:00 A.M. Wednesday morning, Martineau told the agents the FBI had learned from an informant that four snipers planned to shoot Kennedy with high-powered rifles. Their ambush was set to happen along the route of the presidential motorcade, as it came in from O'Hare down the Northwest Expressway and into the Loop on Saturday morning. [133]

The FBI had said "the suspects were rightwing para-military fanatics." The assassination "would probably be attempted at one of the Northwest Expressway overpasses." They knew this from an informant named "Lee." [134] Who was the informant named "Lee"? Could it have been Lee Harvey Oswald? We will return to that question.

The following day, the landlady at a boarding house on the North Side independently provided further information. Four men were renting rooms from her. She had seen four rifles with telescopic sights in one of the men's rooms, together with a newspaper sketch of the president's route. She phoned the FBI. [135]

The FBI told Martineau everything was now up to the Secret Service. James Rowley, head of the Secret Service in Washington, confirmed to Martineau that J. Edgar Hoover had passed the buck. It was the Secret Service's jurisdiction. The FBI would do nothing to investigate or stop the plot against Kennedy.[136]

Martineau set up a twenty-four-hour surveillance of the men's boarding house. He passed out to his agents four photos of the men allegedly involved in the plot.[137] The stakeout reached a quick climax on Thursday night, October 31, at the same time as halfway around the world rebel tanks and troops were preparing to move through the streets of Saigon toward the presidential palace.

In Chicago, Secret Service agent J. Lloyd Stocks in his car spotted two of the suspects driving. Stocks followed them. When the men drove into an alley behind their rooming house, Stocks did, too. He discovered too late that the alley was a dead end. The men had turned their car around and were on their way back out. They squeezed past Stocks's car at an unfortunate moment for the agent—just as his car radio blared out a message from Martineau.[138] The startled men looked his way, then drove off quickly. Stocks reported back to Martineau with chagrin that he'd blown the surveillance.[139]

Martineau ordered that the two men be taken into custody immediately. They were seized and brought to the Secret Service headquarters early Friday morning. Through the early morning hours, J. Lloyd Stocks questioned one of the two men, while his fellow agent Robert Motto questioned the other. The two suspects, who have remained anonymous to this day, stonewalled the questions.[140] In the meantime, their two reported collaborators remained at large. President Kennedy was due to arrive the next day for his motorcade through the streets of Chicago.

In Saigon on Friday morning, November 1, Ambassador Lodge and Admiral Harry Felt, Commander in Chief of the Pacific, met with President Diem, as rebel troops were gathering outside the city. Lodge noticed that Diem spoke to them "with unusual directness." [141] Lodge did not reciprocate the directness.

Felt took note of a particular exchange between Diem and Lodge (that could be seen in retrospect as having happened three hours before the coup began):

Diem said, "I know there is going to be a coup, but I don't know who is going to do it."

Lodge not only knew there was going to be a coup but also who was going to do it. He reassured Diem by saying, "I don't think there is anything to worry about." [142]

When Felt had departed, Diem spoke with Lodge for another fifteen minutes. Diem had asked Lodge in advance to spend this time alone with him. After Lodge heard Diem once again make a series of charges against the United States, the ambassador got up to go. This was the last moment for

Diem to speak his mind. He knew that a coup was imminent (that he hoped to survive). He also knew Lodge was scheduled to leave that weekend on a trip to Washington to consult with President Kennedy. As Lodge stood up, Diem spoke up:

"Please tell President Kennedy that I am a good and a frank ally, that I would rather be frank and settle questions now than talk about them after we have lost everything."

In his report to the State Department, Lodge added here parenthetically, "This looked like a reference to a possible coup," then continued quoting Diem's parting words to him:

"Tell President Kennedy that I take all his suggestions very seriously and wish to carry them out but it is a question of timing." [143]

This was the response from Diem that Kennedy had been waiting for, and Lodge recognized it. In his comment on Diem's statement, Lodge cabled: "If U.S. wants to make a package deal, I would think we were in a position to do it. The conditions of my return [to Washington] could be propitious for it. In effect he said: Tell us what you want and we'll do it." [144]

A milestone had been reached. Diem had finally responded to Kennedy in a hopeful way through a reluctant ambassador, and Lodge had conveyed the message to Washington with a supportive comment.

However, Lodge buried Diem's message to Kennedy near the end of his report. Moreover, he did not send the report on his breakthrough conversation with Diem until 3:00 P.M., an hour and a half after the coup had started. He also chose to send this critical cable by the slowest possible process rather than "Critical Flash," which would have given it immediate attention in Washington. As a result of Lodge's slow writing and transmission of Diem's urgent message to Kennedy, it did not arrive at the State Department until hours after the rebel generals had laid siege to the presidential palace. [145] It was too late.

If President Kennedy had been assassinated in Chicago on November 2 rather than Dallas on November 22, Lee Harvey Oswald would probably be unknown to us today. Instead Thomas Arthur Vallee would have likely become notorious as the president's presumed assassin. For in the Chicago plot to kill Kennedy, Thomas Arthur Vallee was chosen for the same scapegoat role that Lee Harvey Oswald would play three weeks later in Dallas.

While most of the Chicago Secret Service agents were scrambling to locate and arrest all four members of the sniper team before the president's Saturday, November 2, arrival, two agents were acting on another threat. The Secret Service office had also received a tip that Thomas Arthur Vallee, an alienated ex-Marine, had threatened to kill Kennedy in Chicago.

Thomas Arthur Vallee was quickly identified from intelligence sources as an ex-Marine who was a "disaffiliated member of the John Birch Society," [146] a far right organization obsessed with Communist subversion in the United

States. Vallee was also described as a loner, a paranoid schizophrenic, and a gun collector. He fit perfectly the "lone nut" profile that would later be used to characterize ex-Marine Lee Harvey Oswald.

The two Secret Service agents surveilling Vallee broke into his rented North Side room in his absence. They found an M-1 rifle, a carbine rifle, and twenty-five hundred rounds of ammunition. The agents had seen enough. On Friday, November 1, they phoned Chicago Police Department captain Robert Linsky, requesting twenty-four-hour surveillance on Vallee and reportedly asking that he be "gotten off the street." [147]

Two experienced Chicago police officers, Daniel Groth and Peter Schurla, were assigned the task. After watching Vallee for hours, Groth and Schurla arrested him on Saturday, November 2, at 9:10 A.M., two and a half hours before JFK was due in at O'Hare Airport. They stopped Vallee's car at the corner of West Wilson and North Damen Avenues, as Vallee was turning south toward the president's motorcade route. The pretense for the arrest was an improper turn signal. When the police officers found a hunting knife lying on Vallee's front seat, they also charged him with carrying a concealed weapon. [148] More significantly, in Vallee's trunk they found three hundred rounds of ammunition. [149]

Groth and Schurla first took Vallee to Secret Service headquarters. There he was questioned by Special Agent in Charge Maurice Martineau behind closed doors in his office. The police then took Vallee to a Chicago jail. [150] They had succeeded in "getting him off the street" before JFK's visit to Chicago. But as they may have known already from intelligence sources, Vallee was no isolated threat but a pawn being moved in a much larger game.

A first clue to Thomas Arthur Vallee's connections with intelligence agencies was the New York license plate on the 1962 Ford Falcon he was driving: 31-10RF. [151] A few days after President Kennedy's assassination, NBC News in Chicago learned about Vallee's arrest on the same day President Kennedy had been scheduled to come to Chicago. Luke Christopher Hester, an NBC Chicago employee, asked his father-in-law, Hugh Larkin, a retired New York City police officer, to check on Vallee's license plate. Larkin asked his old friends in the New York Police Department if they would run a background check on it. They came back to Larkin saying the license plate information was "frozen," and that "only the FBI could obtain this information." [152] NBC News got no further. The registration for the license plate on the car Thomas Arthur Vallee was driving at the time of his arrest was classified—restricted to U.S. intelligence agencies.

The two Chicago police officers who arrested Vallee, Daniel Groth and Peter Schurla, were themselves destined for prominent roles in police intelligence activities. In 1975 when a reporter tried unsuccessfully to interview Peter Schurla about Vallee's arrest, Schurla was a high-level intelligence official at Chicago police headquarters. [153] His companion Daniel Groth's career in intelligence had by then become more public and more notorious than Schurla's.

At 4:30 A.M. on December 4, 1969, six years after the arrest of Thomas Arthur Vallee, Sergeant Daniel Groth commanded the police team that broke into the Chicago apartment of Black Panther leaders Fred Hampton and Mark Clark. The heavily armed officers shot both men to death.[154] In 1983 the Black Panther survivors of the raid and the families of Hampton and Clark were awarded $1.85 million in a lawsuit against federal, state, and Chicago officials and officers including Daniel Groth.[155] Groth acknowledged under oath that his team of officers had carried out the assault on Fred Hampton and Mark Clark at the specific request of the FBI.[156]

Northeastern Illinois University professor Dan Stern researched Daniel Groth's background. He discovered that Groth had taken several lengthy "training leaves" from the Chicago Police Department to Washington, D.C., where Stern and other researchers believed Groth "underwent specialized counterintelligence training under the auspices of both the FBI and the CIA."[157] According to Stern, "Groth *never* had a normal [Chicago] police assignment, but was deployed all along in a counterintelligence capacity," with an early focus on the Fair Play for Cuba Committee.[158] From his research Stern concluded that "the CIA and the Chicago police were very tight," and that while technically a member of the Chicago police, Daniel Groth probably worked under cover for the CIA.[159] When a journalist confronted Groth and asked him point-blank, "Are you CIA?" Groth just shrugged it off.[160]

If Vallee was arrested by police intelligence officers, one of whom probably worked for the CIA, what was the background of Thomas Arthur Vallee himself?

To learn more about Vallee's past, in late summer 2004 I talked with his sister, Mary Vallee-Portillo, a nurse in Chicago. She reminisced with me about her older brother, who had died sixteen years earlier. She referred to him fondly as "Tommy." Reflecting on his arrest as a potential assassin to President Kennedy, she said, "My brother probably was set up. He was very much used."[161]

Tommy Vallee had grown up as a middle child between his sisters, Margaret, two years older, and Mary, three years younger. Their French Canadian family lived in a German-Irish neighborhood in the northwest part of Chicago.[162] Mary's strongest memory of her brother was of his always wanting to be a Marine like his older cousin, Mike. "All he dreamt of," she said, "was being a Marine."[163] At the age of fifteen, Tommy realized his dream. He ran away from home, lied about his age, and joined the Marine Corps.

Thomas Arthur Vallee was wounded in the Korean War when a mortar shell exploded near him.[164] He suffered a concussion that would affect him the rest of his life. An FBI teletype on Vallee the week after Kennedy's assassination stated that the schizophrenic ex-Marine had a prior history of mental commitment, "allegedly has a metal plate in his scalp," and "received complete disability from the Veterans Administration."[165]

After Vallee was discharged from the Marines at the age of nineteen in November 1952, he used his money to buy a new car. A few days later, he got drunk in a neighborhood bar, then demolished the car in an accident.[166] He suffered another terrible head injury. He was in a coma for a couple of months. His father stayed by his bed. When Thomas finally regained consciousness, he had to go through a complete rehabilitation program, learning all over again how to walk, talk, and hold a knife and fork.[167]

Soon after he returned home, while he was regaining the basic skills of living, his father died of a heart attack. An uncle accused Thomas of killing his father, driving him to death by his errant behavior. Mary said her brother felt deeply guilty about his father's death. "After the accident," she said, "my brother was never the same again."[168]

In spite of his shaky health, Vallee reenlisted for a second term in the Marines in February 1955. It was another unsettling experience. His Marine Corps medical records noted his "extremely abnormal nervousness and periods of excitement in which he cannot talk to anyone. He is also said to be very hyper-active and does not get along well in the barracks . . ."[169] After giving Vallee an extensive psychiatric evaluation, the Marines honorably discharged him in September 1956 for a physical disability diagnosed as "Schizophrenic Reaction, Paranoid Type #3003, Moderate, Chronic."[170] His military records show further that a Naval Speed Letter to the Navy's Bureau of Medicine and Surgery on August 6, 1956, requested a bed for him in a Veterans Administration Hospital near Chicago for an indefinite length of time.[171]

Thomas Vallee had been led along a trail that Lee Oswald would follow after him. In his most revealing interview, Vallee told investigative reporter Edwin Black that he had been assigned by the Marines to a U-2 base in Japan, Camp Otsu.[172] Vallee thereby came under the control of the Central Intelligence Agency, which commanded the U-2, just as Oswald would come under the CIA's control as a radar operator at another CIA U-2 base in Japan.

Vallee also told Black that he later worked with the CIA at a camp near Levittown, Long Island, helping to train Cuban exiles to assassinate Fidel Castro.[173] Oswald participated in a CIA training camp with Cuban exiles by Lake Pontchartrain, near New Orleans.[174] Vallee's close CIA connections, like Oswald's, help to explain how he, too, came to be employed at a site over a presidential parade route. Thomas Arthur Vallee and Lee Harvey Oswald, two men under the CIA's thumb for years, were being set up, one after the other, as scapegoats in two prime sites for killing Kennedy.

In August 1963 as Oswald was preparing to move from New Orleans back to Dallas, Vallee moved from New York City back to Chicago.[175] Just as Oswald got a job in a warehouse right over Kennedy's future motorcade route in Dallas, so, too, did Vallee get a job in a warehouse right over Kennedy's future motorcade route in Chicago. Like Oswald in Dallas (before his summer in New Orleans), Vallee found employment as a printer. He was hired by IPP Litho-Plate, located at 625 West Jackson Boulevard in Chicago.

With the help of a friendly real estate agent, I have stood on the roof of the building in which Thomas Arthur Vallee worked in November 1963. The view from 625 West Jackson was strikingly similar to the view I had from the Texas School Book Depository, during a trip I made to Lee Harvey Oswald's workplace in Dallas.

When I visited 625 West Jackson Boulevard in the summer of 2001, the old eight-storied building had been remodeled for loft apartment dwellers. According to its Chicago building code inspectors' records, the building I was standing on dated back to at least 1913.[176] From its roof I could look down and over to where JFK's presidential limousine had been scheduled to make a slow turn up from the Northwest Expressway (today ironically the Kennedy Expressway) exit ramp onto West Jackson on November 2, 1963. It was analogous to the slow curve the limousine would make in Dallas in front of the Texas School Book Depository three weeks later. In the Chicago motorcade, after proceeding one more block, President Kennedy would have passed by Vallee's workplace, just as he would in fact pass by Oswald's workplace in Dallas three weeks later.

Vallee's location at IPP Litho-Plate actually gave him a nearer, clearer view of the November 2 Chicago motorcade than Oswald's so-called "sniper's nest" did of the November 22 Dallas motorcade. Oswald's job was on the sixth floor. Vallee's work site, three floors lower than Oswald's, put him in the culpable position of having an unimpeded shot at a president passing directly below him. At the same time, the unidentified snipers in the Chicago plot could have shot Kennedy from hidden vantage points and then escaped, leaving Vallee to take the blame.

Thomas Vallee had two people in particular to thank for his not becoming the scapegoat in a presidential assassination that almost occurred beneath his Chicago workplace. Lieutenant Berkeley Moyland, a member of the Chicago Police Department, was the first intervening angel who saved Vallee from suffering what would soon become Oswald's fate. Years after Moyland retired, with his health failing, he confided in his son the story of his salvific encounter with Thomas Arthur Vallee. Even then, he added cautiously, "You probably can't repeat it, but you ought to know it."[177] The U.S. Treasury Department, he said, had for some reason forbidden him to share the experience with anyone.[178] Yet the story seemed innocent enough.

In the fall of 1963, Lieutenant Moyland had the habit of eating at a cafeteria on Wilson Avenue in Chicago, where he knew the manager. One day in late October, the manager alerted the officer in plainclothes to a regular customer who had been making threatening remarks about President Kennedy, due to visit Chicago within the week. The manager told Moyland when the threatening customer usually came in. Moyland decided to wait for him at the appropriate time. When the manager indicated that this was the man, Moyland took his tray over to Thomas Vallee's table, sat down with him, and engaged him in conversation.[179]

Moyland sized up Vallee quickly as a damaged, imbalanced personality. He also realized Vallee probably had weapons in his possession, as would soon be confirmed.[180] He told the man firmly that nothing good could come from the remarks he was making about President Kennedy. His behavior could in fact lead to serious consequences, beginning with anyone like himself who talked and acted in such a way. As Berkeley Moyland described this confrontation later to his son, he said the man across the table listened to him soberly, especially when Moyland identified himself as a police officer.[181]

After leaving the cafeteria, Lieutenant Moyland phoned the Secret Service with a warning about Vallee.[182] He was told that the Secret Service would take care of the situation. As a result of Moyland's tip, Vallee was, as we have seen, investigated and placed under police surveillance. However, it was not Moyland but an FBI informant named "Lee" whose alert disrupted the more critical four-man rifle team that represented the real threat to Kennedy, and thus to potential patsy Vallee as well.

Berkeley Moyland was phoned back by an official in the Treasury Department (with jurisdiction over the Secret Service) who committed him to the absolute silence on the matter that he almost took to his grave. The Treasury Department official gave the police officer stringent orders. He said: "Don't write anything about it. Don't tell anybody about it. Just forget about it."[183] Nevertheless, in his final years, Moyland did finally tell the story to his son, who in turn shared it with me in an interview thirty years later.

Unlike the story of Dallas, Berkeley Moyland's forbidden story had a peaceful conclusion. Lieutenant Moyland and Thomas Vallee met one more time at the cafeteria, under more relaxed circumstances—"just to shoot the bull," Moyland said.[184]

Finally, the retired officer said, ending the story to his son, he received a message in the mail some time later that he believed came from Thomas Arthur Vallee. It was a greeting card that said "thank you." The card bore no signature. Yet Moyland felt certain it came from the disturbed but grateful man he had cautioned over breakfast and then turned in to the Secret Service.[185]

Thanks to the intervention of Berkeley Moyland and the unidentified "Lee," Thomas Arthur Vallee was spared the shame of being identified in the public's mind as President Kennedy's assassin. He was arrested on a pretext two and a half hours before Kennedy's scheduled arrival in Chicago. However, as the Chicago Secret Service knew, with only that much time to go before the president's plane was due to touch down at O'Hare Airport, they still had the responsibility of finding two of the four snipers who remained at large on the streets.

At 4:30 P.M. on Friday, November 1, as rebel military units were encircling the Gia Long Presidential Palace in Saigon, President Diem phoned Ambassador Lodge. When their conversation was over, Lodge reported it in a Flash Telegram to the State Department that was passed to the CIA, the White House, and the Secretary of Defense:

DIEM: "Some units have made a rebellion and I want to know: What is the attitude of the U.S.?"

LODGE: "I do not feel well enough informed to be able to tell you. I have heard the shooting, but am not acquainted with all the facts. [Lodge was in fact receiving Conein's regular reports from the coup command post at Joint General Staff headquarters.] Also it is 4:30 A.M. in Washington and the U.S. Government cannot possibly have a view." [As Lodge knew, CIA, State, White House, and Defense officials were very much awake at that hour in Washington reading his and Conein's reports on the coup they had facilitated.]

DIEM: "But you must have some general ideas. After all, I am a Chief of State. I have tried to do my duty. I want to do now what duty and good sense require. I believe in duty above all."

LODGE: "You have certainly done your duty. As I told you only this morning, I admire your courage and your great contributions to your country. No one can take away from you the credit for all you have done. Now I am worried about your physical safety. I have a report that those in charge of the current activity offer you and your brother safe conduct out of the country if you resign. Had you heard this?"

DIEM: "No. [Then after a pause, as Diem realized from Lodge's words that the U.S. ambassador was in close contact with coup leaders.] You have my telephone number."

LODGE: "Yes. If I can do anything for your physical safety, please call me."

DIEM: "I am trying to re-establish order." [186]

The rebel troops bombarded the presidential guard barracks and the Gia Long Palace through the night. At 3:30 Saturday morning, the generals ordered an assault to overwhelm Diem's loyalist guards.

CIA agent Lucien Conein was beside the generals at Joint General Staff headquarters. He continued to act as their adviser. They had alerted him a few hours before the coup. Conein had at the generals' request brought "all available money" to the coup headquarters from the CIA's operational funds, $42,000 worth of piastres—"for food for the rebel troops," as Conein said,[187] and perhaps, as Lodge had said, "to buy off potential opposition." [188] Conein also brought with him a special voice radio "to relay information about the coup to the [Saigon] station and other CIA officers cut into his net." [189] In addition, the generals had set up for him a direct telephone line to the U.S. Embassy. Conein was at the hub of a coup communications system extending from the generals' command post to CIA headquarters in Langley, Virginia, and to the Situation Room in the White House. The CIA's coup adviser, Lucien Conein, was totally wired to apply covert power from afar.[190] He and the generals knew the "advice" he was relaying to them from elsewhere could never be attributed to its ultimate sources.

Two of Conein's sources of recommendations to the generals were in the White House Situation Room. There in the early morning hours of November 1, while the president was sleeping upstairs, McGeorge Bundy and Roger Hilsman were poring over Conein's blow-by-blow account of the coup. Already looking ahead, they cabled the Saigon Embassy that if the coup should be successful, the generals should justify it publicly by saying that "Nhu was dickering with the Communists to betray the anti-Communist cause. High value of this argument should be emphasized to them at earliest opportunity." [191] The embassy relayed the message through Conein, then cabled back to Bundy and Hilsman, "Point has been made to the generals." [192]

Bundy's and Hilsman's recommendations, which the generals followed after the coup, put another obstacle in the way of Kennedy's withdrawal policy. That anyone might do in Vietnam what Kennedy had already done in Laos was being characterized by Kennedy's own advisers as a betrayal of the anti-communist cause, to be used as the reasonable public justification for a coup d'état in Saigon. Bundy and Hilsman were making it more difficult for Kennedy to negotiate a way out of Vietnam. Moreover, a similar case for "betrayal of the anti-Communist cause" could already be made against JFK to justify a Washington coup.

General Tran Van Don in his circumspect memoir of the Saigon coup reveals another, more urgent mandate that CIA operative Conein passed on to the generals. When General Don told Conein that he suspected the Ngo brothers might no longer be in the presidential palace, Conein said to him with irritation, "Diem and Nhu must be found at any cost." [193]

Diem and Nhu had escaped from the palace in the Friday night darkness, eluding the soldiers surrounding the grounds. They were then driven by an aide to Cholon, where a Chinese businessman gave them overnight refuge in his home. [194] It was from Cholon on Saturday morning that Ngo Dinh Diem made his last phone call to Henry Cabot Lodge. In his descriptions of the coup over the years, Lodge never mentioned his Saturday morning call from Diem. The two men's final exchange was revealed by Lodge's chief aide, Mike Dunn, in an interview in 1986, the year after Lodge's death. [195]

Diem had decided to take seriously the ambassador's parting words to him Friday afternoon: "If I can do anything for your physical safety, please call me." Diem did so Saturday morning.

"That morning," Mike Dunn said, "Diem asked [in his call] if there was something we could do. Lodge put the phone down and went to check on something. I held the line open . . . Lodge told Diem he would offer them asylum and do what he could for them. I wanted to go over—in fact, I asked Lodge if I could go over and take them out. I said, 'Because they are going to kill them.' Told him that right flat out." [196]

Dunn thought if Lodge had forced the issue by sending him over to bring Diem and Nhu out of Cholon, their lives would have been saved—as the man whom Lodge represented, President Kennedy, wanted to happen.

But Lodge said to Dunn, "We can't. We just can't get that involved." [197]

Lucien Conein has said in an interview of his own that Diem also made three final calls to the generals on Saturday, ultimately surrendering and "requesting only safe conduct to the airport and departure from Vietnam." [198] Conein said he then called the CIA station. The CIA told him "it would take twenty-four hours to get a plane with sufficient range to fly the brothers nonstop to a country of asylum." [199] The CIA had made no plans to evacuate Diem and Nhu to avoid their assassinations. Nor, according to the CIA, did the U.S. Air Force in Vietnam have a plane available then with sufficient range to fly Diem and Nhu to asylum, although a plane had apparently been standing by to fly Lodge to Washington. The Ngo brothers would have to remain in Saigon while the generals decided their fate. It did not take long for that to happen.

At 8:00 A.M. Saturday, Diem and Nhu left the house in Cholon to go to a nearby Catholic church. It was All Souls Day. Although the early morning Mass had ended, the brothers were able to receive communion from a priest shortly before a convoy of two armed jeeps and an armored personnel carrier pulled up in front of the church.

After learning the Ngos' location, General Minh had sent a team of five men to pick them up. Two of the men in the personnel carrier were Major Duong Hieu Nghia, a member of the Dai Viet party that was especially hostile to Diem,[200] and Minh's personal bodyguard, Captain Nguyen Van Nhung, described as a professional assassin who had killed forty people.[201]

Diem and Nhu were standing on the church steps. From what Lodge and the generals had told him on the phone, Diem thought he was being taken to the airport for a flight to another country. He asked if he could go by the palace to pick up some of his things. The officers said their orders were to take him at once to military headquarters.[202]

As Diem and Nhu were led to the armored personnel carrier, they expressed surprise that they wouldn't be riding in a car. According to a witness, "Nhu protested that it was unseemly for the president to travel in that fashion." [203] They were shown how to climb down the hatch into the semidarkness of the armored vehicle. Captain Nhung went down with them. He tied their hands behind their backs. Major Nghia remained over them in the turret with his submachine gun. The convoy took off.

When the vehicles arrived at 8:30 at Joint General Staff headquarters, the hatch of the personnel carrier was opened. Diem and Nhu were dead. Both men had been "shot in the nape of the neck," according to Lodge's report two days later.[204] Nhu had also been stabbed in the chest and shot many times in the back.[205] Years later, two of the officers in the convoy described the assassinations of Diem and Nhu: "Nghia shot point-blank at them with his submachine gun, while Captain Nhung . . . sprayed them with bullets before using a knife on them." [206]

On Saturday, November 2, at 9:35 A.M., President Kennedy held a meeting at the White House with his principal advisers on Vietnam. As the meeting began, the fate of Diem and Nhu was unknown. Michael Forrestal walked in with a telegram. He handed it to the president. It was from Lodge.

The message was that "Diem and Nhu were both dead, and the coup leaders were claiming their deaths to be suicide." [207] But Kennedy knew they must have been murdered. General Maxwell Taylor, who was sitting with the president at the cabinet table, has described JFK's reaction:

"Kennedy leaped to his feet and rushed from the room with a look of shock and dismay on his face which I had never seen before. He had always insisted that Diem must never suffer more than exile and had been led to believe or had persuaded himself that a change in government could be carried out without bloodshed." [208]

After he learned of Diem's and Nhu's deaths, Kennedy was "somber and shaken," according to Arthur Schlesinger, who "had not seen him so depressed since the Bay of Pigs." [209]

As in the Bay of Pigs, Kennedy accepted responsibility for the terrible consequences of decisions he had questioned, but not enough. In the case of the coup, he had submitted to the pressures for the August 24 telegram and the downward path that followed, while trying to persuade Lodge to negotiate with Diem, and Diem to change course in time. Both had refused to cooperate. He had sent Torby Macdonald to Saigon to appeal personally to Diem to save his life. Diem had again been unresponsive. When Diem did finally say in effect to Kennedy through Lodge on the morning of November 1, "Tell us what you want and we'll do it," [210] it was the eleventh hour before the coup. Lodge's delayed transmission of Diem's conciliatory message to Kennedy made certain that JFK would receive it too late.

Kennedy knew many, if not all, of the backstage maneuvers that kept him from reaching Diem in time, and Diem from reaching him. But he also knew he should never have agreed to the August 24 telegram in the first place. And he knew he could have thrown his whole weight against a coup from the beginning, as he had not. He had gone along with the push for a coup, while dragging his feet and seeking a way out of it. He accepted responsibility for consequences he had struggled to avoid, but in the end not enough—the deaths of Diem and Nhu.

But again, as in the Bay of Pigs, he blamed the CIA for manipulation, and in this case, assassination. In his anger at the CIA's behind-the-scenes role in the deaths of Diem and Nhu, he said to his friend Senator George Smathers, "I've got to do something about those bastards." He told Smathers that "they should be stripped of their exorbitant power." [211] He was echoing his statement after the Bay of Pigs that he wanted "to splinter the CIA in a thousand pieces and scatter it to the winds." [212]

Kennedy's anguish at Diem's death was foreshadowed by his response to the CIA-supported murder of another nationalist leader.

On January 17, 1961, three days before John Kennedy took office as president, Congo leader Patrice Lumumba was assassinated by the Belgian government with the complicity of the CIA. [213] As Madeleine Kalb, author of *The Congo Cables*, has observed, "much of the sense of urgency in the first few weeks of January [1961] which led to the death of Lumumba came . . .

from fear of the impending change in Washington" that would come with Kennedy's inauguration.[214] It was no accident that Lumumba was rushed to his execution three days before the U.S. presidency was turned over to a man whose most notorious foreign policy speech in the Senate had been a call for Algerian independence. Senator John Kennedy's July 1957 speech in support of the Algerian liberation movement created an international uproar, with more conservative critics (including even Adlai Stevenson) claiming he had gone too far in his support of African nationalism.[215]

In 1959, the year before Kennedy was elected president, he had said to the Senate: "Call it nationalism, call it anti-colonialism, call it what you will, Africa is going through a revolution . . . The word is out—and spreading like wildfire in nearly a thousand languages and dialects—that it is no longer necessary to remain forever poor or forever in bondage."[216] In Africa and Europe, Kennedy had become well known as a supporter of African nationalism. JFK even took his support of the African independence movement into his 1960 presidential campaign, saying then repeatedly, "we have lost ground in Africa because we have neglected and ignored the needs and aspirations of the African people."[217] It is noteworthy that in the index to his 1960 campaign speeches, there are 479 references to Africa.[218]

The CIA took seriously Kennedy's African nationalist sympathies. As his inauguration approached, the CIA's station chief in Leopoldville, Lawrence Devlin, spoke of "the need to take 'drastic steps' before it was too late."[219] CIA analyst Paul Sakwa pointed out in an interview that the decision to put Lumumba in the hands of his assassins was made by men "in the pay of and receiving constant counsel from the CIA station."[220] The CIA succeeded in having Lumumba killed in haste by Belgian collaborators three days before Kennedy took his oath of office.

Four weeks later, on February 13, 1961, JFK received a phone call with the delayed news of Lumumba's murder. Photographer Jacques Lowe took a remarkable picture of the president at that moment. Lowe's photo of Kennedy responding to the news of Lumumba's assassination is on the dust-jacket cover of Richard D. Mahoney's book *JFK: Ordeal in Africa*. It shows JFK horror-stricken. His eyes are shut. The fingers of his right hand are pressing into his forehead. His head is collapsing against the phone held to his ear.

Kennedy was not even president at the time of Lumumba's death. However, he recognized that if as president-elect he had spoken out publicly in support of Lumumba's life, he might have stopped his assassination. After Kennedy had won the November 1960 election, Lumumba under house arrest had smuggled out a telegram congratulating Kennedy and expressing his admiration for the president-elect's support for African independence.[221] JFK had then asked Averell Harriman, "Should we help Lumumba?" Harriman replied that he "was not sure we could help him even if we wanted to."[222]

In spite of his sympathy for Lumumba, Kennedy had not spoken out on the Congo leader's behalf in the weeks leading up to his assassination and Kennedy's inauguration. When JFK received the delayed news of Lumumba's murder a month later, he was anguished by his failure at not having helped him.

His response to the news of Diem's murder was even more pronounced. In the case of Diem, he held himself especially responsible because of his cooperation, albeit reluctant, with the coup. Had he thrown presidential caution to the winds and spoken up decisively, he might have saved Diem's life. A badly compromised Vietnamese leader, with whom he might once have negotiated a withdrawal from the war, was now dead. All of this entered into his disgust with the Vietnam War and the strength of his decision to withdraw from it.

At the last possible moment, at 10:15 A.M. on Saturday, November 2, White House Press Secretary Pierre Salinger announced that President Kennedy's trip to Chicago had been cancelled. The decision to call off his trip was made so late that the press plane had already taken off for Chicago. Salinger said to the media left behind: "The President is not going to the football game." Salinger said the Vietnam crisis would keep Kennedy in Washington.[223]

Chicago Secret Service agents knew that another reason for the last-second cancellation was the warning they had given the White House: Two snipers with high-powered rifles were thought to be waiting along the president's parade route. Three other potential assassins were already in custody or about to be arrested: the two suspected snipers being held at the Secret Service office, and Thomas Arthur Vallee, who was being followed by the Chicago Police.

The time at which Thomas Arthur Vallee was arrested, 9:10 A.M. Central Time (10:10 A.M. Eastern Time),[224] by Chicago Police intelligence officers Daniel Groth and Peter Schurla, is significant. Whereas the press announcement of the Chicago trip's cancellation was made at 10:15 A.M. Eastern (9:15 A.M. Central), even a quick decision to cancel the trip would have been made at least ten minutes before the public announcement—with government authorities therefore being aware of the trip's cancellation by about 10:00 A.M. Eastern (9:00 A.M. Central).

Why did the police officers who had been watching for hours overnight a potential presidential assassin wait until *after* the president had cancelled his trip before they arrested their suspect? The impression given is that the purpose of the two intelligence-connected officers may not have been to restrain Vallee but to shadow him until the president was actually shot. For the success of the assassination plot, the scapegoat Vallee had to remain free—and did remain free—so long as Kennedy was still coming to Chicago and could be shot there. If the officers' purpose was, as claimed, "to get Vallee off the street" and protect the president, why was Vallee's arrest put off until *after* government authorities knew President Kennedy was no longer coming to Chicago?

On the following Monday and Tuesday, Maurice Martineau collected the Chicago plot information from his Secret Service agents. Unlike in their work on other investigations, they were told to prepare no documents of their own. Following Martineau's orders, the Chicago agents dictated oral reports to the office's top secretary, Charlotte Klapkowski, then turned in their notebooks. Secret Service chief James J. Rowley had phoned Martineau from Washington, asking that the Chicago office use a special "COS" (Central Office Secret) file number for this case—a process whose effect, as Bolden explained later to House investigators, was to sequester the Chicago plot documents, making their subterranean existence deniable by the government.[225] In the Chicago office, only Martineau wrote and saw the official, top-secret report. He sent it immediately by special courier to Washington chief James J. Rowley.[226]

Abraham Bolden watched apprehensively the compartmentalized preparation of the super-secret Chicago report. Looking back after Dallas, he would wonder what became of this critical information that could have saved the president's life. In the meantime, he felt, as an already known objector to Kennedy's flawed Secret Service protection, that he had come under added suspicion for the forbidden knowledge he now had of the Chicago plot.

On November 17, Bolden was suddenly ordered to report to Washington, D.C. There the Internal Revenue Service offered him an undercover assignment for an investigation of congressional aides. He would, they said, be given a new identity, that of "David Baker." He was to turn in all his Secret Service identification. He was told that his old identity of Abraham Bolden would be erased, even to the point of the IRS destroying his birth records.

Bolden wondered why he had been singled out for such a special assignment. The IRS had its own black agents. Was he so brilliant that they had to recruit him from the Secret Service? He thought there was something suspicious about it all. He declined the offer.[227]

As I visited with Abraham Bolden one sunny morning in 2001 in his backyard in South Side Chicago, he straightened up from his gardening and said quietly that he thought he had been set up in mid-November 1963 to be killed.[228] As was the case for thousands of Latin American activists when they were about to be abducted and murdered, he was being positioned for his disappearance. Abe Bolden knew far too much in the days after the failed Chicago plot to kill Kennedy. Although Bolden managed to escape a Washington setup on November 17, when he returned to Chicago he was filled with apprehension. He felt something terrible was about to happen. He told both his wife and a secretary at the Secret Service office that he thought the president was going to be assassinated.[229]

On the following Friday afternoon, November 22, he went to a tavern in

Chicago to interview a man about a forged check. A television set suddenly flashed the news that Kennedy had been shot. Bolden's legs seemed to collapse. It had happened, just as he feared.[230]

When Bolden returned to his office, he raised the question with his fellow Secret Service agents about the obvious connections between the Chicago plot and the president's murder that afternoon in Dallas only three weeks later. Most of the agents agreed that they were connected.[231] However, Special Agent In Charge Martineau was quick to shut down any office discussion linking Chicago on November 2 and Dallas on November 22. He told his staff what to believe: Lee Harvey Oswald was a lone gunman. There was no connection with Chicago. Forget November 2 in Chicago.[232]

In January 1964, the Secret Service took the extraordinary step of ordering all its agents to turn in their identification booklets for replacements. Secret Service agents carried small, passport-size booklets holding their identification, known as "commission books." When the order came down requiring each agent to be re-photographed and provided with a newly engraved commission book, Bolden suspected that Secret Service credentials had been used as a cover device in the assassination of President Kennedy.[233] As we shall see, his suspicions would be confirmed.

Bolden continued to reflect on the president's poor security that he had witnessed on the White House detail. He also thought about the connections between Chicago and Dallas, wondering if that information shouldn't be shared with the Warren Commission. He bided his time, waiting for a chance to speak up on forbidden subjects. An opportunity presented itself the following spring.

On May 17, 1964, Bolden arrived in Washington, D.C., for a month-long training program at the Secret Service School. He took advantage of his first afternoon in Washington to try to contact the Warren Commission. His Secret Service superiors had anticipated his initiative. As Bolden became aware, his movements in Washington were being monitored. An accompanying Chicago agent was watching him closely. When he tried unsuccessfully on May 17 to phone Warren Commission counsel J. Lee Rankin, he realized the Chicago agent probably overheard him.[234]

On May 18, as Bolden was attending one of his first classes, the Secret Service ordered him to fly back to Chicago to take part, they said, in an investigation into a black counterfeiting ring. On his return to Chicago, Bolden was arrested by fellow agents. Maurice Martineau accused him of trying to sell Secret Service files to a counterfeiter. Bolden told him the accusation was ridiculous. He was taken before a district judge and charged with the crimes of soliciting money to commit fraud, obstructing justice, and conspiracy.[235]

In a trial on these charges held before District Judge J. S. Perry on July 11–12, 1964, the jury reached an impasse. Judge Perry said he would exercise a rare prerogative by advising the jurors how to rule on the evidence: "In my opinion, the evidence sustains a verdict of guilty on Counts 1, 2, and Count 3." [236] Undeterred by the judge's advice, the jury remained dead-locked. A mistrial was declared.[237]

In a second trial before Judge Perry on August 12, 1964, Abraham Bolden was convicted on all three counts. The prosecution's case featured testimony by indicted counterfeiter Joseph Spagnoli. In his own later trial for counterfeiting, held before the same Judge Perry, Spagnoli shocked the court by confessing on the witness stand that he had perjured himself when he testified against Bolden.[238] He said Prosecutor Richard Sikes had told him he should lie.[239]

In a series of appeals, Abraham Bolden's conviction was never over-turned, in spite of the documented evidence of Judge Perry's prejudice and Spagnoli's perjury. Bolden thought pressures from high within the system accounted for both the rigging of his case and the repeated denials of his appeal. He served three years and nine months in federal prisons.[240]

When he was imprisoned at Springfield Federal Penitentiary, Bolden had prearranged a discreet way to inform his wife and lawyer if he desperately needed help. He would send a letter with a sign only they would recognize, notifying them that the time had come to object strongly to something being done to him.[241]

That urgent time came soon. The prison authorities committed Bolden to a psychiatric unit. A prison official told him, "You won't know who you are any more when we get through with you." [242] He was given mind-numbing drugs. Fortunately other prisoners showed him how to fake swallowing the pills. As his situation worsened, Bolden sent the sign-marked letter to his lawyer, who alerted Barbara Bolden. She went immediately to the prison, where she objected strenuously to her husband's treatment.[243]

"She saved my life," Mr. Bolden said repeatedly in my visits with him and Mrs. Bolden, referring especially to her persistent intercession on his behalf while he was in the Springfield psychiatric unit.

In the years while Abraham Bolden was in prison, Barbara Bolden and their two sons and daughter had to endure a series of anonymously engineered attacks at their South Side Chicago home: an attempt to bomb the house; the burning down of their garage; a shot fired through one of their windows; the following of Mrs. Bolden; a brick tossed through the window of her car.[244]

In December 1967, Bolden was visited at Springfield Penitentiary by three men: his court-appointed attorney, Warren Commission critic Mark Lane, and an assistant to New Orleans District Attorney Jim Garrison, who by then had begun his investigation into the Kennedy assassination. After hearing Bolden's story, his visitors publicized widely his testimony to the parallels between the Chicago and Dallas plots. For thus speaking out to the public on the Kennedy assassination via his visitors, Bolden was placed in solitary confinement.[245]

In the almost four decades since his release from prison in the fall of 1969, Abraham Bolden has continued to speak out to researchers and writers on the Chicago plot against Kennedy, in spite of the chilling consequences he has already suffered. Since his retirement in 2001 as the quality control manager of an industrial firm, Bolden has written his autobiography, whose publication will occur at about the same time as this book's. I can testify personally to Abraham and the late Barbara Bolden's warmth, hospitality, and courageous willingness to speak the truth in the face of powerful efforts to deter them. Because they were witnesses to the unspeakable even before John Kennedy was killed, and because they maintained that witness into the next century, we are able to understand the meaning of the Chicago precedent to Dallas.

The Secret Service investigation of the Chicago plot to kill President Kennedy was initially a success story. By disrupting the Chicago plot, the Secret Service had fulfilled its responsibility to protect the president. The FBI's informant, "Lee," had somehow made the federal security system work in Chicago as it was supposed to work. "Lee" had whistled the key information on the plot far enough into the system for it to function in Chicago as it was meant to function, in spite of the plotters' control over major components of the system. It was as if the security alarm bells that the FBI's Marvin Gheesling had abruptly turned off—by canceling Oswald's security watch—suddenly rang. But they rang only for a short while, and only in one place, Chicago. Then they became deathly silent again, as the plot moved on to Dallas.

The Secret Service investigation that disrupted the Chicago plot to kill President Kennedy should have disrupted the Dallas plot as well. The central elements were the same in both places: a sniper team waiting in the shadows, complemented by a CIA-connected, "lone nut" patsy positioned in a building directly over the motorcade route. What the Secret Service discovered in Chicago should have made impossible what was then done copycat fashion in Dallas.

However, the plotters reasserted their control. This time they cut the wires of the president's security alarms. They placed a blanket over Chicago. They smothered the possible pre-assassination testimony of witnesses such as Abraham Bolden, whose whistleblowing, like that of "Lee," if heard, could have brought the president's security system to life again. The failed plot's total cover-up within the government's police agencies made possible its success the second time around.

Although the failed Chicago plot was hushed up, Thomas Arthur Vallee still became a minor scapegoat. He was the only person arrested in Chicago who was ever identified publicly. Vallee was scapegoated as a threat to the president a month after his arrest and twelve days after Kennedy's murder in Dallas. On December 3, 1963, an article appeared in the *Chicago American* on Vallee's November 2 arrest, "Cops Seize Gun-Toting Kennedy Foe." The unnamed detectives who disclosed Vallee's month-old arrest characterized him as "a gun-collecting malcontent who expressed violent anti-Kennedy views before the assassination of the late President."[246] A similar article on Vallee's arrest, drawing on unidentified federal agents, appeared in the *Chicago Daily News* on the same day.[247]

The anonymous police detectives and federal agents who informed the media after Dallas of Vallee's arrest in Chicago one month earlier never mentioned the Secret Service's detention and questioning of the two suspected snipers. After November 2, 1963, they and their two unapprehended comrades in arms vanished without a trace of their existence. The Dallas plot was then allowed to unfold smoothly, as if it had no Chicago paradigm. Higher orders ensured the necessary amnesia. A Treasury Department official ordered Chicago Police Lieutenant Berkeley Moyland to forget his encounter with Thomas Arthur Vallee. Secret Service Special Agent in Charge Maurice Martineau sent the top-secret report of the four-man sniper team to Washington headquarters, where it was made inaccessible. But even that subterranean existence of the Chicago report created a problem for the Secret Service three decades later. In January 1995, the Secret Service deliberately destroyed all its records of the Chicago plot to kill President Kennedy (with other key JFK security documents) when the Assassination Records Review Board requested access to them.[248]

Once the Chicago plot failed, the Dallas assassination was allowed to happen, unimpeded by the intelligence community's knowledge of its forerunner. After Dallas, Vallee alone was exposed in Chicago, as if the only precedent were that of another gun-toting malcontent like Lee Harvey Oswald. The real parallels between the two CIA-connected scapegoats, both set up with jobs directly over the president's motorcade, vanished along with the snipers behind them.

Just as Chicago was the model for Dallas, Saigon was the backdrop for Chicago. The virtual simultaneity of the successful Saigon plot to assassinate Ngo Dinh Diem and the unsuccessful Chicago plot to assassinate John F. Kennedy strongly suggests their having been coordinated in a single, comprehensive scenario. If Kennedy had been murdered in Chicago on the day after Diem's and Nhu's murders in Saigon, the juxtaposition of the events would have created the perfect formula to be spoon-fed to the public: "Kennedy murdered Diem, and got what he deserved."

The legend created for the Dallas scenario of the gun-toting malcontent Lee Harvey Oswald followed a similar pattern. From the claims made by a series of CIA officers to the authors of widely disseminated books and articles, John Kennedy has been convicted in his grave of having tried to kill Fidel Castro, whose supposedly deranged surrogate, Lee Harvey Oswald, then retaliated. As a successful Chicago plot would have done, the Dallas plot ended up blaming the victim: "Kennedy tried to murder Castro, and got what he deserved."

In the fall of 1963, as the president ordered a U.S. withdrawal from Vietnam, he was being eased out of control, by friends and foes alike, for the sake of an overriding vision of war. They all thought they knew better than he did what needed to be done to win the war in Vietnam, and elsewhere across the globe against an evil enemy. Kennedy's horror of the nuclear war he had skirted during the missile crisis, his concern for American troops in Vietnam, and his turn toward peace with Nikita Khrushchev and Fidel Castro, had, in his critics' eyes, made him soft on Communism.

For our covert action specialists in the shadows, accountable only to their own shadows, what Kennedy's apparent defeatism meant was clear. The absolute end of victory over the evil of Communism justified any means necessary, including the assassination of the president. The failed plot in Chicago had to be followed by a successful one in Dallas.

CHAPTER SIX

Washington and Dallas

A month and a half after the Cuban Missile Crisis, Nikita Khrushchev sent John Kennedy a private letter articulating a vision of peace they could realize together.

"We believe that you will be able to receive a mandate at the next election," Khrushchev wrote with satisfaction to the man who had been his enemy in the most dangerous confrontation in history. The Soviet leader told Kennedy hopefully, "You will be the U.S. President for six years, which would appeal to us. At our times, six years in world politics is a long period of time." Khrushchev believed that "during that period we could create good conditions for peaceful coexistence on earth and this would be highly appreciated by the peoples of our countries as well as by all other peoples."[1]

Khrushchev's son Sergei said the missile crisis had forced his father to see everything in a different light. The same was true of Kennedy. These two superpower leaders had almost incinerated millions, yet they had also turned in that spiritual darkness from fear to trust. Their year-long secret correspondence had laid the foundation. Then JFK's appeal for help in the crisis, Nikita's quick response, and their resulting agreement had forced them to trust each other. Sergei said, "Since he trusted the U.S. president, Father was ready for a long period of cooperation with John Kennedy."[2]

It was during that time of hope that a conversation took place at the Vatican between Pope John XXIII and Norman Cousins, two men who were helping to mediate the Kennedy–Khrushchev dialogue that promised so much. Pope John was dying of cancer. When he and Cousins talked in the pope's study in the spring of 1963, Pope John had just written his encyclical "Peace on Earth," whose theme of deepening trust across ideologies was then being incarnated in the Kennedy–Khrushchev relationship. As Cousins recalled their conversation ten years later, the dying pope kept repeating a single phrase that seemed to sum up his hopeful message of peace on earth:

"Nothing is impossible."[3]

With the help of Pope John, even Kennedy and Khrushchev had begun to believe that nothing was impossible. That was true of both good and evil. They had passed through the mutual threat of an inferno into a sense of interdependence. Through their acceptance of interdependence on the brink of nuclear war, peace had now become possible.

In the American University address, Kennedy appealed to the American people to recognize that, while the United States and the Soviet Union had differences, they were still, in the end, interdependent: "And if we cannot end now our differences, at least we can help make the world safe for diversity. For, in the final analysis, our most basic common link is that we all inhabit this small planet. We all breathe the same air. We all cherish our children's future. And we are all mortal."[4]

Because Kennedy and Khrushchev had recognized their interdependence, nothing was impossible. After Kennedy's peace speech, he and Khrushchev showed their determination to make peace by their remarkably quick signing of the nuclear test ban treaty—to the consternation of the president's military, CIA, and business peers. The powers that be were heavily invested in the Cold War and had an unyielding theology of war. They believed that an atheistic, Communist enemy had to be defeated. Theirs was the opposite of Pope John's vision that we all need to be redeemed from the evil of war itself by a process of dialogue, respect, and deepening mutual trust. The anticommunist czars of our national security state thought the only way to end the Cold War was to win it.

However, moved by the missile crisis, Kennedy and Khrushchev had turned from absolute ideologies. They had caught on to the process of peace. At least equally important was the fact that the people of both their countries had caught on. Ordinary citizens who had felt helpless during the Missile Crisis wanted more steps for peace. Khrushchev knew the Russian people were heartened by the American University address and the test ban treaty. Kennedy felt a significant shift toward peace among the American people, too, by the end of the summer of 1963.

When JFK went on a speaking tour of western states in September 1963, he discovered to his surprise that whenever he strayed from his theme of conservation to mention the test ban treaty, the crowds responded with ovations. He found that his beginning steps toward peace with Khrushchev had become popular in areas normally identified as bastions of the Cold War. When he spoke at the Mormon Tabernacle in Salt Lake City, usually considered the heart of conservatism, he was greeted by a five-minute standing ovation.[5] Intrigued White House correspondents suggested to Press Secretary Pierre Salinger that the president was suddenly tapping the public's newfound desire for peace. Salinger agreed. "We've found that peace is an issue," he said.[6] Kennedy realized from his trip west that he could make peace much more of an election issue than he had thought.

Moreover, he now had a secret political partner in Khrushchev, who had admitted in their correspondence that a second JFK term as president "would appeal to us." Not quite one of the six years Khrushchev said he hoped to work with Kennedy "for peaceful coexistence on earth" had passed. They had made good progress. Nothing was impossible in the five years remaining in Khrushchev's hoped-for time line for their joint peacemaking.

Following the president's successful grassroots organizing with Norman Cousins for Senate ratification of the test ban treaty, the hope for peace was becoming contagious. Kennedy realized from both Khrushchev's readiness to negotiate and the public's support of the test ban treaty that a peaceful resolution of the Cold War was in sight. Nothing was impossible.

To the power brokers of the system that Kennedy ostensibly presided over, his and Khrushchev's turn toward peace was, however, a profound threat. The president's growing connection with the electorate on peace only increased the threat, making JFK's reelection a foregone conclusion. As the Cold War elite knew, Kennedy was already preparing to withdraw from Vietnam. They feared he would soon be able to carry out a U.S. withdrawal from the war with public support, as one part of a wider peacemaking venture with Khrushchev (and perhaps even Castro).

For people of great power in the Cold War, everything seemed to be at stake. From the standpoint of their threatened power and what they had to do, they, too, thought that nothing was impossible.

Lee Harvey Oswald was being systematically set up for his scapegoat role in Dallas, just as Thomas Arthur Vallee had been set up as an alternative patsy in Chicago. Vallee escaped that fate when two whistleblowers, Chicago Police Lieutenant Berkeley Moyland and an FBI informant named "Lee," stopped the Chicago plot. Oswald was not so fortunate in Dallas. His incrimination by unseen hands continued. Oswald, or someone impersonating him, continued to engage in actions evidently designed to draw attention to himself, laying down a trail of evidence that could later be drawn upon to incriminate Lee Harvey Oswald as the president's assassin. However, the Warren Commission ended up ignoring or rejecting much of that evidence, because it indicated the work of intelligence agencies at least as much as it did the guilt of Oswald.

On Friday, November 1, at the same time as the Chicago plot was unraveling, a man bought ammunition for his rifle in a conspicuous way at Morgan's Gun Shop in Fort Worth, Texas. A witness, Dewey Bradford, later told the FBI that the man was "rude and impertinent." The man made an enduring impression on the gun shop's other customers, as he seems to have intended. He made a point of telling Bradford that he had been in the Marine Corps, a detail that fit Oswald's background. Dewey Bradford was in the shop with his wife and brother-in-law. When they later saw Oswald's picture in *Life* magazine, all three of them agreed that the rude "ex-Marine" who had so vocally bought the ammunition for his rifle was Lee Harvey Oswald.[7]

But was it in fact Oswald at the gun shop or instead an impersonator who bore a resemblance to him? Why did the "ex-Marine" seem to deliberately make a scene while buying his ammunition? The *Warren Report* ignored the incident, thereby avoiding the question of a plant.

In mid-afternoon the next day, a young man walked into the Downtown Lincoln-Mercury showroom near Dealey Plaza in Dallas. The young man told car salesman Albert Guy Bogard he was interested in buying a red Mercury Comet. He said his name was Lee Oswald. He told Bogard he didn't have any money then for a down payment, but as the salesman recounted the conversation later to the FBI, "he said he had some money coming in within two or three weeks and would pay cash for the car."[8] "Oswald" accepted Bogard's invitation to test drive a red Comet. He then gave the salesman a memorable ride, accelerating "at speeds up to 75 and 85 miles per hour" on a Stemmons Freeway route that coincided with the scheduled route of JFK's motorcade twenty days later.[9] Back in the showroom, the increasingly flamboyant young man became bitter when Bogard's fellow salesman, Eugene M. Wilson, tried to sell him the Comet on the spot but said he needed a credit rating. "Oswald" then said provocatively, "Maybe I'm going to have to go back to Russia to buy a car."[10]

The *Warren Report* dismissed the provocative behavior of the young man at Downtown Lincoln Mercury, saying he couldn't have been Oswald: Their descriptions didn't match, Oswald couldn't drive, and Oswald was apparently elsewhere that afternoon.[11] But the Warren Commission left unmentioned another possibility—that the "returnee from Russia" who "would soon have the cash" to buy a $3000 automobile was indeed not Lee Harvey Oswald but an imposter, planting fake evidence against the man whose name he was using as his own.

What was going on in the mind of John Kennedy during that time when the plot to kill him intensified? Did he have any intimation that, in Thomas Merton's phrase, he had been "marked out for assassination"?

Merton was a poet and a spiritual writer, not a political analyst. His premise for an assassination was not so much a political plot as it was a spiritual breakthrough, by President Kennedy, to "depth, humanity, and a certain totality of self forgetfulness and compassion, not just for individuals but for man as a whole: a deeper kind of dedication." From his Trappist monastery in Kentucky one year into JFK's presidency, Merton hoped and prayed in a letter to a friend that "maybe Kennedy will break through into that some day by miracle."[12]

Nine months after Merton wrote those words, Nikita Khrushchev, who was no more of a saint than John Kennedy, helped Kennedy "break through into that depth" at the height of the Cuban Missile Crisis "by miracle," just as Kennedy at the same critical time helped Khrushchev break through "by miracle." The form of the miracle, following Pope John's process, was communication, respect, and agreement between two political enemies at the height of the most dangerous conflict in history. The two men then turned together, at the risk of their lives and power, toward the "deeper kind of dedication" Merton described. It was a breakthrough for humanity that, according to Merton's inexorable spiritual logic, marked out Kennedy for assassination. With no knowledge of any plots, Thomas Merton had simply understood that if Kennedy were to experience the deep change that was necessary for humanity's survival, he himself might very well not survive: "such people are before long marked out for assassination." [13]

Set in that spiritual context, as this entire book is, the question of Kennedy's awareness is not whether he knew of any specific plot machinations, which was unlikely. It is rather whether he knew, in the words of another poet, what was blowing in the wind, namely, his own death. When the question is considered in terms of Kennedy's thinking about his own death, we can see he had been listening for a long time to an answer blowing in the wind.

JFK biographer Ralph Martin observed: "Kennedy talked a great deal about death, and about the assassination of Lincoln." [14] Kennedy's conscious model for struggling truthfully through conflict, and being ready to die as a consequence, was Abraham Lincoln. On the day when Kennedy and Khrushchev resolved the Missile Crisis, JFK told his brother, Robert, referring to the assassination of Lincoln, "This is the night I should go to the theater." [15]

Kennedy was preparing himself for the same end Lincoln met during his night at the theater. As we saw from presidential secretary Evelyn Lincoln's midnight discovery of the slip of paper JFK had written on, he had adopted Lincoln's prayer: "I know there is a God—and I see a storm coming. If he has a place for me, I believe that I am ready." [16]

Kennedy loved that prayer. He cited it at the annual presidential prayer breakfast on March 1, 1962,[17] and again in a speech in Frankfurt, Germany, on June 25, 1963.[18] More important, he made the prayer his own. Ever since his graceful journey on the currents of Ferguson Passage, Kennedy had known there was a God. In his deepening conflicts with the CIA and the military, he saw a storm coming. If God had a place for him, he believed that he, too, would be ready for the storm.

In his final months, the president spoke with friends about his own death with a freedom and frequency that shocked them. Some found it abnormal. Senator George Smathers said, "I don't know why it was, but death became kind of an obsession with Jack." [19] Yet if one understood the pressures for war and Kennedy's risks for peace, his awareness of his own death was realistic. He understood systemic power. He knew who his enemies were and what he was up against. He knew what he had to do, from his turn away from the Cold War in his American University address, to negotiating peace with Khrushchev and Castro and withdrawing U.S. troops from Vietnam. Conscious of the price of peace, he took the risk. Death did not surprise him.

For at least a decade, his favorite poem had been "Rendezvous," a celebration of death. "Rendezvous" was by Alan Seeger, an American poet killed in World War I. The poem was the author's affirmation of his own anticipated death. Before the United States entered the war, Alan Seeger, a recent Harvard graduate, volunteered for the French Foreign Legion. He was killed on July 4, 1916, while attacking a German position in northern France.[20]

The refrain of "Rendezvous," "I have a rendezvous with Death," articulated John Kennedy's deep sense of his own mortality. These words of an earlier Harvard graduate, who like Kennedy had volunteered for a war front, became part of JFK's lifelong meditation on death. Kennedy had experienced a continuous rendezvous with death in anticipation of his actual death: from the deaths of his *PT* boat crew members, from drifting in the dark waters of Ferguson Passage toward the open ocean, from the early deaths of his brother Joe and sister Kathleen, and from the recurring near-death experiences of his almost constant illnesses. The words of his American University address were heartfelt: "we are all mortal."

He recited "Rendezvous" to Jacqueline in 1953 their first night home in Hyannis after their honeymoon.[21] She memorized the poem, and recited it back to him over the years. In the fall of 1963, Jackie taught the words of the poem to their five-year-old daughter, Caroline. It was Caroline who then gave "Rendezvous" its most haunting rendition.

On the morning of October 5, 1963, President Kennedy was meeting with his National Security Council in the White House Rose Garden. Caroline suddenly appeared at her father's side. She said she wanted to tell him something. He tried to divert her attention while the meeting continued. Caroline persisted. The president smiled and turned his full attention to his daughter. He told her to go ahead. While the members of the National Security Council sat and watched, Caroline looked into her father's eyes and said:

> I have a rendezvous with Death
> At some disputed barricade,
> When Spring comes back with rustling shade
> And apple-blossoms fill the air—
> I have a rendezvous with Death
> When Spring brings back blue days and fair.
>
> It may be he shall take my hand
> And lead me into his dark land
> And close my eyes and quench my breath—
> It may be I shall pass him still.
> I have a rendezvous with Death
> On some scarred slope of battered hill,
> When Spring comes round again this year
> And the first meadow-flowers appear.
>
> God knows 'twere better to be deep
> Pillowed in silk and scented down,
> Where love throbs out in blissful sleep,

> Pulse nigh to pulse, and breath to breath,
> Where hushed awakenings are dear . . .
> But I've a rendezvous with Death
> At midnight in some flaming town,
> When Spring trips north again this year,
> And I to my pledged word am true,
> I shall not fail that rendezvous.[22]

After Caroline said the poem's final word, "rendezvous," Kennedy's national security advisers sat in stunned silence. One of them, describing the scene three decades later, said the bond between father and daughter was such that "it was as if there was 'an inner music' he was trying to teach her."[23]

John Kennedy had been listening to the music of death for years. He had no fear of it, indeed welcomed hearing that music so long as he could remain faithful to it. From repetition and reflection, "I have a rendezvous with Death," with its anticipated parallel to the end of his own journey, may have become his personal refrain, alongside Lincoln's prayer. Now hearing his own acceptance of death from the lips of his daughter, while surrounded by a National Security Council that opposed his breakthrough to peace, he may have once again deepened his pledge not to fail that rendezvous.

As he had written to himself during a midnight flight two years earlier, Kennedy knew there was a God and saw a storm coming. The storm he feared was nuclear war. If God had a place for him—a rendezvous with death—that might help avert that storm on humanity, he believed that he was ready.

The framing of Lee Harvey Oswald in advance of the assassination continued. From September through November, there were repeated sightings (reported after November 22) of a man who looked like Oswald taking target practice in Dallas with his rifle.

Once again, Oswald, or an imposter, was acting in such a way as to draw attention to himself. Warren Commission witness Malcolm H. Price, Jr., remembered a man who resembled Oswald asking Price's help in adjusting the scope on his rifle at the Sports Drome Rifle Range in Dallas. Price told the Warren Commission that "it was just about dusky dark" one night in late September when he turned on his car headlights on a target at the rifle range, so he could adjust the man's scope. After Price zeroed in the rifle, "Oswald" used it to fire three shots into a bull's eye on the target illuminated by the car's headlights.[24] Price said he saw the same man practicing with his rifle in mid-October at the Sports Drome, and again in November not long before the assassination.[25]

Witness Garland G. Slack remembered a man who looked like Oswald firing his rifle at the Sports Drome on November 10 and 17. Slack recalled him vividly because of the way the man provoked him. On November 17, after Slack put up his own target for shooting, the man turned his rifle and repeatedly fired into Slack's target, "burning up the ammunition." When Slack objected strenuously, the man gave him, Slack said, "a look that I never would forget."[26]

Oswald, or a double, was again making himself easy to remember in situations that in retrospect would suggest he was training for a killing.[27] On the face of it, this evidence of the presumed assassin's rifle practice strengthened the Warren Commission's case against him. However, the testimony pointing to an Oswald in training with his rifle carried its own disturbing question as to how Oswald managed to be in two places at the same time. As we have seen, the CIA had already placed Oswald in Mexico City at the end of September, in another choreographed scenario at least equally damaging to his profile. In the end, the "rifle practice Oswald" had to be subtracted from the official biography of Lee Harvey Oswald that the government composed for the *Warren Report*.

For, according to the *Warren Report*, on September 28, 1963, when Malcolm Price turned his headlights on the Sports Drome target and zeroed in the rifle of the man who looked like Oswald, "Oswald is known to have been in Mexico City." The *Report* went on to observe that "since a comparison of the events testified to by Price and Slack strongly suggests that they were describing the same man, there is reason to believe that Slack was also describing a man other than Oswald."[28]

The *Warren Report* had painted itself into a corner where it was faced by one too many Oswalds doing too many Oswald-like things to arouse people's suspicions, at exactly the same time. If Oswald was "known" to be in Mexico City suspiciously visiting the Russian and Cuban Embassies,[29] then who was the Oswald look-alike suspiciously getting his telescopic sight adjusted at the same time on a Dallas rifle range?

The *Warren Report* sought an escape route from its double-Oswald corner. To try to clarify things, it argued that when Garland Slack saw the same man resembling Oswald whom Malcolm Price had seen, this time firing his rifle at the Sports Drome on November 10, "there is persuasive evidence that on November 10, Oswald was at the Paine's home in Irving and did not leave to go to the rifle range."[30] So then it could not have really been Oswald at the Sports Drome. However, if Lee Harvey Oswald was actually with his wife and daughters at the Paine residence, then who was the Oswald look-alike who at the same time, twelve days before Kennedy's assassination, was again taking target practice at the Dallas rifle range?

It was one week later that the same Oswald look-alike made himself notorious at the Sports Drome by deliberately and repeatedly firing at another man's target, then staring the other man down when he objected. Who was this provocateur who looked like Lee Harvey Oswald? Why was he making himself so obvious, acting obnoxiously and "burning up the ammunition" at a Dallas rifle range just five days before the president's motorcade was due to pass beneath the workplace of the real Lee Harvey Oswald?

More important than the masquerader's own identity was the question of who was behind his provocative actions. Who were the Oswald look-alike's handlers? The Warren Commission never recognized that question. It simply dismissed the case of the man like Oswald who ostentatiously took rifle practice at a public range in Dallas for the two months leading up to the assassination. Although the "rifle practice Oswald" and the "Mexico City Oswald" taken in themselves each added to the government's circumstantial case against Lee Harvey Oswald, they overlapped in time, creating too many Oswalds. There were more Oswalds providing evidence against Lee Harvey Oswald than the *Warren Report* could use or even explain.[31]

As Lee Harvey Oswald was being set up as an individual scapegoat, so too was the Soviet Union, together with its less powerful ally, Cuba, being portrayed as the evil empire behind the president's murder. It was in fact all projection by the actual plotters, but a consciously contrived projection, artfully done for the American public. The brilliantly conceived Kennedy assassination scenario being played out, scene by deadly scene, was based on our Manichean Cold War theology. After a decade and a half of propaganda, the American public had absorbed a systematic demonizing of Communism. Atheistic Communist enemies armed with nuclear weapons were thought to constitute an absolute evil over against God and the democratic West. Against the backdrop of this dualistic theology, a beloved president seeking a just peace with the enemy could be murdered with impunity by the covert-action agencies of his national security state. U.S. intelligence agencies, coordinated by the CIA, carried out the president's murder through a propaganda scenario that projected the scheme's inherent evil onto our Cold War enemies. The Soviet Union, whose leader had become Kennedy's secret partner in peacemaking, was intended to be the biggest scapegoat of all.

On November 18, 1963, the Soviet Embassy in Washington received a crudely typed, badly spelled letter dated nine days earlier and signed by "Lee H. Oswald" of Dallas. The timing of the letter's arrival was no accident. Its contents made it a Cold War propaganda bomb whose trigger would be President Kennedy's assassination. Read in the context of Dallas four days later, the text of the letter seemed to implicate the Soviet Union in conspiring with Oswald to murder the U.S. president. Three paragraphs in particular laid the blame for the assassination at the door of the Russians.

The letter's first paragraph read:

"This is to inform you of recent events sincem [*sic*] my meetings with comrade Kostin in the Embassy of the Soviet Union, Mexico City, Mexico."[32]

"Comrade Kostin" was, as the *Warren Report* noted, "undoubtedly a reference to Kostikov"[33]—Valery Vladimirovich Kostikov, a KGB officer working under the cover of being a consul at the Soviet Embassy in Mexico City. As we have seen, Kostikov was no ordinary KGB agent. According to Clarence M. Kelley, FBI director from 1973 to 1978, Valery Vladimirovich Kostikov was "the officer-in-charge for Western Hemisphere terrorist activities—including and especially assassination."[34] He was, according to Kelley, "the most dangerous KGB terrorist assigned to this hemisphere!"[35]

Thus, on the Monday before the Friday when Kennedy would be assassinated, a letter from "Lee H. Oswald" of Dallas, delivered to the Soviet Embassy in Washington, began by mentioning Oswald's recent meetings at the Soviet Embassy in Mexico City with the U.S.S.R.'s director of assassinations in the Western Hemisphere. This was the same KGB undercover specialist in assassinations, Valery Kostikov, who had already been set up as Oswald's Russian handler in fraudulent "Oswald" phone calls and transcripts.[36] Now the same Oswald-damning connection was being asserted in a (phony) letter to the most important Soviet embassy in the world. This propaganda bomb was being sent into the embassy four days before Kennedy's motorcade would pass beneath Oswald's workplace (while secret snipers would wait elsewhere in Dealey Plaza, just as they had been primed to wait secretly for Kennedy in Chicago near Thomas Arthur Vallee's workplace). The fuse of the propaganda bomb in the Soviet Embassy in Washington stretched to Dallas. When Kennedy was murdered, the incriminating letter with its "Kostin"/Kostikov-Oswald connection could then be revealed to the American people. Lee Harvey Oswald, and his apparent sponsors, the Soviet Union and Cuba, could be scapegoated simultaneously in the assassination of the president. It was a scenario whose intended climax was not only the death of the president but also a victorious preemptive attack against the enemies with whom he was talking peace.

The letter's third paragraph read: "I had not planned to contact the Soviet embassy in Mexico so they were unprepared, had I been able to reach the Soviet embassy in Havana as planned, the embassy there would have had time *to complete our business*."[37]

Here the letter deepens the Soviet involvement in the plot and extends the complicity to Cuba. "Oswald's" original intention had been "to complete our business" at the Soviet Embassy in Cuba, which he says was more prepared to deal with him (prior to his return to Dallas for the plot's countdown). However, in lieu of his failure to obtain a Cuban visa, Oswald is saying he was forced to take up "our business" directly with Soviet assassinations manager Kostikov in Mexico City. As we have already seen, a melodramatic, CIA-monitored Oswald in Mexico City had tried to obtain an immediate Cuban visa. His letter arriving at the Soviet Embassy in Washington on November 18 now attempts to document the presumed assassin's frustrated objective in Mexico City in September—to travel then to the much safer environment of Communist-controlled Havana in order "to complete our business" with the Soviets.

The letter's fourth paragraph states:

"Of corse [*sic*] the Soviet embassy was not at fault, they were, as I say unprepared, the Cuban consulate was guilty of a gross breach of regulations, I am glad he has since been replced [*sic*]."

"Oswald" here displays his insider's awareness of Cuban diplomatic busi-

ness. The Cuban consul, Eusebio Azcue, had vigorously ejected provocateur Oswald (or an impostor) from the Cuban Embassy in Mexico City on
September 27. In his letter to the Russians, the offended Oswald expresses
his righteous indignation at "the Cuban consulate" for his "gross breach
of regulations." However, he is satisfied that Azcue is now no longer the
consul. Eusebio Azcue was in fact replaced as the Cuban consul in Mexico
City on November 18,[38] the same day on which the Oswald letter arrived
at the Soviet Embassy in Washington. Oswald, set up to be the scapegoat in
Dallas, is here telegraphing his accurate foreknowledge of the workings of
Cuba's Communist government—another strike against him.

As was true of all mail sent to the Soviet Embassy, the Oswald letter was
intercepted, opened, and copied by the FBI before its eventual delivery to
the embassy. FBI director J. Edgar Hoover described the secret process to
the new president, Lyndon Johnson, in a phone call at 10:01 A.M., Saturday, November 23. This was the same call in which, as we saw in chapter
2, Hoover presented Johnson with evidence from Mexico City of either a
Cuban-Soviet plot with Oswald to kill Kennedy or (more likely) the CIA's
impersonation of Oswald in its own plot. In the midst of his trying to deal
with those unpalatable alternatives, Johnson also heard Hoover say:

"We do have a copy of a letter which was written by Oswald to the Soviet
Embassy here in Washington inquiring as well as complaining about the
harassment of his wife and the questioning of his wife by the FBI. Now, of
course, that letter information, we process all mail that goes to the Soviet
embassy—it's a very secret operation. No mail is delivered to the Embassy
without being examined and opened by us, so that we know what they
receive." [39]

Hoover may have suspected already that the Oswald letter, like the
Mexico City story that it furthered, was a CIA fabrication with dangerous implications. In his conversation with Johnson, he soft-pedals the letter by characterizing it in terms of its less significant passages, in which
"Oswald" complains about the FBI's "questioning of his wife." [40] Hoover
leaves unmentioned the presumed assassin's "Kostin"/Kostikov connection
in Mexico City that on the face of it indicates a Soviet-Oswald conspiracy.

When Lee Harvey Oswald was arrested in Dallas and was fingered by
the U.S. media as the president's assassin, top-level Soviet officials realized
that the Oswald letter that had arrived at their Embassy on November 18
had probably been designed to set them up. The Soviets' response to the
predicament that they recognized right after Dallas was not revealed until
the end of the twentieth century, after the Soviet Union had fallen. It was the
highlight of long-secret Soviet documents on the JFK assassination that Russian president Boris Yeltsin unexpectedly gave to U.S. president Bill Clinton
at their meeting in Germany in June 1999.[41]

As revealed by those archival Soviet documents that Clinton received,
it was on Tuesday, November 26, 1963, the day after President John F.
Kennedy's funeral, that Soviet ambassador Anatoly Dobrynin sent a "Top

Secret/Highest Priority" telegram from Washington to Moscow. Its subject was the suspicious Oswald letter received by the Soviet Embassy four days before the assassination.

Dobrynin cabled Moscow:

"Please note Oswald's letter of November 9, the text of which was transmitted to Moscow over the line of nearby neighbors [for security reasons].

"*This letter was clearly a provocation*: it gives the impression we had close ties with Oswald and were using him for some purposes of our own. It was totally unlike any other letters the embassy had previously received from Oswald. Nor had he ever visited our embassy himself. The suspicion that the letter is a forgery is heightened by the fact that it was typed, whereas the other letters the embassy had received from Oswald before were handwritten.

"One gets the definite impression that the letter was concocted by those who, judging from everything, are involved in the President's assassination. It is possible that Oswald himself wrote the letter as it was dictated to him, in return for some promises, and then, as we know, he was simply bumped off after his usefulness had ended.

"The competent U.S. authorities are undoubtedly aware of this letter, since the embassy's correspondence is under constant surveillance. However, they are not making use of it for the time being. Nor are they asking the embassy for any information about Oswald himself; perhaps they are waiting for another moment." [42] (emphasis in Russian original)

"The competent U.S. authorities," beginning with Lyndon Johnson and J. Edgar Hoover, were indeed aware of the provocative letter that the Soviets, for their part, knew had passed under U.S. intelligence agencies' constant surveillance of their correspondence. As we know, Hoover brought the letter to Johnson's attention in the midst of LBJ's first morning as president. Dobrynin not only identified the letter as a clear provocation, forged by Kennedy's assassins (or perhaps dictated to Oswald "in return for some promises" before "he was simply bumped off"). The Soviet ambassador also discerned the momentary uncertainty in "the competent U.S. authorities" as to how to handle the dubious Mexico City evidence represented by the letter. Would the U.S. government, now under Lyndon Johnson's leadership, go along with scapegoating the Soviet Union for Kennedy's assassination, as the planners of the murder scenario had apparently arranged?

While the Soviet leaders pondered this question and their own response to having been set up, Johnson decided to reject the CIA-doctored Mexico City evidence of a Soviet plot. He was intensely aware of the pressures for war that the disclosure of a Communist plot to murder Kennedy would bring. Just how much Mexico City was on Johnson's mind his first full day as president is revealed in a memorandum that CIA director John McCone dictated two days later.[43] After Hoover's disturbing phone call at 10:01 A.M., the new president met at 12:30 P.M. with McCone specifically to be filled in further on "the information received from Mexico City." [44] Mexico City became Johnson's jumping off point for the Warren Commission. Johnson cited the Mexico City information as the basis for his fear of nuclear war and his need for a Special Commission to both Supreme Court Chief Justice Earl Warren and newly appointed Warren Commission member, Senator Richard Russell.[45] He told Russell: "And we've got to take this [question of Kennedy's assassination] out of the [Mexico City] arena where they're testifying that Khrushchev and Castro did this and did that and kicking us into a war that can kill forty million Americans in an hour."[46]

The Warren Commission would ensure a lone-assassin cover-up of the conspiracy evidence the new president was facing. That would free Johnson from his dilemma arising from the Mexico City evidence of having to confront either the Soviet Union as the assassination's biggest scapegoat or the CIA as its actual perpetrator. To Johnson's credit, he refused to let the Soviets take the blame for Kennedy's murder; to his discredit, he decided not to confront the CIA over what it had done in Mexico City. Thus, while the secondary purpose of the assassination plot was stymied, its primary purpose was achieved. The presidency was returned to the control of Cold War interests, priorities, and profits. Not only was JFK dead, but so was his breakthrough with Khrushchev. In allowing the assassination to go unchallenged, Kennedy's successor in the White House consented to the total cover-up of both JFK's murder and his turn toward peace with the Communists.

Ambassador Dobrynin recommended in his November 26 telegram to Moscow that the Soviet government pass on to U.S. authorities Oswald's last letter, "because if we don't pass it on, the organizers of this entire provocation could use this fact to try casting suspicion on us."[47]

Anastas I. Mikoyan, first deputy chairman of the Soviet council of ministers, wired back his agreement with Dobrynin:

"You may send [U.S. Secretary of State Dean] Rusk photocopies of the correspondence between the embassy and Oswald, including his letter of November 9, but without waiting for a request by the U.S. authorities. When sending the photocopies, say that the letter of November 9 was not received by the embassy until November 18; obviously it had been held up somewhere. The embassy had suspicions about this letter the moment it arrived; either it was a forgery or was sent as a deliberate provocation. The embassy left Oswald's letter unanswered."[48]

By turning over the "Oswald letter" to the United States, the Soviets overturned its potential propaganda damage. The Soviet leaders served notice they would not be intimidated. The letter was an obvious counterfeit that pointed a finger in the opposite direction from the letter's recipients. Langley had more to fear from its public disclosure than did Moscow.

The U.S. government had already recognized that unfortunate fact. Once Johnson and his government in tow had decided to reject the Mexico City evidence as too explosive, the Warren Commission was given a contradictory mandate. What Johnson told Russell he wanted the Special Commission to do was to "look at the facts and bring in any other facts you want in here and determine who killed the president."[49] However, as he emphasized to Russell, Johnson wanted even more to take the question of Kennedy's assassination "out of the [Mexico City] arena," where the evidence apparently implicated the Soviet Union in the foreground but in reality the CIA in the background. The Warren Commission's impossible task, "for the sake of national security" (meaning the protection of U.S. intelligence agencies from national disgrace and their leaders from criminal indictments), was to make a convincing, heavily documented case for a lone-assassin conclusion. To do so, the commission would have to cover up especially the critical Mexico City evidence that had so alarmed Lyndon Johnson in his first hours as president.

The CIA-planted "Oswald letter" dated November 9, that the Soviet Embassy received on November 18 and recognized as a fraud, had backfired. The Soviet ambassador's formal diplomatic return of the letter to the U.S. government made the document a part of the official record. If the Soviet leaders chose to do so, they could make that diplomatic process, and the letter itself, public. The U.S. government was in a bind. The (more and more obviously) phony letter had to be covered up or explained away. The American public it was originally designed to fool might be led instead to the real assassins. How could that cover-up, or cover explanation of a CIA-planted letter, be accomplished?

The Warren Commission's star witness against Lee Harvey Oswald, other than his widow, Marina, was Ruth Paine. As we saw, it was Ruth and Michael Paine who became the Oswalds' benefactors after George de Mohrenschildt left Dallas. It was Ruth Paine who arranged for Oswald's job at the Texas School Book Depository in October 1963. And it was Ruth Paine whose Warren Commission testimony also put a different spin on the Oswald letter that was threatening to uncover the CIA in the president's assassination.

In March 1964, four months after the Soviet Embassy turned over the letter to the United States, identifying it as a forgery or a deliberate provocation, Ruth Paine testified that on Saturday, November 9, 1963, she had seen Oswald type the letter in her home on her typewriter. Besides giving an eyewitness account of Oswald actually writing the letter, her testimony placed on record a different version of the letter from the one the Soviets had received. The new, U.S.-government-preferred version of the letter came, in Paine's testimony, in the form of a rough draft that she said Oswald left accidentally on her secretary desk.

Paine testified that, although "my tendency is to be very hesitant to look into other people's things,"[50] she secretly read Oswald's folded, handwritten draft of the letter left on her desk, while he was out of the room on the morning after he typed the final version. She copied the rough draft by hand while he was taking a shower. She said that, while "I am not used to subter-fuge in any way," [51] she subsequently took his draft of the letter and hid it in her desk, so she could give it to the FBI the next time they came to see her.[52]

Paine said she became curious about the letter in the first place because Oswald had moved something over his handwritten draft, apparently to keep her from reading it while he was typing. Yet she then describes him as having left the draft sitting out on her desk for days, thereby giving her the opportunity to copy it, take it, and hide it until she could give it to the FBI. According to Paine, Oswald had become oblivious of the draft he had sup-posedly been anxious to keep her from seeing.[53]

Apart from the inconsistencies in Ruth Paine's story, there is a more seri-ous question at issue. The draft of Oswald's letter that Paine claimed she hid from him and gave to the FBI has, as a result, been put on record by the Warren Commission as the more definitive version of the letter that was received by the Soviet Embassy four days before President Kennedy's assas-sination. The words that the writer crossed out in the draft have been used to reinterpret the typed letter, in terms of Oswald's intentions. Yet the draft stands in significant contrast to the provocative letter that was sent to the Soviets. Moreover, the draft shows internal evidence of having been written by someone other than Oswald, perhaps even months after the typed version of the letter. The purpose of such a forged, more innocuous "draft" would have been to defuse the explosive Oswald–Soviet Mexico City connection that Lyndon Johnson rejected and that, on close examination, could lead dangerously back to the CIA.

In an article comparing the letter that the Soviet Embassy received with its supposed draft, researcher Jerry Rose pointed to an odd reversal of the differences in spelling between the two documents, both supposedly written by the notoriously bad speller, Oswald.[54] While the handwritten version has only three errors that are corrected in the typed letter, there are twice as many changes from correct to faulty spelling. The results are the opposite of what one would expect to see in the transition from a draft to a more carefully done, typed version. In terms of composition, it looks as if the typewritten version preceded the draft.

More significantly, the paragraphs in the draft are rearranged so as to de-emphasize Oswald's contacts with the Soviet and Cuban embassies, empha-sizing instead his differences with the FBI.[55] The draft has also replaced words that suggested a Soviet conspiracy, "time to complete our business" (conjuring up a sinister "business" with "comrade Kostin"/Kostikov and the Soviet Embassy that was never explained in the typewritten letter) with words that provide an innocent explanation, "time to assist me" (an "assis-tance" whose nonconspiratorial travel purpose is explained in the draft with the crossed-out words, "would have been able to get the necessary docu-ments I required").[56]

Using the draft as its means of interpretation, the *Warren Report* tried to explain away the all-too-revealing Oswald letter that the Soviet Embassy received on November 18: "Some light on [the letter's] possible meaning can be shed by comparing it with the early draft. When the differences between the draft and the final document are studied, and especially when crossed-out words are taken into account, it becomes apparent that Oswald was intentionally beclouding the true state of affairs in order to make his trip to Mexico sound as mysterious and important as possible.

". . . In the opinion of the Commission, based upon its knowledge of Oswald, the letter constitutes no more than a clumsy effort to ingratiate himself with the Soviet Embassy." [57]

By reading the typed letter in terms of its very different draft, the Warren Commission tried to reduce the explosive meaning of the letter sent to the Soviet Embassy to nothing more than an Oswald ego-trip. What could be seen as a probably fraudulent, dangerously revealing letter was explained away in retrospect by another probably fraudulent, also revealing draft of the same letter.

The equally suspicious, "original" handwritten draft that had become the interpretive key to what Oswald wrote to the Soviet Embassy then became accessible to only one person. The members of the Warren Commission decided to give the original document, supposedly written by Oswald, back to Ruth Paine, at her request. They did so in May 1964, four months before they issued their official report drawing on that same document as key evidence. [58]

The Warren Commission included some of the shrewdest lawyers in the country, headed by the Chief Justice of the Supreme Court. They knew the legal importance of preserving the evidence in the assassination of the president of the United States. They nevertheless authorized almost immediately, at the request of the privileged witness who introduced it into evidence, the return to her of a handwritten letter she claimed to have taken secretly from the reputed assassin, just before he (supposedly) sent its conspiratorial, typed version to the Soviet Embassy.

The Warren Commission then cited in its *Report* the draft it no longer possessed to cover up the fraudulent Oswald letter that was designed to set up the Soviets. However, because it left too obvious a trail, the letter to the Soviet Embassy still threatened ultimately to blow open the CIA's conspiracy against both President Kennedy and the Soviet Union.

How real was the threat to use President Kennedy's assassination as the justification for an attack on Cuba and the Soviet Union?

When we take off our Warren Commission blinders, we can see that the letter sent to the Soviet Embassy was designed to implicate the Soviets and Cubans in the murder of the president of the United States. That was the apparent tactic of a twofold, winner-take-all plot: a plot to assassinate the president who was prepared to negotiate an end to the Cold War, inter-twined with a deeper plot to use fraudulent proof of the U.S.S.R.'s and

Cuba's responsibility for that assassination so as to justify the option of preemptive strikes on those same two Communist nations.

President Kennedy encountered that kind of push for a nuclear first strike against the Soviet Union from the beginning of his presidency. While such a "winning strategy" was becoming a top-secret, military priority, the pressures on Kennedy to approve it were so intense that it took a contemplative monk in the silence of his Kentucky monastery to recognize and articulate the truth.

In the first half of 1962 as the Cuban Missile Crisis drew nearer, Thomas Merton shared his intuition about the increasing danger of a U.S. preemptive strike with as many people as he could. It was a recurring theme in his mimeographed manuscript, *Peace in the Post-Christian Era*, that he sent to a host of friends (including Ethel Kennedy). He wrote in that prophetic text: "There can be no question that at the time of writing what seems to be the most serious and crucial development in the policy of the United States is this indefinite but growing assumption of the necessity of a first strike." [59]

As Merton sensed rightly from the hills of Kentucky, the Joint Chiefs of Staff in Washington, D.C., were in fact pressing their young commander-in-chief, John F. Kennedy, to support the strategic necessity of a first strike. They first did so in the summer of 1961, in a National Security Council meeting whose significance remained deeply hidden until the declassification of a top-secret document in 1994. Economist James K. Galbraith, the son of Kennedy's friend and ambassador to India, John Kenneth Galbraith, co-authored an article that used the newly disclosed document to expose the nuclear first-strike agenda of Kennedy's military chiefs. [60]

At the July 20, 1961, NSC meeting, General Hickey, chairman of the "Net Evaluation Subcommittee" of the Joint Chiefs of Staff, presented a plan for a nuclear surprise attack on the Soviet Union "in late 1963, preceded by a period of heightened tensions." [61] Other presenters of the preemptive strike plan included General Lyman Lemnitzer, chairman of the Joint Chiefs of Staff, and CIA director Allen Dulles. Vice President Lyndon Johnson's military aide, Howard Burris, wrote a memorandum on the meeting for Johnson, who was not present.

According to the Burris memorandum, President Kennedy raised a series of questions in response to the first-strike presentation he heard. He asked about a preemptive attack's likely damage to the U.S.S.R., its impact if launched in 1962, and how long U.S. citizens would have to remain in fallout shelters following such an attack. [62] While the Burris memorandum is valuable in its revelation of the first-strike agenda, it does not mention Kennedy's ultimate disgust with the entire process. We know that fact first from its disclosure in an oral history by Roswell Gilpatric, JFK's Deputy Secretary of Defense. Gilpatric described the meeting's abrupt conclusion: "Finally Kennedy got up and walked right out in the middle of it, and that was the end of it." [63]

Kennedy's disgusted reaction to this National Security Council meeting was also recorded in books written by Arthur Schlesinger, Jr., McGeorge Bundy, and Dean Rusk.[64] None of them, however, identified the first-strike focus of the meeting that prompted the disgust. They describe the meeting in only the most general terms as "the Net Evaluation, an annual doomsday briefing analyzing the chances of nuclear war" (Schlesinger)[65] or "a formal briefing on the net assessment of a general nuclear war between the two superpowers" (Bundy).[66] However, as much as JFK was appalled by a general nuclear war, his walkout was in response to a more specific evil in his own ranks: U.S. military and CIA leaders were enlisting his support for a plan to launch a nuclear attack on the Soviet Union.

Kennedy didn't just walk out. He also said what he thought of the entire proceeding. As he led Rusk back to the Oval Office, with what Rusk described as "a strange look on his face," Kennedy turned and said to his Secretary of State, "And we call ourselves the human race."[67]

"And we call ourselves the human race" was directed especially at the "we," himself included, who had been seriously discussing a preemptive nuclear strike on millions of other humans, at least until he was so revolted by the process that he had to leave the room. His walkout could not have pleased his military and CIA chiefs.

Nevertheless, the judgment Kennedy made, "And we call ourselves the human race," continued to apply to himself, as he became increasingly ensnared in his national security state's nuclear war plans.

In the late winter of 1962, Thomas Merton was finishing writing *Peace in the Post-Christian Era*, at the same time as Kennedy was being overcome by mounting Cold War pressures. Merton could see what was happening. He wrote then that "the influence of the hard school is more and more evident. Whereas President Kennedy used to assert that the United States would 'never strike first' he is now declaring that 'we may have to take the initiative' in the use of nuclear weapons."[68]

What Merton was alluding to was an alarming statement Kennedy had made in March 1962 to journalist Stewart Alsop for a *Saturday Evening Post* article. What Alsop wrote from his JFK interview was:

"Khrushchev must *not* be certain that, where its vital interests are threatened, the United States will never strike first. As Kennedy says, 'in some circumstances we might have to take the initiative.'"[69]

Kennedy's statement shocked Khrushchev. As soon as JFK's first-strike quote was headlined across the world, the Kremlin ordered a special military alert.[70] When Kennedy's press secretary, Pierre Salinger, visited Khrushchev in Moscow in May, the chairman told Salinger how disturbed he was by the statement.

Salinger replied that Kennedy had meant only "our options in the event of a major conventional attack [by the Soviet Union] on Western Europe."[71] It was true the article had placed Kennedy's remarks in that context. Even so, the implications of a first use of nuclear weapons in any conflict went far beyond Europe.

Khrushchev, who had spoken warmly of Kennedy up to that point, dismissed Salinger's defense of him. He said, "Not even Eisenhower or Dulles would have made the statement your president made. He now forces us to reappraise our own position." [72]

Khrushchev then made just such a "reappraisal." Two days after Salinger left Moscow, while Khrushchev was on a trip to Bulgaria, he thought for the first time of installing nuclear missiles in Cuba. [73] His idea was, first of all, to deter the United States from invading Cuba. After all, the United States had its missiles in Turkey, on the border of the Soviet Union. [74] But it was Kennedy's first-strike statement that helped spark Khrushchev's reappraisal of the Soviet position.

During Salinger's long talks with Khrushchev in May 1962, the Soviet leader also made it clear that he and Kennedy could choose together a different path from the perilous one they were then taking (which would climax five months later in the Missile Crisis). He recounted for Salinger with satisfaction his and Kennedy's peaceful resolution of the tanks crisis at the Berlin Wall in 1961, which we have already seen.

Khrushchev said he had told his Defense Minister, Marshal Rodion Malinovsky, "to back up our tanks a little bit and hide them behind buildings where the Americans couldn't see them. If we do this, I said to Malinovsky, the American tanks will also move back within twenty minutes and we will have no more crisis."

Khrushchev grinned at Salinger. "It was just as I said it would be. We pulled back. You pulled back. Now that's generalship!" [75]

Khrushchev's generous retreat at the Berlin Wall, made in response to a back-channel appeal by Kennedy, [76] would be repeated in the Cuban Missile Crisis.

As we saw, the pressures on Kennedy for an attack on the Soviet missile sites in Cuba were overwhelming, from both his military and civilian advisers. He resisted those pressures and instead worked out the mutual concessions with Khrushchev that resolved the crisis. The Joint Chiefs of Staff were infuriated by his steadfast refusal to launch an attack.

The president said to Arthur Schlesinger, "The military are mad. They wanted to do this." [77] By "this" he meant an attack on Cuba, perhaps involving also a preemptive strike on the Soviet Union. For the Joint Chiefs, Kennedy's peaceful resolution of the crisis with Khrushchev meant a lost opportunity to defeat the enemy, the best opportunity they ever had to "win" the Cold War.

Following the peaceful outcome of the Missile Crisis, during the year Kennedy had left as president, he resisted his military command's continuing pressures for a preemptive strike strategy.

One month after the Missile Crisis, the Joint Chiefs pushed for a buildup in U.S. strategic forces to a disarming first-strike capability. On November 20, 1962, they sent a memorandum to Secretary of Defense McNamara stating: "The Joint Chiefs of Staff consider that a first-strike capability is both feasible and desirable . . ." [78]

McNamara, reflecting what he knew was Kennedy's position, wrote the president on the same day about the challenge they faced: "It has become clear to me that the Air Force proposals, both for the RS-70 [Bomber] and for the rest of their Strategic Retaliatory Forces, are based on the objective of achieving a first-strike capability." [79] McNamara told the president what was at issue with the Air Force was whether U.S. forces should "attempt to achieve a capability to start a thermonuclear war in which the resulting damage to ourselves and our Allies could be considered acceptable on some reasonable definition of the term." [80] McNamara said he believed that a first-strike capability "should be rejected as a U.S. policy objective," and that the U.S. should not augment its forces for a first-strike capability. [81]

Two months before Kennedy's assassination, the president was given another "Net Evaluation Subcommittee Report" on preemptive war planning. This time around, Kennedy was prepared by two years of struggle with his military commanders for what he was about to hear. This time he was not about to walk out on them.

State Department historians have reported that the "Net Evaluation Subcommittee Report" that was presented to President Kennedy at the September 12, 1963, National Security Council Meeting "has not been found." [82] However, we do have a revealing record of the meeting's discussion. [83] As in 1961, the evident premise of the report is a U.S. first strike against the Soviet Union.

After he heard the Net Subcommittee Report from General Maxwell Taylor, chairman of the Joint Chiefs of Staff, Kennedy engaged in a cat-and-mouse game with his generals. He opened the discussion with a question whose premise was the first-strike strategy he knew they wanted in place. Yet its judge, under his euphemism, "political leaders," was himself, their deeply resistant commander-in-chief.

The president asked, "Even if we attack the USSR first, would the loss to the U.S. be unacceptable to political leaders?"

Air Force general Leon Johnson, representing the Net Subcommittee, answered, "It would be. Even if we preempt, surviving Soviet capability is sufficient to produce an unacceptable loss in the U.S." [84]

Kennedy could only have been relieved by Johnson's reply. The window of opportunity for a "successful" U.S. preemptive strike on the Soviets by Kennedy's generals was apparently closed. The U.S.S.R. had by now apparently deployed too many missiles in hardened underground silos for superior U.S. forces to be able to destroy a retaliatory force in a first strike. That meant Kennedy's military command could not pressure him with the same urgency for a preemptive strike. However, as we shall see, Johnson's answer was deceptive in terms of the time span it covered.

Kennedy pressed his advantage by asking Johnson, "Are we then in fact in a period of nuclear stalemate?"

General Johnson admitted that we were.

The President said, "I have read the statement in this morning's paper by the Air Force Association recommending nuclear superiority. What do they mean by 'nuclear superiority versus nuclear stalemate'? How could you get superiority?" [85]

Kennedy knew very well what the Air Force Association meant by "nuclear superiority versus nuclear stalemate." The Committee of the Air Force Association was pushing for the same first-strike capability that the Joint Chiefs of Staff had long advocated. Kennedy wanted Johnson's comment on a policy that the Air Force Association, like the Joint Chiefs, was pursuing without saying so against a resistant president.

General Johnson said carefully, measuring his words, "I believe the members of the Committee of the Air Force Association which drafted the resolution did not have the facts as brought out in the report being presented at this time." [86]

According to the minutes of the meeting, General Johnson, under the president's persistent questioning, then "acknowledged that it would be impossible for us to achieve nuclear superiority." [87]

Defense Secretary McNamara interjected to reinforce the president's case against a preemptive strike. He said, "Even if we spend $80 billion more [for shelters and increased weapons systems] than we are now spending, we would still have at least 30 million casualties in the U.S. in the 1968 time period, even if we made the first strike against the USSR." [88]

The president said, "Those fatality figures are much higher than I heard recently in Omaha. As I recall, SAC [Strategic Air Command] estimated that, if we preempt, we would have 12 million casualties." [89]

Kennedy was probing his military command for the truth behind their statistical efforts to advance a first-strike policy. In the Vietnam War, their figures had been manufactured to fit their arguments for the deployment of U.S. troops.

He pressed on, saying, "Why do we need as much as we've got? De Gaulle believes even the small nuclear force he is planning will be big enough to cause unacceptable damage to the USSR." [90]

General Johnson tried to explain to his skeptical commander-in-chief that they could bring down the number of casualties "by undertaking additional weapons programs." Kennedy wasn't buying it.

"Doesn't that just get us into the overkill business?" he asked. [91]

General Johnson countered, "No, sir. We can cut down U.S. losses if we knock out more Soviet missiles by having more U.S. missiles and more accurate U.S. missiles. The more Soviet missiles we can destroy the less the loss to us." [92]

Kennedy's questions were smoking out the underlying purpose of the "additional weapons programs" the Joint Chiefs were urging on him. The "more missiles and more accurate missiles" they wanted would be further steps toward a U.S. capability to destroy the Soviet retaliatory force in a disarming first strike before it could be launched.

Under Kennedy's questioning gaze, Johnson then made explicit the consequences and the purpose of the Joint Chiefs' thinking. He said, "Each of the

[Net report] strategies used against the USSR *resulted in at least 140 million fatalities in the USSR. Our problem* is *how to catch more of the Soviet missiles before they are launched* and how to destroy more of the missiles in the air over the U.S." [93]

This was roughly the point at which Kennedy had walked out in disgust two years earlier, saying to Rusk, "And we call ourselves the human race." Both then and now, it had become clear that a nuclear first strike meant genocide to the people attacked. Now in September 1963, the National Security Council had once again reached the point of blandly considering the killing of 140 million Soviet citizens in a U.S. effort to beat their leaders to the nuclear punch.

However, this time Kennedy did not walk out on his military commanders. He continued to probe their preemptive-war planning. He wanted to know as much as he could, for a purpose different from theirs. His purpose in terms of people, as opposed to their purpose in terms of missiles, was how to keep such a slaughter from ever happening.

McNamara reiterated, on behalf of Kennedy, that "there was no way of launching a no-alert attack against the USSR which would be acceptable. No such attack, according to the calculations, could be carried out without 30 million U.S. fatalities—an obviously unacceptable number." [94]

McNamara added, "The President deserves an answer to his question as to why we have to have so large a force."

The painfully obvious answer was that the Joint Chiefs wanted to be able to preempt the Soviets. Kennedy, on the other hand, saw such an option as a danger within his own government.

McNamara, caught between his president and his military chiefs, tried to explain away their conflict. He said, "The answer lies in the fact that there are many uncertainties in the equations presented in today's report." [95]

The president shifted gears. He asked why the Soviet Union "does have a smaller force" than the U.S., implying that the U.S. might want to follow their example rather than vice versa.

After granting that the Soviets might think they had enough to deter the U.S., General Johnson said apprehensively, "I would be very disturbed if the President considered this report indicated that we could reduce our forces and/or not continue to increase to those programmed. If a reduction should take place, the relative position of the U.S. and Soviets would become less in our favor." [96]

Kennedy, who wanted to negotiate an end to the Cold War with the Soviets, said to his general, "I understand."

After further discussion, JFK summed up the meeting in as hopeful a way as he could to his entrenched military command: "Preemption is not possible for us. This is a valuable conclusion growing out of an excellent report." [97]

He also said, "This argues in favor of a conventional force [rather than nuclear weapons]." [98]

General Johnson differed, saying, "I have concluded from the calculations [showing U.S. nuclear dominance] that we could fight a limited war using nuclear weapons without fear that the Soviets would reply by going to all-out war." [99]

Kennedy was familiar with arguments designed to lure him past the point of no return. He said, "I have been told that if I ever released a nuclear weapon on the battlefield, I should start a pre-emptive attack on the Soviet Union as the use of nuclear weapons was bound to escalate and we might as well get the advantage by going first." [100]

If the president's listeners did not agree with where he came out on the Net report, his questions had at least brought their preemptive-war thinking to the surface. However, he had also raised one particular question to which the National Security Council gave no answer at all. It bore on the strategic situation in the fall of 1963.

Kennedy had asked, in the middle of the discussion, "What about the case of preempting *today* with the Soviets in a low state of alert?" [101]

McNamara was the only person who ventured a reply. He said, "In the studies I have had done for me, I have not found a situation in which a preempt during a low-alert condition would be advantageous . . ." [102]

An unidentified reporter of this National Security Council meeting added a parenthetical comment, after McNamara's name and before his above statement: "(Today's situation not actually answered.)" [103]

Nor did any of Kennedy's other advisers offer an opinion in response to his question about a U.S. preemptive strike at the particular time in which they were then living. Moreover, their discussion of a preemptive war had been carried out, from beginning to end, in relation to a projected time scheme of 1964 through 1968. The situation in the remaining three and one-half months of 1963 was a question left untouched, even after Kennedy explicitly raised it.

As JFK may have recalled from the National Security Council meeting he walked out of in July 1961, the first Net Evaluation Subcommittee report had focused precisely on "a surprise attack in late 1963, preceded by a period of heightened tensions." [104] Kennedy was a keen reader and listener. In the second preemptive-war report, he may also have noticed the slight but significant discrepancy between its overall time frame, *1963–1968*, and the extent of its relatively reassuring conclusion, which covered only *1964* through 1968.

Although the Net report itself "has not been found," according to State Department historians,[105] nevertheless a memorandum that described it has been discovered. Addressed to National Security Adviser McGeorge Bundy two weeks before the September 12, 1963, NSC meeting, the memorandum by Colonel W. Y. Smith stated: "the [Net] briefing will cover the results of the studies of a series of general wars initiated earlier during the period *1963* through 1968 . . . Probably the major NESC conclusion is that during the years *1964* through 1968 neither the US nor the USSR can emerge from a full nuclear exchange without suffering very severe damage and high casualties, no matter which side initiates the war." [106]

In his cat-and-mouse questioning of his military chiefs, President Kennedy had built upon the report's apparently reassuring conclusion in such a way as to discourage preemptive-war ambitions. However, given the "late 1963" focus in the first Net Report that that was the most threatening time for a preemptive strike, Kennedy had little reason to be reassured by a second report that implicitly confirmed that time as the one of maximum danger. The personally fatal fall JFK was about to enter, in late 1963, was the same time his military commanders may have considered their last chance to "win" (in their terms) a preemptive war against the Soviet Union. In terms of their second Net Report to the president, which passed over the perilous meaning of late 1963, the cat-and-mouse game had been reversed. It was the generals who were the cats, and JFK the mouse in their midst.

The explicit assumption of the first Net Report was "a surprise attack in late 1963, preceded by a period of heightened tensions."[107] The focus of that first-strike scenario corresponded to the Kennedy assassination scenario. When President Kennedy was murdered in late 1963, the Soviet Union had been set up as the major scapegoat in the plot. If the tactic had been successful in scapegoating the Russians for the crime of the century, there is little doubt that it would have resulted in "a period of heightened tensions" between the United States and the Soviet Union.

Those who designed the plot to kill Kennedy were familiar with the inner sanctum of our national security state. Their attempt to scapegoat the Soviets for the president's murder reflected one side of the secret struggle between JFK and his military leaders over a preemptive strike against the Soviet Union. The assassins' purpose seems to have encompassed not only killing a president determined to make peace with the enemy but also using his murder as the impetus for a possible nuclear first strike against that same enemy.

The incrimination of Lee Harvey Oswald in advance of the assassination continued, even to the point of trying to charter a plane for his apparently intended escape to Cuba, an escape that would never happen.

On Wednesday morning, November 20, 1963, a car with three people in it drove into Red Bird Air Field, on the outskirts of Dallas. The car parked in front of the office of American Aviation Company, a private airline. A heavy-set young man and a young woman got out of the car and entered the office, leaving a second young man sitting in the right front passenger seat.

The man and the woman spoke with American Aviation's owner, Wayne January, who rented out small planes. They said they wanted to rent a Cessna 310 on the afternoon of Friday, November 22. Their destination would be the Yucatan Peninsula, in southeast Mexico near Cuba.[108]

The couple asked January unusually detailed questions about the Cessna: How far could it go without refueling? What was its speed? Under certain wind conditions, would it be able to go on to another location?

Wayne January became suspicious. He knew from experience that people didn't ask those kinds of questions when they chartered an airplane.[109] January decided not to rent the Cessna to the couple. He said later that he suspected from their questions that they might have had in mind hijacking the plane to Cuba, just east of the Yucatan Peninsula.[110] That may have been exactly what they wanted him to think.

As the couple left his office, expressing irritation at his rejection of their deal, January was curious as to why the other man hadn't come in with them. He took a good look at the man sitting in the front passenger seat of the car. The following weekend, he recognized on television and in the newspapers the man he'd seen with the couple he suspected of wanting to hijack a plane to Cuba. Their companion had been Lee Harvey Oswald (or someone who bore an exact resemblance to him).

As was the case when he stood on Sylvia Odio's doorstep between Leopoldo and Angel, Oswald at the Red Bird Air Field was nothing more than a prop in a scene being played out by two other characters. Yet the scene was designed once again to implicate him. Red Bird Air Field was located just five miles south of Oswald's apartment, a short drive away on the freeway connection. The apparent purpose of the plane-chartering scene, two days before the assassination, was to identify Oswald with a covert plan to fly to Cuba right after the president's murder.

Because Lyndon Johnson blocked the scapegoating of the Soviet Union and Cuba but failed to confront the CIA, the government also had to cover up the Red Bird incident. Like the Odio incident, it was obvious evidence of a conspiracy—if not by Soviet or Cuban agents, then by U.S. agents.

In 1991, when British author Matthew Smith was examining Kennedy assassination scholar Harold Weisberg's government documents (obtained under the Freedom of Information Act) in the basement of Weisberg's Maryland home, he discovered Wayne January's FBI report on the episode at Red Bird Air Field. Smith then visited Dallas and showed the FBI report to January, who was astounded by what he was described as saying.[111] The FBI claimed he said the incident took place in late July 1963, four months before the assassination rather than two days. In that greatly lengthened time span, the FBI also claimed January was uncertain in his identification of Oswald.[112]

January told Smith that, contrary to the FBI, "It was the Wednesday before the assassination." With only two days between his look at the man in the car and Oswald's arrest, January said he was so certain of his identification of Oswald that he "would give it nine out of ten."[113]

When Smith commented that the Kennedy assassination was a mystery, he met with resistance. January leaned back in his chair, his hands behind his head. He said, "The CIA was behind this."[114]

Smith said there were other possible involvements to consider. He began listing them. January just looked at him, saying nothing.

When Smith reflected back on January's quiet certitude, he wondered how he could be so sure the CIA was behind the assassination.[115] He would learn later, as we shall, that Wayne January knew much more than he was saying.

The assassination of John F. Kennedy was like the sudden coming of a tornado that sucked people up into death, both Kennedy's death and their own. One such victim was a woman who predicted the killing of Kennedy, Rose Cheramie.

A half day after the incident at Red Bird Air Field, on the night of Wednesday, November 20, Louisiana State Police lieutenant Francis Fruge was called to Moosa Memorial Hospital in Eunice, Louisiana. There he was given custody of Rose Cheramie (also known as Melba Christine Marcades), a heroin addict who was experiencing withdrawal symptoms. One of two men with whom she was traveling had thrown her out of the Silver Slipper Lounge in Eunice earlier that evening. Cheramie had then been hit by a car, suffering minor abrasions.[116]

Fruge took Cheramie in an ambulance to East Louisiana State Hospital in Jackson for treatment of her withdrawal symptoms. During the two-hour trip, she responded to his questions.

She said she had been driving with the two men from Miami to Dallas before they stopped at the lounge in Eunice. She stated: "We're going to kill President Kennedy when he comes to Dallas in a few days."[117] Their combined purpose, she said, was "to number one, pick up some money, pick up her baby [being kept by another man], and to kill Kennedy."[118] Because of Cheramie's condition, Fruge did not take her words seriously.

At the East Louisiana State Hospital on November 21, Rose Cheramie said again, this time to hospital staff members, that President Kennedy was about to be killed in Dallas.[119]

Immediately after Kennedy's assassination, Lieutenant Fruge called the hospital, telling them not to release Cheramie until he could question her further. When he did so on Monday, November 25, Cheramie described the two men driving with her from Miami to Dallas as either Cubans or Italians.[120]

As Fruge related Cheramie's story to the House Select Committee on Assassinations, "The men were going to kill Kennedy [in Dallas] and she was going to check into the Rice Hotel [in Houston], where reservations were already made for her, and pick up 10 kilos of heroin from a seaman coming into Galveston. She was to pick up the money for the dope from a man who was holding her baby. She would then take the dope to Mexico."[121]

How reliable was Rose Cheramie as a witness? The Louisiana State Police decided to find out.

The police checked on parts of Cheramie's story with Nathan Durham, the Chief Customs Agent in the Texas region that included Galveston. Durham confirmed that the ship with the seaman Cheramie said had the heroin was about to dock in Galveston.[122] The seaman was on it. The police checked out the man holding the money and Cheramie's baby. He was identified as a suspected dealer in drug traffic.[123] Working with Cheramie, the police and customs agents tried to follow and trap the seaman when he disembarked from his ship in Galveston, but the man eluded them.[124] In any case, key details in Cheramie's story had been confirmed by the police and customs authorities.

Colonel Morgan of the Louisiana State Police phoned Captain Will Fritz of the Dallas Police to tell him about Cheramie's prediction of the assassination, the confirmed parts of her story, and that the Chief Customs Agent in Houston was holding her for further questioning. When Morgan hung up from his conversation with Fritz, he turned to the other officers in the room and said, "They don't want her. They're not interested."[125] By that time Oswald had been captured, jailed, and shot to death by Jack Ruby. The Dallas police wanted no further witnesses to the president's assassination.

The Chief Customs Agent called FBI agents to pass on the information received from Cheramie: Did they want to talk to her? The FBI said it also did not want to question Rose Cheramie.[126]

As Cheramie's story was being confirmed, she also told Francis Fruge that she used to work for Jack Ruby as a nightclub stripper. She said that as a result of her employment by Ruby, she knew Lee Harvey Oswald. Rose Cheramie was a witness not only to participants in the Kennedy assassination traveling to Dallas but also to Ruby and Oswald knowing each other. She said she knew that the two of them had an intimate relationship "for years."[127] Her testimony, if heard, would have contradicted the *Warren Report*'s assertions that Ruby and Oswald were lone killers and had never met.

After both Dallas and federal investigative authorities refused to question Rose Cheramie, the Chief Customs Agent released her in Houston, and she disappeared.

On September 4, 1965, Rose Cheramie's body was found at 3:00 A.M. on Highway 155, 1.7 miles east of Big Sandy, Texas. Cheramie had reportedly been run over by a car.[128] Jerry Don Moore, the driver of the car in question, said he'd been driving from Big Sandy to his home in Tyler. He suddenly saw three or four suitcases lined up in the center of the road. As researcher James DiEugenio summarized Moore's story, "He swerved to his right to avoid hitting [the suitcases]. In front of him was the prone body of a woman lying at a 90-degree angle to the highway with her head toward the road. Moore applied the brakes as hard as he could."[129]

The investigating officer, J. A. Andrews, stated that Moore said, "although he had attempted to avoid running over her, he ran over the top part of her skull, causing fatal injuries."[130] Moore, on the contrary, swore he never hit Cheramie.[131] He came close to her, stopped, then drove her to the nearest doctor in Big Sandy. An ambulance took her from the doctor's to Gladewater Hospital, where she was declared dead on arrival. Although Officer Andrews expressed uncertainty as to what happened to Cheramie, "due to the fact that the relatives of the victim did not pursue the investigation, he closed it as accidental death."[132]

Yet how did Rose Cheramie happen to be lying at a 90-degree angle across Highway 155 at three in the morning, near suitcases that seemed to be positioned to direct an oncoming car over her body?

Cheramie may in fact have been shot in the head before Jerry Don Moore found her on the highway. Records at Gladewater Hospital describe a "deep punctate stellate" (starlike) wound to her right forehead. Dr. Charles A. Crenshaw commented in his book, *JFK: Conspiracy of Silence*: "The wound to Cheramie's forehead as described, according to medical textbooks, occurs in contact gunshot wounds—that is, when a gun barrel is placed against a victim's body and discharged. It is especially applicable to a gunshot wound of the skull . . ." [133]

Cheramie's autopsy "cannot be found" according to the responsible authorities. [134] Because of the unanswered questions about Cheramie's death, New Orleans District Attorney Jim Garrison wanted to exhume her body. The local Texas authorities refused to cooperate with Garrison's request. [135]

Following Rose Cheramie's death, her life continued to be a source of information on John Kennedy's death. In 1967 the Louisiana State Police assigned Lieutenant Francis Fruge to work with Jim Garrison in his investigation of JFK's murder. Fruge then interviewed the owner of the Silver Slipper Lounge, where Cheramie had been thrown out and hit by a car November 20, 1963, before she predicted Kennedy's murder that night. Mac Manual had continued to be the owner of the Silver Slipper, a known house of prostitution.

Manual remembered well the night at the Silver Slipper when the two men and Rose Cheramie got into a fight. Manual said they had several drinks when they arrived. Cheramie "appeared to be intoxicated when she got there. She started raising a ruckus. One of the men kind of slapped her around and threw her outside." [136]

Manual told Fruge he recognized the two men with Cheramie as soon as they walked into the Silver Slipper. He should have. He worked with them. They were, he said, "pimps who had been to my place before, hauling prostitutes from Florida and hauling them back." [137]

Lieutenant Fruge had brought with him a stack of photographs from the New Orleans District Attorney's office. From the photographs, Mac Manual picked out his two business associates in prostitution. They were more than that. The two men he identified as having accompanied Rose Cheramie to the Silver Slipper were Sergio Arcacha Smith and Emilio Santana, two anti-Castro Cuban exiles with CIA credentials. [138]

Emilio Santana admitted in an interview with Jim Garrison's office that the CIA hired him on August 27, 1962, the evening of the day he arrived in Miami as an exile from his native Cuba. [139] Santana was immediately employed by the Agency as a crewmember on a boat sailing back to Cuba, carrying weapons and electronic equipment for CIA-sponsored guerrilla actions. He was a CIA employee, he said, during 1962 and 1963. [140] As a Cuban fisherman, he had intimate knowledge of the Cuban coastline, which made him a valuable asset in piloting boats that smuggled CIA operatives in and out of Cuba.[141] He acknowledged piloting a boat with a CIA team that was off the coast of Cuba for twenty days at the time of the Cuban Missile Crisis.[142] Santana's boat would have been carrying one of the unauthorized commando teams that CIA Special Operations organizer William Harvey dispatched to Cuba at the height of the Missile Crisis, igniting the fury of Robert Kennedy for the CIA's covert provocation of nuclear war.[143] President Kennedy's refusal then, as at the Bay of Pigs, to attack Cuba, and his crisis-resolving pledge to Khrushchev never to do so, provoked a counter-anger in the CIA extending down into the exile community that included Emilio Santana.

The CIA's version of its employment of Santana is more modest. When Jim Garrison investigated Emilio Santana, a CIA document acknowledged that the Agency had in fact recruited him—in October 1962, it said, corresponding to the time of the Missile Crisis. The document claimed that the Agency had terminated Santana's contract after he took part in an infiltration operation in May 1963.[144]

The man Mac Manual identified as Rose Cheramie's other companion, Sergio Arcacha Smith, had a more commanding role in the CIA's anti-Castro network.

Sergio Arcacha Smith had been a prominent Cuban diplomat for the Batista regime before it was overthrown by the Cuban revolution led by Fidel Castro. As Arcacha stated on his personal resume, he was Cuba's diplomatic consul in Madrid, Rome, Mexico City, and Bombay (at the latter station under Batista).[145] After he left the diplomatic service, Arcacha had by 1959 prospered enough as a business executive in Latin America to have his own factory in Caracas, Venezuela.[146] He became active there in an anti-Castro group, which may have initiated his involvement with the CIA. On June 29, 1960, he was arrested by the government of Venezuela and charged with plotting to assassinate Venezuelan President Ernesto Betancourt.[147] He was released on July 14, 1960.[148] The American Embassy came to his immediate assistance, issuing nonimmigrant visitor visas to him and his family so they could depart from Venezuela.[149]

After arriving in the U.S., Arcacha Smith became the New Orleans delegate of the FRD (Frente Revolucionario Democratico), which a CIA document on Arcacha states "was organized and supported by the Agency."[150] The FRD "was used," the CIA noted, "as a front for recruitment of Brigade 2506 for the [Bay of Pigs] invasion."[151] Arcacha admitted in a 1967 polygraph test that he and David Ferrie, while working for the CIA, "helped train the Bay of Pigs invasion force with M-1 rifles."[152] When the FRD was phased out, Arcacha established a New Orleans chapter of the Cuban Revolutionary Council,[153] the Cuban "government in exile" organized by the CIA.[154]

Guy Banister, the detective/intelligence agent who would guide Oswald in the summer of 1963 in New Orleans, also worked closely with Arcacha Smith in 1961–62. Banister helped set up an organization to raise funds for

Arcacha Smith's branch of the Cuban Revolutionary Council.[155] Banister
and Smith both had their offices in the Balter Building in New Orleans.[156]
They moved together in early 1962 to the Newman Building at 544 Camp
Street,[157] the same address that Oswald used for one of his Fair Play for
Cuba leaflets when he was arrested in New Orleans on August 9, 1963, for
disturbing the peace.[158] According to Arcacha's New Orleans public relations man, Richard Rolfe, Arcacha said frankly to him that he was under
the thumb of the CIA, which in public he always referred to as the "State
Department." [159]

Sergio Arcacha Smith was also seen with Lee Harvey Oswald. David
Lewis, a former employee of Guy Banister, stated to the New Orleans District Attorney's Office that he witnessed a meeting in the late summer of
1963 at Mancuso's Restaurant in New Orleans between Sergio Arcacha
Smith, Lee Harvey Oswald, and a man named Carlos whose last name Lewis
didn't know (who may have been Arcacha's and Oswald's mutual friend,
Carlos Quiroga).[160] Lewis said Arcacha, Oswald, and Carlos "were involved
in some business which dealt with Cuba," and that Arcacha "appeared to
be the boss." [161]

As we have seen, "Arcacha" was the name given by CIA double agent
Richard Case Nagell to identify one of the participants besides Nagell and
Oswald in a late August 1963 planning meeting for killing Kennedy.[162]
There is just one man with the name, Arcacha, who keeps reappearing in
the assassination plot: Sergio Arcacha Smith.[163]

Sergio Arcacha Smith's identification by Mac Manual as one of Rose
Cheramie's companions, who she said told her they were going to Dallas to
kill Kennedy, is further evidence that the CIA played an operational role in
the assassination. Sergio Arcacha Smith in particular had an extensive CIA
background, including working relationships with Guy Banister, David Ferrie, and Lee Harvey Oswald. Claiming she had been an employee of Jack
Ruby, Rose Cheramie also testified to Ruby and a man she identified as Lee
Oswald knowing each other well. Rose Cheramie lived and died as a witness
to the Unspeakable.

At the risk of his political future (and his life), John Kennedy continued
to pursue a secret dialogue toward a rapprochement with Fidel Castro.
On November 5, 1963, at the White House, U.S. diplomat William
Attwood briefed National Security Adviser McGeorge Bundy on Premier
Castro's warm response to the process developing behind the scenes at the
United Nations between Attwood, a deputy to U.S. ambassador Adlai Ste-
venson, and Cuban ambassador Carlos Lechuga. Castro's righthand man,
Rene Vallejo, said in a phone call to intermediary Lisa Howard that the
Cuban leader was ready to negotiate with Kennedy's representative "any-
time and appreciated the importance of discretion to all concerned." [164] Cas-
tro enthusiastically offered to expedite the process by sending a plane to

pick up Attwood in Mexico. Attwood would be flown to a private airport in Cuba where he would talk confidentially with Castro and then be flown back immediately.[165]

"In this way," Castro hoped, "there would be no risk of [Attwood's] identification at the Havana airport." [166]

After meeting with Attwood, Bundy updated Kennedy on Castro's concrete proposal. Fortunately for history, Kennedy pushed a button under his desk to record the private conversation with his National Security Adviser.[167]

Bundy told the president of Castro's invitation to Attwood "to go down completely on the QT and talk with Fidel about the chances and conditions on which he would be interested in changing relations with the United States."

JFK said, "Can Attwood get in and out of there very privately?"

Bundy shared Castro's logistical planning for the meeting. He acknowledged the danger of Attwood's close connection with the president. He added—to Kennedy's approval—that Attwood as his representative would have the advantage of already knowing Castro, having met with him in Cuba in the late 50s.

Kennedy said, "We'd have to have an explanation of why Attwood was there. Can we get Attwood off the [government] payroll . . . before he goes?"

At this point in their conversation, Kennedy's and Bundy's attention was diverted by their receiving word of the Russians holding up a British convoy on its way to West Berlin. When they returned to the subject of the Castro meeting, the president repeated, "I think we ought to have [Attwood] off the payroll, because otherwise it's much more difficult."

The two men agreed. Given the risk of the Attwood–Castro meeting being discovered by the press, Attwood should sever his formal relation with the government. Thanks to his reputation as a journalist before his diplomatic career, Attwood should carry out his secret mission to Castro "as a newsman." [168]

As Kennedy knew, the greatest risk of the politically explosive meeting lay not with the press but with the CIA. However, the CIA already knew— and was letting others know. As Cuban government intelligence would learn, the CIA had not only closely monitored Kennedy's secret turn toward Castro from the beginning, as could have been expected. The Agency had also divulged the Kennedy–Castro connection to its Cuban exile network in Miami, thereby inflaming the exiles' anti-Kennedy sentiment that went back to the Bay of Pigs.[169] From the CIA's command center in Langley to its largest hub of activity in Miami, President Kennedy in his developing détente with Fidel Castro was now regarded as a total traitor to the anti-communist cause.

Having taken the momentous step of approving the secret talks with Castro, during the final week of his life President Kennedy sent a hopeful message to the Cuban premier. It came in his November 18 address in Miami to the Inter-American Press Association. William Attwood said he was told by Arthur Schlesinger, Jr., who co-authored Kennedy's speech, that "it was intended to help me by signaling to Castro that normalization was possible if Cuba simply stopped doing the Kremlin's work in Latin America (such as trying to sabotage—vainly as it turned out—the upcoming Venezuelan elections)." [170]

In his November 18 speech, the president first emphasized that the Alliance for Progress did "not dictate to any nation how to organize its economic life. Every nation is free to shape its own economic institutions in accordance with its own national needs and will." [171]

Kennedy then issued a challenge and a promise to Castro. He said that "a small band of conspirators" had made "Cuba a victim of foreign imperialism, an instrument of the policy of others, a weapon in an effort dictated by external powers to subvert the other American Republics. This, and this alone, divides us. As long as this is true, nothing is possible. Without it, everything is possible. Once this barrier is removed, we will be ready and anxious to work with the Cuban people in pursuit of those progressive goals which a few short years ago stirred their hopes and the sympathy of many people throughout the hemisphere." [172]

Kennedy's final message to Castro was a promise that if he stopped what Kennedy regarded as Cuba's covert action in support of Soviet policies in Latin America, then "everything was possible" between the United States and Cuba. On the same day he made this pledge, November 18, his representative Attwood took a further step toward détente by agreeing with Vallejo by phone (with Castro listening in) to set an agenda for a Kennedy–Castro dialogue. [173] Attwood said that when he reported on the call to the White House the next day, he was told by Bundy that "once an agenda had been agreed upon, the president would want to see me and decide what to say to Castro. [Bundy] said the president would be making a brief trip to Dallas but otherwise planned to be in Washington." [174] Kennedy was ready to work out the specific elements of his dialogue with Castro as soon as he returned from Dallas.

However, the CIA was just as dedicated to undermining the words John Kennedy had already spoken as it was to making sure he would never speak again. The Agency immediately began propagating its own version of the November 18 speech, in combination with its efforts to kill both Kennedy and Castro.

In early September, the CIA set in motion yet another assassination plot against Castro, this one meant to serve ultimately as a way to blame Robert Kennedy for the killing of his own brother. The CIA's Castro/RFK scheme utilized its key undercover agent in Cuba, Rolando Cubela, who was known by the code-name AM/LASH. Rolando Cubela was no ordinary agent but a

Cuban political figure whom Fidel Castro trusted. Cubela had fought beside Castro in the Cuban Revolution. He then held various posts in the revolutionary government but became disillusioned by Castro's alliance with the Soviet Union. In 1961 he was recruited by the CIA, which nurtured carefully its secret relationship with a Castro associate who also had experience as an assassin. In 1959 Cubela had shot to death Batista's head of military intelligence.[175] Thus, the CIA's Cubela plot was, as Castro assessed it years later, "one that had many possibilities of success because that individual had access to us."[176]

On October 29, 1963, Rolando Cubela met at a CIA safe house in Paris with Desmond Fitzgerald, chief of the CIA's Special Affairs staff. In one of the CIA's most blatant attempts to destroy both Kennedy brothers, Fitzgerald, using a false name, posed as a U.S. senator representing Attorney General Robert Kennedy.[177] The Church Committee, following the CIA's top-secret *Inspector General's Report*, discovered that the Deputy Director of Plans, Richard Helms, had "agreed that Fitzgerald should hold himself out as a personal representative of Attorney General Robert Kennedy."[178] As the CIA's own internal report admitted blandly, Helms had also decided "it was not necessary to seek approval from Robert Kennedy for Fitzgerald to speak in his name."[179] The CIA's impersonation worked, convincing Cubela that he had been authorized by the Attorney General's representative to assassinate Castro. Fitzgerald then put in a special order for Cubela of a poison pen device from the CIA's Operations Division of the Office of Medical Services: "a ball-point rigged with a hypodermic needle . . . designed to be so fine that the victim would not notice its insertion."[180]

On November 22, according to the *Inspector General's Report*, "it is likely that at the very moment President Kennedy was shot, a CIA officer was meeting with a Cuban agent in Paris and giving him an assassination device for use against Castro"[181]—acting falsely once again in the name of Attorney General Robert Kennedy. As the Church Committee discovered, Cubela's CIA handler told him that Desmond Fitzgerald, whom Cubela knew as "Robert Kennedy's representative," had helped write the president's speech that was delivered in Miami on November 18. Cubela was informed "that the passage about the 'small band of conspirators' was meant as a green light for an anti-Castro coup."[182]

The CIA, by reversing the meaning of Kennedy's speech to motivate its own hired assassin, created a dogma of disinformation that it would disseminate for decades—that the Miami speech meant an encouragement to murder, not dialogue. The CIA's further device of hiring Cubela in the name of Robert Kennedy to assassinate Castro laid the foundation for the repeated claim that Castro, to preempt the threat on his own life, ordered JFK's murder—and that RFK had therefore triggered his own brother's assassination.

When Arthur Schlesinger, Jr., learned years later of the murderous twist the CIA had put on the speech he helped write, he commented: "On its face the passage was obviously directed against Castro's extracontinental ties and signaled that, if these were ended, normalization was possible; it was meant in short as assistance to Attwood [for a dialogue with Castro], not to Fitzgerald [for assassinating him]. This was the signal that Richard Goodwin, the chief author of the speech, intended to convey." [183]

President Kennedy stated the purpose of his Miami speech when he first spoke to his speechwriter, Theodore Sorensen, about it. The speech's audience would be the Inter-American Press Association, which Sorensen knew was "a very tough anti-Castro group." [184] Yet Kennedy told Sorensen he had another audience in mind: Fidel Castro. Sorensen said later that the president specifically wanted "a speech that would open a door to the Cuban leader." [185]

That is precisely the way in which Fidel Castro understood Kennedy's words—as an open door.

In a speech in Cuba on November 23, 1963, Premier Castro reflected on President Kennedy's death the day before. He took a special interest in JFK's November 18 Miami speech, recognizing that it signaled an opening to himself and thus posed a threat to those opposed to rapprochement. Citing wire service reports, he noted the exile community's hostile reaction to the speech:

"And so, a series of cables. Here 'Miami, Florida—The Cuban exiles waited tonight in vain for a firm promise from President Kennedy to take energetic measures against the communist regime of Fidel Castro.'

"It says: 'They waited tonight in vain for a firm promise' . . . Many met in the offices of the revolutionary organizations and in their homes, to listen to President Kennedy over the radio . . . They listened when the President said: 'We in this hemisphere must also use every resource at our command to prevent the establishment of another Cuba in this hemisphere.'[186] That is, they did not accept the fact he said 'to prevent the establishment of another Cuba in this hemisphere,' because they thought that it carried with it the idea of accepting one Cuba. Many exiles had hopes of more vigorous statements to liberate Cuba from communism . . . " [187]

Like the exiles, Castro understood at once the nuance of the carefully written phrase, "to prevent the establishment of *another* Cuba in this hemisphere" (emphasis added). What was cause for bitterness in the exiles was cause for hope in Castro, the hope of dialogue with the enemy, and peace. He continued his commentary on the press reports of the president's speech:

" 'Miami Beach: Latin American newspaper publishers and editors in response to the speech delivered by President Kennedy tonight . . . said that he had not taken a strong enough position against the communist regime of Fidel Castro.'

"[Another newspaper says:] 'Kennedy now refuses to allow Cuban exiles to launch attacks against Cuba from U.S. territory, and in fact uses U.S. air and naval power to maintain Castro in power.' . . . That is to say, they accuse Kennedy of using naval and air power to maintain Castro in power.

"... The UPI overflowed with information as it had never done before, picking up all the criticisms of Kennedy because of his Cuban policy ...

"How strange it is really that the assassination of President Kennedy should take place at a time when there was unanimous agreement of opinion against certain aspects of his policy. How strange all this is." [188]

Castro also commented on the strangeness of the wire service reports the day before that had instantly identified Lee Harvey Oswald as the assassin. On November 23, 1963, he asked brilliantly obvious questions about Oswald that have been suppressed in the U.S. media from then until now.

"Can anyone who has said that he will disclose military secrets [as Oswald said to the Soviet Union] return to the United States without being sent to jail? ...

"How strange that this former marine should go to the Soviet Union and try to become a Soviet citizen, and that the Soviets should not accept him, that he should say at the American Embassy that he intended to disclose to the Soviet Union the secrets of everything he learned while he was in the U.S. service and that in spite of this statement, his passage is paid by the U.S. Government ... He goes back to Texas and finds a job. This is all so strange!" [189]

Fidel Castro recognized "CIA" written all over Lee Harvey Oswald and the disinformation on him that was being sent around the world soon after the assassination. The Dallas setup was obvious to someone as familiar with CIA plots as Fidel Castro was. On the night before Oswald was killed and silenced forever, Castro's questions pointed beyond Oswald to an unspeakable source of the crime:

"Who could be the only ones interested in this murder? Could it be a real leftist, a leftist fanatic, at a moment when tensions had lessened, at a moment when McCarthyism was being left behind, or was at least more moderate, at a moment when a nuclear test ban treaty is signed, at a moment when [presidential] speeches [that] are described as weak with respect to Cuba were being made?" [190]

In the years to come, Fidel Castro would conclude that Nikita Khrushchev and John Kennedy had negotiated a correct way out of the missile crisis, in spite of his own opposition. He would then admit honestly that he had been too blind to see a liberating way out at the time. In a 1975 interview, he acknowledged that he had been "enormously irritated" by the way in which the crisis was resolved, with no guarantee of Cuba's security against a U.S. invasion. "But if we are realistic," he added, "and we go back in history, we realize that ours was not the correct posture." [191] Upon further reflection he had come to feel "history has proven that the Soviet position [of withdrawing its missiles in return for a no-invasion pledge] was the correct one" and that Kennedy's "promise not to invade Cuba [turned out to be] a real promise and everyone knows that. That is the truth." [192] JFK's successors in the White House adhered to that promise, even though they failed to follow up on his beginning negotiations with Castro.

Castro had seen Kennedy change as president: "I have an impression of

Kennedy and of Kennedy's character, but I formed it over the years that he was President from different gestures, different attitudes. We mustn't forget the speech he made at American University several months prior to his death, in which he admitted certain truths and spoke in favor of peace and relaxation of tensions. It was a very courageous speech and it took note of a series of international realities . . . This was Kennedy after two years in the presidency, who felt sure of his reelection, a Kennedy who dared make decisions—daring decisions . . .

"One of the characteristics of Kennedy was courage. He was a courageous man. A man capable of taking a decision one way or another, a man capable of revising a policy, because he had the courage to do so." [193]

Speaking to members of Congress who visited Cuba in 1978, Castro said of his former enemy, "I can tell you that in the period in which Kennedy's assassination took place Kennedy was changing his policy toward Cuba . . . To a certain extent we were honored in having such a rival . . . He was an outstanding man." [194]

Julia Ann Mercer, a twenty-three-year-old employee of Automat Distributors in Dallas, drove into Dealey Plaza at about 11:00 A.M. on Friday, November 22, 1963. It was an hour and a half before the president's motorcade would pass through. While Mercer's car was stalled by heavy traffic in what would soon become a killing zone, her attention was drawn to a green pickup truck parked up on the curb to her right.

As Mercer watched, a man walked around to the back of the pickup. He reached in and pulled out a rifle case wrapped in paper. The man carried what was apparently a rifle up a slope that would soon become known as the grassy knoll.[195]

Mercer looked up at the bridge that formed an arch over the street ahead of her. Three police officers were standing talking beside a motorcycle. She wondered why they took no interest in the man carrying the rifle up the hill.

Mercer eased her car forward, until she was parallel to a second man, who was driving the pickup. The driver turned his head, looking straight into the eyes of Julia Ann Mercer. The man had a round face. He turned away, then looked back at her. Their eyes locked again. Two days later, while watching television, Mercer would recognize the driver of the truck, Jack Ruby, in the act of shooting Lee Harvey Oswald.[196]

After Mercer drove away from Dealey Plaza, she stopped to eat at a favorite restaurant. She told friends there about the man she'd seen carrying the rifle up the hill. She guessed he had to be a member of the Secret Service. "The Secret Service is not very secret," she said.[197]

When she continued her drive to work, a police car pulled her over. Two officers who had overheard her in the restaurant said she was needed for questioning in Dallas. President Kennedy had been shot in Dealey Plaza, where she had seen the man with the rifle.[198]

For several hours that afternoon and the next morning, Julia Ann Mercer was questioned by the Dallas police and the FBI. Four years later, she saw the statements they attributed to her. She was unable to recognize them as her own.

It was in January 1968, during Jim Garrison's investigation of the Kennedy assassination, that Julia Ann Mercer's husband phoned Garrison. He said he and his wife were in New Orleans and wanted to talk with Garrison. When Garrison met them in their hotel suite, he was confronted, as he would write, by "a most impressive couple. A middle-aged man of obvious substance, he had been a Republican member of Congress from Illinois. Equally impressive, she was intelligent and well-dressed, the kind of witness any lawyer would love to have testifying on his side in front of a jury." [199]

Garrison showed Mercer her statements as printed in the Warren Commission Exhibits. Reading them carefully, she shook her head.

"These have all been altered," she said. "They have me saying just the opposite of what I really told them." [200]

She said that on Saturday, November 23, the day after the president's assassination, FBI agents showed her an assortment of pictures. She selected four of the pictures as looking like the driver of the green pickup truck. When they turned one over, she read the name "Jack Ruby" on the back. [201]

She told Garrison, "I had no doubts about what the driver's face looked like. I do not know whether the other three pictures shown me were other men who looked like Ruby or whether they were three other pictures of Jack Ruby. But they definitely showed me Jack Ruby, and I definitely picked him out as looking like the driver." [202]

Her identification of Jack Ruby as the driver had occurred on *the day before* Ruby shot Oswald. If her testimony on Ruby delivering a man with a gun case to the grassy knoll had become public, it would have created a major problem for the government's argument that there was no conspiracy. Perhaps not surprisingly, the FBI version of her statement claimed "Mercer could not identify any of the photographs" with the driver. [203]

Julia Ann Mercer wrote down, on Garrison's copy of the FBI report, a description of her identification of Ruby's picture. She added: "I again recognized Jack Ruby when I saw him shoot Oswald and I said to my family, who were watching TV with me, 'That was the man I saw in the truck.'" [204]

After seeing Ruby's murder of Oswald, Mercer notified the FBI that she had again recognized Ruby as the driver of the truck. [205] That is not in the FBI report. According to it, she never identified Ruby at all, much less a second time. The FBI report acknowledges only that she had been shown a picture of Ruby (without disclosing that this happened on the day before Ruby shot Oswald). The FBI again claims "she could not identify him as the person [driving the truck]." [206]

Pointing this out to Garrison, she laughed and said, "He was only a few feet away from me [in Dealey Plaza]. How could I not recognize Jack Ruby when I saw him shoot Oswald on television?" [207]

The FBI and Dallas Sheriff's Department versions of Mercer's statement not only denied her identification of Ruby as the driver. They also claimed she said the truck had a sign on its side in black, oval letters that read "Air Conditioning."[208] Mercer told Garrison she said the opposite: "Every time I was questioned—which included at least two times by the FBI—I clearly stated that there was no printing on the truck."[209]

The FBI's and Sheriff's Department's false description of the truck as having an "Air Conditioning" sign on its side resulted in a charade. FBI agents then conducted a thorough but irrelevant search throughout Dallas for the driver of such a truck.[210]

The government's documents on Julia Ann Mercer are, on close examination, not only deceptive. They are also fraudulent.

The Sheriff Department's statement was signed by "Julia Ann Mercer" and notarized. However, in Garrison's presence, Mercer signed her name below the written corrections she had just made to the statement. She showed him the difference between her signature and the forgery someone had done in her name on the original document.[211]

She stated: "Neither of the signatures on the two pages of this affidavit is mine although they are fairly close imitations (except for the way the capital A is written in my second name, Ann. I have always used a pointed capital A and whoever signed my name on these two pages used a round capital A each time).

"Also I note that a woman has signed her name as a Notary Public and has indicated that this alleged statement was 'sworn to and subscribed' before her. This also is untrue." Mercer said she was the only woman present during any of her questioning.[212]

Julia Ann Mercer has been a key witness in the assassination of John F. Kennedy from the beginning. The government knows that. So does she. For that reason, she has been almost impossible to locate for decades.

Jim Garrison, "conscious of the sudden deaths of some witnesses who appeared to have seen too much for their own survival,"[213] thought she should continue to use her maiden name on her New Orleans statements, just as she had in Dallas. She followed his suggestion, and thereby became inaccessible. Nevertheless, because of the critically important nature of her testimony, in the late 1970s Garrison offered to locate her for the House Select Committee on Assassinations, "if they intended to call her as a witness and would assure me that there would be a serious effort to protect her."[214] He never heard from them. He later read in the HSCA's published report that he had sent them statements on the "allegation" made by Julia Ann Mercer, but that the "committee has been unable to locate Ms. Mercer."[215]

From reading her own definitive statements, countering the government's claims of what she said, I have sometimes felt like I knew her. Of course, I don't. However, I once talked to someone who did—her stepdaughter. She described her in the same way anybody might who has read Julia Ann Mercer's own words, as opposed to their government revision. She said her stepmother was "very dynamic, very straightforward, and very determined."[216] She also made it clear that her stepmother knew the meaning of witness intimidation and had chosen to disappear from public view. Since 1983 when Mercer granted an interview to author Henry Hurt,[217] she has remained hidden and anonymous.

From the moment on November 22, 1963, when Julia Ann Mercer was caught in traffic beside the grassy knoll, she has been very dynamic, very straightforward, and very determined to see and tell the truth. For some, that has made her a very dangerous person. It has also placed her in danger. However, she has never repudiated or compromised her testimony.

Julia Ann Mercer summarized her response to the repeated government claims that she could not identify the driver of the pickup truck from which the rifle had been taken up the grassy knoll: "That is not true. I saw the driver very clearly. I looked right in his face and he looked at me twice. It was Jack Ruby."[218]

At a White House meeting the evening of Tuesday, November 19, JFK's second-to-last night in Washington, the president said he was willing to visit the developing nation of Indonesia the following spring.[219] Kennedy was thereby endorsing a long-standing invitation from President Sukarno, the fiery Indonesian leader. Sukarno was notorious in Washington for his anti-American rhetoric and militant third world nationalism. Although Sukarno said he was a neutralist in terms of the Cold War, U.S. analysts saw him favoring Soviet policies, as shown by his acceptance of Soviet military aid to Indonesia.

Yet Kennedy, who had been an outspoken senator in support of newly liberated third world nations, welcomed Sukarno to the White House in 1961. Sukarno had in turn hoped to host Kennedy in Indonesia. When the Indonesian leader repeated his invitation in November 1963, he said he would give the U.S. President "the grandest reception anyone ever received here."[220]

Kennedy's openness to Sukarno and the nonaligned movement he represented once again placed the president in direct conflict with the Central Intelligence Agency. The CIA's Deputy Director for Plans, Richard Bissell, wrote to Kennedy's National Security Adviser, McGeorge Bundy, in March 1961:

"Indonesia's growing vulnerability to communism stems from the distinctive bias of Sukarno's global orientation, as well as from his domestic policies . . . That his dictatorship may possibly endure *as long as he lives* strikes us as the crux of the Indonesian problem."[221]

The CIA wanted Sukarno dead, and what the Agency saw as his pro-communist "global orientation" obliterated. Still justifying the CIA's assassination efforts in an interview long after his retirement, Richard Bissell put Congo leader Patrice Lumumba and Sukarno in the same disposable category: "Lumumba and Sukarno were two of the worst people in public

life I've ever heard of. They were mad dogs . . . I believed they were dangerous to the United States." [222]

Assassination plots against such men, Bissell conceded, may at times
have shown "bad judgment," but only when they were unsuccessful. He
insisted that plotting to kill such "mad dogs" was "not bad morality." He
regretted only that certain CIA assassination plots had failed and become
public.[223]

The CIA's coup plotting against Sukarno became public during the Eisenhower administration. In the fall of 1956, the CIA's then-Deputy Director
for Plans, Frank Wisner, said to his Far East division chief, "I think it's time
we held Sukarno's feet to the fire." [224] The Agency then fomented a 1957–58
army rebellion in Indonesia, supplied arms shipments to the rebels, and even
used a fleet of camouflaged CIA planes to bomb Sukarno's government
troops.[225] The CIA's covert role was exposed after one of its hired pilots,
Allen Pope, bombed a church and a central market, killing many civilians.
Pope was shot down and identified as a CIA employee.[226] Sukarno freed
Pope from a death sentence four years later in response to a personal appeal
by Robert Kennedy, when the Attorney General visited Indonesia on behalf
of the president, thereby strengthening the bonds Sukarno felt with both
Kennedys.

Unlike the CIA, President Kennedy wanted to work with Sukarno, not
kill or overthrow him. In 1961–62, the president brokered an agreement
between Indonesia and its former colonial master, the Netherlands, on the
eve of war between them. JFK's peaceful resolution of the Indonesian-Dutch
crisis through the United Nations ceded the contested area of West Irian
(West New Guinea) from the Netherlands to Indonesia, giving the people of
West Irian the option by 1969 of leaving Indonesia. The CIA felt Kennedy
was thereby aiding and abetting the enemy. As Bissell put it, "by backing
Indonesia's claim to sovereignty over West Irian, we may inadvertently help
to consolidate a regime which is innately antagonistic toward the United
States." [227]

Kennedy looked at the situation instead through Sukarno's eyes. He
said, "When you consider things like CIA's support to the 1958 rebellion
[against his government], Sukarno's frequently anti-American attitude is
understandable." [228]

Citing this statement, an adviser to the president noted: "This remark
seems somehow to have worked its way back to Sukarno, who found the
generosity and understanding that prompted it confirmed when he met the
President himself." [229] Through his empathy with an apparent ideological
opponent, Kennedy was able to acknowledge the truth behind Sukarno's
words, establish a mutual respect with him, and prevent Indonesia and the
Netherlands from going to war.

At the same time that Kennedy diplomatically resolved the Indonesian–
Netherlands conflict, the president countered the CIA's plots against Sukarno
by issuing his National Security Action Memorandum 179 on August 16,

1962. Addressing NSAM 179 to the heads of the State Department, Defense Department, CIA, AID, and the U.S. Information Agency, JFK ordered them to take a positive approach to Indonesia:

"With a peaceful settlement of the West Irian dispute now in prospect, I would like to see us capitalize on the US role in promoting this settlement to move toward a new and better relationship with Indonesia. I gather that with this issue resolved the Indonesians too would like to move in this direction, and will be presenting us with numerous requests.

"To seize this opportunity, will all agencies concerned please review their programs for Indonesia and assess what further measures might be useful. I have in mind the possibility of expanded civic action, military aid, and economic stabilization and development programs, as well as diplomatic initiatives. The Department of State is requested to pull together all relevant agency proposals in a plan of action and submit it to me no later than September 15th.

John F. Kennedy" [230]

As in the case of newly independent African nations, the CIA's deep-seated opposition to Kennedy's openness to Sukarno arose from something more basic than Cold War ideology. As in the Congo, Indonesia was rich in natural resources. If its natural resources were developed, Indonesia would become the third or fourth richest nation in the world.[231] U.S. corporations were determined to exploit Indonesia for their own profits, whereas Sukarno was busy protecting the wealth of his country for the people by expropriating all foreign holdings. With the corporation-friendly Dutch out of the picture thanks to Kennedy's diplomacy, Sukarno could now block foreign control of West Irian resources as well.[232]

From the ruling standpoint of corporate profits and Cold War ideology, it was clear Sukarno had to go. The CIA was committed to achieving that goal, as Sukarno was well aware. On November 4, 1963, he told U.S. ambassador Howard Jones "he had been given evidence of a CIA plan to topple him and his government."[233] Jones reported to the State Department: "Sukarno acknowledged he was convinced that President Kennedy and the U.S. Ambassador were not working against him. However, he was aware from the past that CIA often participated in activities of which the Ambassador was not aware and which even perhaps the White House was not aware."[234]

On the evening of November 19, 1963, when JFK said he was willing to accept Sukarno's invitation to visit Indonesia the following spring, he was setting in motion a radically transforming process that could dramatize in a very visible way Kennedy's support of third world nationalism. That sea change in U.S. government policy would be terminated three days later. The fate of Sukarno himself would be decided, in effect, in Dallas. As would be revealed by post-Dallas events, the primary factor that had kept Sukarno's independent government alive amid the hostile forces trying to undermine it was the personal support of President John F. Kennedy.

The assassins of the president controlled the crime scene, Dealey Plaza, from the beginning. When witnesses instinctively stormed the grassy knoll to chase a shooter who was apparently behind the fence at the top, they immediately encountered plainclothesmen identifying themselves as Secret Service agents. These men facilitated and covered up the escape of the triggermen, if they were not themselves the triggermen shielded by Secret Service credentials.

The Warren Commission acknowledges in effect that the men behind the fence on the grassy knoll could not have been genuine Secret Service agents. The *Warren Report* states that the Secret Service agents "assigned to the motorcade remained at their posts during the race to the hospital. None stayed at the scene of the shooting, and none entered the Texas School Book Depository Building at or immediately after the shooting . . . Forrest V. Sorrels, special agent in charge of the Dallas office, was the first Secret Service agent to return to the scene of the assassination, approximately 20 or 25 minutes after the shots were fired." [235]

The men in Dealey Plaza who said they were Secret Service agents played an important role in the assassination. However, in so doing, they themselves became part of the evidence. This was thanks to the testimony of the witnesses whom they were trying to control.

After President Kennedy was shot when his limousine passed through Dealey Plaza, Dallas Police Officer Joe Marshall Smith was one of the first people to rush up the grassy knoll and behind its stockade fence. As he reported to his superiors, he smelled gunpowder right away.[236] He told the Warren Commission that when he encountered a man in the parking lot behind the fence, "I pulled my pistol from my holster, and I thought, this is silly, I don't know who I am looking for, and I put it back. Just as I did, he showed me that he was a Secret Service agent." [237]

The "Secret Service agent" was well prepared to discourage anyone like Officer Smith who might challenge his being behind the fence where someone had just shot at the president. "He saw me coming with my pistol," Smith said, "and right away he showed me who he was." [238]

"The man, this character," Smith said in an interview, "produces credentials from his hip pocket which showed him to be Secret Service. I have seen those credentials before, and they satisfied me and the deputy sheriff." [239]

However, especially when Officer Smith learned later that there were no real Secret Service agents there, he realized that the man he had confronted, with the smell of gunpowder in the air, didn't look the part of a Secret Service agent.

"He looked like an auto mechanic." Smith said. "He had on a sports shirt and sports pants. But he had dirty fingernails, it looked like, and hands that looked like an auto mechanic's hands. And afterwards it didn't ring true for the Secret Service." [240]

Another witness who met a man behind the fence with Secret Service identification was Gordon L. Arnold, a twenty-two-year-old soldier in uniform. Arnold confronted a "Secret Service agent" at about the same place as Officer Smith did. In Arnold's case, the encounter happened shortly before the assassination.

Infantryman Gordon Arnold was on leave in Dallas after having completed his basic training. He had brought a movie camera to Dealey Plaza to film the presidential motorcade. He thought the railroad bridge over the triple underpass would give him the best vantage point. To get there, Arnold started walking behind the fence on top of the grassy knoll.[241]

He found his way blocked quickly by a man in a civilian suit wearing a sidearm.[242] The man in the suit told the young soldier he shouldn't be there. When Arnold challenged the man's authority, the man pulled out a large identification badge[243] and held it toward Arnold. He said, "I'm with the Secret Service. I don't want anybody up here." [244]

Arnold said all right and began walking back along the fence. He could feel the man following him. Arnold stopped halfway down the fence. He looked over it with his camera. It was an ideal place to shoot his film.

The man in the suit came up again.

"I told you," he said, "to get out of this area."

Arnold said okay. He walked the complete length of the fence and went around to the top of the grassy knoll. A few minutes later, when the presidential limousine approached, Arnold began filming the president. As he stood with his back to the fence that was three feet behind him, he found himself in the line of fire.

"Just after the car turned onto Elm and started toward me," he recalled, "a shot went off from over my left shoulder. I felt the bullet, rather than heard it, and it went right past my left ear . . . You don't really hear the whiz of a bullet; you feel it. You feel something go by, and then you hear a report just behind it . . . It was like a crack, just like I was standing there under the muzzle." [245]

Arnold hit the dirt. He felt a second shot pass over his head and heard its crack. He knew the feeling. During basic training, he had crawled under live machine gun fire.

When the shooting stopped, while Arnold was still lying on the ground, he felt a sharp kick.

"Get up," said a policeman standing over him.

A second policeman appeared. He was crying and shaking. In his hands was a long gun that he was waving nervously at Arnold. The two men demanded Arnold's film.

When Gordon Arnold described his experience years later, he said, "I thought [the man with the gun] was a police officer, because he had the uniform of a police officer. He didn't wear a hat, and he had dirty hands. But it didn't really matter much at that time [whether he was a police officer or not]. With him crying like he was, and with him shaking, and with the weapon in his hand, I think I'd have given him almost anything . . ." [246]

Arnold tossed the movie camera to the first "police officer." The man opened it, pulled out the film, and threw the camera back to Arnold. The two men in police uniforms left quickly with his film. Arnold would never see or hear of his film again. He ran to his car. Two days later, he was on a plane reporting for duty at Fort Wainwright, Alaska. Terrified by his experience on the grassy knoll, he did not report it to authorities.

The deep fear Gordon Arnold felt from the "Secret Service agent," the two "police officers," and the bullets that were fired by an assassin a few feet behind him, silenced him for years. He heard about the mysterious deaths of witnesses to the assassination. He had been one of the closest witnesses. He did not want to become one of the dead ones. [247]

Arnold shared his experience on the grassy knoll with very few people. His story finally became public in 1978 when a Dallas reporter heard about it, and persuaded Arnold to be interviewed. [248]

According to the testimony of other witnesses, men claiming to be Secret Service agents were collecting critically important evidence immediately after the president was shot. Witness Jean Hill said that when she ran behind the fence of the grassy knoll, men who identified themselves as Secret Service agents held her while they took from her coat pocket all the motorcade pictures she had just put there from her friend Mary Moorman's Polaroid camera. [249] Deputy Constable Seymour Weitzman, who told the Warren Commission he met up with Secret Service agents behind the wall that adjoined the stockade fence, said he turned over "to one of the Secret Service men" what he believed was a portion of the president's skull that he had found on Elm Street. [250] The counterfeit Secret Service agents who took vital evidence from Hill and Weitzman, like the equally questionable men in police uniforms who took Gordon Arnold's movie film, were cleaning up the crime scene only seconds after the president was murdered. It was a pattern that would be followed with other critical evidence for the rest of the day.

No one had a more revealing view than did witness Ed Hoffman of what the phony Secret Service agents were facilitating and covering up. Ed Hoffman was uniquely qualified to serve as an eyewitness. He had trained himself to see more sharply than most people because he lacked one sense they had—hearing. Ed Hoffman was a deaf-mute. His keen eyewitness testimony has given us eyes to see behind the fence.

On the morning of November 22, Ed Hoffman, twenty-seven years old, was excused from his job in a machine shop at Texas Instruments in North Dallas because he had broken a tooth. While he was driving to the dentist, he was reminded by seeing the crowds of people along the street that President Kennedy was visiting Dallas that day. Hoffman momentarily forgot about his tooth and decided to stop and see the president, who was expected in a little less than an hour. He parked his car on the broad shoulder of Stemmons Freeway just west of Dealey Plaza, and walked to a point where he would be able to look down from the freeway into the president's car when it passed below him. He found he also had a panoramic view of the railroad bridge at Dealey Plaza and the area adjoining it behind the wooden fence at the top of the grassy knoll.[251]

Although he was standing beside a freeway roaring with traffic, he heard none of it. He explained later his attention to what he was seeing: "I think my vision is much sharper than a hearing person's, because I concentrate totally on what I'm seeing and there are no sounds to distract me. I was really enjoying the view."[252]

In the forty-five minutes before the presidential motorcade arrived, Ed Hoffman became completely absorbed in watching the activities of two men behind the stockade fence at the top of the grassy knoll. He saw a stocky man in a dark blue business suit and black hat standing near the fence. In Ed Hoffman's mind, this was the "suit man." The second man Hoffman observed was tall, thin, and dressed like a railroad worker. The "railroad man" stood waiting by the switch box at the railroad tracks, where the tracks, after passing across the bridge, ran perpendicular to the fence. Hoffman was puzzled by the fact that the two men, although dressed quite differently, seemed to be working together. The "suit man" kept walking back and forth between the fence and the switch box, where he would confer with the "railroad man."[253]

Hoffman also noticed two cars drive into the parking lot behind the fence: first, a white four-door; then a light green Rambler station wagon. Hoffman thought the drivers were looking for parking spaces. After driving through the parking lot, the Rambler station wagon parked near a railroad switching tower. Ed Hoffman's sharp eye had just spotted a vehicle that he and other witnesses would identify as a getaway vehicle in the hour ahead.[254]

When Hoffman sensed that the presidential limousine (which he could not see) was approaching, he saw the "suit man" walk over to the "railroad man" a final time, speak briefly, and return to the fence. The "suit man" crouched down and stood up, apparently picking something up. He looked over the fence. In the silent drama Ed Hoffman was watching, he then saw a puff of smoke by the "suit man." He assumed it was from a cigarette.[255] He soon realized the smoke had come from the firing of a rifle he was unable to hear.

Hoffman saw the "suit man" turn suddenly with a rifle in his hands. He ran to the "railroad man," tossing the rifle to him over a thin, horizontal pipe about four feet off the ground. The "railroad man" caught the rifle, breaking it down with a twist. He thrust it in a railroad worker's soft brown tool bag and ran north along the tracks. The "suit man" turned back, assumed a casual pose, and began strolling alongside the fence.[256]

A police officer came quickly around the fence and confronted the "suit man" with a revolver. The "suit man" held out his empty hands. He then took what was apparently identification out of his coat pocket and showed it to the police officer. The officer put his gun away. The "suit man" mingled with the crowd of people that was coming around the fence.[257] He then "walked over to the Rambler wagon and got in on the passenger side. The Rambler station wagon drove out of the parking lot along the north side of the [Texas School Book Depository]. Hoffman last saw this vehicle as it made a right turn onto Houston Street."[258]

Ed Hoffman's attention switched to the presidential limousine, as it was then being driven below him onto Stemmons Freeway. He looked down on President Kennedy's body sprawled across the back seat, with a gaping wound in his right rear skull. It looked like bloody Jello.[259]

Hoffman was unable to see anything more behind the fence. A slowly moving freight train had crossed the railroad bridge and was blocking his view. Realizing he had witnessed the assassination of the president, he became overwhelmed by the need to let people know that he had seen the man with the rifle. He ran to his car. He made visits to Dallas Police Headquarters and the FBI office that proved futile. In the wake of the assassination, no one was patient enough to understand a seemingly obsessed man who was unable to speak.

Hoffman's biggest hope was to communicate what he had seen to his father. Frederick Hoffman, a florist, was his son's best friend and a hearing person who knew sign language. Ed hoped his father would help him tell his story to the authorities. However, when Ed finished telling Frederick excitedly in sign how he had seen the man who killed the president, his father was strangely resistant to the idea of phoning the police. (Ed would realize later that his father recognized Ed was in a dangerous position and was trying to protect him.) After Oswald was arrested and shown on television, Ed insisted the police had the wrong man from the wrong place, the Texas School Book Depository, not the man with the rifle he had seen behind the fence. Yet his father continued to put him off. He finally agreed to help Ed tell his story to his Uncle Bob—Lieutenant Robert Hoffman, a Dallas Police detective—during the Hoffman family's Thanksgiving gathering, six days after the assassination.[260]

After Frederick Hoffman had interpreted Ed's story in detail on Thanksgiving Day, detective Robert Hoffman stood up for emphasis and spoke seriously to his nephew. What Ed saw from his father's translation was:

"Your father is right. You should keep quiet about this. You might be in danger."

Ed argued against his uncle and father. He signed in protest to them: "The real killers got away! The authorities don't know about the shot from behind the fence. They have to be notified!"

The Dallas Police lieutenant's response, through the signing of Ed's father, was even more emphatic: "You stay-down. Hush! You talk, you get-shot!"[261]

For three and a half years, Ed Hoffman followed his father's and his uncle's counsel that he keep quiet about the assassination. Then, compelled by his conscience and without his father's knowledge, Hoffman made an appointment with the Dallas FBI office for June 28, 1967. With no sign language interpreter present, he tried to give his testimony on what he had seen behind the fence to Special Agent Will Hayden Griffin by means of gestures, sketches, and notes made up of sentence fragments. Griffin's subsequent report was so filled with transcription errors, if not deliberate misrepresentations, that it ultimately had Hoffman saying he "could not have seen the [two] men running because of a fence west of the Texas School Book Depository building." [262]

Nevertheless, Griffin did understand Hoffman well enough to think it advisable to offer him a bribe to remain silent about what he knew.

After Hoffman had used every means at his command to communicate his knowledge of the assassination, Agent Griffin smiled at him. He pointed his index finger at Hoffman, for the word, "you." Griffin put his finger to his mouth, meaning "hush." He mimed taking his wallet from his hip pocket and giving Hoffman something from it. To indicate what that would be, he held out his hand with his fingers extended—for the number 5—then closed his hand twice into a fist, for "00."

Hoffman was shocked. He immediately gestured to Griffin his refusal of the bribe.

Griffin's smile passed into a stern, almost angry expression. He gestured more earnestly to Hoffman, "You hush!" [263]

After Ed Hoffman left, agent Griffin phoned Frederick Hoffman about his son's visit to the FBI office. Frederick was appalled at what Ed had done. When Ed stopped by his father's flower shop, Frederick told him in despair, "I can't do anything about it if they shoot you, too!" [264]

A week later, the FBI interviewed Frederick Hoffman, asking him to assess his son's testimony. Hoffman continued to fear that Ed would be killed if he were identified as an assassination witness. He was therefore not about to confirm the likely truth of Ed's story. Yet he could not deny his son's integrity. Ed's brother, Fred, who was present at their father's FBI interview, claimed that Frederick ended up making a confusing, agnostic statement to the FBI: "I don't know if Ed saw what he saw." [265]

Frederick Hoffman may have realized the FBI would give his words a negative twist in their report, as they did: "The father of Virgil [Edward] Hoffman stated that he did not believe that his son had seen anything of value . . ." [266]

After his father's death in 1976, Ed Hoffman made a final attempt on March 25, 1977, with the partial help of interpreters, to communicate his knowledge to the FBI. The FBI's report was again so full of errors that it bore little resemblance to Hoffman's testimony. [267] It was only in 1989 with the publication of Jim Marrs's book *Crossfire*, containing Hoffman's story as given through an interpreter, that Ed Hoffman was finally able to tell an attentive audience what he had seen behind the fence of the grassy knoll. [268]

Ed Hoffman had witnessed a critically important scene in the assassination scenario. The "suit man," who tossed the rifle to the "railroad man" for rapid disposal, had been equipped beforehand with a powerful means of identification. His just showing it at the murder scene, with the smell of gunpowder still in the air, had so reassured a suspicious police officer, Joe Marshall Smith, that he immediately put his gun away and let the suspect go without detaining or questioning him.[269] The man, whose credentials passed him off as a Secret Service agent, was in fact a methodical assassin in an orchestrated killing of the president. Moments before, as Hoffman had seen, the documented "Secret Service agent" had fired his rifle at President Kennedy before tossing it to an assistant. Thus, the assassins were not only well prepared to identify themselves as government agents. They also seemed confident that they would not be exposed from their bold use of Secret Service credentials to assure their escape. They were right. The Warren Commission went out of its way to ignore the obvious evidence of Secret Service imposters at a source of the shots.

As we learned from Secret Service agent Abraham Bolden, the Secret Service took the extraordinary step of withdrawing and replacing all of its agents' commission books a month and a half following the assassination, moving Bolden to suspect that Secret Service identification had been used as a cover by the assassins of President Kennedy. Officer Joe Marshall Smith, who was familiar with Secret Service credentials, said he had confronted a man behind the fence at the top of the grassy knoll who showed him such credentials. That raises the question: What was the source of the Secret Service identification displayed by JFK's assassins?

In June 2007, in response to a fifteen-year-old Freedom of Information Act request, the CIA finally declassified its "Family Jewels" report. Buried in the 702-page collection of documents was a memorandum written by Sidney Gottlieb, chief of the CIA's Technical Services Division (TSD). Gottlieb was the notorious designer of the CIA's contaminated skin diving suit intended in the spring of 1963 for the assassination of Castro, the scapegoating of Kennedy, and the destruction of an incipient Cuban–American rapprochement.

In his secret May 8, 1973, CIA memorandum, Sidney Gottlieb stated that "over the years" his Technical Services Division "furnished this [Secret] Service" with "gate passes, security passes, passes for presidential campaign, emblems for presidential vehicles; a secure ID photo system."[270] The Secret Service supposedly received its identifying documents from the Bureau of Engraving and Printing, as Abraham Bolden said it did in the replacement of its agents' commission books in January 1964.[271] Since the Bureau of Engraving and Printing is, like the Secret Service, a part of the Treasury Department, it is reasonable in terms of in-house security and accessibility that it—and especially not the CIA—would provide the Secret Service commission books. Yet here is the CIA's Sidney Gottlieb acknowledging that "over the years" his Technical Services Division "furnished" such identification to the Secret Service—identification that could just as easily have been given at any time, as might prove useful, to CIA operatives using a Secret Service cover. The source was the same.

There is a certain criminal consistency between Gottlieb's having prepared a poisoned diving suit meant for Castro's murder and his perhaps having furnished as well the Secret Service credentials used by the assassins on the grassy knoll. However, Gottlieb was only a CIA functionary who carried out higher orders. The more responsible assassins were above him.

What does the phenomenon of a sniper team supplied with official government credentials for an immediate cover-up tell us about the forces behind the crime?

Would an innocent government, in its investigation of the murder of its president, ignore such evidence of treachery within its own ranks? [272]

A key to John Kennedy's presidency, and to its end in Dallas, was his extraordinary, ongoing communication with his Communist adversary, Nikita Khrushchev.

According to the official State Department record, *Kennedy-Khrushchev Exchanges*, the last such exchange between Chairman Khrushchev and President Kennedy happened on October 10, 1963. [273] On that day in Moscow, after a ceremony in which Khrushchev proudly signed the historic Limited Test Ban Treaty, Soviet Deputy Foreign Minister Valerian Zorin handed U.S. ambassador Foy Kohler a letter from Khrushchev to Kennedy.

Foy Kohler was not an ambassador on the same wave length as his president. JFK had appointed Kohler, a rigid Cold Warrior recommended by the Foreign Service, [274] only when Robert Kennedy, who strongly opposed him, was unable to come up with an alternative. [275] When Kohler wired to the State Department what would turn out to be the final Khrushchev–Kennedy letter, he characteristically dismissed its significance in a way that Kennedy would not have. Kohler's telegram stated that the Khrushchev letter contained "nothing new of substance." [276] While that may have been technically true, Khrushchev considered his letter to Kennedy, issued on the occasion of their greatest mutual achievement, at least important enough for the Soviet leader to have it broadcast over Moscow Radio that same evening. Kennedy would have thought it important enough, at the very least, for Khrushchev to receive a reply from him. That was not to happen.

In Khrushchev's letter to the president, the Soviet chairman followed Kennedy's lead in his UN address by proposing in turn that they together use the test ban treaty, that "has injected a fresh spirit into the international atmosphere," as their opening "to seek solutions of other ripe international questions." He then singled out projects that the two of them could work on: "conclusion of a non-aggression pact between countries of NATO and member states of the Warsaw Pact, creation of nuclear free zones in various regions of the world, barring the further spread of the nuclear weapon, banning of launching into orbit objects bearing nuclear weapons, measures for the prevention of surprise attack, and a series of other steps." [277]

"Their implementation," Khrushchev wrote, "would clear the road to general and complete disarmament, and, consequently, to the delivering of peoples from the threat of war." [278]

Khrushchev's vision, as inspired by the test ban treaty, corresponded in a deeply hopeful way to Kennedy's American University address. In his letter, Khrushchev was signaling his readiness to work with Kennedy on a host of projects. If the two leaders should succeed as they had on the test ban treaty, in only a few of Khrushchev's suggested projects, they would end the Cold War.

However, following Ambassador Kohler's negative comment, the State Department doubted if Khrushchev's letter even deserved a response from the president. A State Department memorandum sent from "Mr. Klein" to National Security Adviser McGeorge Bundy again dismissed the Khrushchev letter: "With reference to the message from Khrushchev on the signing of the test ban treaty, the Department generally is reluctant to make a substantive reply. Should there be a polite response?" [279]

Someone, presumably McGeorge Bundy, wrote "Yes" under the typed question.

The State Department then prepared a "polite," two-paragraph "Suggested Reply from the President to Khrushchev," and sent it back on October 20 to McGeorge Bundy. He scribbled, "Approved, let's get it out" on the cover memorandum. But, unlike other documents seen and approved by the president himself, there is no indication on this one that it was seen by anyone except National Security Adviser Bundy.

It is at this point that the final Khrushchev-to-Kennedy letter, and the president's minimal response approved by McGeorge Bundy, were filed into limbo by the State Department. For the month remaining until Kennedy's death, nothing at all was sent to Khrushchev. His hopeful, open-ended letter to Kennedy on their next possible steps together was simply left hanging.

Two and one-half weeks after Kennedy's assassination, a terse, official explanation was put on record for this abrupt ending of a correspondence that, if allowed to continue, could have ended the Cold War. A White House "Memo for Record" was typed up on December 9, 1963. It stated that the draft reply approved by Bundy was never sent to Khrushchev "due to clerical misunderstanding in the State Department." [280]

The unsigned memorandum then observed: "When it was learned on December 4, 1963 that a reply had not gone forward, the State Department recommended, and Mr. McGeorge Bundy concurred, that no reply need be made at this time." [281]

Since John Kennedy was dead, it would have been difficult for the State Department and Bundy to send Khrushchev an apology in Kennedy's name (or anyone else's), attempting to explain the "clerical misunderstanding" that had ended their correspondence. Moreover, had Khrushchev learned of this "clerical misunderstanding," he would have had further reason to question just what kind of support the president was getting from his own government in the month before his assassination.

After following the baffling trail of this aborted end to the Kennedy–Khrushchev correspondence, historian Michael Beschloss commented: "Waiting in Moscow for Kennedy's reply, Khrushchev might have wondered why Kennedy had not responded to his cordial letter about new opportunities for peace. As the weeks passed in silence, his dark imagination may have begun to take over: was the president about to turn his back on the emerging détente?" [282]

Fortunately, however, Khrushchev knew better than that, because Kennedy had used a surreptitious means to reassure him. The Soviet chairman knew through a back-channel message from Kennedy that the president had not given up at all on their mutual hopes for peace. Kennedy let Khrushchev know at the end of September that he did indeed want to move forward with the Soviets on disarmament talks, but that he had to do so secretly.

Thanks to the opening of Moscow archives following the fall of the Soviet Union, we can now begin to see the Soviet side of this subterranean tale of Cold War leaders in communication. Drawing on previously top-secret Soviet documents, authors Aleksandr Fursenko and Timothy Naftali discovered that "on September 30, 1963, John Kennedy through his press secretary, Pierre Salinger, had attempted to reestablish a confidential channel to the Soviet leadership." [283]

As we recall, it was Pierre Salinger who in the fall of 1961 received for Kennedy the first secret letter from Khrushchev, rolled up in a newspaper by a Soviet "magazine editor" who was in reality a member of the KGB, the Soviet secret police. Now Kennedy, through Salinger, was reversing the process.

Vladimir Semichastny, the Moscow head of the KGB, reported to Nikita Khrushchev on October 2, 1963, that Kennedy wanted to reopen the secret channel between them, using Salinger and a Washington-based KGB agent as the conduit. Kennedy's people had recommended Colonel G. V. Karpovich, a known KGB officer in the U.S.S.R.'s Washington Embassy, as an undercover messenger between JFK and Khrushchev.[284] As Fursenko and Naftali confirmed from the Soviet documents, Khrushchev then "approved the use of the KGB as an intermediary to exchange proposals [with Kennedy] that could not go through regular diplomatic channels." [285]

Kennedy's secret September 30 initiative to Khrushchev preempted in a shrewd way the State Department's (deliberate or inadvertent) termination of his formal correspondence with the Soviet leader. The president was well aware of how few people in his administration he could trust with his peacemaking messages to their Communist enemies. As he was forced to do repeatedly with his Cold War bureaucracy, he simply bypassed the State Department's resistance to his dialogue with Khrushchev in the fall of 1963 by creating an alternative means of communication.[286]

Nevertheless, although the tactic was a familiar one for Kennedy, the means he sought out for his final effort to explore peace with Khrushchev is startling. For JFK to have to rely in the end not on his own State Department but on the Soviet secret police to convey secure messages of peace between himself and Khrushchev speaks volumes. Because of his turn toward peace, the president had become almost totally isolated in his own government before he made his trip to Dallas.

At 10:30 A.M. on November 22, 1963, Sheriff Bill Decker held a meeting in preparation for the President's visit to Dallas that day. Decker had called together all his available deputies, about one hundred men.[287] They included the plainclothes men and detectives who were especially important to the president's safety as he passed through the streets of Dallas. Decker gave his assembled officers an unusual order.

The Sheriff said they "were to take *no* part whatsoever in the security of that [presidential] motorcade." The Sheriff told his officers they were simply "to stand out in front of the building, 505 Main Street, and represent the Sheriff's Office."[288]

Sheriff Decker gave the order of noninvolvement to his security teams just two hours before the president's assassination in Dealey Plaza, which was just outside the window of the sheriff's office.[289] As Deputy Sheriff Roger Craig later reflected back on the sheriff's words, he realized that Decker had withdrawn the Dallas County component of President Kennedy's security at the motorcade's most vulnerable location only a few feet away.[290]

Dealey Plaza was characterized by tall buildings, fences, and sewer openings. Sniper teams could take their pick. The hairpin turn from Houston to Elm Street would slow the limousine to a crawl, making the president an almost stationary target for crossfire from many possible angles. What was in effect a sniper's gallery represented a tremendous challenge for security police. The withdrawal of JFK's security made Dealey Plaza the ideal ambush site, set up with the help of those responsible for the president's protection.

Dallas Police Chief Jesse Curry, like Sheriff Bill Decker, gave a critical order that would also keep his officers away from Dealey Plaza during the president's perilous passage through it. William Manchester, in his book *The Death of a President*, noted that Curry told his officers "to end supervision of Friday's crowd at Houston and Main, a block short of the ambush, on the ground that traffic would begin to thin out there."[291]

The truth lay deeper. Chief Curry, in his book *JFK Assassination File*, gave a more authoritative reason than the anticipation of light traffic for his cutting short the president's security one block too soon. He said he was simply following the orders of the Secret Service: "The Dallas Police Department carefully carried out the security plans which were laid out by Mr. Lawson, the Secret Service representative from Washington, D.C."[292]

Chief Curry and Sheriff Decker gave their orders withdrawing security from the president *in obedience* to orders they had themselves received from the Secret Service. Curry and Decker in Dallas were carrying out orders from

Washington. As the House Select Committee on Assassinations put it, it was the Secret Service that "defined and supervised the functions of the police during Kennedy's visit [to Dallas]."[293]

The Secret Service also made a critical change in the protection the president would normally receive from his motorcycle escorts. Following past precedents, the Dallas Police had made plans at a preliminary meeting (not attended by the Secret Service) to assign motorcycle escorts "alongside the President's car,"[294] thereby partially screening the president from any gunfire. However, at a Dallas Police Department/Secret Service coordinating meeting held on November 21, the Secret Service changed the plan. The motorcycle escorts were pulled back from their positions alongside the limousine (where they shielded the president) to positions in the rear (where they were not a hindrance to snipers).[295]

The reason given for this stripping of security from the president was that he didn't want his motorcycle security. Police Captain Perdue W. Lawrence, the Dallas officer for escort security, testified to the Warren Commission on the Secret Service rationale for the change made at the November 21 meeting: "I heard one of the Secret Service men say that President Kennedy did not desire any motorcycle officer directly on each side of him, between him and the crowd, but he would want the officers to the rear."[296]

The Secret Service advance man from Washington, Winston G. Lawson, who attended the November 21 meeting, explained to the Warren Commission: "It was my understanding that [the president] did not like a lot of motorcycles surrounding the car . . . if there are a lot of motorcycles around the President's car, I know for a fact that he can't hear the people that are with him in the car talking back and forth, and there were other considerations I believe why he did not want them completely surrounding his car."[297]

It is puzzling, however, why JFK had the "desire," explained by the Secret Service after his death, to withdraw his motorcycle security only in Dallas. The day before in Houston, he apparently had no such desire, since the Secret Service (according to its own report on the Houston presidential visit) deployed motorcycles there in its normal way alongside the presidential limousine.[298] The House Select Committee on Assassinations drew the reluctant conclusion:

"Surprisingly, the security measure used in the prior motorcades during the same Texas visit show that the deployment of motorcycles in Dallas by the Secret Service may have been uniquely insecure . . . it may well be that by altering Dallas Police Department Captain Lawrence's original motorcycle plan, the Secret Service deprived Kennedy of security in Dallas that it had provided a mere day before in Houston."[299]

Even more critically, the Secret Service withdrew the protection of its agents normally stationed on the back of the presidential limousine. If the agents had been at their usual posts on the limousine, holding the hand rails on the car, they could have obstructed gunfire or thrown themselves on the president when the shooting began. But they, too, had been withdrawn in Dallas. They were reassigned to the car following the limousine, where they were useless in preventing the assassination. During the shooting of the president, the Special Agent in Charge of the follow-up car, Emory Roberts, actually ordered his agents "not to move even after recognizing the first shot as a shot."[300] To his credit, Agent Clint Hill disobeyed Roberts's order by instead running after the limousine and climbing on it, but too late to help the president.[301]

The reason given for the further stripping of agents from the limousine was that the president also didn't want his limousine security. According to Secret Service documents submitted to the Warren Commission, the president had said "he did not want agents riding on the back of his car."[302]

To investigate this claim, researcher Vincent Palamara interviewed a series of former Secret Service agents and White House aides to Kennedy. They all agreed that, on the contrary, "Kennedy did not restrict agents from riding on the rear of the limousine."[303]

Agent Gerald A. Behn, the initially cited source of the official Secret Service/Warren Commission claim that JFK stripped away his limousine security, told Palamara the exact opposite: *"I don't remember Kennedy ever saying that he didn't want anybody on the back of the car."*[304]

Contrary to the Secret Service claim that it had to deal with a difficult president who opposed having agents on his limousine, former agent Robert Lilly said, "Oh, I'm sure he didn't. He was very cooperative with us once he became President. He was extremely cooperative. Basically, 'whatever you guys want is the way it will be.'"[305]

Even agent Floyd Boring, the most frequently used source for the Warren Commission claim, said instead of the president: "He didn't tell them anything . . . JFK was a very easy-going guy . . . he didn't interfere with our actions at all."[306]

From Palamara's interviews, it soon became obvious that the withdrawal of agents from the presidential limousine in Dallas "was a Secret Service decision, not a JFK desire as 'official' history (Warren Commission/[Jim] Bishop/ [William] Manchester/ Secret Service) has told us all. The Secret Service lied, using JFK as a scapegoat."[307]

Besides withdrawing security from Dealey Plaza and the presidential limousine, the Secret Service also planned the turn that slowed Kennedy's limousine to a crawl. That forced slowdown completed the setup for the snipers in waiting. The Secret Service advance man, Winston G. Lawson, approved the fatal dogleg turn in Dealey Plaza when he and the Dallas Special Agent in Charge, Forrest V. Sorrels, did their dry run over the motorcade route on November 18.[308]

Thus, not only did the Secret Service plan and coordinate a turn that flagrantly violated its own security rule of a forty-four-mile-an-hour minimum speed for the presidential limousine.[309] Through orders from Washington, the agency responsible for the president's security created a vacuum of security—in Dealey Plaza, all around the presidential limousine, and on the surrounding buildings as well.

Air Force Colonel Fletcher Prouty, who helped supervise security for President Eisenhower's visit to Mexico City, said it was a Secret Service rule for an obviously dangerous site like Dealey Plaza "to order all the windows to be closed and sealed. Put a seal on it that says to anyone working in the building: 'Do NOT open this window.' Then you say, yes, but how are you going to control maybe hundreds of people? It's not hard. You put a man on the roof with a radio. You put others in strategic positions with snipers' rifles. You put another man down in the middle of the plaza on the grass, looking up, and he's got a radio. If he sees a window open, he broadcasts immediately: 'third floor, fourth window over.' The snipers cover the window and one of the team on the roof runs down there, sees why the window's up—some secretary opened the window to see the President go by—and he says: 'Close that window!' And it's closed. You have radios. It can be done."[310]

Yet, as we have seen, the only "Secret Service Agents" in Dealey Plaza when the shots were fired were imposters and killers, bearing false credentials to facilitate their escape and coerce witnesses into handing over vital evidence that would vanish. The vacuum created by orders from Washington was immediately filled. When the president's security was systematically withdrawn from Dealey Plaza, his assassins moved swiftly into place.

Unaware of Washington's plans for Dealey Plaza, Deputy Sheriff Roger Craig, on hearing the first shot, also moved swiftly. Craig had been following Sheriff Decker's orders, standing passively with the other deputy sheriffs in front of the courthouse at 505 Main Street. At 12:30 P.M., President Kennedy was driven in his limousine past the courthouse and four feet away from Roger Craig. The limousine turned from Main onto Houston. It finally made the agonizingly slow turn from Houston onto Elm. Then Craig heard a rifle shot. He instinctively broke ranks and began running into Dealey Plaza. Before he could reach the corner, he heard two more shots.[311]

John Kennedy was already gone, but Roger Craig's work on his behalf had just begun.

For the next ten minutes, Craig questioned witnesses and looked for bullet marks along the street. While scanning the south curb of Elm Street at 12:40 P.M., he heard a shrill whistle from the opposite side of the street. In an unpublished memoir, *When They Kill a President*, Roger Craig described what he saw when alerted by the whistle:

"I turned and saw a white male in his twenties [whom Craig would later identify, to the dismay of the Warren Commission, as Lee Harvey Oswald] running down the grassy knoll from the direction of the Texas School Book Depository Building. A light green Rambler station wagon was coming slowly west on Elm Street. The driver of the station wagon was a husky looking Latin, with dark wavy hair, wearing a tan wind breaker type jacket. He was looking up at the man running toward him. He pulled over to the north curb and picked up the man coming down the hill. I tried to cross Elm Street to stop them and find out who they were. The traffic was too heavy and I was unable to reach them. They drove away going west on Elm Street." [312]

Craig was struck by the two men's rush to leave the scene of the assassination. Everyone else around him was rushing to the scene to see what they could. Craig thought the incident suspicious enough to report to authorities at the police command post. He ran to the front of the Texas School Book Depository and asked for anyone involved in the investigation. A man on the steps dressed in a gray business suit turned to Craig. He said, "I'm with the Secret Service." [313]

Roger Craig gave his information to the man in the suit, naively believing, as he said later, that everyone at the command post was an actual officer. "The Secret Service Agent" seemed strangely uninterested in what Craig had to say about the two departing men. Then his interest suddenly picked up. He began taking notes on his little pad while Craig told him about the station wagon, an automobile whose description Craig would soon learn seemed to correspond to a station wagon then owned by Marina Oswald's hostess, Ruth Paine. [314]

Later in the afternoon, Roger Craig learned the Dallas Police were holding a man suspected of involvement in the president's murder. Craig thought immediately of the man running down the grassy knoll. He phoned the homicide chief, Captain Will Fritz, who asked him to come look at the suspect.

Shortly after 4:30 P.M., Craig looked into Captain Fritz's office and identified the man being held there as the same man he had seen running down the grassy knoll to the station wagon—Lee Harvey Oswald. [315]

As Fritz and Craig entered the office together, Fritz said to Oswald, "This man saw you leave."

Oswald became a little excited. He said, "I told you people I did."

Fritz said in a soothing tone of voice, "Take it easy, son. We're just trying to find out what happened."

Then Fritz asked Oswald, "What about the *car?*"

Oswald leaned forward and put both hands on Fritz's desk. He said, "That *station wagon* belongs to Mrs. Paine. Don't try to drag her into this."

Then he leaned back in his chair. He said in a low voice, "Everybody will know who I am now."

Craig has emphasized that Oswald made this statement in a dejected tone of voice. He said, "Everybody will know who I am now," as if his cover had just been blown. [316]

At this point Fritz ushered Craig from the office. It was too late—for both the government and Roger Craig. Deputy Sheriff Craig had seen and heard too much.

It was also at this time that Captain Fritz received an urgent phone request from Sheriff Decker to come see him immediately. Decker's need to talk with Fritz in person, not by phone, was so great that the homicide chief suspended his questioning of Oswald so as to travel the fifteen blocks to the sheriff's office and meet with him privately.[317]

Why did Decker cause such a strange break at an early, critical stage of Fritz's questioning of Oswald? In the rush of all the commotion and chaos, when evidence of the assassination had to be gathered quickly, why did Sheriff Decker not just talk on the phone with Captain Fritz instead of having Fritz traipse halfway across town to confer with him in person?[318] Apparently the sheriff needed to talk in absolute secrecy with the homicide chief, without any risk of their conversation being overheard on the phone.

Although we do not know what Decker said to Fritz behind closed doors, Penn Jones, Jr., the courageous local journalist who explored Dallas's darkest alleys, made the observation "that knowledge of the assassination was on a 'need to know' basis. When Oswald was not killed in the Texas Theater, and was now in the hands of Captain Will Fritz, did Fritz move into the circle of those who 'needed to know'?"[319]

What Deputy Sheriff Roger Craig would testify to in the years ahead, as his piece of the truth of Dallas, was corroborated by a parade of other witnesses. Ed Hoffman had already seen the "suit man" get in a light green Rambler station wagon, which drove him out of the parking lot by the Depository. Additional witnesses saw either the Nash Rambler or someone suspicious who would be picked up by the station wagon. Together with Craig's testimony, these witnesses' stories have given us a picture of the Rambler's function as an escape vehicle—which leads in turn to an insight into the enigma of Lee Harvey Oswald.

Carolyn Walther, a worker in a dress factory, stood on Houston Street at the edge of Dealey Plaza a few minutes before the president's arrival. As she waited for the motorcade, Walther looked up at the Texas School Book Depository. On one of its upper floors,[320] she saw a man in a white shirt leaning out the southeast corner window with a rifle in his hands pointed down, as if for all the world to see. The man, who had blonde or light-brown hair, was looking down the street where the motorcade was about to come around the corner—a posed, public portrait of the assassin waiting for his target to come into view.[321]

However, Carolyn Walther also spied a second, more mysterious man, standing by the man with the rifle. The second man's head was blocked from view by the dirty glass in the upper half of the window. She could see his body from his waist to his shoulders. Her clothing worker's eye took note of the headless man's apparel. Before she turned her eyes to the approaching motorcade, she had seen that the second man in the window was wearing a brown suit coat.[322]

Up the street from Carolyn Walther was another witness about to see a man in such a coat. Standing four feet from the Texas School Book Depository was James Richard Worrell, Jr., a twenty-year-old high school dropout. After the president was driven past him, Worrell heard a shot. He looked straight up at the building over him. He saw the barrel of a rifle sticking out a window in the fifth or sixth floor, pointing in the direction of the limousine. It seemed to be firing—an assassin's weapon in public view. Worrell looked ahead. He saw the president slumping down in his seat.[323]

Terrified, Worrell pivoted and ran up the street as he heard a gun fire two more times. After he heard a fourth shot (thereby contradicting what would be the government's three-shot case against Oswald) and continued running, Worrell paused a block away to catch his breath. He looked back.[324] He saw a man in a sport coat running out the back of the Texas School Book Depository. As the man ran, Worrell could see his coat open and flapping in the breeze. James Worrell turned. Like the man in the sport coat, he fled the scene.[325]

A third witness connected the man in the coat with a Rambler station wagon. High above Carolyn Walther, James Worrell, and the president in his limousine was Richard Randolph Carr, an unemployed steelworker who was ascending the stairway of the partially constructed new courthouse building. He was looking for the foreman on the ninth floor to inquire about work. When he reached the sixth floor, Richard Carr stopped for a rest. He gazed across at the Texas School Book Depository. He saw a man looking out the second window from the southeast corner of the top floor. Carr later described the man as "a heavy set individual, who was wearing a hat, a tan sport coat and horn-rimmed glasses." [326]

About a minute later, Carr heard what he thought was a car's backfire or a firecracker. Then he heard two more such reports in quick succession. From his perch above Dealey Plaza, he looked toward the triple underpass where he thought the noises were coming from and saw people falling to the ground.[327]

Carr descended the stairway to see what had happened. On Houston Street, he was surprised to see the same man in the sport coat who had been at the Depository window. The man was walking quickly toward Carr, looking back over his shoulder.[328] Carr watched him turn and walk a block east very fast. Then the man in the sport coat got into a 1961 or 1962 Rambler station wagon, parked on Record Street. The driver was "a young negro man." [329] The Rambler drove off to the north.

The station wagon then apparently headed two blocks north, made a left turn onto Elm Street, and continued a block and a half down Elm. It was soon spotted there, by Roger Craig and four other witnesses, as it stopped abruptly in front of the Texas School Book Depository.

Helen Forrest witnessed the same scene Roger Craig did but from the opposite side of the street. Forrest told historian Michael Kurtz she was on the incline by the grassy knoll, when she "saw a man suddenly run from the rear of the Depository building, down the incline, and then enter a Rambler station wagon." [330] Like Roger Craig, Helen Forrest was clear in identifying the running man. "If it wasn't Oswald," she said, "it was his identical twin." [331] Forrest's account was corroborated by another eyewitness, James Pennington.[332]

Craig's, Forrest's, and Pennington's stories of the Rambler's grassy knoll pick-up were supported by the testimony of two passing drivers, Marvin C. Robinson and Roy Cooper.

Shortly after the assassination, Marvin Robinson had to jam on his Cadillac's brakes in front of the Texas School Book Depository. The light-colored Rambler just ahead of him had pulled over suddenly beside the curb. It was about to pick up a man coming down the grass from the Depository.[333] Robinson's employee, Roy Cooper, driving just behind him, told the FBI he saw the near-accident. Cooper said the man coming down the incline waved at the Rambler, then jumped into it. The Rambler sped off ahead of Cooper and Robinson in the direction of the Oak Cliff section of Dallas,[334] where Dallas Police Officer J. D. Tippit would soon be killed, and where Lee Harvey Oswald would then be arrested in the Texas Theater.

The Warren Commission rejected Roger Craig's testimony on Oswald and the getaway Rambler, supported by a chorus of eyewitnesses, since the Commission decided by that time that Oswald must have escaped from the scene on a city bus.[335] The *Warren Report* also rejected Craig's account of the dialogue with Oswald in Fritz's office, because Fritz denied Craig was even there.[336] As we have seen, the same Captain Will Fritz, perhaps after moving into the circle of those who "needed to know," told the Louisiana State Police he had no interest in questioning Rose Cheramie as a witness, excluding her testimony just as effectively as he discredited Craig's. Deputy Sheriff Craig would also be attacked on the basis of an FBI report that seemed to show Ruth Paine did not own a Nash Rambler but rather a 1955 Chevrolet station wagon.[337] Judged in terms of its source, the report proved nothing. The FBI agent who wrote it would later confess to a Congressional committee, as we shall see, that he was guilty of deliberately destroying key assassination evidence in obedience to his FBI superior's orders.[338]

By rejecting Roger Craig's testimony, the Warren Commission could ignore the significance of Oswald's words to his interrogator, Captain Fritz. According to Roger Craig, it was Oswald who said the car that picked him up was a station wagon, and who identified the owner of the station wagon as Mrs. Paine, whom Oswald then defended. Moreover, as a result of the incident and his own comments on it, he acted as if he had just blown his cover. Thus he said bleakly, "Everybody will know who I am now," implying his involvement as an undercover intelligence agent.

He was, of course, wrong in thinking now everybody would know who he was. Two days after his remark, Oswald would be dead. And no one beyond a secret circle would know the details about just who he had been. The mouth that was beginning to blurt out the truth of his undercover life would be quickly sealed.

The person nearest to President Kennedy when he was shot to death was his wife, Jacqueline. Her presence in Dallas beside her husband was a sign of the couple's deepening support for each other since the death in August 1963 of their infant son, Patrick Bouvier Kennedy, which had devastated both of them. In his response to the death of their son, we can discern a hidden truth in the life of John Kennedy.

Although Kennedy was a Cold Warrior who had taken the world to the very brink of nuclear war, there was a more peaceful element in his character from which God could create something new. What was the seed of his transformation? As an author trying to understand his turnaround with Nikita Khrushchev from the depths of the Missile Crisis, I have puzzled over what it was in Kennedy's character that made possible his turn toward peace. What was the seed of his change from the president of a national security state into a leader with a more universal humanity, which, as Thomas Merton foresaw, would then mark him out for assassination?

At least one natural component of that seed for change was, I believe, his love for his children, and his ultimately transcending ability to see in them everyone's children. In reading his story, one is struck by the depth of love he had for Caroline and John, the global lessons he repeatedly drew from his feeling for their lives and the lives of all children, and the deep pain he and Jacqueline experienced at the death of Patrick.

On August 7, 1963, in the same morning Jacqueline Kennedy began to have premature birth pains, John Kennedy was in a meeting with Norman Cousins and a group of organizers to mobilize the public to urge Senate ratification of the Atmospheric Test Ban Treaty.[339] As we have seen, Kennedy understood the test ban treaty as an absolutely crucial issue for his presidency, yet one whose success he remained pessimistic about, even after his negotiation of the treaty with Khrushchev. Its biggest obstacle, Kennedy knew, lay not in Moscow but in Washington. Now that he and Khrushchev had come to terms on the treaty, how was he to get the Senate to approve it?

Given the Cold War's continuing hold on the United States and Congress in particular, the president thought getting the Senate's necessary two-thirds approval of the treaty would be "almost in the nature of a miracle."[340] Nevertheless, he told his advisers, he was committed to waging an all-out campaign to win the Senate's approval of the treaty, even if it cost him the 1964 election.[341]

The reason for his total commitment to the test ban treaty, a critical first step toward peace, was apparent in what Kennedy repeated to friends about his dread of nuclear war: "I keep thinking of the children, not my kids or yours, but the children all over the world."[342]

Robert Kennedy, who knew his brother's deepest concerns better than anyone else on earth did, said that in the Cuban Missile Crisis "the thought that disturbed him the most, and that made the prospect of war much more fearful than it would otherwise have been, was the specter of the death of the children of this country and all the world—the young people who had no role, who had no say, who knew nothing even of the confrontation, but whose lives would be snuffed out like everyone else's. They would never have a chance to make a decision, to vote in an election, to run for office, to lead a revolution, to determine their own destinies." [343]

President Kennedy was also becoming more deeply conscious that children all over the world were already innocent victims of the radioactive fallout from his and other governments' testing of nuclear weapons.

As we have seen, Kennedy was a keen listener. Sometimes a single sentence with a momentous truth was all he needed to hear.

One afternoon in his office, he was talking with his science adviser, Jerome Wiesner, about the contamination from the U.S. and Soviet nuclear testing. While rain fell outside the White House windows, Kennedy asked Wiesner how nuclear fallout returned to the earth from the atmosphere.

"It comes down in rain," Wiesner said.

The president turned around. He looked out the windows at the rain falling in the White House's Rose Garden.

"You mean there might be radioactive contamination in that rain out there right now?" he said.

"Possibly," Wiesner said.

Wiesner left the office. Kennedy sat in silence for several minutes, looking at the rain falling in the garden. His appointments secretary Kenny O'Donnell came and went quietly. O'Donnell had never seen Kennedy so depressed. [344]

Nor later, in August 1963, had his advisers ever seen Kennedy so determined as he was to win Senate confirmation of the test ban treaty. He gave the reason for his determination in his televised appeal for the treaty on July 26, 1963:

"This treaty is for all of us. It is particularly for our children and our grandchildren, and they have no lobby here in Washington."

He emphasized what was especially at stake: "children and grandchildren with cancer in their bones, with leukemia in their blood, or with poison in their lungs."

In retrospect, one of his most memorable statements was: "The malformation of even one baby—who may be born long after we are gone—should be of concern to us all." [345] He said these words two weeks before his own newborn baby would die.

On the morning of August 7, at the same time as Kennedy was meeting at the White House with Norman Cousins and the Citizens Committee for a Nuclear Test Ban, Kenny O'Donnell "received word from Hyannis Port that Jackie was undergoing emergency surgery at the Otis Air Base hospital for a delivery, five weeks premature of a baby boy." [346]

A minute later, Evelyn Lincoln, the president's secretary, came into the test ban meeting and handed Kennedy a note. Norman Cousins watched JFK's face become clouded as he read the note. Kennedy got up from his chair, and disappeared through the door to his own office, abruptly ending the meeting. [347] He then flew quickly to Otis Air Base to be with Jackie.

By the time he arrived, his four-pound, ten-and-one-half-ounce son, Patrick Bouvier Kennedy, had been delivered by Caesarean section and was in an oxygen-fed incubator. The premature baby "was suffering from hyaline membrane disease, a lung condition that blocked the supply of oxygen to the bloodstream." [348] The base chaplain immediately baptized him. While Jackie was still in surgery, her husband agreed with doctors to move Patrick to the better-equipped Children's Hospital in Boston. While an ambulance pulled up, JFK wheeled Patrick's incubator into Jackie's room for the only look she would ever have of her son. [349]

As Patrick's breathing failed over the next day, doctors moved him again, this time to a high-pressure oxygen chamber in Harvard's School of Public Health, where JFK stayed overnight in a waiting room. At 2:00 A.M. on August 9, the president was awakened and summoned to the side of his son's oxygen chamber. When the doctors knew Patrick was about to die, they brought him out of the chamber to be with his father. Patrick died at 4:04 A.M. on August 9, at the age of thirty-nine hours and twelve minutes, with his father holding his fingers. [350]

JFK went back to his room, sat on the bed, and wept. A helicopter took him to the Otis Air Base hospital, where he and Jackie spent an hour alone together. [351]

In his own dying child, Kennedy saw other afflicted children. While he was waiting to see Patrick for the last time, he noticed a badly burned child in another hospital room. He asked for the mother's name, borrowed pen and paper, and wrote an encouraging note to be given to her when she came to visit her child. [352] When he returned to the White House, now with an even deeper sense of the death of children, he worked with renewed determination for passage of the test ban treaty. Thanks to the mobilization campaign of Norman Cousins and the Citizens Committee, as overseen by the president, public opinion turned around.

On August 28, Cousins sent a progress report to President Kennedy "on your specific suggestions for the public campaign to ratify the test ban treaty." In his memorandum to the president, Cousins ticked off a series of recommendations JFK had given the Citizens Committee in the August 7 meeting. Cousins also listed the follow-up the committee had accomplished in the three weeks since then. It comprised an outreach program to the nation through business leaders, scientists, religious leaders, farmers, scholars and university presidents, unions, newspapers, key states, and liberal organizations such as SANE (National Committee for a Sane Nuclear Policy), UWF (United World Federalists), and ADA (Americans for Democratic Action). [353] They had all been specified by Kennedy in the August 7 meeting, just before he was given word of Jacqueline's emergency and departed quickly from the White House. As the result of a whirlwind August campaign managed by Cousins, summarized in his memorandum to the man behind it, the American public reversed course on a critical Cold War issue. The people, and their president, were more open to change than Congress was. But senators could also feel new winds of peace blowing. They, too, turned toward a new possibility.

The Senate approved the treaty by a decisive margin, 80 to 19, in September. The miracle had happened. It did so with such apparent ease, through a unique coalition created by the president, that future historians would view Kennedy's success with the test ban treaty, less than a year after the Cuban Missile Crisis, as no great accomplishment.

John and Jacqueline Kennedy's closest friends said Patrick's death affected them profoundly and brought them closer together[354]—eventually in Dallas. In late October, Jackie surprised her husband by agreeing readily to go with him to Texas,[355] on a political trip she did not look forward to happily— into a part of the country where they anticipated a hostile reception. She surprised him again on the trip, after their warm receptions in San Antonio, Houston, and Fort Worth, by saying she'd go anywhere with him that year.

JFK smiled, turned to Kenny O'Donnell, and said, "Did you hear *that*?"[356] Then they prepared to board their plane to Dallas.

Three hours later, Jackie Kennedy was sitting beside JFK in the back seat of the limousine as it was driven into Dealey Plaza. The following week, she described to writer Theodore H. White the death of her husband, as seen by the closest witness, herself. Her immediate description of the assassination would not be released to the American public until 1995:

"They were gunning the motorcycles; there were these little backfires; there was one noise like that; I thought it was a backfire. Then next I saw [Governor] Connally [in the seat in front, who had just been shot] grabbing his arms and saying 'no no nononono,' with his fist beating—then Jack turned and I turned—all I remember was a blue gray building up ahead; then Jack turned back, so neatly; his last expression was so neat; he had his hand out, I could see a piece of his skull coming off; it was flesh colored not white—he was holding out his hand—and I can see this perfectly clean piece detaching itself from his head . . . "[357]

Her instinctive response to the fatal shot that blew out the back of his head was to climb on the trunk of the car to try to retrieve a portion of his skull. Secret Service Agent Clint Hill, who ran from the car behind and climbed on the limousine, testified to Jacqueline Kennedy's instinctive effort to put her husband's head back together.

After "the second noise that I had heard had removed a portion of the President's head," Hill said, "Mrs. Kennedy had jumped up from the seat and was, it appeared to me, reaching for something coming off the right rear bumper of the car."[358] Hill grabbed her, put her back in her seat, and crawled up on top of the back seat. From his position looking down at the President's head, he saw, as they arrived at Parkland Hospital, that "the right rear portion of his head was missing."[359]

If "the right rear portion of his head was missing," as the Parkland doctors and nurses would soon confirm, then the shot causing that massive exit wound must have come from the front—not from the Texas School Book Depository in the rear where Oswald was.

Jacqueline Kennedy recalled vividly what she was doing in the car on the way to the hospital:

"I was trying to hold his hair on. But from the front there was nothing. I suppose there must have been. But from the back, you could see, you know, you were trying to hold his hair on, and his skull on." [360]

However, this description of her attempt to hold her husband's hair and skull together over a gaping wound was deleted from her Warren Commission testimony, ostensibly because it would have been "in poor taste." [361] Perhaps more important to the censors, it could also have led to widespread recognition of evidence for a shot from the front.

At least part of the "something" that Clint Hill said Mrs. Kennedy was reaching for so desperately from the trunk of the limousine may have been found the next day by a Dallas premedical student. At 5:30 P.M. on Saturday, November 23, William Allen Harper was taking photographs in the triangular grassy area in the center of Dealey Plaza. About twenty-five feet behind and to the left of the point on Elm Street where a shot had blown out the back of the president's skull, Harper discovered a large bone fragment in the grass. He took what would become known as the "Harper fragment" to his uncle, Dr. Jack C. Harper, at Methodist Hospital, who turned it over to Dr. A. B. Cairns, the hospital's chief pathologist. [362]

Dr. Cairns, Dr. Harper, and another pathologist, Dr. Gerard Noteboom, examined closely the five-by-seven-centimeter bone fragment. They agreed that it came from the occiput, the lower back part of a human skull. [363] The pathologists also noted evidence of a lead deposit on the fragment, suggesting the impact of a bullet. [364] Their fortuitous examination of the bone, and identification of its origin, would become a critical clue to a government cover-up.

Nine years later, a UCLA graduate student in physics named David Lifton compared the Dallas pathologists' identification of the Harper fragment with the official government X-rays of the slain president's head. Lifton was puzzled, then electrified by what the comparison revealed. He realized that if Dr. Cairns and his colleagues were correct, "the X-rays could not possibly be authentic, for nature provides us with only one occipital bone, and President Kennedy's occipital bone could not be lying on the grass of Dealey Plaza, and appear simultaneously in the X-rays of his skull taken that night at Bethesda [Naval Hospital]." [365]

The autopsy X-rays had been used as incontrovertible proof that there was no exit wound in the rear of the skull—and therefore no assassin in front. Yet twenty-one doctors, nurses, and Secret Service agents at Parkland Hospital in Dallas had all, in their earliest statements, said they had seen a large wound in the right rear portion of JFK's skull. [366] According to the X-rays' "more scientific" proof, they all had to be wrong. On the other hand, the Warren Commission had ignored Dr. Cairns's statement in an FBI interview that the Harper fragment "looked like it came from the occipital region of the skull," [367] precisely where the X-rays showed an intact skull. Something strange was going on in the X-ray darkroom.

After comparing the Harper fragment's place in the skull with what the president's X-rays showed was supposedly still there, David Lifton wrote to Dr. Cyril Wecht, a Warren Commission dissenter, that the Harper fragment "was the medical equivalent of the legendary piece-of-a-dollar-bill which one carries to a rendezvous with an unknown person, where the trustworthiness of one's counterpart is vouched for by the fact that he can produce the other half . . . [W]hen one goes to a rendezvous with one-half of a dollar bill, and the other party produces the *same* half, that can only mean one thing." [368]

Dr. David W. Mantik, a radiation oncologist with a Ph.D. in physics, tested the autopsy X-rays at the National Archives in 1993–95 to determine their authenticity. He used an optical densitometer to measure the levels of light on different areas of the official X-rays, in which the denser parts of the skull would ordinarily produce whiter images on the X-rays and the more vacant parts would produce darker images. Mantik was puzzled by the X-rays' remarkable contrast between the front and back of Kennedy's skull, apparent even to the naked eye. By taking optical density measurements of the X-rays, what he discovered was, as he put it, "quite astonishing. The posterior white area transmits almost one thousand times more light than the dark area!" [369] There was far too much bone density being shown in the rear of JFK's skull relative to the front. The X-ray had to have been a composite. The optical density data indicated a forgery in which a patch had been placed over an original X-ray to cover the rear part of the skull— corresponding to the gap left in part by the Harper fragment, evidence of an exit wound. The obvious purpose was to cover up evidence of a shot from the front that, judging from the original Parkland observations, had created an exit hole the size of one's fist in the back of the head. [370]

Dr. Mantik's optical density tests confirmed a radical hypothesis. The autopsy's skull X-rays, in which the Harper fragment had so wondrously rejoined a dead president's skull in spite of the fragment's simultaneous existence elsewhere, had indeed been cleverly altered. Precisely where the government had rested its case for a lone assassin on a claim of scientific evidence—in its autopsy X-rays—the public could now see for itself was evidence of fakery. The scientific evidence claimed by Warren Commission apologists had been forged in the X-ray darkroom. Thanks to Dr. Mantik's experiments conducted during his visits to the National Archives (now available to anyone who Googles "Twenty Conclusions after Nine Visits"), the unspeakable has been probed, verified, and documented.

In the case of the government's X-rays, their exact duplication of the Harper fragment, as if that bullet-blasted bone were still in the slain president's skull, has turned out to be a revelation of the cover-up. When the government's "best evidence" was finally examined independently, the tests showed the X-rays were a hoax. The bottom line of the *Warren Report* was a forgery. A fragment of the head that Jacqueline Kennedy had tried unsuccessfully to put together again has come back decades later to haunt the government's cover-up.

Where was Lee Harvey Oswald when President John F. Kennedy was shot in Dealey Plaza?[371]

According to *The Warren Report*'s record of Oswald's interrogation, when he was asked "what part of the building he was in at the time the president was shot," "he said that he was having his lunch about that time on the first floor."[372] Oswald added that "he went to the second floor where the Coca Cola machine was located and obtained a bottle of Coca Cola for his lunch."[373]

A key witness, whose testimony was covered up by the FBI, placed Oswald in fact in the second floor lunchroom (which had the Coca Cola machine) at 12:15 P.M.

Carolyn Arnold was the secretary to the Depository vice president. She knew Oswald because he was in the habit of stopping by her desk on the second floor, asking her for change in nickels and dimes.[374]

In an interview with Dallas reporter Earl Golz, Arnold said "she saw Oswald in the second-floor lunchroom as she was on her way out of the Depository to watch the presidential motorcade Nov. 22, 1963."[375]

Arnold told author Anthony Summers the time of her seeing Oswald was "about 12:15. It may have been slightly later."[376] She told Earl Golz she actually left the building at 12:25 P.M., five minutes before the president was shot.[377]

Carolyn Arnold was especially conscious of what she was doing at the time because she was pregnant. Before she went outside to see the president, she had a craving for a glass of water. When she walked into the lunchroom to quench her thirst, she saw Oswald.[378] In retrospect, it was her most memorable experience in an unforgettable day.

"I do not recall that he [Oswald] was doing anything," she said. "I just recall that he was sitting there in one of the booth seats on the right hand side of the room as you go in. He was alone as usual and appeared to be having lunch. I did not speak to him but I recognized him clearly."[379]

The motorcade was running late. The president had been scheduled to pass the Depository at 12:25 P.M.,[380] ten minutes after Carolyn Arnold saw Oswald sitting in the booth seat of the second-floor lunchroom. If an assassin planned to shoot President Kennedy from a sixth-floor window at 12:25, would he have been sitting in the second-floor lunchroom at 12:15?

At 12:31 P.M., Dallas Patrolman M. L. Baker, accompanied by Depository superintendent Roy Truly, rushed up the Depository stairs. About a minute and a quarter to a minute and a half after the first shot was fired in Dealey Plaza, Baker pushed open the door of the second-floor lunchroom.[381] With his revolver drawn, he confronted Lee Harvey Oswald, who was walking toward a Coca Cola machine.[382]

"Come here," Baker said. Oswald turned and walked toward him.[383]

Baker turned to Truly and said, "Do you know this man? Does he work here?" [384]

Truly said yes. Baker turned around, went out, and continued climbing the stairs. Oswald apparently finished buying a drink from the vending machine. Within a minute, Mrs. R. A. Reid, clerical supervisor for the Depository, saw him walk through the clerical office on the second floor. He was holding a bottle of Coca Cola. [385]

The Warren Commission decided Oswald had just barely enough time, after he supposedly shot the president and Governor Connally, to hide his rifle and go down four flights of stairs into the lunchroom. Yet, according to both Baker and Truly, Oswald was remarkably composed. In response to questions from the Warren Commission, Baker affirmed that Oswald "did not seem to be out of breath" and "did not show any evidence of any emotion." [386] Truly said Oswald "didn't seem to be excited or overly afraid or anything," [387] after having just accomplished the crime of the century and a quick trip down the stairs.

How is one to explain the presumed assassin's composure? Carolyn Arnold's testimony would have helped. Her encounter with Oswald in the lunchroom, a few minutes before Baker and Truly confronted him in the same place, indicates they found him finishing what she saw him doing—not killing the president but eating lunch. That was not the explanation desired. Arnold was not asked to testify before the Warren Commission.

Fifteen years after the assassination, Carolyn Johnston, whose name had changed from Carolyn Arnold, was surprised to learn about the FBI report of her November 26, 1963, interview. The FBI had, as she put it, "misquoted" her statement about seeing Oswald in the second-floor lunchroom just before she went out to see the president. [388] Instead the FBI report claimed that, after she left the Depository and "was standing in front of the building" to watch the motorcade, she "thought she caught a fleeting glimpse of Lee Harvey Oswald standing in the hallway" off the first floor. [389]

"This is completely foreign to me," she told the *Dallas Morning News*. "It would have forced me to have been turning back around to the building when, in fact, I was trying to watch the parade. Why would I be looking back inside the building? That doesn't make any sense to me." [390]

As in Julia Ann Mercer's experience, what Carolyn Arnold saw on November 22, 1963—Oswald eating lunch on the second floor, not preparing to shoot the president from the sixth—did not fit the government's story. Carolyn Arnold was a witness to the unspeakable.

Warren Commission counsel David Belin wrote: "The Rosetta Stone [the key to Egyptian hieroglyphics] to the solution of President Kennedy's murder is the murder of Officer J. D. Tippit." [391] From the Warren Commission's standpoint, the killing of Tippit, who presumably challenged the assassin's flight after he killed Kennedy, was said to prove "that Oswald had the capacity to kill."[392]

Warren Commission critic Harold Weisberg saw Tippit's murder instead as the government's way of poisoning the public mind against Lee Harvey Oswald: "Immediately the [flimsy] police case [against Oswald] required a willingness to believe. This was provided by affixing to Oswald the opprobrious epithet of 'cop-killer.' "[393]

According to the *Warren Report*, the tracking of Oswald from Dealey Plaza to Tippit's murder began with eyewitness Howard Brennan, a forty-five-year-old steamfitter who was standing across the street from the Texas School Book Depository watching the presidential motorcade. Brennan told a police officer right after the assassination that he saw a man standing in a sixth-floor window of the Depository fire a rifle at the president's car.[394] The *Warren Report* says Brennan described the standing shooter as "white, slender, weighing about 165 pounds, about 5'10" tall, and in his early thirties," a description matching Oswald that was radioed to Dallas Police cars at approximately 12:45 P.M.[395] Yet, as Mark Lane pointed out, "There could not have been a man standing and firing from [the sixth-floor window] because, as photographs of the building taken within seconds of the assassination prove, the window was open only partially at the bottom, and one shooting from a standing position would have been obliged to fire through the glass."[396] Moreover, Brennan's testimony that the man firing the rifle "was standing up and resting against the left windowsill"[397] was also impossible because the windowsill was only a foot from the floor, with the window opened about fourteen inches.[398] So if key witness Howard Brennan could not have provided such a description accurately, and if the Warren Commission could cite only him as a source for the 12:45 P.M. police description, who put out that Oswald-like alert if not the conspirators?

Supposedly on the basis of nothing more than that radioed description, Officer Tippit stopped his car at 1:15 P.M. to confront a man walking on East 10th Street in the Oak Cliff area of Dallas. The man then shot Tippit to death. The murderer fled the scene on foot. Half an hour later, the man was reported sneaking into the Texas Theater, which the Dallas police then stormed, arresting a man who was soon identified as Lee Harvey Oswald.

As Weisberg pointed out, the killing of Tippit provided a dramatic reinforcement of Oswald's assumed killing of Kennedy. At the same time, the killing of a fellow police officer helped motivate the Dallas police to kill an armed Oswald in the Texas Theater, which would have disposed of the scapegoat before he could protest his being framed.

Once again, however, the assassination script was imperfectly carried out. Oswald survived his arrest in the theater. And as in a flawed movie where scene variations are shot, doubles are used, and the director is in a hurry, the final version of this film for our viewing doesn't add up. The Warren Commission's attempt to squeeze it all into a lone-gunman explanation has resulted in an implausible narrative.

According to the *Warren Report*, between President Kennedy's assassination at 12:30 P.M. and Officer Tippit's murder at 1:15 P.M., Lee Harvey Oswald did the following:

After the lone assassin shot the president to death and wounded Governor Connally from a sixth-floor window in the Texas School Book Depository,[399] he hid his rifle and stepped quickly down four flights of stairs to the lunchroom, where he was seen calmly preparing to buy a bottle of Coca Cola from a vending machine.[400] He escaped from the building and walked seven blocks.[401] He took a bus that was headed back toward the Texas School Book Depository, got stuck with the bus in a traffic jam, and got off it. He walked three to four blocks to hire a taxi.[402] He offered to give up his taxi to an old lady when she asked his driver for help finding a cab (an offer she refused, allowing him to continue his escape without changing taxis).[403] He rode 2.4 miles in the taxi, taking him five blocks too far past his rooming house.[404] He paid his fare, got out, and walked five blocks back to his rooming house.[405] "He went on to his room and stayed about 3 or 4 minutes,"[406] picked up his jacket and a revolver, and departed.[407] The housekeeper saw him standing in front of the house by the stop for a *north*bound bus.[408] He apparently gave up on the bus and instead walked *south* another remarkably brisk nine-tenths mile.[409] All of these actions, following his killing of the president, were, by the Commission's timetable, accomplished in forty-five minutes.[410] Oswald then, we are told, used his revolver to calmly murder Officer J. D. Tippit on a quiet street in the Oak Cliff neighborhood of Dallas, "removing the empty cartridge cases from the gun as he went,"[411] helpfully leaving a trail of ballistic evidence for the police to collect. He thereby aborted his escape and became a magnet for a massive police chase. The police arrested him in the Texas Theater at 1:50 P.M.[412]

This jam-packed scenario was created by more than one man bearing Oswald's likeness, with help from behind the scenes. At 12:40 P.M., exactly the same time that Deputy Sheriff Roger Craig and Helen Forrest saw Oswald get into a Rambler station wagon in front of the Book Depository, Oswald's former landlady, Mary Bledsoe, saw him board a bus seven blocks east of the Depository.[413] Oswald told Captain Will Fritz he rode the bus, until its holdup in traffic made him switch to a taxi.[414] A bus transfer found in his shirt pocket at his arrest seemed to confirm the short bus trip.[415] Yet when Fritz told Oswald that Craig had seen him depart by car, Oswald said defensively, "That station wagon belongs to Mrs. Paine. Don't try to drag her into this."[416]

When he added dejectedly, "Everybody will know who I am now," Oswald seemed to imply that his (or a double's) departure in the station wagon, and the vehicle's association with Mrs. Paine, were keys to his real identity.

If he was not the man picked up by the station wagon, then Roger Craig and Helen Forrest had seen, in Forrest's words, "his identical twin."[417] The man spirited away by the Nash Rambler had been either Oswald or a double; driven, Craig said, by "a husky looking Latin."[418]

Besides the mysterious Nash Rambler that was in the end spotted by so many mutually supportive witnesses—Craig, Forrest, Pennington, Carr, Robinson, and Cooper—there may have been two more cars even more deeply in the shadows that helped Lee Harvey Oswald make his otherwise unlikely transitions that climactic afternoon in the assassination plot. Another car appeared out of nowhere when he arrived at his rooming house.

After Oswald went to his room at 1:00 P.M., the housekeeper, Mrs. Earlene Roberts, saw a police car stop directly in front of the house. She told the Warren Commission that two uniformed policemen were in the car. The driver sounded the horn, "just kind of a 'tit-tit'—twice," [419] an unmistakable signal, then eased the car forward and went around the corner.[420]

After "about three or four minutes," [421] Oswald returned from his room and went outside. Before Mrs. Roberts turned her attention elsewhere, she saw him standing in front of the house by a northbound bus stop—to be heard from next in the *Warren Report* twelve minutes later as the apparent killer of Officer Tippit near the corner of Tenth and Patton, almost one mile away in the opposite direction. How he got there in time to kill Tippit, or even *if* he did, has never been clearly established.[422]

He may have been picked up by the Dallas police car that parked briefly in front of the house, beeped its horn twice lightly—tap, tap—in a signal, and drove around the corner (perhaps only to circle the block and return for him). Earlene Roberts told the Warren Commission that the number on the police car was 107.[423] As the Commission's staff would discover, the Dallas Police Department no longer had a car 107. It had sold its car 107 on April 17, 1963, to a used car dealer. The Dallas Police would not resume using the number 107 until February 1964, three months after the assassination.[424] If Mrs. Roberts had the car's number right, then the horn signal to Oswald came from two uniformed men in a counterfeit police car. Their likely destination, with Oswald as their passenger, was the Texas Theater, where they would drop off Oswald for a setup for his arrest and murder—while the Oswald impostor in the Nash Rambler was being let off for a short walk to meet Officer Tippit in a fatal encounter at Tenth and Patton.

The *Warren Report* describes the murder of Officer Tippit "at approximately 1:15 P.M.," after he confronted a man walking east along the south side of Patton: "The man's general description was similar to the one broadcast over the police radio. Tippit stopped the man and called him to his car. He approached the car and apparently exchanged words with Tippit through the right front or vent window. Tippit got out and started to walk around the front of the car. As Tippit reached the left front wheel the man pulled out a revolver and fired several shots. Four bullets hit Tippit and killed him instantly. The gunman started back toward Patton Avenue, ejecting the empty cartridge cases before reloading with fresh bullets." [425]

As the gunman walked and trotted away from the murder scene while still holding the revolver, the *Warren Report* says he was seen by at least twelve persons: "By the evening of November 22, five of them had identified Lee Harvey Oswald in police lineups as the man they saw. A sixth did so the next day. Three others subsequently identified Oswald from a photograph. Two witnesses testified that Oswald resembled the man they had seen. One witness felt he was too distant from the gunman to make a positive identification."[426]

The fleeing man identified later as Oswald was seen finally by Johnny Calvin Brewer, manager of Hardy's Shoestore, located a few doors east of the Texas Theater. After spotting the man acting suspiciously in the recessed area in front of his store, Brewer went outside. He saw the man ducking into the theater up the block. The ticket-seller, Julia Postal, confirmed to Brewer that the man had not bought a ticket. She called the police.[427]

However, the man who shot Tippit, fled the murder scene, sneaked into the Texas Theater just before 1:45 P.M., and was identified as Lee Harvey Oswald, posed another bi-location problem. Oswald once again seemed to be in two places at the same time.

According to Warren H. "Butch" Burroughs, the concession stand operator at the Texas Theater, Lee Harvey Oswald entered the theater sometime between 1:00 and 1:07 P.M., several minutes before Officer Tippit was slain seven blocks away.[428] If true, Butch Burroughs's observation would eliminate Oswald as a candidate for Tippet's murder. Perhaps for that reason, Burroughs was asked by a Warren Commission attorney the apparently straightforward question, "Did you see [Oswald] come in the theater?" and answered honestly, "No, sir; I didn't."[429] What someone reading this testimony would not know is that Butch Burroughs was unable to see anyone enter the theater from where he was standing at his concession stand, unless that person came into the area where he was working. As he explained to me in an interview, there was a partition between his concession stand and the front door. Someone could enter the theater, go directly up a flight of stairs to the balcony, and not be seen from the concession stand.[430] That, Burroughs said, is what Oswald apparently did. However, Burroughs still knew Oswald had come into the theater "between 1:00 and 1:07 P.M." because he saw him inside the theater soon after that. As he told me, he sold popcorn to Oswald at 1:15 P.M.[431]—information that the Warren Commission did not solicit from him in his testimony. When Oswald bought his popcorn at 1:15 P.M., this was exactly the same time the *Warren Report* said Officer Tippit was being shot to death[432]—evidently by someone else.

Butch Burroughs was not alone in noticing Oswald in the Texas Theater by then. The man who would soon be identified as the president's assassin drew the attention of several moviegoers because of his odd behavior.

Edging into a row of seats in the right rear section of the ground floor, Oswald had squeezed in front of eighteen-year-old Jack Davis. He then sat down in the seat right next to him. Because there were fewer than twenty people in the entire nine-hundred-seat theater, Davis wondered why the man chose such close proximity to him. Whatever the reason, the man didn't stay there long. Oswald (as Davis would later identify him) got up quickly, moved across the aisle, and sat down next to someone else in the almost deserted theater. In a few moments, he stood up again and walked out to the lobby.[433]

Davis thought it obvious Oswald was looking for someone.[434] Yet it must have been someone he didn't know personally. He sat next to each new person just long enough to receive a prearranged signal, in the absence of which he moved on to another possible contact.

Back out in the lobby at 1:15 P.M., Oswald then bought popcorn from Butch Burroughs at the concession stand.[435] Burroughs told author Jim Marrs and myself that he saw Oswald go back in the ground floor of the theater and sit next to a pregnant woman[436]—in another apparently fruitless effort to find his contact. Several minutes later, "the pregnant woman got up and went to the ladies washroom," Burroughs said. He "heard the restroom door close just shortly before Dallas police came rushing into the theater."[437] Jack Davis said it may have been "twenty minutes or so" after Oswald returned from the lobby (when Burroughs saw Oswald sit by the pregnant woman) that the house lights came on and the police rushed in.[438]

The police arrested Oswald in a curious way. They entered the theater from the front and back, blocking all exits and surrounding Oswald. Officer M. N. McDonald and three other officers came in from behind the movie screen. With the theater lights on, McDonald scanned the audience.[439] Johnny Brewer, who had seen the man who looked like Oswald duck into the theater, showed McDonald where the man was sitting—in the third row from the rear of the ground floor.[440]

With the suspect identified and located, McDonald and an accompanying officer, instead of apprehending the man in the rear of the theater, began searching people between him and them.[441] As the police proceeded slowly toward Oswald, it was almost as if they were provoking the suspected police-killer to break away from his seat. His attempt to escape would have given Tippit's enraged fellow officers an excuse to shoot him.[442]

When McDonald finally reached his suspect in the third row from the back, Oswald stood up and pulled out his pistol. While he struggled with McDonald and the other officers who had converged on the scene, they heard the snap of the hammer on his gun misfiring.[443] However, Oswald, instead of being shot to death on the spot, was wrestled into submission by the police and placed under arrest. The police hustled him out to a squad car. They drove him to Dallas Police Headquarters in City Hall.

Butch Burroughs, who witnessed Oswald's arrest, startled me in his interview by saying he saw a second arrest occur in the Texas Theater only "three or four minutes later."[444] He said the Dallas Police then arrested "an Oswald lookalike." Burroughs said the second man "looked almost like Oswald, like he was his brother or something."[445] When I questioned the comparison by asking, "Could you see the second man as well as you could see Oswald?" he said, "Yes, I could see both of them. They looked alike."[446] After the officers half-carried and half-dragged Oswald to the police car in front of the theater, within a space of three or four minutes, Burroughs saw the second

Oswald placed under arrest and handcuffed. The Oswald look-alike, however, was taken by police not out the front but out the back of the theater.[447]

What happened next we can learn from another neglected witness, Bernard Haire.[448]

Bernard J. Haire was the owner of Bernie's Hobby House, just two doors east of the Texas Theater. Haire went outside his store when he saw police cars congregating in front of the theater.[449] When he couldn't see what was happening because of the crowd, he went back through his store into the alley out back. It, too, was full of police cars, but there were fewer spectators. Haire walked up the alley. When he stopped opposite the rear door of the theater, he witnessed what he would think for decades was the arrest of Lee Harvey Oswald.

"Police brought a young white man out," Haire told an interviewer. "The man was dressed in a pullover shirt and slacks. He seemed to be flushed, as if he'd been in a struggle. Police put the man in a police car and drove off."[450]

When Haire was told in 1987 that Lee Harvey Oswald had been brought out the *front* of the theater by police, he was shocked.

"I don't know who I saw arrested," he said in bewilderment.[451]

Butch Burroughs and Bernard Haire are complementary witnesses. From their perspectives both inside and outside the Texas Theater, they saw an Oswald double arrested and taken to a police car in the back alley only minutes after the arrest of Lee Harvey Oswald. Burroughs's and Haire's independent, converging testimonies provide critical insight into the mechanics of the plot. In a comprehensive intelligence scenario for Kennedy's and Tippit's murders, the plan culminated in Oswald's Friday arrest and Sunday murder (probably a fallback from his being set up to be killed in the Texas Theater by the police).

There is a hint of the second Oswald's arrest in the Dallas police records.

According to the Dallas Police Department's official Homicide Report on J. D. Tippit, "Suspect was later arrested *in the balcony* of the Texas theatre at 231 W. Jefferson."[452]

Dallas Police detective L. D. Stringfellow also reported to Captain W. P. Gannaway, "Lee Harvey Oswald was arrested *in the balcony* of the Texas Theater."[453]

To whom are the Homicide Report and Detective Stringfellow referring? Lee Harvey Oswald was arrested in the orchestra, not the balcony. Are these documents referring to the Dallas Police Department's second arrest at the Texas Theater that afternoon? Was Butch Burroughs witnessing an arrest of the Oswald look-alike that actually began in the balcony? That would have likely been the double's hiding place, after he entered the theater without paying, thereby drawing attention to himself and leading the police to the apprehension of his likeness, Lee Harvey Oswald (who was already inside). As Butch Burroughs pointed out, anyone coming in the front of the theater could head immediately up the stairs to the balcony without being seen from the concession stand.

The Oswald double, after having been put in the police car in the alley, must have been driven a short distance and released on higher intelligence orders. Unfortunately for the plotters, he was seen again soon. With the scapegoat, Lee Harvey Oswald, now safely in custody, we can presume that the double was not supposed to be seen again in Dallas—or anywhere else. Had he not been seen, the CIA's double-Oswald strategy in an Oak Cliff shell game might have eluded independent investigators forever. But thanks to other key witnesses who have emerged, we now have detailed evidence that the double was seen again—not just once but twice.

At 2:00 P.M., as Lee Harvey Oswald sat handcuffed in the back seat of a patrol car boxed in by police officers on his way to jail, Oswald knew what final role had been chosen for him in the assassination scenario. That night, while being led through police headquarters, he would shout out to the press, "I'm just a patsy!" [454]

Also at about 2:00 P.M., a man identified as Oswald was seen in a car eight blocks away from the Texas Theater, still very much at large and keeping a low profile.[455] A sharp-eyed auto mechanic spotted him.

T. F. White was a sixty-year-old, longtime employee of Mack Pate's Garage in the Oak Cliff section of Dallas. While White worked on an automobile the afternoon of the assassination, he could hear police sirens screaming up and down Davis Street only a block away. He also heard radio reports describing a suspect then thought to be in Oak Cliff.[456] The mechanic looked out the open doors of the garage. He watched as a red 1961 Falcon drove into the parking lot of the El Chico restaurant across the street. The Falcon parked in an odd position after going a few feet into the lot. The driver remained seated in the car.[457] White said later, "The man in the car appeared to be hiding." [458] White kept his eye on the man in the Falcon.

When Mack Pate returned from his lunch break a few minutes later, T. F. White pointed out to his boss the oddly parked Falcon with its waiting driver who seemed to be hiding. Pate told White to watch the car carefully, reminding him of earlier news reports they had heard about a possible assassination attempt against President Kennedy in Houston the day before involving a red Falcon.[459]

T. F. White walked across the street to investigate. He halted about ten to fifteen yards from the car. He could see the driver was wearing a white t-shirt.[460] The man turned toward White and looked at him full face. White stared back at him. Not wanting to provoke a possible assassin, White began a retreat to the garage. However, he paused, took a scrap of paper from his coveralls pocket, and wrote down the Texas license plate of the car: PP 4537.[461]

That night, while T. F. White was watching television with his wife, he recognized the Dallas Police Department's prisoner, Lee Harvey Oswald, as the man he had seen in the red Falcon in El Chico's parking lot. White was unfazed by what he did not yet know—that at the same time he had seen one Oswald sitting freely in the Falcon, the other Oswald was sitting handcuffed in a Dallas police car on his way to jail. Mrs. White, fearing the encompassing arms of a conspiracy, talked her husband out of reporting his information to the authorities.[462] Thus, the Oswald sighted in the parking lot might have escaped history, but for the fact White was confronted by an alert reporter.

On December 4, 1963, Wes Wise, a Dallas newscaster whose specialty was sports, gave a luncheon talk to the Oak Cliff Exchange Club at El Chico's restaurant. At the urging of his listeners, he changed his topic from sports to the president's assassination, which Wise had covered. He described to his luncheon audience how he, as a reporter, had become a part of Jack Ruby's story. Wise's encounter with the man he knew as a news groupie came on the grassy knoll, the day before Ruby shot Oswald. Wise had just completed a somber, day-after-the-assassination radio newscast from the site banked with wreaths.

While he sat in his car in silent reflection beside the Texas School Book Depository, he heard a familiar voice call out, "Hey, Wes!"

As Wise told the story, "I turned to see the portly figure of a man in a dark suit, half-waddling, half-trotting, as he came toward me. He was wearing a fedora-style hat which would later become familiar and famous." Jack Ruby was making his way along the grassy knoll "from the direction of the railroad tracks," precisely where the day before, as Ed Hoffman watched, another man in a suit had fired a rifle at the president—an hour and a half after Julia Ann Mercer saw a man, dropped off by Jack Ruby, carry a rifle up the same site.

Ruby leaned into Wise's car window and said, his voice breaking and with tears in his eyes, "I just hope they don't make Jackie come to Dallas for the trial. That would be terrible for that little lady." [463]

In retrospect, Wise wondered if Ruby was trying to set him up for a radio interview—to go on record the day before with his famous "motive" for murdering Oswald. Although Wise had no interest then in interviewing Jack Ruby, he had already just been told enough for him to be called as a witness in Ruby's trial. He would be subpoenaed as a Ruby witness by both the prosecution and the defense.[464] His testimony at the trial, quoting what Ruby said to him the day before Ruby murdered Oswald, would then be cited in *Life* magazine.[465]

At the end of Wise's talk to his absorbed audience at the Oak Cliff Exchange Club, Mack Pate, who had walked across the street from his garage to listen, gave the newscaster a new lead. He told Wise about his mechanic having seen Oswald. Wise asked to go immediately with Pate to speak with his employee.[466]

As Wes Wise told me in an interview four decades later, he then "put a little selling job on Mr. White" to reveal what he had seen. Wise said to the reluctant auto mechanic, "Well, you know, we're talking about the assassination of the president of the United States here." [467]

Convinced of his duty, T. F. White took Wise into El Chico's parking lot and walked him step by step through his "full face" encounter with Oswald.

Wise realized the car had been parked at the center of Oswald's activity in Oak Cliff that afternoon: one block from where Oswald got out of the taxi, six blocks south of his rooming house, eight blocks north of his arrest at the Texas Theater, and only five blocks from Tippit's murder on a route in between.[468]

Taking notes on his luncheon invitation, Wise said, "I just wish you had gotten the license number."

White reached in his pocket and took out a scrap of paper with writing on it. He handed it to Wise.

"This is it," he said.[469]

Newscaster Wes Wise notified the FBI of White's identification of Oswald in the car parked in the El Chico lot, and cited the license plate number. FBI agent Charles T. Brown, Jr., reported from an interview with Milton Love, Dallas County Tax Office: "1963 Texas License Plate PP 4537 was issued for a 1957 Plymouth automobile in possession of Carl Amos Mather, 4309 Colgate Street, Garland, Texas."[470] Agent Brown then drove to that address. He reported that the 1957 Plymouth bearing license plate PP 4537 was parked in the driveway of Mather's home in Garland, a suburb of Dallas.[471] Thus arose the question of how a license plate for Carl Amos Mather's Plymouth came to be seen on the Falcon in El Chico's parking lot, with a man in it who looked like Oswald.

The FBI had also discovered that Carl Amos Mather did high-security communications work for Collins Radio, a major contractor with the Central Intelligence Agency. Three weeks before Kennedy's assassination, Collins Radio had been identified on the front page of the *New York Times* as having just deployed a CIA raider ship on an espionage and sabotage mission against Cuba.[472] Collins also held the government contract for installing communications towers in Vietnam.[473] In 1971, Collins Radio would merge with another giant military contractor, Rockwell International.[474] In November 1963, Collins was at the heart of the CIA-military-contracting business for state-of-the-art communications systems.

Carl Mather had represented Collins at Andrews Air Force Base by putting special electronics equipment in Vice President Lyndon Johnson's Air Force Two plane.[475] Given the authority of his CIA-linked security clearance, Carl Mather refused to speak to the FBI.[476] The FBI instead questioned his wife, Barbara Mather, who stunned them. Her husband, she said, was a good friend of J. D. Tippit. In fact, the Mathers were such close friends of Tippit and his wife that when J. D. was murdered, Marie Tippit phoned them. According to his wife, Carl Mather left work that afternoon at 3:30 and returned home.[477] Carl and Barbara Mather then drove to the Tippit home, where they consoled Marie Tippit on the death of her husband (killed by a man identical to the one seen a few minutes later five blocks away in a car bearing the Mathers' license plate number).

Fifteen years after the assassination, Carl Mather did finally consent to an interview for the first time—with the House Select Committee on Assassinations, but on condition that he be granted immunity from prosecution.[478]

The electronics specialist could not explain how his car's license number could have been seen on the Falcon with its Oswald-like driver in the El Chico lot.[479]

The HSCA dismissed the incident as "the Wise allegation," [480] in which a confused auto mechanic had jotted down a coincidentally connected license plate, as "alleged" by a reporter. The odds against White having come up with the exact license plate of a CIA-connected friend of J. D. Tippit were too astronomical for comment, and were given none.

What kept "the Wise allegation" from sinking into total oblivion over the years was the persistent conscience of Wes Wise, who in 1971 was elected mayor of Dallas. During his two terms as mayor (1971–76), Wise guided Dallas out from under the cloud of the assassination and at the same time saved the Texas School Book Depository from imminent destruction, preserving it for further research into the president's murder.[481]

In the fall of 2005, I interviewed Wes Wise, who recalled vividly T. F. White's description of his confrontation with a man looking like Oswald in the El Chico parking lot. Wise said he was so struck by the incident that he returned to the El Chico lot on a November 22 afternoon years later to reenact the scene with similar lighting and a friend sitting in an identically parked car. Standing on the spot where T. F. White had and with the same degree of afternoon sunlight, Wise confirmed that one could easily recognize a driver's features from a "full face" look at that distance, irrespective of whether the car's window was up or down.[482]

The possible significance of what he had learned stayed with Wise during his years as a reporter and as Dallas mayor, in spite of its repeated dismissal by federal agencies. Knowing the value of evidence, Mayor Wise preserved not only the Texas School Book Depository but also the December 4, 1963, luncheon invitation on which he had immediately written down T. F. White's identification of the license plate on the Oswald car. Producing it from his files during our interview, Wise read to me over the phone T. F. White's exact identification of the license plate, as the auto mechanic had shown it to the reporter on the scrap of paper taken from his coveralls pocket, and as Wise had then copied it down on his luncheon invitation: "PP 4537." [483]

At the end of our conversation, Mayor Wise reflected for a moment on the question posed by Lee Harvey Oswald's presence elsewhere at the same time as T. F. White saw him in El Chico's parking lot (in a car whose license plate could now be traced, thanks to the scrupulous note-taking of White and Wise, to the employee of a major CIA contractor).

"Well," he said, "You're aware of the idea of two Oswalds, I guess?" [484]

I was especially aware of "the idea of two Oswalds" from the testimony of U.S. Air Force sergeant Robert G. Vinson of the North American Air Defense Command (NORAD).[485] Vinson not only saw the second Oswald on the afternoon of November 22 soon after T. F. White did. He actually witnessed the Oswald double escaping from Dallas in a CIA plane. Sergeant Vinson was already on the CIA getaway plane when the second Oswald boarded it. Vinson also got off the plane at the same CIA base as Oswald's double did, a few moments after him. Robert Vinson is a unique witness to the CIA's secret movement of an Oswald double out of Dallas on the afternoon of the assassination.

On November 20, 1963, Sergeant Robert Vinson took a trip to Washington, D.C., from Colorado Springs, where he was stationed at Ent Air Force Base on the staff of NORAD. The thirty-four-year-old sergeant had decided for the first time in his sixteen-year military career to go over his superiors' heads. His purpose in traveling to Washington was to ask why he had not received an overdue promotion. Vinson's rise in rank had been delayed in spite of his having received outstanding job evaluations at NORAD, where he served as administrative supervisor of the electronics division and held a crypto security clearance.[486] Sergeant Vinson was known by his NORAD commanders as a mild-mannered subordinate who could be counted on not to raise uncomfortable questions. But after discussing at length the problem of his stalled promotion with his wife, Roberta, Robert Vinson decided now was the time to depart from his usual pattern of compliance.[487]

On Thursday, November 21, in a basement office of the Capitol Building, Sergeant Vinson met with a Colonel Chapman, who served as a liaison officer between Congress and the Pentagon. While he looked over Vinson's papers, Chapman engaged in a phone conversation Vinson would not forget.

Col. Chapman told the person on the other end of the line he "would highly recommend that the President not go to Dallas, Texas, on Friday because there had been something reported."[488] Chapman said the president should cancel his Dallas trip, even though an advance group of Congressmen whom Chapman was coordinating had already left the capital.[489] Vinson did not hear what the "something" was that moved Col. Chapman to urge the last-second cancellation of President Kennedy's Dallas trip (that would have followed by less than three weeks the last-second cancellation of his Chicago trip, where a four-man sniper team and an assassination scapegoat had been discovered).

Col. Chapman referred Sergeant Vinson's promotion question to an office at the Pentagon. A personnel officer there scanned Vinson's records. The officer was puzzled at why he hadn't been promoted. He assured him their office would look into the situation.

The next day, November 22, Vinson took a bus to Andrews Air Force Base. He planned to hitch a ride home on the first available flight going to Colorado Springs or its vicinity.

When an airman at the check-in counter told him there was nothing scheduled that day going his way, Vinson still wrote his name and serial number on the check-in sheet. He said he was going for breakfast in the cafeteria and asked the airman to let him know "if anything should come through that you don't have a notice on."[490] A loudspeaker paged him fifteen minutes later. He left his breakfast sitting on the table, grabbed his bag, and ran for a plane that was pointed out by the airman, who said it was about to depart for Lowry Air Force Base in Denver.

The plane down the runway that Vinson climbed aboard was a propeller-driven C-54, a large cargo plane. Unlike all the other planes Vinson had hitched a ride on, the C-54 bore no military markings or serial numbers. Its only identification was on its tail—a rust-brown graphic of an egg-shaped earth, crossed by white grid marks.[491]

The plane's door was open. When Vinson got in the C-54, he found it empty. He took a seat over the right wing. Through the window, he could see two men in olive drab coveralls walking around under the plane. Their coveralls bore no markings.

In a minute, the two men got on the plane. They walked past Vinson without saying a word. The men closed the cockpit door. The engines started up, and the plane took off.

Looking out the window at the runway disappearing beneath him, Vinson reflected on the flight's strange beginning and his own anonymity. Whenever he had hitched a ride before with the Air Force, the crew chief had always asked him to sign the "manifest," or log. This flight didn't even have a crew chief, much less a manifest.[492] Nor did the pilot or co-pilot (if that's what the second man in the cockpit was) give him the usual friendly greeting. His reception had been total silence from the two men now flying the C-54 due west.

At a location Vinson thought was somewhere over Nebraska, he suddenly heard an unemotional voice say over the intercom:

"The president was shot at 12:29."[493]

Immediately after the flatly given announcement, the plane banked into a sharp left turn. It began heading south.

About 3:30 P.M. Central Time, Vinson saw on the horizon the skyline of a city he was familiar with: Dallas.

The plane turned and came in over Dallas in a southeast direction. It landed abruptly in a rough, sandy area alongside the Trinity River. It was not a runway. Vinson thought it looked like a road under construction. Dust blew up, as the C-54 taxied around in a U-turn and came to a stop. The engines kept running.

Through the window Vinson saw a tool shed of the type used by highway construction crews, perhaps four by six feet in size, in a large, open, sandy area. Low cliffs stood at a distance. Across the river to the north was the Dallas skyline. Two men were running toward the plane from a jeep, which then backed out of Vinson's sight.[494]

One of the plane's pilots came back and unlatched the passenger door. The two men came aboard. Vinson watched as the men passed his seat without looking or speaking to him. They were wearing off-white, beige coveralls, the type used by highway workers. They carried nothing. The men sat down right behind the cockpit. They said nothing to the man who let them on the plane or to each other. To Vinson it was obvious they were following orders, which must have included keeping silent about what they were doing.[495]

The taller of the two men, 6' to 6'1", weighing 180 to 190 pounds, looked Latino. Vinson thought he was Cuban. The shorter man, 5'7" to 5'9", weighing about 150 to 160 pounds, was Caucasian. When Vinson watched the televised events from Dallas later that weekend, he recognized Lee Harvey Oswald as identical to the shorter man he had seen board the plane.[496]

Without ever having stopped its engines, the C-54 took off from the sandy area in a northwest direction. Carrying the man who looked like Oswald, the plane soon left Dallas—and the jailed, about-to-be-killed Lee Harvey Oswald—far behind.

A little after dusk, the C-54 landed on a runway. Going by what he was told at Andrews, Robert Vinson continued to think the plane's destination was Lowry Air Base in Denver.

As soon as the C-54's engines were shut off, the two men in the cockpit emerged quickly. They rushed past Vinson out the door of the plane. The two passengers from Dallas hastened after them. Vinson was left alone in the aircraft, just as he had been at the beginning.

"That was strange, very strange," Vinson said years later in an interview. "I couldn't understand why they were in such a rush. They just bailed out."[497]

Robert Vinson descended from the plane into the gathering darkness. There was no one in sight. Nothing looked familiar. Across the runway he could see a building with lights in it. Inside he found a lone Air Policeman on duty.

"Hi," said Vinson, "Can you tell me where I am?"

"You're at Roswell Air Force Base in New Mexico," the AP said.[498]

"I thought I was going to Denver, Colorado. How can I get downtown and catch a bus?"

The Air Policeman told him he couldn't go anywhere because the base was on alert. No one could come in or go out.

Vinson thought that was strange because the C-54 had just come in. How had their plane managed to enter a base that no one was allowed to enter? It didn't occur to him that the arrival of their plane could have been the reason for the base's closure to everyone else. That would explain why Vinson found the runway area deserted. At least one of the C-54 passengers was not supposed to be seen by anyone. But Vinson had seen him and had even flown out of Dallas with him, though he didn't know the significance of the man whom he had seen.

The AP said there was nothing for Vinson to do except take a seat in the waiting room until the alert was lifted. After a couple of hours, the AP told him the alert was over and gave him directions to a bus stop.[499]

By the next morning, Saturday, November 23, Robert Vinson was at home in Colorado Springs, telling Roberta the story of his strange flight. Although they didn't understand what lay behind it all, they both felt it could be dangerous. They agreed not to discuss it with anyone else.

That night, while watching the TV coverage from Dallas, Robert shook his head in disbelief. He said to Roberta, "That guy looks just like the little guy who was on the airplane."

"Are you nuts?" she said. "It couldn't be him. He's in jail."

"I swear that's the little guy who got on the plane."

"Well," she said, "keep quiet about it." [500]

After Lee Harvey Oswald was murdered the following day, Robert Vinson kept quiet for thirty years about the little guy he saw get on the plane in Dallas. However, his silence could not erase the name and serial number he had given the airman at the Andrews check-in counter the morning of November 22. No doubt the two men who got on the plane in Dallas, and the two in the cockpit, were thoroughly debriefed. They would have referred to the other member of their team, a man as silently obedient to the plan as they had been, who was on the C-54 before any of them got on and until after they got off. One can imagine the debriefer's shock: What other man?

The subsequent discovery that it was Air Force Sergeant Robert Vinson who was the unauthorized passenger in the flight from Dallas led, the Vinsons suspected, to further developments in their lives.

In the spring of 1964, after Vinson was promoted to technical sergeant, a friend told Robert and Roberta that their neighbors were being questioned by the FBI about what kind of people the Vinsons were and what they talked about. Not long after, Robert was ordered by his commanding officer to sign a new secrecy agreement. Roberta was also asked to fill out a personal history statement and sign a secrecy agreement, the first time she was ever required to do so as an Air Force wife. [501]

On November 25, 1964, Robert Vinson received orders to go to Washington, D.C., and report to a telephone number "in conjunction with a Special Project." [502] When he arrived in D.C. and phoned the number, he received instructions that resulted in his spending five days at CIA Headquarters in Langley, Virginia. The CIA put him through a series of psychological and physical tests. At their conclusion, he was interviewed in a conference room by a half-circle of men in semi-darkness. They asked Vinson to work for them. He refused, saying he wanted to retire from the Air Force and take a job in Colorado Springs. The CIA men offered him lucrative inducements, which he again refused. They finally let him go. [503]

As it turned out, they had not let him go at all.

Three months later, Robert Vinson was again ordered to report to a telephone number for the CIA, this time in Las Vegas, Nevada. The difference was he was no longer being *asked* to work for the CIA. He was *told* to work for the CIA. The Air Force had reassigned him to a top-secret CIA project, the Blackbird SR 71 spy plane, at an air base hidden in the Nellis Mountains, forty miles northwest of Las Vegas.[504] In more recent years, after the base was closed especially because of radioactive contamination from the Nevada Test Site, this former CIA testing area was identified as Site 51.[505]

On his new assignment, Vinson would soon learn that the CIA's projects out of Site 51 included experimental aircraft shaped like saucers. The same was true at the CIA's other base at Roswell, New Mexico, where the C-54 carrying the second Oswald had landed. Both Site 51 and Roswell were home to the "flying saucers" that people saw periodically in the area. They in fact came not from outer space but from the CIA, which encouraged the flying saucer reports as a convenient cover story for U.S. experimental aircraft.[506]

For the final year and a half of his Air Force enlistment, Vinson served as the administrative supervisor for base supply of the CIA's SR-71/Blackbird spy plane project at Site 51.[507] It was obvious to Vinson he was not so uniquely qualified for this position that the CIA would for that reason alone pluck him out of the NORAD staff in Colorado Springs, only eighteen months before his retirement, and insert him into their Nevada project. The Agency had other reasons for asking the Air Force to reassign him. He and Roberta agreed the CIA was keeping both of them under close observation, while paying Vinson off for his continuing silence with the CIA's monthly cash payments as a bonus to his Air Force salary.[508] Nothing explicit, however, was ever said to him about his inadvertent presence on the flight from Dallas.

While Robert Vinson was working at Site 51, he saw a C-54 like the one that flew the second Oswald out of Dallas. On its tail was the same rust-brown graphic of an egg-shaped earth, crossed by white grid marks, that he had seen on the C-54 he boarded at Andrews. An Air Force sergeant at Site 51 confirmed the source of the plane he was looking at.

"CIA," he said.[509]

Robert Vinson's CIA employment ceased with his retirement from the Air Force on October 1, 1966.[510] Although the CIA had paid him well to keep silent, he and Roberta "felt as if they'd been freed from a plush prison."[511]

Out of fear for his life and concern for his military retirement benefits, Vinson maintained his silence during the twenty years he worked in Wichita, Kansas, first as an accountant, then as an administrative assistant and supervisor in the Wichita Public Works Department. In 1976 when he asked a lawyer friend in Wichita if he should reveal his secret, the lawyer said, "Don't tell a soul. For your own safety."[512] Yet Vinson's conscience continued to push him toward speaking out on what he knew.

After Congress passed the JFK Records Act in 1992, mandating the disclosure of government records on the assassination, Vinson consulted with his member of Congress. Representative Dan Glickman of Wichita said to his relief that the new law freed him from his secrecy agreement when it came to assassination information.[513]

On November 23, 1993, Robert Vinson told the story of his flight from

Dallas to news anchor Larry Hatteberg on Wichita's KAKE-TV Channel 10 News. Viewers gave "an incredible response" to Vinson's story, Hatteberg told me, as they have to its several re-runs on the Wichita channel.[514] One of those responding initially to Vinson was Wichita civil liberties lawyer James P. Johnston, who had studied the Kennedy assassination. Johnston volunteered his legal assistance to Vinson to help bring his testimony to the public's and the government's attention. Vinson then offered to testify before the Assassination Records Review Board created by the JFK Act, but was never called to do so. In 2003 James Johnston and journalist Jon Roe co-authored their book *Flight from Dallas*, describing Robert Vinson's experience in detail.

On a Dallas map sent to him by Johnston, Vinson identified the C-54's landing area as "the Trinity River Flood Plain just south of downtown Dallas."[515] The particular location he marked out as the landing strip, between Cadiz Street Viaduct and Corinth Street Viaduct, was 4,463 feet long.[516]

James Johnston found a C-54 expert to consult, retired Air Force Major William Hendrix, who flew the C-54 on over one hundred missions during the Berlin airlift. In response to Johnston's query on what the C-54 could do, Hendrix wrote: "It is my personal opinion that a C-54 could easily have landed in the Trinity Flood Plain and have taken off therefrom, the depicted area."[517]

In a colossal CIA blunder, Robert Vinson's providential presence on the second Oswald's flight from Dallas has enabled us to see the planning for the Oak Cliff follow-up to the assassination. First, in Dealey Plaza, came the killing of JFK by snipers firing from the grassy knoll and the Texas School Book Depository. Then in Oak Cliff, the scenario continued with Oswald's "escape" in a taxi, while the second Oswald was driven into the same area in the Rambler station wagon by the man Roger Craig described as "a husky looking Latin"[518]—corresponding to Robert Vinson's description of the Oswald companion who got on the C-54, standing 6' to 6'1", weighing 180 to 190 pounds, whom Vinson, like Craig, said looked Latino, probably Cuban.[519] Officer J. D. Tippit was then shot to death by a man who witnesses said looked like Oswald. After Tippit's murder and Oswald's capture, in a shell game featuring the Oswald lookalike, he and his Cuban-looking companion flew out of Oak Cliff on the CIA plane.

The C-54's landing strip by the Trinity River was on the perimeter of Oak Cliff. Where the CIA plane taxied in a half-circle and paused to pick up the second Oswald and his Cuban-looking partner was 1.3 miles from El Chico's parking lot. The man like Oswald whom T. F. White saw sitting in the CIA-connected car on El Chico's lot at 2:00 P.M. was a five-minute drive from the point where the CIA plane would meet him at 3:30 P.M. He had plenty of time to reconnect with his handler, change into his highway worker coveralls, and rendezvous with the C-54, while his more visible counterpart went to jail—and two days later, to death.

Robert Vinson has said that since November 22, 1963, "Every time I'd see an article on the assassination, I stop and wonder if I have the answer to this puzzle. Could this small piece of information fit into the larger picture to help us learn what happened?"[520] Thanks to the pieces of information presented by Mayor Wes Wise, auto mechanic T. F. White, concession stand operator Butch Burroughs, hobby shop owner Bernard Haire, and Air Force Sergeant Robert Vinson, we now have a larger picture of the way in which two men played the role of Lee Harvey Oswald in the Oak Cliff section of Dallas on the afternoon of November 22, 1963. The interlocking testimonies of Wise, White, Burroughs, Haire, and Vinson have given us a back-stage view of the double Oswald drama directed by the CIA.

The man who announced President Kennedy's death to the world at Parkland Hospital on the afternoon of November 22 was Assistant Press Secretary Malcolm Kilduff. Shortly before his own death four decades later, Malcolm Kilduff told me in an interview that President Kennedy made a powerful statement to him on Vietnam just before they departed for Texas.[521]

Kilduff said he came into the Oval Office the morning of November 21 to prepare the president for a press briefing. Kilduff discovered that JFK's mind was instead on Vietnam.

Kennedy said to Kilduff: "I've just been given a list of the most recent casualties in Vietnam. We're losing too damned many people over there. It's time for us to get out. The Vietnamese aren't fighting for themselves. We're the ones who are doing the fighting.

"After I come back from Texas, that's going to change. There's no reason for us to lose another man over there. Vietnam is not worth another American life."[522]

What Kennedy meant was clear, Kilduff said:

"There is no question that he was taking us out of Vietnam. I was in his office just before we went to Dallas and he said that Vietnam was not worth another American life. There is no question about that. There is no question about it. I know that firsthand."[523]

In his final hour at the White House, Kennedy was focused on his decision to withdraw from Vietnam, a process he had already begun by National Security Action Memorandum 263 on October 11, 1963. As he told his friend Larry Newman in Hyannis Port on October 20, "This war in Vietnam—it's never off my mind, it haunts me day and night."[524] Vietnam would leave his mind only when a bullet entered it.

Precisely how Kennedy would have followed up on NSA 263 to continue his Vietnam withdrawal we don't know. But there are clues to his thinking.

The first clue is his discovery that peace was an election issue. The ovations he received on his September speaking tour from even conservative audiences whenever he mentioned the test ban treaty showed him the people were ahead of the government on peace. The terror of the Missile Crisis, followed by the hope of the test ban treaty, had disrupted Cold War propaganda and ideology. Kennedy saw that, at least outside Washington, D.C., people were living with a deeper awareness of the ultimate choice they faced. Nuclear weapons were real. So, too, was the prospect of peace. Shocked by the Cuban Missile Crisis into recognizing a real choice, people preferred peace to annihilation.

Kennedy knew a Vietnam withdrawal was vital to his détente with Khrushchev. Now thanks to popular support for the test ban, he was coming to see how a withdrawal could even help spark his campaign for reelection, especially against his most likely opponent, the notoriously bellicose Barry Goldwater.

Looking back at that hopeful time five years later, *New York Times* writer Tom Wicker observed that Goldwater offered "a natural opening for Kennedy to sound a peace theme that could be greatly amplified if a settlement in Vietnam allowed some or all" of the U.S. soldiers there to return home in an election year.[525] As Goldwater began to emerge as the Republican presidential candidate, Kennedy could see the election shaping up as a referendum on war and peace. His withdrawal from Vietnam would fit right into such a scenario.

JFK's private statements for the withdrawal he had already authorized were becoming more forceful and concrete by the day. After telling his Marine Corps Chief of Staff General David Shoup on November 11 he was "getting out of Vietnam,"[526] the next day he said to his most vocal critic on Vietnam, Senator Wayne Morse, that Morse was "absolutely right" in his rejection of the war, adding:

"I'm in the midst of an intensive study which substantiates your position on Vietnam. When I'm finished, I want you to give me half a day and come over and analyze it point by point. Wayne, I've decided to get out. Definitely!"[527]

JFK's statement to Kilduff on the day before the assassination, that "Vietnam is not worth another American life," and that "after I come back from Texas, that's going to change," combined passion with urgency. Kennedy seemed on the verge of making his withdrawal a matter of public policy.

He knew that he had a ripe international moment to make his stand public. In a little-noticed article, UN Secretary General U Thant revealed later that after the fall of the Diem government in November 1963, "he suggested to the United States that it promote a coalition government in Saigon that would include a number of non-Communist Vietnamese political exiles, especially those who had taken refuge in Paris."[528] The *New York Times* reported: "this suggestion did not bear fruit, one reason being that the Paris group of exiles decided against returning to Saigon."[529] Another, unmentioned reason was that the president who was open to U Thant's suggestion was then assassinated. His successor had no interest in it.

The annual report *The United States in World Affairs*, published for the Council on Foreign Relations, noted for the period just before Kennedy's assassination the emergence of "new proposals for a negotiated settlement involving the reunification of all of Vietnam, as envisaged in the 1954 agreements, and its neutralization on something like the Laotian pattern." [530]

The neutralization proposals came not only from U Thant but also from the Communist government of North Vietnam. The *Manchester Guardian* reported that after the fall of Diem, Hanoi "was willing to discuss the establishment of a coalition neutralist government in Saigon." [531] The National Liberation Front in South Vietnam supported and encouraged such negotiation to end the war. On November 8, 1963, the NLF's radio station broadcast an appeal for the "opening of negotiations between various interested groups in South Vietnam, in order to arrive at a cease-fire and a solution to the great problems of the country." [532]

Looking back at these proposals, which Kennedy would have weighed carefully, U Thant later commented: "In my view, there was a very good possibility in 1963 of arriving at a satisfactory political solution." [533]

To get a sense of JFK's attitude toward these neutralization proposals the week before he went to Dallas, we can recall the strict instructions he gave repeatedly to Roger Hilsman the previous spring and summer. Hilsman said:

"[Kennedy] began to instruct me, as Assistant Secretary for Far Eastern Affairs, to position ourselves to do in Vietnam what we had done in Laos, i.e., to negotiate the neutralization of Vietnam. He had made a decision on this. He did not make it public of course, but he had certainly communicated it to me as I say, in four-letter words, good earthy anglo-saxon four-letter words, and every time that I failed to do something [in a way] he felt endangered this position, he let me know in very clear language." [534]

Toward the end of November 1963, the time had suddenly become ripe for an end to the Vietnam War, along the lines envisioned by John F. Kennedy and in a way that seemed politically feasible in both a national and international context. This was the concrete situation in which JFK told Malcolm Kilduff, in disgust at more American casualties and only minutes before his departure for Dallas, "Vietnam is not worth another American life," and "after I come back from Texas, that's going to change."

When Malcolm Kilduff announced the death of President Kennedy at Parkland Hospital the next day, he was announcing also in effect the death of over 50,000 American soldiers and three million Vietnamese, Laotians, and Cambodians from a war that would continue until 1975.

Who or what assassinated President John F. Kennedy? In the course of experimenting in the dark truth of JFK's death, the ongoing, deepening historical hypothesis of this book has been that the CIA coordinated and carried out the president's murder. That hypothesis has been strengthened as the documents, witnesses, and converging lines of inquiry have pointed more conclusively at the CIA. Yet understanding that the CIA coordinated the assassination does not mean that we can limit the responsibility to the CIA. To tell the truth at the heart of darkness in this story, one must see and accept a responsibility that goes deeper and far beyond the Central Intelligence Agency.

The CIA was the coordinating instrument that killed the president, but the question of responsibility is more systemic, more personal, and more chilling. Thomas Merton described it rightly as the unspeakable. Let us continue to follow the story as far as we can, in the hope that the unspeakable, if not spoken, can at least be glimpsed in the shadows.

At 12:38 P.M. on Friday, November 22, 1963, Doctor Charles Crenshaw burst into Trauma Room One of Parkland Hospital where a mortally wounded President Kennedy had just been brought in on a gurney. Dr. Crenshaw, a resident surgeon, had been alerted by phone that the president had been shot and was on his way to Parkland.

The first person Crenshaw saw in Trauma Room One was Jacqueline Kennedy.

"She was standing," he said, "just inside the door in pensive quietness, clutching her purse, her pillbox hat slightly askew. She turned and gazed at me, then refocused her attention on her husband. The look on her face forever marked my memory. Anger, disbelief, despair, and resignation were all present in her expression . . .

"Drying blood caked the right side of Jacqueline's dress and down her leg. Her once-white gloves were stained almost completely crimson. If she hadn't been standing, I would have thought she had been shot, too." [535]

Crenshaw said decades later that of all the people he had seen in his career grieving over trauma victims, he "never saw or sensed more intense and genuine love than Jacqueline showed at that moment toward her dying husband." [536]

While Crenshaw assisted the other doctors, he stood by the president's waist. It was then that he "noticed a small opening in the midline of his throat. It was small, about the size of the tip of my little finger. It was a bullet entry wound. There was no doubt in my mind," he said, "about that wound, as I had seen dozens of them in the emergency room." [537] Because the wound was impairing JFK's ability to breathe, Dr. Malcolm Perry "decided to perform a tracheotomy [a surgical incision followed by the insertion of a tube] on the President's throat, where the bullet had entered his neck." [538]

When the doctors had exhausted their ways to save the president's life, Crenshaw walked behind John Kennedy's head. He was shocked by what he saw. The right rear of Kennedy's brain was gone.

"It looked," he said, "like a crater—an empty cavity. All I could see there was mangled, bloody tissue. From the damage I saw, there was no doubt in my mind that the bullet had entered his head through the front . . ." [539]

At 12:52 P.M., even the most sensitive machine in Trauma Room One could detect no sign of a heartbeat in the president. Dr. Crenshaw helped two other doctors cover the body with a sheet.

Twenty-one out of twenty-two witnesses at Parkland Hospital—most of them doctors and nurses, trained medical observers—agreed in their earliest statements that JFK's massive head wound was located in the right rear of his skull, demonstrating a fatal head shot from the front.[540] The exit wound in the back of his skull was unforgettable. Crenshaw said it "resembled a deep furrow in a freshly plowed field." [541]

As Crenshaw also recognized, the hole in JFK's throat was an entry wound. Doctors Malcolm Perry and Kemp Clark drew that same conclusion at a press conference in a classroom at Parkland Hospital at 3:15 that afternoon, cited in the *New York Times* the following day.[542]

Dr. Perry said repeatedly at the press conference that the throat wound he had seen was an entrance wound:

> QUESTION: "Where was the entrance wound?"
> PERRY: "There was an *entrance* wound in the neck."
> QUESTION: "Which way was the bullet coming on the neck wound? At him?"
> PERRY: "It appeared to be *coming at him*." (emphasis added)
>
> QUESTION: "Doctor, describe the entrance wound. You think from the front in the throat?"
> PERRY: "The wound appeared to be an *entrance* wound in the front of the throat; yes, that is correct." (emphasis added)[543]

With the suspect, Lee Harvey Oswald, having already been located in the Texas School Book Depository to the rear of Kennedy, the implication of an entrance wound in the throat was obvious. Someone other than Oswald had shot the president from the front.

Inspired by the doctors' testimony, historian Staughton Lynd and Jack Minnis, research director for the Student Nonviolent Coordinating Committee, wrote the first published critique of the JFK assassination. Appearing in the December 21, 1963, issue of the *New Republic*, their article concluded: "The central problem—the fact that the President was wounded in the front of the throat, 'the midsection of the front part of his neck,' according to 'staff doctors' at Parkland Hospital on November 23 (*New York Times*, November 24)—remains." [544]

The problem that the throat wound raised, which Lynd and Minnis underscored, remains to this day.

After the doctors had covered JFK's body with a sheet, the Secret Service took over. Somber men in suits led by Agent Roy Kellerman took possession of the coffin containing the president's body. They almost ran over Dallas Coroner Earl Rose when he tried to block their way. Rose resisted them, saying that Texas law and the chain of evidence required him to perform an autopsy before the body left Parkland. Kellerman and the Secret Service pushed ahead with the coffin. Rose stood aside. The body was taken away.[545]

When the government took charge with its official story of a lone assassin firing from the rear, the doctors were pressured by the Warren Commission to change their initial observations of Kennedy's body. The Warren Commission's staff counsel Arlen Specter, a future U.S. senator, confronted the Dallas doctors with a question that contained the answer the Commission was seeking:

"*Assuming* . . . that the bullet passed through the President's body, going in between the strap muscles of the shoulder without violating the pleura space and *exited at a point in the midline of the neck,* would the hole which you saw on the President's throat *be consistent with an exit point*, assuming the factors which I have just given to you?" [546]

As Charles Crenshaw (who was not asked to testify) pointed out later, Specter had asked the doctors, "If the bullet *exited* from the front of Kennedy's throat, could the wound in the front of Kennedy's throat have been an *exit* wound?" [547]

The doctors went along with Specter's show of logic: Yes, assuming the bullet exited from the front of Kennedy's throat, that wound could indeed have been an exit wound. Pressed further by Warren Commission member Gerald Ford, who would later become president, Dr. Malcolm Perry repudiated as "inaccurate" the press reports of his clear description of the hole in the throat as an entrance wound. [548]

This was not enough for Allen Dulles, who wanted the Warren Commission to draw extensively on the doctors' denial of their earliest press statements as a way to counteract the "false rumors" of the hole in the throat as an entrance wound. The Commission, Dulles felt, needed "to deal with a great many of the false rumors that have been spread on the basis of false interpretation of these appearances before television, radio, and so forth." [549]

Dr. Perry's retraction was not only manipulated but given under stress. He had been threatened beforehand by "the men in suits," specifically the Secret Service. As Dallas Secret Service agent Elmer Moore would admit to a friend years later, he "had been ordered to tell Dr. Perry to change his testimony." Moore said that in threatening Perry, he acted "on orders from Washington and Mr. Kelly of the Secret Service Headquarters." [550]

Moore confessed his intimidation of Dr. Perry to a University of Washington graduate student, Jim Gochenaur, with whom he became friendly in Seattle in 1970. Moore told Gochenaur he "had badgered Dr. Perry" into "making a flat statement that there was no entry wound in the neck." [551] Moore admitted, "I regret what I had to do with Dr. Perry." [552] However, with his fellow agents, he had been given "marching orders from Washington." He felt he had no choice: "I did everything I was told, we all did everything we were told, or we'd get our heads cut off." [553] In the cover-up, the men in suits were both the intimidators and the intimidated.

With the power of the government marshaled against what the Parkland doctors had seen, they entered into what Charles Crenshaw called "a conspiracy of silence." [554] When Crenshaw finally broke his own silence in 1992, he wrote:

"I believe there was a common denominator in our silence—a fearful perception that to come forward with what we believed to be the medical truth would be asking for trouble. Although we never admitted it to one another, we realized that the inertia of the established story was so powerful, so thoroughly presented, so adamantly accepted, that it would bury anyone who stood in its path . . . I was as afraid of the men in suits as I was of the men who had assassinated the President . . . I reasoned that anyone who would go so far as to eliminate the President of the United States would surely not hesitate to kill a doctor." [555]

In the case of Dr. Crenshaw, the cost of speaking up almost thirty years later was the assassination of his character.

In April 1992, Crenshaw came out with his book *JFK: Conspiracy of Silence*, which revealed what he had seen of President Kennedy's wounds, contradicting the *Warren Report*. The book rose to number one on the *New York Times* best-seller list. Crenshaw was then attacked in print by the director of the FBI's Dallas office, who claimed "the documentation does not show that the doctor was involved in any way," [556] and by a former Warren Commission attorney, who said the press should demand "full financial disclosure [of Crenshaw] because hundreds of thousands and millions have been made out of the assassination." [557] Then, to his surprise, Crenshaw was denounced by the prestigious *Journal of the American Medical Association (JAMA)*.

In its May 27, 1992, issue, *JAMA* published two articles suggesting Dr. Crenshaw was not even in Trauma Room One with President Kennedy.[558] *JAMA*'s editor promoted the articles by a New York press conference that received massive press coverage. Dr. Crenshaw submitted to *JAMA* a series of articles and letters responding to the charge that he was a liar. He pointed out that in testimony before the Warren Commission five different doctors and nurses had specifically mentioned seeing him working with them to revive the president.[559] They made it clear Crenshaw had been in Trauma Room One, doing exactly what he said he did in *Conspiracy of Silence*.[560]

All of Dr. Crenshaw's written efforts to set the record straight on *JAMA*'s pages were rejected by the editor. Crenshaw then sued the journal. In 1994, through court-ordered mediation, *JAMA* agreed to pay Dr. Crenshaw and his co-author, Gary Shaw, a sum of money. *JAMA* also agreed to publish their rebuttal article, which eventually appeared in an abbreviated version.[561] Then *JAMA* published still another piece attacking Crenshaw, Shaw, and their book.[562]

However, even though Crenshaw's rebuttal reached fewer readers than *JAMA*'s widely publicized attacks on his character, his book's impact coincided with the public outcry created by Oliver Stone's movie *JFK*. As a result, Charles Crenshaw's witness to the truth of what he had seen in

Trauma Room One helped create the Assassinations Records Review Board and its release of hundreds of thousands of assassination-related government documents to the American public.[563]

Late Friday afternoon, November 22, 1963, Dr. Robert B. Livingston made a phone call from his home in Bethesda, Maryland, to the Bethesda Naval Hospital. Dr. Livingston was scientific director for two of the National Institutes of Health. Because his scientific responsibilities related to the president's wounds and autopsy, Dr. Livingston paid careful attention to the news reports from Dallas. He learned that "there was a small frontal wound in the President's throat." [564]

Dr. Livingston's call was put through at Bethesda Hospital to Commander James Humes, the naval doctor chosen to head the autopsy team. Livingston has described their conversation:

"Dr. Humes said he had not heard much reporting from Dallas and Parkland Hospital because he had been occupied preparing to conduct the autopsy. I told him about reports describing the small wound in the President's neck. I stressed that, in my experience, that would have to be a wound of entrance. I emphasized the importance of carefully tracing the path of this projectile and of establishing the location of the bullet or any fragments. I said carefully, that if that wound were confirmed as a wound of entrance, that would prove beyond peradventure of doubt that a bullet had been fired from in front of the President—hence that if there were shots from behind, there had to have been more than one gunman. At just that moment, there was an interruption in our conversation. Dr. Humes returned after a pause to say, 'Dr. Livingston, I'm sorry, but I can't talk with you any longer. The FBI won't let me.' " [565]

Dr. Livingston then wondered aloud to his wife, who had overheard his end of the conversation, "why the FBI would want to interfere with a discussion between physicians relating to the important problem of how best to investigate and interpret the President's wounds." [566]

The FBI's disruption of Dr. Livingston's phone call to Dr. Humes was a sign of things to come. The autopsy itself would be totally disrupted by government authorities. The military control over the president's autopsy from start to finish has been described by several of its participants.

Lieutenant Colonel Pierre Finck was the army doctor who assisted Humes and another navy doctor, Commander J. Thornton Boswell, in the autopsy. Finck became a reluctant witness to the military control over the doctors' examination of the president's body. Subpoenaed by New Orleans district attorney Jim Garrison, Colonel Finck was questioned under oath about the president's autopsy:

QUESTION: "Was Dr. Humes running the show?"
FINCK: "Well, I heard Dr. Humes stating that—he said, 'Who is in charge here?' and I heard an Army General, I don't remember his name,

stating, 'I am.' You must understand that in those circumstances, there were law enforcement officials, military people with various ranks, and you have to co-ordinate the operation according to directions."

QUESTION: "But you were one of the three qualified pathologists standing at that autopsy table, were you not, Doctor?"

FINCK: "Yes, I was."

QUESTION: "Was this Army General a qualified pathologist?"

FINCK: "No."

QUESTION: "Was he a doctor?"

FINCK: "No, not to my knowledge."

QUESTION: "Can you give me his name, Colonel?"

FINCK: "No, I can't. I don't remember." [567]

Finck described an autopsy carried out in strict obedience to military commands, watched by an audience from the entire panoply of national security agencies:

QUESTION: "How many other military personnel were present at the autopsy in the autopsy room?"

FINCK: "That autopsy room was quite crowded. It is a small autopsy room, and when you are called in circumstances like that to look at the wound of the President of the United States who is dead, you don't look around too much to ask people for their names and take notes on who they are and how many there are. I did not do so. The room was crowded with military and civilian personnel and federal agents. Secret Service agents, FBI agents, for part of the autopsy, but I cannot give you a precise breakdown as regards the attendance of the people in that autopsy room at Bethesda Naval Hospital."

QUESTION: "Colonel, did you feel that you had to take orders from this Army General that was there directing the autopsy?"

FINCK: "No, because there were others, there were Admirals."

QUESTION: "There were Admirals?"

FINCK: "Oh, yes, there were Admirals, and when you are a Lieutenant Colonel in the Army you just follow orders, and at the end of the autopsy we were specifically told—as I recall it, it was by Admiral Kenney, the Surgeon General of the Navy—this is subject to verification—we were specifically told not to discuss the case." [568]

As the prosecutor zeroed in on the entrance wound in the president's neck, Dr. Finck had more and more difficulty in responding to the questions:

QUESTION: "Did you have an occasion to dissect the track of that particular bullet in the victim as it lay on the autopsy table?"

FINCK: "I did not dissect the track in the neck."

QUESTION: "Why?"

FINCK: "This leads us into the disclosure of medical records."

QUESTION: "Your Honor, I would like an answer from the Colonel and I would ask The Court so to direct."

THE COURT: "That is correct, you should answer, Doctor."

FINCK: "We didn't remove the organs of the neck."

QUESTION: "Why not, Doctor?"

FINCK: "For the reason that we were told to examine the head wounds and that the . . ."

QUESTION: "Are you saying someone told you not to dissect the track?"

THE COURT: "Let him finish his answer."

FINCK: "I was told that the family wanted an examination of the head, as I recall, the head and chest, but the prosecutors in this autopsy didn't remove the organs of the neck, to my recollection."

QUESTION: "You have said they did not. I want to know why didn't you as an autopsy pathologist attempt to ascertain the track through the body which you had on the autopsy table in trying to ascertain the cause or causes of death? Why?"

FINCK: "I had the cause of death."

QUESTION: "Why did you not trace the track of the wound?"

FINCK: "As I recall I didn't remove these organs from the neck."

QUESTION: "I didn't hear you."

FINCK: "I examined the wounds but I didn't remove the organs of the neck."

QUESTION: "You said you didn't do this; I am asking you why you didn't do this as a pathologist?"

FINCK: "From what I recall I looked at the trachea, there was a tracheotomy wound the best I can remember, but I didn't dissect or remove these organs."

QUESTION: "Your Honor, I would ask Your Honor to direct the witness to answer my question.

"I will ask you the question one more time: Why did you not dissect the track of the bullet wound that you have described today and you saw at the time of the autopsy at the time you examined the body? Why? I ask you to answer that question."

FINCK: "As I recall I was told not to, but I don't remember by whom."

QUESTION: "You were told not to, but you don't remember by whom?"

FINCK: "Right."

QUESTION: "Could it have been one of the Admirals or one of the Generals in the room?"

FINCK: "I don't recall."

QUESTION: "Do you have any particular reason why you cannot recall at this time?"

FINCK: "Because we were told to examine the head and the chest cavity, and that doesn't include the removal of the organs of the neck."

QUESTION: "You are one of the three autopsy specialists and pathologists at the time, and you saw what you described as an entrance wound in the neck area of the President of the United States who had just been assassinated, and you were only interested in the other wound but not interested in the track through his neck, is that what you are telling me?"

FINCK: "I was interested in the track and I had observed the conditions of bruising between *the point of entry in the back of the neck* and *the point of the exit at the front of the neck*, which is *entirely compatible with the bullet path*." [emphasis added to Finck's unsupported statement, in contradiction to the known evidence]

QUESTION: "But you were told not to go into the area of the neck, is that your testimony?"

FINCK: "From what I recall, yes, but I don't remember by whom."[569]

Navy medical corpsman Paul O'Connor, who helped the doctors with the president's autopsy, was dismayed, he said, by "the fact that we weren't able to do certain critical things like probe the throat wound that we thought was a bullet wound. We found out it was a bullet wound years later."[570]

In an interview years later, O'Connor described how the military command kept the three Bethesda doctors from probing the throat wound, which had been identified in Dallas to the world's press as an entrance wound:

"It got very tense. Admiral [Calvin] Galloway [the chief of the hospital command] started getting very agitated again, because there was a wound in his neck . . . and I remember the doctors were going to check that out when Admiral Galloway, told them, 'Leave it alone. Don't touch it. It's just a tracheotomy.'

"He stopped anybody from going further. Drs. Humes and Boswell, Dr. Finck, were told to leave it alone, let's go to other things."[571]

Paul O'Connor's fellow hospital corpsman, James Jenkins, who also assisted in the autopsy, confirmed that the doctors were obeying military orders. Jenkins, too, said the pathologists' failure to probe the president's wounds was done at the command of Admiral Calvin Galloway, the hospital commander, who directed the autopsy from the morgue's gallery.[572]

Jenkins thought it odd the autopsy would even be done at Bethesda, rather than by the civilian doctors at Parkland Hospital in Dallas:

"In retrospect, I think it was a controlling factor. They could control Humes, Boswell, and Finck because they were military . . . I think they were controlled. So were we. We were all military, we could be controlled. And if we weren't controlled, we could be punished and that kept us away from the public."[573]

Jenkins said his experience of the president's autopsy changed forever his view of his own government:

"I was 19 or 20 years old, and all at once I understood that my country was not much better than a third world country. From that point on in time, I have had no trust, no respect for the government."[574]

The process of killing President Kennedy and covering up the conspiracy relied on parties whom the plotters knew in advance they could count on to enter into a conspiracy of silence. Those few witnesses who courageously broke the silence, such as Dr. Charles Crenshaw, suffered the consequences of being isolated and singled out. But the Dallas and Bethesda doctors who changed their testimony under stress, who lied out of fear for their lives, or who followed orders in not probing wounds and then stonewalling questions, were not alone. They joined in a larger conspiracy of silence that would envelop our government, our media, our academic institutions, and virtually our entire society from November 22, 1963, to the present.

The promoters of the systemic evil involved in killing President Kennedy counted on our repression and denial of its reality. They knew that no one would want to deal with the elephant in the living room. The Dallas and Bethesda doctors who saw the truth staring up at them from the president's dead body, and who then backed away from it, were not unique. They are symbolic of us all.

Those who dared to break the conspiracy of silence risked consequences more severe than the assassination of one's character. Dr. Crenshaw said he "reasoned that anyone who would go so far as to eliminate the President of the United States would surely not hesitate to kill a doctor." [575]

Or would surely not hesitate to kill a photographer who had taken pictures of what the doctors had seen. There was in fact such a photographer, documenting for history the wounds that the doctors saw—and would eventually deny seeing.

At 4:30 P.M. Eastern Time on Friday, November 22, 1963, three hours after President Kennedy was shot in Dallas, Lieutenant Commander William Bruce Pitzer received a phone call at his home in Takoma Park, Maryland. Lt. Cmdr. Pitzer was the head of the Audio-Visual Department of the Naval Medical School. In his audio-visual expertise, Pitzer worked closely with Bethesda Naval Hospital, where the president's autopsy was about to take place.

After listening to his caller, Bill Pitzer hung up. He excused himself from his family's dinner table, and said he was going to work. Pitzer took with him his 35 mm camera. He did not return home until the next afternoon. He did not discuss with his family the work he had done in the meantime. [576]

On the Monday or Tuesday following the assassination, First Class Hospital Corpsman Dennis David stopped by the office of his good friend and mentor, Lt. Cmdr. Pitzer. David found Pitzer crouched over a film-editing machine.

"Come here," said Pitzer, "I want to show you something." [577]

As Pitzer hand-cranked a sixteen-millimeter, black-and-white film through the machine, David watched the short movie on a small screen. What he saw was the body of President Kennedy viewed from the waist up, being touched by the hands of unseen individuals. He saw the hands roll the body onto its side and back. [578]

Pitzer was editing the film. David watched him work on several reels. He got the impression, he said, that Pitzer "was pulling some of the frames off of the films to make slides with."[579] In addition to the movie film, Pitzer had pictures and slides on his desk. They showed the president's body from different aspects. Pitzer shared his photographic evidence with David. The two men talked over what they were seeing.

David recalled to an interviewer his and Pitzer's conclusions: "Number one, it was our distinct impression—impression, hell, it was our opinion, actual opinion—that the shot that killed the President had to have come from the front."

Asked why, David said, "Because we both noted a small entry wound here [interviewer notes that David points to the right side of his forehead] from another photo, and a large exit wound back in this area [indicates right rear of head]. I had seen gunshot wounds before, and so had Bill. I've seen a lot of them since, and I can assure you that it definitely was an entry wound in the forehead."[580]

That he and Pitzer were looking at an exit wound in the rear of Kennedy's head was even more obvious: "It is inconceivable that anyone even vaguely acquainted with gunshot wounds would conclude that the massive wound in the *rear* of JFK's skull could have occurred from a rear-entry projectile, unless it was from grenade or mortar shrapnel, which tears and rends flesh and bone rather than pierces it."[581]

Pitzer did not tell David he had taken the film he was editing, but David assumed he had. "I never asked him," David said. "He was head of the Audio-Visual Department. I just assumed he had done it, he had taken it."[582]

What Dennis David says was on Bill Pitzer's film contradicts not only the Warren Report but also the increasingly challenged official photographs and X-rays of the autopsy, as well as the questionable testimony of Drs. Humes, Boswell, and Finck. If David is right, the Pitzer film and photographs would constitute powerful evidence of a systematic government cover-up of the gunshot wounds. Pitzer himself would be a critical witness to the process whereby he either took or obtained the government-incriminating movie and photographs of the president's body.

Bill Pitzer was shot to death on October 29, 1966. His body was discovered at 7:50 P.M. on the floor of the TV production studio of the National Naval Medical Center, Pitzer's working area. The estimated time of his death was approximately 4:00 P.M.[583] As an FBI teletype reported early the next morning, the victim was found dead with a gunshot wound in his head and a thirty-eight caliber revolver lying close to his body.[584] Pitzer's body was found lying face down "with the head extending under the lower rung of two aluminum step ladders which were leaning against a foundation post."[585] Following a joint investigation by the Naval Investigative Service (NIS) and the FBI, the Navy ruled that Bill Pitzer had committed suicide.[586] The members of his family were certain that he had not.

The Navy investigative board's verdict of suicide rested on its claim that Pitzer "was experiencing marital difficulty and was intimately associated with another woman." [587] Bill Pitzer's friends and family resisted the board's theory of suicide and Pitzer's supposed motivation, both of which contradicted their knowledge of the man. [588]

Dennis David had "a gut feeling" that Pitzer would not have committed suicide: "He had been through too many stressful situations in his life. Second world war—he had been in and out of Vietnam for various and sundry reasons . . . you know, he was not a weak personality type, or type of person who would ever run into anything he couldn't handle . . ." [589]

The Navy's claim that Pitzer had an ultimately fatal affair was based on "an unsigned, undated summary report of two interviews [with an unnamed woman] conducted by unnamed NIS agents." [590] The obscurity of the investigation, whose interviews were kept secret and inaccessible until they had been "routinely destroyed," [591] made it impossible to scrutinize the Navy's allegation of the character defect that presumably caused Pitzer's suicide. If Pitzer was instead killed by government forces, the Navy was adding to that crime its assassination of his character.

Bill Pitzer had been about to leave the military for a new career, whose promise implied peril. Four days before he died, Pitzer told a colleague he was ready to submit his retirement letter to the Navy. [592] He had confided in Dennis David that he "had some very lucrative offers from a couple of the national networks like ABC, CBS, to go to work for them." David thought the offers were connected with Pitzer's assassination film. [593] Joyce Pitzer, his widow, said that on the Saturday he was shot Bill had gone to his office to write a speech he was scheduled to deliver the next Wednesday at Montgomery Junior College, a nearby campus where he was enthused about a job offer to teach educational television. [594]

Bill Pitzer was on the verge of an exciting new vocation drawing on his television skills. At the same time, once he retired from the Navy, his opportunity to broadcast his film on Kennedy's wounds represented a threat to the forces covering up the assassination.

When Dennis David was asked why he suspected Bill Pitzer had been assassinated, he said, "I think it was because, with him retiring, they—and I don't know who they are—were afraid that he would take these pictures that he and I had seen, these 35-millimeter [slides] and the 16-millimeter film, that he would take them [with him]. And if he went to work for a major studio, that they would use them, or he would have them aired.

"That would really have blown some people out of the water, if that would have transpired." [595]

Bill Pitzer's film of John F. Kennedy's body has never been found. One investigator hypothesized that Pitzer had stored the film in his TV production studio's false ceiling. The upright ladder under which his head was found after his death was seen as a clue. It could have been the means by which Pitzer, or an assassin, climbed up to retrieve the film from its hiding place the final afternoon of Pitzer's life. He was then shot to death, and the film vanished. [596]

Joyce Pitzer believed strongly her husband's death was no suicide. However, she was pressured into silence by Navy intelligence officials who came to her home after Bill's death. "They told me," she said, "not to talk to anyone . . . the Navy intelligence [people] were here, and—at the house, and everything—and for twenty-five years, I did not really discuss it." [597]

When in 1995 at the age of eighty, Mrs. Pitzer described the Navy's pressure on her, she was still afraid that if she questioned her husband's death, "my [Navy] compensation might be stopped." [598]

The man to whom Joyce Pitzer revealed this fear was Retired Army Special Forces lieutenant colonel Daniel Marvin. He had phoned her with shocking news. In August 1965, Marvin told her, the CIA had asked him as an elite Special Forces officer, a Green Beret, to assassinate her husband, an assignment he then refused but that someone else apparently accepted. [599] A government plot that Bill Pitzer's family and friends had long feared was the cause of his death was now finally being filled in, three decades later, by a man who almost participated in it.

Colonel Daniel Marvin told a story that has subsequently caused him to be dismissed by skeptics, denounced and expelled by the Special Forces Association of retired soldiers, and begged by his family to retreat into silence. Yet, as a born-again Christian, Marvin has insisted on the need to repent of his covert-action past, partly by acknowledging to Joyce Pitzer—and to the American public—how close he came to assassinating her husband.

Dan Marvin was an ironic candidate to assassinate a JFK witness. Marvin had volunteered for the Special Forces on November 22, 1963. It was "out of my respect for President Kennedy," he said, "and because of his respect for the U.S. Army's Special Forces." [600] The curriculum that Marvin then followed at the Special Warfare School, Fort Bragg, North Carolina, included, he said, "training not only in guerrilla warfare, but also in assassination and terrorism. I believed that extreme measures were sometimes necessary 'in the interests of national security.' " [601]

For their top-secret training in assassinations, Dan Marvin and his Green Beret classmates were taken, he said, "to a different building that had a double barbed-wire fence, surrounded by guard dogs."

The instruction they received in the high-security compound gave them a different view of recent history:

"On the John F. Kennedy situation, that was brought to our attention as a classic example of the way to organize a complete program to eliminate a nation's leader, while pointing the finger at a lone assassin. It involved also the cover-up of the assassination itself. We had considerable detail. They had a mock lay-out of the plaza and that area, and showed where the shooters were, and where the routes were to the hospital . . .

"They had quite a bit of movie, film coverage—it seemed like, thinking back to that time—and some still photos of the Grassy Knoll and places like that. They told us that Oswald was not involved in the shooting at all. He was the patsy. He was the one who was set up.

"We did, myself and a friend of mine, form a very distinct impression that the CIA was involved in Kennedy's assassination. During the coffee break, we overheard one of the CIA instructors say to the other, 'Things really did go well in Dealey Plaza, didn't they?' Or something to that effect.

"And that just reinforced, or really added to our suspicions. And we really felt, before the end of the training was over, that one of those instructors may have been involved himself in the assassination of John F. Kennedy." [602]

Marvin said, as a result of his CIA primer on the Kennedy assassination, he "had to do a lot of re-thinking. And perhaps it's the way soldiers of fortune are. I don't know. But I just then convinced myself, as did my friend, that it somehow had to be in the best interests of the United States government that Kennedy was killed. Otherwise, why would our own people have done it?" [603]

In the first week of August 1965, Colonel Clarence W. Patten, commanding officer of the 6th Special Forces Group, summoned then-captain Dan Marvin to an office in Fort Bragg headquarters. Marvin says Colonel Patten told him to "meet a 'Company' man in an area adjacent to headquarters." [604]

Marvin has described this meeting, "in the shade of some nearby pine trees," with "a slender man of about 5'10":

"Dressed casually in short sleeves, light slacks and sunglasses appropriate for the August heat, he flashed his ID and took me aside. Would I terminate a man who was preparing to give state's secrets to the enemy—a traitor in the making?" [605]

Marvin, already trained as an assassin, said he would. He assumed his target would be in Southeast Asia, where he was on orders to go in December 1965. [606]

Marvin asked the CIA man who the traitor was.

"I was told," Marvin said, "he was a Navy officer—a Lieutenant Commander William Bruce Pitzer. The agent told me that Pitzer worked at Bethesda Naval Hospital. He said nothing of a link with the JFK autopsy and I just assumed that Pitzer was one of those sorry types that went wrong and was going to sell secrets to our enemy. The job had to be done at Bethesda before the man retired from the Navy." [607]

It was only at this point that Dan Marvin refused the trigger role in the plot against Pitzer. He had no objection, he confessed later, to killing Lt. Cdr. Pitzer, so long as the deed were to be done abroad, not in the United States.

According to Marvin, "It was common knowledge in Mafia and CIA circles that Green Berets were tapped by the Company to terminate selected 'targets' in foreign countries, whereas the Mafia provided the CIA's pool of able assassins for hits in the U.S." [608]

Marvin's assassination skills, he had been taught, "would be used overseas—not on our home turf. So—I refused the mission after he'd already told me the guy's name which is not a good thing." [609]

Marvin and the CIA agent parted with the understanding "that the name would be as good as forgotten by me . . .

"The agent then simply turned around and walked over to meet Captain [David] Vanek who was waiting just out of earshot and I headed back to my office. Whether or not that agent offered Vanek [with whom Marvin had taken assassination training] the same mission or whether or not he accepted the mission is only for him to say; I have neither seen him nor heard of him these past twenty-nine years." [610]

Dan Marvin began trying to find David Vanek in April 1993. Following his conversion to the Christian faith, Marvin began speaking out against the CIA's and Special Forces' training in assassination. He hoped Vanek would corroborate the assassination classes they attended together at Fort Bragg and would help him bring that evil to light. [611] Drawing on Army orders for a training assignment that included both Vanek and himself, Marvin provided Vanek's Army service number in a query to the Veterans Services Directorate of the Army Reserve Personnel Center. For over a year, he got no response.

In the meantime, he was given a shocking revelation.

While watching a documentary on the Kennedy assassination in November 1993, Marvin "suddenly felt extremely ill" when he saw the name of William Bruce Pitzer flash across his screen. [612] Pitzer's name was one in a list of violent deaths linked with the JFK assassination and cover-up. Marvin was transported back to the shade of Fort Bragg pine trees where the CIA man in dark glasses asked him to kill the "traitor," William Bruce Pitzer, a man "who was preparing to give state's secrets to the enemy." Marvin realized the assignment he refused under those trees must have been carried out by someone else. That could have been his Green Beret classmate, David Vanek, to whom the CIA agent had spoken next.

Following the revelation of Pitzer's death, Marvin redoubled his efforts to find Vanek. After informing the Veterans Services Directorate that he might have to seek the help of members of Congress, Marvin finally received a reply in December 1994. It stated their office had "been unable to identify a service of record for the person concerned." [613] Marvin feared Vanek was dead—that there had been a second murder through a CIA doublecross. He worried that his Green Beret comrade, David Vanek, had not only killed William Pitzer, but that he had been killed in turn and his records obliterated to complete a cover-up. [614]

However, in 1996 the Assassination Records Review Board (ARRB), following the leads of researchers, located David Vanek. ARRB staff members interviewed him by phone. Doctor David Vanek was by then a colonel in the U.S. Army Reserve Medical Corps. He had indeed attended the same January-April 1964 session of the Special Warfare School that Daniel Marvin had, but said he could not remember Marvin: "I'm not familiar with that name." [615]

Asked if he recalled attending any course where movie film or still photos of the JFK assassination were shown, he said, "Jesus, I don't remember that at all." [616]

When he was read Marvin's account of their alleged encounter with the CIA "Company man," Vanek said he did not recall the incident. He denied even being at Fort Bragg in August 1965, when he "may no longer have been in the military." [617]

Nevertheless, he did admit that, while in the Army, he worked under cover in Vietnam in 1964 "as a civilian 'employee' at a provincial office of the Agency for International Development" [618] (a CIA front). According to David Vanek's Curriculum Vitae, his military duty included "Special Assignment on Loan from US Army to Agency for International Development (South Vietnam)—1964–1965." [619] He was then in Bangkok from 1965–1967 as a civilian "Counterinsurgency Warfare Specialist (GS 13) for Advanced Research Projects, Agency of Office Secretary Defense (Thailand Field Unit)." [620]

Vanek was apparently well versed in CIA cover stories and covert warfare. However, when asked if he recognized the name William Bruce Pitzer, he said, "No, not at all." [621]

Regardless of who may have been involved in Pitzer's death, Dan Marvin remains convinced that the assignment he turned down at Fort Bragg was carried out by another assassin. For Marvin, the key to William Pitzer's murder was given in the words of the Company man under the trees. Yet Marvin did not comprehend their meaning until almost three decades later, when he learned of Pitzer's death. Only when the name of William Bruce Pitzer flashed across Marvin's television screen did he understand that the CIA's designated "traitor" was in fact a JFK witness, and "the enemy" to whom Pitzer "was preparing to give state's secrets" was the American people.

John Kennedy was turning. The key to understanding Kennedy's presidency, his assassination, and our survival as a species through the Cuban Missile Crisis is that Kennedy was turning toward peace. The signs of his turning are the seeds of his assassination.

Marcus Raskin worked in the Kennedy administration as an assistant to National Security Adviser McGeorge Bundy. Not long after the Bay of Pigs, Raskin witnessed an incident in the Oval Office that tipped him off to Kennedy's deep aversion to the use of nuclear weapons.

During the president's meeting with a delegation of governors, New York governor Nelson Rockefeller, expressing his irritation at the guerrilla tactics of the Viet Cong, said, "Why don't we use tactical nuclear weapons against them?"

Raskin, watching Kennedy closely, was in a position to see what happened next. The president's hand began to shake uncontrollably.

JFK said simply, "You know we're not going to do that." [622]

But it was the suddenly shaking hand that alerted Raskin to Kennedy's profound uneasiness with nuclear weapons, a mark of conscience that would turn later into a commitment to disarmament.

Nevertheless, in the year leading up to the Cuban Missile Crisis in October 1962, Kennedy was responsible, as we have seen, for belligerent Cold

War policies. Khrushchev was rightly shocked when he read what Stewart Alsop wrote in the *Saturday Evening Post* after interviewing Kennedy: "Khrushchev must *not* be certain that, where its vital interests are threatened, the United States will never strike first. As Kennedy says, 'in some circumstances we might have to take the initiative.'" [623]

Kennedy had also intensified the arms race with the Soviet Union, "doubling the production of Polaris missile submarines from ten a year to twenty, increasing the number of Strategic Air Command nuclear-armed bombers in the air on alert at all times from 33 percent to 50 percent, signing off on one thousand new U.S. intercontinental ballistic missiles, each one with a charge eighty times more powerful than the atomic bomb dropped at Hiroshima." [624] During these disastrous decisions that moved the United States closer to the brink of nuclear war over Cuba in October, Kennedy also gave hints of the turning he would experience with his enemy Khrushchev in the midst of that crisis.

On the morning of May 1, 1962, President Kennedy met in the Oval Office with a delegation of Quakers dedicated to a process of total disarmament and world order. The six members of the Society of Friends who saw the president represented one thousand Friends who had been vigiling for peace and world order outside the White House and the State Department during the previous two days.

As Kennedy was well aware, the Quakers were adamantly opposed to his ever exercising his function as commander-in-chief of the armed forces, unless he should choose to order the troops to convert their bombs into ploughshares. The six Friends submitted to him a statement urging the government to change direction "from headlong preparation for nuclear war to a total foreign policy geared to the peace race [a term Kennedy himself had used in his September 25, 1961, address to the United Nations]," so as to achieve a "speedy transition from a precarious balance of terror to general and complete disarmament." [625]

What was Kennedy doing, meeting with a group of peacemakers committed to "general and complete disarmament"?

The Quakers had drawn shrewdly and sympathetically on JFK's own vision and language. In his UN speech challenging the Soviet Union to a peace race, he had described the process and goal of such a race: "to advance together step by step, stage by stage, until general and complete disarmament has actually been achieved." [626]

The Quakers were aware that, five days before JFK's UN speech, his disarmament representative, John McCloy, and Khrushchev's representative, Valerian Zorin, had signed an agreement outlining a "program for general and complete disarmament." [627] The McCloy-Zorin Agreement had then been quickly adopted by the UN General Assembly.[628] The Quakers were simply asking Kennedy to be true to what he had already agreed to in the United Nations.

The president began the meeting by responding positively to a Quaker appeal. He said, "I've received a number of letters from Quakers objecting to the government's announcement that a Polaris submarine would be named the 'William Penn.'" He smiled wryly, recognizing the irony of putting a great pacifist's name on a nuclear weapons system.

"I can assure you," he said, "that this will not be done." [629]

The six Friends, sitting in a half-circle with JFK in his rocking chair, were surprised. The president, by personally sinking the Navy Department's hypocritical choice of name for its Polaris submarine, had just made clear that he was more prepared to listen to the Quakers than they had assumed. They were accustomed to speaking truth to power, but not to having someone in power listen.

Samuel Levering, chair of the Friends Committee on National Legislation, told the president that Friends believed the alternative to an arms race leading to our total destruction was "world order which meant general and complete disarmament, peacefully enforced by a developed and strengthened United Nations." [630]

Kennedy nodded in agreement.

As we know, the young reporter John F. Kennedy, while witnessing the founding of the United Nations in San Francisco, had then already understood that the solution to war was world order, while recognizing the difficulty in attaining it. He had written in his notebook:

"Admittedly world organization with common obedience to law would be solution. Not that easy. If there is not the feeling that war is the ultimate evil, a feeling strong enough to drive them together, then you can't work out this internationalist plan." [631]

At that same time, having just lost close friends, his brother, and his brother-in-law to war, JFK had written to a *PT* boat friend a prophetic understanding of the problem whose formulation could have come straight from the Quakers:

"Things cannot be forced from the top. The international relinquishing of sovereignty would have to spring from the people—it would have to be so strong that the elected delegates would be turned out of office if they failed to do it . . . War will exist until that distant day when the conscientious objector enjoys the same reputation and prestige that the warrior does today." [632]

As president, John F. Kennedy was now in a position to push for a realization of the vision of disarmament and world order that he shared with the Quakers. But he also understood with them the truth, as experienced day by day in his presidency, that "things cannot be forced from the top."

He continued to listen intently to the visitors seated around him.

Dorothy Hutchinson, president of the U.S. section of the Women's International League for Peace and Freedom, said, "We're here to suggest a completely different orientation in foreign policy—a whole series of initiatives for peace." The U.S. could, for example, dismantle a foreign base or halt nuclear testing. [633]

Hutchinson was challenging Kennedy on his resumption of nuclear testing in the South Pacific only one week before. The U.S. test on April 25, 1962, had been the first of a series of twenty-four atmospheric tests that would continue until the following November.

Kennedy nodded in response to her suggestion that he begin instead a series of initiatives for peace. However, he knew that to take such steps for peace he had to overcome obstacles in his own government. He said, "All virtue does not reside on our side."

It was a heretical, anti–Cold War statement that he would develop the following year in his American University address, where he would insist that it wasn't just the Russians who were to blame for the nuclear threat to life on earth. First of all, for there to be any hope at all for peace, we had to examine our own attitudes as Americans. Self-examination was the foundation of peace. "All virtue does not reside on our side."

As JFK spoke of having already taken steps for peace that he admitted were small, the Quakers broke in to suggest a bolder initiative—food for China. The United States should offer its surplus food to the People's Republic of China, then considered an enemy nation but one whose people were in a famine.

Kennedy said, "Do you mean you would feed your enemy when he has his hands on your throat?"

The Quakers said they meant exactly that. Sam Levering said pointedly, "As Quaker Christians, we know that Jesus said, 'If your enemy hungers, feed him.' As a Catholic, you know that."

Kennedy said, "I do know that. I'd propose making food available immediately if it were politically possible. But the China lobby is strong. There's no point in my marching up Capitol Hill to defeat, like [President] Wilson did." [634]

The Friends were equally uncompromising with the president when it came to disarmament. While affirming Kennedy's support for the United Nations, they stressed the need for real steps toward general and complete disarmament. The Arms Control and Disarmament Agency, they felt, was a disappointment. Its Advisory Board members lacked any past commitment to disarmament.

The president did not argue the point. He had not appointed any pacifists to the board. His appointments were in fact often more conservative than he himself was, as had been the case with Arms Control and Disarmament Agency director William C. Foster, a Republican. But his reasoning was, as the Quakers stated in their confidential record of the meeting, "If skeptical people on the Board become convinced of the necessity and feasibility of disarmament, you have a better chance [in Congress] than if the Board is made up of people known to have had long time convictions in favor of disarmament." [635]

Kennedy said with a smile, "You believe in redemption don't you?"

He added, "The Pentagon opposes every proposal for disarmament." [636]

David Hartsough, at the age of twenty-two the youngest Quaker in the group, said the essence of what Kennedy then told them was: "The military-industrial complex is very strong. If you folks are serious about trying to get our government to take these kinds of steps, you've got to get much more organized, to put pressure on the government to move in this direction."[637]

The members of the delegation agreed afterward on the striking fact that John Kennedy seemed to feel more boxed in by adversaries near at home than he did by enemies abroad. Henry Cadbury, the group's elder and a distinguished theologian, saw the president as "frustrated and trapped," especially by the power of the Pentagon.[638]

"He seemed to indicate," Dorothy Hutchinson thought, "that he had gone as far as he can alone."[639]

Yet the plain-speaking Quakers, who challenged the president in unique ways to go much farther than he had, paradoxically made JFK feel less alone. When Kenny O'Donnell came in to point out that his next appointment was waiting, Kennedy replied, "Let them wait. I'm learning things from these Quakers."[640]

After keeping the Friends another five minutes, he was still talking while walking them to the door. In saying goodbye to Henry Cadbury, he mentioned that he had known of him as a beloved professor at the Harvard Divinity School, when JFK was an undergraduate.

"I never spent much time at the Divinity School," he said. "Now it's maybe regrettable that I didn't."[641]

The Quakers, on the basis of beliefs and scriptures they held in common with Kennedy, had sympathetically yet truthfully pushed the president toward bold initiatives for peace, such as halting nuclear testing and sharing food with China. They had also encouraged him toward the seemingly impossible, yet necessary, goal in a nuclear age of general and complete disarmament.

What struck them as amazing was that Kennedy listened to them.

David Hartsough said, "He didn't just let you say something for a minute, and then go on to his next agenda item. His humanity really impressed me. Here's the president of the United States, sitting in his rocking chair, listening to this bunch of Quakers. And he was listening at least as much as he was talking."[642]

Dorothy Hutchinson said, "I think it's fair to say that he was positively friendly, and the interview was in excellent spirit and informal . . . and I would say, if it hadn't been such a serious interview, delightful."[643]

George Willoughby, a pioneer in nonviolent action who had been jailed for sailing into a nuclear test site, noticed Kennedy treated them as equals: "Really he was very friendly and warm to us, as prevailed through the entire twenty minutes. He listened, spoke when he wanted to . . . But when you interrupted him [as Willoughby confessed to having done "once or twice"], he didn't get mad or pull rank on us or anything."[644]

Edward Snyder, executive secretary of the Friends Committee on National Legislation, said, "I think he was really listening. There was a real dialogue."[645]

Kennedy's dialogue with the Quakers was a hopeful sign of what would come in the last year of his presidency, when he would make a crucial turn toward peace.

From a perspective in the administration working under McGeorge Bundy, Marcus Raskin saw the Cuban Missile Crisis as the event that was the catalyst in JFK's change. Reflecting decades later on the shift he had seen then in Kennedy's attitude, Raskin said:

"After the Cuban Missile Crisis, it became clear to him that there had to be a way out of the arms race. He really was frightened, truly frightened of it in ways he understood before, but not in an existential way. I would argue that it was at that moment when very serious discussions began going on internally within the administration." [646]

Raskin credits Jerome Wiesner, Kennedy's science adviser, with playing an important role in this dynamic. Five weeks after the Missile Crisis, on December 4, 1962, Wiesner sent Kennedy a memorandum stating that, as Raskin puts it, "the McNamara defense build-up was an unmitigated disaster for the national security of the United States, that it forced the Soviets to follow the United States in the arms race, thereby making the United States less secure." [647] Having been shaken by the October crisis into a deeper awareness of impending nuclear war, Kennedy realized Wiesner was right.

With the help of Marcus Raskin and JFK Library Archives Technician Sharon Kelly, I found Wiesner's December 4, 1962, memorandum for the president in the JFK Library's National Security Files. Although much of the memorandum remains classified, we can see in its opening paragraphs why Wiesner's critique of McNamara would have convinced Kennedy, for Wiesner takes up McNamara's own argument on behalf of the president against the Joint Chiefs' first-strike policy. However, using McNamara's logic, Wiesner says that unfortunately the Defense Secretary's actual force recommendations end up playing into the Joint Chiefs' logic, thereby heightening Soviet fears of a first strike—justifiably so. Wiesner writes:

"There is no question but that the recommended force levels are greatly in excess of those required to maintain a secure deterrent ... Despite Secretary McNamara's assertion, with which I am in full agreement, that a really acceptable first strike posture cannot be achieved, the size and rate of build-up of the recommended force levels could easily be interpreted by the Soviets as an attempt on our part to achieve such a posture. The distinction between a 'creditable first strike' capability and a strong second strike counterforce capability is very difficult for an enemy with inferior forces to judge ... I believe that the net effect of the resulting build-up of Soviet missile forces will be an over-all reduction in this country's security in the years to come." [648]

Wiesner's convincing critique of McNamara left the president significantly to the left of the Defense Secretary, the same man he was relying on to control the Joint Chiefs' ambitions for a Cold War "victory" that could destroy the world. Kennedy felt he could not afford to veto his loyal but wrong Defense Secretary's force recommendations simply on the basis of his science adviser's more astute reading of nuclear strategy. JFK's position was becoming increasingly untenable. Yet with an insight that went to the heart of the symptoms plaguing his presidency in Cuba, Vietnam, and on every Cold War front, Kennedy decided to transform the context of spreading global illnesses by ending the Cold War itself.

I know of no evidence that the president ever even referred again to the radical counsel he received from his six Quaker critics, who pushed him to act consistently with his own underlying vision of world order. Yet he in effect adopted the Quakers' recommendations as a strategy for his goal of ending the Cold War.

To work his way out of the arms race (and free from the kind of dilemma that arose from his science adviser knowing more about nuclear war, even its strategy, than his Defense Secretary), Kennedy decided to create a series of peace initiatives. He began with the American University address, the Partial Nuclear Test Ban Treaty, National Security Action Memorandum 263 withdrawing U.S. troops from Vietnam, and a covert dialogue with Fidel Castro.

During his final months in office, he went further. Compelled by the near-holocaust of the Missile Crisis, he tried to transcend the government's (and his own) disastrous Cold War assumptions by taking a visionary stand for general and complete disarmament.

On May 6, 1963, President Kennedy issued National Security Action Memorandum Number 239, ordering his principal national security advisers to pursue both a nuclear test ban and a policy of general and complete disarmament. NSAM 239 reads in full:

Washington, May 6, 1963.

TO
The Director, U.S. Arms Control and Disarmament Agency
The Committee of Principals [namely the already-mentioned Director of the Arms Control and Disarmament Agency, Secretary of State, Secretary of Defense, Chairman of the Joint Chiefs of Staff, Chairman of the Atomic Energy Committee, Director of Central Intelligence, Special Assistant to the President for National Security Affairs, and Special Assistant to the President for Science and Technology][649]

SUBJECT
U.S. Disarmament Proposals

1. Discussions in the 18 Nation Disarmament Conference at Geneva on both *general and complete disarmament* and a *nuclear test ban treaty* have unfortunately resulted in almost no progress. There has been no serious discussion of *general and complete disarmament* for some time. While discussions of a *test ban treaty* have shown important developments since the beginning of the 18 Nation Conference, they are now stalled.

2. I have in no way changed my views of the desirability of a *test ban*

treaty or the value of our proposals on *general and complete disarmament*. Further, the events of the last two years have increased my concern for the consequences of an un-checked continuation of the arms race between ourselves and the Soviet Bloc.

3. We now expect the 18 Nation Disarmament Committee in Geneva to recess shortly for six weeks to two months. I should like the interval to be used for an urgent re-examination of the possibilities of new approaches to significant measures short of *general and complete disarmament* which it would be in the interest of the United States to propose in the resumed session of the Geneva Conference. ACDA will, in accordance with its statutory responsibilities, take the leadership in this effort and coordinate with the other agencies concerned through the usual procedures of the Committee of Principals. I should like to review the results at an appropriate time in the process.

John F. Kennedy[650]

Marcus Raskin has commented on the meaning of this document: "The President said, 'Look, we've really got to figure out how to get out of this arms race. This is just impossible. Give me a plan, the first stage at least of how we're going to get out of the arms race.'

"This would be a 30% cut of arms. Then move from that stage to the next stage. He was into that. There's no question about it."[651]

In the three paragraphs of NSAM 239, Kennedy uses the phrase "general and complete disarmament" four times—twice in the opening paragraph, once each in the final two paragraphs. It is clearly the central focus of the order he is issuing.

The president's accompanying, secondary emphasis is on "a nuclear test ban treaty," which he mentions three times. It is his secondary focus that shows just how strongly he is committed to NSAM 239's higher priority, general and complete disarmament. For we know that in the three months after NSAM 239 was issued, JFK concentrated his energy on negotiating a nuclear test ban agreement with Khrushchev, a goal he accomplished.

General and complete disarmament is the more ambitious project in which he says he wants immediate steps to be taken: "an urgent re-examination of the possibilities of new approaches to significant measures short of general and complete disarmament," such as the 30 percent cut in arms mentioned by Raskin.

In his American University address the following month, he reiterates: "Our primary long-range interest [in the Geneva talks] is general and complete disarmament—designed to take place by stages, permitting parallel political developments to build the new institutions of peace which would take the place of arms."[652]

The American University address and the test ban treaty opened the door to the long-range project that was necessary for the survival of humanity in the nuclear age. The test ban treaty was JFK's critically important way to initiate with Khrushchev the end of the Cold War and their joint leadership in the United Nations for the redemptive process of general and complete disarmament.

In NSAM 239, Kennedy said why he was prepared to pursue such a radical program: "the events of the last two years have increased my concern for the consequences of an un-checked continuation of the arms race between ourselves and the Soviet Bloc."

Having been shaken and enlightened by the Cuban Missile Crisis, Kennedy had the courage to recognize, as head of the most disastrously armed nation in history, that humanity could not survive the nuclear age unless the United States was willing to lead the world to general and complete disarmament.

"You believe in redemption don't you?" Kennedy had said to his Quaker visitors. As usual, his irony told the truth and doubled back on himself. Ted Sorensen observed that when it came to disarmament, "The President underwent a degree of redemption himself." [653]

JFK took no action on the Quakers' other major recommendation to him—food for China. However, in the fall of 1963, when the Soviet Union experienced a severe grain shortage, Kennedy decided to sell wheat to the Russians. Taking a leaf from the Quakers' book (which was his book as well), he chose to help feed the same Cold War enemies whom the year before he had struggled with on the brink of nuclear war. Others in the government said in effect to him what he had said to the Quakers: Would you feed an enemy who has his hands on your throat?

Vice President Lyndon Johnson said to Kenny O'Donnell, "Selling this wheat to Russia would be the worst political mistake he ever made." [654]

The members of Kennedy's political staff, led by O'Donnell, were dead set against the grain sale to Russia. They were certain that, as O'Donnell put it, "lending such a helpful hand to Khrushchev would bring strong political repercussions against the administration, particularly from the anti-Communist Americans of German and Polish descent, as well as from Irish Catholics." [655] The president granted that his staff's political fears were justified.

Nevertheless, Kennedy went ahead with the wheat sale "to the enemy." Today an almost forgotten act at the end of his presidency, at the time neither the decision nor the process was easy. Yet, as Sorensen noted, "In time he overcame attempted Congressional restrictions, attempted longshoreman boycotts, Soviet haggling about freight rates, disagreements between Agriculture and State, disagreements between Labor and Commerce, disputes over financing and a host of other obstacles." [656]

Now marching to a different drummer than his advisers were, Kennedy had chosen the wheat sale as still another initiative for peace. It was not only the right thing to do, as proclaimed in the ancient scriptures he heard in church on Sunday. It was also another way to mark an end to the Cold War.

JFK had reached a point in his presidency where a popular groundswell had begun to support his initiatives for peace. As in the case of the Atmospheric Test Ban Treaty, the American public supported the wheat sale as another hopeful step with the Russians. Peace had become an issue that would not hinder the president's reelection, but would ensure it. Unlike Kennedy's Cold War government, Americans in the heartland were increasingly prepared to walk with the president toward a more livable future.

In that hopeful fall of 1963, it was not only President John F. Kennedy who was turning toward peace. The people were turning with him.

Discerning what the scapegoat of the assassination, Lee Harvey Oswald, was thinking in his jail cell on Friday, November 22, and Saturday, November 23, is no easy task. Yet we have clues. They include his few public statements, his attitude toward his interrogators, and his attempt Saturday night to make a critical phone call. From these clues we can see the awakening and turning of a mind trained by his government to obey orders blindly. Oswald was resisting the role into which he had been maneuvered in the execution of the president. He may have pondered in his cell the strange irony of his now having been accused of assassinating a president he admired.

Lee Oswald had become personally interested in the life and vision of Kennedy. On July 1, 1963, as library records reveal, he checked out of the New Orleans Public Library William Manchester's cameo of Kennedy, *Portrait of a President*.[657] He followed it up two weeks later by reading JFK's own *Profiles in Courage*.[658] He became so interested in Kennedy that when he returned *Portrait of a President* to the library he took out another book, *The White Nile* by Alan Moorehead, only because Manchester mentioned in passing that the president had read it recently.[659]

Oswald told his wife, Marina, as she revealed later, that he "liked and approved of the President and believed that for the United States in 1963, John F. Kennedy was the best President the country could hope to have."[660] He listened intently on their radio to Kennedy's speeches that summer, especially his July 26 address to the nation on the test-ban agreement.[661] JFK warned of a war that would not only end the country but would leave "a world so devastated by explosions and poison and fire that today we cannot even conceive of its horrors."[662] Lee explained to his non–English-speaking wife that the president was making an appeal for disarmament.[663] He told her "some critics blamed Kennedy for 'losing' Cuba," whereas in fact the president "would like to pursue a better, more gentle policy toward Cuba but was not free to do as he wished,"[664] as Oswald knew personally from seeing the CIA's marshaling of anti-Castro, anti-Kennedy sentiment among its paid Cuban exiles.

On the night after he heard JFK warn the country of an inconceivable war, Oswald gave a talk of his own warning of an inconceivable danger within the country. His cousin, Eugene Murret, had invited Lee to speak at the Jesuit House of Studies, Spring Hill College, in Mobile, Alabama, where

Eugene was a seminarian. The topic, as suggested by Eugene, was "contemporary Russia and the practice of Communism there." [665]

As Lee outlined his speech in advance, he found himself going beyond his topic. Thanks to the preservation of his handwritten notes, we can understand the speech better than his actual audience did, several of whom recalled from it months later for the Warren Commission only Oswald's mundane description of life in Russia.[666] Oswald may not even have said in his speech what he wrote more boldly in private. He laid out there the danger to the country (which he served secretly as an intelligence agent) of its being overcome by a military coup.

Understood in terms of his notes, this may have been, in contrast to his statements to the New Orleans media, the only non–CIA-dictated speech of Oswald's summer. He at least planned to say what he actually believed, not what he was ordered to say in public to create a pro-Castro, pro-Soviet image of himself. In fact, what he wrote in the text of his speech to the seminarians warned against the implications of what he was acting out in public. He began:

"Americans are apt to scoff at the idea that a military coup in the U.S., as so often happens in Latin American countries, could ever replace our government. But that is an idea that has grounds for consideration." [667]

In his thinking, Oswald was flying below the radar of his intelligence handlers. He had broken through their thought barriers. He pushed ahead to ask where in the armed forces a prospective coup d'état against the elected government would most likely originate:

"Which military organization has the potentialities of executing such action? Is it the army with its many conscripts, its unwieldy size, its scores of bases scattered across the world? The case of Gen. [Edwin] Walker shows that the army, at least, is not fertile enough ground for a far right regime to go a very long way." [668]

Oswald was familiar with the case of General Edwin Walker, an army general relieved of his command by the Kennedy administration for indoctrinating his troops with an anti-communist program of speeches and literature. After he was admonished for propagandizing his soldiers, Walker resigned from the army and retired to Dallas, where he became a leader in the anticommunist John Birch Society.[669] Soon after Oswald's death, the president's presumed assassin would be accused on shaky grounds of having tried to kill Walker the previous spring—an allegation then used by the Warren Commission to shore up the equally shaky evidence supporting Oswald's capacity to kill Kennedy.[670] In his speech notes, Oswald dismissed the danger of an army coup led by a demagogue such as Walker as being too unwieldy.

He continued: "For the same reasons of size and disposition the Navy and air force is also to be more or less disregarded. Which service then, can qualify to launch a coup in the USA? Small size, a permanent hard core of officers and few bases is necessary. Only one outfit fits that description and the U.S.M.C. is a right wing infiltrated organization of dire potential consequences to the freedoms of the U.S. I agree with former President Truman when he said that 'The Marine Corps should be abolished.'"[671]

Although Oswald had been in the Marines, his description of a likely institution for a coup fits the CIA, which was then manipulating him, more than it does the Marine Corps. In a similar way, his inaccurate Truman quotation conveys Truman's (and Oswald's) sense of a very real danger to democracy that lay elsewhere than in the Marines. Although President Truman was wrongly accused by critics of wanting to abolish the Marine Corps,[672] he did in fact speak up later—after Oswald's death—as if the CIA presented the same kind of internal threat to freedom that Oswald warned against. In his thoughts, Oswald was again skirting an unspeakable truth in a strangely prophetic way.

On December 22, 1963, one month to the day after JFK's assassination, Former President Truman published a very carefully worded article in the *Washington Post* warning the American people about the danger of the CIA taking over the government. He wrote:

"I think it has become necessary to take another look at the purpose and operations of our Central Intelligence Agency—CIA . . .

"For some time I have been disturbed by the way the CIA has been diverted from its original assignment. It has become an operational and at times a policy-making arm of the Government. This has led to trouble and may have compounded our difficulties in several explosive areas.

"We have grown up as a nation, respected for our free institutions and for our ability to maintain a free and open society. There is something about the way the CIA has been functioning that is casting a shadow over our historic position and I feel that we need to correct it."[673]

Truman's warning, with its ominous post-assassination timing, was greeted by total silence.[674] Had it been noticed and heeded, the controversial ex-president might have been accused more justly this time of trying to abolish the CIA, since he did indeed want to abolish its covert activities. President Harry Truman had himself established the CIA in 1947, but not, he thought, to do what he saw it doing in the fall of 1963.

Allen Dulles, whom Kennedy had fired as CIA director, was alarmed that Truman's CIA warning might get noticed.[675] On April 17, 1964, Dulles took a break from his Warren Commission business. He met privately with Truman at the Truman Library in Independence, Missouri, and urged him to retract his CIA critique. Dulles put his own version of the meeting on record for the CIA. On April 21, he sent a secret memorandum to his longtime CIA colleague, General Counsel Lawrence Houston.[676] He alleged that Truman had disowned the article published over his name as being foreign to his thinking. Dulles claimed that when he showed the president the *Washington Post* piece, Truman "seemed quite astounded by it. In fact, he said that this was all wrong. He then said that he felt it had made a very unfortunate impression. . . .

"At no time did Mr. Truman express other than complete agreement with the viewpoint I expressed and several times said he would see what he could do about it, to leave it in his hands. He obviously was highly disturbed at the *Washington Post* article." [677]

Dulles was lying for the record. The plainspoken president meant what he wrote about the CIA and would repeat it. Truman's published words were faithful to the preliminary notes (preserved in the Truman Library) that he had written by hand on December 1, 1963, three weeks before his article appeared:

"[The CIA] was not intended as a 'Cloak & Dagger Outfit'! . . .

"It was intended merely as a center for keeping the President informed on what was going on in the world at large and the United States and its dependencies in particular.

"It should not be an agency to initiate policy or to act as a spy organization. That was never the intention when it was organized." [678]

Ignoring the pressures of Allen Dulles, President Truman restated his radical critique of the CIA in a letter written six months after the *Washington Post* article. [679] The managing editor of *Look* magazine had sent Truman the latest *Look* featuring a piece on the CIA. Truman wrote back:

"Thank you for the copy of *Look* with the article on the Central Intelligence Agency. It is, I regret to say, not true to the facts in many respects.

"The CIA was set up by me for the sole purpose of getting all the available information to the president. It was not intended to operate as an international agency engaged in strange activities." [680]

Lee Harvey Oswald was caught up totally in what Truman termed the CIA's "strange activities." Yet, as we can see from Oswald's admiration of John Kennedy and his notes for his speech to the Jesuits, he rejected the idea of a coup against the president. He in fact warned against one. As his intelligence mentors were pulling him more deeply into the plot against Kennedy, Oswald in his own mind was moving in the opposite direction—in support not of the plotters but of the president.

What, then, was Oswald to do?

In the light of his awakening conscience, his strange request from his New Orleans jail cell on August 8 to speak with an FBI agent after his leafleting arrest takes on further meaning. By that time, two weeks after he wrote his speech notes warning of a coup d'état, Oswald was working in the midst of the CIA's Kennedy-hating Cuban exile community, some of whose key members such as Sergio Arcacha Smith had been commandeered by the Agency for the assassination of the president. Oswald himself was being led step by step into his scapegoat role, with his New Orleans arrest as a pro-Castro leafleter serving as a key element in the scenario.

Whatever Oswald's reason for requesting an FBI interview from jail, it would not have been, as FBI agent John Quigley, who met with him, said lamely to the Warren Commission: "to explain to me why he was distributing this literature." [681] As an agent provocateur, Oswald may have been reporting to the FBI as well as the CIA on his subversion of the public image of the Fair Play for Cuba Committee. But given his closely held pro-Kennedy, anti-coup state of mind, he may also have decided to blow the whistle on the CIA's deepening assassination plot.

As we saw, the Warren Commission in its January 27, 1964, meeting became acutely aware of what its general counsel J. Lee Rankin called "a dirty rumor" that Oswald was an FBI informant.[682] The FBI denied it, but could the Bureau be believed?

Allen Dulles told the other commission members at their top-secret January meeting that if Oswald worked for the FBI and CIA, their officials would have to lie under oath if questioned about it.[683] FBI clerk William Walter, who in 1963 worked in the Bureau's New Orleans office, viewed the matter more independently. He told the House Select Committee on Assassinations that Oswald did indeed have "an informant's status with our office."[684] Other witnesses have filled in this picture of Oswald and the FBI.

New Orleans bar owner Orest Pena, who was an FBI informant himself, stated "he had seen Oswald with FBI agent [Warren] deBrueys on 'numerous occasions' and that deBrueys had threatened him physically before his Warren Commission appearance, warning him to keep quiet about what he had observed."[685]

Adrian Alba, a friend of Oswald who managed a New Orleans garage that looked after FBI and Secret Service cars, saw Oswald walk up one day to an FBI car that stopped outside his workplace. Through a window Oswald was handed a white envelope that he hid under his shirt. Oswald, Alba said, "met the car again a couple of days later and talked briefly with the driver," who Alba knew was an "FBI agent visiting New Orleans from Washington."[686]

From Oswald's support for Kennedy and his expressed opposition to a coup, it is possible he was not only an FBI informant but also one trying to save the life of the president. He may have been alerting the Bureau as early as August 8 from jail about the actual coup against Kennedy, which he had warned against as a possibility only two weeks earlier.

If Oswald thought he could help the FBI stop a CIA plot to kill the president, he was seriously mistaken. At the time the FBI may not have known key details of the plot. Nevertheless, the plan to kill Kennedy and cover up the conspiracy went to the top ranks of our national security state, harnessing to its treasonous purpose not only the CIA but ultimately Hoover and the FBI as well, who were crucial to the cover-up. To appeal to the FBI against the CIA was only to crawl more deeply into the spider's web.

However, Oswald's path is too littered with disinformation for us to know yet what he really thought he was doing. At this point we are given nothing more than a few mid-summer hints as to his actual state of mind. As summer turns to fall and "Oswald" appearances proliferate, the evidence of one man's thinking seems to disappear in smoke and mirrors.

We have seen already how the person Lee Harvey Oswald disappeared down a black hole during the Warren Commission–reported trip to Mexico

City September 27–October 2, 1963. The CIA used "Oswald's" highly dramatized visits to the Cuban and Soviet consulates, plus the Agency's transcripts of fraudulent "Oswald" phone calls, to link him in retrospect with the KGB's head of assassinations in the Western Hemisphere. The Oswald who in July read Kennedy books, listened to Kennedy speeches, and warned of a right-wing coup may not even have gone to Mexico City in September.[687] If he did, he was given a less active role in the scenario than he had in New Orleans. He was replaced by impostors in many if not all of the phone calls and visits made in his name to the Communist consulates to implicate him, Cuba, and the Soviet Union in the assassination.

As we also saw, during October and November in Dallas, Oswald (or more likely someone impersonating him) engaged in a series of provocative actions that would incriminate him in retrospect: at a gun shop flaunting his self-proclaimed past as a Marine by rudely buying ammunition for his rifle;[688] at a car dealership test-driving a Mercury Comet at high speeds, and when confronted by the absence of a credit rating, saying he might "have to go back to Russia to buy a car";[689] at a rifle range firing obnoxiously at another man's target, then in response to the man's objections giving him a look the man said he would never forget;[690] at Red Bird Air Field showing up with two companions to charter a small plane "to the Yucatan Peninsula" for the afternoon of November 22, for what could be seen later as evidence of advance planning for an escape by air to Cuba.[691]

Yet the Warren Commission was forced to cover up all this planted evidence against Oswald. It proved too much—implicating Cuba and the USSR (both set up by the CIA but exonerated by the new president, Lyndon Johnson, as shown by his recorded phone calls). It went too far—revealing the activities of the CIA's second Oswald (whom a CIA plane flew secretly out of Dallas on November 22, as witnessed by Air Force sergeant Robert Vinson). What the Oswald appearances conveyed willy-nilly was that, in an overambitious plot, the scapegoat wound up being in too many places at the same time. An Oswald other than the man working at the Texas School Book Depository and visiting his family at Ruth Paine's home was simultaneously laying down an overly obvious, false trail of assassination evidence elsewhere. The FBI, on behalf of the Warren Commission, doubled back in its investigation to sanitize the unduly revealing story, as we saw in the case of the Red Bird Air Field incident. The FBI's report pre-dated the incident to the previous summer to make it seem less likely Wayne January could have remembered and identified Oswald.[692]

In a more blatantly criminal act, FBI officials also ordered the destruction of a written note left at their Dallas office two weeks before the assassination by a man they identified as Lee Harvey Oswald.

Around noon on a day estimated to be Wednesday, Thursday, or Friday, November 6–8, 1963, the receptionist for the Dallas FBI office, Nannie Lee Fenner, watched a man get off the elevator and approach her desk. The man, whom she would refer to later in a congressional hearing as "Mr. Oswald," said to her, "S. A. Hosty, please."[693]

"S. A." was a shorthand designation for "Special Agent" that only some-one familiar with the FBI would use. The man, Fenner said, "had a wild look in his eye, and he was awfully fidgety, and he had a 3 × 5 envelope in his hand." [694] Fenner noticed that a folded piece of paper extended from the envelope.

When she replied that S. A. Hosty was not in the office, the man threw the envelope on her desk, saying, "Well, get this to him." He then turned and left.

Fenner could see the bottom part of a handwritten message sticking out of the envelope—a virtual invitation to read the last two lines. She did. They said: "I will either blow up the Dallas Police Department or the FBI office." [695]

Since it was an obvious threat, Fenner took the letter out of the envelope and read it from the top. Twelve years later, she told members of Congress who were investigating the incident, "I don't remember the exact words, but it was something about [them] speaking to his wife and what he was going to do if they didn't stop" [696]—"blow up the Dallas Police Department or the FBI office." The letter was signed: "Lee Harvey Oswald." [697]

The man to whom this threatening letter was addressed was FBI special agent James P. Hosty, Jr., who had been assigned to investigate Oswald as a possible Soviet agent.[698] Hosty had visited Ruth Paine's home on November 1 and 5 in Oswald's absence. He questioned both Ruth Paine and Marina Oswald about Lee Oswald.[699] The threat Nannie Lee Fenner read was apparently Oswald's angry response to Hosty's questioning of his wife.

In terms of the assassination plot, Oswald's letter to Hosty served a deeper purpose. In keeping with other provocative Oswald scenes created in New Orleans, Mexico City, and Dallas, the letter's dramatic delivery and contents were hard for a witness to forget. The letter thereby added to the false trail of evidence incriminating Oswald. Whether the man who threw it down on Fenner's desk was Oswald or an impostor, the letter's purpose was obvious from the words left visible extending outside its envelope. By threatening to blow up the Dallas Police Department or the FBI office, the letter's signer, "Lee Harvey Oswald," had documented his capacity for lethal violence—two weeks before the president's trip to Dallas.[700]

In throwing down a written threat to the FBI in November, "Oswald" also dramatized a distinctly different attitude toward the Bureau than that of the prisoner in the New Orleans jail in August, who at his own request conferred privately with an FBI agent for an hour and a half.[701] Oswald's initiative in arranging a conference with the FBI in jail is consistent with the reports of witnesses who saw him meeting or accompanying FBI agents in New Orleans that summer.[702] The Oswald–FBI connection had to be covered up. The assassin's legend laid down after New Orleans therefore emphasized "Oswald's" animosity toward the FBI.

For example, on September 28, 1963, during his visit to the Soviet Embassy in Mexico City, "Oswald" spoke of FBI surveillance and persecution. He then dramatically pulled out a revolver and put it on a table, saying, "See? This is what I must carry now to protect my life." [703]

In the same vein, the "Oswald" letter dated November 9, 1963, received by the Soviet Embassy in Washington on November 18, devoted two paragraphs to alleged FBI harassment of the Oswalds, concluding, "I and my wife strongly protested these tactics by the notorious FBI." [704]

In both cases, "Oswald" was simultaneously demonstrating his allegiance to the Soviet Union and his antipathy to the FBI. The anti-FBI statements attributed to Oswald were a necessary distancing of his public persona from the Bureau after the real Oswald's cozy relationship with the FBI in New Orleans. The tracks of an FBI informant could be covered over by the legend of an anti-FBI assassin.

Yet both the delivery and contents of the Oswald-Hosty letter, like "Oswald's" Mexico City activities, raised too many questions after the assassination. At an initial level, the evidence of the letter to Hosty implicated the FBI, which, after receiving a threat from Oswald, had failed to warn the Secret Service about a potential assassin in Dallas before the president's visit. If one saw through the cover story and identified the "Oswald" in the incident as an impostor, the evidence of the letter could even expose the plot itself.

The FBI therefore destroyed the evidence.

On the afternoon of Sunday, November 24, three hours after Oswald died of a gunshot wound, James Hosty was summoned to the office of chief Dallas FBI agent J. Gordon Shanklin.

When Hosty entered the office, Shanklin reached into the lower right hand drawer of his desk. He took out Oswald's letter and a memorandum Hosty had written about receiving it.

Shanklin told Hosty to get rid of the letter and the memorandum.

Hosty took the letter. He began tearing it up.

"No, get it out of here." Shanklin said, "I don't even want it in this office. Get rid of it." [705]

Then, as Hosty told a Congressional investigating committee in 1975, he took Oswald's letter and the memorandum into the washroom. There he flushed them down the toilet. [706]

Hosty also admitted to members of Congress that, when he testified before the Warren Commission, he did not divulge his destruction of the Oswald letter. When asked why not, Hosty said he had been instructed by FBI officials in Washington and Dallas to answer only the questions put to him by the Warren Commission, with no elaboration. [707] He followed orders and maintained a discreet silence before the Commission about his destruction of critically important evidence.

Following the lead of a Dallas newspaper, an investigative reporter for the *New York Times* helped bring the letter's destruction to light with a September 17, 1975, front-page article. Citing a high-level FBI source, the *Times* article said the decision to destroy the Oswald letter "was taken at a meeting of top FBI officials in Washington," almost certainly including Director J. Edgar Hoover, "on the weekend after Kennedy was murdered in Dallas on Friday, Nov. 22, 1963." [708]

"The order to destroy the letter was relayed to Dallas, where the letter was on file, by one of Mr. Hoover's assistants, but the assistant would never have ordered the destruction of possible evidence except on Mr. Hoover's expressed order, the source said." [709]

Special Agent Hosty was not simply obeying orders from his Dallas chief, J. Gordon Shanklin. When Hosty flushed the Oswald letter down the toilet, then withheld that criminal fact from the Warren Commission, he was obeying the FBI's chain of command. Everyone familiar with the FBI knew J. Edgar Hoover ruled it with an iron fist. Hosty was serving as Hoover's instrument when he destroyed critically important evidence, from either Oswald or an impostor, three hours after Oswald was killed.

The Oswald letter to the FBI, if exposed and investigated, could have quickly unraveled the plot that had just killed Kennedy. That was not an option. J. Edgar Hoover and the FBI made certain the evidence would never be seen again.

After the FBI's destruction of the letter became public in 1975, the House investigating committee referred it to the Justice Department for possible prosecution. The Justice Department chose not to pursue the matter against its own agency, the Federal Bureau of Investigation.

Although John Kennedy was in deepening conflict with his own Cold War government, he was supported in his turn toward peace by two improbable companions, a dying pope and a beleaguered Communist. In the final year of Kennedy's life, Pope John XXIII and Prime Minister Nikita Khrushchev became the president's greatest allies in his pursuit of peace. They made all the difference. Without them, his isolation would have been almost complete.[710] With them, he could begin to lay the foundations for a more peaceful world.

The unlikely trio of the capitalist president, the dying pope, and the Communist premier began to conspire for peace in the midst of an equally unlikely event for such collaboration, the Cuban Missile Crisis. Because the Missile Crisis shocked and sobered Kennedy and Khrushchev, in spite of themselves they joined hands and began an about-face from war—with the active support of the pope and his secret peacemaking agent, a New York journalist, Norman Cousins. It was Cousins who, because of the behind-the-scenes cooperation of this odd trio, later dubbed them "the improbable triumvirate." [711]

In October 1962, a group of leading Soviet academicians, writers, and scientists and a corresponding group of Americans converged at a secluded site in Andover, Massachusetts. They had journeyed secretly from mutually distant locations for a frowned-upon exercise in the frigid atmosphere of Cold War politics—seeking peace. Their quiet purpose in a weeklong dialogue was to begin to overcome East–West conflicts. In an unofficial context that encouraged honest talk, genuine peace initiatives could emerge. Norman Cousins, editor of the *Saturday Review* and a founder of SANE

(National Committee for a Sane Nuclear Policy), was a prime mover of this peacefully subversive process.[712]

On their first night together, the Russians and Americans huddled around a television set. They had met just in time to hear President Kennedy speak to the nation on October 22, 1962. His speech defined, in U.S. terms, the Cuban Missile Crisis. Kennedy said, because Soviet missiles had been secretly delivered to Cuba, creating an intolerable situation, he had ordered the U.S. Navy to intercept further Soviet shipments.[713]

Confronted by an apocalyptic conflict that called into question their even being together, the national delegations agreed unanimously to continue their meeting. The U.S. and U.S.S.R. delegates then spent the week debating intensely but respectfully the questions involved in the Soviet placement of missiles in Cuba and the U.S. blockade in response. While sharply divided along national lines, they shared a deep desire to find a way out of the crisis.[714]

Into this volatile, peace-seeking community came a Vatican visitor, Father Felix Morlion, an adviser to Pope John XXIII. Norman Cousins had met Father Morlion earlier that year. The Dominican priest had told Cousins about the pope: "All the world will come to acclaim and love this gentle man, Pope John. He is not arbitrary or fixed. He has a profound respect for people of all faiths. He wants to help save the peace."[715]

At Andover, Father Morlion asked the members of both delegations, "Might a papal intervention in the Cuban crisis—even if only in the form of an appeal for greater responsibility—serve an important purpose? Would a proposal to both nations be acceptable that called for a withdrawal both of military shipping and the blockade?"[716]

Cousins phoned the White House. He spoke with Ted Sorensen, who consulted with President Kennedy. Sorensen told Cousins: "The President welcomes the offer of Pope John's intervention." However, Sorensen added, "The President cannot encourage Pope John to believe that his proposal meets the central issue. That issue is not so much the shipping but the presence of Russian missiles on Cuban soil. Those missiles have to be removed— and soon—if the consequences of the crisis are to be averted."[717]

After a member of the Soviet delegation phoned Moscow, he reported, "The Pope's proposal calling for withdrawal both of the military shipping and the blockade is completely acceptable to Premier Khrushchev."[718]

Father Morlion relayed the Washington and Moscow reports to the Vatican.

The next day, Pope John issued a public plea for moral responsibility and peace that was delivered to the U.S. and Soviet Embassies: "We implore all rulers not to remain deaf to the cry of humanity for peace . . . to reassume negotiations . . . To set in motion, encourage and accept discussions at all levels and at any time is a maxim of wisdom and prudence."[719]

Cousins noted: "In line with President Kennedy's reservations, [the Pope] made no specific reference to the military shipments or the block-ade. Instead, he directed himself to the clear obligation of political leaders to avoid taking those steps that could lead to a holocaust. He said that not just the Americans and Russians but all the world's peoples were involved, and that their fate could not be disregarded. He said that history would praise any statesman who put the cause of mankind above national considerations."[720]

"This message," Khrushchev said later, "was the only gleam of hope."[721]

The pope's appeal was headlined around the world, including Moscow. *Pravda*, not known for its endorsement of papal statements, carried a front-page, banner headline citing Pope John's plea to the Cold War leaders "not to remain deaf to the cry of humanity for peace."[722] When Khrushchev announced on October 28 that he would withdraw the Soviet missiles from Cuba, *Pravda* printed the pope's message as a commentary on the resolution of the Missile Crisis, praising the "realism of the Pope concerning the question of peace."[723]

At the Andover meeting, Father Morlion raised with Soviet delegates the idea of further communications between Rome and Moscow on peace. He suggested Norman Cousins would be an acceptable intermediary, "unofficial and unattached," for the Vatican. Would he be acceptable also to Moscow? The Russians said they would find out.[724]

In late November 1962, Norman Cousins received a phone call in New York from Soviet ambassador Anatoly Dobrynin in Washington. Father Morlion's project was approved. Premier Khrushchev had invited Cousins to meet with him in Moscow in mid-December.[725]

When Cousins notified the White House of his upcoming Vatican–Moscow mission, he was invited to meet with President Kennedy. The president told Cousins that Khrushchev "will probably say something about his desire to reduce tensions, but will make it appear there's no reciprocal interest by the United States. It is important that he be corrected on this score. I'm not sure Khrushchev knows this, but I don't think there's any man in American politics who's more eager than I am to put Cold War animosities behind us and get down to the hard business of building friendly relations."[726]

When Norman Cousins arrived in Moscow, he was briefed by government representatives on how critically necessary it was for Khrushchev "to vindicate his basic policy of coexistence and to demonstrate that the Cuban situation, far from representing capitulation, could lead to agreements with the United States . . . Khrushchev's supporters felt that the decision to withdraw from Cuba was an act of statesmanship and high responsibility, and could represent a vital turning point in the Cold War. Others, however, reserved judgment, saying it would be necessary to come up with specific agreements, before such an optimistic interpretation could be sustained."[727]

In his meeting with Khrushchev, Cousins learned how much Pope John had impressed the Soviet premier.

"I am not religious," Khrushchev said, "but I can tell you I have a great liking for Pope John . . . There's something very moving to me about a man like him struggling despite his illness to accomplish such an important goal before he dies. His goal, as you say, is peace. It is the most important goal in the world."

Khrushchev spoke of the impossibility after a nuclear war of distinguishing "Communists or Catholics or capitalists or Chinese or Russians or Americans. Who could tell us apart? Who will be left to tell us apart?"

Cousins found himself suddenly looking at a man whose "eyes were in a vacant stare." The Soviet leader had retained an enlightened awe of nuclear weapons from the near-holocaust in October.

"During that week of the Cuban crisis," he said, "the Pope's appeal was a real ray of light. I was grateful for it."

Cousins asked, "How did it feel to have your fingers so close to the nuclear trigger?"

Khrushchev said, "The Chinese say I was scared. Of course I was scared. It would have been insane not to have been scared. I was frightened about what could happen to my country—or your country and all the other countries that would be devastated by a nuclear war. If being frightened meant that I helped avert such insanity then I'm glad I was frightened. One of the problems in the world today is that not enough people are sufficiently frightened by the danger of nuclear war.

"Anyway, most people are smart enough to understand that it is ridiculous to talk in terms of another war. Pope John understands this. I would like to express my appreciation to him for what he did during the crisis of the Cuban week. Do you have any suggestions?"[728]

Cousins raised the prickly issue of religious freedom in the Soviet Union. He said Pope John was hopeful Archbishop Slipyi of the Ukraine could be released after eighteen years of internment.

Khrushchev stiffened.

"You know," he said, "I'm rather familiar with the Slipyi case. I'm from the Ukraine. The entire matter is still fresh in my mind."

Cousins said the point was not to reargue the case. The pope only hoped Archbishop Slipyi might be granted the freedom to live out his life in a distant seminary.

Khrushchev shook his head. "It is not a good idea. I would like to have improved relations with the Vatican, but this is not the way to do it. In fact, it would be the worst thing we could do. It would make a terrible stink."[729]

"In what respect?" Cousins asked.

Khrushchev said if Slipyi were freed, banner headlines would proclaim falsely, "Bishop Reveals Red Torture." Reporters would be certain to exploit his release. In the end, it would worsen relations with the Vatican.

Cousins assured Khrushchev that Pope John was acting in good faith. He would not exploit Archbishop Slipyi's release for propaganda purposes. Khrushchev remained skeptical.

Cousins pushed Khrushchev for several minutes on the issue of anti-Semitism in the Soviet Union. The American then stood up to leave, feeling he might have overstayed his welcome. Yet he had still not raised other matters that concerned President Kennedy.

"Please sit down," Khrushchev said. Reading Cousin's mind, he asked, "How is President Kennedy?"

Assured by Cousins that the president was in good health and spirits, Khrushchev proceeded to explore with Kennedy's unofficial intermediary the prospects for a test ban treaty and the Soviet premier's fear of a re-armed Germany. When Cousins said in conclusion that there was no aspirant to the presidency in the United States more eager than Kennedy to end the Cold War, Khrushchev said, "If that's the case, he won't find me running second in racing toward that goal." [730]

Cousins flew to Rome and met with Pope John, giving him warm written messages from both Kennedy and Khrushchev. The two Cold War leaders were deeply aware of Pope John's pain and approaching death. The pope was becoming a dying bridge between them.

"Pain is no foe of mine," the pope said. "Wonderful memories give me great joy now and fill my life. There is really no room for the pain."

Cousins reported on his visit with Khrushchev.

Pope John smiled and said, "Much depends now on keeping open and strengthening all possible lines of communication. As you know, I asked the statesmen [in October] to exercise the greatest restraint and to do all that had to be done to reduce the terrible tension. My appeal was given prominent attention inside the Soviet Union. I was glad that this was so. This is a good sign.

"World peace is mankind's greatest need. I am old but I will do what I can in the time I have." [731]

In early January 1963, Norman Cousins was invited by Ambassador Dobrynin to have lunch with him at the Soviet Embassy in Washington. Dobrynin then informed him that Archbishop Slipyi was about to be released.

"The Chairman," Dobrynin said, "has undertaken this action in the spirit of his conversation with you, in which the importance of strengthening the peace was recognized, and as a manifestation of his high regard for Pope John and the efforts being made by His Holiness in behalf of world peace." [732]

Two days after Archbishop Slipyi's release, Dobrynin phoned Cousins again, this time to read to him a news story just published under the headline: "BISHOP TELLS OF RED TORTURE." [733]

Cousins was appalled. He phoned the Vatican. He was assured Slipyi had spoken with no reporters. The following day, the Vatican newspaper, *Osservatore Romano*, carried the pope's front-page statement repudiating the news stories about Archbishop Slipyi. Cousins pointed all this out in an apologetic letter to Khrushchev. The Soviet leader did not respond to Cousins in the three months before he agreed to see him again. [734]

To the discouragement of both Kennedy and Khrushchev, the late winter and early spring of 1963 marked a cooling off of their dialogue. Their distancing was accomplished partly by militant Cold War forces in the U.S. government. From Cuba to Vietnam, the CIA was systematically undermining Kennedy's peace initiatives and antagonizing Khrushchev.

Directed by the CIA's David Atlee Phillips, the Cuban exile group Alpha 66 repeatedly attacked Soviet ships in Cuban waters in March. The avowed purpose of the CIA-sponsored attacks, as revealed later by Alpha 66 leader Antonio Veciana, was "to publicly embarrass Kennedy and force him to move against Castro." [735] Khrushchev naturally held Kennedy responsible for what he suspected rightly were CIA-directed attacks on Soviet ships. He raised angry objections until the president abruptly cracked down on the exiles' raids, arresting their leaders and confining them to the Miami area. [736]

In Vietnam, Kennedy's plans for a U.S. withdrawal, complemented by Ngo Dinh Diem's growing desire for the same, were disrupted by a CIA-planted plastic bomb in Hue, killing Buddhist demonstrators. [737] The explosion, attributed to the Diem government, deepened and widened the Buddhist Crisis. The popular Buddhist uprising destroyed Diem's already impaired ability to govern, setting the stage for his CIA-facilitated assassination in the fall. The CIA's Saigon maneuvers set back Kennedy's hope to neutralize Vietnam in parallel to Laos, a plan that JFK repeatedly emphasized to his aide on Vietnam, Roger Hilsman. [738]

Kennedy saw a nuclear test ban as an overarching way to redirect U.S.–Soviet relations toward peace, defuse each of these conflicts, and initiate an end to the Cold War. Although Khrushchev shared that hope, the Soviet leader was adamant on a sticking point that blocked further test-ban negotiations. Convinced that inspections were only an excuse for espionage, Khrushchev felt double-crossed after he got his government to concede a U.S. demand for three annual inspections. U.S. negotiators then said they hadn't meant three and really needed eight to verify compliance with a test ban. Kennedy said the conflicting interpretations must have been due to an honest misunderstanding, which Khrushchev insisted was impossible. In any case, Kennedy knew—as he told Cousins to inform Khrushchev in their next meeting—that he could never get the Senate to ratify a treaty that called for only three inspections per year.

With the test-ban negotiations stalled, Kennedy and Khrushchev were under mounting political pressures from each of their governments to conduct more nuclear tests as soon as possible. A new cycle of poisonous atmospheric testing, with an accompanying escalation in the nuclear arms race, seemed imminent. A deeply alarmed Pope John prepared to respond to the threat with the most important statement of his papacy, an encyclical letter given the title of his primary concern, "Peace on Earth" (or *Pacem in Terris* in the original Latin).

When Cousins met with Khrushchev in April at the Soviet leader's estate by the Black Sea, they dealt with questions of mistrust. Cousins repeated the regrets of Vatican officials at "what had appeared to be a breach of faith in some of the news coverage that followed [Archbishop Slipyi's] release."

Khrushchev voiced no skepticism. He said he understood. He asked about Pope John's health, adding, "I have often thought of, and been inspired by,

Pope John's desire to contribute to world peace in whatever time remains to him."

Cousins thought this an appropriate time to present to Khrushchev from Pope John an advance copy, translated into Russian, of *Pacem in Terris*. The premier of the Soviet Union would perhaps be the first person outside the Vatican to read the pope's great letter on peace.

After expressing his pleasure, Khrushchev asked, "Are there any parts of the encyclical that ought to be discussed now?" [739]

Cousins then brought to the attention of his Communist partner in dialogue the key passages of *Pacem in Terris*. They included: "If [disarmament] is to come about, the fundamental principle on which our present peace depends must be replaced by another, which declares that the true and solid peace of nations can consist, not in equality of arms, but in mutual trust alone." [740]

Khrushchev nodded. He again praised "Pope John's service to world peace." He said he would study the encyclical carefully. Thus challenged by the pope to deepen in trust, Khrushchev and Cousins turned to an issue of mutual distrust between their nations, the continuing stalemate on inspections.

"Frankly," Khrushchev said, "We feel we were misled. If you can go from three [inspections] to eight, we can go from three to zero."

The Russian leaned forward in his chair.

"As you know, we have already successfully tested a 100-megaton bomb [the largest weapons blast in history], but [Soviet scientists and generals] want to follow this up with more variations. They say the United States has carried out seventy percent more tests than the Soviet Union and that the world will understand if we seek to reduce this gap. My scientists want a green light to go ahead; I think I may decide to give it to them."

Cousins remained silent.

"Well?" said Khrushchev.

"You are looking at a depressed man," Cousins said. "I came here for the purpose of bearing witness to the President's good faith. You have apparently placed little weight on this. Your final response is that you are probably going to resume atmospheric tests. If you do, I cannot imagine that the United States will stand still and let its lead dwindle. So we will test again, and you will test, and we will test, and so on. This destroys any possibility that other nations can be persuaded not to test. The poisons in the air will multiply. None of this adds either to American or Russian security.

"There is something else that occurs to me at this point," Cousins continued. He decided to risk making an undiplomatic parallel. "Last summer President Kennedy was informed by a Soviet representative that missile bases were not being installed in Cuba. Perhaps it will be said that this was a misunderstanding. Under the circumstances, perhaps one misunderstanding can cancel out another."

Khrushchev looked at Cousins severely.

"Very well," he said, "You want me to accept President Kennedy's good faith? All right, I accept President Kennedy's good faith. You want me to believe that the United States sincerely wants a treaty banning nuclear tests? All right, I believe the United States is sincere. You want me to set all mis-understandings aside and make a fresh start? All right, I agree to make a fresh start."

Khrushchev sighed and sat back in his chair.

He said, "You can tell the President I accept his explanation of an honest misunderstanding and suggest that we get moving. But the next move is up to him." [741]

On April 22, eleven days after *Pacem in Terris* was published in Rome, Cousins reported to Kennedy in the White House on his conversation with Khrushchev. A large part of their dialogue, he said, had been "directed to the misunderstanding over the number of inspections." Cousins recounted Khrushchev's adamant interpretation of the apparent U.S. change in the number of inspections and the premier's unwillingness to consider any more than three. To the listening president, the Soviet position ruled out any chance of a treaty that could be passed by the U.S. Senate. He and Khrushchev had reached an impossible negotiating situation that Khrush-chev, through Cousins, had just tossed back to Kennedy: "the next move is up to him."

Kennedy, sitting in his rocker, listened quietly. "His feeling," Cousins wrote later in a note to himself, "seemed to be one of considerable sadness." [742]

Then the president said: "You know, the more I learn about this business, the more I learn how difficult it is to communicate on the really important matters."

Cousins described the mounting pressures being put on Khrushchev from his own government to adopt a hard line.

Kennedy said: "One of the ironic things about this entire situation is that Mr. Khrushchev and I occupy approximately the same political positions inside our governments. He would like to prevent a nuclear war but is under severe pressure from his hard-line crowd, which interprets every move in that direction as appeasement. I've got similar problems. Meanwhile, the lack of progress in reaching agreements between our two countries gives strength to the hard-line boys in both, with the result that the hard-liners in the Soviet Union and the United States feed on one another, each using the actions of the other to justify its own position." [743]

Cousins told the president he regretted deeply that he had failed in his mission to Moscow.

Kennedy said, "I can't accept the fact of failure. We have to try and find some way of getting through and breaking the deadlock."

He was looking intently at Cousins.

"Do you have any suggestions?" he asked.

Cousins said, "I feel the stage may be set now for what might be the most important single speech since you came into office. Perhaps what is needed is a breathtaking new approach toward the Russian people, calling for an end to the Cold War and a fresh start in American-Russian relationships."

The president lit a thin cigar.

"I'd like to think about it," he said. He asked Cousins to write a memorandum for him on the subject.[744]

Norman Cousins's memorandum was sent as a letter to President Kennedy on April 30, 1963. It expanded on his response to the president's request for suggestions:

"The moment is now at hand for the most important single speech of your Presidency. It should be a speech which, in its breathtaking proposals for genuine peace, in its tone of friendliness for the Soviet people and its understanding of their ordeal during the last war, in its inspired advocacy of the human interest, would create a world groundswell of support for American leadership.

"More than anything else, it would create a whole new context for the pursuit of peace. I doubt that there is any issue that reaches more deeply into the American people—indeed, all peoples—than this. There is a terrible sense of foreboding and ominous drift. The advocacy of powerful ideas directed to the peace produces vast new sources of energy.

"One of the striking achievements of your September 1961 speech before the United Nations [in which Kennedy challenged the Soviet Union to "a peace race," a term he had in turn adopted from Cousins's anti-nuclear organization, SANE][745] was that it created a surging tide that swept along many of the hard-liners . . . In any case, a re-definition right now of our peace aims, including an inspiring offer to the peoples on the other side, would blanket the opposition, internal and external." [746]

Two weeks after Cousins sent his letter-memorandum to the president, he was invited to meet at the White House with Ted Sorensen, Kennedy's speechwriter. Sorensen said the president had given him Cousins's memorandum about a speech with a dramatic peace offer. "He wants to pursue it," Sorensen said. "He would like you to send in some ideas for the text of a commencement talk he'll be giving at American University on June 10." [747]

While John Kennedy was deciding to risk everything in a groundbreaking speech on peace, Nikita Khrushchev was risking his alliance with Fidel Castro by encouraging him to trust Kennedy.

After Cousins's visit with Khrushchev in April, Castro became the Soviet leader's guest in May for an entire month. Castro was still angry with Khrushchev for having apparently sold him out in the Missile Crisis. When Khrushchev averted disaster by announcing his abrupt decision to withdraw the Soviet missiles, he infuriated Castro.[748] Without consulting the Cuban government, Khrushchev had taken away Cuba's deterrent to a U.S. invasion only days after the missiles were put in place. In return Khrushchev got nothing more for Cuba than a noninvasion pledge by a capitalist president. Now Khrushchev was trying to mollify Castro while taking him on a friendship tour of the Soviet Union. Nevertheless, for the sake of a larger peace, Khrushchev once again risked a strain in his relationship with the Cuban premier. He urged Castro to see the practical wisdom of trusting their enemy, John F. Kennedy.

Castro has described the remarkable month-long tutorial he received from Khrushchev, who schooled him patiently on just how the Missile Crisis was resolved peacefully: "for hours [Khrushchev] read many messages to me, messages from President Kennedy, messages sometimes delivered through Robert Kennedy . . . There was a translator, and Khrushchev read and read the letters sent back and forth." [749]

As Sergei Khrushchev described Nikita's conversations with Fidel, "Father tried to persuade Castro that the U.S. president would keep his word and that Cuba was guaranteed six years of peaceful development, which was how long Father thought Kennedy would be in the White House. Six years! Almost an eternity!" [750]

In the end, Castro chose to follow his Communist elder's advice. He freed himself from his attachment to an almost disastrous effort to deter the United States with Soviet missiles. He turned instead to Pope John's (and now Nikita Khrushchev's) alternate principle of peace, the prospect of avoiding war not by threatening the use of massive weapons but by building trust. As CIA covert-action director Richard Helms noted in a June 5 memorandum, "at the request of Khrushchev, Castro was returning to Cuba with the intention of adopting a conciliatory policy toward the Kennedy administration 'for the time being.'" [751]

At the same time, John Kennedy was preparing to talk peace. On June 10 at American University, JFK took Norman Cousins's idea of a visionary peacemaking speech and made it his own. A saintly pope, whose influence the Catholic president, John Kennedy, could never acknowledge, was also in the background of the speech.[752] After *Pacem in Terris* appeared that spring of 1963, there was a hopeful shift in the East–West spiritual climate, as seen in Khrushchev's dialogue with Castro on making peace with Kennedy. The president had felt the change. He chose that moment to take a huge risk for global peace.

The American University address owed much to *Pacem in Terris*. The papal encyclical had stated, in a clear reference to working with Communists: "teachings [that may be false regarding the nature, origin, and destiny of humanity], once they are drawn up and defined, remain always the same, while the movements, working in constantly evolving historical situations, cannot but be influenced by these latter and cannot avoid, therefore, being subject to changes, even of a profound nature. Besides, who can deny that those movements, insofar as they conform to the dictates of right reason and are interpreters of the lawful aspirations of the human person, contain elements that are positive and deserving of approval?

"It can happen, then, that meetings for the attainment of some practical end, which formerly were deemed inopportune or unproductive, might now or in the future be considered opportune and useful." [753]

The pope knew from Norman Cousins just how "opportune and useful" such "meetings for the attainment of some practical end" could be. It was that same month when Cousins gave Nikita Khrushchev the pope's gift of an advance, Russian-language copy of *Pacem in Terris*. The Cousins–Khrushchev dialogue, followed by Khrushchev's study of the encyclical, strengthened the Russian's resistance to his own bomb-makers and renewed his commitment to making peace with Kennedy.

The U.S. president in his greatest speech echoed the call of *Pacem in Terris* for cooperation with an ideological opponent. In the American University address, Kennedy made the same kind of distinction the pope did:

"No government or social system is so evil that its people must be considered as lacking in virtue. As Americans, we find communism profoundly repugnant as a negation of personal freedom and dignity. But we can still hail the Russian people for their many achievements—in science and space, in economic and industrial growth, in culture and in acts of courage."

Kennedy then took the pope's theme and ran with it. He first cited Russians' and Americans' mutual disgust with war, reminding his American audience of what war had done to the Soviet Union and what it could do now to the entire planet:

"Among the many traits the peoples of our two countries have in common, none is stronger than our mutual abhorrence of war. Almost unique, among the major world powers, we have never been at war with each other. And no nation in the history of battle ever suffered more than the Soviet Union suffered in the course of the Second World War. At least 20 million lost their lives. Countless millions of homes and farms were burned or sacked. A third of the nation's territory, including nearly two thirds of its industrial base, was turned into a wasteland—a loss equivalent to the devastation of this country east of Chicago.

"Today, should total war ever break out again—no matter how—our two countries would become the primary targets. It is an ironic but accurate fact that the two strongest powers are the two in the most danger of devastation. All we have built, all we have worked for, would be destroyed in the first 24 hours."

Following up Pope John's support of "meetings [with ideological opponents] for the attainment of some practical end," Kennedy praised agreements with the Soviet Union as essential to ending the arms race before it was too late:

"In short, both the United States and its allies, and the Soviet Union and its allies, have a mutually deep interest in a just and genuine peace and in halting the arms race. Agreements to this end are in the interests of the Soviet Union as well as ours—and even the most hostile nations can be relied upon to accept and keep those treaty obligations, and only those treaty obligations, which are in their own interest."

Then came the heart of the speech, the most eloquent statement of John F. Kennedy's presidency:

"So, let us not be blind to our differences—but let us also direct attention to our common interests and to the means by which those differences can be resolved. And if we cannot end now our differences, at least we can help make the world safe for diversity. For, in the final analysis, our most basic common link is that we all inhabit this small planet. We all breathe the same air. We all cherish our children's future. And we are all mortal." [754]

Because we all share this small planet, because we all hope for our children's future, and because we are all mortal, Kennedy asked us all to "reexamine our attitude toward the Cold War, remembering that we are not engaged in a debate, seeking to pile up debating points. We are not here distributing blame or pointing the finger of judgment."

Given everything we shared and our common need to leave the finger of judgment behind, it was not strange where he hoped to go in the Geneva arms negotiations: "general and complete disarmament—designed to take place by stages, permitting parallel political developments to build the new institutions of peace which would take the place of arms."

A first act in the process was at hand, "a treaty to outlaw nuclear tests." To jump-start that process, Kennedy made a unilateral pledge:

"To make clear our good faith and solemn convictions on the matter, I now declare that the United States does not propose to conduct nuclear tests in the atmosphere so long as other states do not do so. We will not be the first to resume." [755]

When Kennedy talked peace from his heart at American University, Khrushchev had ears to hear. He said it was "the greatest speech by any American President since Roosevelt." [756] They were now on the same wavelength. Within two months, they signed the Atmospheric Test Ban Treaty. In less than a year after they had brought the world to the edge of destruction, the same two men, chastened by their experience, were beginning to work together for a peaceful future.

Pope John XXIII died of cancer on June 3, 1963, one week before Kennedy gave his American University address. With the publication of *Pacem in Terris*, the pope's work for world peace was done. On his deathbed, he felt it was far too little. He feared that his family, all of humanity, would experience the agony of another terrible war. His private secretary, Monsignor Loris Capovilla, said, "That one avoid war was the thought that assailed the dying Pontiff." [757] Had Pope John lived two more months, he would have rejoiced in the test ban treaty as a sign of hope.

Norman Cousins, the pope's "unofficial and unattached" emissary of peace, had not, as he feared, been a failure—to either Khrushchev or Kennedy. By conveying to the two Cold War leaders a courageous vision of "Peace on Earth," based on honest dialogue and a growing trust of one's opponent, Norman Cousins—and the dying pope behind him—strengthened the mutual resolve of Kennedy and Khrushchev to wage peace rather than war. The immediate legacy of *Pacem in Terris* was the increasingly hopeful Kennedy–Khrushchev détente. The two surviving members of "the improbable triumvirate" were on the verge of shifting their policies from a suicidal reliance on nuclear arms to a step-by-step realization of the pope's principle of disarmament, mutual trust alone.

However, Kennedy's and Khrushchev's days were also numbered. Their more peaceful visions of the future had set them at odds with their respective military establishments, which began to plot their demise.

The previous February Khrushchev had proposed to his Defense Council a complete restructuring of the Soviet military. When the commander-in-chief of the Warsaw Pact forces, Marshal Andrei Grechko, argued with Khrushchev that he should equip the Army with tactical nuclear weapons, the Soviet leader refused for a concrete reason. "I don't have the money," he said.[758]

He then unveiled his radical vision for the Soviet armed forces. To reduce sharply an economically self-destructive defense budget, what he wanted was "only a very small, but very highly qualified, army." Beyond a nucleus of strategic missile forces, he said, "the rest of the army should be organized on the basis of regional militias. Its soldiers could live at home, do useful work, and spend some time on military training. They would be mobilized only if the country was really in danger."

Even the Soviet missile forces could be reduced to a minimum, Khrushchev said. The factories that made the missiles could then be converted to the peaceful production of ships for Soviet rivers.[759]

Khrushchev's February 1963 proposal for a radically reorganized Army, and for the peace conversion of Soviet missile factories, astonished his Defense Council. To the consternation of his generals, he continued to return to his peace conversion plan as late as October 1964, the month before the generals helped remove him from power.[760] By then, however, the premier's proposal was little more than a relic. It had rested on the hope of a reign of peace through mutual trust with a now-dead president, John F. Kennedy. After the murder of the president whom he had counted on being in office for another six years, Khrushchev's hope for an end to the Cold War collapsed. The end of his own rule came eleven months later.

In the case of Kennedy, after Pope John's death, the president's break with his military establishment was even more consequential than Khrushchev's. Kennedy's declaration of peace at American University, his successful negotiation of the Nuclear Test Ban Treaty, his opening to Fidel Castro, and his decision to withdraw from Vietnam added up to a presidency that was no longer acceptable to power. Kennedy had traveled beyond the Cold War point of no return. His journey of peace would mean his soon experiencing firsthand the truth he stated at American University—that we are all mortal.

Norman Cousins was right in foreseeing the transforming effect Kennedy's speech would have in the Soviet Union, but wrong in imagining a similar impact in the president's own country. At the same time that the American University address was highlighted by the Soviet media, it was ignored or downplayed in the United States.[761] Few Americans even knew Kennedy had given a groundbreaking speech on peace, much less what was in it. That has remained true to this day. The American media response to the speech was, and has been, almost total silence. It was as if someone had unplugged the president's microphone as soon as he began talking about peace.

At American University, in a speech to his fellow citizens, President John

F. Kennedy declared peace with our Cold War enemies. But only our enemies were able to hear him.

The assassination of President Kennedy continued to suck innocent people
into its whirlwind. One was a man who was kind enough to pick up a
hitchhiker in Dallas. He was then caught up in darkness for the rest of his
life.

Ralph Leon Yates was a refrigeration mechanic for the Texas Butcher
Supply Company in Dallas, making his rounds to meat outlets on Wednesday, November 20, 1963. At 10:30 A.M. Ralph Yates was driving on the
R. L. Thornton Expressway. He noticed a man hitchhiking in Oak Cliff near
the Beckley Avenue entrance to the expressway. Yates stopped to pick up
the man.

When the hitchhiker got into Yates's pickup truck, he was carrying what
Yates described later, in a statement to the FBI, as "a package wrapped in
brown wrapping paper about 4 feet to 4½ feet long." [762]

Yates told the man he could put the package in the back of the pickup.
The man said the package had curtain rods in it, and he would rather carry
it with him in the cab of the truck. [763]

Yates mentioned to the man that people were getting excited about the
president's upcoming visit. He had broached a subject the man was eager to
talk about. The man had a remarkable sense, as seen later, of what would
become the government's case against Lee Harvey Oswald. The man also
looked so much like Oswald that he was in effect his double. Or was he
actually Oswald?

As cited by the FBI, Ralph Yates recalled the hitchhiker's comments:
"Yates stated the man then asked Yates if he thought a person could assassinate the President. Yates replied that he guessed such a thing could be
possible. The man then asked Yates if it could be done from the top of a
building or out of a window, high up, and Yates said he guessed this was
possible if one had a good rifle with a scope and was a good shot.

"Yates advised about this time the man pulled out a picture which showed
a man with a rifle and asked Yates if he thought the President could be killed
with a gun like that one. Yates said he was driving and did not look at the
picture but indicated to the man that he guessed so.

"Yates said that the man then asked if he knew the President's route for
the parade in Dallas and Yates replied that he did not know the route but
that it had been in the paper. He said the man then said that he had misunderstood him and that actually he had asked Yates if he thought that the
President would change his route. Yates said he replied that he doubted it
unless they might for safety reasons." [764]

The hitchhiker asked to be let off along Houston Street. Yates dropped
him off at Elm and Houston, the stoplight by the Texas School Book Depository. He last saw the man carrying his package of "curtain rods" across Elm
Street—perhaps into the Book Depository. [765]

When Ralph Yates returned to his workplace at the Texas Butcher Supply Company, he told his co-worker, Dempsey Jones, about his strange conversation with the man he picked up in Oak Cliff and dropped off at Elm and Houston who was carrying the package. Dempsey Jones thereby became a supporting witness to Yates's account. He confirmed in an FBI interview that it was before President Kennedy was assassinated that Yates described picking up the hitchhiker, "who discussed the fact with him that one could be in a building and shoot the President as he, the President, passed by." [766]

After Yates saw the pictures in the media of Lee Harvey Oswald, he said the man he gave the ride to was "identical with Oswald." [767]

However, the FBI was not happy with the statement Ralph Leon Yates volunteered to them on November 26, repeated at the FBI's request on December 10, and repeated yet again at their further requests on January 3 and 4, 1964, finally during an FBI polygraph examination. Although Yates's statement seemed to be a thorough incrimination of the now dead Oswald, once again—as in other "Oswald" appearances—it proved too much for the government's case, even placing that case in jeopardy. As the FBI would make clear, the witness wasn't wanted. They kept recalling him only in order to discredit his story.

What was so unacceptable about Ralph Yates's testimony?

In terms of the hitchhiker's looks, itinerary, and comments, he was either Lee Harvey Oswald or a well-informed double. The Beckley Avenue entrance to the Thornton Expressway was on the same street as Oswald's rooming house, located at 1026 North Beckley. The man looking like Oswald had hitched a ride from the vicinity of Oswald's rooming house to the location of Oswald's workplace, the Texas School Book Depository.

The man's comments were, like "Oswald's" behavior in the series of self-incriminating incidents we have already seen, an obvious attempt to draw attention to himself as a potential presidential assassin.

Most significant in this instance was the package in brown wrapping paper that the man insisted on keeping with him in the cab, which he said contained "curtain rods." The package of "curtain rods" carried by Yates's hitchhiker corresponds to Oswald's notorious cover story in the *Warren Report* for sneaking his rifle into the Book Depository.

As the *Warren Report* describes this incident, it was on Thursday, November 21, that Lee Oswald asked his co-worker, Buell Wesley Frazier, if he could ride home with him that afternoon. Frazier lived in Irving half a block from Ruth Paine's house, where Oswald's wife, Marina, and their two daughters were then staying. Frazier asked Oswald why he wanted to ride with him on Thursday rather than Friday, when Lee normally went to the Paine household to stay with his family over the weekend. Lee's answer reportedly was: "I'm going home to get some curtain rods . . . [to] put in an apartment." [768]

According to Frazier and his sister, Linnie Mae Randle, the next morning Oswald brought a brown paper package "about 2' long" [769] with him when he rode in Frazier's car back to the Book Depository. Frazier told the Warren Commission that when he asked Oswald what was in the package, he replied, "Curtain rods." [770]

Despite the fact that the package Frazier and Randle claimed they saw was too small to hold even a rifle that was broken down, and although no one else saw Oswald with any package at all that morning, the Warren Commission concluded that Oswald must have used such a ruse to smuggle his rifle from Ruth Paine's garage into the Depository Building. In the *Warren Report*, the "curtain rod story" is the critical lie that supposedly enabled Oswald to carry secretly the weapon he then used to murder the president. [771]

What, then, are we to make of Ralph Yates's Oswald-like hitchhiker who prophetically acted out the "curtain rod story" two days before Lee Oswald reportedly reenacted it, in his ride with Buell Wesley Frazier to the Texas School Book Depository the morning of November 22?

Had there been no second curtain rod/rifle delivery by Oswald to the Depository, the first as done by the "Oswald" Ralph Yates picked up could have served the *Warren Report* quite well. Oswald could have been portrayed as smuggling the rifle into the Depository on Wednesday, then hiding it on the sixth floor of the building until he used it to shoot the president on Friday. In that version of the story, Yates could have been a valuable witness for the government against an already dead, media-convicted assassin.

However, just as there was once again a problem of too many Oswalds—with one working his regular hours in the Book Depository, while the other was hitchhiking with Yates—so, too, was there a problem of too many curtain rod deliveries to account for one rifle being smuggled into the building. The trail of duplicating curtain rod stories led not to a lone assassin but to an intelligence operation tripping over itself while working overtime to scapegoat Oswald.

Ralph Yates was a stubborn witness to what turned out to be unwanted evidence. On his second trip to the Dallas FBI office on December 10, 1963, he repeated and signed his statement about picking up the hitchhiker with the curtain rods. From his first contact with the FBI, Yates, who had pointed out that he was married with five children, said he "would appreciate not receiving any type of publicity from the fact he was furnishing this information." [772] About that concern he need not have worried. The FBI would make certain his testimony to another Oswald with a second curtain rods story would be buried from public view.

On January 2, 1964, FBI director J. Edgar Hoover sent a teletype marked "URGENT" to Dallas Special Agent in Charge J. Gordon Shanklin on Ralph Leon Yates. Hoover noted that a previous FBI investigation into whether Yates may have been at his company at the same time he said he picked up the Oswald-like hitchhiker provided insufficient evidence "to completely discredit Yates' story." Hoover therefore ordered the Dallas FBI office to "reinterview Yates with polygraph," [773] the instrument more commonly known as a "lie detector."

On January 4 in another "URGENT" teletype, Shanklin reported back to Hoover on Yates's polygraph examination that day: "Results of test were inconclusive as Yates responded to neither relevant or control type questions."[774] Because his lie-detector test was inconclusive, Yates had still not been discredited. But there was more to come.

During his final, January 4 trip to the FBI office, Ralph Yates was accompanied by his wife, Dorothy. He had asked her to come with him. In an interview forty-two years later, she told me what happened next to her husband. After he completed his (inconclusive) lie-detector test, she said, the FBI told him he needed to go immediately to Woodlawn Hospital, the Dallas hospital for the mentally ill. He drove there with Dorothy. He was admitted that evening as a psychiatric patient. From that point on, he spent the remaining eleven years of his life as a patient in and out of mental health hospitals.[775]

A crucial transition in the psychic health of Ralph Yates seems to have occurred at the FBI office on January 4, 1964. Something the FBI said after Ralph's polygraph test puzzled and disturbed Dorothy:

"They told me that he was telling the truth [according to the polygraph machine], but that basically he had convinced himself that he was telling the truth. So that's how it came out. He strongly believed it, so it came out that way."[776]

According to what the FBI told Dorothy Yates, the data that registered on the polygraph machine, as then read in the normal way by the polygraph examiner, showed that Ralph Yates was telling the truth. His test was officially recorded as "inconclusive" (meaning the examiner wasn't sure if Yates was telling the truth) only because J. Edgar Hoover and the FBI had decided what the truth had to be for Yates. The FBI-defined truth was that Yates had not picked up the Oswald-like hitchhiker with the "curtain rods" package, because for the FBI there could be no such hitchhiker. Therefore Ralph Leon Yates, by being so definitive (as shown by his polygraph chart) in knowing that he did precisely that—picked up a nonexistent hitchhiker— could only have lost touch with reality. What for any other polygraphed person would serve as proof of truth-telling was, in the case of Yates, proof only of an illusory divorce from reality. The wrenching but undeniable truth for Yates, that he helped a man he thought was the president's assassin deliver what could have been his weapon to the Book Depository, was what compelled him to contact the FBI in the first place. Now he was being told his experience was nothing but an illusion. The FBI said so. Because of Yates's unswerving, polygraphed conviction to the contrary, that he knew what really happened, J. Edgar Hoover and the FBI knew what they had to do. They told him to report at once to a psychiatric hospital.

Exactly what happened to Ralph Yates in the following days as a patient at Woodlawn Hospital, Dorothy Yates did not witness and does not know.[777]

She does know that early one morning about a week later, Ralph broke out of Woodlawn. At 4:00 A.M. she opened the front door of their house to find Ralph standing barefoot on the steps in his white hospital clothes.

Snow was swirling around him. Ralph told Dorothy he had escaped from the mental institution. He said he tied sheets together and climbed down from a window. He had then stolen a car and driven home.[778]

Ralph was tormented by fear in a way Dorothy would see repeated for years. He told his wife someone was trying to kill them and their children because of what he knew about Oswald. She quickly bundled up their five sleepy children, the oldest of whom was six. Ralph drove his family away from their house in the stolen car. Within a few hours, Dorothy was more alarmed by her husband's frantic efforts to evade their murder at every turn than she was by any unidentified killers. She returned the car and reported his whereabouts to the Woodlawn Hospital authorities.[779]

Ralph was picked up and returned to Woodlawn. He was soon transferred to Terrell State Hospital, a psychiatric facility about thirty miles east of Dallas, where he lived for eight years. He was then transferred to the Veterans Hospital in Waco for a year and a half, and finally to Rusk State Hospital for the final year and a half of his life. While a patient at all three hospitals, he spent intermittent periods of from one to three months at home with his wife and children. He was never able to work again.

In the course of Ralph's psychiatric treatment, Dorothy said, he was given the tranquilizing drugs Thorazine and Stelazine to the point where "they made him walk around like a zombie."[780] He learned to resist the process. Just as Abraham Bolden had done in the Springfield Penitentiary psychiatric unit, Ralph faked swallowing the pills.

More difficult to avoid were the shock treatments. He received over forty of them. The impact of the shock treatments on his long-range memory was, his wife said, "evidently nothing, because he didn't forget what he was there for," his encounter with the hitchhiker he had dropped off at Elm and Houston.[781]

Ralph told Dorothy, "I don't know if they're trying to make me forget what's happened, or what. But I'm always going to say those things happened."[782]

To the end of his life Ralph held on to the truth of his experience with the hitchhiker carrying the curtain rods. "He never backed down," Dorothy said.[783]

Ralph died at Rusk State Hospital on September 3, 1975, from congestive heart failure. He was thirty-nine years old.

Over three decades later, Dorothy continues to ponder her husband's stubborn adherence to a strange story that in effect made him a prisoner in mental hospitals, took him away from a family he loved, and impoverished all of them. He was haunted by an experience he couldn't forget, for which he then suffered the rest of his life because of his unwillingness to recant it.

Other relatives and friends dismissed Ralph's account of the Oswald-like hitchhiker with the curtain rods package as pure fantasy.

His uncle, J. O. Smith, who went with him on his first trip to the FBI office, said of his nephew's story, "I really thought that was all just imagination."[784]

His cousin, Ken Smith, remembers Ralph before Kennedy's death as nothing more than "a chain-smoker who watched football games." [785] Once Ralph had what he thought was his Oswald experience, Ken said, he became a man obsessed:

"He wouldn't let it go. He believed it to be true. This consumed Ralph. His thinking didn't go beyond that afterwards. This just totally destroyed his life.

"Ralph blamed himself for Kennedy's assassination. He said, 'I was the reason the President got killed.'

"If he had shut up, his life wouldn't have been so bad. Everybody thought he was crazy. So he became crazy." [786]

Even Ralph's co-worker and corroborating witness, Dempsey Jones, who confirmed to the FBI that Yates told him at least one day before the assassination about the hitchhiker's talk on shooting the president, was skeptical. As the FBI liked to point out, he added a disclaimer: "[Jones] said Yates is a big talker who always talks about a lot of foolishness." [787]

Only the FBI knew why Ralph Yates needed to be taken seriously. Not even Yates himself, who had no sense of an Oswald double, understood the significance of what he felt compelled to say for the rest of his life. Only the Federal Bureau of Investigation recognized the importance of his testimony, with the threat it posed to the government's case against Oswald. If evidence surfaced of the Oswald-like hitchhiker, who delivered his "curtain rods" to the Depository two days before the assassination, it would have preempted and brought into question the government-endorsed curtain rods story, as given by Buell Wesley Frazier. Thanks to the bungling redundancy of cover stories, the plot to kill the president was again in danger of exposure.

There were too many Oswalds in view, with too many smuggled rifles, retelling a familiar story to too many witnesses. At least one curtain rods story, and the disposable witness who heard it, had to go. The obvious person to be jettisoned was the hapless Ralph Yates. His stubborn insistence on what he knew he had seen and heard, from the man he had given a ride, had to be squelched.

Ralph Yates then went through eleven years of hell. Yet he could not forget, and would not stop speaking about, what he witnessed when he picked up the man he thought was Lee Harvey Oswald. Without ever understanding the full meaning of the experience he refused to renounce, Ralph Leon Yates was a witness to the unspeakable.

The deepening sense John Kennedy had of his assassination was, as in everything he faced, laced with irony.

While in church waiting for Mass to begin one Sunday morning, the president turned to the reporters sitting behind him and said, "Did you ever stop and think, if anyone tried to take a shot at me, they'd get one of you guys first?" [788]

He had both a detachment about death and an urgency about life. He told one of his friends, "I have no fear of death . . . You know, during my experience out in the Pacific, I really wasn't afraid to die. And I wasn't afraid of dying when I was in the hospital in New York . . . Maybe I'm not that religious. I feel that death is the end of a hell of a lot of things. But I've got too many things to do. And I just hope the Lord gives me the time to get all these things done!" [789]

Two things that he wanted to get done in October 1963, while he still had the time, were to visit his infant son's grave and his bedridden father.

On Saturday, October 19, Kennedy's friends and aides, Kenny O'Donnell and Dave Powers, went with him to the Harvard–Columbia football game in Boston. As halftime approached, the president fell silent. He seemed oblivious to the game on the field.

He turned to O'Donnell and said, "I want to go to Patrick's grave and I want to go there alone, with nobody from the newspapers following me." [790]

Helped by a Boston police officer, who kept reporters' cars from leaving a parking lot in time to follow, the president, O'Donnell, and Powers went to the Brookline cemetery.

JFK stood at his son's headstone, inscribed simply "Kennedy." He said, "He seems so alone here." [791]

He spent the next day with his father at their Hyannis Port, Cape Cod, home. Joseph Kennedy had been incapacitated by a stroke in December 1961. His right side was paralyzed, and his speech garbled. The president, ignoring a house full of guests, sat by his father's bed through the morning and afternoon. Although Joseph Kennedy could say almost nothing comprehensible to his son, he loved being with him. For long periods the two men just sat quietly together.

The president postponed his usual Sunday afternoon time of return to the White House, lingering with his father until late in the evening. As dusk fell, the presidential helicopter landed outside the bedroom window. JFK finally rose to depart. He kissed his father goodbye on the forehead. He said he'd be back to see him after a trip he had to make to Texas. [792]

Years later, Dave Powers remembered Mr. Kennedy's farewell to his son with his eyes—speechless, but "Oh, that look," said Powers. [793]

After the president left, Joseph Kennedy's nurse and an assistant wheeled his bed to the balcony doors, so he could watch his son board the helicopter. Mr. Kennedy waited impatiently for him to appear on the lawn.

Suddenly JFK was back in the room. Mr. Kennedy, still straining to see his son outside, didn't realize he had returned. The president touched his father on the back of his shoulder.

"Look who's here, Dad," he said. [794]

He put his arms around his father and kissed him all over again. Then the president departed a second time, giving his father a high, wide wave from the lawn. In the helicopter, as Kennedy looked back at the balcony doors framing his father in his bed, Dave Powers saw the president's eyes glistening with tears. [795]

One month later, on the Air Force One flight from Dallas to Washington after JFK was killed, Powers described this scene to Jacqueline Kennedy. He said he had never known the president to make such a return to his father. It was as if he sensed he was seeing him for the last time.[796]

For whatever reasons, JFK seemed to be saying goodbye to the two people he loved who were least capable of saying goodbye to him, his buried son and his stricken father.

What was the process whereby nightclub owner Jack Ruby came to murder Lee Harvey Oswald two days after President Kennedy's assassination?

Jack Ruby's first known involvement with the Central Intelligence Agency came in the late 1950s, when he was smuggling guns from Florida and Texas to a young Cuban revolutionary, Fidel Castro, and his band of rebels. Ruby, a Chicago mob functionary transplanted to Dallas, ran guns to Fidel, so that the Mafia could hedge its bets on the next Cuban government by supporting both the dictator Batista and the insurrectionist Castro.[797] The CIA monitored the shipments. According to gun smuggler and CIA operative Edward Browder, "During the pre-Castro-[government] years, the CIA and Customs would not oppose gun shipments to Castro. After Castro turned Communist, the CIA and Customs encouraged shipments to anti-Castro forces."[798] Ruby was no more in sympathy with Castro's cause than were his sponsors and monitors. As a friend of his put it, he "was in it for the money. It didn't matter what side, just one that would pay him the most."[799]

In 1957, Ruby commuted between Dallas and the Houston suburb of Kemah on Galveston Bay. In Kemah, according to his poker-playing friend, car dealer James E. Beaird, Ruby stored guns and ammunition in a two-story house near the waterfront. Beaird saw Ruby and his associates load "many boxes of new guns, including automatic rifles and handguns" on pickup trucks, transporting them to "what looked like a 50-foot surplus military boat." With Ruby in command, the boat would then carry the guns across the Gulf of Mexico to Castro's rebel army in Cuba.[800]

After Castro overthrew Batista in January 1959, the easily bought Ruby began to provide weapons, now with CIA support, to anti-Castro Cubans. Ruby was working with another CIA-connected gunrunner, Thomas Eli Davis III. It was an association that would later haunt him. When Ruby was preparing for his trial for killing Oswald, it was the name of Davis that he feared might be brought up by the prosecution. He told his first attorney, Tom Howard, that he "had been involved with Davis, who was a gunrunner entangled in anti-Castro efforts."[801]

For robbing a bank in June 1958, Thomas Eli Davis III had received a sentence of five years probation, during which time he went to work for the CIA. Ruby's biographer, Seth Kantor, discovered Davis helped "in training anti-Castro units in Florida and at another site in South America."[802] When JFK was assassinated, Thomas Davis was in a jail cell in Algiers, "charged with running guns to the secret army terrorist movement then attempting to assassinate French Premiere Charles de Gaulle." [803] Davis was released through the intervention of the CIA's foreign agent code-named "QJ/WIN," identified by the top-secret CIA Inspector General's Report as the "principal asset" in the Agency's assassination program known as ZRRIFLE. [804]

Jack Ruby knew his CIA involvement with Thomas Eli Davis in running guns against Castro and Davis's ongoing CIA assassination ties were dynamite. When Ruby warned his lawyer about his association with Thomas Davis, he was tiptoeing through a minefield. If a witness or investigative reporter had revealed the Ruby–Davis connection, it could have blown open not only Ruby's trial but also the Agency's behind-the-scenes role in the assassination plot. Ruby's CIA background may have been the lead that nationally syndicated columnist Dorothy Kilgallen told friends she was following when she attended the trial, gained a private meeting with Ruby behind closed doors, and then, while being hounded for months by the FBI, died mysteriously in her Manhattan home. [805]

Another Ruby–CIA connection that lay just beneath the surface was Ruby's friendship with Gordon McLendon, the owner of Dallas radio station KLIF. In an FBI interview, Jack Ruby identified Gordon McLendon as one of his six closest friends. [806] When Ruby was arrested for shooting Oswald, he shouted out that he wanted the help of Gordon McLendon. [807] Why radio station owner McLendon?

In 1978 the House Select Committee on Assassinations discovered that Gordon McLendon was then working closely with JFK assassination suspect David Atlee Phillips on a CIA propaganda front. McLendon, a World War II Naval intelligence officer in the Pacific Ocean Joint Intelligence Center at Pearl Harbor, [808] was a leader in the Association of Former Intelligence Officers. Phillips, after "retiring" from being the Western Hemisphere chief of the CIA, had founded the group. Its purpose was to counter the widening, post-Watergate critique of the CIA that helped push Congress to reinvestigate the JFK and Martin Luther King assassinations. McLendon worked hand in hand with master propagandist Phillips at creating a less critical image of the CIA. On March 3, 1978, McLendon, Phillips, and Hollywood producer Fred Weintraub met with CIA director Admiral Stansfield Turner in his office to explore the idea of a TV series that would "fight back in defense of the CIA and other U.S. intelligence organizations." [809]

In November 1963, Gordon McLendon was a less visible supporter of the CIA, but his Liberty Radio Network with its Dallas station was known for promoting a hard-line anti-communism. McLendon told the HSCA he "could not recall" if he had consciously provided a cover job for a particular CIA agent employed at one of his stations. He would, he added, have been happy to have his company serve as a CIA cover. [810] He denied any knowledge of a plot to kill JFK. He also disclaimed being a friend of Jack Ruby, saying he was only "a close acquaintance" of the man whose first cry for help after murdering Oswald had been to Gordon McLendon. [811]

Most crucial to understanding Ruby's killing of Oswald is Ruby's involvement in the killing of Kennedy. Thanks to Julia Ann Mercer's unflinching
testimony, which the government covered up, we know that Ruby delivered
a man with a rifle to the grassy knoll an hour and a half before the assassination. As we have seen, Jim Garrison interviewed Mercer, who showed
him how the government revised her testimony and forged her signature.
Garrison then made the connection between Ruby's role in the killing of
Kennedy and his subsequent killing of Oswald:

"When you understand that that part of the Mafia which was the ally in
the late Fifties, early Sixties, of the CIA is working with the agency like it
used to before, as Ruby was doing, actually the evidence is overwhelming
that he was working for the intelligence community. Not as agent No. 352
with a gold badge, but as a member of the Mafia, part of which had become
subservient to the CIA.

"That was Ruby's involvement from the beginning. That's why he was
actively engaged in the assassination. He delivered one of the riflemen to the
grassy knoll, as one witness observed; although the government, the FBI,
changed her testimony, I subsequently got the true testimony from her . . .
Apparently, that's one of the ways they persuaded Ruby it was the better
part of valor for him to be the one to remove Oswald. Because a few days
earlier, he had delivered a gunman to the grassy knoll. It wasn't a case of
saying, 'Say, Jack, would you mind doing this little project for us?' By the
time Sunday after the assassination rolled around, they were in a position to
say, 'Jack, do you realize what you did the other day?' That's why he was
crying the next few days. He wasn't crying about the president. He was crying because he knew what he had to do." [812]

Jack Ruby knew what he had to do to Oswald because he was already a
key player in the assassination plot. He had carried out the dangerously visible task of delivering a gunman to the grassy knoll. Ruby was ideal for such
a role because he was tied in with the CIA's anti-Castro Mafia underlings,
making him and the Mob the perfect backup scapegoats behind Oswald, the
Soviet Union, and Cuba—an alternative scapegoat role Ruby and the Mob
have continued to play to the present. The CIA could hold Ruby in reserve
for the murder of Oswald, in case Oswald was not killed by the Dallas police
in the Texas Theater, as turned out to be the case. When Oswald survived
his arrest and was taken to jail instead of to the morgue, Ruby acted as if he
knew what he had to do next.

Jack Ruby was everywhere on the weekend of the assassination. After
Ruby-aided gunmen shot President Kennedy, Ruby showed an ability not
only to keep pace with the post-assassination drama but also to anticipate its
unfolding events. Although the Warren Commission did its best to obscure
the fact, Ruby was always on top of the breaking news, appearing on the
spot of an event just after or even before it happened.

At about 1:30 P.M. on November 22, 1963, Seth Kantor, a White House
correspondent who was a passenger in the motorcade, saw Jack Ruby in

Parkland Hospital. Press Secretary Malcolm Kilduff had just told Kantor and other reporters to follow him to the site of what would turn out to be the press conference announcing the president's death. As Kantor was hurrying up a hospital stairway, he felt a tug on his coat. He turned around. It was Jack Ruby.

As a reporter in Dallas until 1962, Seth Kantor was well acquainted with Ruby, who had tried to enlist him in doing feature stories on Ruby's interests. On the hospital stairs, Ruby called Kantor by his first name and shook his hand. Kantor has described his impression of Ruby at that moment:

"He looked miserable. Grim. Pale. There were tears brimming in his eyes. He commented on the obvious—how terrible the moment was—and did I have any word on the President's condition? There was nothing I knew to tell him and I only wanted to get away. Kilduff was disappearing up the steps. Certainly there was nothing unusual about seeing Jack Ruby there. He regularly turned up at spectacles in Dallas. In a subdued voice he asked me if I thought it was a good idea for him to close his places for three nights because of the tragedy. Instead of shrugging, I told him I thought it was a good idea and then took off on the run, up the steps." [813]

When Jack Ruby denied he had been at Parkland Hospital the afternoon of the assassination, the Warren Commission accepted his version of events over that of Seth Kantor.[814] It was a remarkable act of trust in Ruby. The Commission was supporting the claim of Oswald's killer over against the word of a trained journalist who already knew Ruby, who had a vivid encounter with him at Parkland, and who then reported it in an article he wrote two days later right after seeing Ruby shoot Oswald.[815] The disparity between the trustworthiness of the two men was so great, and the Commission's decision so arbitrary, that its acceptance of Ruby's word over Kantor's in itself destroyed the credibility of the *Warren Report* for early critics.[816]

A pioneer among the critics, Sylvia Meagher, asked, "Why was it so urgent to repress reports that Ruby was at Parkland Hospital shortly after the assassination?"[817] She answered that a clue may have been the title of the *Warren Report*'s chapter that included Kantor's testimony: "Possible Conspiracy Involving Jack Ruby."[818]

Jack Ruby's appearance at Parkland Hospital was a beginning sign of his knowledge of the plot. Once we know that Ruby delivered a gunman to the grassy knoll an hour and a half before the shooting began, we can see how he knew enough to be only half a step behind Seth Kantor going up the Parkland Hospital stairway. Jack Ruby was wired to the assassination plot. Ruby knew where to be because he knew the assassination scenario before the actors took the stage.

As Johnny-on-the-spot as Ruby was in following Kantor up the Parkland stairs, his presence there could still be attributed to the quick movements of an experienced news hound. However, Ruby had to know the assassination plot's script to show up where he did twenty minutes later—at the Texas Theater to watch the police close in on Oswald.

George J. Applin, Jr., was an off-duty crane operator attending the movie at the Texas Theater the afternoon of November 22, 1963. When the lights came on and police officers started coming down the aisle, the first carrying a shotgun, Applin got up from his seat.[819] He retreated to the rear of the theater, while the officers prepared to move in on Oswald. While standing in the rear, Applin warned a man sitting in a back-row seat—whom he later identified as Ruby—that it would be smart to move.

In an interview with investigative reporter Earl Golz, Applin described his encounter with Ruby:

"Ruby was sitting down, just watching them. And when Oswald pulled the gun and snapped it at his [a policeman's] head and missed and the darn thing wouldn't fire, that's when I tapped him [Ruby] on the shoulder and told him he had better move because those guns were waving around.

"He just turned around and looked at me. Then he turned around and started watching them." [820]

When Applin was questioned by Dallas police later that day, he did not mention the man in the back row. He could not have identified him in any case, because he did not know Ruby by sight. Two days later, thanks to the television news, he knew that the man in the back row of the Texas Theater on Friday afternoon was the same man who shot Oswald to death on Sunday morning, Jack Ruby.[821] He also realized it could be dangerous to divulge that truth.

In his Warren Commission testimony four months later, Applin did bring up his encounter with the man in the back row, but denied any later recognition of him. In response to the question, "Ever seen the man since?," he said, "No, sir; didn't." [822]

In a 1979 interview, George Applin finally identified Jack Ruby as the man he had seen at Oswald's arrest. He said fear had kept him from making his knowledge public:

"I'm a pretty nervous guy anyway, because I'll tell you what: After I saw that magazine where all those people they said were kind of connected with some of this had come up dead, it just kind of made me keep a low profile." [823]

After Oswald was jailed on Friday afternoon, Ruby managed to gain increasing access to Dallas Police Department headquarters and to Oswald himself. Media and police witnesses saw Ruby early Friday evening on the third floor of police headquarters. He was near Captain Will Fritz's office, where Oswald was being questioned.[824] As witnessed by a reporter, Ruby then went so far as to attempt to enter Fritz's office while Oswald was inside: "[Ruby] put his hand on the knob, turned it, opened the door and started in, probably not more than a step or a step and a half before the officers reacted and pulled him back." [825]

At about 11:30 P.M. Friday, Ruby reentered police headquarters. He attended the televised midnight press conference on the third floor at which District Attorney Henry Wade presented the prisoner Oswald to the media and the world. This strange event was in effect a dry run of Oswald's murder on Sunday morning. About five minutes before Oswald was brought in, UPI photographer Pete Fisher noticed Jack Ruby standing near the room's entrance. In an FBI interview, Fisher described the preview he was given then of Oswald's murder on Sunday:

"The Dallas Police brought Oswald through this entrance and Oswald passed not more than three feet from Ruby as he was led up on the stage. Fisher pointed out that if Ruby had wanted to shoot Oswald at that time he could easily have done it because of the fact that he was so close to Oswald." [826] Ruby also had the means to shoot Oswald. At the time he "was carrying a loaded, snub-nosed revolver in his right-hand pocket," as he would admit to the FBI a month later. [827] Why he passed up that chance to kill Oswald is unclear, although we will be given clues to the reason from his behavior early Sunday morning.

Ruby missed his moment of opportunity Friday night, but he would be given an even better one Sunday.

While the police were exposing their prisoner to a waiting assassin, the prisoner was pondering his plight. He was seeking a way out of it.

We have seen mounting evidence that Lee Harvey Oswald, an admirer of President Kennedy, was an FBI informant trying to stop the CIA plot to kill the president. In late July, in the notes he wrote for his speech to the Jesuits, Oswald warned of a coup d'état against the U.S. government. He attributed that threat especially to the Marine Corps—in a way, however, that pointed more specifically at the CIA, into whose ranks he had passed from the Marine Corps.

In August, according to New Orleans FBI employee William Walter and other witnesses, Oswald was acting as an FBI informant. [828] While Oswald was in jail in New Orleans for the ruckus caused by his pro-Castro leafleting, he met for an hour and a half with FBI agent John Quigley. [829] Given his Kennedy sympathies, his warning against a coup, and his recent recruitment (with deeper designs) into the plot to kill the president, it is reasonable to suppose Oswald at this point in his FBI contacts was trying to save Kennedy's life—and in the process, risking his own.

He apparently kept on trying. The Chicago plot to kill Kennedy on November 2 was, as we saw, disrupted by Chicago Police lieutenant Berkeley Moyland and by an otherwise unidentified FBI informant named "Lee." Lee Harvey Oswald, the most likely candidate to have been the FBI informant "Lee," had strong similarities to the intended Chicago scapegoat, Thomas Arthur Vallee. Government sources characterized both men unsympathetically as psychopathic loners with extremist political views—in effect, perfect patsies. Both were Marine veterans. Both had served at U-2 bases in Japan under the Joint Technical Advisory Group (JTAG), the CIA's cover name for its U-2 spy plane surveillance as well as "other covert operations in Asia." [830]

Both of their U-2 bases were prime recruitment stations for the CIA. Both men had recent intelligence connections with anti-Castro Cuban exiles.

Yet Oswald's and Vallee's most striking parallel came from their places of employment in November 1963. After they had relocated in the late summer and fall—Vallee to Chicago, Oswald back to Dallas—each potential scapegoat fortuitously found work in a building overlooking the street of an upcoming presidential motorcade near a dogleg turn. There each could be identified as a lone assassin, while covert snipers killed the president. Who had the power to place Oswald and Vallee in the same position of suspicion for the motorcades scheduled to pass beneath their workplace windows?

Lee Harvey Oswald and Thomas Arthur Vallee had traveled the same, punishing road of CIA covert action. They were disposable pawns in a high-risk game. As a result of his medical history, Vallee was the more disposable of the two. As Mary Vallee-Portillo told me, "My brother probably was set up. He was very much used." [831] Thomas Vallee like Lee Oswald was a vulnerable, low-level intelligence asset, intensely loyal to the government he served, on the verge of being jettisoned alongside the president. However, unlike Oswald, Vallee survived. Whoever informed on the Chicago plot's sniper team, saving Kennedy's life for three more weeks, was, like Berkeley Moyland, someone who saved Vallee's life in the process.

If the FBI informant named "Lee" who blew the whistle on the Chicago plot was indeed Lee Harvey Oswald, it would help explain why Oswald was, at least on the surface, such a pliant patsy prior to the assassination. If he knew he had already succeeded in stopping the Chicago plot at the eleventh hour, he would have expected to do the same in Dallas. Even while he was eating lunch in the Book Depository on Friday, November 22, at 12:15 P.M.—"alone as usual," as Carolyn Arnold described him[832]—Oswald may have anticipated the imminent arrest of assassins whom he had identified to the FBI. Any such hopes were in vain. The FBI had become part of the plot. If he was the "Lee" who saved Kennedy and Vallee in Chicago, Oswald had risked becoming what he in fact became—the ultimate scapegoat in Dallas, where there was no one to save Kennedy and himself. The young man who was "alone as usual" in the Depository lunchroom had become totally alone.

While being questioned as a prisoner at Dallas Police headquarters, Oswald acted as if he had suddenly lost his cover as a U.S. agent. The turning point was his confrontation by Deputy Sheriff Roger Craig. With several other witnesses, Craig had seen Oswald (or more likely, a man looking just like him) run down the grassy knoll to the Rambler station wagon, scramble in, and be driven away by "a husky looking Latin." [833] Oswald had already told Captain Will Fritz he rode the bus home, until a traffic tie-up forced him to switch to a taxi.

When Craig joined Fritz outside his Homicide Bureau office shortly after 4:30 P.M., the Deputy Sheriff looked through the open door at the prisoner.

He told Fritz that Oswald was the man he had seen run down the grassy knoll and depart in the station wagon. Fritz and Craig then entered the office together. When Fritz told Oswald that Craig had seen him leave, he asked his prisoner, "What about the *car*?" Oswald said defensively, "That *station wagon* belongs to Mrs. Paine. Don't try to drag her into this." [834]

Oswald then said dejectedly, "Everybody will know who I am now," [835] with the implication that a double's (or less likely, his) departure in the station wagon, and the vehicle's association with Mrs. Paine, were keys to his real identity. Given what Craig had seen, Oswald thought his cover was blown.

Oswald then began to resist the role he had been given that was assuming overwhelming scapegoat proportions. At 6:00 P.M. Friday when Captain Will Fritz showed him a picture of himself holding a rifle in one hand, Communist publications in the other, and wearing a pistol on his hip, Oswald said the ridiculously incriminating photo (which would soon appear on the cover of *Life* magazine) was not of him. Fritz told Oswald the picture had been found in the garage at Mrs. Paine's house. Oswald said it had never been in his possession. He had never seen it before. The face was his, he said, but someone had superimposed it on another man's body. Oswald said he knew a lot about photography, and that in time, he would show how it was not his picture. He would never have that time. [836]

At 7:55 P.M., as Oswald was being taken down a hall in Dallas Police headquarters, he made it clear—to those who had ears to hear—that he was not going down quietly. He called out to reporters, "I'm just a patsy!" [837] That rebellious shout may have been the immediate source of the decision to give Ruby his first chance to kill Oswald, on the prisoner's way into the hastily called press conference four hours later. However, when Oswald was led to his armed assassin at the doorway, Ruby froze. Oswald in passing was given another few hours of life.

From his arrest Friday afternoon until he was shot to death late Sunday morning, he sought legal counsel he could trust. He appealed repeatedly for the help of New York lawyer John Abt, well known for his defense of political prisoners in Smith Act cases. [838] If Abt was not available, as proved to be the case, Oswald said he wanted to see a member of the American Civil Liberties Union. ACLU representatives came to the jail Friday night but were then told wrongly that Oswald did not want an attorney. [839]

As his situation grew more desperate, on late Saturday night Oswald tried to make a mysterious long-distance phone call to Raleigh, North Carolina.

That night in the Dallas City Hall, Mrs. Alveeta A. Treon and Mrs. Louise Sweeney were working as switchboard operators when two law enforcement officials came into the room. The men said they wanted to listen to a call Oswald was about to make. They were shown to an adjoining room where they could monitor the prisoner's conversation. [840]

At 10:45 P.M. Mrs. Sweeney took a call from the jail. Notifying the men in the next room that it was Oswald, she wrote down the information he gave her on the number he wanted to reach. What transpired then, apparently in obedience to the men's orders, has been described by Sweeney's co-worker, Alveeta Treon:

"I was dumbfounded at what happened next. Mrs. Sweeney opened the key to Oswald and told him, 'I'm sorry, the number doesn't answer.' She then unplugged and disconnected Oswald without ever really trying to put the call through. A few moments later, Mrs. Sweeney tore the page off her notation pad and threw it into the wastepaper basket." [841]

After Mrs. Sweeney left work at 11:00 p.m., Mrs. Treon retrieved the slip of paper. She copied the information onto a message slip as her souvenir of the event. In 1970, a copy of the slip came into the possession of Chicago researcher Sherman H. Skolnick during a Freedom of Information Act suit. [842]

According to the phone message, Oswald was trying to call a "John Hurt" in Raleigh, North Carolina, at "834-7430 or 833-1253." In November 1963, John David Hurt was listed as having the first number in Raleigh, and John William Hurt as having the second. Of the two Hurts, the first, John David Hurt, had a military intelligence background. During World War II, John David Hurt served as a U.S. Army Counterintelligence Special Agent. [843] House Select Committee on Assassinations lawyer Surell Brady, who was in charge of investigating the Raleigh call, described the fact that John David Hurt had served in U.S. Army Counterintelligence as "provocative." [844] In a brief 1980 interview, John David Hurt denied knowing why Oswald was trying to phone him on the night of November 23, 1963. [845]

Although Oswald's purpose in making the Raleigh call has never been disclosed, former CIA officer Victor Marchetti thought he knew why. After fourteen years with the CIA, during which he became executive assistant to the Deputy Director, Victor Marchetti resigned in disillusionment in 1969. [846] He then co-authored *The CIA and the Cult of Intelligence*, a Book-of-the-Month Club Alternate that the CIA censored, leaving 339 blank spaces in the text. [847]

Marchetti said he thought Oswald was following the standard intelligence practice of trying to contact his case officer through a "cut-out," a "clean" intermediary with no direct involvement in an operation. As to why Oswald's call was made to North Carolina, Marchetti pointed out that the Office of Naval Intelligence had an operations center in Nags Head, North Carolina, for agents who had been sent as fake expatriates to the Soviet Union—corresponding to Oswald's background. [848]

In an interview, Marchetti said, "[Oswald] was probably calling his cut-out. He was calling somebody who could put him in touch with his case officer. He couldn't go beyond that person. There's no way he could. He just had to depend on this person to say, 'Okay, I'll deliver the message.' Now, if the cut-out has already been alerted to cut him off and ignore him, then . . ." [849]

The interviewer asked Marchetti about the plight of an undercover agent in trouble who was desperately seeking help, as Oswald seemed to be doing:

> INTERVIEWER: "Okay, if someone were an agent, and they were involved in something, and nobody believes they are an agent. He is arrested, and trying to communicate, let's say, and he is one of you guys. What is the procedure?"
>
> MARCHETTI: "I'd kill him."
>
> INTERVIEWER: "If I were an agent for the Agency, and I was involved in something involving the law domestically and the FBI, would I have a contact to call?"
>
> MARCHETTI: "Yes."
>
> INTERVIEWER: "A verification contact?"
>
> MARCHETTI: "Yes, you would."
>
> INTERVIEWER: "Would I be dead?"
>
> MARCHETTI: "It would all depend on the situation. If you get into bad trouble, we're not going to verify you. No how, no way."
>
> INTERVIEWER: "But there is a call mechanism set up."
>
> MARCHETTI: "Yes."
>
> INTERVIEWER: "So it is conceivable that Lee Harvey Oswald was . . ."
>
> MARCHETTI: "That's what he was doing. He was trying to call in and say, 'Tell them I'm all right.'"
>
> INTERVIEWER: "Was that his death warrant?"
>
> MARCHETTI: "You betcha. Because this time he went over the dam, whether he knew it or not, or whether they set him up or not. It doesn't matter. He was over the dam. At this point it was executive action." [850]

"Executive action" was a CIA code phrase for assassination.

Lee Harvey Oswald had been going over the dam for months, possibly years. As we saw, James Jesus Angleton's Special Investigations Group (SIG) in CIA Counterintelligence held a 201 file on Oswald in the three years leading up to JFK's assassination. That meant, as we learned from Angleton's assistant, Ann Egerter, in her House Select testimony, that Oswald was a CIA employee or asset who had come under suspicion by the Agency as a counterintelligence risk.[851] Angleton apparently had Oswald under internal CIA investigation. Former CIA finance officer Jim Wilcott confirmed that Oswald was indeed a CIA double agent to the Soviet Union. Wilcott had issued the paychecks for Oswald's counterespionage project under a cryptonym.[852] Moreover, as Wilcott's Tokyo CIA station knew, Oswald was a disgruntled spy.

"One of the reasons given for the necessity to do away with Oswald," Wilcott said, "was the difficulty they had with him when he returned. Apparently, he knew the Russians were on to him from the start, and this made him very angry."[853]

In short, Lee Harvey Oswald was a questioning, dissenting CIA operative, who had become a security risk. His investigation by assassinations specialist Angleton was the beginning of his end. Oswald thereby became the ideal scapegoat for the president's assassination. From the standpoint of the assassins, Dallas eliminated two Cold War security risks, Kennedy and Oswald, in the same weekend, blaming the second for the murder of the first. Drawing CIA dissenter Oswald into the plot in such a way that he thought he was blowing a whistle on the CIA to the FBI would, from Angleton's standpoint, have made for poetic counterintelligence irony. As a soon-to-be-murdered scapegoat, Oswald would become a double victim of the conspiracy.

Although Jack Ruby was being given easy access to Dallas Police headquarters—and at the Friday night press conference even proximity to Oswald—he seemed reluctant to shoot him. Ruby knew that by following orders (funneled to him from powerful forces) and killing Oswald, he, too, would likely become a disposable shield of those forces. Only hours before he did shoot Oswald, Ruby was apparently trying to make that murder impossible by warning law enforcement authorities that it was about to happen.

At 3:00 A.M. Sunday a phone call was received by Dallas Police Officer Billy Grammer. He later identified the voice as Ruby's. The caller said, "If you move Oswald the way you are planning, we are going to kill him." [854]

Billy Grammer knew Jack Ruby. On a Central Independent TV program broadcast in England, Grammer said in an interview that Ruby was warning the police to transfer Oswald secretly to the county jail: "He knew me, and I knew him. He knew my name," Grammer said. "It [Oswald's shooting] was not a spontaneous event." [855]

Warnings from a male caller saying Oswald would be killed in the morning were also received twice by the Dallas County Sheriff's office around 2:15 A.M. Sunday[856] and once by the Dallas FBI office at 2:30 A.M.[857] In spite of this series of warning calls to the FBI, the Dallas Police, and the Sheriff's Department, perhaps all from Jack Ruby, the authorities, instead of transferring Oswald secretly, repeated the process of the midnight press conference. The prisoner's transfer to the county jail became a second media circus, this one ending in an ambush. Through a press gauntlet, Oswald's police guards once again led him (whether knowingly or not) right into the vicinity of a waiting Ruby.

If the purpose of Ruby's phoning the police had been to obstruct his ability to carry out a higher order, the Dallas authorities did not prove helpful. They, too, seem to have had higher orders.[858] They in effect gave Ruby an even easier opportunity to kill Oswald Sunday morning than they had Friday night. This time Ruby did not hesitate.

Kennedy was warned repeatedly in the days before Dallas about going into its hostile political environment. His friend Larry Newman said later, "You know, they talked for three weeks about him being shot in Texas! And they tried to talk him out of it, right to the last minute. But he just said, 'If this is the way life is, if this is the way it's going to end, this is the way it's going to end.'" [859]

On the danger of his being assassinated, Kennedy liked to quote the passage in Ecclesiastes, "There is a time to be born, and a time to die." [860]

However, at other moments the president was less stoical about what he felt might happen on his trip to Texas. As the day approached, he kept repeating his apprehensions to Senator George Smathers: "God, I hate to go out to Texas. I just hate to go. I have a terrible feeling about going. I wish I could get out of it." [861]

On the night of November 20, the eve of his departure, John and Jacqueline Kennedy held their annual judicial reception at the White House. Early in the evening, while over five hundred employees from the Department of Justice and the White House waited their turn downstairs, the Kennedys received the Supreme Court Justices and their wives upstairs. The guests came in their finest formal attire. The gala event would be John Kennedy's last in the White House. As described by William Manchester in *The Death of a President*, it reminds one of the Russian ball on the eve of war in Tolstoy's *War and Peace*. The light of that last night at the Kennedy White House, like the glitter of the waltzing Russian aristocracy, could not hold back the darkness.

Ethel Kennedy watched her brother-in-law, the president, from across the room. While JFK made the requisite social comments to the circle around him, Ethel realized, as she told Manchester later, "that something very grave must be on his mind. He had leaned back in the rocker, his hand cupped under his chin, and was gazing out with hooded gray eyes." [862]

At that moment Chief Justice Earl Warren called over to him, "Texas is going to be rough, Mr. President!" [863]

Kennedy made no response. As his sister-in-law could see, he had withdrawn to a place in his mind.

"Why," she wondered, "is Jack so preoccupied?"

Ethel walked over and greeted him. As long as she had known Jack Kennedy, no matter how great the stress he was under, he had always responded to her.

"Not now," she said. "For the first time in thirteen years he was looking right through me." [864]

To what degree Kennedy was then preoccupied with his trip to Texas, we do not know. We do know that on the trip itself he kept talking about his death as imminent, while adding there was nothing to be done about it.

On Friday morning, November 22, while he and Jacqueline were in their Fort Worth hotel suite, JFK read a threatening full-page advertisement addressed to him in the *Dallas Morning News*. Under a bold headline, "*WELCOME MR. KENNEDY*," the ad was bordered in black, like a funeral notice. It stated:

"Because of your policy, thousands of Cubans have been imprisoned, are starving and being persecuted—with thousands already murdered and thousands more awaiting execution and, in addition, the entire population of almost 7,000,000 Cubans are living in slavery."

Hatred, in response to his decisions in the Bay of Pigs and the Cuban Missile Crisis, was staring up at him.

The ad went on to ask Kennedy: "Why have you approved the sale of wheat and corn to our enemies when you know the Communist soldiers 'travel on their stomachs' just as ours do? Communist soldiers are daily wounding and/or killing American soldiers in South Viet Nam." [865]

His wheat sale to the Soviet Union had come back to haunt him.

He finished reading the ad, placed by a group calling itself "The American Fact-Finding Committee." [866] He handed it to his wife.

As Jacqueline read it, the blood draining from her face, he said to her, "We're heading into nut country today. But, Jackie, if somebody wants to shoot me from a window with a rifle, nobody can stop it, so why worry about it?" [867]

"You know," he said, "last night would have been a hell of a night to assassinate a president." He paused.

"I mean it. There was the rain, and the night, and we were all getting jostled. Suppose a man had a pistol in a briefcase." Kennedy pointed his right hand like a pistol at the wall, moving his thumb as the hammer. "Then he could have dropped the gun and the briefcase, and melted away in the crowd." [868]

In two subliminal scenes, JFK had sketched the assassinations of both himself that same day in Dealey Plaza and of another president (in the making) four and a half years later, his brother, Bobby, the night he would get jostled by the crowd in the pantry of the Ambassador Hotel in Los Angeles.

The extent to which our national security state was systematically marshaled for the assassination of President John F. Kennedy remains incomprehensible to us. When we live in a system, we absorb a system and think in a system. We lack the independence needed to judge the system around us. Yet the evidence we have seen points toward our national security state, the systemic bubble in which we all live, as the source of Kennedy's murder and immediate cover-up.

Intelligence agencies in that state have advantages over us ordinary citizens in controlling our government. The CIA, FBI, and their intelligence affiliates in the armed forces have resources and aspirations, as revealed by the president's assassination, that go far beyond our moral imagination. In his increasingly isolated presidency, John Kennedy had a diminishing power over them. Partly because of our naiveté as citizens, he was killed by covert-action agencies and the conspiracy covered up by them, with relative ease and legal impunity. It was the beginning of a deadly process. Even before his assassination took place, there was evidence that those in command of our security agencies may have already been thinking about whom they might have to kill next for the sake of the nation.

A prime candidate was the president's brother—his possible successor in the White House in the years to come, Attorney General Robert F. Kennedy.

On Thursday, November 21, as John and Jacqueline Kennedy were arriving on Air Force One in Houston to begin their Texas tour, Wayne January was at Red Bird Air Field in Dallas preparing a DC-3 aircraft for flight. In this narrative, we have already encountered January, who the day before had refused to charter a flight for November 22 to a suspicious young couple, accompanied by a man January later identified as Lee Harvey Oswald.

Wayne January was working on the DC-3 all day Thursday with the pilot who was scheduled to fly it out of Dallas on Friday afternoon.[869] It was their third day on the job. Working together on a project they both enjoyed—preparing an extraordinary machine for flight—the two men had become friends. Wayne had also become curious about the background of his friend, who said he had been born in Cuba, though Wayne could detect no trace of an accent. The man said he had been in the Cuban Air Force, where he achieved a high rank.[870]

Except for his work with January, the pilot kept totally to himself, refusing Wayne's invitations to eat out with him. The pilot confined himself to eating sandwiches with Wayne by the plane.[871]

Wayne became more curious. He asked the pilot about the well-dressed man who had bought the plane from a company January co-owned. The man had carried out the transaction with January's partner by phone. The buyer had made only one appearance at the airfield, when he came with the pilot on Monday.

The pilot described his boss as "an Air Force colonel who deals with planes of this category."[872] The colonel had bought the plane on behalf of a company known as the "Houston Air Center." January would learn later that the Houston Air Center was a front for the CIA.[873] As revealed by the plane's archived papers, the aircraft had originally been a troop transport version of the DC-3, also known as a C-47, made in the Second World War and sold by the government to a private airline after the war.[874] It was now being sold back to the government for use as a covert CIA aircraft.

As Wayne and the pilot continued talking during their lunch break Thursday, Wayne suddenly found himself in a twilight zone, learning more about secret government operations than he ever wanted to know. The moment of transition came after a pause in their conversation. The other man sat leaning against a wheel of the plane, eating his sandwich. He was silent for a time, mulling over something in his mind.

Then he looked up and said, "Wayne, they are going to kill your president."[875]

As Wayne January described this scene three decades later in a remarkable faxed letter to British author Matthew Smith, he tried to convey his utter incomprehension of the man's words. When Wayne asked the pilot what he meant, the man repeated, "They are going to kill your president."

Wayne stared at him.

"You mean President Kennedy?"

The man said yes.

While Wayne kept trying to make sense of his words, his co-worker revealed that he had been a pilot for the CIA. He was with the CIA in the planning of the Bay of Pigs. When many of his friends died there, the planners and survivors of the operation bitterly blamed John and Robert Kennedy for not providing the air cover the CIA claimed they had promised.

Wayne asked if that was why he thought they were going to kill the president.

The man said, "They are not only going to kill the President, they are going to kill Robert Kennedy and any other Kennedy who gets into that position." [876]

Wayne thought he was beginning to catch on. His friend had gone off the deep end. Wayne tried to say so in a polite, circumspect way.

The pilot looked at him. "You will see," he said.

The two men went back to work. They were behind schedule, with less than twenty-four hours left to complete their task. "My boss wants to return to Florida," the pilot said. There was room in the plane for more passengers than his boss. Wayne and the pilot were reinstalling twenty-five seats in it. [877] The DC-3 had to be ready to take off from Dallas by early afternoon the next day, Friday, November 22.

In the course of their work, the pilot made another memorable remark. "They want Robert Kennedy real bad," he said.

"But what for?" Wayne asked.

"Never mind," the man said, "You don't need to know." [878]

Thanks to the two men's joint efforts, they succeeded in having the plane ready to go early Friday afternoon. By 12:30 P.M., all the DC-3 lacked was fuel—and whoever would soon get aboard it to depart from Dallas.

As they finished up their work, there was a commotion by the terminal. A police car took off at high speed. Wondering what was up, Wayne walked back to the terminal building. The driver of a passing car slowed down and shouted at him, "The President has been shot!"

Wayne went into the building. He listened to a radio until he heard the announcement that President John F. Kennedy was dead.

He walked back to the DC-3. It had received its fuel. The pilot was putting luggage on the plane. Wayne asked him if he had heard what had happened. Without pausing from his loading, the pilot said he had, the man on the fuel truck had told him.

Then he said, "It's all going to happen just like I told you." [879]

Wayne said goodbye to the pilot. With a sense of profound sickness, he left work to find a television set where he could watch the news of the president's assassination unfold.

Until 1992, Wayne January lived alone with the nightmare of what the pilot had told him. Because of what he knew, he feared for his life and the lives of his wife and family. When the FBI and a few researchers asked him questions related to the assassination, he told them only about the couple with Oswald whom he had turned down when they tried to charter a plane for Friday the 22nd.[880] Without his knowledge, the FBI then discredited him by dating the incident four months earlier, minimizing its importance and making a more delayed Oswald identification seem less plausible.

However, Wayne remained silent about the CIA pilot who knew the president was going to be killed, the colonel representing "Houston Air Center," and the newly purchased CIA plane that took off from Red Bird Air Field the afternoon of November 22. He also kept secret the pilot's prediction of what would happen to Robert Kennedy, as fulfilled by his murder in June 1968, "and any other Kennedy who gets into that position."

In 1992 Wayne January broke his silence about the pilot's revelation. As we have seen, author Matthew Smith had already interviewed him the year before about the couple with Oswald. After Smith showed him the FBI report that claimed falsely the incident occurred the previous July, the two men became good friends. January realized he had finally found someone he could trust with his long-held secret. He faxed to Smith at his home in Sheffield, England, a complete account of what the CIA pilot had said to him. Smith had been puzzled in Dallas at how January could be so sure in saying the CIA was behind the Kennedy assassination. Now he knew.

January told Smith that sending his faxed statement after thirty years of silence "seems to be a release of some kind that I don't understand," "a relief that seems to make me more relaxed."[881] He gave the British author permission to publish the story on the condition that he not be identified, because "he still feared for his life and for that of his wife."[882] Smith agreed. He used a pseudonym for January's name and changed a few details to avoid identifying him.

The story of "Hank Gordon's" experience with the CIA pilot at Red Bird Air Field subsequently appeared in Matthew Smith's books, *Vendetta: The Kennedys* (1993) and *Say Goodbye to America* (2001).[883] After Wayne January died in 2002, Smith obtained permission from his widow to reveal his name.[884] He did so at a November 2003 conference in Dallas and in his book, *Conspiracy—The Plot to Stop the Kennedys* (2005).[885]

Thanks to Wayne January's friendship with a CIA pilot who risked confiding in him,[886] and to January's deeper friendship with Matthew Smith, in whom he risked confiding, we can now see more than we may want to see. We can see a possible commitment to a chain of covert-action murders that would extend from JFK to RFK and any other Kennedy liable to become president: "They are not only going to kill the President, they are going to kill Robert Kennedy and any other Kennedy who gets into that position."

The Kennedy family has been well aware since John F. Kennedy's murder as president, mirrored by Senator Robert F. Kennedy's murder as a presidential candidate, how dangerous it is for one of them to aspire to the presidency. Others have attributed that peril to the office of the presidency, combined with the legendary hazard of being a Kennedy. When the danger is seen as more specific, however, from evidence that government agencies have conspired in their deaths, it is a peril not only for the Kennedys but for every U.S. citizen who believes in the right to change the government. JFK and RFK were targeted because they refused to comply with national security demands imposed upon them from the Bay of Pigs to the Cuban Missile Crisis and Vietnam. Two and a half years into his presidency, enlightened by the Missile Crisis and emboldened by the hope of peace, JFK had reached a point where he began to transcend the ruling assumptions of national security. He was inspired to seek peace with such enemies of the state as Nikita Khrushchev and Fidel Castro.

In short, the Kennedys believed in seeking a just, negotiated peace with the enemy. Their more secret, domestic enemies thought peace with justice was impossible or even undesirable. Having faced the total darkness on the planet that was its alternative, John and Robert Kennedy were prepared to wage peace with the same kind of dedication that we normally associate with waging war—a willingness to give their lives for the good of the country. If seeking peace in the resolute way they did is what makes one an enemy of our national security state, we have all become at least potential enemies of the state. Anyone can, and perhaps should, become a peacemaker, thereby becoming the natural enemy of a state whose purpose has become intertwined with waging war.

What does the nature of the assassination of President John F. Kennedy reveal about ourselves? What does it reveal about a national security state we have allowed to assume control over our lives? Have we reached the point where the state itself has become an enemy of the people, at least until we the people can manage to change, even revolutionize, its purpose?

Can we transform our lives, and the state of the United States of America, so as to practice the truth that waging peace is our only real security?

JFK's death in Dallas preempted several decisions he was ready to make in Washington the following week. The first was the question of how to deal with his rebellious ambassador to South Vietnam, Henry Cabot Lodge, who wanted to escalate and "win" the war the president had decided to withdraw from.

Robert Kennedy has commented on his brother's loss of patience with an ambassador who would not carry out his instructions or even give him the courtesy of a response to those instructions: "The individual who forced our position at the time of Vietnam was Henry Cabot Lodge. In fact, Henry Cabot Lodge was being brought back—and the President discussed with me in detail how he could be fired—because he wouldn't communicate in any way with us . . . The President would send out messages, and he would never really answer them . . . [Lodge] wouldn't communicate. It was an impossible situation during that period of time." [887]

According to RFK, the president in consultation with the Attorney General had already made the decision to fire Lodge: "We were going to try to get rid of Henry Cabot Lodge." It was only a matter of "trying to work out how he could be fired, how we could get rid of him." [888]

President Kennedy was scheduled to meet with Lodge on Sunday afternoon, November 24, as soon as JFK returned from his trip to Texas and Lodge from his post in Vietnam. [889] Kennedy had prepared for his encounter with Lodge by inviting to it a strong dissenter to the Vietnam War, Under Secretary of State George Ball. He talked to Ball by phone on Wednesday night, November 20, right after the White House reception for the judiciary, [890] making sure the most antiwar member of his administration would attend the Sunday meeting with Lodge.

It was George Ball who had warned Kennedy prophetically as early as November 1961 on Vietnam: "Within five years we'll have three hundred thousand men in the paddies and jungles and never find them again. That was the French experience. Vietnam is the worst possible terrain both from a physical and political point of view." [891]

JFK responded: "George, you're just crazier than hell. That just isn't going to happen." [892]

However, George Ball was right, even underestimating by two hundred thousand the number of American soldiers who would be sent at one time (by Lyndon Johnson) to the paddies and jungles of Vietnam. Kennedy knew his own resistance to introducing combat troops in Vietnam, but not that he would be killed before he could effectively reverse course there.

It was his successor as president, Lyndon B. Johnson, who instead presided over the Sunday, November 24, meeting with returning ambassador Henry Cabot Lodge. As New York Times reporter Tom Wicker described the relationship between the two men, LBJ had a much less critical view of Lodge than did JFK, who planned to fire him: "Lodge [was] an old friend of Johnson's from their Senate days, whom Johnson once had recommended to Eisenhower for Secretary of Defense, and who was thus close enough to the new President to speak his mind." [893] Johnson, a firm believer in an anticommunist theology, put faith in the counsel of his old friend Lodge, who was among the Cold War elite.

Lodge told Johnson, "If Vietnam is to be saved, hard decisions will have to be made. Unfortunately, Mr. President, you will have to make them." [894]

Unlike Kennedy, Johnson was an unrepentant Cold Warrior. Given Lodge's authoritative shove toward a wider war, the new president thought he knew what had to be done. A person present at the meeting said Johnson scarcely hesitated.

"I am not going to lose Vietnam," he said. "I am not going to be the President who saw Southeast Asia go the way China went." [895]

To keep making the hard decisions for war that Lodge recommended,

Johnson would have to win the presidential election less than a year away, when he would run shrewdly and successfully as the "peace candidate" against Senator Barry Goldwater. However, in the course of his campaign rhetoric for peace, Johnson did not want his military advisers to confuse him with his predecessor's fatal turn in that direction. He made clear to them that he and they were definitely on the same page.

One month after his meeting with Lodge, at a White House reception on Christmas Eve 1963, Johnson told the Joint Chiefs of Staff: "Just let me get elected, and then you can have your war." [896]

JFK's murder kept him from being the one to make critical decisions in Washington that would decide the fate of not only Vietnam but also Indonesia.

As we have seen, when he left for Texas, Kennedy had said he was willing to accept an invitation from President Sukarno to visit Indonesia in the spring of 1964. Such a turn of events, sought strongly by Sukarno, would have signaled in a dramatic way Kennedy's support for independent third world nations. As one analyst pointed out, Sukarno was "the most outspoken proponent of Third World neutralism in the Cold War." Sukarno had himself coined the term "third world" at the first Conference of Non-Aligned Nations that he hosted at Bandung, Indonesia, in 1955. [897]

Kennedy's support for Sukarno was another sign of how out of step he was with his national security state. Sukarno was a close ally in the Non-Aligned Movement with Ghana's president Kwame Nkrumah, a leading African nationalist whom Kennedy was also helping—to the dismay of advisers opposed to Nkrumah, including even Robert Kennedy. When JFK challenged the National Security Council in November 1961 by announcing he had decided to lend Kwame Nkrumah the money for his Volta Dam project in Ghana, he added, "The Attorney General has not yet spoken, but I can feel the hot breath of his disapproval on the back of my neck." [898] However, regardless of who opposed him in his support for Nkrumah, the president was determined "to dramatize the new American attitude toward non-alignment throughout Africa." [899] Sukarno's invitation to him to visit Indonesia gave JFK the further opportunity to support the leader of the nonaligned bloc in Southeast Asia.

A presidential visit to Sukarno would have been a major setback to the corporate leaders with a heavy stake in third world resources, particularly in oil-and-mineral-rich Indonesia, where they accused Sukarno of having gone Communist by expropriating their holdings. Yet Sukarno had received a warm welcome from Kennedy at the White House. In his invitation to JFK to visit Indonesia, Sukarno promised him in return "the grandest reception anyone ever received here." [900] In visiting Indonesia, Kennedy would cross a threshold by demonstrating publicly his long-held support of third world nationalism. In terms of the policies he was forging in Indonesia, Ghana, and the Congo, with their adverse impact on multinational corporations, the president was being seen increasingly as a class traitor and a Cold War heretic.[901]

Sitting on Kennedy's desk for his signature when the Oval Office was taken over by Johnson was a document critical to the future of United States–Indonesian relations. It was a presidential determination, required by an act of Congress, that said continuing U.S. economic aid to Indonesia was essential to the national interest. As Kennedy aide Roger Hilsman observed, "Since everyone down the line had known that President Kennedy would have signed the determination routinely, we were all surprised when President Johnson refused." [902]

When Johnson repeated his refusal to sign into law the necessary presidential support for aid to Indonesia at a National Security Council meeting on January 7, 1964,[903] it became clear that Sukarno no longer had a friend in the White House. Its new occupant was in fact hostile to Sukarno and the independent nationalist policies he espoused. In the months following Johnson's accession to the presidency, the U.S. government cut off economic aid to Indonesia.[904] However, a significant exception to the end of U.S. funding was military aid to the Indonesian Army under the rising control of Major General Haji Mohammad Suharto.[905] With the covert support of the U.S. military, Suharto was preparing to overthrow Sukarno.

In 1964, when Kennedy had planned to make a friendship visit to Indonesia, under Johnson, "the level of hostility and mutual recrimination between the United States and Indonesia rose." [906] In the year following, as economic aid for Sukarno's projects ceased, the Pentagon funneled new military aid for CIA-connected operations in the Indonesian Army under the control of Sukarno's "least loyal components." [907]

As the CIA and the Pentagon built up Sukarno's opponents in the army, corporate leaders sensed a new day for business in Indonesia. In April 1965, the U.S.-based corporation, Freeport Sulphur, anticipated Sukarno's overthrow by half a year, reaching "a preliminary arrangement with Indonesian officials for what would become a $500 million investment in West Papua copper." [908]

In October 1965, the enemy that Sukarno had learned to fear most, the CIA, finally succeeded in toppling his government. Ralph W. McGehee, a CIA agent for 25 years, has summarized in his book, *Deadly Deceits*, the CIA's elimination in 1965–66 of both the government of Sukarno and the Communist Party of Indonesia that was represented in it:

"The Agency seized this opportunity [of a failed October 1965 coup attempt by junior Indonesian military officers] to overthrow Sukarno and to destroy the Communist Party of Indonesia (PKI), which had three million members. As I wrote in *The Nation*, 'Estimates of the number of deaths that occurred as a result of this CIA [one word deleted by the CIA, which censored McGehee's article] operation run from one-half million to more than one million people.' " [909]

The U.S. government quickly provided weapons in response to the Indonesian army's November 6, 1965, request "to arm Moslem and nationalist youth in Central Java for use against the PKI." The army's stated purpose, shown by U.S documents and interviews with Indonesian army intelligence chief, General Sukendro, was "to eliminate the PKI."[910]

As admitted later by the former deputy CIA station chief in Indonesia, the CIA had helped U.S. Embassy officials in Jakarta compile death lists of thousands of members of the Communist Party of Indonesia.[911] The death lists were then turned over to the Indonesian army command, which used them for its systematic massacre. The CIA, working through the U.S. Embassy in Indonesia, kept track of those who were killed or captured, checking off the names on the list one by one.[912]

Robert Martens, a political officer at the U.S. Embassy in Jakarta, stated twenty-five years after taking part in this process: "It really was a big help to the army. They probably killed a lot of people, and I probably have a lot of blood on my hands, but that's not all bad. There's a time when you have to strike hard at a decisive moment."[913]

Sukarno was at first made a figurehead in the new military government, then placed under house arrest until he died in 1970.[914]

In the year between John Kennedy's assassination and the CIA-instigated overthrow of the Indonesian government and massive purge of suspected Communists, President Sukarno received a second visit from U.S. Attorney General Robert Kennedy. At Kennedy's urging, Sukarno agreed to a politically difficult cease-fire in a dispute with Malaysia.[915] When RFK had left, Sukarno's American biographer, Cindy Adams, asked the Indonesian president what he thought of Bobby Kennedy. She reported his response, which included his opinion of John Kennedy as well:

"Sukarno's face lit up. 'Bob is very warm. He is like his brother. I loved his brother. He understood me. I designed and built a special guest house on the palace grounds for John F. Kennedy, who promised me he'd come here and be the first American President ever to pay a state visit to this country.' He fell silent. 'Now he'll never come.'

"Sukarno was perspiring freely. He repeatedly mopped his brow and chest. 'Tell me, why did they kill Kennedy?' "[916]

In the years that followed, as he witnessed the subversion of his government and the slaughter of his people, Sukarno must have extended his question: Why did they kill Kennedy? Why did they kill my people? Why did so many cooperate in the killing?

These are questions for us all.

When John Kennedy died, Nikita Khrushchev was left without a partner in his hope to end the Cold War. In their public statements and secret communications, Kennedy and Khrushchev had engaged in a deeply contentious but ultimately transforming dialogue. The Soviet leader was emptied of hope by the loss of the man he had thought, as he wrote to him after the Missile Crisis, would "be able to receive a mandate at the next election."[917] It would have given them a total of six more years of struggle and work for peace. "At our times," he said hopefully to Kennedy after their improbable coming together in the worst of times, "six years in world politics is a long period of time." [918] But it was to be only a year, part of which they squandered. After resolving the Missile Crisis, they struggled again for precious months over a test ban, accomplished it with the help of Pope John and Norman Cousins, then struggled again—but always with an eye to the future. When the year passed and Kennedy was suddenly struck dead, there was no future. Khrushchev knew the hope he and his great adversary had realized together, at a moment of peril, was also dead.

That hope included a trip by John Kennedy to the Soviet Union. Indonesia was not the only controversial country JFK had decided to visit. In his last conversation with his old friend, British ambassador David Ormsby-Gore, the president said he "had made up his mind to visit the Soviet Union at the first suitable moment." [919] In another final conversation with a close friend, artist William Walton on November 19, the president said "he intended to be the first U.S. president to visit the Kremlin, as soon as he and Khrushchev reached another arms control agreement." [920]

President Kennedy knew the political impact his visiting the Soviet Union would have on the Cold War. It would end it. Jacqueline Kennedy would have accompanied her husband on such a journey of reconciliation. [921] The Kennedys would have been greeted by Nikita Khrushchev and the Russian people with the kind of welcome that would have ended the Cold War resoundingly, fulfilling Kennedy's and Khrushchev's hopes and those of the majority of people in the United States and the U.S.S.R. The people of both countries had been shaken by the Missile Crisis, then inspired by the test ban treaty. They were eager for peace. However, at the end of November 1963, Khrushchev, instead of standing with Kennedy at the gateway of realizing that hope, stood alone.

Soon after Kennedy's murder, a man Press Secretary Pierre Salinger described as "a high official of the Soviet Embassy in Washington" [922] told Salinger over a private lunch how Khrushchev had reacted to the assassination. He had first wept, then withdrew into a shell. "He just wandered around his office for several days, like he was in a daze," the Soviet official said. [923]

The president's assassination placed the Kennedy family in the peculiar position of feeling they could trust the Russians, supposedly their enemies, more than they could their own government. Their new sense of where their real friends lay had followed the president's own realization of what was, for him, a fatal truth. He had known for some time he had more in common with his enemy, Nikita Khrushchev, than he had with his own people in the CIA and the Pentagon. Kennedy and Khrushchev knew their world had turned upside down following the Missile Crisis, making their outward belligerence a thin cover for their having become secret allies. They were still struggling on many fronts but now had a new, shared mission—to end a conflict, the Cold War, that neither wanted and that they now knew, from their immersion together in an imminent holocaust, could doom the human race. In the process of their collaboration, friends had become enemies, and enemies friends. The Kennedy family's quiet shift of trust in the same direction immediately after Dallas has been revealed by recently unearthed evidence of their having then sent a secret messenger to Moscow. He was JFK's close friend, painter William Walton, in whom he had confided his decision to visit the Soviet Union.

William Walton, artist and former journalist, was a unique intimate of both John and Jacqueline Kennedy. He was also close to Robert Kennedy, having been a key political organizer with him on behalf of his brother. During the 1960 presidential campaign, Walton gave several months of his life to working full-time with RFK for JFK.[924] John Kennedy so trusted his writer-artist friend that he invited Walton to be his only companion in a critical pre-election meeting with Eleanor Roosevelt.[925] At the same time, Jacqueline so enjoyed Walton's company that he often spent time with both Kennedys in their home. The three of them watched the 1960 presidential election returns together.[926] On the day before Kennedy's inauguration, the president-elect used Walton's Washington home as his office for his final appointments and meetings before moving into the White House.[927]

In early December 1963, William Walton traveled to Moscow on behalf of Robert and Jacqueline Kennedy to convey a secret message to the Soviet leaders about President Kennedy's assassination. Walton used an already scheduled trip, at JFK's request "to visit Moscow to meet Soviet artists," [928] as a cover for his revised purpose of telling the Russians what the Kennedys thought lay behind Dallas. The Kennedys' message to the Russians was retained in top-secret Soviet intelligence archives. It was discovered in the 1990s by researcher-writers Aleksandr Fursenko and Timothy Naftali, who then reported it in their 1997 book on the Cuban Missile Crisis, *"One Hell of a Gamble."* [929]

Walton conveyed the Kennedys' secret assessment of the assassination to Georgi Bolshakov, the journalist/intelligence agent who had been their most trusted Soviet confidant in the months around the time of the Missile Crisis. In Washington, working out of the Soviet Embassy, Georgi Bolshokov had met repeatedly with Attorney General Robert Kennedy in secret to convey questions and concerns between Chairman Khrushchev and President Kennedy.[930] In Moscow after the assassination, he was in a corresponding position to relay Walton's discreet information to Chairman Khrushchev.

The Kennedys informed Bolshakov through Walton that, "despite Oswald's connections to the communist world," they believed "there was a large political conspiracy behind Oswald's rifle" that came from a different source. In their view, "the President was felled by domestic opponents." He had been, the Kennedys thought, "the victim of a right-wing conspiracy." [931]

Walton added that the Russian leaders should have no illusions that Lyndon Johnson would continue JFK's work for peace. Johnson, Walton said, would be "incapable of realizing Kennedy's unfinished plans." [932] The new president's "close ties to big business would bring many more of its representatives into the administration," whose adverse impact on hopes for peace Chairman Khrushchev would understand.[933]

Walton also conveyed to the Kremlin leadership through Bolshakov that Robert Kennedy would remain as attorney general only through 1964, then seek an elective office. Walton mentioned the governorship of Massachusetts, whereas RFK would actually be elected a New York senator the next fall. In any case, it would be in preparation, Walton said, "for an eventual run for the presidency." As the archived Soviet notes for their conversation recorded, "Walton, and presumably Kennedy, wanted Khrushchev to know that only RFK could implement John Kennedy's vision and that the cooling that might occur in U.S.–Soviet relations because of Johnson would not last forever." [934]

On Monday, November 25, 1963, Deputy Soviet Premier Anastas Mikoyan was Nikita Khrushchev's personal representative at John Kennedy's funeral in Washington. At the White House afterwards, Jacqueline Kennedy noticed Mikoyan moving toward her in the reception line—and as she recounted later, he "was trembling all over" and "looked terrified." [935]

She reached out for his hand and greeted him warmly. There are two accounts of what she said then to Mikoyan. As she recalled her words, they were: "Please tell Mr. Chairman President that I know he and my husband worked together for a peaceful world, and now he and you must carry on my husband's work." [936]

Secretary of State Dean Rusk's memory of what Jacqueline Kennedy said to Mikoyan was more succinct: "My husband's dead. Now peace is up to you." [937]

That essence of her message is appropriate to us all. John F. Kennedy is dead. Now peace is up to us.

Afterword

The "why" of President Kennedy's murder can be a profound source of hope to us all.

Now how can that be? The reason for his murder as a source of hope?

In a time when the Cold War has given way to a war on terror, hope comes from walking through the darkness of our history. We can find hope at that point of total denial and darkness where we don't want to go. Hope comes from confronting the unspeakable truth of the assassination of President Kennedy.

The seeds of that unimaginable hope lie, first of all, in our acknowledgment of the covert origins in our history for what happened in Dallas on November 22, 1963.

The doctrine of "plausible deniability" in an old government document was a key enabler of the assassination of President Kennedy. The document was issued in 1948, one year after the CIA was established, fifteen years before JFK's murder. That document, National Security Council directive 10/2, on June 18, 1948, "gave the highest sanction of the [U.S.] government to a broad range of covert operations"[1]—propaganda, sabotage, economic warfare, subversion of all kinds, and eventually assassinations—all seen as necessary to "win" the Cold War against the Communists. The government's condition for those covert activities by U.S. agencies, coordinated by the CIA, was that they be "so planned and executed that . . . if uncovered the US government can plausibly disclaim any responsibility for them."[2]

The man who proposed this secret, subversive process in 1948, diplomat George Kennan, said later, in light of its consequences, that it was "the greatest mistake I ever made."[3] President Harry Truman, under whom the CIA was created, and during whose presidency the plausible deniability doctrine was authorized, came to have deep regrets. One month to the day after JFK's assassination, Truman said he was "disturbed" because the CIA had "become an operational and at times a policy-making arm of the Government. This has led to trouble . . . There is something about the way the CIA

381

has been functioning that is casting a shadow over our historic position and I feel that we need to correct it." [4]

What George Kennan and Harry Truman realized much too late was that, in the name of national security, they had unwittingly allowed an alien force to invade a democracy. As a result, we and the world had to deal with a U.S. government agency authorized to carry out a broad range of covert, criminal activities on an international scale, theoretically accountable to the president but with no genuine accountability to anyone. One assumption behind Kennan's proposal unleashing the CIA for its war against Communism was that the agency's criminal power could be confined to covert action beyond the borders of the United States, with U.S citizens granted immunity to its lethal power. That assumption proved to be wrong.

The CIA's plausible deniability for crimes of state, as exemplified by JFK's murder, corresponds in our politics to what Thomas Merton called "the Unspeakable." For Merton, the unspeakable was ultimately a void, an emptiness of any meaning, an abyss of lies and deception. He wrote the following description of the unspeakable shortly after the publication of *The Warren Report,* which he could have been describing: "[The Unspeakable] is the void that contradicts everything that is spoken even before the words are said; the void that gets into the language of public and official declarations at the very moment when they are pronounced, and makes them ring dead with the hollowness of the abyss." [5]

We encounter the void of the unspeakable at the heart of our national security state's murder of President Kennedy. And that is where hope begins.

In the Cuban Missile Crisis, JFK had to confront the unspeakable in the form of total nuclear war. At the height of that terrifying conflict, he felt the situation spiraling out of control, especially because of the pressures and provocations of his generals.[6] At a moment when the world was falling into darkness, Kennedy did what his generals thought was unforgivable. He not only rejected their pressures for war. Even worse, the president reached out to the enemy for help. That could be considered treason.

Nikita Khrushchev saw it as hope. When Khrushchev received Kennedy's plea for help in Moscow, he turned to his foreign minister, Andrei Gromyko, and said, "We have to let Kennedy know that we want to help him."

Khrushchev hesitated when he heard himself say "help." Just when the U.S. president seemed to be at his wit's end, did he, Khrushchev, really want to help his enemy? Yes, he did. He repeated the word "help" to his foreign minister:

"Yes, help. We now have a common cause, to save the world from those pushing us toward war." [7]

How can we understand that moment? The two most heavily armed leaders in history, on the verge of total nuclear war, suddenly joined hands against those on both sides pressuring them to attack. Khrushchev ordered the immediate withdrawal of his missiles in return for Kennedy's public pledge never to invade Cuba and his secret promise to withdraw U.S. missiles from Turkey—as he would in fact do. The two Cold War enemies had turned, so that each now had more in common with his opponent than either had with his own generals. As a result of that turn toward peace, one leader would be assassinated thirteen months later. The other, left without his peacemaking partner, would be overthrown the following year. Yet because of their turn away from nuclear war, today we are still living and struggling for peace on this earth. Hope is alive. We still have a chance.

What can we call that transforming connection when Kennedy asked his enemy for help and Khrushchev gave it?

From a Buddhist standpoint, it was enlightenment of a cosmic kind. Others might call it a divine miracle. In terms of the Hebrew Scriptures, it was the *teshuvah,* "turning" or repentence. Readers of the Christian Gospels could say that Kennedy and Khrushchev were only doing what Jesus said: "Love your enemies." That would be "love" as Gandhi understood it, love as the other side of truth, a respect and understanding of our opponents that goes far enough to integrate their truth into our own. In the last few months of Kennedy's life, he and Khrushchev were walking that extra mile where each was beginning to see the other's truth.

Neither John Kennedy nor Nikita Khrushchev was a saint. Each was deeply complicit in policies that brought humankind to the brink of nuclear war. Yet, when they encountered the void, then by turning to each other for help, they turned humanity toward the hope of a peaceful planet.

In November 2009, a year and a half after the publication of this book's hardcover edition, I interviewed Sergei Khrushchev about an important late development in the relationship between his father and President Kennedy. In his interview, Mr. Khrushchev confirmed that his father had finally decided, not long before President Kennedy's death, to accept Kennedy's proposal that the United States and the Soviet Union go to the moon together.[8] In Kennedy's September 20, 1963, speech to the United Nations, he had once again stated his hope for such a joint expedition to the moon. However, both American and Soviet military leaders, jealous of their rocket secrets, resisted his initiative. Nikita Khrushchev, siding with his rocket experts, felt he again had to decline Kennedy's proposal.

JFK was looking beyond the myopia of the generals and scientists on both sides of the East-West struggle. He knew merging their missile technologies in a peaceful project would defuse the Cold War. It was part of his day-to-day strategy of peace.

Sergei Khrushchev said his father talked to him about a week before Kennedy's death about the president's idea for a joint lunar mission.[9] Nikita Khrushchev had broken ranks with his rocket scientists. He said he now thought the Soviet Union should accept Kennedy's invitation to go to the moon together, as a further, decisive step in peaceful cooperation.

In Washington, Kennedy acted as if he already knew about Khrushchev's change of heart. JFK went ahead in ordering NASA to begin work on a joint U.S.-Soviet lunar mission. On November 12, 1963, JFK issued his National Security Action Memorandum 271, ordering NASA to implement "my September 20 proposal for broader cooperation between the United States and the USSR in outer space, including cooperation in lunar landing programs."[10]

That further visionary step to end the Cold War also died with President Kennedy. The United States went to the moon alone. U.S. and Soviet rockets continued to be pointed at their opposite countries rather than joined in a project that could have brought the Cold War to an end. Sergei Khrushchev said, "I think if Kennedy had lived, we would be living in a completely different world."[11]

So if that is the case, how does the why of his murder give us hope?

How can we take hope from a peacemaking president's assassination by his own national security state?

President Kennedy's courageous turn from global war to a strategy of peace provides the why of his assassination. Because he turned toward peace with our enemies, the Communists, he found himself at odds with his own national security state. Peacemaking was at the top of his agenda as president. That was not the kind of leadership the CIA, the Joint Chiefs of Staff, and the military-industrial complex wanted in the White House. Given the Cold War dogmas that gripped those dominant powers, and given Kennedy's turn toward peace, his assassination followed as a matter of course.

The story of why John Kennedy died encircles the earth. Because JFK chose peace on earth at the height of the Cold War, he was executed. But because he turned toward peace, in spite of the consequences to himself, humanity is still alive and struggling. That is hopeful, especially if we understand what he went through and what he has given us as his vision.

At the climax of his presidency in the missile crisis, John Kennedy turned a corner. Although JFK was already in conflict with his national security managers, the missile crisis was the breaking point. At that most critical moment for us all, he turned from the remaining control his security managers had over him toward a deeper ethic, a deeper vision in which the fate of the earth became his priority. Without losing sight of our own best hopes in this country, he began to home in, with his new partner, Nikita Khrushchev, on the hope of peace for everyone on this earth—Russians, Americans, Cubans, Vietnamese, Indonesians, everyone—no exceptions. He made that commitment to life at the cost of his own.

What a transforming story that is.

And what a propaganda campaign has been waged to keep us Americans from understanding that story, from telling it, and from re-telling it to our children and grandchildren.

Because that's a story whose telling can transform a nation. But when a nation is under the continuing domination of an idol, namely war, it is a story that will be covered up. When the story can liberate us from our idolatry of war, then the worshippers of the idol are going to do everything they can to keep the story from being told. From the standpoint of a belief that war is the ultimate power, that's too dangerous a story. It's a subversive story. It shows a different kind of security than always being ready to go to war. It's unbelievable—or we're supposed to think it is—that a president was murdered by our own government agencies because he was seeking a more stable peace than relying on nuclear weapons. It's unspeakable. For the sake of a nation that must always be preparing for war, that story must not be told. If it were, we might learn that peace is possible without making war. We might even learn there is a force more powerful than war. How unthinkable! But how necessary if life on earth is to continue.

That is why it is so hopeful for us to confront the unspeakable and to tell the transforming story of a man of courage, President John F. Kennedy. It is a story ultimately not of death but of life—all our lives. In the end, it is not so much a story of one man as it is a story of peacemaking when the chips are down. That story is our story, a story of hope.

I believe it is a providential fact that the anniversary of President Kennedy's assassination always falls around Thanksgiving, and periodically on that very day. Thanksgiving is a beautiful time of year, with autumn leaves falling to create new life. Creation is alive, as the season turns. The earth is alive. It is not a radioactive wasteland. We can give special thanks for that. The fact that we are still living—that the human family is still alive with a fighting chance for survival, and for much more than that—is reason for gratitude to a peacemaking president, and to the unlikely alliance he forged with his enemy. So let us give thanks for John F. Kennedy, and for his partner in peacemaking, Nikita Khrushchev.

Their story is our story, a story of the courage to turn toward the truth. Let us remember what Gandhi said that turned theology on its head. He said truth is God. That is the truth: Truth is God. We can discover the truth and live it out. There is nothing more powerful than the truth. The truth will set us free.

Jim Douglass
January 6, 2010

APPENDIX

Commencement Speech at American University

President John F. Kennedy
June 10, 1963

President Anderson, members of the faculty, board of trustees, distinguished guests, my old colleague, Senator Bob Byrd, who has earned his
degree through many years of attending night law school, while I am earning mine in the next 30 minutes, distinguished guests, ladies and gentlemen:

It is with great pride that I participate in this ceremony of the American
University, sponsored by the Methodist Church, founded by Bishop John
Fletcher Hurst, and first opened by President Woodrow Wilson in 1914.
This is a young and growing university, but it has already fulfilled Bishop
Hurst's enlightened hope for the study of history and public affairs in a city
devoted to the making of history and to the conduct of the public's business. By sponsoring this institution of higher learning for all who wish to
learn, whatever their color or their creed, the Methodists of this area and
the Nation deserve the Nation's thanks, and I commend all those who are
today graduating.

Professor Woodrow Wilson once said that every man sent out from a
university should be a man of his nation as well as a man of his time, and I
am confident that the men and women who carry the honor of graduating
from this institution will continue to give from their lives, from their talents,
a high measure of public service and public support.

"There are few earthly things more beautiful than a university," wrote
John Masefield in his tribute to English universities—and his words are
equally true today. He did not refer to spires and towers, to campus greens

and ivied walls. He admired the splendid beauty of a university, he said, because it was "a place where those who hate ignorance may strive to know, where those who perceive truth may strive to make others see."

I have, therefore, chosen this time and place to discuss a topic on which ignorance too often abounds and the truth is too rarely perceived—yet it is the most important topic on earth: world peace.

What kind of peace do I mean? What kind of peace do we seek? Not a Pax Americana enforced on the world by American weapons of war. Not the peace of the grave or the security of the slave. I am talking about genuine peace, the kind of peace that makes life on earth worth living, the kind that enables men and nations to grow and to hope and to build a better life for their children—not merely peace for Americans but peace for all men and women—not merely peace in our time but peace for all time.

I speak of peace because of the new face of war. Total war makes no sense in an age when great powers can maintain large and relatively invulnerable nuclear forces and refuse to surrender without resort to those forces. It makes no sense in an age when a single nuclear weapon contains almost ten times the explosive force delivered by all of the allied air forces in the Second World War. It makes no sense in an age when the deadly poisons produced by a nuclear exchange would be carried by wind and water and soil and seed to the far corners of the globe and to generations yet unborn.

Today the expenditure of billions of dollars every year on weapons acquired for the purpose of making sure we never need to use them is essential to keeping the peace. But surely the acquisition of such idle stockpiles—which can only destroy and never create—is not the only, much less the most efficient, means of assuring peace.

I speak of peace, therefore, as the necessary rational end of rational men. I realize that the pursuit of peace is not as dramatic as the pursuit of war—and frequently the words of the pursuer fall on deaf ears. But we have no more urgent task.

Some say that it is useless to speak of world peace or world law or world disarmament—and that it will be useless until the leaders of the Soviet Union adopt a more enlightened attitude. I hope they do. I believe we can help them do it. But I also believe that we must reexamine our own attitudes—as individuals and as a Nation—for our attitude is as essential as theirs. And every graduate of this school, every thoughtful citizen who despairs of war and wishes to bring peace, should begin by looking inward—by examining his own attitude toward the possibilities of peace, toward the Soviet Union, toward the course of the cold war and toward freedom and peace here at home.

First: Let us examine our attitude toward peace itself. Too many of us think it is impossible. Too many think it is unreal. But that is a dangerous, defeatist belief. It leads to the conclusion that war is inevitable—that mankind is doomed—that we are gripped by forces we cannot control.

We need not accept that view. Our problems are manmade—therefore, they can be solved by man. And man can be as big as he wants. No problem of human destiny is beyond human beings. Man's reason and spirit have often solved the seemingly unsolvable—and we believe they can do it again.

I am not referring to the absolute, infinite concept of universal peace and good will of which some fantasies and fanatics dream. I do not deny the value of hopes and dreams but we merely invite discouragement and incredulity by making that our only and immediate goal.

Let us focus instead on a more practical, more attainable peace—based not on a sudden revolution in human nature but on a gradual evolution in human institutions—on a series of concrete actions and effective agreements which are in the interest of all concerned. There is no single, simple key to this peace—no grand or magic formula to be adopted by one or two powers. Genuine peace must be the product of many nations, the sum of many acts. It must be dynamic, not static, changing to meet the challenge of each new generation. For peace is a process—a way of solving problems.

With such a peace, there will still be quarrels and conflicting interests, as there are within families and nations. World peace, like community peace, does not require that each man love his neighbor—it requires only that they live together in mutual tolerance, submitting their disputes to a just and peaceful settlement. And history teaches us that enmities between nations, as between individuals, do not last forever. However fixed our likes and dislikes may seem, the tide of time and events will often bring surprising changes in the relations between nations and neighbors.

So let us persevere. Peace need not be impracticable, and war need not be inevitable. By defining our goal more clearly, by making it seem more manageable and less remote, we can help all people to see it, to draw hope from it, and to move irresistibly toward it.

Second: Let us reexamine our attitude toward the Soviet Union. It is discouraging to think that their leaders may actually believe what their propagandists write. It is discouraging to read a recent authoritative Soviet text on military strategy and find, on page after page, wholly baseless and incredible claims—such as the allegation that "American imperialist circles are preparing to unleash different types of war . . . that there is a very real threat of a preventive war being unleashed by American imperialists against the Soviet Union . . . [and that] the political aims of the American imperialists are to enslave economically and politically the European and other capitalist countries . . . [and] to achieve world domination . . . by means of aggressive wars."

Truly, as it was written long ago: "The wicked flee when no man pursueth." Yet it is sad to read these Soviet statements—to realize the extent of the gulf between us. But it is also a warning—a warning to the American people not to fall into the same trap as the Soviets, not to see only a distorted and desperate view of the other side, not to see conflict as inevitable, accommodation as impossible, and communication as nothing more than an exchange of threats.

No government or social system is so evil that its people must be considered as lacking in virtue. As Americans, we find communism profoundly repugnant as a negation of personal freedom and dignity. But we can still hail the Russian people for their many achievements—in science and space, in economic and industrial growth, in culture and in acts of courage.

Among the many traits the peoples of our two countries have in common, none is stronger than our mutual abhorrence of war. Almost unique among the major world powers, we have never been at war with each other. And no nation in the history of battle ever suffered more than the Soviet Union in the Second World War. At least 20 million lost their lives. Countless millions of homes and farms were burned or sacked. A third of the nation's territory, including two thirds of its industrial base, was turned into a wasteland—a loss equivalent to the destruction of this country east of Chicago.

Today, should total war ever break out again—no matter how—our two countries would become the primary targets. It is an ironic but accurate fact that the two strongest powers are the two in the most danger of devastation. All we have built, all we have worked for, would be destroyed in the first 24 hours. And even in the cold war, which brings burdens and dangers to so many countries, including this Nation's closest allies—our two countries bear the heaviest burdens. For we are both devoting massive sums of money to weapons that could be better devoted to combat ignorance, poverty, and disease. We are both caught up in a vicious and dangerous cycle, in which suspicion on one side breeds suspicion on the other, and new weapons beget counter-weapons.

In short, both the United States and its allies, and the Soviet Union and its allies, have a mutually deep interest in a just and genuine peace and in halting the arms race. Agreements to this end are in the interests of the Soviet Union as well as ours—and even the most hostile nations can be relied upon to accept and keep those treaty obligations, and only those treaty obligations, which are in their own interest.

So, let us not be blind to our differences—but let us also direct attention to our common interests and to the means by which those differences can be resolved. And if we cannot end now our differences, at least we can help make the world safe for diversity. For, in the final analysis, our most basic common link is that we all inhabit this small planet. We all breathe the same air. We all cherish our children's futures. And we are all mortal.

Third: Let us reexamine our attitude toward the cold war, remembering that we are not engaged in a debate, seeking to pile up debating points. We are not here distributing blame or pointing the finger of judgment. We must deal with the world as it is, and not as it might have been had the history of the last 18 years been different. We must, therefore, persevere in the search for peace in the hope that constructive changes within the Communist bloc might bring within reach solutions which now seem beyond us. We must conduct our affairs in such a way that it becomes in the Communists' interest to agree on a genuine peace. Above all, while defending our own vital interests, nuclear powers must avert those confrontations which bring an adversary to a choice of either a humiliating retreat or a nuclear war. To adopt that kind of course in the nuclear age would be evidence only of the bankruptcy of our policy—or of a collective death-wish for the world.

To secure these ends, America's weapons are nonprovocative, carefully controlled, designed to deter, and capable of selective use. Our military forces are committed to peace and disciplined in self-restraint. Our diplomats are instructed to avoid unnecessary irritants and purely rhetorical hostility.

For we can seek a relaxation of tensions without relaxing our guard. And, for our part, we do not need to use threats to prove that we are resolute. We do not need to jam foreign broadcasts out of fear our faith will be eroded. We are unwilling to impose our system on any unwilling people—but we are willing and able to engage in peaceful competition with any people on earth.

Meanwhile, we seek to strengthen the United Nations, to help solve its financial problems, to make it a more effective instrument for peace, to develop it into a genuine world security system—a system capable of resolving disputes on the basis of law, of insuring the security of the large and the small, and of creating conditions under which arms can finally be abolished.

At the same time we seek to keep peace inside the non-Communist world, where many nations, all of them our friends, are divided over issues which weaken Western unity, which invite Communist intervention or which threaten to erupt into war. Our efforts in West New Guinea, in the Congo, in the Middle East, and in the Indian subcontinent, have been persistent and patient despite criticism from both sides. We have also tried to set an example for others—by seeking to adjust small but significant differences with our own closest neighbors in Mexico and Canada.

Speaking of other nations, I wish to make one point clear. We are bound to many nations by alliances. Those alliances exist because our concern and theirs substantially overlap. Our commitment to defend Western Europe and West Berlin, for example, stands undiminished because of the identity of our vital interests. The United States will make no deal with the Soviet Union at the expense of other nations and other peoples, not merely because they are our partners, but also because their interests and ours converge.

Our interests converge, however, not only in defending the frontiers of freedom, but in pursuing the paths of peace. It is our hope—and the purpose of allied policies, to convince the Soviet Union that she, too, should let each nation choose its own future, so long as that choice does not interfere with the choices of others. The Communist drive to impose their political and economic system on others is the primary cause of world tension today. For there can be no doubt that, if all nations could refrain from interfering in the self-determination of others, the peace would be much more assured.

This will require a new effort to achieve world law—a new context for world discussions. It will require increased understanding between the Soviets and ourselves. And increased understanding will require increased contact and communication. One step in this direction is the proposed arrangement for a direct line between Moscow and Washington, to avoid on each side the dangerous delays, misunderstandings, and misreadings of the other's actions which might occur at a time of crisis.

We have also been talking in Geneva about other first-step measures of arms control, designed to limit the intensity of the arms race and to reduce the risk of accidental war. Our primary long range interest in Geneva, however, is general and complete disarmament—designed to take place by stages, permitting parallel political developments to build the new institutions of peace which would take the place of arms. The pursuit of disarmament has been an effort of this Government since the 1920's. It has been urgently sought by the past three administrations. And however dim the prospects may be today, we intend to continue this effort—to continue it in order that all countries, including our own, can better grasp what the problems and possibilities of disarmament are.

The one major area of these negotiations where the end is in sight, yet where a fresh start is badly needed, is in a treaty to outlaw nuclear tests. The conclusion of such a treaty, so near and yet so far, would check the spiraling arms race in one of its most dangerous areas. It would place the nuclear powers in a position to deal more effectively with one of the greatest hazards which man faces in 1963, the further spread of nuclear arms. It would increase our security—it would decrease the prospects of war. Surely this goal is sufficiently important to require our steady pursuit, yielding neither to the temptation to give up the whole effort nor the temptation to give up our insistence on vital and responsible safeguards.

I'm taking this opportunity, therefore, to announce two important decisions in this regard.

First: Chairman Khrushchev, Prime Minister Macmillan, and I have agreed that high-level discussions will shortly begin in Moscow looking toward early agreement on a comprehensive test ban treaty. Our hopes must be tempered with the caution of history—but with our hopes go the hopes of all mankind.

Second: To make clear our good faith and solemn convictions on the matter, I now declare that the United States does not propose to conduct nuclear tests in the atmosphere so long as other states do not do so. We will not be the first to resume. Such a declaration is no substitute for a formal binding treaty, but I hope it will help us achieve one. Nor would such a treaty be a substitute for disarmament, but I hope it will help us achieve it.

Finally, my fellow Americans, let us examine our attitude towards peace and freedom here at home. The quality and spirit of our own society must justify and support our efforts abroad. We must show it in the dedication of our own lives—as many of you who are graduating today will have an opportunity to do, by serving without pay in the Peace Corps abroad or in the proposed National Service Corps here at home.

But wherever we are, we must all, in our daily lives, live up to the age-old faith that peace and freedom walk together. In too many of our cities today, the peace is not secure because freedom is incomplete.

It is the responsibility of the executive branch at all levels of government—local, State, and National—to provide and protect that freedom for all of our citizens by all means within their authority. It is the responsibility of the legislative branch at all levels, wherever that authority is not now adequate, to make it adequate. And it is the responsibility of all citizens in all sections of this country to respect the rights of all others and to respect the law of the land.

All this is not unrelated to world peace. "When a man's ways please the Lord," the Scriptures tell us, "he maketh even his enemies to be at peace with him." And is not peace, in the last analysis, basically a matter of human rights—the right to live out our lives without fear of devastation—the right to breathe air as nature provided it—the right of future generations to a healthy existence?

While we proceed to safeguard our national interests, let us also safeguard human interests. And the elimination of war and arms is clearly in the interest of both. No treaty, however much it may be to the advantage of all, however tightly it may be worded, can provide absolute security against the risks of deception and evasion. But it can—if it is sufficiently effective in its enforcement, and if it is sufficiently in the interests of its signers—offer far more security and far fewer risks than an unabated, uncontrolled, unpredictable arms race.

The United States, as the world knows, will never start a war. We do not want a war. We do not now expect a war. This generation of Americans has already had enough—more than enough—of war and hate and oppression. We shall be prepared if others wish it. We shall be alert to try to stop it. But we shall also do our part to build a world of peace where the weak are safe and the strong are just. We are not helpless before that task or hopeless of its success. Confident and unafraid, we must labor on—not toward a strategy of annihilation but toward a strategy of peace.

Acknowledgments

I am deeply grateful to the friends who read and critiqued this work in progress: Bob and Janet Aldridge, Robert Aitken, Marya Barr, Karol Schulkin, Sandy Bishop, Rhea Miller, Frank Bognar, Robert Bonazzi, Clare Carter, Jim Crosby, John Dear, Ronnie Dugger, Dot and John Fisher-Smith, Gaeton Fonzi, Michael Green, Elizabeth Hallett, Leon Holman, Steve Jones, Chester Layman, Barbara Ledingham, Roger Ludwig, Anne Fullerton, Staughton and Alice Lynd, Gerald McKnight, Emmanuel Charles McCarthy, William Hart McNichols, Marietta Miller, Don Mosley, David Oliver, Laurie Raymond, Bert Sacks, Vince Salandria, Marty Schotz, Peter Dale Scott, Ladon Sheats (during his last days on earth), Paul Smith, John Stewart, Mark Taylor, Terry Taylor, Louie Vitale, Kim and Bill Wahl, Edward Walsh, Patrick Walsh, John Williams, Don Wilson, Jonathan Wilson-Hartgrove, Howard Zinn, and Barrie Zwicker. What I have seen through their eyes, questioning mine, has helped me reconsider and revise many points along the way. They are not responsible for my enduring mistakes.

Terry Taylor gave me my first computer. Sisters Mary McGehee and Genevieve Sachse gave me its successor, and John Fievet the successor's successors. Rick Ambrose, Jerry Levin, and John Fievet have been my computer doctors and advisers. Deepest thanks to them all. Were it not for Rick, his Internet searches, and his and Lexie's patience through my countless consultations, much of the research for this book would not have occurred.

The first person who peppered me with questions about JFK's death, while we watched a Seattle Mariners' baseball game decades ago, was my friend Joe Martin. He has never stopped pursuing those questions. I thank you, Joe, for not giving up on me when I didn't see the connections you were making between Dallas and a succession of disturbing events since then.

For out-of-town research, I give thanks to Tim Murphy, a constant source of help, Tom Brejcha, Craig Tews, and the Thomas More Society in Chicago—and to Kathy Kelly, Voices in the Wilderness, and Voices for Creative Nonviolence for warm hospitality on my trips to Chicago to interview key witnesses.

Archivists and librarians have sustained this project at every step. At the

393

National Archives in College Park, Maryland, Marty McGann answered patiently my many early morning phone requests for help. Stephen Plotkin and Sharon Kelly of the Research Room at the JFK Library in Boston helped graciously at long distance and during my visit there. Maura Porter and Michelle DeMartino of the JFK Library's Declassification Unit facilitated my Mandatory Review Requests for Kennedy administration documents. Jim Lesar at the Assassination Archives and Research Center in Washington, DC, provided unpublished materials and documents, as did Regina Greenwell and Linda Seelke at the LBJ Library in Austin. Margaret Goodbody of the D.C. Public Library found for me old articles in Washington newspapers. At the Birmingham Public Library, Johnny Coley, Richard Grooms, and Jim Murray in Social Sciences, and Shirley Nichols in Inter Library Loans, were especially helpful. At the Swarthmore College Peace Collection, Curator Wendy Chmielewski copied for me documents from their file folder on the six Friends' meeting with President Kennedy on May 1, 1962, and facilitated the transfer of a reel-to-reel tape about the meeting. Diana Peterson shared with me documents from the Quaker Collection of Haverford College on the same meeting, as did Gwen Gosney Erickson, drawing on the archives of the Friends Historical Collection at Guilford College.

Andy Winiarczyk of the Last Hurrah Bookshop (937 Memorial Ave., Williamsport, PA 17701; phone: 570-321-1150) has been my constant friend and resource for books and queries. Dave Hawkins at The Collector's Archives (Box 2, Beaconsfield, QUE, Canada H9W 5T6; phone: 514-685-4319) has sent many otherwise inaccessible articles and publications. John Judge of the Coalition on Political Assassinations and Tom Jones of JFK Lancer provided helpful references and documents, as did Steve Jones, John Williams, Bob Aldridge, John Armstrong, Jerry Robertson, Edwin Black, Malcolm Blunt, Abraham Bolden, Curtis A. Bolden, Frank Bognar, Kai Bird, Jim Botelho, Frank DeBenedictis, Jeff Dietrich, Clara Solis, Bill Davy, Len Desroches, Sister Alice Godin, Sister Terry Horvath, Daniel Ellsberg, Gaeton Fonzi, H. Bruce Franklin, Jim Gochenaur, Earl Golz, Kathlee Fitzgerald, David Hartsough, Ed Snyder, George and Lillian Willoughby, Vince Palamara, James Johnston, John Kelin, Bill Kelly, Paul Krassner, Barbara LaMonica, Staughton Lynd, Pat McCormick, Bill Sulzman, Gerald McKnight, David McReynolds, Hal Verb, Ray Marcus, Jim Marrs, Peter DeMott, Dan Marvin, Jo Maynes, Herbert S. Parmet, Lisa Pease, Bill Pulte, Marcus Raskin, David Ratcliffe, Peter Dale Scott, Martin Shackleford, Elizabeth Shanklin, Gary Shaw, Matthew Smith, William Weston, Sue Wheaton, Wes Wise, Sherman Skolnick, Grace P. Vale, Tom Vondra, Lawrence S. Wittner, Carl Kaysen, and the late R. B. Cutler, Norb Drouhard, Mary Ferrell, Phil Melanson, and Arthur M. Schlesinger, Jr. Jerry Rose shared with me articles from *The Third Decade* and *The Fourth Decade* after it ceased publication. And I am grateful to Jim DiEugenio for sending every issue of *Probe* magazine as well as his own JFK files.

Bob Corley loaned me his twenty-six volumes of the Warren Commission Hearings and Exhibits—a priceless resource, without which I could not have done much of my research into the government's case. Thank you, Bob.

Mohandas Gandhi's and Thomas Merton's spirit and writings have formed this experiment in truth since its conception. I am grateful to the International Thomas Merton Society for inviting me to deliver the keynote address at its June 13, 1997, meeting in Mobile, Alabama. That talk on "Compassion and the Unspeakable" provided the framework for this book. I also wish to thank Jim Allen, Judy Cumbee, and Project Hope to Abolish the Death Penalty for publishing the text of "Compassion and the Unspeakable," as both a Project Hope fund-raiser and an initial way to test these thoughts with readers.

Jacques Lowe took the stunning photograph of John Kennedy on the cover (used by permission of Woodfin Camp Associates), with cover design by Roberta Savage of Orbis Books and the help of a key question from Tom Douglass.

Two pilgrims into the truth of JFK's assassination whom I admire greatly and who passed into the communion of saints while the work was in progress are Elmer Maas and Steve Orel. I then asked their assistance, and I thank them for giving it, as I do everyone else in the communion of saints who helped, especially my mother, Madalin Douglass, who led me out of many dead ends.

I have the grace of living with the best writer I know. Unlike the author, Shelley knew when the last line of the story was written – also how to write better many of the previous sentences and paragraphs. Living through the research and writing of this story while carrying out a Catholic Worker ministry of hospitality, as she has with grace and love, has not been easy. Her morning prayer may be the answer to how that and many other gifts in our lives have happened.

The subject of this book, and the approach taken to it, call for a courageous editor and publisher. Robert Ellsberg, who combines those functions at Orbis Books, has been the answer to that prayer. Robert has a vision and skills that are unique in the world of publishing. He is a gift to work with.

Shane and Mary-Ellen Creamer were the inspiration for the paperback publication of the book by Simon & Schuster/Touchstone. After reading *JFK and the Unspeakable*, they told their daughter, Stacy Creamer, that she had to read it. She did, and passed it on with her recommendation to editor Michelle Howry, who then facilitated beautifully the paperback process from beginning to end with her Touchstone team. I am grateful to them all.

For all the witnesses in this story, beginning with John Kennedy and Nikita Khrushchev, I thank God. They each paid a price. The witnesses to JFK's assassination have shared their own critical parts of the truth. Because of their decisions to speak the truth as they saw it, not counting the cost, we can know the truth.

Most of my acknowledgments are in the endnotes. In addition to the documents and witnesses, the notes identify a multitude of researchers and writers, many of whom were seeking answers to President Kennedy's assassination long before I knew the questions. I am profoundly grateful to them all. Vince Salandria and Marty Schotz have been special guides on my path. I dedicate this book to Vince and Marty, my teachers and friends.

NOTES

Introduction

1. Thomas Merton, "Chant to Be Used in Processions around a Site with Furnaces," in *The Nonviolent Alternative*, edited by Gordon C. Zahn (New York: Farrar, Straus & Giroux, 1980), p. 262.

2. Thomas Merton, *Peace in the Post-Christian Era* (Maryknoll, N.Y.: Orbis Books, 2004), p. 119. Merton's forbidden book was finally published by Orbis Books forty-two years after it was written. If we simply substitute "terrorist" for "communist" in Merton's text, *Peace in the Post-Christian Era* is as relevant today as when it was written.

3. From Thomas Merton's January 18, 1962, letter to W. H. Ferry, in *Letters from Tom: A Selection of Letters from Father Thomas Merton, Monk of Gethsemani, to W. H. Ferry, 1961–1968*, edited by W. H. Ferry (Scarsdale, N.Y.: Fort Hill Press, 1983), p. 15.

4. Thomas Merton, *Raids on the Unspeakable* (New York: New Directions, 1966), p. 5 (Merton's emphasis).

5. Ibid., p. 4.

6. Peter Grose, *Gentleman Spy: The Life of Allen Dulles* (New York: Houghton Mifflin, 1994) p. 293.

7. William Blum, *Killing Hope: U.S. Military and CIA Interventions since World War II* (Monroe, Me.: Common Courage Press, 1995).

8. James W. Douglass, "The King Conspiracy Exposed in Memphis," in *The Assassinations*, edited by James DiEugenio and Lisa Pease (Los Angeles: Feral House, 2003), pp. 492–509. Also available at *Probe* magazine Web site. The trial transcript for the wrongful death lawsuit of the Martin Luther King Jr. family versus Loyd Jowers "and other unknown co-conspirators," held in Memphis, November 15-December 8, 1999, is online at www.thekingcenter.com.

9. Thomas Merton, *The Sign of Jonas* (New York: Harcourt, Brace & Company, 1953), p. 334.

10. As biblical scholars John L. McKenzie and Walter Wink have pointed out, the excessively literal translation "the son of the man" for Jesus' Aramaic phrase was as meaningless in Greek as it is in English. The Aramaic idiom Jesus uses eighty-two times in the Gospels to identify himself, *bar nasha*, means humanity, personally and collectively. What he says about himself as "the human being," he says also about humanity. His story is meant to be our story. See John L. McKenzie, *The New Testament without Illusion* (Chicago: Thomas More Press, 1980), pp. 114–24; James W. Douglass, *The Nonviolent Coming of God* (Maryknoll, N.Y.: Orbis Books, 1991), pp. 29–59; and Walter Wink, *The Human Being: Jesus and the Enigma of the Son of the Man* (Minneapolis: Fortress Press, 2003).

11. Mark 9:31; 10:32–34; Matthew 17:22–23; 20:17–19; Luke 9:22; 9:44; 18:31–33.

1. A Cold Warrior Turns

1. *Dorothy Day: Selected Writings,* edited by Robert Ellsberg (Maryknoll, N.Y.: Orbis Books, 1983, 1992, 2005), p. 266.

2. Nigel Hamilton, *JFK: Reckless Youth* (New York: Random House, 1992), pp. 42, 104, 147–52; Robert Dallek, "The Medical Ordeals of JFK," *Atlantic Monthly* (December 2002), pp. 49–61.

3. Quoted by George Smathers in an interview by Peter Collier and David Horowitz for their book *The Kennedys: An American Drama* (New York: Warner Books, 1984), p. 208.

4. Robert J. Donovan, *PT 109* (New York: McGraw-Hill, 1961), p. 166.

5. John Hersey, "Survival," *New Yorker* (June 17, 1944), pp. 34–37.

6. Joan and Clay Blair, Jr., *The Search for J.F.K.* (New York: G. P. Putnam's Sons, 1976), p. 376.

7. Robert F. Kennedy, foreword to John F. Kennedy, *Profiles in Courage* (New York: HarperPerennial, 1964), p. xii.

8. The Melanesian islanders continued to remember him, as he did them. On September 25, 1962, Barney Ross accompanied their Solomon Islands rescuer Benjamin Kevu to the White House, where he and President Kennedy embraced. Kennedy also invited two of the other rescuers to visit him, but to their grief he was killed before they could see him again. Hamilton, *JFK,* p. 602.

9. Cited by Helen O'Donnell, *A Common Good: The Friendship of Robert F. Kennedy and Kenneth P. O'Donnell* (New York: William Morrow, 1998), p. 48.

10. Kenneth P. O'Donnell and David F. Powers, *"Johnny, We Hardly Knew Ye"* (Boston: Little, Brown, 1970), p. 46.

11. Hamilton, *JFK,* p. 698.

12. Arthur M. Schlesinger, Jr., *A Thousand Days* (Boston: Houghton Mifflin, 1965), p. 88.

13. Ibid.

14. Ibid.

15. *Prelude to Leadership: The European Diary of John F. Kennedy*, ed. Deirdre Henderson (Washington, D.C.: Regnery, 1995), p. 20.

16. Ibid., p. 7.

17. Michael J. Hogan, *A Cross of Iron: Harry S. Truman and the Origins of the National Security State, 1945–1954* (Cambridge/New York: Cambridge University Press, 1998), p. 413.

18. Gregg Herken interview of Jerome Wiesner, February 9, 1982. Cited by Christopher A. Preble, "Who Ever Believed in the 'Missile Gap'? John F. Kennedy and the Politics of National Security," *Presidential Studies Quarterly* 33, no. 4 (December 2003), p. 816.

19. Gareth Porter, *Perils of Dominance* (Berkeley: University of California Press, 2005), p. 14.

20. Marcus G. Raskin, *Essays of a Citizen* (Armonk, N.Y.: M. E. Sharpe, 1991), p. 52.

21. *"Let the Word Go Forth": The Speeches, Statements, and Writings of John F. Kennedy* (New York: Delacorte, 1988), pp. 370–71.

22. Herbert S. Parmet, *Jack: The Struggles of John F. Kennedy* (New York: Dial, 1980), p. 286.

23. Schlesinger, *A Thousand Days*, p. 553.

24. Ibid., pp. 553–54.

25. Ibid.

26. Richard D. Mahoney, *JFK: Ordeal in Africa* (New York: Oxford University Press, 1983).

27. Hugh Sidey, introduction to *Prelude to Leadership*, pp. xxiv-xxv.

28. Ibid., p. xxix.

29. *Public Papers of the Presidents: John F. Kennedy, 1961,* "Inaugural Address" (Washington: U.S. Government Printing Office, 1962), p. l.

30. Thomas Merton, *Cold War Letters* (Maryknoll, N.Y.: Orbis Books, 2006), p. 4.

31. Ibid., p. 6.

32. From Thomas Merton's January 18, 1962, letter to W. H. Ferry, in *Letters from Tom: A Selection of Letters from Father Thomas Merton, Monk of Gethsemani, to W. H. Ferry, 1961–1968,* edited by W. H. Ferry (Scarsdale, N.Y.: Fort Hill Press, 1983), p. 15.

33. Evelyn Lincoln, *My Twelve Years with John F. Kennedy* (New York: Bantam Books, 1966), p. 230.

34. Sidey, introduction to *Prelude,* p. xxxii.

35. Lincoln, *My Twelve Years,* p. 230.

36. Paul B. Fay, Jr., *The Pleasure of His Company* (New York: Dell, 1966), pp. 162–63.

37. Theodore C. Sorensen, *Kennedy* (New York: Konecky & Konecky, 1965), pp. 606–7.

38. Ibid., p. 606.

39. Arthur M. Schlesinger, Jr., *Robert Kennedy and His Times* (New York: Ballantine Books, 1978), p. 485.

40. Charles Higham and Joel Greenberg, *The Celluloid Muse: Hollywood Directors Speak* (New York: New American Library, Signet reprint, 1972), p. 92; cited by Schlesinger, *Robert Kennedy.*

41. "The Bay of Pigs Invasion: A Comprehensive Chronology of Events," in *Bay of Pigs Declassified,* edited by Peter Kornbluh (New York: New Press, 1998), pp. 269–70.

42. Ibid., p. 275.

43. Ibid., p. 293.

44. Ibid., p. 296.

45. Ibid., p. 303.

46. Ibid., p. 305.

47. Ibid., pp. 319–22.

48. O'Donnell and Powers, *"Johnny, We Hardly Knew Ye,"* p. 274.

49. Schlesinger, *Robert Kennedy,* p. 486.

50. Lucien S. Vandenbroucke, "The 'Confessions' of Allen Dulles: New Evidence on the Bay of Pigs," *Diplomatic History* 8, no. 4 (Fall 1984): p. 369; citing Allen W. Dulles Papers, handwritten notes, Seeley G. Mudd Manuscript Library, Princeton University, Princeton, New Jersey.

51. Noah Adams, *All Things Considered,* March 26, 2001, hour l, National Public Radio.

52. Daniel Schorr, *All Things Considered,* March 26, 2001, hour l, National Public Radio.

53. Haynes Johnson with Manuel Artime, Jose Perez San Roman, Emeido Oliva, and Enrique Ruiz-Williams, *The Bay of Pigs* (New York: Dell, 1964), p. 74.

54. Ibid.

55. *Robert Kennedy in His Own Words,* edited by Edwin O. Guthman and Jeffrey Shulman (New York: Bantam, 1988), p. 245. RFK also said, "In fact, we found out later that, despite the President's orders that no American forces would be used, the first two people who landed in the Bay of Pigs were Americans. The CIA sent them in." Ibid.

56. Tom Wicker, John W. Finney, Max Frankel, E. W. Kenworthy, "C.I.A.: Maker of Policy, or Tool?" *New York Times* (April 25, 1966), p. 20.

57. Schlesinger, *Robert Kennedy,* p. 486.

58. David T. Ratcliffe, *Understanding Special Operations: 1989 Interview with L. Fletcher Prouty* (Santa Cruz, CA: rat haus reality press, 1999), pp. 170–71.

59. Schlesinger, *Thousand Days,* p. 428.

60. In addition to former CIA director Allen W. Dulles, President Lyndon B. Johnson

on November 30, 1963, appointed six other members to the President's Commission on the Assassination of President Kennedy: Earl Warren, Chief Justice of the Supreme Court, Chairman of the Commission; Georgia Senator Richard B. Russell; Kentucky Senator John Sherman Cooper; Representative Hale Boggs of Louisiana; Representative Gerald R. Ford of Michigan, the future U.S. president; John J. McCloy, who had been a World War II Assistant Secretary of War, President of the World Bank, and U.S. Military Governor and High Commissioner for Germany. LBJ's first choice for the commission had been Allen Dulles, who would be its most influential member, but "he needed Warren to deflect any future criticism of the investigation from the liberal establishment." Gerald D. McKnight, *Breach of Trust: How the Warren Commission Failed the Nation and Why* (Lawrence, Kans.: University Press of Kansas, 2005), p. 41.

61. Willie Morris, *New York Days* (Boston: Little, Brown, 1993), p. 36.

62. Cited by L. Fletcher Prouty, *The Secret Team* (New York: Ballantine, 1974), p. 472.

63. Cold War Letter 9, to Archbishop Thomas Roberts, S.J., London, December, 1961; in *Cold War Letters*, p. 26.

64. Thomas Merton, *Witness to Freedom: Letters in Times of Crisis*, edited by William H. Shannon (New York: Harcourt Brace, 1994), p. 77.

65. Merton, *Cold War Letters*, p. 65.

66. Ibid., p. 165.

67. Gaeton Fonzi, *The Last Investigation* (New York: Thunder's Mouth, 1994), pp. 53–59.

68. Merton, *Cold War Letters*, p. 43.

69. Ibid.

70. Ibid., p. 44.

71. Merton, *Cold War Letters*, p. 26.

72. *Public Papers of the Presidents: John F. Kennedy, 1961*, "Address in Seattle at the University of Washington's 100th Anniversary Program," November 16, 1961 (Washington: U.S. Government Printing Office, 1962), p. 726.

73. Thomas Merton, *Peace in the Post-Christian Era* (Maryknoll, N.Y.: Orbis Books, 2004), pp. 121–22.

74. Ibid., p. 122.

75. Merton, *Cold War Letters*, p. 29.

76. Ibid.

77. *Public Papers of the Presidents: John F. Kennedy, 1961*, "Radio and Television Report to the American People on the Soviet Arms Buildup in Cuba," October 22, 1962, p. 807.

78. *Khrushchev Remembers*, with introduction, commentary, and notes by Edward Crankshaw (Boston: Little, Brown, 1970), p. 492.

79. Ibid., p. 493.

80. Ibid., p. 494.

81. Merton, *Cold War Letters*, p. 96.

82. "Now the question *really* is what action we take which *lessens* the chances of a nuclear exchange, which obviously is the final failure." President John F. Kennedy, October 18, 1962, 11:00 A.M., Cabinet Room. Sheldon M. Stern, *Averting "The Final Failure"* (Stanford, Calif.: Stanford University Press, 2003), pp. 95, 105–6.

83. In 1997 Ernest R. May and Philip D. Zelikow edited and published transcripts of the Cuban Missile Crisis tapes in their book *The Kennedy Tapes* (Cambridge, Mass.: Harvard University Press, 1997). In 2000 the accuracy of their transcripts was challenged in two articles by Sheldon M. Stern, historian at the JFK Library from 1977 to 1999: "What JFK Really Said," *Atlantic Monthly* 285 (May 2000): pp. 122–28, and "Source Material: The 1997 Published Transcripts of the JFK Cuban Missile Crisis Tapes: Too Good to Be True?" *Presidential Studies Quarterly* 30 (September 2000): pp. 586–93. When Zelikow, May, and Timothy Naftali brought out a revised set of missile crisis tran-

scripts, *The Presidential Recordings: John F. Kennedy: Volumes 1–3, The Great Crises* (New York: W.W. Norton, 2001), Stern critiqued their revision for further inaccuracies in his article "The JFK Tapes: Round Two," *Reviews in American History* 30 (2002): pp. 680–88. Sheldon M. Stern has written a comprehensive narrative account of the missile crisis deliberations of President Kennedy and the Executive Committee of the National Security Council (ExComm), citing his own transcripts of the tapes, *Averting "The Final Failure": John F. Kennedy and the Secret Cuban Missile Crisis Meetings* (Stanford, Calif.: Stanford University Press, 2003). My citations of the tapes are taken from *Averting "The Final Failure."*

84. Stern, *Averting "The Final Failure,"* pp. 123–24.

85. Ibid., p. 126.

86. Ibid., p. 128.

87. Ibid., p. 129.

88. Robert Kennedy, *Thirteen Days* (New York: Signet, 1969), p. 31.

89. Ibid., pp. 69–70.

90. Paul Wells, "Private Letters Shed Light on Cold War," *Montreal Gazette* (July 24, 1993), p. A1. The private letters between Kennedy and Khrushchev, known as the "Pen Pal Correspondence," were published with the Cold War leaders' more formal, public letters in the State Department volume *Foreign Relations of the United States [FRUS], 1961–1963, Volume VI: Kennedy-Khrushchev Exchanges* (Washington: U.S. Government Printing Office, 1996).

91. Wells, "Private Letters," p. A4.

92. *FRUS 1961–1963*, vol. VI, p. 25.

93. Ibid., pp. 25–26.

94. Ibid., p. 26.

95. Ibid., p. 35.

96. Ibid., pp. 38–39.

97. R. Kennedy, *Thirteen Days*, p. 97.

98. Ibid., p. 98.

99. Ibid., p. 106.

100. *Khrushchev Remembers*, pp. 497–98.

101. From Ambassador Anatoly Dobrynin's cable to the Soviet Foreign Ministry, October 27, 1962. Reprinted in translation in Richard Ned Lebow and Janice Gross Stein, *We All Lost the Cold War* (Princeton, NJ: Princeton University Press, 1994), pp. 523–26. Cited by Jim Hershberg, "Anatomy of a Controversy: Anatoly F. Dobrynin's Meeting with Robert F. Kennedy, Saturday, 27 October 1962," *The Cold War International History Project Bulletin* (Issue 5, Spring 1995), available at http://www.gwu.edu/~nsarchiv/nsa/ cuba_mis_cri/

102. Schlesinger, *Robert Kennedy*, pp. 561–62.

103. Scott D. Sagan, *The Limits of Safety* (Princeton, N.J.: Princeton University Press, 1993), p. 79.

104. Richard Rhodes, "The General and World War III," *New Yorker* (June 19, 1995), pp. 58–59.

105. *FRUS 1961–1963*, vol. VI, p. 57.

106. *Khrushchev Remembers*, p. 498.

107. Letter from Fidel Castro to Nikita Khrushchev, October 26, 1962, cited by Carlos Lechuga, *In the Eye of the Storm* (Melbourne: Ocean Press, 1995), p. 88.

108. *Khrushchev Remembers*, p. 498.

109. It is true that in a less intense sense the crisis continued until November 20, when President Kennedy announced at a press conference that two outstanding issues had been resolved: In addition to its nuclear missiles, the Soviet Union had agreed to remove from Cuba its IL-28 bombers, which the U.S. regarded as offensive weapons. Although there would be no UN inspections because Premier Fidel Castro would not cooperate in a process verifying the missiles' and bombers' removal, the Soviets agreed to leave the

weapons on the decks of their departing ships for observation by the United States. *Kennedy Tapes*, pp. 664–65.

110. Robert Kennedy had in fact been more explicit in his diary about the missile trade-off between the United States and the Soviet Union than the edited text of his posthumous work, *Thirteen Days*, revealed. In a Moscow conference in January 1989, former Kennedy speechwriter Theodore Sorensen stated: "Ambassador Dobrynin felt that Robert Kennedy's book did not adequately express that the 'deal' on the Turkish missiles was part of the resolution of the crisis. And here I have a confession to make to my colleagues on the American side, as well as to others who are present. I was the editor of Robert Kennedy's book. It was, in fact, a diary of those thirteen days. And his diary was very explicit that this was part of the deal; but at that time it was still a secret even on the American side, except for the six of us who had been present at that [preliminary White House] meeting. So I took it upon myself to edit that out of his diaries, and that is why the Ambassador is somewhat justified in saying that the diaries are not as explicit as his conversation." Sorensen's "confession" is cited in Hershberg, "Anatomy of a Controversy."

111. Because Rusk was ill and unable to attend the March 1987 Hawk's Cay (Florida) meeting of former ExComm members, his revelation was made in a letter read to the conference participants by Kennedy's National Security Adviser, McGeorge Bundy. Cited by James G. Blight and David A. Welch, *On the Brink* (New York: Noonday, 1990), pp. 83–84.

112. Dorothy Day and the Catholic Worker house had been a stopping point two decades earlier on John Kennedy's journey of conscience. In her book *Loaves and Fishes*, published in 1963 shortly before the president's assassination, Dorothy Day recalled a night in the forties when "two members of the Kennedy family" visited her at the Catholic Worker house on Mott Street in New York. The Kennedys, Dorothy, and several others went to an all-night restaurant and talked until the small hours. "I remember," she wrote, "only that we talked of war and peace and of man and the state. I do not remember which of the Kennedy boys were there, but those who do remember tell me it was our President, John Kennedy, and his older brother Joseph, who lost his life in the war." Dorothy Day, *Loaves and Fishes* (New York: Curtis Books, 1963), p. 159.

Dorothy Day's longtime co-worker Stanley Vishnewski remembered the Kennedy brothers' visit more vividly. He said they spent the afternoon with others at the Worker before seeing Dorothy. "And of course, they were just the Kennedys to us, just young people that we thought were coming slumming." Recalling the young John Kennedy's reaction to what he was seeing, Vishnewski told Bill Moyers in a 1973 television interview, "I remember distinctly how bewildered he was by the sight of the poverty and the misery of the place. And then Dorothy came in. She talked to him. Then Dorothy says, 'Come and have supper with us.' And Kennedy looked at her, a little startled, and says, 'No, come out and have dinner with us instead.' So Dorothy, and Joe and John Kennedy . . . We went out to a little restaurant around the corner. We had a wonderful conversation." (From "Still a Rebel," a program on Dorothy Day, *Bill Moyers' Journal*, February 20, 1973, Public Broadcasting Service.)

John Kennedy's visit to the Mott Street Catholic Worker took place in the summer of 1940. Marquette University's Catholic Worker archivist Phil Runkel has sent to me copies of several pages from the Mott Street Catholic Worker's Guest Book for 1940. Included in the signatures between July 29 and August 4, 1940, is a somewhat illegible "John F. Kennedy, Hyannisport—Cape Cod, Ma."

Author Michael Harrington, who spent two years with the Catholic Worker, wrote a book entitled *The Other America: Poverty in the United States* (New York: Macmillan, 1962), which had a powerful impact on JFK. Arthur Schlesinger wrote that *The Other America* helped crystallize Kennedy's determination in 1963 to enact a poverty program (*Thousand Days*, p. 1010). Stanley Vishnewski thought the combination of what Kennedy saw that day at the Catholic Worker, heard that night from Dorothy Day, and read years later in *The Other America* "planted the idea of the poverty program" (*Bill Moyers'*

Journal, February 20, 1973). Perhaps the conversation into the early morning hours "of war and peace and of man and the state," as Day remembered it, also helped plant the idea of peace in the future president.

113. Stern, *Averting "The Final Failure,"* pp. 123, 125.

114. O'Donnell and Powers, *"Johnny, We Hardly Knew Ye,"* p. 318.

115. John Kenneth Galbraith, *A Life in Our Times* (Boston: Houghton Mifflin, 1981), p. 388.

116. Robert S. McNamara, *In Retrospect* (New York: Random House, 1995), p. 341.

117. Rhodes, "General and World War III," p. 58.

118. Schlesinger, *Robert Kennedy,* p. 565.

119. Ibid.

120. Dave Powers, interview by Ted O'Brien, "Dave Powers & JFK," WGBH-TV (1990).

121. Thomas Merton, letter to Daniel Berrigan, November 27, 1962; in *The Hidden Ground of Love: The Letters of Thomas Merton on Religious Experience and Social Concerns,* edited by William H. Shannon (New York: Farrar, Straus & Giroux, 1985), p. 75.

122. Merton, *Cold War Letters,* p. 190.

123. Thomas Merton, letter to Ethel Kennedy, May 14, 1963; in *Hidden Ground of Love,* p. 447.

124. R. Kennedy, *Thirteen Days,* p. 110.

125. Norman Cousins, *The Improbable Triumvirate* (New York: W. W. Norton, 1972), p. 9.

126. Richard Reeves, *President Kennedy: Profile of Power* (New York: Touchstone, 1993), pp. 312, 339, 514.

127. Cousins, *Improbable Triumvirate,* p. 101.

128. Gar Alperovitz, *Atomic Diplomacy* (New York: Penguin Books, 1985), p. 8.

129. Ibid., p. 58.

130. Daniel Ellsberg, "Call to Mutiny," in *Protest and Survive,* edited by E. P. Thompson and Dan Smith (New York: Monthly Review, 1981), pp. i–ii; citing January 1980 *Time* article.

131. Michael J. Hogan, *A Cross of Iron: Harry S. Truman and the Origins of the National Security State, 1945–1954* (New York: Cambridge University Press, 1998), p. 65.

132. Ibid., p. 56.

133. Peter Grose, *Gentleman Spy: The Life of Allen Dulles* (New York: Houghton Mifflin, 1994), p. 293.

134. Ibid.

135. Ibid., citing NSC 10/2.

136. *Alleged Assassination Plots Involving Foreign Leaders: An Interim Report; November 20, 1975* (Washington: U.S. Government Printing Office, 1975), pp. 74–77.

137. Ibid., pp. 79–82.

138. Richard M. Bissell, interview by Lucien S. Vandenbroucke, Farmington, Connecticut, May 18, 1984; cited in Vandenbroucke "'Confessions' of Allen Dulles," p. 374.

139. *Alleged Assassination Plots,* p. 151.

140. Ibid., p. 150.

141. Ibid., p. 151.

142. Ibid., p. 135.

143. Tad Szulc, "Cuba on Our Mind," *Esquire* (February 1974), p. 90. David Talbot has pointed out that, although "Kennedy critics charge that JFK staged this dialogue with Szulc to give himself cover in case the murder plots [against Castro] were later revealed," others find this far-fetched. Kennedy adviser Richard Goodwin found it hard to imagine that, if JFK were in fact plotting to kill Castro, he would then bring up the subject to a

New York Times reporter, "who the day after Castro was killed would be sitting on the biggest story in the world!" Richard Goodwin interview by David Talbot in David Talbot, *Brothers* (New York: Free Press, 2007), p. 94. Fidel Castro has assured both Tad Szulc and Ethel Kennedy that he knows John and Robert Kennedy "had nothing to do with the CIA attempts on his life." Ibid., p. 94.

144. Thomas Powers, *The Man Who Kept the Secrets: Richard Helms and the CIA* (New York: Alfred A. Knopf, 1979).

145. Schlesinger, *Thousand Days*, p. 900.

146. Sorensen, *Kennedy*, p. 731.

147. *Public Papers of the Presidents: John F. Kennedy, 1963*, p. 460. All subsequent citations of the American University address are from pp. 460–64.

148. President Dwight D. Eisenhower, "Farewell Address," January 17, 1961, in *The President Speaks: From William McKinley to Lyndon B. Johnson*, edited by Louis Filler (New York: Capricorn Books, 1965), pp. 367–68.

149. *The Warren Commission Report* (New York: St. Martin's Press, 1992, from U.S. Government printing in 1964), p. 747.

150. Ibid., p. 748.

151. Ibid., p. 393.

152. Interviews with Marines who served with Oswald at Atsugi Air Force Base, including James R. Persons, Joseph Macedo, Miguel Rodriguez, George Wilkins, Jerry E. Pitts, Pete F. Connor, Richard Cyr, Peter Cassisi, and John E. Donovan. Cited by Edward Jay Epstein, *The Assassination Chronicles* (New York: Carroll & Graf, 1992), pp. 343–46, 355, 617–19. See also Philip H. Melanson, *Spy Saga: Lee Harvey Oswald and U.S. Intelligence* (New York: Praeger, 1990), pp. 7–9, 16–18. McKnight, *Breach of Trust*, p. 300.

153. *Warren Commission Hearings* (hereafter cited as *WCH*), vol. 8, p. 298.

154. John Donovan, interview with John Newman, July 19, 1994; cited by John Newman, *Oswald and the CIA* (New York: Carroll & Graf, 1995), p. 45.

155. Francis Gary Powers with Curt Gentry, *Operation Overflight* (New York: Holt, Rinehart & Winston, 1970), pp. 357–59.

156. *Warren Report*, p. 712. U.S. Consul Richard E. Snyder at the Moscow Embassy stated in a State Department telegram: "I was sole officer handling Oswald case" (Commission Exhibit 909, *WCH*, vol. 18, p. 100). According to CIA documents, Richard E. Snyder had joined the CIA on March 27, 1950, only to "resign" six months later to begin a career of overseas U.S. embassy assignments for the State Department (CIA letter to Richard E. Snyder, March 27, 1950. JFK Record Number 104-10276-10270; also Secret Memorandum to Chief Personnel Security Branch, CIA, September 26, 1950; records of House Select Committee on Assassinations: Segregated CIA Collection). Snyder's official change of jobs corresponded to the standard CIA practice of its employees using a State Department cover while stationed at U.S. embassies. Through Richard Snyder's handling, Lee Harvey Oswald was under the effective control of the CIA in all his Moscow Embassy contacts.

Snyder apparently treated Oswald as a privileged visitor to the Moscow Embassy. Joan Hallett, a receptionist at the embassy who was married to the assistant naval attaché, recalled in a 1994 interview that, in contrast to the official story, Oswald had come "several times" to the embassy in 1959. Hallett said Snyder and the security officer "took him upstairs to the working floors, a secure area where the Ambassador and the political, economic, and military officers were. A visitor would never get up there unless he was on official business. *I* was never up there." Anthony and Robbyn Summers, "The Ghosts of November," *Vanity Fair* (December 1994).

157. Ibid., p. 658.

158. Melanson, *Spy Saga*, p. 21, citing *WCH*, vol. 22, p. 12, and vol. 24, p. 509.

159. Sylvia Meagher, *Accessories after the Fact* (New York: Vintage Books, 1992), pp. 328–29.

160. McKnight, *Breach of Trust*, p. 300. McKnight's research into Oswald's security clearances determined the fact that "when he served overseas at Cubi Point, the Philippines, and Atsugi, Japan, Oswald had 'Crypto' clearance, probably one of a dozen or more special clearances at that time higher than 'Top Secret' . . . The Warren Commission knew about Oswald's 'Crypto' clearance but suppressed it from being included in the record."

161. *Warren Report*, p. 423.

162. Ibid.

163. Ibid.

164. Anthony Summers, *Conspiracy* (New York: Paragon House, 1989), pp. 144–45.

165. James Botelho, interview by Mark Lane, cited by Jim Marrs, *Crossfire: The Plot That Killed Kennedy* (New York: Carroll & Graff, 1990), p. 110. When I spoke with James Botelho by phone in June 2007 and read to him his earlier statements on Oswald now cited in this text, he confirmed their accuracy. He added, "I still feel that way [that Oswald was on an assignment in Russia for American intelligence]." Botelho said he liked Oswald: "He was the best roommate I ever had. He pretty much let me alone. He was quiet. We both liked classical music." So far as Oswald's being violent, Botelho said, "He didn't like violence. The thought of it repulsed him. He wasn't afraid of it. He just thought of it as being primitive. He wouldn't do to others what he didn't like done to him." Author's interview of James Anthony Botelho, June 16, 2007.

166. Ibid., pp. 110–11.

167. Merton, *Cold War Letters*, pp. 47–48.

168. Pope John XIII, *Pacem in Terris* (New York: America Press, 1963), p. 50.

169. Ibid., pp. 50–51.

170. Norman Cousins, *The Improbable Triumvirate: John F. Kennedy, Pope John, Nikita Khrushchev* (New York: W. W. Norton, 1972), pp. 80, 91.

171. Ibid., p. 108.

172. *Public Papers of the Presidents: John F. Kennedy, 1963*, pp. 468–69.

173. Sorensen, *Kennedy*, p. 733.

174. Schlesinger, *Thousand Days*, p. 904.

175. Ibid., pp. 904–5.

176. Max Frankel, "Harriman to Lead Test-Ban Mission to Soviet [Union] in July," *New York Times* (June 12, 1963), p. 1.

177. *Warren Report*, p. 713.

178. Jim Garrison, *On the Trail of the Assassins* (New York: Warner Books, 1988), p. 58.

179. Jim Marrs, *Crossfire* (New York: Carroll & Graf, 1989), pp. 200, 279. See also Epstein, *Assassination Chronicles*, pp. 463–64.

180. Epstein, *Assassination Chronicles*, p. 559.

181. Ibid., p. 558.

182. Ibid., p. 559.

183. Henry Hurt, *Reasonable Doubt* (New York: Henry Holt, 1985), p. 220.

184. Summers, *Not in Your Lifetime*, p. 158.

185. Hurt, *Reasonable Doubt*, p. 221.

186. *Warren Report*, p. 403.

187. Hurt, *Reasonable Doubt*, p. 219.

188. Ibid., pp. 219, 221.

189. Epstein, *Assassination Chronicles*, pp. 559, 566.

190. According to a memorandum in de Mohrenschildt's CIA file, he and his Haitian partner Clemard Joseph Charles were to meet in Washington on May 7, 1963, with CIA staff officer Tony Czaikowski and Assistant Director of Army Intelligence and CIA liaison Dorothe Matlack. Matlack confirmed the May 7 meeting in her testimony before the House Select Committee on Assassinations (HSCA) on September 4, 1978. She said de Mohrenschildt "dominated" Charles. *Appendix to Hearings before the Select Com-*

mittee on Assassinations of the U.S. House of Representatives (HSCA) (Washington: U.S. Government Printing Office, 1979), vol. 12, pp. 56–57.

191. *Warren Report*, p. 283.

192. Ibid., pp. 283–84.

193. Garrison, *On the Trail of the Assassins*, p. 64.

194. Ibid.

195. Gaeton Fonzi, *The Last Investigation* (New York: Thunder's Mouth Press, 1994), p. 192.

196. Garrison, *On the Trail of the Assassins*, p. 64.

197. Schlesinger, *Thousand Days*, p. 896.

198. Glenn T. Seaborg, *Kennedy, Khrushchev, and the Test Ban* (Berkeley: University of California Press, 1981), p. 195.

199. *Public Papers of the Presidents: John F. Kennedy, 1963*, p. 107.

200. On May 20, 1963; cited by Seaborg, *Kennedy, Khrushchev, and the Test Ban*, p. 199.

201. Schlesinger, *Thousand Days*, p. 899.

202. *Kennedy Khrushchev, and the Test Ban*, p. 200 (emphasis in original).

203. Cousins, *Improbable Triumvirate*, p. 128.

204. Schlesinger, *Thousand Days*, p. 734.

205. Ibid.

206. Reeves, *President Kennedy: Profile of Power*, pp. 545, 740.

207. Ibid., pp. 548–49.

208. Ibid., p. 550.

209. *Public Papers of the Presidents: John F. Kennedy, 1963*, p. 602; all subsequent citations of the Test Ban Treaty address are from pp. 603–6.

210. Cousins, *Improbable Triumvirate*, pp. 128–29.

211. Ibid., p. 129.

212. "Is U.S. Giving up in the Arms Race?" *U.S. News and World Report* (August 5, 1963), p. 37.

213. "If Peace Does Come—What Happens to Business?" *U.S. News and World Report* (August 12, 1963).

214. Reeves, *President Kennedy: Profile of Power*, p. 554.

215. Cousins, *Improbable Triumvirate*, pp. 113–14.

216. Sergei Khrushchev, "Commentary on 'Thirteen Days, *New York Times* (Sunday, February 4, 2001), OP-ED, p. 17.

217. Sorensen, *Kennedy*, p. 739.

218. Ibid.

219. Schlesinger, *Thousand Days*, p. 911.

220. Sorensen, *Kennedy*, p. 740.

221. Schlesinger, *Thousand Days*, pp. 909–10.

2. Kennedy, Castro, and the CIA

1. Thomas Merton, Cold War Letter 111, to Rabbi Everett Gendler, Princeton, October 1962; in Thomas Merton, *Witness to Freedom: Letters in Times of Crisis,* edited by William H. Shannon (New York: Harcourt Brace, 1994), p. 69.

2. Peter Kornbluh, "JFK & Castro: The Secret Quest For Accommodation," *Cigar Aficianado* (October 1999), p. 90.

3. Ibid., p. 91.

4. March 4, 1963, Memorandum for the Record on "Mr. Donovan's Trip to Cuba," written at the request of National Security Adviser McGeorge Bundy by his deputy, Gordon Chase.

5. Evan Thomas, *Robert Kennedy: His Life* (New York: Simon & Schuster, 2000),

p. 239; citing March 14, 1963, RFK to JFK memorandum, Theodore Sorensen Papers, John F. Kennedy Library.

6. Ibid., citing March 26, 1963, RFK to JFK memorandum, Assassination Records Review Board, John F. Kennedy Library.

7. Max Frankel, "Exiles Describe 2 New Cuba Raids," *New York Times Western Edition* (March 20, 1963), p. 2.

8. Gaeton Fonzi, *The Last Investigation* (New York: Thunder's Mouth Press, 1994), p. 132.

9. Dick Russell, "Three Witnesses," *New Times* (June 24, 1977), p. 34.

10. Fonzi, *Last Investigation*, pp. 117–71, 271–365.

11. Ibid.

12. "New Attack Reported," *New York Times* (March 28, 1963), p. 3.

13. Fonzi, *Last Investigation*, pp. 389–90.

14. "Memorandum from Attorney General Kennedy to President Kennedy," April 3, 1963, *Foreign Relations of the United States (FRUS), 1961–1963, Volume VI: Kennedy-Khrushchev Exchanges*, p. 263.

15. "U.S. Curbs Miami Exiles to Prevent Raids on Cuba," *New York Times* (April 1, 1963), p. 1. Antonio Veciana told journalist Dick Russell that he was among those whom President Kennedy had ordered confined to Dade County. Dick Russell, *The Man Who Knew Too Much* (New York: Carroll & Graf, 1992), p. 297.

16. "Seized Boat's Owner Says U.S. Knew in Advance of Cuba Raids," *New York Times* (April 3, 1963), p. 3.

17. Ibid.

18. "U.S. Strengthens Check on Raiders," *New York Times* (April 6, 1963), p. l.

19. "Castro Sees a Gain in U.S. Bar to Raids," *New York Times* (April 11, 1963), p. 10.

20. Tad Szulc, "Cuban Exile Leader Out in Rift With U.S.," *New York Times* (April 10, 1963), p. 8.

21. "Spending Figure Disputed," *New York Times* (April 18, 1963), p. 12.

22. "Cuban Exile Chief Quits With Attack on Kennedy," *New York Times* (April 19, 1963), p. 1.

23. "Statement by Dr. Miro Cardona on His Resignation From Cuban Exile Council," published in full in the *New York Times* (April 19, 1963), p. 14.

24. Associated Press, "Cuban Exile Chief Accuses the U.S. of Defaming Him," *New York Times* (April 18, 1963), p. 1.

25. *FRUS 1961–1963*, vol. VI, p. 267.

26. *Memorandum for the Record: Subject: Report on Plots to Assassinate Fidel Castro*, prepared by the Inspector General and delivered in installments to the Director of Central Intelligence in April-May 1967; from Section 6, "Schemes in Early 1963." In an introduction to the report as printed by Prevailing Winds Research, Peter Dale Scott has written: "The IG Report was the result of an investigation ordered in 1967 by President Johnson, after a Drew Pearson–Jack Anderson column of March 7, 1967, had published for the first time details of 'a reported CIA plan in 1963 to assassinate Cuba's Fidel Castro.' However, Johnson never got to see the actual report: [CIA Director] Helms merely spoke to him from a set of notes which excluded the key events of late 1963."

27. Ibid.

28. Ibid.

29. Arthur M. Schlesinger, *Robert Kennedy and His Times* (New York: Ballantine Books, 1978), p. 583. See also introduction by Peter Kornbluh to "Kennedy and Castro: The Secret Quest for Accommodation; An Electronic Briefing Book" at the National Security Archive's web site: www.seas.gwu.edu/nsarchive.

30. Schlesinger, *Robert Kennedy*, p. 584.

31. From Richard Helm's secret May 1, 1963, CIA Memorandum on "Interview of U.S. Newswoman with Fidel Castro Indicating Possible Interest in Rapprochement with

the United States," which was declassified on June 19, 1996. Peter Kornbluh posted the document as part of his "Electronic Briefing Book."

32. Ibid.

33. Kornbluh, "JFK & Castro," p. 93.

34. Cited by Kornbluh, "JFK & Castro," p. 93.

35. Anthony Summers, *Not in Your Lifetime* (New York: Marlowe, 1998), pp. 220–21.

36. CIA memo to file from M. D. Stevens, dated January 31, 1964, document #1307-475. Cited by William Davy, *Let Justice Be Done: New Light on the Jim Garrison Investigation* (Reston, Va.: Jordan Publishing, 1999), p. 36.

37. New Orleans District Attorney interview of Gerald Patrick Hemming, May 8, 1968, as described by Davy, *Let Justice Be Done.*

38. Jim Garrison, *On the Trail of the Assassins* (New York: Warner Books, 1988), pp. 29–31, 46, 68.

39. Ibid., p. 46.

40. Anthony Summers, *Conspiracy* (New York: Paragon House, 1989), p. 291.

41. Daniel Campbell interview by Jim DiEugenio, September 3, 1994; cited by Davy, *Let Justice Be Done*, pp. 40 and 288.

42. Summers, *Not in Your Lifetime*, p. 229.

43. Ibid.

44. Ibid.

45. Ibid. Banister made a similar remark to George Higginbotham, another one of his infiltrators into suspect groups. When Higginbotham alerted his boss to Oswald's leafleting, Banister responded, "Cool it. One of them is one of mine." New Orleans District Attorney interviews with George Higginbotham, April 12, 16, 17, 1968; cited by Davy, *Let Justice Be Done*, pp. 41 and 288.

46. *Warren Commission Hearings (WCH)*, vol. 20, p. 515.

47. John Newman, *Oswald and the CIA* (New York: Carroll & Graf, 1995), pp. 312–13.

48. CIA memo, CI/R&A, Garrison and the Kennedy Assassination, June 1, 1967; cited by Newman, *Oswald and the CIA*, p. 325.

49. *Appendix to Hearings before the Select Committee on Assassinations of the U.S. House of Representatives* (HSCA), vol. 10, Anti-Castro Activities and Organizations, Investigation of the Assassination of President John F. Kennedy (Washington: U.S. Government Printing Office, 1979), p. 82.

50. Summers, *Not in Your Lifetime*, p. 216; citing HSCA testimony of Howard Hunt, Pt. II, November 3, 1978, p. 29, released under JFK Records Act.

51. *WCH*, vol. 10, p. 36.

52. Ibid., p. 37.

53. Ibid., pp. 37–38.

54. *WCH, Exhibits*, vol. 20, p. 527.

55. *WCH*, vol. 4, p. 435.

56. *President's Commission on the Assassination of President Kennedy: Report of Proceedings Held at Washington, D.C., Monday, January 27, 1964*; published by Harold Weisberg as *Whitewash IV: Top Secret JFK Assassination Transcript* (Frederick, Md.: 1974), p. 38; p. 129 of original transcript.

57. Ibid.

58. Ibid., p. 48; p. 139 of transcript.

59. *The Warren Commission Report* (New York: St. Martin's Press, 1992, from U.S. Government printing in 1964), p. 327.

60. Weisberg, *Whitewash IV*, p. 62; p. 153 of transcript.

61. Ibid., p. 52; p. 143 of transcript.

62. CIA memo dated May 23, 1968, part of the JFK collection at the National Archives; cited by Davy, *Let Justice Be Done*, p. 81.

63. *WCH*, vol. 11, pp. 167–68.

64. Ibid., p. 168.

65. *WCH, Exhibits*, vol. 21, p. 634.

66. Ibid., pp. 634–41.

67. Barbara Tomlinson, an early sixties organizer of the Seattle Fair Play for Cuba Committee, has described the means used to destroy her own FPCC chapter long before Oswald carried out his New Orleans charade. Over a year before JFK's assassination, Tomlinson received a mailing from the FPCC's New York headquarters promoting the speaking tour of a professor of anthropology and musicology who had visited Cuba, defying the U.S. embargo. The FPCC-sponsored professor would lecture and show slides on Afro-Cuban dance. When Tomlinson organized a Seattle meeting for the speaker, he began his presentation by insulting her. He then showed tourist slides from Brazil at a frantic pace, while garbling an unintelligible script that had no connection to Cuba. The impostor's presentation and behavior so disrupted Tomlinson's fragile coalition of Old Left activists and a few liberal Democrats that they managed only one more meeting before breaking up permanently. Tomlinson feels the FPCC national office must have been taken over by government agents even at that early stage for it to have been promoting a nationwide speaking tour by a provocateur. If so, the CIA would have known that it had no real FPCC to target in the summer and fall of 1963. Tomlinson's Seattle perspective supports the view that whatever Guy Banister told Oswald, the underlying purpose for Oswald's New Orleans theater would have had to lie beyond discrediting a sham organization. From Barbara Tomlinson's June 7 and 14, 2001, statements in Seattle to James Douglass.

68. *FRUS, 1961–1963*, Volume XI, *Cuban Missile Crisis & Aftermath October 1962– December 1963*, pp. 828–34, 837–38; also Mark J. White, *The Kennedys and Cuba: The Declassified Documentary History* (Chicago: Ivan R. Dee, 1999), pp. 324–31.

69. Carlos Lechuga, *In the Eye of the Storm* (Melbourne: Ocean Press, 1995), p. 104.

70. Sergei Khrushchev, *Nikita Khrushchev and the Making of a Superpower* (University Park, Pa.: Pennsylvania State University Press, 2000), p. 642.

71. Fidel Castro, Address to the Tripartite Conference on the Cuban Missile Crisis, January 11, 1992; Laurence Chang and Peter Kornbluh, editors, *The Cuban Missile Crisis, 1962* (New York: New Press, 1992), p. 343.

72. Nikita Khrushchev's January 31, 1963, Letter to Fidel Castro; Chang and Kornbluh, *Cuban Missile Crisis*, p. 319.

73. Ibid.

74. Ibid.

75. Ibid., p. 327.

76. S. Krushchev, *Nikita Khrushchev and the Making of a Superpower*, p. 659.

77. Castro's January 11, 1992, Address, Chang and Kornbluh, *Cuban Missile Crisis*, p. 344.

78. S. Krushchev, *Nikita Khrushchev and the Making of a Superpower*, p. 659.

79. Chang and Kornbluh, *Cuban Missile Crisis*, p. 344.

80. Richard Helms, Memorandum for the Director of Central Intelligence on "Reported Desire of the Cuban Government for Rapprochement with the United States," June 5, 1963; Peter Kornbluh, "Electronic Briefing Book."

81. United States Senate Select Committee to Study Governmental Operations with Respect to Intelligence Activities (Church Committee), *The Investigation of the Assassination of President John F. Kennedy: Performance of the Intelligence Agencies: Final Report* (Washington: U.S. Government Printing Office, 1976), p. 14.

82. Ibid. "Fidel Says Cuba Will Fight Back," *Miami Herald* (September 9, 1963), p. 1A.

83. "Interview of Fidel Castro Ruz," *Investigation of the Assassination of President John F. Kennedy: Hearings before the HSCA* (Washington: U.S. Government Printing Office, 1978–79), vol. 3, p. 216.

84. Lisa Howard, "Castro's Overture," *War/Peace Report* (September 1963), pp. 3–5; cited by Kornbluh, "JFK & Castro," p. 90.

85. Ibid.

86. United States Senate Select Committee to Study Government Operations with Respect to Intelligence Activities, Executive Session, July 10, 1975, Testimony of William Attwood.

87. "Memorandum by William Attwood," Washington, September 18, 1963, *FRUS, 1961–1963*, vol. XI, p. 870.

88. Ibid.

89. William Attwood noted President Kennedy's September 20 approval for him to make the initial "discreet contact" with Cuba's UN ambassador Carlos Lechuga in his November 8, 1963, memorandum to Gordon Chase of the National Security Council staff, *FRUS, 1961–1963*, vol. XI, p. 880.

90. William Attwood, *The Twilight Struggle: Tales of the Cold War* (New York: Harper & Row, 1987), p. 259.

91. Lechuga, *In the Eye of the Storm*, p. 197.

92. Ibid., p. 198.

93. Ibid., p. 199.

94. Ibid., p. 200.

95. Attwood, *Twilight Struggle*, pp. 259–60.

96. Ibid., p. 260.

97. Ibid. See also Attwood's November 8, 1963, Memorandum to Gordon Chase. *FRUS, 1961–1963*, vol. XI, p. 881.

98. Attwood, *Twilight Struggle*, p. 260.

99. Attwood's Memorandum to Chase, *FRUS, 1961–1963*, vol. XI, p. 881.

100. Attwood, *Twilight Struggle*, p. 260.

101. Ibid. Also Lechuga, *In the Eye of the Storm*, p. 205.

102. Attwood to Chase, *FRUS, 1961–1963*, vol. XI, p. 882.

103. Ibid.

104. William Attwood, *The Reds and the Blacks: A Personal Adventure* (London: Hutchinson, 1967), p. 261.

105. Jean Daniel, "Unofficial Envoy: An Historic Report from Two Capitals," *New Republic* (December 14, 1963), p. 16.

106. Ibid.

107. Ibid.

108. Ibid., p. 17.

109. Ibid.

110. Fonzi, *Last Investigation*, pp. 141–42. Veciana also described the Bishop–Oswald meeting to author Dick Russell, who included it in *The Man Who Knew Too Much*, p. 417.

111. Fonzi, *Last Investigation*, p. 142.

112. Ibid., p. 396. In *The Last Investigation* Gaeton Fonzi proved through witnesses who knew David Atlee Phillips and a wealth of circumstantial evidence that he was indeed Maurice Bishop (pp. 304–65).

113. Author's interview of Antonio Veciana, Sr., November 14, 2007. Translation by Antonio Veciana, Jr. On the assassination of President Kennedy, Mr. Veciana said, "For me there is no question that it was a conspiracy, and Fidel Castro had nothing to do with it." Ibid.

114. Fonzi, *Last Investigation*, p. 266.

115. Ibid., p. 428.

116. *Warren Report*, pp. 733–36.

117. Dan Hardway and Edwin Lopez, *Lee Harvey Oswald, the CIA and Mexico City* (top secret HSCA report declassified gradually in the mid-nineties and known to researchers as the *Lopez Report*), pp. 12, 31.

118. Ibid., p. 53.

119. The following analysis of CIA documents on Oswald in Mexico City draws especially on the work of John Newman, particularly his "Mexico City—a New Analysis," a

presentation made at the "November in Dallas" JFK Lancer Conference, November 19, 1999; at www.jfk lancer.com/backes/newman. See also Newman, *Oswald and the CIA,* pp. 352–419.

120. Cable from Mexico City to Director, CIA, October 8, 1963; CIA 201-289248; JFK 104-10015-10047. Newman, *Oswald and the CIA,* p. 509. Also James P. Hosty, Jr., *Assignment, Oswald* (New York: Arcade, 1996), p. 279. Unless stated otherwise, the documents I have cited in this analysis are linked, according to their JFK numbers, to the above Newman transcript.

121. Clarence M. Kelley and James Kirkpatrick Davis, *Kelley: The Story of an FBI Director* (Kansas City: Andrews, McMeel & Parker, 1987), p. 268.

122. Marina Oswald thought her husband's Russian was "colloquial and idiomatic." Priscilla Johnson McMillan, *Marina and Lee* (New York: Bantam, 1978), p. 156. McMillan's book explains Lee Oswald's proficiency in Russian, by the time he met Marina, by his previous year and a half in the Soviet Union, where his co-workers at the Minsk Radio Plant had especially helped him with the language. However, the Warren Commission's general counsel J. Lee Rankin told the commission members at a closed-door meeting that "we are trying . . . to find out what [Oswald] studied at the Monterey School of the Army in the way of languages," suggesting Oswald received the kind of expert assistance in Russian given to the U.S. military's counterintelligence agents. January 27, 1964, Meeting; Weisberg, *Whitewash IV,* p. 101; p. 192 of original transcript. As Harold Weisberg notes, "Neither the [Warren] Report nor Oswald's service records refer to this language schooling." Ibid.

123. Newman, *Oswald and the CIA,* p. 509.

124. CIA Director to Mexico City, October 10, 1963. Reproduced in Newman, *Oswald and the CIA,* p. 512.

125. Cable from CIA to Department of State, FBI, and Navy, October 10, 1963; CIA 201-289248; JFK 104-10015-10052.

126. Memorandum from CIA Deputy Director, Plans, to Director, FBI, November 23, 1963; CIA 201-289248; JFK 104-10004-10257.

127. The witnesses are divided on whether it was the real Oswald or not who visited the two consulates. The Cuban consul Eusebio Azcue, who had argued with the man in the consulate, saw a newsreel film two or three weeks after the assassination that showed Jack Ruby shooting Oswald (Summers, *Not in Your Lifetime,* pp. 265–66). Azcue told the HSCA on April 1, 1978, that "the man Jack Ruby shot in the Dallas Police Station was not the same individual who had visited the Cuban Consulate in 1963" (*Lopez Report,* p. 202).

Alfredo Mirabal, Azcue's colleague and successor, had "caught only glimpses of the man" at the consulate. Nevertheless he thought "the person whose picture appears on Lee Harvey Oswald's visa application [a genuine photo of Oswald] was the same Lee Harvey Oswald who visited the Consulate" (Alfredo Mirabal Diaz to the HSCA, September 18, 1978; *Lopez Report,* pp. 205–6).

Silvia Duran, the Mexican employee at the Cuban Consulate who had dealt with Oswald at length, was arrested by the Mexican government at the request of the CIA's Mexico City Station on November 23, 1963. Duran was held incommunicado and questioned intensively (*Lopez Report,* pp. 184–85). Her signed statement to the Mexican police that was forwarded to the Mexico City Station on November 27, 1963, stated in part: "When she became aware [from news reports] that the assassin was Lee Harvey Oswald, she ascertained that it was the same man who approximately two months prior had been to the Cuban Consulate to solicit an intransit visa to Russia. Having taken his name from the special documentation he presented she knew that he was married to a Russian woman and belonged to the 'Fair Play for Cuba Committee.' She checked the data in the Consulate archives and became certain that it was the same individual who was blonde, short, dressed unelegantly and whose face turned red when angry" (*Lopez Report,* p. 186). She also said she gave Oswald her business phone number but "he never called back" (ibid., p. 187).

When the CIA in turn forwarded a copy of Duran's statement to the Warren Commission, it had deleted her description of Oswald as blond and short (which was in conflict with the Oswald arrested in Dallas, who had brown hair and was five feet nine inches tall). It had also changed her strong statement that "he never called back" to "she does not recall whether or not Oswald later telephoned her at the Consulate number that she gave him." When the authors of the *Lopez Report* noted these changes, they observed, "Had the [original] statements been included, the Warren Commission's conclusions would not have seemed as strong" (*Lopez Report*, pp. 186–87, 90).

In 1979 after watching the film of an Oswald interview in New Orleans, Silvia Duran told author Anthony Summers she was not sure if that was the same man she had interviewed or not (Summers, *Not in Your Lifetime*, p. 267).

Col. Oleg Nechiporenko, the KGB's vice consul at the Soviet Consulate, thought "the Oswald he met in Mexico City was the same one who was in Dallas" (Gerald Nadler, "The KGB Spies Who Came in for the Gold," *Washington Times*, May 27, 1992, p. A1). In his memoir *Passport to Assassination*, Nechiporenko's view is supported by his fellow KGB officer at the consulate who also met Oswald, the notorious Valery Kostikov (Col. Oleg Maximovich Nechiporenko, *Passport to Assassination: The Never-Before-Told Story of Lee Harvey Oswald by the KGB Colonel Who Knew Him* [New York: Birch Lane Press, 1993], p. 76).

128. Memorandum from FBI Liaison to Liaison Section Chief, September, 18, 1963; cited by Church Committee, *Investigation of the Assassination of President John F. Kennedy*, p. 65.

129. The FBI memorandum continued: "CIA is also giving some thought to planting deceptive information which might embarrass the [Fair Play for Cuba] Committee in areas where it does have some support.

"Pursuant to a discussion with the Liaison Agent, [censored name of a middle level CIA official working on anti-Castro propaganda] advised that his Agency will not take action without first consulting with the Bureau, bearing in mind that we wish to make certain the CIA activity will not jeopardize any Bureau investigation." Ibid. This assurance of CIA cooperation with the FBI in what turned out to be a Mexico City subplot of President Kennedy's assassination was, as J. Edgar Hoover would soon learn, without any foundation.

130. Summers, *Not in Your Lifetime*, p. 263.

131. *Lopez Report*, p. 192.

132. Ibid., p. 194.

133. Summers, *Not in Your Lifetime*, p. 264.

134. *Lopez Report*, p. 194.

135. Nechiporenko, *Passport*, p. 67.

136. Ibid., p. 70.

137. Ibid.

138. Ibid., p. 77.

139. Ibid., p. 81.

140. Silvia Duran to the Mexican Police, November 23, 1963, in Newman, *Oswald and the CIA*, p. 407; Silvia Duran's HSCA testimony, HSCA, vol. III, pp. 30–31, 49–51, cited in Newman, *Oswald and the CIA*, pp. 409–12; Silvia Duran to author Anthony Summers, January 31, 1995, in Newman, *Oswald and the CIA*, p. 368.

141. Nechiporenko, remarks in a special interview with American researchers at the 1993 Assassination Symposium on John Kennedy, in Newman, *Oswald and the CIA*, p. 368.

142. CIA 201-289248; JFK 104-10004-10257. For legibility I have added paragraph indentations to the CIA's run-on transcript.

143. Newman, "Mexico City—A New Analysis."

144. Michael R. Beschloss, editor, *Taking Charge: The Johnson White House Tapes, 1963–64* (New York: Simon & Schuster, 1997), p. 22.

145. Commission Exhibit 15, *WCH*, vol. 16, p. 33.

146. Beschloss, *Taking Charge*, p. 23.

147. Emphasis added. A copy of the FBI memorandum with Hoover's written comment on it is on p. 5 of John Newman's article, "Oswald, the CIA and Mexico City: Fingerprints of Conspiracy," *Probe* (September-October 1999).

148. The CIA also claimed in retrospect that its surveillance cameras had failed to photograph Oswald on any of his five trips to the Cuban and Soviet Embassies. HSCA investigators were blocked by the CIA from access to its surveillance photos (*Lopez Report*, pp. 90–91). Yet even CIA witnesses were skeptical of the agency's claim: "CIA officers who were in Mexico in 1963 and their Headquarters counterparts generally agreed that it would have been unlikely for the photosurveillance operations to have missed ten opportunities to have photographed Oswald" (ibid., p. 91).

Also arguing against the CIA's claim was its surveillance cameras' success in taking pictures at the Soviet Embassy in October 1963 of the mystery man who was not Oswald, yet who corresponded to the October 8 CIA cable's wrong description of Oswald as "apparent age 35, athletic build, circa 6 feet, receding hairline, balding top." Freedom of Information lawsuits have forced the CIA to surrender twelve photographs of this man. These photos provide further evidence of an Oswald impostor. The CIA has never identified the man. Bernard Fensterwald, Jr., *Coincidence or Conspiracy?* (New York: Zebra Books, 1977), p. 400.

149. CIA 201-289248; JFK 104-10015-10124. See also *Lopez Report*, p. 164, with reference to MEXI 7023, November 23, 1963, para. 2.

150. CIA 201-289248; JFK 104-11015-10082. See also *Lopez Report*, p. 164, with reference to MEXI 7054, November 24, 1963, para. 3.

151. *Lopez Report*, pp. 164, 183–84.

152. Nicholas deB. Katzenbach, "Memorandum for Mr. Moyers," November 25, 1963; in E. Martin Schotz, *History Will Not Absolve Us: Orwellian Control, Public Denial and the Murder of President Kennedy* (Brookline, Mass.: Kurtz, Ulmer & DeLucia, 1996), p. 188. Also *Investigation of the Assassination of President John F. Kennedy: Hearings before the HSCA,* vol. 3, pp. 566–67.

153. Ibid., p. 189.

154. Beschloss, *Taking Charge*, p. 72 (emphasis in original).

155. Ibid., pp. 67, 69.

156. Attwood's Memorandum to Chase, *FRUS, 1961–1963,* vol. XI, p. 882.

157. Ibid.

158. Ibid.

159. Ibid.

160. Ibid.

161. "Memorandum from William Attwood to Gordon Chase of the National Security Council Staff," November 22, 1963, *FRUS, 1961–1963,* vol. XI, p. 892.

162. Ibid., pp. 892–93.

163. Ibid., p. 893.

164. Ibid.

165. Attwood, *Twilight Struggle*, p. 262.

166. Daniel, "Unofficial Envoy," p. 17.

167. Ibid., pp. 17–18.

168. Ibid., pp. 18–19 (emphasis in original).

169. Ibid., p. 19.

170. Ibid.

171. Ibid., p. 20; Jean Daniel, "When Castro Heard the News," *New Republic* (December 7, 1963), p. 7.

172. Daniel, "When Castro Heard the News," p. 7.

173. Ibid.

174. Ibid.

175. Ibid.

176. Ibid.

177. Beschloss, *Twilight Struggle*, p. 263.

178. Ibid.

179. Memorandum from Gordon Chase of the National Security Council Staff to the President's Special Assistant for National Security Affairs (Bundy), November 25, 1963, *FRUS, 1961–1963*, vol. XI, p. 890.

180. Ibid.

181. Ibid.

182. Attwood, *Twilight Struggle*, p. 263.

183. Ibid.

184. Kornbluh, "JFK and Castro," p. 97 (emphasis in original). These are the paragraphs that are numbered 3, 4, and 6 in the six-paragraph Castro memorandum. Of the other paragraphs, 1 asks Howard to assure Johnson of Castro's desire that he win the presidential election (against a presumably more conservative opponent), adding the ironic comment: "if there is anything I can do to add to his majority (aside from retiring from politics), I shall be happy to cooperate." Paragraph 2 is Castro's offer to cancel a Cuban act of retaliation to any "necessary" act of hostility by the president while seeking election, a paragraph I am about to quote. Paragraph 5 cautions Johnson that "he should not interpret my conciliatory attitude, my desire for discussions, as a sign of weakness. Such an interpretation would be a serious miscalculation . . ." Ibid.

185. Ibid., pp. 97–98. Castro showed his good faith behind this extraordinary no-retaliation proposal by his response to an incident described by Peter Kornbluh: "When a Marine at Guantanamo shot a Cuban on the base, Castro used this channel [via Lisa Howard and Adlai Stevenson] to inquire if the incident had been an isolated act or a provocation. After informing President Johnson, Bundy authorized Stevenson to tell Howard to tell Castro that there was no plan of provocation at the base, and the episode was contained."

186. Ibid.

187. Ibid., p. 98.

188. Ibid.

189. Frank Mankiewicz and Kirby Jones, *With Fidel: A Portrait of Castro and Cuba* (Chicago: Playboy Press, 1975), p. 173.

3. JFK and Vietnam

1. Richard D. Mahoney, *JFK: Ordeal in Africa* (New York: Oxford University Press, 1983), p. 108.

2. From an interview with Edmund Gullion by Richard Reeves, *President Kennedy: Profile of Power* (New York: Touchstone, 1993), p. 254.

3. National Security Action Memorandum No. 263, October 11, 1963, *Foreign Relations of the United States (FRUS), 1961–1963, Volume IV: Vietnam: August-December 1963* (Washington: U.S. Government Printing Office, 1991), p. 396.

4. *Pacific Stars and Stripes* (October 4, 1963), p. 1.

5. *New York Times* (November 16, 1963), p. 1.

6. *The Pentagon Papers: The Defense Department History of United States Decision Making on Vietnam, Senator Gravel Edition*, 5 vols. (Boston: Beacon Press, 1972), vol. 2, p. 303.

7. From Thomas Merton's January 18, 1962, letter to W. H. Ferry, in *Letters from Tom: A Selection of Letters from Father Thomas Merton, Monk of Gethsemani, to W. H. Ferry, 1961–1968*, edited by W. H. Ferry (Scarsdale, N.Y.: Fort Hill Press, 1983), p. 15.

8. Paul B. Fay, Jr., *The Pleasure of His Company* (New York: Dell, 1966), pp. 162–63.

9. Drew Pearson, "Kennedy Has Chance to End the Cold War," *Washington Merry-Go-Round* (January 23, 1963; syndicated in numerous U.S. newspapers).

10. *Public Papers of the Presidents: John F. Kennedy, 1963* (Washington: U.S. Government Printing Office, 1964), p. 268.

11. Memorandum for the Secretary of Defense, March 13, 1962; "Subject: Justification for US Military Intervention in Cuba (Top Secret)"; L. L. Lemnitzer, Chairman, Joint Chiefs of Staff; pp. 7–9. Available at http://www.gwu.edu/~nsarchiv/news/20010430/northwoods.pdf.

12. Ibid.

13. Ibid., p. l.

14. James Bamford, *Body of Secrets: Anatomy of the Ultra-secret National Security Agency: From the Cold War through the Dawn of a New Century* (New York: Doubleday, 2001), pp. 86–87. It was Bamford who discovered and first cited parts of "Operation Northwoods." Ibid., pp. 82–86.

15. *Foreign Relations of the United States (FRUS), 1961–1963, Volume X, Cuba 1961–1962* (Washington: U.S. Government Printing Office, 1997), p. 771.

16. Bamford, *Body of Secrets*, p. 87.

17. *Foreign Relations of the United States (FRUS), 1961–1963, Volume XXIV, Laos Crisis* (Washington: U.S. Government Printing Office, 1994), p. 21.

18. Ibid., pp. 19, 21.

19. Kenneth P. O'Donnell and David F. Powers, *"Johnny, We Hardly Knew Ye"* (Boston: Little, Brown, 1970), p. 244.

20. *Pentagon Papers*, vol. 2, p. 18.

21. Ibid.

22. Winthrop Brown, oral history interview in 1968 by Larry J. Hackman, 14–15, JFK Library. Cited by Edmund F. Wehrle, "'A Good, Bad Deal': John F. Kennedy, W. Averell Harriman, and the Neutralization of Laos, 1961–1962," *Pacific Historical Review* (August 1998), p. 355.

23. Roger Hilsman, *To Move a Nation: The Politics of Foreign Policy in the Administration of John F. Kennedy* (New York: Delta, 1964), p. 115.

24. *FRUS, 1961–1963*, vol. XXIV, pp. 45–47.

25. Wehrle, "Good, Bad Deal," p. 355.

26. *FRUS, 1961–1963*, vol. XXIV, p. 74.

27. Ibid., p. 77.

28. Ibid., p. 80, text for March 10, 1961, meeting between Khrushchev and Thompson; also footnote 2.

29. Ibid.

30. Ibid., p. 100.

31. Ibid.

32. Theodore C. Sorensen, *Kennedy* (New York: Konecky & Konecky, 1966), p. 641.

33. Chalmers M. Roberts, *First Rough Draft: A Journalist's Journal of Our Times* (New York: Praeger, 1973), p. 194.

34. Sorensen, *Kennedy*, p. 643.

35. Charles A. Stevenson, *The End of Nowhere: American Policy toward Laos since 1954* (Boston: Beacon Press, 1972), p. 151.

36. Arthur M. Schlesinger, Jr., *A Thousand Days* (Boston: Houghton Mifflin, 1965), p. 339.

37. Lawrence Freedman, *Kennedy's Wars: Berlin, Cuba, Laos, and Vietnam* (Oxford: Oxford University Press, 2000), p. 302.

38. Ibid.

39. *FRUS, 1961–1963*, vol. XXIV, p. 153.

40. Schlesinger, *Thousand Days*, p. 338.

41. Ibid.

42. Stevenson, *End of Nowhere*, p. 150.

43. Schlesinger, *Thousand Days*, p. 339.

44. Arthur M. Schlesinger, Jr., *Robert Kennedy and His Times* (New York: Ballentine Books, 1978), p. 760.

45. JFK, memorandum of conversation, April 28, 1961, JFK Papers; cited by Schlesinger, Robert Kennedy, p. 759.

46. Bernard Fensterwald, "The Case of Secret Service Agent Abraham W. Bolden," *Computers and Automation* (June 1971), p. 41.

47. Ibid.

48. Abraham Bolden, interview by author, July 2, 1998.

49. Ibid.

50. Abraham Bolden, interview by author, June 16, 2001. Also Fensterwald, "Case of Secret Service," p. 41.

51. Stevenson, *End of Nowhere*, p. 154.

52. Evelyn Lincoln, *My Twelve Years with John F. Kennedy* (New York: Bantam Books, 1966), p. 230.

53. *FRUS, 1961–1963*, vol. XXIV, p. 226.

54. Ibid., p. 228.

55. Ibid.

56. Ibid., p. 234.

57. Averell Harriman, interview by Charles A. Stevenson; cited in Stevenson, *End of Nowhere*, p. 154.

58. William J. Rust, *Kennedy in Vietnam* (New York: Charles Scribner's Sons, 1985), pp. 3, 13.

59. *Pentagon Papers*, vol. 2, p. 22.

60. Ibid.

61. Ibid., pp. 56–57.

62. Ibid., p. 59.

63. Ibid., p. 65.

64. Ibid., p. 66.

65. Ibid., p. 67.

66. Ibid.

67. Schlesinger, *Thousand Days*, p. 544.

68. *Pentagon Papers*, vol. 2, p. 70.

69. Ibid., p. 88.

70. Ibid., p. 90.

71. Ibid., pp. 90–91.

72. Ibid., p. 108.

73. Maxwell Taylor, in recorded interview by L. J. Hackman, November 13, 1969, 47; cited by Schlesinger, *Robert Kennedy*, p. 761.

74. Cited in Schlesinger, *Robert Kennedy*, p. 82.

75. Ibid.

76. Schlesinger, *Thousand Days*, p. 547.

77. Daniel Ellsberg, *Secrets: A Memoir of Vietnam and the Pentagon Papers* (New York: Viking, 2002), p. 193.

78. Ibid., p. 194.

79. Ibid., p. 195.

80. Ibid., p. 196 (emphasis in original).

81. Ibid.

82. Reeves, *President Kennedy: Profile of Power*, p. 222.

83. From Richard Reeves's interview of Roswell Gilpatric, in ibid.

84. Raymond L. Garthoff, "Berlin 1961: The Record Corrected," *Foreign Policy* no. 84 (Fall 1991), p. 147.

85. Reeves, *President Kennedy: Profile of Power*, p. 249.

86. Garthoff, "Berlin 1961," pp. 147–48, 152.

87. Sergei Khrushchev, *Nikita Khrushchev and the Creation of a Superpower* (University Park, Pa.: Pennsylvania State University, 2000), p. 464.

88. Ibid., p. 461.

89. Pierre Salinger, *With Kennedy* (Garden City, N.Y.: Doubleday, 1966), p. 191.

90. Ibid.

91. Ibid., p. 192.

92. Ibid., p. 193.

93. Ibid., p. 194.

94. *Public Papers of the Presidents: John F. Kennedy, 1961*, p. 387.

95. S. Khrushchev, *Nikita Khrushchev*, p. 464.

96. Michael R. Beschloss, *The Crisis Years: Kennedy and Khrushchev* (New York: Edward Burlingame Books, 1991), p. 335.

97. Ibid., p. 334.

98. *Robert Kennedy in His Own Words*, edited by Edwin O. Guthman and Jeffrey Shulman (New York: Bantam Books, 1988), pp. 259–60. See also Garthoff, "Berlin 1961," p. 150, and S. Khrushchev, *Nikita Khrushchev*, p. 466.

99. Clay-Rusk telegram, November 13, 1961; in *FRUS, 1961–1963, Volume XIV: Berlin Crisis, 1961–1962* (Washington: U.S. Government Printing Office, 1994), p. 586.

100. *Public Papers of the Presidents: John F. Kennedy, 1961*, p. 1.

101. Ibid., p. 2.

102. *FRUS, 1961–1963*, vol. VI, p. 43.

103. Ibid., p. 37.

104. Ibid., p. 44.

105. Ibid.

106. Ibid., p. 60.

107. Ibid., p. 63.

108. Ibid.

109. *FRUS, 1961–1963*, vol. XXIV, pp. 398–99.

110. Schlesinger, *Thousand Days*, p. 428.

111. Cited by Timothy N. Castle, *At War in the Shadow of Vietnam: U.S. Military Aid to the Royal Lao Government, 1955–1975* (New York: Columbia University Press, 1993), p. 54.

112. Schlesinger, *Thousand Days*, p. 427.

113. Walt Haney, "The Pentagon Papers and the United States Involvement in Laos," in *Pentagon Papers*, vol. 5, p. 264.

114. Hugh Toye summarizing the *Times*' articles of May 24 and 31, 1962, in his *Laos: Buffer State or Battleground* (London: Oxford University Press, 1968), p. 184.

115. *The Times* (May 31, 1962), cited by Toye, *Laos*, pp. 184–85.

116. Haney, "Pentagon Papers," p. 264.

117. Stevenson, *End of Nowhere*, p. 170.

118. Ibid., p. 154.

119. Rudy Abramson, *Spanning the Century: The Life of W. Averell Harriman, 1891–1986* (New York: William Morrow, 1992), pp. 586–87.

120. Ibid., p. 587.

121. Ibid.

122. From the journal of Arthur M. Schlesinger, Jr., May 14, 1962; cited in *Robert Kennedy and His Times*, p. 758.

123. *FRUS, 1961–1963, Volume II, Vietnam 1962* (Washington: U.S. Government Printing Office, 1990), p. 298.

124. Ibid., p. 297.

125. Cited by John M. Newman, *JFK and Vietnam: Deception, Intrigue, and the Struggle for Power* (New York: Warner Books, 1992), p. 236.

126. *FRUS, 1961–1963*, vol. II, p.327.

127. Ibid., p. 309.

128. Ibid.

129. The official State Department volume that published the memorandum recording the Kennedy–Harriman conversation on April 6, 1962, states in a footnote: "The instructions referred to here [as ordered by the President] have not been found." *FRUS, 1961–1963,* vol. II, p. 309.

130. Gareth Porter, *Perils of Dominance* (Berkeley: University of California Press, 2005), p. 158.

131. Ibid., p. 159.

132. John Kenneth Galbraith confirmed to a *Boston Globe* reporter in 2005 that he never received President Kennedy's instructions for the mutual de-escalation proposal for North Vietnam. Bryan Bender, "Papers Reveal JFK Efforts on Vietnam," *Boston Globe* (June 6, 2005).

133. *FRUS, 1961–1963,* vol. II, p. 310.

134. George Allen, interview by John M. Newman, August 10, 1987; cited by Newman, *JFK and Vietnam,* pp. 254, 264–66. Also George Allen, *The Indochina Wars: 1950–1975* (unpublished manuscript).

135. Newman, *JFK and Vietnam,* p. 265.

136. Allen interview cited by Newman, *JFK and Vietnam,* p. 254.

137. Ibid.

138. Ibid.

139. Allen, *Indochina Wars,* p. 192; cited by Newman, *JFK and Vietnam,* p. 254.

140. John Kenneth Galbraith, *A Life in Our Times* (Boston: Houghton Mifflin, 1981), p. 469.

141. Ibid., p. 406.

142. *FRUS, 1961–1963,* vol. II, p. 549.

143. *Pentagon Papers,* vol. 2, p. 175.

144. Ibid., p. 176.

145. Unlike the military chiefs ordered to draw up Kennedy's withdrawal plan, the *Pentagon Papers* identify it explicitly as "Phased Withdrawal of U.S. Forces, 1962–1964." Ibid., pp. 160–200.

146. *FRUS, 1961–1963,* vol. II, pp. 673–75.

147. Ibid., p. 607.

148. Ibid., p. 566.

149. Ibid., p. 587.

150. Ibid., p. 675.

151. Ibid., p. 690.

152. Gregory Allen Olson, *Mansfield and Vietnam: A Study in Rhetorical Adaptation* (East Lansing: Michigan State University Press, 1995), p. 2.

153. *FRUS, 1961–1963,* vol. II, p. 779.

154. Ibid., p. 782.

155. Ibid., pp. 782–83.

156. O'Donnell and Powers, *"Johnny, We Hardly Knew Ye,"* p. 15.

157. Isaiah Berlin oral history, John F. Kennedy Library. Cited by David Kaiser, *American Tragedy: Kennedy, Johnson, and the Origins of the Vietnam War* (Cambridge: Belknap Press of Harvard University Press, 2000), p. 41.

158. John Kenneth Galbraith, *Ambassador's Journal: A Personal Account of the Kennedy Years* (Boston: Houghton Mifflin, 1969), p. 632.

159. Cited by Roberts, *First Rough Draft,* p. 221.

160. Roger Hilsman, letter to the *New York Times,* January 20, 1992.

161. *FRUS, 1961–1963,* Volume III: *Vietnam, January-August 1963* (Washington: U.S. Government Printing Office, 1991), p. 63. Hilsman letter to the *New York Times.*

162. Hilsman Letter, ibid. *FRUS, 1961–1963,* vol. III, p. 63.

163. O'Donnell and Powers, *"Johnny, We Hardly Knew Ye,"* p. 16.

164. *FRUS, 1961–1963,* vol. III, p. 268.

165. *Pentagon Papers,* vol. 2, p. 180.

166. Ibid.

167. April 3, 1963, Memorandum by Assistant Secretary of State-designate Roger Hilsman to Frederick G. Dutton, Assistant Secretary of State for Congressional Affairs. *FRUS, 1961–1963,* vol. III, p. 124.

168. Ibid., p. 153.

169. Ibid.

170. Ibid., pp. 208, 211.

171. Ibid. Also Francis X. Winters, *The Year of the Hare: America in Vietnam, January 25, 1963-February 15, 1964* (Athens: University of Georgia Press, 1999), p. 26.

172. Ibid., p. 208.

173. *FRUS, 1961–1963,* vol. III, p. 224; Winters, *Year of the Hare,* p. 27.

174. *FRUS, 1961–1963,* vol. III, p. 223.

175. *Pentagon Papers,* vol. 2, p. 724.

176. William Colby, *Honorable Men: My Life in the CIA* (New York: Simon & Schuster, 1978), p. 178.

177. Cited by Do Tho, Diem's aide-de-camp, in *Hoa Binh* (July 5, 1970); Ellen J. Hammer, *A Death in November: America in Vietnam, 1963* (New York: E. P. Dutton, 1987), p. 121.

178. Marguerite Higgins, *Our Vietnam Nightmare* (New York: Harper & Row, 1965), p. 91.

179. Hammer, *Death in November,* p. 112; Higgins, *Our Vietnam Nightmare,* p. 93.

180. *Report of the United Nations Fact-Finding Mission to South Viet-Nam* (United Nations Document A/5630, December 7, 1963).

181. Cited by Higgins, *Our Vietnam Nightmare,* pp. 90–91.

182. *UN Report,* p. 74.

183. Hammer, *Death in November,* p. 114.

184. "A Bomb Makes a Shambles of a Sunny Saigon Square," *Life* (January 28, 1952), p. 19.

185. Tillman Durdin, "Reds' Time Bombs Rip Saigon Center," *New York Times* (January 10, 1952), p. 2.

186. Graham Greene, *Ways of Escape* (New York: Simon & Schuster, 1980), p. 171.

187. H. Bruce Franklin explained the historical events underlying *The Quiet American* in his article "Our Man in Saigon," *The Nation* (February 3, 2003), pp. 43–44.

188. In the 2002 Penguin paperback edition of *The Quiet American,* Greene's references to the CIA's plastic explosive appear on pages 72, 74, 96, 129, 133, 143 (twice), 154, 160, and 183. At the time of the Saigon bombing in 1952, the CIA was only five years old and virtually unknown. Thus, the novel's narrator, Fowler, at one point asks a well-informed Saigon contact what U.S. agency the quiet American, Pyle, is really working for:

"What is he? O.S.S.?" [Office of Strategic Services, U.S. predecessor to the CIA]

The man responds:

"The initial letters are not very important. I think now they are different" (Penguin edition, p. 173).

When Greene discussed *The Quiet American* in 1979 in his conversations with French writer Marie-Francoise Allain (published later in English as *The Other Man*), he named the CIA as the source of the Saigon bomb: "One could put a finger on a number of operations set in hand by the CIA (the CIA was behind the bomb attack in the Saigon square which I mentioned in the novel, for example)." Marie-Francoise Allain, *The Other Man: Conversations with Graham Greene* (New York: Simon & Schuster, 1983), p. 96.

189. Lemnitzer, March 13, 1962, Memorandum to McNamara; p. 9. See note 11 in this chapter for "Operation Northwoods."

190. Hammer on the Catholic newspaper *Hoa Binh*'s reconstruction of the May 8, 1963, events; *Death in November,* p. 116.

191. Ibid. Hammer wrote that she had "been unable to prove or disprove the truth of this account."

192. *FRUS, 1961–1963,* vol. III, pp. 311–12; Hammer, *Death in November,* pp. 117–18.

193. Warren Unna, "Viet-Nam Wants 50% of GIs Out," *Washington Post* (May 12, 1963), p. A1.

194. Ibid.

195. Ibid.

196. Ibid., p. A14.

197. Ibid., p. A1.

198. Ibid., p. A14.

199. Ibid., pp. A1, A14.

200. Editorial, "U.S. and South Viet-Nam," *Washington Post* (May 14, 1963), p. A18.

201. *FRUS, 1961–1963,* vol. III, p. 295.

202. Ibid.

203. *Public Papers of the Presidents: John F. Kennedy, 1963,* p. 421.

204. Ibid. (emphasis added).

205. David Halberstam, *The Making of a Quagmire* (New York: Random House, 1965), p. 202 (emphasis in original).

206. *FRUS, 1961–1963,* vol. III, pp. 310–12.

207. Michael Charlton and Anthony Moncrieff, *Many Reasons Why: The American Involvement in Vietnam* (New York: Hill & Wang, 1978), p. 84.

208. O'Donnell and Powers, *"Johnny, We Hardly Knew Ye,"* p. 18.

4. Marked Out for Assassination

1. Robert F. Kennedy, "Foreword to the Memorial Edition," December 18, 1963; John F. Kennedy, *Profiles in Courage* (New York: Harper Perennial, 1988), p. xii.

2. Benjamin C. Bradlee, *Conversations with Kennedy* (New York: W. W. Norton, 1975), p. 150.

3. RFK, "Foreword," p. xi.

4. Ibid., p. xv.

5. JFK, *Profiles,* p. xix.

6. Ibid., p. 244.

7. Dwight D. Eisenhower, "Farewell Address"; Louis Filler, editor, *The President Speaks: From William McKinley to Lyndon B. Johnson* (New York: Capricorn Books, 1965), pp. 367–68.

8. Hugh Brogan, *Kennedy* (Harlow, England: Pearson Education Limited, 1996), p. 105.

9. *Public Papers of the Presidents: John F. Kennedy, 1962* (Washington: U.S. Government Printing Office, 1963), p. 284.

10. Theodore C. Sorensen, *Kennedy* (New York: Konecky & Konecky, 1966), p. 447.

11. Bradlee, *Conversations with Kennedy,* p. 76.

12. Richard Reeves, *President Kennedy: Profile of Power* (New York: Touchstone, 1993), p. 296.

13. Bradlee, *Conversations with Kennedy,* p. 76.

14. Arthur M. Schlesinger, Jr., *A Thousand Days* (Boston: Houghton Mifflin, 1965), p. 635.

15. Roy Hoopes, *The Steel Crisis* (New York: John Day, 1963), p. 23, n. 1.

16. Reeves, *President Kennedy: Profile of Power,* p. 296.

17. Ibid., p. 298.

18. Ibid.

19. Clark Clifford, *Counsel to the President: A Memoir* (New York: Random House, 1991), p. 377.

20. *Robert Kennedy in His Own Words*, edited by Edwin O. Guthman and Jeffrey Shulman (New York: Bantam Books, 1988), pp. 333–34.

21. *Public Papers of the Presidents: JFK, 1962*, pp. 315–16.

22. Ibid., p. 317.

23. Reeves, *President Kennedy: Profile of Power*, p. 301; Clifford, *Counsel to the President*, p. 376.

24. Clifford, *Counsel to the President*, p. 377.

25. Ibid.

26. Hoopes, *Steel Crisis*, p. 165.

27. Sorensen, *Kennedy*, p. 459.

28. Ibid.

29. *Public Papers of the Presidents: JFK, 1962*, pp. 379–80.

30. John H. Davis, *The Kennedys: Dynasty and Disaster* (New York: S.P.I. Books, 1992), pp. 78–80.

31. *Public Papers of the Presidents: JFK, 1962*, p. 380.

32. Hoopes, *Steel Crisis*, p. 17. Also Donald Gibson, *Battling Wall Street: The Kennedy Presidency* (New York: Sheridan Square Press, 1994), p. 17.

33. "Steel: The Ides of April," *Fortune* (May 1962), p. 98.

34. Ibid.

35. Ibid.

36. Schlesinger, *Thousand Days*, p. 636 footnote.

37. *Wall Street Journal*, April 19, 1962, cited by Arthur M. Schlesinger, Jr., *Robert Kennedy and His Times* (New York: Ballentine Books, 1978), p. 437.

38. Michael Calder, *JFK vs CIA: Death to Traitors: The Assassination of President John F. Kennedy—An Analysis of the Social, Political, and Economic Factors Which Led to His Assassination by the Central Intelligence Agency* (Los Angeles: West LA Publishers, 1998), pp. 106–7.

39. *Public Papers of the Presidents: JFK, 1962*, p. 364.

40. Ibid., pp. 364–65.

41. Schlesinger, *Thousand Days*, p. 641.

42. Kenneth P. O'Donnell and David F. Powers, *"Johnny, We Hardly Knew Ye"* (Boston: Little, Brown, 1970), p. 407.

43. Abraham Bolden, interview by author, June 16, 2001.

44. *The Warren Commission Report* (New York: St. Martin's Press, 1992, from U.S. Government printing in 1964), p. 748.

45. Ibid., p. 393.

46. June 28, 1984, deposition of Joseph Trento to Mark Lane; in Lane's *Plausible Denial: Was the CIA Involved in the Assassination of JFK?* (New York: Thunder's Mouth Press, 1992), p. 164. Cf. Lisa Pease, "James Angleton," in *The Assassinations*, edited by James DiEugenio and Lisa Pease (Los Angeles: Feral House, 2003), p. 164.

47. Evan Thomas, *The Very Best Men: Four Who Dared: The Early Years of the CIA* (New York: Touchstone, 1995), p. 85.

48. "Hunt Says C.I.A. Had Assassin Unit," *New York Times* (December 26, 1975), p. 9, cited by Lisa Pease in *Assassinations*, p. 164.

49. Trento deposition cited in Lane, *Plausible Denial*, p. 164.

50. David C. Martin, *Wilderness of Mirrors* (New York: Ballantine Books, 1980), p. 121.

51. The CIA's *Clandestine Services Handbook* stated that a 201 file was one opened on a person "of active operational interest at any given point in time." *Clandestine Services Handbook*, 43-1-1, February 15, 1960, Chapter III, Annex B, "PERSONALITIES—201 and IDN NUMBERS," p. 43; NARA JFK Files, box 13, folder 29. Cited by John Newman, *Oswald and the CIA* (New York: Carroll & Graf, 1995), p. 537 note 2.

52. William Harvey's notes for "ZR/RIFLE" are cited in Martin, *Wilderness of Mirrors*, pp. 122–24, and in Pease, *Assassinations*, p. 162.

53. Martin, *Wilderness of Mirrors*, p. 124.

54. Joseph B. Smith, *Portrait of a Cold Warrior* (New York: Ballantine Books, 1981), p. 389.

55. Martin, *Wilderness of Mirrors*, p. 16.

56. The CIA document that opened Oswald's 201 SIG file on December 9, 1960, signed by Ann Egerter, is on page 463 of Newman's *Oswald and the CIA*.

57. *President's Commission on the Assassination of President Kennedy: Report of Proceedings Held at Washington, D.C. Monday, January 27, 1964*; published by Harold Weisberg as *Whitewash IV: Top Secret JFK Assassination Transcript* (Frederick, Md.: 1974), p. 62; p. 153 of transcript.

58. HSCA Deposition of Ann Elizabeth Goldsborough Egerter, p. 8. Cited by Lisa Pease, "James Angleton," in *Assassinations*, p. 146 (emphasis added).

59. Egerter, HCSA Deposition, p. 9 (emphasis added).

60. Ibid., pp. 9–10.

61. Pease, *Assassinations*, p. 147.

62. Preliminary HSCA Interview of Ann Egerter by Dan Hardway and Betsy Wolf, March 31, 1978, p. 3. JFK Record Number 180-10142-10298.

63. Egerter HSCA Deposition, May 17, 1978, p. 20. JFK Record Number 180-10131-10333.

64. Ibid., p. 21. Egerter's HSCA interviewer, Michael Goldsmith, also asked her about the suggestive letters "AG" (meaning "AGENT"?) printed in an identification box on the December 9, 1960, form by which Egerter had opened Oswald's 201 file:

> GOLDSMITH: "What does the term 'AG' stand for?"
> EGERTER: "I have forgotten."
> GOLDSMITH: "Is that your handwriting?"
> EGERTER: "I don't think so. I forget."
> GOLDSMITH: "Would that have stood for agent?"
> EGERTER: "No. I forget what 'AG' meant." Ibid., pp. 58–59.

Lacking an independent authority to interpret the CIA form, Goldsmith accepted Egerter's inability to remember what "AG" meant or if she had written those letters on the form, and moved on to other questions.

65. James B. Wilcott's Testimony before the House Select Committee on Assassinations, March 22, 1978, p. 48. JFK Record Number 180-10116-10096.

66. Warren Hinckle, "Couple Talks about Oswald and the CIA," *San Francisco Chronicle* (September 12, 1978).

67. Bob Loomis, "Ex-CIA Couple Tell of Disillusion," *Oakland Tribune* (September 18, 1978), p. B14. Also Hinckle, "Couple Talks about Oswald."

68. Loomis, "Ex-CIA Couple."

69. Wilcott HSCA Testimony, p. 11. The House Select Committee evaluated Jim Wilcott's testimony by interviewing "several present and former CIA employees selected on the basis of the position each had held during the years 1954–64," including "a broad spectrum of areas" at the Tokyo Station. Perhaps not surprisingly, given the consequences of saying otherwise, the CIA employees all denied having any knowledge of Oswald's having been a CIA agent. Accordingly, "the committee concluded that Wilcott's allegation was not worthy of belief" (*HSCA Report*, March 29, 1979, pp. 199–200). Jim Wilcott's HSCA testimony was then sealed and became inaccessible to the public. It was finally released in 1998 under the JFK Records Act, passed by Congress as a result of the public pressure generated by Oliver Stone's film *JFK*.

70. Wilcott HSCA Testimony, p. 47.

71. Hinckle, "Couple Talks about Oswald."

72. Jim Wilcott, "The Assassination of John F. Kennedy: A C.I.A. Insider's View," *Stray Magazine* (February 1989), p. 38.

73. Wilcott HSCA Testimony, p. 35.

74. Ibid., pp. 35–37.

75. Author's interview of Jim and Elsie Wilcott's friend and neighbor, Bill Callison, August 31, 1997.

76. Gracia Fay Ellwood, "A Concord Vigil," *Reformed Journal* (February 2, 1989).

77. Callison interview.

78. "Current Intelligence Memorandum," Central Intelligence Agency, Washington, June 3, 1963. *FRUS, 1961–1963, Volume III: Vietnam, January-August 1963* (Washington: U.S. Government Printing Office, 1991), p. 345.

79. Ibid.

80. Ellen Hammer on the Catholic newspaper *Hoa Binh*'s reconstruction of the May 8, 1963, events, *A Death in November: America in Vietnam, 1963*, p. 116.

81. Richard Reeves, *President Kennedy: Profile of Power* (New York: Touchstone, 1993), p. 517.

82. *FRUS, 1961–1963*, vol. III, pp. 381–83.

83. Ibid., pp. 386–87, footnote 5.

84. Schlesinger, *Thousand Days*, p. 904.

85. *Public Papers of the Presidents: John F. Kennedy, 1963* (Washington: U.S. Government Printing Office, 1964), p. 469.

86. Reeves, *President Kennedy: Profile of Power*, pp. 522–23.

87. John Kenneth Galbraith, "A Communication," originally published in the *Washington Post* (November 25, 1963); in *Ambassador's Journal: A Personal Account of the Kennedy Years* (Boston: Houghton Mifflin, 1969), pp. 631–32.

88. Ibid., p. 629.

89. Reeves, *President Kennedy: Profile of Power*, p. 526.

90. Richard D. Mahoney, *JFK: Ordeal in Africa* (New York: Oxford University Press, 1983), p. 108.

91. Ibid., pp. 114, 246–48.

92. Herbert S. Parmet interview of Edmund Gullion, August 18, 1980, cited in Herbert S. Parmet, *JFK: The Presidency of John F. Kennedy* (New York: Dial Press, 1983), p. 320.

93. Mahoney, *JFK: Ordeal in Africa*, p. 246.

94. Ibid., p. 81.

95. Ibid., p. 246.

96. Kennedy's biographer, Richard Reeves, confirmed the president's first choice of Gullion by interviews with both Edmund Gullion and the man who blocked his appointment, Dean Rusk. Reeves, *President Kennedy: Profile of Power*, p. 736, endnote for p. 526.

97. Anne E. Blair, *Lodge in Vietnam: A Patriot Abroad* (New Haven: Yale University Press, 1995), pp. 12–13.

98. Ibid., p. 5.

99. Reeves, *President Kennedy: Profile of Power*, p. 429.

100. Blair, *Lodge in Vietnam*, p. 10.

101. Ibid., pp. 4, 162 note 7.

102. *Robert Kennedy in His Own Words*, p. 301.

103. O'Donnell and Powers, *"Johnny, We Hardly Knew Ye,"* p. 16.

104. Cited in Martin, *Wilderness of Mirrors*, p. 124.

105. Dick Russell, *The Man Who Knew Too Much* (New York: Carroll & Graf, 1992), p. 45.

106. Ibid., p. 101.

107. Ibid., p. 104.

108. Ibid., pp. 170–72. At a meeting with Nagell, Dick Russell told him he had concluded from his own research and Nagell's oblique comments that the "HID" part of Oswald's alias was derived from a Korean intelligence unit Nagell had worked with for the Army, and the "ELL" part had come from the last three letters of Nagell's own name. Nagell "stared back at me, did not deny it, and quickly changed the subject." Ibid., p. 172.

109. Nagell emphasized the word "large" when he spoke of the assassination plot to

New Orleans District Attorney Jim Garrison. *On the Trail of the Assassins* (New York: Warner Books, 1988), p. 214.

110. Russell, *Man Who Knew Too Much*, p. 294.

111. Ibid., pp. 294, 331.

112. Ibid., p. 429.

113. Ibid., p. 437.

114. Letter from Richard Case Nagell to Dick Russell, cited in *Man Who Knew Too Much*, p. 442. Nagell said he signed his letter to Hoover with the alias "Joseph Kramer" because it was "an alias of a known Communist (Soviet) agent then residing in Canada" and an alias Nagell had himself used in a meeting with FBI agents. From Nagell's November 21, 1975, affidavit sent to U.S. Representative Don Edwards, Chairman of the House Judiciary Subcommittee on Civil and Constitutional Rights, cited in *Man Who Knew Too Much*, pp. 56–57.

115. Richard Case Nagell, letter to *The New Yorker* (November 14, 1968); cited in *Man Who Knew Too Much*, p. 442.

116. Nagell, November 21, 1975, affidavit in *Man Who Knew Too Much*, p. 56.

117. Ibid.

118. *WCH*, vol. 20, p. 270.

119. *WCH*, vol. 19, p. 577.

120. *WCH*, vol. 20, p. 271.

121. Jim Garrison's CIA-connected staff member William R. Martin reported back to Garrison on his prison interview of Nagell: "When questioned as to the identity of the persons speaking on the tape the subject stated openly that one of them was 'Arcacha' and another individual whom the subject would only identify as 'Q.' The subject did not wish to go into more detail concerning the tape at that time since he, all during our previous conversations, had indicated that our conversation could possibly be bugged." William R. Martin Memorandum to Jim Garrison, April 18, 1967. Cited by James DiEugenio in *Assassinations*, p. 237. In Nagell's own written comments on another Martin memorandum to Garrison, he described further the four persons on the audiotape as: (1) Oswald; (2) Nagell himself, who served as Oswald's interpreter for the predominately Spanish conversation; (3) an unidentified person; (4) Angel. Cited by Russell in *Man Who Knew Too Much*, p. 425.

122. Russell, *Man Who Knew Too Much*, pp. 424, 642–44.

123. Ibid., p. 46.

124. Ibid., p. 47.

125. Ibid., p. 670.

126. Ibid., p. 695.

127. Nagell finally came to believe his immediate CIA contact was a double agent working for the Soviets, and that he'd been misled by him into "basically operating for the Soviets since signing his CIA contract the year before." Russell concluded "that when Nagell found himself left out in the cold [in September 1963] by not only his CIA controllers, but by his contacts within Soviet intelligence as well, something in him snapped. Coming to the realization that he was being used, already aware that Oswald had long been in a similar boat, Nagell found himself backed into a lonely, terrifying and extremely dangerous corner. He was essentially a man without a country." Dick Russell, *The Man Who Knew Too Much* (1992; updated ed., New York: Carroll & Graf, 2003), pp. 463–64.

128. Ibid., p. 447 (Russell's emphasis).

129. Ibid., pp. 447, 451–52.

130. Ibid., pp. 449, 452.

131. Ibid., p. 452.

132. Ibid.

133. Ibid., p. 451.

134. Ibid., p. 465.

135. *WCH*, vol. 11, p. 370. Gaeton Fonzi, *The Last Investigation* (New York: Thun-

der's Mouth Press, 1994), p. 111. Anthony Summers, *Conspiracy* (New York: Paragon House, 1989), p. 387.

136. Fonzi, *Last Investigation*, pp. 382, 385. Also Silvia Odio interview by Gaeton Fonzi, January 16, 1976.

137. Ibid., p. 109.

138. Ibid., p. 111.

139. George Michael Evica, *And We Are All Mortal: New Evidence and Analysis in the John F. Kennedy Assassination* (West Hartford, Conn.: University of Hartford, 1978), pp. 119–20.

140. Ibid., pp. 109–10. Also Odio interview by Fonzi.

141. *WCH*, vol., 11, p. 381.

142. The author of a State Department memorandum, written on the eve of the Cuban Missile Crisis, noted that JURE was "opposed by most of the established exile groups." *Foreign Relations of the United States (FRUS), 1961–1963, Volume XI, Cuban Missile Crisis and Aftermath, October 1962-December 1963* (Washington: U.S. Government Printing Office, 1997), p. 25.

143. E. Howard Hunt, *Give Us This Day* (New York: Popular Library, 1973), p. 185.

144. *Bay of Pigs Declassified: The Secret CIA Report on the Invasion of Cuba*, edited by Peter Kornbluh (New York: New Press, 1998), p. 223.

145. Jean Daniel, "Unofficial Envoy: An Historic Report from Two Capitals," *New Republic* (December 14, 1963), p. 16.

146. Hunt, *Give Us This Day*, p. 94.

147. Ibid.

148. CIA dispatch, July 22, 1963; cited by Gaeton J. Fonzi and Elizabeth J. Palmer, "Junta Revolucionaria Cubana (JURE)," *Appendix to Hearings Before the Select Committee on Assassinations of the U.S. House of Representatives (HSCA) Vol. 10: Anti-Castro Activities and Organizations, Investigation of the Assassination of President John F. Kennedy* (Washington: U.S. Government Printing Office, 1979), p. 78.

149. CIA cables, October 11, 1963, and September 7, 1963; ibid.

150. *WCH*, vol. 11, p. 371.

151. Odio interview. Also Fonzi, *Last Investigation*, p. 111.

152. Odio interview.

153. *WCH*, vol. 11, p. 379.

154. Fonzi, *Last Investigation*, p. 112.

155. Odio interview.

156. *WCH*, vol. 11, p. 372.

157. Fonzi, *Last Investigation*, p. 112.

158. *WCH*, vol. 11, pp. 372–73.

159. Ibid., p. 373.

160. Silvia Odio interview. Annie Laurie Odio Mallo interview by Gaeton Fonzi, September 19, 1978.

161. Ibid.

162. Edward Jay Epstein, *Inquest: The Warren Commission and the Establishment of Truth* (New York: Viking Press, 1966), p. 105.

163. *Warren Report*, pp. 322–24. The *Warren Report* also claimed that a Cuban exile, Loran Eugene Hall, said that he and two companions (one of whom Hall said resembled Oswald) were the visitors at Odio's door. Ibid., p. 324. However, Hall denied having made such a statement. Fonzi, *Last Investigation*, p. 115. And once again the *Warren Report*'s argument ignored the at least equally sinister implications of the incident if it was not Oswald himself at the door.

164. Sylvia Meagher, *Accessories after the Fact: The Warren Commission, the Authorities, and the Report* (New York: Vintage Books, 1992), p. 379.

165. William P. Bundy, unpublished manuscript on the Vietnam War Decisions, chap-

ter 9, "The Decline and Fall of Diem (May to November 1963)," p. 8; Papers of William P. Bundy, Box Number 1, Lyndon Baines Johnson Library.

166. *FRUS, 1961–1963*, vol. III, p. 591.

167. Ibid., p. 629.

168. "Steel: The Ides of April," *Fortune* (May 1962), p. 97.

169. Charles Mohr, "Vietnam—Where We Stand and Why," *Time* (May 2, 1963); cited by Blair, *Lodge in Vietnam*, p. 21.

170. Blair, *Lodge in Vietnam*, pp. 21, 165 note 49.

171. *FRUS, 1961–1963*, vol. III, p. 634.

172. Reeves, *President Kennedy: Profile of Power*, p. 563, p. 744 note for p. 563.

173. Kai Bird, *The Color of Truth: McGeorge Bundy and William Bundy, Brothers in Arms: A Biography* (New York: Simon & Schuster, 1998), p. 254.

174. William J. Rust, *Kennedy in Vietnam* (New York: Charles Scribner's Sons, 1985), p. 119.

175. *FRUS, 1961–1963*, vol. III, p. 645.

176. Rust, *Kennedy in Vietnam*, p. 110. Colonel Lucien Conein's CIA expertise included a working knowledge of the CIA's staple in covert operations, plastic explosives. One of Conein's covert action scenarios was designed for the Hanoi mansion where he was living in 1954 when the French withdrew from Vietnam. Assuming that a Communist Party official would soon take over the house, Conein filled the refrigerator with plastic explosives. He then wired them with an electric detonator, so that when the refrigerator was plugged in, the explosion would obliterate not only the house but most of the neighborhood. Conein's plot was interrupted by the U.S. consul in Hanoi, who ordered that the CIA's huge plastic bomb be dismantled.

177. *FRUS, 1961–1963, Volume IV, Vietnam, August–December 1963* (Washington: U.S. Government Printing Office, 1991), p. 16.

178. Ibid., p. 20.

179. Ibid., pp. 33–34.

180. Ibid., pp. 38–39.

181. Ibid., p. 105.

182. Ibid., p. 107.

183. Thomas Powers, *The Man Who Kept the Secrets: Richard Helms and the CIA* (New York: Alfred A. Knopf, 1979), p. 187. Cf. Roger Hilsman, *To Move a Nation: The Politics of Foreign Policy in the Administration of John F. Kennedy* (New York: Delta, 1967), p. 488, where Hilsman states: "The Acting Director of CIA also went over the draft, and he too decided to approve without disturbing his chief's vacation—adding the comment that the time had clearly come to take a stand." Hilsman revealed that Helms responded enthusiastically to the opportunity for what was in effect a CIA-State united front on the telegram (with McCone out of the loop): "Helms phoned me immediately after signing the cable to say that it was about time the United States tried to do something about the situation caused by Brother Nhu." Helms knew McCone did not agree with the coup that the cable encouraged. Roger Hilsman, "McNamara's War—Against the Truth: A Review Essay," *Political Science Quarterly* (Spring 1996), p. 157.

William Colby, former Saigon station chief who would become the CIA director in 1973, wrote misleadingly about Helms's approval of the August 24 telegram: "I later heard that Helms, who was the Agency's duty officer that day, had seen the message and cleared it, regarding it as a policy rather than an intelligence matter, in which the Agency thus had no formal role." William Colby, *Honorable Men: My Life in the CIA* (New York: Simon & Schuster, 1978), p. 210. Colby seems to be trying to avoid the implications of Helms's clearance. Helms simply had no problem clearing his own freedom as Deputy Director of Plans to guide and follow (through his agent Lucien Conein) a coup in South Vietnam.

When McCone was informed personally by Colby about the August 24 telegram (on a special trip Colby made to McCone's California home), he returned quickly to Washington to voice his anger at the State officers' manipulation of the decision-making process. Colby, *Honorable Men*, p. 210; Powers, *Man Who Kept the Secrets*, p. 187. But there is no record of McCone having confronted his deputy, Richard Helms, for a more obvious usurpation of his own authority as DCI.

184. Torbert Macdonald background from Herbert S. Parmet, *Jack: The Struggles of John F. Kennedy* (New York: Dial Press, 1980), pp. 45–48, 352.

185. Seymour M. Hersh, *The Dark Side of Camelot* (Boston: Little, Brown and Company, 1997), p. 433.

186. Herbert S. Parmet, *JFK: The Presidency of John F. Kennedy* (New York: Dial Press, 1983), pp. 335, 390 endnotes 50 and 51.

187. Ibid., p. 335.

188. Joe Croken interview by Seymour Hersh, *Dark Side of Camelot*, p. 432. Unlike Eleanore Carney and Torbert Macdonald, Jr., Joe Croken was not told about the message Macdonald was delivering to Diem. Ibid.

189. Herbert S. Parmet's handwritten notes from interview with Michael V. Forrestal, February 17, 1981.

190. Parmet, *JFK*, p. 335.

191. Ibid. Colonel Edward Lansdale, Diem's CIA adviser when he took power in 1954, told Daniel Ellsberg a story about another possible JFK mission to Diem—which Lansdale said he turned down. Lansdale said that in late September 1963, in a private meeting between President Kennedy, Lansdale, and Robert McNamara, Kennedy "said he wanted [Lansdale] to go over to try to influence Diem to send his brother Ngo Dinh Nhu out of the country, along with his wife Madame Nhu. He asked if Lansdale was willing to go, with that mission. Lansdale said yes.

"Then Kennedy said to him, 'But if that didn't work out, or I changed my mind and decided that we had to get rid of Diem himself, would you be able to go along with that?'

Lansdale told Ellsberg he thought Kennedy meant Diem's assassination, so he responded, "No, Mr. President. I couldn't do that. Diem is my friend."

Lansdale said the president "seemed to understand his response and didn't say anything unfriendly or express disappointment. But the discussion was over." Unpublished memoir by Daniel Ellsberg, "Edward G. Lansdale Story File," October 24, 2000.

Lansdale may have misunderstood what Kennedy meant. One can also question Lansdale's reliability as a witness to the truth.

As a CIA operative, Colonel Edward Lansdale was responsible for securing Saigon for the beginning of Diem's rule in June 1954. He did so by employing General Trinh Minh The, the same CIA-sponsored warlord whose terrorist bombing with plastic explosives in Saigon two years earlier was exposed in Graham Greene's novel, *The Quiet American*. Because the title character's role in the plot corresponds to Lansdale's covert activities in Saigon and his employment of Trinh Minh The, Lansdale has long been identified as the prototype for the Quiet American. H. Bruce Franklin, "Our Man in Saigon," *The Nation* (February 3, 2003), p. 44.

Although Greene denied Lansdale was his model, Lansdale did all he could for the CIA to destroy the truth of *The Quiet American* in its first film version. When Joseph Mankiewicz bought the novel's movie rights in 1956, Lansdale wrote the director a letter, assuring him that no "more than one or two Vietnamese now alive know the real truth of the matter [of Trinh Minh The's terrorist bombing and his claiming credit for it on the radio], and they certainly aren't going to tell it to anyone." Therefore, Lansdale urged, Mankiewicz should "just go right ahead and let it be finally revealed that the Communists did it after all, even to faking the radio broadcast." Following Lansdale's lead, Mankiewicz returned to the CIA's scapegoat scenario but in an altered Graham Greene context, depicting the Communists as the bombers, the Quiet American as an innocent hero, and the narrator Fowler as "a writhing, loathsome and self-loathing stand-in for Graham Greene." Franklin, "Our Man in Saigon," p. 44.

192. *WCH*, vol. 11, p. 396. See also transcript of Ruth Paine's testimony before the Orleans Parish Grand Jury, April 18, 1968, pp. 2–4.

193. *WCH*, vol. 9, p. 258.

194. Ibid., p. 257.

195. *WCH*, vol. 2, p. 436.

196. *WCH*, vol. 9, p. 258.

197. Ibid.

198. Edward Jay Epstein, *The Assassination Chronicles* (New York: Carroll & Graf, 1992), pp. 559, 564.

199. Ibid., pp. 559, 566.

200. Ibid., p. 567.

201. *Appendix to Hearings before the HSCA*, vol. 12, pp. 56–57.

202. J. Edgar Hoover Letter to J. Lee Rankin, October 23, 1964. FBI Record Number 124-10147-10006. Agency File Number 105-126128-1ST NR 120.

203. *WCH*, vol. 2, p. 385.

204. Ibid.

205. Bruce Campbell Adamson, *Oswald's Closest Friend: The George de Mohrenschildt Story*, 11 volumes (Aptos, Calif.: self-published, 1993, 1995), vol. 6, pp. l, 31. William Kelly, "Arthur Young and Ruth Forbes Young—the Crux of the Matter," Conference Abstract, Coalition on Political Assassinations, *Opening the Files: JFK, MLK, RFK*; Washington, D.C., October 18–20, 1996.

206. Adamson, *Oswald's Closest Friend*, vol. 6, pp. 31–35. Mary Bancroft, *Autobiography of a Spy* (New York: William Morrow, 1983).

207. *Oral History of Mary Bancroft* (Columbia University, 1972), p. 243. Cited by Adamson, *Oswald's Closest Friend*, p. 34. Bancroft also refers to her friendship with Ruth Forbes Paine (later Young) in *Autobiography of a Spy*, pp. 54–61.

208. *WCH*, vol. 2, p. 386.

209. It was at Allen Dulles's repeated suggestion in the 1960s that Mary Bancroft wrote her *Autobiography of a Spy*, memorializing their covert work together in a plot to assassinate Hitler. Bancroft's book was based on her OSS reports written specifically for Dulles, her spy mentor and lover in Switzerland during the war. When Dulles was fired as CIA director by Kennedy in 1961, he took Bancroft's reports with him into retirement, placing them in a filing cabinet in his home.

After his death in 1969, the CIA confiscated the filing cabinet and everything in it. Two years later, in response to Bancroft's personal appeal, then CIA director Richard Helms returned her OSS spy reports. Bancroft then wrote her World War II memoir, mentioning only fleetingly in a final chapter her continuing contacts with Allen Dulles up to his death. *Autobiography of a Spy*, pp. 290–91.

Mary Bancroft's *Oral History* acknowledges her simultaneous postwar alliances with Allen Dulles and *Time-Life-Fortune* magnate Henry Luce: "Mary enjoyed seeing Dulles mad over Luce. One night Mary creeped back to Dulles' apartment when Allen called to Mary: 'Have you been with Luce all this time?' Mary fired back: 'Yes!'" Drawn from *Oral History*, p. 310. Cited by Adamson, *Oswald's Closest Friend*, p. 29.

210. *WCH*, vol. 3, p. 3.

211. Barbara LaMonica, "All in the Family (the Paines)," Conference Abstract, Coalition on Political Assassinations, *Opening the Files: JFK, MLK, RFK*; Washington, D.C., October 18–20, 1996.

212. George Cotter, "Spies, Strings and Missionaries," *The Christian Century* (March 25, 1981), p. 321.

213. "Executive Agents are business people, religious personnel, technical experts or scholars sent abroad to collect intelligence on matters bearing upon issues of particular importance to American foreign interests." Barbara LaMonica, "William Avery Hyde," *The Fourth Decade* (November 1997), p. 11.

214. William A. Hyde, "End of-Tour Report," August 8, 1967; located by researcher

Steve Jones in the AID Library, Washington, D.C.; LaMonica, "William Avery Hyde," p. 10.

215. "Security File on Sylvia Hyde Hoke," 7/30/71; CIA File Number 348 201; Inclusive Dates: 1955–1971; NARA Document ID Number 1993.07.24.08:39:37:560310.

216. The inclusive dates on Sylvia Hyde Hoke's CIA Security File, 1955–1971, indicate she had already been employed by the CIA for eight years by the time of her sister Ruth's September 1963 visit at her Falls Church, Virginia, home. Ibid.

217. WCH, vol. 3, pp. 3–4.

218. Ruth Paine's Testimony before the Orleans Parish Grand Jury, April 18, 1968, p. 57.

219. Ibid., p. 58.

220. Ibid., 56–57.

221. Warren Report, pp. 14–15. The neighbor identified by Ruth Paine as having mentioned the job opening, Linnie Mae Randle, said, contrary to Paine's testimony, "I didn't know there was a job opening over there [at the Texas School Book Depository]." WCH, vol. 2, p. 247.

222. Affidavit of Robert L. Adams, August 4, 1964. WCH, vol. 11, p. 481.

223. Ibid.

224. Ibid. There is evidence that if Lee Oswald had been informed about the much higher-paying, permanent job at Trans Texas, he would probably have applied for it. Marina Oswald testified that after Lee took the Book Depository job, he was still answering want ads because he "wanted to get something better." WCH, vol. 1, p. 68.

225. WCH, vol. 9, pp. 389–90.

226. Adams Affidavit, ibid.

227. Marina Oswald Porter's Testimony before the Orleans Parish Grand Jury, February 8, 1968, pp. 69–70.

5. Saigon and Chicago

1. Sergei N. Khrushchev, Nikita Khrushchev and the Creation of a Superpower (University Park, Pa.: Pennsylvania State University, 2000), p. 630.

2. Ibid.

3. Ibid., pp. 618–19.

4. Khrushchev Remembers, ed. Edward Crankshaw (Boston: Little, Brown, 1970), p. 498.

5. S. Khrushchev, Nikita Khrushchev, p. 622.

6. Public Papers of the Presidents: John F. Kennedy, 1963, p. 694.

7. Ibid.

8. Ibid., p. 695.

9. Ibid.

10. Ibid., p. 696.

11. Ibid., p. 462.

12. Ibid., p. 696.

13. Ibid., p. 698.

14. FRUS, 1961–1963, Volume XI, Cuban Missile Crisis and Aftermath, October 1962-December 1963 (Washington: U.S. Government Printing Office, 1997), p. 880.

15. William Attwood, The Twilight Struggle: Tales of the Cold War (New York: Harper & Row, 1987), p. 264. Arthur Schlesinger agreed with Attwood that the CIA was monitoring the Attwood–Lechuga communications: "I think the CIA must have known about this initiative. They must certainly have realized that Bill Attwood and the Cuban representative to the UN were doing more than exchanging daiquiri recipes when they met. They had all of the wires tapped at the Cuban delegation to the United Nations." Cited by Anthony Summers, Conspiracy (New York: Paragon House, 1989), p. 401.

16. Cited by Summers, *Conspiracy*, p. 394.

17. James P. Hosty, Jr., *Assignment, Oswald* (New York: Arcade, 1996), p. 166.

18. John Newman, "Oswald, the CIA and Mexico City: Fingerprints of Conspiracy," *Probe* (September-October 1999), p. 4.

19. Lee Harvey Oswald Wanted Notice Card, FBI Jacket No. 327 925 D; Ref. Memo dated 11-4-59, Branigan to Belmont. Document on CD-ROM for John Armstrong, *Harvey and Lee: How the CIA Framed Oswald* (Arlington, Tex.: Quasar, 2003), Oct, 63–08.

20. Ibid., with the addition to the document: "FLASH CANCELLED: Information Received 10-9-63 (per v/s from Gheesling Div 5) DL 10/15/63."

21. Classified Message from Central Intelligence Agency to Federal Bureau of Investigation on Lee Henry [*sic*] Oswald, October 10, 1963. On page 513 of John Newman, *Oswald and the CIA* (New York: Carroll & Graf Publishers, 1995). The CIA sent the same 10/10/63 message to the Department of State and the Department of the Navy.

22. Newman, "Oswald, the CIA and Mexico City," p. 4.

23. Cited by John Newman, "Mexico City—A New Analysis," Presentation at the "November in Dallas" JFK Lancer Conference, November 19, 1999; transcript at jfklancer.com/backes/newman, p. 35.

24. Hosty, *Assignment, Oswald*, p. 166. Hoover was reacting defensively to the Warren Commission's criticisms that "the FBI took an unduly restrictive view of its responsibilities in preventive intelligence work, prior to the assassination" and had failed "to list Oswald as a potential threat to the safety of the President." *The Warren Commission Report* (New York: St. Martin's Press, 1992, from U.S. Government printing in 1964), p. 443. The FBI director imposed disciplinary transfers on Marvin Gheesling and four other agents who had key responsibilities for the Oswald information before the assassination. Hoover sent letters reprimanding twelve more agents for their not having been more alert regarding Oswald. Hosty, *Assignment, Oswald*, p. 167.

25. The FBI memorandum with Hoover's written comment on it is reproduced on page 5 of Newman, "Oswald, the CIA and Mexico City" (emphasis added).

26. Church Committee, *The Investigation of the Assassination of President John F. Kennedy: Performance of the Intelligence Agencies*, Book V, Final Report (Washington: U.S. Government Printing Office, 1976), p. 65. See also Newman, *Oswald and the CIA*, p. 394.

27. Summers, *Conspiracy*, pp. 335–36. When Anthony Summers found and interviewed William Gaudet at a retirement home fifteen years later, the CIA man claimed that his proximity to Oswald in line at the consulate and their simultaneous trips to Mexico were only coincidences. Gaudet did admit to Summers that he worked secretly for the CIA for more than twenty years. He also said he knew Oswald in New Orleans, though he quickly changed his statement to his having merely observed Oswald handing out leaflets. Ibid., pp. 336–37.

28. Ibid., p. 336.

29. Cited by Howard Hughes's assistant John Meir; interviewed by Lisa Pease, "The RFK Plot Part II: Rubik's Cube," in *The Assassinations*, edited by James DiEugenio and Lisa Pease (Los Angeles: Feral House, 2003), p. 608. Hoover was commenting on the assassination of Robert Kennedy.

30. Nancy Zaroulis and Gerald Sullivan, *Who Spoke Up? American Protest against the War in Vietnam 1963–1975* (Garden City, N.Y.: Doubleday, 1984), p. 12.

31. Ibid., pp. 12–13.

32. "National Security Action Memorandum No. 263," October 11, 1963, *Foreign Relations of the United States (FRUS), 1961–1963, Volume IV: Vietnam: August-December 1963* (Washington: U.S. Government Printing Office, 1991), p. 396.

33. Lodge cable on September 11, 1963, calling for the overthrow of Diem in *FRUS, 1961–1963*, vol. IV, pp. 171–74; McGeorge Bundy's supportive response in his September 11 telephone call to Secretary of State Dean Rusk, ibid., p. 176. See also John M.

Newman, *JFK and Vietnam: Deception, Intrigue, and the Struggle for Power* (New York: Warner Books, 1992), pp. 379–80. Kennedy ordered a noncommittal response to Lodge saying "we are considering his cable" and urging him once again to concentrate on communicating with Diem. *FRUS, 1961–1963*, vol. IV, p. 193.

34. Chalmers M. Roberts, *First Rough Draft: A Journalist's Journal of Our Times* (New York: Praeger, 1973), pp. 195–96.

35. Charles Bartlett, "Portrait of a Friend," in *The Kennedy Presidency: 17 Intimate Perspectives of John F. Kennedy*, edited by Kenneth W. Thompson (Lanham, Md.: University Press of America, 1985), p. 16.

36. John Aloysius Farrell, *Tip O'Neill and the Democratic Century* (Boston: Little, Brown, 2001), p. 193.

37. Ralph G. Martin, *A Hero for Our Time: An Intimate Story of the Kennedy Years* (New York: Ballantine Books, 1983), p.465. Date of Kennedy's last visit to Hyannis Port from Michael Desmond's inspection of JFK's Appointments Index at the John Fitzgerald Kennedy Library.

38. Tristram Coffin, "CIA: Tales of a Rogue Elephant," *The Washington Spectator* (October 1, 1987), p. 2.

39. Author's interview of Mrs. Zola Shoup, September 9, 1999. Stephen Plotkin, Reference Archivist at the Kennedy Library, confirmed from the White House Appointments Book that President Kennedy met with General Shoup at 10:52 a.m. on November 11, 1963, and walked over with him to the wreath-laying ceremony.

40. Coffin, "CIA: Tales," p. 2.

41. Wayne Morse, interview by David Nyhan, "We've Been a Police State a Long Time," *Boston Globe* (June 24, 1973), pp. A1–2. Wayne Morse remained courageously true to his antiwar convictions after his speeches' target and converted listener, John Kennedy, was murdered and the prowar Lyndon Johnson took his place as president. Morse of Oregon and Ernest Gruening of Alaska were the only two senators who voted against the Tonkin Gulf Resolution in 1964 that "legitimized" the Vietnam War. They were both defeated for reelection. Ibid., p. A–1.

42. Coffin, "CIA: Tales," p. 2.

43. Henry Brandon, *Anatomy of Error: The Inside Story of the Asian War on the Potomac, 1954–1969* (Boston: Gambit, 1969), p. 30.

44. Michael Forrestal quote cited from a 1971 NBC television program by Roberts, *First Rough Draft*, p. 221.

45. *FRUS, 1961–1963,* vol. IV, p. 143.

46. Ibid., p. 252.

47. Ibid., p. 254.

48. Ibid., p. 255.

49. Ibid.

50. Harriman defined the president's "disaster" by saying that Kennedy was sending "two men opposed to our policy [McNamara and Taylor], plus one who wouldn't stand up [Deputy Undersecretary of State U. Alexis Johnson], to carry out policy." Memorandum of a Telephone Conversation Between the Under Secretary of State for Political Affairs (Harriman) and Michael V. Forrestal of the National Security Council Staff, Washington, September 17, 1963, 4:20 p.m. *FRUS, 1961–1963*, vol. IV, p. 256.

51. Ibid., p. 256.

52. William Colby, *Honorable Men: My Life in the CIA* (New York: Simon & Schuster, 1978), p. 178.

53. *The Pentagon Papers: The Defense Department History of the United States Decision Making on Vietnam,* Senator Gravel Edition, 5 vols. (Boston: Beacon Press, 1972), vol. 2, p. 724.

54. David T. Ratcliffe, *Understanding Special Operations and Their Impact on the Vietnam War Era: 1989 Interview with L. Fletcher Prouty Colonel USAF (Retired)* (Santa Cruz, Calif.: rat haus reality press, 1999), pp. 68–70.

55. Arthur Krock, "In the Nation: The Intra-Administration War in Vietnam," *New York Times* (October 3, 1963), p. 34.

56. Ibid.

57. Richard Starnes, "'Arrogant' CIA Disobeys Orders in Viet Nam," *Washington Daily News* (October 2, 1963), p. 3.

58. *FRUS, 1961–1963*, vol. IV, p. 205.

59. Ibid.

60. By a symbolic act, Lodge made certain the CIA in Vietnam knew he had taken over its command post for "changing governments." He moved into the deposed station chief's former home. Peer de Silva, *Sub Rosa: The CIA and the Uses of Intelligence* (New York: Times Books, 1978), p. 211.

Peer de Silva, John Richardson's successor as Saigon station chief after Johnson became president, wrote in his memoir *Sub Rosa* that Lodge's newly commandeered home had one serious drawback, its notoriety from its use by the Diem government for torture: "The house had been used as an interrogation center for Vietcong suspects and it was common knowledge among the Vietnamese that a number of them had gone to their reward under interrogation in the house." Ibid.

61. Thomas Powers, *The Man Who Kept the Secrets: Richard Helms and the CIA* (New York: Alfred A. Knopf, 1979), p. 187.

62. *FRUS, 1961–1963*, vol. III: *Vietnam, January-August 1963* (Washington: U.S. Government Printing Office, 1991), p. 268.

63. Ibid., p. 591.

64. Ibid.

65. Fletcher Prouty, interview by David Ratcliffe, *Understanding Special Operations and Their Impact of the Vietnam War Era* (Santa Cruz, Calif.: rat haus reality press, 1999), pp. 71–72.

66. Ibid., p. 72.

67. *FRUS, 1961–1963*, vol. IV, pp. 395–96.

68. Robert S. McNamara, *In Retrospect: The Tragedy and Lessons of Vietnam* (New York: Times Books, 1995), p. 79.

69. Ibid., p. 80.

70. *FRUS, 1961–1963*, vol. IV, p. 351.

71. Ibid.

72. McNamara, *In Retrospect*, p. 80.

73. Kenneth P. O'Donnell and David F. Powers with Joe McCarthy, *"Johnny, We Hardly Knew Ye"* (Boston: Little, Brown, 1970), p. 17.

74. *FRUS, 1961–1963*, vol. IV, pp. 396, 338.

75. Bartlett, "Portrait of a Friend," p. 16.

76. See Newman, *JFK and Vietnam*, p. 410.

77. *FRUS, 1961–1963*, vol. IV, p. 396.

78. "Vietnam Victory by the End of '65 Envisaged by U.S.," *New York Times* (October 3, 1963), p. 1. *Times* published the October 2 White House statement on Vietnam, including the paragraph:

"[Secretary McNamara and General Taylor] reported that by the end of this year the United States program for training Vietnamese should have progressed to the point where 1,000 United States military personnel assigned to South Vietnam can be withdrawn." Ibid., p. 4.

"White House Report: U.S. Troops Seen Out of Viet by '65", *Pacific Stars and Stripes* (October 4, 1963), p. 1.

79. *Public Papers of the Presidents: JFK, 1963*, pp. 651–52.

80. Ibid., p. 652.

81. Ibid.

82. According to the Vietnam Memorial Web site, the number of U.S. combat deaths in Vietnam was 8 during the Eisenhower Administration (1957–60). During the Kennedy

years, 16 died in 1961, 53 in 1962, and 118 in the entire year of 1963, including the five weeks when Lyndon Johnson was president.

83. *Public Papers of the Presidents: JFK, 1963*, p. 660.

84. Anne E. Blair, *Lodge in Vietnam: A Patriot Abroad* (New Haven: Yale University Press, 1995), p. 52

85. Joseph Alsop, "Very Ugly Stuff," *Washington Post* (September 18, 1963), p. A17.

86. Mieczyslaw Maneli, *War of the Vanquished* (New York: Harper & Row, 1971), pp. 112–31.

87. *FRUS, 1961–1963*, vol. IV, p. 240.

88. Ibid., p. 254.

89. Ibid., p. 260.

90. Ibid., p. 282.

91. David Halberstam, *The Best and the Brightest* (New York: Random House, 1972), p. 283. Halberstam wrote that the "high-level meeting" at which AID administrator David Bell had his exchange with the president took place "in early September [1963]." He probably meant a September 10, 1963, White House meeting in which a State Department memorandum identifies Bell as one of the participants. *FRUS, 1961–1963*, vol. IV, p. 161. Besides President Kennedy, those who heard Bell's comments on the commodity aid cutoff would then have included Secretary of State Dean Rusk, Attorney General Robert Kennedy, Defense Secretary Robert McNamara, and CIA director John McCone.

92. Ellen J. Hammer, *A Death in November: America in Vietnam, 1963* (New York: E. P. Dutton, 1987), p. 190.

93. Marguerite Higgins, *Our Vietnam Nightmare* (New York: Harper & Row, 1965), p. 208.

94. Ibid.

95. Ibid.

96. *FRUS, 1961–1963*, vol. IV, p. 346.

97. Ibid., p. 369.

98. Ibid., p. 372.

99. Ibid., pp. 372–73.

100. Ibid., p. 374.

101. Ibid., pp. 385–86.

102. Ibid., p.386.

103. Ibid., p. 385.

104. Ibid.

105. Starnes, "'Arrogant' CIA," p. 3.

106. *FRUS, 1961–1963*, vol. IV, p. 352.

107. At the October 2, 1963, National Security Council meeting, Kennedy answered his own question, "What should we say about the news story attacking CIA which appeared in today's *Washington Daily News*?" He read aloud a drafted paragraph for a press release that presented a very different picture from Richard Starnes's report that CIA agents had "penetrated every branch of the American community in Saigon, until non-spook Americans here almost seem to be suffering a CIA psychosis." The draft paragraph claimed instead that "there are no differences of view among the various U.S. agencies represented in Saigon." Kennedy looked up from the press release and said, "That's too fluffy. No one would believe that." He deleted the paragraph from the White House statement issued that night which announced the beginning fall withdrawal from Vietnam. *FRUS, 1961–1963*, vol. IV, p. 352.

108. Starnes, "'Arrogant' CIA," p. 3.

109. Ibid.

110. Prouty interview by Ratcliffe, *Understanding Special Operations*, p. 122.

111. Ibid., p. 123.

112. Ibid.

113. *FRUS, 1961–1963,* vol. IV, p. 434.

114. *Report of the United Nations Fact-Finding Mission to South Viet-Nam* (United Nations Document A/5630, December 7, 1963), pp. 6–7.

115. Ibid., p. 10.

116. Hammer, *Death in November,* p. 261.

117. *FRUS, 1961–1963,* vol. IV, p. 438.

118. Ibid., pp. 443–44.

119. Ibid., p. 444.

120. Ibid., p. 443.

121. Ibid., p. 445.

122. Tran Van Don, *Our Endless War: Inside Vietnam* (Novato, Calif.: Presidio Press, 1987), p. 99.

123. *FRUS, 1961–1963,* vol. IV, pp. 484–85.

124. Ibid., p. 472.

125. Ibid., p. 473.

126. Ibid., p. 449.

127. Ibid., p. 450. Lodge also referred to General Don's awareness of the withdrawal order in reports on October 28 and October 30. Ibid., pp. 449 and 493.

128. Ibid., p. 487.

129. Author's interviews with Abraham Bolden on July 2, 1998; July 22, 1999; January 7, 2000; March 4, 2001; June 16, 2001; July 13, 2003; October 1, 2004.

130. Abraham W. Bolden, Sr., E-mail to Family and Friends on "Death of My Beloved Wife, Barbara," December 27, 2005.

131. Investigative journalist Edwin Black wrote a breakthrough article, "The Plot to Kill JFK in Chicago November 2, 1963," in the November 1975 issue of the *Chicago Independent* magazine. Edwin Black would later become famous for his series of books on the Holocaust: *The Transfer Agreement* (New York: Macmillan, 1984), *IBM and The Holocaust* (New York: Crown Publishers, 2001), and *War against the Weak* (New York: Four Walls Eight Windows, 2003). Black's revealing JFK article, accessible only to the readers of a short-lived magazine and ignored by the national media, soon disappeared from public view. (I found a copy in the basement of the University of Chicago Library a quarter of a century later.) The article drew on the initial research of Chicago court investigator Sherman Skolnick. Black devoted eight months to interviewing witnesses and digging through government documents. Crucial to his article was the firsthand information provided at great risk by an unidentified Secret Service agent—Abraham Bolden.

132. "1,300 Policemen To Guard Routes of Kennedy Here," *Chicago Sun-Times* (November 1, 1963), p. 1.

133. Author's interview of Abraham Bolden, July 13, 2003. Also Black, "Plot to Kill JFK," p. 4.

134. Black, "Plot to Kill JFK," p. 5.

135. Author's July 13, 2003, interview with Bolden.

136. Author's July 13, 2003, interview with Bolden. Also Black, "Plot to Kill JFK," p. 5.

137. Sherman Skolnick's Suit against the National Archives and Records Service, filed on April 6, 1970, in the United States District Court for the Northern District of Illinois Eastern Division, p. 2.

138. Author's interview with Bolden, July 13, 2003.

139. Ibid. Also Black, "Plot to Kill JFK," p. 5.

140. Author's interview with Bolden, July 13, 2003. Also Black, "Plot to Kill JFK," p. 5. Also House Select Committee on Assassinations Interview of Abraham Bolden, January 19, 1978, p. 3. JFK Record Number 180-10070-10273.

141. Hammer, *Death in November,* p. 282.

142. William J. Rust, *Kennedy in Vietnam* (New York: Charles Scribner's Sons, 1985), p. 162.

143. *FRUS, 1961–1963*, vol. IV, p. 517.

144. Ibid.

145. Blair, *Lodge in Vietnam*, p. 68. Hammer, *Death in November*, p. 284.

146. Vallee described himself as a "disaffiliated member of the John Birch Society." "Quiz North Sider on Weapons Count," *Chicago Daily News* (December 3, 1963).

147. Black, "Plot to Kill JFK," p. 6.

148. November 2, 1963, Chicago Police Department Record of Arrest of Thomas Arthur Vallee "for traffic violation and carrying concealed weapon."

149. "Information Concerning Thomas Vallee," November 30, 1963, FBI Teletype "To Director and SACS [Special Agents In Charge], Dallas and New York, From SAC, Chicago," p. 5.

150. Author's interview with Abraham Bolden, July 13, 2003.

151. "Information Concerning Thomas Vallee," November 30, 1963, FBI Teletype, p. 6. Also Record of Arrest for Thomas Arthur Vallee, November 2, 1963, Chicago Police Department.

152. "Information Concerning Thomas Vallee," November 30, 1963, FBI Teletype, pp. 1–2. Author's interview with Luke Christopher Hester, August 24, 2004. When the FBI's red flag on the license plate of the car Vallee was driving came up, the very fact that Hugh Larkin was raising such a question made his old friends in the New York police suspicious of him. They asked him why he was checking it. They evidently also notified the FBI that Larkin and his son-in-law were inquiring about the license plate. FBI agents then showed up at the apartment door of Luke Christopher Hester and his family in Chicago on Thanksgiving morning 1963. They questioned Hester extensively concerning the reasons for his, his father-in-law's, and NBC's interest in Vallee. Hugh Larkin then asked his son-in-law on the phone, "What the hell have you gotten me into?" Author's interview with Luke Christopher Hester, August 23, 2004.

Hugh Larkin's daughter, Mary Larkin Ivino, was so curious about the car's license plate that she conducted her own investigation. She somehow managed to obtain the address for the license plate. It was a location on Long Island. She knew from her brother, who was a firefighter, that the fire department had a registry of addresses. At her request, members of the fire department checked their registry for more information concerning the Long Island address for the license plate of the car Vallee had been driving at his arrest. They told Mary Larkin Ivino, "That address is a vacant lot." Whoever registered the license plate for the car had given an address that would frustrate any quest for further information. Author's interview with Luke Christopher Hester, August 24, 2004.

153. Black, "Plot to Kill JFK," p. 33.

154. Ward Churchill and Jim Vander Wall, *Agents of Repression: The FBI's Secret Wars against the Black Panther Party and the American Indian Movement* (Boston: South End Press, 1990), pp. 66, 71.

155. Ibid., pp. 76–77.

156. Ibid., p. 401 endnote 73.

157. Ibid., p. 398 endnote 27.

158. Ibid.

159. Author's interview with Dan Stern, August 14, 2002.

160. Ibid.

161. Author's interview with Mary Vallee-Portillo, August 14, 2004.

162. Author's interview with Mary Vallee-Portillo, August 17, 2004.

163. Vallee-Portillo interview, August 14, 2004.

164. Ibid. Also FBI Report by Leonard Lewis, St. Louis, Missouri, December 4, 1963; File #SL 105–3665.

165. "Information Concerning Thomas Vallee," November 30, 1963, FBI Teletype, p. 6.

166. Author's interview of Patricia Rish, cousin by marriage of Thomas Arthur Vallee, August 20, 2004.

167. Vallee-Portillo interview, August 14, 2004.

168. Ibid.

169. From a letter in Vallee's Marine Corps medical records dated February 23, 1956, "Subject: Psychiatric evaluation of VALLEE, Thomas Arthur, Corporal, 111 44 55, United States Marine Corps." Cited in Leonard Lewis FBI Report. Also FBI notation at the bottom of copy of letter from John Edgar Hoover, FBI Director, to Thomas A. Vallee, February 15, 1968. FBI Files, JFK Record Number 124-10335-10278.

170. Ibid.

171. Cited in Leonard Lewis FBI Report.

172. Black, "Plot to Kill JFK," pp. 5, 34.

173. Ibid.

174. Robert K. Tanenbaum, who was initially in charge of the House Select Committee on Assassinations investigation of JFK's murder, has described a film he saw (in the HSCA evidence) of Cuban exiles in training near Lake Ponchartrain, with scenes that included CIA officer David Atlee Phillips, CIA pilot David Ferrie, and Lee Harvey Oswald. Jim DiEugenio, "The *Probe* Interview: Bob Tanenbaum," *Probe* (July-August 1996), p. 24; with reference to the film depicted in Robert Tanenbaum's fictionalized account of his HSCA experience, *Corruption of Blood* (New York: Signet Books, 1996), pp. 168–71. When an orchestrated media campaign forced HSCA director Richard Sprague to resign, Tanenbaum also left the HSCA rather than participate in "American history that I knew to be absolutely false." Tanenbaum *Probe* interview, p. 16.

175. "Vallee said he returned to his native Chicago from New York City last August [1963] . . ." From "Quiz North Sider on Weapons Count."

176. Inspector's Copy of December 15, 1913, Building Repair Permit for 625 West Jackson. City of Chicago—Department of Buildings. I am grateful to Craig Tews of the Thomas More Society for his research into the history of 625 West Jackson Boulevard.

177. Berkeley F. Moyland, Jr., citing Berkeley F. Moyland, Sr. Author's interview with Berkeley F. Moyland, Jr., January 2, 2005.

178. Moyland interview.

179. Ibid.

180. Special Agent Francis F. Uteg, United States Secret Service Report on Thomas Arthur Vallee, June 23, 1966, re Lieutenant Berkeley Moyland's description of Vallee. JFK Record Number 180-10080-10131.

181. Moyland interview.

182. Uteg Report.

183. Moyland interview.

184. Ibid.

185. Ibid.

186. *FRUS, 1961–1963*, vol. IV, p. 513.

187. Rust, *Kennedy in Vietnam*, p. 163; with reference to Church Committee, *Alleged Assassination Plots Involving Foreign Leaders* (Washington: U.S. Government Printing Office, 1975), p. 222. Conein said the CIA money he brought with him was also for "death benefits to the families of those [rebel soldiers] killed in the coup." Ibid.

188. *FRUS, 1961–1963*, vol. IV, p. 487.

189. Rust, *Kennedy in Vietnam*, p. 163.

190. Hammer, *Death in November*, pp. 284–85. Rust, *Kennedy in Vietnam*, p. 163. Zalin Grant, *Facing the Phoenix* (New York: W.W. Norton, 1991), p. 209.

191. Kai Bird, *The Color of Truth: McGeorge Bundy and William Bundy, Brothers in Arms: A Biography* (New York: Simon & Schuster, 1998), p. 263.

192. Ibid.

193. Don, *Our Endless War*, p. 107.

194. Hammer, *Death in November*, pp. 292–93; Don, *Our Endless War*, p. 107.

195. John Michael ("Mike") Dunn was interviewed by Zalin Grant on November 6,

1986, for Grant's book, *Facing the Phoenix*. Henry Cabot Lodge died on February 27, 1985.

196. Grant, *Facing the Phoenix*, p. 211.

197. Ibid.

198. Zalin Grant interview of Lucien Conein, September 24, 1986, in *Facing the Phoenix*. Although Don suspected earlier that Diem had escaped, the generals thought he must have remained in the palace, after all, because he was still talking with them on the telephone. The coup leaders had cut most of the phone lines in the Saigon area, but left open a palace line to negotiate Diem's surrender. Unknown to them, in preparation for such an emergency, Diem had run a secret phone line from the palace switchboard to the house of his friend in Cholon. On Saturday morning when the generals thought they were talking to Diem cornered in the palace, he was actually speaking from his hiding place in Cholon. Grant, *Facing the Phoenix*, p. 212. Rust, *Kennedy in Vietnam*, p. 171.

General Don has claimed that Diem in effect then made his and Nhu's murders easy by disclosing their location in Cholon to the generals and inviting them to pick them up. Don, *Our Endless War*, p. 108. After interviewing both Dunn and Conein, journalist Zalin Grant suggested another possibility. In describing Diem's final call to Lodge, Dunn said Lodge "put the phone down and went to check on something," an odd response to a man's appeal for his life. Grant pointed out that Lodge's leaving the line at such a moment "would have given him time to get in touch with Lou Conein," to pass on a location that Diem may have given to Lodge for a ride to the airport but not to the generals. Grant, *Facing the Phoenix*, p. 213. Grant's hypothesis is "that Lodge gave Diem up that morning" to Conein, and (through him) to the generals. Ibid., p. 214.

199. Grant, *Facing the Phoenix*, p. 211.

200. Hammer, *Death in November*, p. 298.

201. Brigadier General Nguyen Khanh characterized Captain Nguyen Van Nhung as a professional assassin in an interview with William J. Rust on April 12, 1982. Rust, *Kennedy in Vietnam*, p. 172. When Khanh carried out his own coup d'état in January 1964, he arrested Captain Nhung for resisting it. Don, *Our Endless War*, p. 112. Khanh then investigated Diem's and Nhu's assassinations. He said Nhung was responsible. But Nhung "did not live long enough to reveal on whose orders he was acting" and was soon "found dead in his jail cell, apparently a suicide victim by hanging." Rust, *Kennedy in Vietnam*, p. 172. According to the other alleged assassin, Major Nghia, "the fate of President Diem was decided by the majority of the members of the Revolutionary Committee." Ibid., p. 173.

202. Higgins, *Our Vietnam Nightmare*, p. 218.

203. Hammer, *Death in November*, p. 298; Rust, *Kennedy in Vietnam*, p. 172.

204. *FRUS, 1961–1963,* vol. IV, p. 559.

205. Higgins, *Our Vietnam Nightmare*, p. 219.

206. Don, *Our Endless War*, p. 112.

207. *FRUS, 1961–1963*, vol. IV, p. 533. Maxwell D. Taylor, *Swords and Plowshares* (New York: W. W. Norton, 1972), p. 301.

208. Taylor, *Swords and Plowshares*, p. 301.

209. Arthur M. Schlesinger, Jr., *A Thousand Days* (Boston: Houghton Mifflin, 1965), p. 997.

210. *FRUS, 1961–1963*, vol. IV, p. 517.

211. Herbert S. Parmet, *JFK: The Presidency of John F. Kennedy* (New York: Dial Press, 1983), pp. 334–35.

212. Tom Wicker, John W. Finney, Max Frankel, E. W. Kenworthy, "C.I.A.: Maker of Policy, or Tool?" *New York Times* (April 25, 1966), p. 20.

213. Ludo De Witte, *The Assassination of Lumumba* (New York: Verso, 2001). De Witte cites CIA head Allen Dulles's August 26, 1960, letter concluding that Lumumba's "removal must be an urgent and prime objective and that under existing conditions this

should be a high priority of our covert action." Ibid., p. 17. Richard Bissell, then head of the CIA's covert action, said, "The Agency had put a top priority, probably, on a range of different methods of getting rid of Lumumba in the sense of either destroying him physically, incapacitating him, or eliminating his political influence." Ibid. As De Witte shows, it was the Belgian government that actually carried out Lumumba's assassination on January 17, 1961, three days before Kennedy became president.

214. Madeleine G. Kalb, *The Congo Cables: The Cold War in Africa—from Eisenhower to Kennedy* (New York: Macmillan, 1982), p. 196.

215. Schlesinger, *Thousand Days*, pp. 553–54.

216. Ibid., p. 554.

217. Ibid.

218. Ibid.

219. Richard D. Mahoney, *JFK: Ordeal in Africa* (New York: Oxford University Press, 1983), p. 69.

220. Richard D. Mahoney interview of Paul Sakwa, May 2, 1978, Washington, D.C. Summarized by Mahoney, *JFK: Ordeal in Africa*, p. 266, endnote 58.

221. Mahoney, *JFK: Ordeal in Africa*, p. 59.

222. Ibid.

223. "Kennedy Cancels Trip Here: Viet Crisis Keeps Him in Capital," *Chicago Daily News* (November 2, 1963), p. 1.

224. Record of Arrest for Thomas Arthur Vallee, Chicago Police Department: "DATE & TIME 2 Nov 63 0910."

225. House Select Committee on Assassinations interview with Abraham Bolden, January 19, 1978. JFK Record Number 180-10070-10273.

226. Author's interview with Bolden, July 13, 2003.

227. Author's interview with Abraham Bolden, June 16, 2001.

228. Ibid.

229. Ibid.

230. Ibid.

231. Author's interview with Bolden, July 13, 2003.

232. Ibid.

233. Author's conversation with Abraham Bolden, August 11, 2007.

234. Author's interview with Bolden, July 13, 2003.

235. Testimony of Abraham Bolden. *United States of America vs. Abraham W. Bolden*. Appeal from the United States District Court for the Northern District of Illinois, Eastern Division, No. 14907; pages 44–45, 59.

236. Ibid., p. 61.

237. Bernard Fensterwald, "The Case of Secret Service Agent Abraham W. Bolden—Who Wanted to Tell the Warren Commission about a Chicago Plot to Kill President Kennedy and Was Jailed Six Years for Trying," *Computers and Automation* (June 1971), p. 42.

238. Ibid., p. 43.

239. Testimony by Joseph Spagnoli on January 20, 1965. Appendix in Bolden Appeal, pp. 4–9. Abraham Bolden said Joseph Spagnoli was not the only witness who committed perjury in Bolden's trial. When Bolden had been released from prison, one day he ran into a former Secret Service agent whom he once trusted. Bolden asked the man why he had told such lies about him in his sworn testimony. The fellow agent said he was under enormous pressure to do so. Bolden said that was no excuse. The ex-agent said, "They would have done the same thing to me that they did to you." Author's interviews with Bolden, June 16, 2001, and July 13, 2003.

240. Author's interview with Abraham Bolden, July 22, 1999.

241. Author's interview with Abraham Bolden, October 1, 2004.

242. Author's interview with Abraham Bolden, July 2, 1998.

243. Author's interviews with Bolden, July 2, 1998, and October 1, 2004.

244. Fensterwald, "Case of Bolden," p. 43. Sherman Skolnick Suit, p. 4 (see n. 137 above).

245. Fensterwald, "Case of Bolden," p. 43.

246. "Cops Seize Gun-Toting Kennedy Foe," *Chicago American* (December 3, 1963).

247. "Quiz North Sider on Weapons Count," *Chicago Daily News* (December 3, 1963). After Thomas Arthur Vallee escaped the fate of Lee Harvey Oswald in November 1963, he left his Chicago job at IPP Litho-Plate in December and moved to New York City. During the remaining twenty-four years of his life, he drifted from one printer's job to another in a series of moves from Long Island to Indianapolis to Columbus, Ohio, to Houston. In each locale the U.S. Secret Service kept Vallee aware that he was being watched through their periodic phone calls, visits, and inquiries to his employers. When I requested Vallee's available files from the National Archives, they included many such Secret Service reports on him spanning the rest of his life. He was always living alone in an apartment or trailer, pursuing his profession as a printer, having no apparent contact with any political groups or government agencies other than his Secret Service checkups. His relatives whom I interviewed seldom saw him. Mary Vallee-Portillo believed her brother chose such isolation because he did not want his problems, including his strange link to the Kennedy assassination, to burden members of his family. They almost invariably described him as "a lost soul." Thomas Arthur Vallee died of cancer in Maywood, Illinois, on March 26, 1988. He was fifty-four years old.

248. Douglas P. Horne, the Assassination Records Review Board's Chief Analyst for Military Records, has made public the story of the Secret Service's shredding of what the Review Board suspected were incriminating documents: "In 1995, the Review Board Staff became aware that the U.S. Secret Service had destroyed protective survey reports related to John F. Kennedy's Presidency, and that they had done so well after the passage of the JFK Records Act, and well after having been briefed by the National Archives (NARA) on the Act's requirements to preserve all Assassination Records from destruction until the ARRB had made a determination that any such proposed destruction was acceptable." Douglas P. Horne, *Inside the Assassination Records Review Board: The U.S. Government's Final Attempt to Reconcile the Conflicting Medical Evidence in the Assassination of JFK,* Vol. V (Amazon.com, 2009; also available from Mary Ferrell Foundation website), p. 1451.

The protective survey reports destroyed by the Secret Service covered all of JFK's trips from September 24 through November 8, 1963, including three folders on his cancelled November 2, 1963, trip to Chicago. (Ibid., pp. 1453–54.) Faced by a legal mandate to produce specified evidence in the assassination of the president, the Secret Service had instead shredded two boxes of critical documents.

On August 7, 1995, the ARRB's Executive Director David G. Marwell sent a letter to Secret Service officials spelling out the criminal nature of their action: "The President John F. Kennedy Assassination Records Collection Act (JFK Act) forbids the destruction of any documents 'created *or made available for use by, obtained by, or [that] otherwise came into the possession of . . . the Select Committee on Assassinations . . . of the House of Representatives.' It is our understanding that the records in Accession 87–75–0004 that the Secret Service destroyed were examined by the House Select Committee on Assassinations and thus were 'assassination records' under the JFK Act and they apparently were destroyed in violation of law.*

"We see the destruction of these assassination records as particularly ominous in light of the fact that the Secret Service revised its destruction schedule *after* passage of the JFK Act and that it targeted for destruction records that, at the time the law was passed, were slated to be held 'permanently.'" [emphasis in original] Cited by Horne, ibid., p. 1456.

Douglas Horne reported that ARRB officials were then "considering holding public hearings in which the Secret Service officials responsible for said destruction would be called to account and castigated, in an open forum, with the media present." Ibid., p. 1451.

Secret Service officials quickly arranged a truce with the ARRB, promising they would destroy no more records "related to Presidential protection for the years 1958–1969" without ARRB approval and would grant "full access to all Secret Service records upon demand." (Ibid., p. 1457.) However, the Chicago plot documents and many others were no longer accessible to anyone. They had already been criminally destroyed.

ARRB staff member Horne commented: "The Review Board itself consciously soft-pedaled the dispute in its Final Report, devoting only one paragraph (and virtually no details whatsoever) to the incident." Ibid., p. 1451.

6. Washington and Dallas

1. "Message From Chairman Khrushchev to President Kennedy," December 11, 1962. *Foreign Relations of the United States, 1961–1963, Volume VI: Kennedy-Khrushchev Exchanges* (Washington: U.S. Government Printing Office, 1996), p. 228.

2. Sergei N. Khrushchev, *Nikita Khrushchev and the Creation of a Superpower* (University Park, Pa.: Pennsylvania State University Press, 2000), p. 695.

3. Norman Cousins, "Pope John's Optimism on Peace: Nothing Is Impossible," *Seattle Times* (April 1, 1973).

4. *Public Papers of the Presidents: John F. Kennedy, 1963* (Washington: U.S. Government Printing Office, 1964), p. 462.

5. David Halberstam, *The Best and the Brightest* (New York: Random House, 1972), pp. 295–96.

6. Ibid., p. 296.

7. FBI Report from San Antonio Office by John M. Kemmy, April 30, 1964; Warren Commission Exhibit Number 2129; *WCH, Exhibits,* vol. 24, p. 704.

8. Written statement by Albert Guy Bogard to Dallas FBI Agents C. Ray Hall and Maurice J. White, December 9, 1963; Warren Commission Exhibit No. 2969; *WCH, Exhibits,* vol. 26, p. 451. Albert Guy Bogard said he thought the date of the Oswald visit to Downtown Lincoln-Mercury was November 9, 1963. It was a date the FBI and the Warren Commission locked onto. However, another key witness, car salesman Eugene M. Wilson, said the incident definitely occurred on Saturday, November 2. Wilson was able to identify the date because "Oswald" test drove the red Mercury Comet before "Wilson used the same vehicle later that day to drive his wife and friends home after a meeting of the Lone Star Bulldog Club." Wilson confirmed the date of the meeting, and thus of the young man's test drive, as November 2. Earl Golz, "Salesman Insists FBI Discounted Facts on Oswald," *Dallas Morning News* (May 8, 1977), p. 12A. On CD-ROM for John Armstrong, *Harvey and Lee* (Arlington, Tex.: Quasar, 2003), November, 63-01.

9. *WCH, Exhibits,* vol. 26, p. 451. When "Oswald" and Bogard returned to the showroom, the young man refused to give his address and phone number, so Bogard just wrote the name "Lee Oswald" on the back of one of his cards and put it in his pocket. On November 22 when he heard on the radio that Oswald had been picked up as a suspect, Bogard showed co-workers the card with "Lee Oswald" written on the back, said "He isn't a prospect [for a sale] any more," and threw the card in the waste basket. Ibid.

10. Golz, "Salesman Insists," p. 12A. The *Warren Report* dismissed witness Eugene M. Wilson's citation of the young man's statement, "Maybe I'm going to have to go back to Russia to buy a car," on the grounds that "the statement is not consistent with Bogard's story. Indeed, Bogard has made no mention that the customer ever spoke with Wilson while he was in the showroom. More important, on November 23, a search through the showroom's refuse was made, but no paper bearing Oswald's name was found." *The Warren Commission Report* (New York: St. Martin's Press, 1992, from U.S. Government printing 1964), p. 321.

Based on the Warren Commission's own documents, Bogard and Wilson appear to be complementary, not contradictory, witnesses, supported by two other witnesses, Frank

Pizzo and Oran Brown. See the point-by-point analyses of the testimony of all four men by Sylvia Meagher, *Accessories after the Fact: The Warren Commission, the Authorities, and the Report* (New York: Vintage Books, 1992), pp. 351–56, and by Mark Lane, *Rush to Judgment* (New York: Thunder's Mouth Press, 1992), pp. 331–33. Oran Brown also told Mark Lane: "You know, I am afraid to talk. Bogard was beaten by some men so badly that he was in the hospital for some time, and this was after he testified. Then he left town suddenly and I haven't heard from him or about him since." *Rush to Judgment*, p. 333 footnote. When Brown spoke with Lane on April 4, 1966, he was unaware that Bogard had already died two months earlier, on February 14, 1966, an apparent suicide victim from carbon monoxide poisoning in his car in a Hallsville, Louisiana, cemetery. Craig Roberts and John Armstrong, *JFK: The Dead Witnesses* (Tulsa, Okla.: Consolidated Press International, 1995), p. 37. Michael Benson, *Encyclopedia of the JFK Assassination* (New York: Checkmark Books, 2002), p. 63.

11. *Warren Report*, p. 321.

12. From Thomas Merton's January 18, 1962, letter to W. H. Ferry, in *Letters from Tom: A Selection of Letters from Father Thomas Merton, Monk of Gethsemani, to W. H. Ferry, 1961–1968*, edited by W. H. Ferry (Scarsdale, New York: Fort Hill Press, 1983), p. 15.

13. Ibid.

14. Ralph G. Martin, *A Hero for Our Time: An Intimate Story of the Kennedy Years* (New York: Ballantine Books, 1983), p. 500.

15. Robert F. Kennedy, *Thirteen Days: A Memoir of the Cuban Missile Crisis* (New York: Signet, 1969), p. 110.

16. Evelyn Lincoln, *My Twelve Years with John F. Kennedy* (New York: Bantam Books, 1966), p. 230.

17. T. S. Settel, editor, *The Faith of JFK* (New York: E. P. Dutton, 1965), p. 92.

18. Nicholas A. Schneider, *Religious Views of President John F. Kennedy* (St. Louis: B. Herder, 1965), p. 99.

19. Martin, *Hero for Our Times*, p. 503.

20. Geoffrey Perret, *Jack: A Life like No Other* (New York: Random House, 2001), p. 197.

21. Ibid.

22. The formal title of Alan Seeger's most famous poem seems to have been "Rendezvous," as it is identified at www.emory.edu/ENGLISH/LostPoets/Seeger. However, in *The Oxford Book of American Verse*, Seeger's poem is titled by its refrain, *"I Have a Rendezvous with Death." The Oxford Book of American Verse*, chosen and edited by Bliss Carman (New York: Oxford University Press, 1927), pp. 624–25.

23. Richard D. Mahoney interview of Samuel E. Belk III. Richard D. Mahoney, *Sons & Brothers: The Days of Jack and Bobby Kennedy* (New York: Arcade, 1999), p. 281.

24. *WCH*, vol. 10, p. 370.

25. Ibid., pp. 371–72.

26. Ibid., p. 380.

27. Other witnesses added their own vivid descriptions of a man looking like Oswald taking target practice at the Sports Drome in Dallas in November. See the Warren Commission testimony of Sterling Charles Wood and his father, Dr. Homer Wood. Ibid., pp. 385–98.

28. *Warren Report*, p. 319.

29. Ibid., pp. 734–35.

30. Ibid., p. 319.

31. The Warren Commission also had to deal with the fact that some witnesses to the rifle-firing Oswald "said he was accompanied by one or more other persons." *Warren Report*, p. 318. Garland Slack, for example, told his wife that Oswald was brought to the Sports Drome on one occasion "by a man named 'Frazier' from Irving, Texas." *WCH*,

Exhibit No. 3077; *WCH*, vol. 26, p. 681. Buell Wesley Frazier, Ruth Paine's neighbor in Irving, was Lee Harvey Oswald's co-worker at the Texas School Book Depository. Frazier denied to the FBI that he had ever taken Oswald to a rifle range. Ibid. If it was indeed Frazier and either an impersonator or the real Oswald, their joint involvement immediately introduced the issue of conspiracy—another subject the Warren Commission tried to avoid. The *Warren Report* concluded that "the allegations pertaining to the companions who reportedly accompanied the man believed to be Oswald" were "inconsistent among themselves," thus dismissing also the troubling evidence of collaborators. *Warren Report*, p. 319. Besides too many Oswalds, there were too many Oswald companions. Once President Johnson (and the Warren Commission) had backed away from the implications of a conspiracy, even one Oswald companion was too many.

32. *WCH, Exhibit* 15; vol. 16, p. 33.

33. *Warren Report*, p. 734.

34. Former FBI director Clarence M. Kelley was stressing the importance of Kostikov, "which cannot be overstated," by citing this statement by former Dallas FBI agent Jim Hosty. Clarence M. Kelley and James Kirkpatrick Davis, *Kelley: The Story of an FBI Director* (Kansas City: Andrews, McMeel & Parker, 1987), p. 268.

35. Kelley citing Hosty, ibid.

36. See chapter 2 of this book.

37. *WCH, Exhibit* 15, vol. 16, p. 33 (emphasis added).

38. *WCH, Exhibit* 3126, vol. 26, p. 790.

39. Transcript of Telephone Conversation between Lyndon B. Johnson and J. Edgar Hoover, November 23, 1963, 10:01 AM; p. 2; Box 1, LBJ Library. Just how sensitive this phone conversation was can be seen from its tape and transcript history. After the call from Hoover was transcribed from the audiotape by a member of LBJ's secretarial staff, that specific conversation was erased from the tape, leaving a fourteen-minute gap in the midst of eleven other non-erased calls made on November 23, 1963. Rex Bradford, "The Fourteen-Minute Gap," *Kennedy Assassination Chronicles* (Spring 2000), p. 29.

According to acoustics experts hired in 1998 by the Johnson Library and the National Archives and Records Administration, "the erasure was most likely intentional and is irreversible." Max Holland, *The Kennedy Assassination Tapes* (New York: Alfred A. Knopf, 2004), p. 69.

Fortunately the transcript of the conversation has survived, but not without at least one challenge to its Soviet Embassy references. In the upper righthand corner of my LBJ Library copy of the transcript, there can be read the hand-printed words: "DELETE P. 2 ref. To Soviet Embassy." Below these words are the circled initials: "TJ." In response to my phone query of February 18, 2005, to the LBJ Library, senior archivist Claudia Anderson said that "TJ" was probably Tom Johnson, President Johnson's longtime assistant. Tom Johnson (no relation to LBJ) could have made the notation on the transcript any time between late November 1963 through his years as Johnson's post-presidential aide from 1969 until LBJ's death in 1973. The most likely period for the note to have been written would seem to be soon after the transcribing of the November 23 tape, when the Mexico City issue was most alarming and when the tape itself was probably erased on the orders of Lyndon Johnson. If there was a further reference to the Soviet Embassy (either the embassy in Mexico City or the one in Washington) that was in fact deleted, then the Hoover-Johnson conversation was even more sensitive than the transcript reveals.

40. Hoover was also soft-pedaling the letter's two paragraphs complaining about the FBI. In the first such paragraph (the fifth paragraph of the letter), "Oswald" stated:

"Agent James P. Hasty [Hosty] warned me that if I engaged in F.P.C.C. [Fair Play for Cuba Committee] activities in Texas the F.B.I. will again take an 'interrest' [*sic*] in me." *WHC, Exhibit* 15, vol. 16, p. 33.

In the second FBI-related paragraph (the sixth paragraph of the letter), the text continued:

"This agent also 'suggested' to Marina Nichilayeva that she could remain in the United

States under F.B.I. 'protection,' that is, she could defect from the Soviet uion [*sic*], of couse [*sic*], I and my wife strongly protested these tactics by the notorious F.B.I." Ibid.

"Oswald" (or the CIA in the name of Oswald) has thereby given the FBI alibis for its pre-assassination contacts with the Oswalds, while at the same time making the FBI uncomfortable for having been put up front and on record for even its "innocent" contacts with "the assassin." Meanwhile, to Hoover's annoyance, the manipulating CIA has remained invisible both in the letter and in the larger Oswald story, while the FBI has been exposed to public scrutiny for its documented contacts with Lee and Marina Oswald.

41. "From the Mainstream Press: 'Soviets Believed Oswald Letter Fake' and 'More On All This, *Fair Play Magazine* Web site (September 1, 1999).

42. A. Dobrynin, Cipher Telegram, Special no. 2005, November 26, 1963. Russian original and English translation (by Office of Language Services, Department of State) in National Archives, College Park, Maryland.

43. John A. McCone, "Memorandum for the Record," November 25, 1963. Copy from LBJ Library.

44. Ibid. McCone in his memorandum notes that National Security Adviser McGeorge Bundy also attended the 12:30 P.M., November 23, 1963, briefing of Johnson on Mexico City. McCone then went over the Mexico City information again in a phone conversation that evening with Secretary of State Dean Rusk. Ibid.

45. Michael R. Beschloss, editor, *Taking Charge: The Johnson White House Tapes, 1963–64* (New York: Simon & Schuster, 1997), p. 72. Cf. Holland, *Kennedy Assassination Tapes*, p. 205.

46. Beschloss, *Taking Charge*, p. 67. Cf. Holland, *Kennedy Assassination Tapes*, p. 197.

47. Dobrynin, November 26, 1963, Cipher Telegram.

48. Anastas I. Mikoyan, Telegram to the Soviet Ambassador, Washington; included with Dobrynin's November 26, 1963, telegram in packet of documents given to President Bill Clinton by President Boris Yeltsin in June 1999. Russian original and English translation in National Archives, College Park, Maryland.

49. Beschloss, *Taking Charge*, p. 72. Cf. Holland, *Kennedy Assassination Tapes*, p. 206.

50. WCH, vol. 3, p. 13.

51. Ibid., p. 15.

52. Ibid., pp. 14–17. Ruth Paine testified to the Warren Commission that she gave the "original" handwritten draft of the letter to "an FBI person" who appeared at her house on November 23, 1963. She said she also gave the FBI her copy of that draft in her own hand, probably the next day. Ibid., p. 17.

53. Ibid., pp. 13–18.

54. Jerry D. Rose, "Gifts from Russia: Yeltsin and Mitrokhin," *The Fourth Decade* (November 1999), p. 5. Rose reproduces both the typed letter and the draft in his article, so that readers can compare the two. Both versions of the letter are also included on p. 311 of the *Warren Report*, but in too illegible a form for any comparisons to be made. The typed letter is reproduced more clearly twice in the Warren Commission Hearings: WCH, vol. 16, p. 33, as Commission Exhibit 15; vol. 18, p. 539, as Commission Exhibit 986. The handwritten "draft" can be read in its reproduction as Commission Exhibit 103, WCH, vol. 16, pp. 443–44.

55. In the "draft," Oswald's complaints about the FBI have been moved up to become the third and fourth paragraphs, thereby replacing the suggestion of a Soviet/Cuban conspiracy as the main subject of the letter. The Soviet/Cuban material in the typed letter's third and fourth paragraphs has been dropped down and merged into a final paragraph in the "draft." The de-emphasized Soviet/Cuban connection has then been rendered innocuous by the "draft's" crossed-out words, now made available to the Warren Commission for its overall exegesis of the letter.

56. Peter Dale Scott noted the "draft's" neutralizing of the letter's conspiratorial lan-

guage, especially in its description of Kostikov's role, in his essay, "The CIA, the Drug Traffic, and Oswald in Mexico," p. 13, from the on-line book, *It's the Economy, Stupid!*, edited by Kent Heiner (Bellingham, WA: Mem Publishing, 2002).

57. *Warren Report*, p. 310.

58. On April 17, 1964, J. Lee Rankin, general counsel of the Warren Commission, wrote a letter to J. Edgar Hoover saying the Commission had approved Mrs. Ruth Hyde Paine's request for "the return to her" of the "rough draft of a letter in the handwriting of Lee Harvey Oswald which Mrs. Paine testified she found in her residence." The Commission also approved at the same time Paine's request for the return of her personally annotated 1963 date book and calendar. Letter from J. Lee Rankin to J. Edgar Hoover, April 17, 1964. FBI Files, JFK Record Number 124-10147-10029.

When she was notified at the end of April that the Warren Commission had approved her request, Ruth Paine may have thought she had gone too far in asking for the return of a letter that had become important government evidence in the assassination of President Kennedy. The "draft" letter then became a hot potato. When the Dallas FBI office tried to return it to Paine by order of the Commission, she immediately gave it back to the Commission, saying now that it would be "more proper" to keep it in the public archives. But she restated, as the Dallas FBI reported to Hoover, that "if this item is not made public property by the Commission after their hearings are recessed, and it is to be returned to the private property domain, she would like to have it back at that time." Letter from SAC, Dallas, to Director, FBI, April 28, 1964; FBI Files, JFK Record Number 124-10147-10022.

At that point the Warren Commission had no intention of preserving for any future critical examination, as to its source and authenticity, the original document Ruth Paine said she wanted back. On May 4, 1964, Hoover sent back again the "original rough draft letter in the handwriting of Oswald" to the Dallas FBI office for its return once and for all to Paine. Hoover said with finality that the Commission had ruled that it was "advisable to give it to Mrs. Paine," which the FBI then did. Message from Director, FBI, to SAC, Dallas, May 4, 1964; FBI Files, JFK Record Number 124-10147-10022.

59. Thomas Merton, *Peace in the Post-Christian Era* (Maryknoll, N.Y.: Orbis Books, 2004), p. 119.

60. Heather A. Purcell and James K. Galbraith, "Did the U.S. Military Plan a Nuclear First Strike for 1963?," *The American Prospect* (Fall 1994), pp. 88–96.

61. Memorandum for Vice President Lyndon Johnson, "Notes on National Security Council Meeting, July 20, 1961," by Colonel Howard Burris, Johnson's military aide; reproduced in Purcell and Galbraith, "Did the U.S. Military Plan," p. 89.

62. Ibid.

63. Roswell Gilpatric, in recorded interview by D. J. O'Brien, August 12, 1970, p. 117; JFK Library Oral History Program. Cf. Arthur M. Schlesinger, Jr., *Robert Kennedy and His Times* (New York: Ballantine Books, 1978), p. 483.

64. Schlesinger, *Robert Kennedy*, p. 483; McGeorge Bundy, *Danger and Survival: Choices about the Bomb in the First Fifty Years* (New York: Random House, 1988), p. 354. Dean Rusk, *As I Saw It* (New York: W. W. Norton, 1990), pp. 246–47.

65. Schlesinger, *Robert Kennedy*, p. 483.

66. Bundy, *Danger and Survival*, p. 354.

67. Rusk, *As I Saw It*, pp. 246–47; Bundy, *Danger and Survival*, p. 354.

68. Merton, *Peace in the Post-Christian Era*, p. 16.

69. Stewart Alsop, "Kennedy's Grand Strategy," *Saturday Evening Post* (March 31, 1962), p. 14 (Alsop's emphasis).

70. Pierre Salinger, *With Kennedy* (Garden City, N.Y.: Doubleday, 1966), p. 227.

71. Ibid.

72. Ibid.

73. Pierre Salinger was in Moscow May 11–15, 1963. *With Kennedy*, p. 220. On May 17, while Nikita Khrushchev was visiting Bulgaria, he got the idea of placing Soviet missiles in Cuba. *Khrushchev Remembers*, edited by Strobe Talbott (Boston: Little, Brown,

1970), p. 493. Sergei N. Khrushchev, *Nikita Khrushchev and the Creation of a Super-power* (University Park, Pa.: Pennsylvania State University Press, 2000), p. 483.

74. Talbott, *Khrushchev Remembers*, p. 493.

75. Salinger, *With Kennedy*, p. 228.

76. Either Khrushchev did not mention in his story, or Salinger did not include in his narration of it, that JFK had specifically asked the Soviet Leader (via Robert Kennedy's back-channel meeting with Soviet Embassy attaché Georgi Bolshakov) to pull back his tanks from the confrontation at the Wall. That part of the tanks story was revealed by Robert Kennedy in his oral history, *Robert Kennedy in His Own Words*, edited by Edwin O. Guthman and Jeffrey Shulman (New York: Bantam Books, 1988), pp. 259–60.

77. Schlesinger, *Robert Kennedy*, p. 565.

78. *Foreign Relations of the United States (FRUS), 1961–1963, Volume VIII: National Security Policy* (Washington: U.S. Government Printing Office, 1996), p. 388.

79. Ibid., p. 403.

80. Ibid.

81. Ibid., pp. 403, 405.

82. Ibid., p. 499, footnote 1.

83. The State Department history, *National Security Policy* (for 1961–1963), provides both a Summary Record and a Resume of Discussion for the September 12, 1963, meeting of the National Security Council. Each document helps to illuminate the other, and the two together enable us to follow the meeting's discussion. Ibid., pp. 499–503, 503–7.

84. Ibid., pp. 499–500.

85. Ibid., pp. 500, 503.

86. Ibid., p. 503.

87. Ibid., p. 500.

88. Ibid., pp. 500, 503.

89. Ibid.

90. Ibid., pp. 500, 504.

91. Ibid.

92. Ibid., pp. 500–501.

93. Ibid., p. 501 (emphasis added).

94. Ibid.

95. Ibid.

96. Ibid., p. 505.

97. Ibid., p. 502.

98. Ibid., p. 506.

99. Ibid., p. 502.

100. Ibid., p. 509.

101. Ibid., p. 506 (emphasis added).

102. Ibid.

103. Ibid.

104. Burris Memorandum, Purcell and Galbraith, "Did the U.S. Military Plan," p. 89.

105. *FRUS, 1961–1963*, vol. VIII, p. 499, footnote 1.

106. Memorandum for Mr. Bundy by W. Y. Smith, Subject: Net Evaluation Sub-Committee (NESC), August 28, 1963, p. 1 (emphasis added). National Defense University, Maxwell D. Taylor Papers, Box 27, Folder E, WYS Chron File (Apr.-Sept. 63), Item 24. This important, top-secret document was completely declassified by the National Security Council on December 16, 2005, and by the Department of Defense on January 13, 2006, in response to a Freedom of Information Act request made by the author on March 11, 2005.

Colonel Smith's memorandum made a recommendation that was at direct odds with the president: "The study raises one major and interesting issue: our offensive and defensive weapons currently programmed will not reduce damage from a full nuclear exchange to an acceptable level. Consequently, there is a need for development of new offensive and defensive weapons." Ibid.

The specific "need" Smith identifies, on behalf of the Joint Chiefs of Staff, is the need for an updated first-strike system, a combination of "offensive and defensive weapons" that could both preempt and deflect the fewer Soviet missiles that constituted the U.S.S.R. deterrent to a U.S. attack. If Pentagon strategists were able to reduce such damage "to an acceptable level" in their prewar planning, they would thereby nullify the Soviet deterrent. The war system's constant purpose after the death of Kennedy, who rejected first-strike planning, would be to regain a first strike capability over newer Soviet weapons. The strategic factor behind the nuclear arms race until the breakup of the Soviet Union was the unrelenting U.S. push for a first-strike capability and Cold War dominance. See Robert C. Aldridge, *First Strike! The Pentagon's Strategy for Nuclear War* (Boston: South End Press, 1983).

Colonel Smith's memorandum also reflects his awareness that the president wanted no more first-strike reports or recommendations, and in fact wanted to abolish the Net Evaluation Sub-Committee that was coming up with them. Smith notes an observer's impression from a previous meeting "that Secretary McNamara [representing the president's view] believed the NESC had largely fulfilled its usefulness." Ibid.

As a result of the Kennedy/McNamara opposition to the sub-committee and its first-strike scenarios, its head, General Johnson, had already given his staff other "useful things" to do, as Smith states in his memorandum. He specifies this presumed change of focus: "The NESC staff was given the task of conducting a 4-month study (*to be completed in November*) on the termination of war problems . . . " (ibid., p. 2; emphasis added), another study that was in fact complementary to a first-strike plan.

How to deal with the "termination of war problems" was critical to a "successful" preemptive attack that would involve the "acceptable" loss of several million U.S. citizens, as well as 140 million Soviet citizens. There would indeed be "problems" involved in the "termination" of such a war. The four-month study's November 1963 completion corresponded to Kennedy's assassination and to the "late 1963" time line that the generals in their first Net Report had projected for a preemptive attack on the Soviet Union, before their window of opportunity closed as the Russians developed their missile force into a more effective deterrent.

107. Burris Memorandum, Purcell and Galbraith, "Did the U.S. Military Plan," p. 89.

108. Richard H. Popkin, *The Second Oswald* (New York: Avon, 1966), p. 92; Matthew Smith, *JFK: The Second Plot* (Edinburgh: Mainstream, 1992), p. 269.

109. Smith, *JFK: The Second Plot*, p. 269.

110. Popkin, *Second Oswald*, p. 92; Smith, *JFK: The Second Plot*, p. 270.

111. Author's interview of Matthew Smith, January 3, 2007.

112. Matthew Smith has reproduced the report of Wayne January's November 29, 1963, FBI interview on pp. 272–73 of *JFK: The Second Plot*. A separate FBI memorandum which conveys the same misrepresentation of January's interview is reproduced by John Armstrong on his CD-Rom for *Harvey and Lee*, "1963 November 1–21," image 19.

113. Smith, *JFK: The Second Plot*, p. 273.

114. Smith interview.

115. Ibid.

116. Interview with Francis Louis Fruge, April 7, 1978, pp. 1–2; House Select Committee on Assassinations; JFK Record Number 180-10106-10014.

117. Ibid., p. 3.

118. Testimony of Francis Fruge, April 18, 1978, p. 9; House Select Committee on Assassinations; JFK Record Number 180-10105-10330.

119. "Rose Cheramie," Staff Report of the House Select Committee on Assassinations; *Appendix to Hearings before the Select Committee on Assassinations of the U.S. House of Representatives* (HSCA) (Washington: U.S. Government Printing Office, 1979), vol. 10, p. 200. Memorandum from Frank Meloche to Louis Ivon, Chief Investigator, New Orleans District Attorney's Office, May 22, 1967. JFK Record Number 180-10112-10310.

120. Fruge interview, p. 3.

121. Ibid.

122. Report by Frederick U. Turner, Customs Agent, to Chief Agent Customs, Port Arthur, Texas, December 10, 1963, p. 1. JFK Record Number 180-10105-10003.

123. Ibid., p. 2.

124. Fruge interview, pp. 4–5. Fruge testimony, pp. 20, 22–23.

125. Fruge testimony, p. 20. Fruge interview, p. 4.

126. Fruge interview, p. 5.

127. Ibid., p. 5. Fruge testimony, p. 19.

128. Interview of Officer J. A. Andrews, Texas Highway Patrol, by Lt. F. L. Fruge, April 4, 1967, p. 1. JFK Record Number 180-10112-10057. James DiEugenio, "Rose Cheramie: How She Predicted the JFK Assassination," in *The Assassinations*, edited by James DiEugenio and Lisa Pease (Los Angeles: Feral House, 2003), p. 229.

129. DiEugenio, *Assassinations*, p. 229.

130. Andrews interview, p. 1.

131. Charles A. Crenshaw, with Jens Hansen and J. Gary Shaw, *JFK: Conspiracy of Silence* (New York: Signet, 1992), p. 44. Besides swearing that he didn't hit Rose Cheramie with his car, Jerry Don Moore "also stated that upon stopping to render aid and to transport the victim to medical facilities, he saw a late-model red Chevrolet parked nearby. Cheramie's sister confirms the red Chevy story. She was told by investigating authorities that they too had seen the automobile at the scene shortly before the accident as they made their usual patrol of the area." Ibid., pp. 44–45. Cheramie's family, however, was reluctant to pursue any questions in a follow-up probe. Andrews interview, p. 1.

132. Andrews interview, p. 1. Interviewer Fruge raised other questions concerning Cheramie's "accidental" death: "It should be noted that Hwy. #155 is a Farm to Market Road, running parallel to US Hwys. #271 and #80. It is our opinion, from experience, that if a subject was hitch-hiking, as this report wants to indicate, that this *does not* run true to form" (emphasis in original).

Fruge also "found it unusual that a person would be hit by an auto and only have a fracture of the skull without breaking any other bones in the body." Fruge interview, p. 7.

133. Crenshaw, *JFK: Conspiracy of Silence*, p. 44.

134. Ibid.

135. DiEugenio, *Assassinations*, p. 229.

136. Fruge testimony, p. 28.

137. Ibid., pp. 27–28.

138. In his deposition for the House Select Committee on Assassinations, Francis Fruge identified the same photographs that Mac Manual had said to him were of the two men who were with Rose Cheramie. The photos were of Sergio Arcacha Smith and Emilio Santana. Fruge testimony, pp. 28–30; together with S. Jonathan Blackmer's "Summary of Deposition of Francis Louis Fruge Taken on April 18, 1978, in Baton Rouge, Louisiana," p. 1. JFK Record Number 180-10089-10046.

Fruge also stated that Mac Manual "was shot to death in 1974–1975 in Villeplatte, Louisiana." Fruge interview, p. 6.

139. September 1, 1967, Memorandum to District Attorney Jim Garrison from Assistant D. A. William R. Martin on August 25, 1967, Interview with Emilio Santana; p. 2. I am grateful to researcher Bill Davy for sharing with me this Emilio Santana interview and the Santana interviews cited in the next three notes, all of which he obtained from the Assassination Archives and Research Center, Washington, D.C.

140. Ibid. Also February 15, 1967, Memorandum to District Attorney Jim Garrison from Assistant D.A. James L. Alcock on February 14, 1967, Interview with Emilio Santana, p. 1.

141. February 14, 1967, Santana Interview, p. 1.

142. February 17, 1967, Memorandum to District Attorney Jim Garrison from Investigator Lynn Loisell on February 16, 1967, Interview of Emilio Santana, pp. 4–5.

143. David C. Martin, *Wilderness of Mirrors* (New York: Ballantine Books, 1980),

p. 144. Robert Kennedy demanded that the CIA's William Harvey tell him on whose authority Harvey had sent sixty commandos "into Cuba at a time when the slightest provocation might unleash a nuclear holocaust." Kennedy described Harvey's response: "[Harvey] said we planned it because the military wanted it done, and I asked the military and they never heard of it." When RFK demanded a better explanation and Harvey floundered, Kennedy walked out on him while he was still talking. Ibid.

144. CIA Memorandum on "Garrison Investigation; Emilio SANTANA Galindo," July 9, 1967. JFK Record Number 104-10170-10146.

145. "Resume of Sergio Arcacha," JFK Record Number 180-10085-10408.

146. Ibid.

147. "File Review of Sergio Arcacha Smith," Immigration and Naturalization Service, May 5, 1978; p. 3. JFK Record Number 180-10078-10412. "File Review of Sergio Arcacha Smith and Frank Sturgis," Department of Defense, May 26, 1978; p. 1. JFK Record Number 180-10091-10175.

148. DOD "File Review of Sergio Arcacha Smith and Frank Sturgis," p. 1.

149. INS "File Review of Sergio Arcacha Smith," p. 3.

150. CIA Reference Memorandum on Sergio Vicente Arcacha Smith. JFK Record Number 104-10130-10011.

151. Ibid.

152. From the notes of reporter Dick Billings, 2/21/67. Cited by DiEugenio, *Assassinations,* p. 232.

153. "Cuban Revolutionary Council (CRC): New Orleans Chapter," *Appendix to HSCA Hearings,* vol. 10, p. 61.

154. E. Howard Hunt, *Give Us This Day* (New York: Popular Library, 1973), pp. 182–89.

155. "David Ferrie," *Appendix to HSCA Hearings,* vol. 10, p. 110; "544 Camp Street and Related Events," pp. 126–27.

156. Ibid., p. 110.

157. Ibid. It was Guy Banister who "talked [building-owner] Sam Newman into leasing 544 Camp Street to the Cuban Revolutionary Council" office of Sergio Arcacha Smith. Ibid., p. 127.

158. Ibid., p. 123.

159. Gary Sanders Interview of Richard Rolfe, Memorandum to Louis Ivon, January 13, 1968; p. 1. From the National Archives, Garrison Investigative Papers, Folder: Sanders, Gary; Box 10. By 1963 Sergio Arcacha Smith had moved to Texas, first to Houston, then Dallas, where he was reportedly living at the time of Kennedy's assassination. DiEugenio, *Assassinations,* p. 233. Also INS "File Review of Sergio Arcacha Smith," p. 3.

160. Statement of David F. Lewis, Jr., December 15, 1966, New Orleans District Attorney's Office, p. 1. JFK Record Number 180-10070-10356. In a Secret Service interview in December 1963, Arnesto M. Rodriguez, Sr., a seventy-two-year-old Cuban exile living in New Orleans, said that Carlos Quiroga "knew Arcacha well and was with him frequently (very close connection) at 544 Camp Street." December 1, 1963, Interview of Arnesto M. Rodriguez, Sr., United States Secret Service, Treasury Department. JFK Record Number 180-10078-10417. Quiroga acknowledged his friendship and financial help to Arcacha in his interview by Jim Garrison on January 21, 1967. JFK Record Number 180-10078-10418. Carlos Quiroga visited Lee Harvey Oswald at Oswald's apartment in New Orleans in August 1963. The stack of pamphlets, about 5 or 6 inches high (according to Oswald's landlady), that Quiroga brought to Oswald indicates Quiroga was an intelligence asset delivering pamphlets to his fellow agent, Oswald. *WCH,* vol. 10, p. 269. Ray and Mary La Fontaine, *Oswald Talked: The New Evidence in the JFK Assassination* (Gretna, La.: Pelican, 1996), p. 162.

161. Lewis statement, pp. 1–2.

162. William R. Martin Memorandum to New Orleans District Attorney Jim Garrison, April 18, 1967, p. 10. Richard Case Nagell identified one of the other participants

in the late August 1963 assassination meeting he attended as simply "Q." Ibid. "Q" may have again meant Sergio Arcacha Smith's and Lee Harvey Oswald's mutual friend, Carlos Quiroga. If that is the case, then the same three men Nagell plotted with were seen meeting together around the same time in New Orleans by David Lewis: Sergio Arcacha Smith, Lee Harvey Oswald, and Carlos Quiroga.

163. Sergio Arcacha Smith died on July 5, 2000, in Miami. "Passages," *Kennedy Assassination Chronicles*, vol. 6, no. 2 (Summer 2000), p. 8.

164. Memorandum from William Attwood to Gordon Chase of the National Security Council staff, November 8, 1963, citing Castro's righthand man, Rene Vallejo, speaking on behalf of the premier. *FRUS, 1961–1963*, vol. XI, p. 882.

165. Ibid., pp. 882–83.

166. Ibid., p. 882.

167. Conversation between President John F. Kennedy and National Security Adviser McGeorge Bundy. Oval Office audio tape, November 5, 1963. From the National Security Archive www.gwu.edu/~nsarchiv.

168. Ibid.

169. General Fabian Escalante, director of Cuba's investigation into the assassination of President Kennedy, his assistant Arturo Rodriguez, and former Cuban ambassador Carlos Lechuga met with a group of JFK historians on December 7–9, 1995, in Nassau, Bahamas. Escalante told the group that the original source of the CIA's information that Kennedy had "a plan to dialogue with Cuba" was none other than Henry Cabot Lodge, who learned of JFK's consideration of a détente with Cuba as early as December 1962, half a year before Lodge became Kennedy's ambassador to Vietnam. When CIA operative Felipe Vidal Santiago informed the Miami exile community of Kennedy's plan, Escalante said, "it was almost like a bomb in those meetings," infuriating the exiles against a president they already hated because of what they regarded as his betrayal of their cause at the Bay of Pigs. "Transcript of Proceedings between Cuban Officials and JFK Historians: Nassau Beach Hotel, December 7–9, 1995," (published by JFK Lancer, 332 NE 5th Street, Grand Prairie, TX 75050), p. 33.

170. William Attwood, *The Twilight Struggle: Tales of the Cold War* (New York: Harper & Row, 1987), p. 262.

171. *Public Papers of the Presidents: John F. Kennedy, 1963*, p. 875.

172. Ibid., p. 876.

173. Castro told Attwood years later that he had been listening in on the Vallejo–Attwood phone conversation about setting an agenda for his secret meeting with Attwood. Atwood, *Twilight Struggle*, p. 262.

174. Ibid.

175. Evan Thomas, *The Very Best Men: Four Who Dared: The Early Years of the CIA* (New York: Touchstone, 1995), p. 299.

176. "Interview of Fidel Castro Ruz," *Investigation of the Assassination of President John F. Kennedy: Hearings Before the HSCA*, vol. 3 (1978), p. 240.

177. Anthony Summers, *Conspiracy* (New York: Paragon House, 1989), p. 323.

178. United States Senate Select Committee to Study Governmental Operations With Respect to Intelligence Activities (Church Committee), *Alleged Assassination Plots Involving Foreign Leaders: An Interim Report; November 20, 1975* (Washington: U.S. Government Printing Office, 1975), p. 87; based on *Inspector General's Report*, p. 89 (p. 39 of Prevailing Winds Research text; see above, chapter 2, n. 26).

179. *Inspector General's Report*, pp. 88–89 (p. 39 of Prevailing Winds Research text), cited by Church Committee, *Alleged Assassination Plots*, p. 174.

180. Church Committee, *Alleged Assassination Plots*, p. 88; Thomas, *Very Best Men*, p. 303.

181. *Inspector General's Report*, p. 94 (p. 41 of Prevailing Winds Research text); cited by the Church Committee, *Alleged Assassination Plots*, p. 89.

182. Schlesinger, *Robert Kennedy and His Times*, p. 598; citing the Church Commit-

tee, *The Investigation of the Assassination of President John F. Kennedy: Performance of the Intelligence Agencies* (Washington: U.S. Government Printing Office, 1976), p. 20.

183. Schlesinger, *Robert Kennedy and His Times*, p. 598. In addition to President Kennedy and Theodore Sorensen, five of the president's advisers were involved in discussions about the purpose and content of his November 18 speech in Miami: Schlesinger, Richard Goodwin, McGeorge Bundy, Gordon Chase, and Ralph Dungan. From both Schlesinger's direct knowledge of the speech-writing process and a search of the JFK Papers, "no evidence was uncovered of any contribution from Fitzgerald and the CIA." Ibid.

184. Michael R. Beschloss, citing Theodore Sorensen's Oral History, Columbia Oral History Project; in *The Crisis Years: Kennedy and Khrushchev, 1960–1963* (New York: Edward Burlingame Books, 1991), p. 659.

185. Ibid. Cf. Theodore C. Sorensen, *Kennedy* (New York: Konecky & Konecky, 1965), p. 723.

186. See *Public Papers of the Presidents: John F. Kennedy, 1963*, p. 876.

187. Fidel Castro, "Concerning the Facts and Consequences of the Tragic Death of President John F. Kennedy, November 23rd, 1963," in E. Martin Schotz, *History Will Not Absolve Us: Orwellian Control, Public Denial, and the Murder of President Kennedy* (Brookline, Mass.: Kurtz, Ulmer & DeLucia, 1996), pp. 74–75.

188. Ibid., pp. 75–79.

189. Ibid., p. 81.

190. Ibid.

191. Frank Mankiewicz and Kirby Jones, *With Fidel: A Portrait of Castro and Cuba* (Chicago: Playboy Press, 1975), p. 173.

192. Ibid., p. 174.

193. Ibid., pp. 163–64.

194. "Interview of Fidel Castro Ruz," pp. 221, 227–28.

195. Statement of Julia Ann Mercer, New Orleans, Louisiana; January 16, 1968. From the Files of Jim Garrison at the Assassination Archives and Research Center, Washington, D.C. Cf. Decker Exhibit No. 5323, *WCH*, vol. 19, p. 483.

Julia Ann Mercer was not the only person who saw a man carrying a gun in Dealey Plaza the morning of the assassination. Between 9:30 and 10:00 A.M. on November 22, Julius Hardie was driving his electrical equipment company truck east on Commerce Street when he saw three men on the railroad overpass bridge. Two of the men, he told a reporter, were "carrying guns, long guns." Hardie looked at the men twice, "because even in Texas it's unusual to see people carrying long guns. Now I can't tell you whether it was rifles, shotguns, or what. But two of them had long guns." Earl Golz, "SS 'Imposters' Spotted by JFK Witnesses," *Dallas Morning News* (August 27, 1978), p. 4A.

The men with the long guns were dressed conservatively, like most of the men who posed as Secret Service agents in Dealey Plaza that day. Hardie said two of them had on dark business suits and the third an overcoat. After the assassination, Hardie reported his sighting of the men with the long guns to authorities. Two FBI agents visited him a week or two later to take down his story, but he said he "never heard from them after that." Ibid.

196. Jim Garrison, *On the Trail of the Assassins* (New York: Warner Books, 1991), p. 252.

197. Henry Hurt interview with Julia Ann Mercer, 1983. Cited in Henry Hurt, *Reasonable Doubt: An Investigation into the Assassination of John F. Kennedy* (New York: Henry Holt, 1985), p. 115.

198. Ibid.

199. Garrison, *On the Trail of the Assassins*, p. 252. Years after first reading Garrison's description of Julia Ann Mercer and her husband, I discovered that he had slightly changed details in their background for the sake of Mercer's anonymity and security.

200. Ibid.

201. Julia Ann Mercer's written comment to Jim Garrison on the bottom of 11/28/63

FBI Report by Louis M. Kelley. From the National Archives, Garrison Papers, Special Collection, Box 9, Folder: Mercer, J.A. Why would the FBI show Mercer photos of Jack Ruby? As J. Edgar Hoover became aware, the CIA was laying down a trail—for the FBI to document—of Oswald as a Cuban-and-Soviet-connected assassin. Jack Ruby is known today for his Mafia connections. However, as we shall see, he had also been a gunrunner to Fidel Castro in the 1950s. The young man whom Julia Ann Mercer saw carrying a gun case up the grassy knoll could have been the second Oswald, designed to link Lee Harvey Oswald via Ruby to either Castro or the Mafia, as the need arose. Author Henry Hurt claimed that, when he interviewed Mercer in 1983, she said Oswald was the man with the rifle. Hurt, *Reasonable Doubt*, p. 115. In a CIA scenario that initially involved multiple story lines implicating Oswald, the FBI may have already been put on Ruby's trail as a possible Cuban-and-Mafia-related accomplice to the assassination. However, once Lyndon Johnson settled on a lone assassin story, Julia Ann Mercer's testimony implicating Ruby before he murdered Oswald had to be totally suppressed.

202. Mercer Statement, January 16, 1968.

203. Ibid.

204. Ibid.

205. Garrison, *On the Trail of the Assassins*, p. 253.

206. Mercer Statement, January 16, 1968.

207. Garrison, *On the Trail of the Assassins*, p. 253.

208. *WCH*, vol. 19, Decker Exhibit No. 5323, p. 483.

209. Julia Ann Mercer's written comment to Jim Garrison on the bottom of CD-205, the 11/23/63 FBI Report. From the National Archives, Garrison Papers, Special Collection, Box 9, Folder: Mercer, J.A.

210. Investigation by Special Agents Henry J. Oliver and Louis M. Kelley, November 27, 1963. From the National Archives, Garrison Papers, Special Collection, Box 9, Folder: Mercer, J.A.

211. Garrison, *On the Trail of the Assassins*, p. 253.

212. Mercer Statement, January 16, 1968.

213. Garrison, *On the Trail of the Assassins*, p. 253.

214. Ibid., p. 255.

215. Ibid. Cf. *Appendix to HSCA Hearings*, vol. 12, p. 16.

216. Author's March 27, 2005, phone conversation with Julia Ann Mercer's stepdaughter.

217. Hurt, *Reasonable Doubt*, pp. 114–16.

218. Mercer Statement, January 16, 1968.

In an FBI document, Dallas Police Officer Joe Murphy, who was stationed on the triple underpass the morning of November 22, 1963, offered a rebuttal to Julia Ann Mercer's testimony. He said there was a stalled truck in Dealey Plaza at that time, but claimed it belonged to a construction company (whose name he was unable to recall). The truck, he said, had three men in it.

"Murphy further stated it was probable that one of these men had taken something from the rear of this truck in an effort to start it."

According to Murphy, "these persons were under observation all during the period they were stalled on Elm Street," and "it would have been impossible for any of them to have had anything to do with the assassination of President Kennedy." Statement of Dallas Police Officer Joe Murphy to the FBI, December 9, 1963, CD 205. Also from the National Archives, Garrison Papers.

However, if these persons were under observation all that time, why doesn't Murphy know in fact whether or not one of them took something from the rear of the truck?

How does he know, on the other hand, that it would have been impossible for men from an anonymous construction company to have had anything to do with the assassination of President Kennedy? Cf. Millicent Cranor, "The Other Side of *Six Seconds in Dallas*," *Probe* (September-October 1999), p. 7.

If Officer Joe Murphy is vague in providing critical details, even more so is a key Secret Service agent in giving testimony on the same incident before the Warren Commission.

Forrest Sorrels, the Special Agent in Charge of the Dallas Secret Service office, had been in the lead car of the motorcade. He returned to Dealey Plaza about twenty minutes after the assassination in order to gather evidence. He told the Warren Commission that during his investigation that afternoon, he came across a man whose name he couldn't recall who "saw a truck down there—this is before the parade ever got there—that apparently had stalled down there on Elm Street. And I later checked on that, and found out that the car had gone dead, apparently belonged to some construction company, and that a police officer had come down there, and they had gone to the construction company and gotten somebody to come down and get the car out of the way.

"Apparently it was just a car stalled down there.

"But this lady said she thought she saw somebody that looked like they had a guncase. But then I didn't pursue that any further—because then I had gotten the information that the rifle had been found in the building and shells and so forth." *WCH*, vol. 7, pp. 351–52.

As a Secret Service investigator at the crime scene within an hour of the president's assassination, Forrest Sorrels is less than precise in his testimony about the "apparently stalled" truck or car that "apparently belonged to some construction company." He does not even explain to the Commission the connection between the truck or car and the lady. In any case, the head of the Dallas Secret Service office knew already, on the afternoon of the assassination, not to "pursue any further" Julia Ann Mercer's having observed "somebody that looked like they had a guncase." The government had already solved the president's murder a few minutes after it occurred, since "the rifle had been found in the building and shells and so forth." Ibid.

219. *Foreign Relations of the United States (FRUS), Volume XXIII: Southeast Asia* (Washington: U.S. Government Printing Office, 1995), p. 695.

220. President Sukarno, cited by U.S. ambassador Howard Jones in telegram to the Department of State, November 4, 1963. *FRUS, 1961–1963*, vol. XXIII, p. 694.

221. "Memorandum From the Deputy Director for Plans, Central Intelligence Agency (Bissell) to the President's Special Assistant for National Security Affairs (Bundy)," March 27, 1961. *FRUS, 1961–1963*, vol. XXIII, p. 329 (emphasis added).

222. Richard Bissell, cited in Evan Thomas, *Very Best Men*, pp. 232–33.

223. Ibid., p. 233.

224. Frank Wisner, the CIA's Deputy Director for Plans, to Al Ulmer, CIA Far East division chief; cited by Joseph B. Smith, *Portrait of a Cold Warrior* (New York: Ballantine Books, 1976), p. 197.

225. Ibid., pp. 216–41. Audrey R. and George McT. Kahin, *Subversion as Foreign Policy: The Secret Eisenhower and Dulles Debacle in Indonesia* (New York: New Press, 1995).

226. Smith, *Portrait of a Cold Warrior*, p. 240. Kahin and Kahin, *Subversion as Foreign Policy*, p. 179.

227. *FRUS, 1961–1963*, vol. XXIII, p. 331.

228. Roger Hilsman, *To Move a Nation: The Politics of Foreign Policy in the Administration of John F. Kennedy* (New York: Dell, 1964), p. 363.

229. Ibid.

230. National Security Action Memorandum No. 179, August 16, 1962. *FRUS, 1961–1963*, vol. XXIII, p. 627.

231. Hilsman, *To Move a Nation*, p. 382.

232. Forbes Wilson, a U.S. mining executive whose company had been poised to take over a mountain of copper ore in West Irian with Dutch cooperation, condemned the consequences of Kennedy's turn toward Sukarno:

"Not long after Indonesia obtained control over Western New Guinea in 1963, then-President Sukarno, who had consolidated his executive power, made a series of moves which would have discouraged even the most eager prospective Western investor. He expropriated nearly all foreign investments in Indonesia. He ordered American agencies, including the Agency for International Development [a CIA front], to leave the country. He cultivated close ties with Communist China and with Indonesia's Communist Party, known as the PKI." Forbes Wilson, Freeport Sulphur Director, cited by Lisa Pease in her article "Indonesia, President Kennedy & Freeport Sulphur," *Probe* (May-June, 1996), p. 21.

233. Ambassador Howard Jones, Telegram from the Embassy in Indonesia to the Department of State, November 4, 1963. *FRUS, 1961–1963,* vol. XXIII, p. 692.

234. Ibid.

235. *Warren Report*, p. 52. Warren Commission critic Sylvia Meagher agrees in this case with the Commission. Using their documents, she extends their conclusion to cover all the Secret Service agents in the Dallas field office as well as the traveling members of the White House detail. Meagher, *Accessories after the Fact,* p. 25. All the evidence points to the conclusion that there were no genuine Secret Service agents in Dealey Plaza immediately after the assassination, only imposters bearing Secret Service credentials.

236. Interviews of Joe Marshall Smith by Anthony Summers; cited by Summers, *Conspiracy,* p. 29.

237. *WCH*, vol. 7, p. 535.

238. Ibid. Warren Commission attorney Wesley Liebeler, who was questioning Officer Joe Marshall Smith, knew from other witnesses and documents that there were no Secret Service agents who could be accounted for in Dealey Plaza at that time. Yet he avoided asking Smith any follow-up questions about precisely how the man showed Smith that he was a Secret Service agent. That would have raised for the Warren Commission the critical issue of Secret Service credentials being used by an imposter at the crime scene.

239. Interviews of Smith by Summers, *Conspiracy,* p. 50.

240. Ibid.

241. Earl Golz, "SS 'Imposters' Spotted by JFK Witnesses," *Dallas Morning News* (August 27, 1978), p. 1A.

242. Interview of Gordon Arnold by Henry Hurt, May 1982; cited in Hurt, *Reasonable Doubt*, p. 112.

243. Ibid.

244. Golz, "SS 'Imposters, p. 1A.

245. Interview of Gordon Arnold by Jim Marrs, summer 1985; cited by Jim Marrs, *Crossfire: The Plot That Killed Kennedy* (New York: Carroll & Graf, 1989), p. 78. Interview of Arnold by Hurt, *Reasonable Doubt*, p. 112.

246. Interview of Gordon Arnold on *The Men Who Killed Kennedy: Part Two—"The Forces of Darkness"*; a Nigel Turner film (C.G. Communications, 1992).

247. Golz, "SS 'Imposters, p. 4A.

248. In 1978 reporter Earl Golz persuaded a still-fearful Gordon Arnold to be interviewed anonymously for a story in the *Dallas Morning News*. Because of the last-minute insistence of Golz's editor, Arnold wound up being identified in the story, "SS 'Imposters' Spotted by JFK Witnesses," *Dallas Morning News* (August 27, 1978), p. 1A. Interview of Earl Golz by Henry Hurt, 1983, cited in Hurt, *Reasonable Doubt*, p. 113.

After the story appeared, former U.S. Senator Ralph Yarborough contacted Golz. Yarborough said he had seen a man behaving like Gordon Arnold on the grassy knoll. Senator Yarborough had been riding with Vice President Lyndon Johnson two cars behind the presidential limousine. Yarborough told Golz: "Immediately on the firing of the first shot I saw the man you interviewed throw himself on the ground. He was down within a second of the time the shot was fired and I thought to myself, 'There's a combat veteran who knows how to act when weapons start firing.'" Earl Golz, "Panel Leaves Question of Imposters," *Dallas Morning News* (December 31, 1978), p. 2A.

249. Bill Sloan with Jean Hill, *JFK: The Last Dissenting Witness* (Gretna, La.: Pelican, 1991), p. 26.

250. *WCH*, vol. 7, p. 107. Bogus Secret Service agents were also behind the Texas

School Book Depository by 12:36 P.M. Dallas Police Sergeant D.V. Harkness said that at 12:36 when he went around to the back of the Depository to seal it off: "There were some Secret Service agents there. I didn't get them identified. They told me they were Secret Service." WCH, vol. 6, p. 312. Stewart Galanor, "The Grassy Knoll," Kennedy Assassination Chronicles (Spring, 1999), p. 42.

251. Ed Hoffman and Ron Friedrich, Eye Witness (Grand Prairie, Tex.: JFK Lancer, 1996), pp. 5–6.

252. Bill Sloan, JFK: Breaking the Silence (Dallas: Taylor, 1993), p. 15.

253. Hoffman and Friedrich, Eye Witness, pp. 6–7.

254. Casey J. Quinlan and Brian K. Edwards, Beyond the Fence Line: The Eyewitness Account of Ed Hoffman and the Murder of President Kennedy (Southlake, Texas: JFK Lancer, 2008), pp. 28, 30–31, 33, 40–41, 157–58. "Ed has been asked many times how he was able to distinguish the make of this station wagon from such a distance. He communicated that his best friend, Lucien Pierce, owned a Rambler station wagon exactly like the one he saw driving in the parking lot." Ibid., p. 28.

255. Hoffman and Friedrich, Eye Witness, p. 8. Lee Bowers, Jr., a railroad supervisor in a fourteen-foot tower, was looking behind the fence at the same time as Ed Hoffman but from a different angle. Bowers told Mark Lane he saw "some unusual occurrence—a flash of light or smoke or something which caused me to feel like something out of the ordinary had occurred there." Interview of Lee Bowers, Jr., by Mark Lane, filmed in Arlington, Texas, March 31, 1966; The Plot to Kill JFK: Rush to Judgment (MPI Home Video, 1988), a film by Emile de Antonio and Mark Lane.

On August 9, 1966, four months after he was interviewed by Mark Lane, Lee Bowers, Jr., was killed in a single-car accident in Midlothian, Texas. Benson, Encyclopedia of the JFK Assassination, p. 28.

256. Hoffman and Friedrich, Eye Witness, pp. 8, 25; Marrs, Crossfire, p. 82.

257. Hoffman and Friedrich, Eye Witness, p. 9.

258. Quinlin and Edwards, Beyond the Fence Line, p. 33.

259. Hoffman and Friedrich, Eye Witness, p. 10.

260. Ibid., pp. 11–12.

261. Ibid., p. 12. Author Bill Sloan interviewed retired police detective Robert Hoffman in 1992 about his memories of his twenty-nine-year-old Thanksgiving Day conversation with his nephew through the interpretation of his brother, Frederick Hoffman, who had died in 1976. Robert Hoffman claimed he had misunderstood the details of the story: ". . . all I knew at the time was that someone in a car had pointed a gun at him . . . His father was very, very concerned that Eddie knew anything about the assassination at all." Sloan, JFK: Breaking the Silence, p. 30.

Robert Hoffman vouched for his nephew's character and truthfulness: "Maybe it's better that I didn't understand what he had seen. I know that Eddie's a very bright person and always has been, and I can't think of any reason that he would make up something like this. It would be completely out of character for him to change his story or add to it at a later date."

Sloan asked Robert Hoffman if he believed "Ed would have been putting himself in physical danger by making his story public."

He replied, "I don't know. A lot of witnesses obviously did [put themselves in danger], because some of them died. The same thing could have happened to Eddie." Ibid., pp. 30–31.

262. June 28, 1967, Dallas FBI Report on "Assassination of President John Fitzgerald Kennedy, Dallas, Texas, November 22, 1963," p. 2. Appendix A, Hoffman and Friedrich, Eye Witness, p. 32.

263. Hoffman and Friedrich, Eye Witness, pp. 16–17.

264. Ibid., p. 18.

265. Ibid.

266. Ibid. When the FBI's report of its July 1967 interview with Frederick Hoffman

was finally released and it was then claimed that "Ed's [deceased] father thought that he was lying," Ed's mother, brother, wife, and other family members all insisted that, on the contrary, Frederick Hoffman believed his son from the beginning. He had simply tried to keep Ed quiet out of fear for his son's life. Hoffman and Friedrich, *Eye Witness*, pp. 18–19.

267. April 5, 1977, Dallas FBI Report on "Assassination of President John Fitzgerald Kennedy, November 22, 1963, Dallas, Texas," pp. 1–9. Appendix B, Hoffman and Friedrich, *Eye Witness*, pp. 36–44.

268. Marrs, *Crossfire*, pp. 81–85. Even Marrs's generally accurate interview of Ed Hoffman contains sign-language interpreter errors. The best statements of Ed Hoffman's testimony have been given in *Eye Witness*, written by Ed Hoffman with his pastor and translator, Ron Friedrich, and in *Beyond the Fence Line*, written by Casey J. Quinlan and Brian K. Edwards in close consultation with Ed Hoffman.

During the activity Hoffman has described, his view of the area behind the fence at Dealey Plaza was, contrary to some critics, unobstructed. Pictures taken just after the assassination establish that, as Hoffman says, the train that would soon become a barrier to his vision had not yet appeared. See the pictures on pp. 42, 43, 46, 50, and 51 of Robert J. Groden's *The Killing of a President: The Complete Photographic Record of the JFK Assassination, the Conspiracy, and the Cover-Up* (New York: Viking Studio Books, 1993). The billboard that now blocks one's view was extended vertically to its present height after 1963, and the trees have grown considerably from the time when Hoffman looked over them. Hoffman and Friedrich, *Eye Witness*, pp. 14–15. Groden, pp. 16–17. Quinlin and Edwards, *Beyond the Fence Line*, pp. 152–53.

269. Two books about Ed Hoffman *(Eyewitness,* p. 9; *Beyond the Fence Line,* p. 33) and the hardcover text of this book (p. 265) have identified the "suit man" seen by Hoffman with the man whom Dallas police officer Joe Marshall Smith confronted with a gun behind the stockade fence. However, Smith said the man he confronted "had on a sports shirt and sports pants," so how could it have been the same man? (I am grateful to reader Norman J. Granz for raising this question.)

Hoffman communicated that, in addition to the "suit man" and the "railroad man," he saw two other men behind the fence just before the shooting:

"a) A man in a plaid shirt, labeled 'P' (dotted black line on Photo 23) [in *Beyond the Fence Line,* p. 34], stepped around from the north end of the fence, walked up to the man in the business suit 'A' and spoke to him for a few seconds.

"b) After this brief encounter, the man in the plaid shirt turned and walked back around the east side of the fence and out of Ed's view (solid black line on Photo 23).

"c) The police officer 'F' (Photo 23), who had been standing at the east end of the fence, followed the man in the plaid shirt as he walked around the east side of the fence." *(Beyond the Fence Line,* p. 32)

The "suit man" walked over to the "railroad man" a final time, spoke with him briefly, and returned to the fence where he bent over, picked something up, and looked over the fence. Hoffman then saw a puff of smoke by the "suit man," after which the "suit man" turned suddenly with a rifle in his hands. The "suit man" ran to the "railroad man," tossed the rifle to him, then walked casually back alongside the fence until a police officer came quickly around the fence and confronted him with a revolver. (This is *not* the officer who was at the east end of the fence before who, unlike the officer coming around the fence, had not been wearing a hat. *Beyond the Fence Line,* p. 33.)

To return to the question, how could the man Officer Joe Marshall Smith confronted, who he said "had on a sports shirt and sports pants," have been the "suit man" Ed Hoffman was watching?

After the shooting, Officer Smith came around the fence at the same point where Hoffman's "man in a plaid shirt" had been just moments before. "The man in a plaid shirt" may be the man in "a sports shirt and sports pants" who Smith said showed him Secret Service credentials. Officer Smith may have then confronted a moment later "the suit man," merging the two men in his memory in an interview fifteen years later. *(Conspiracy,* p. 50.)

Other witnesses said they encountered plainclothesmen behind the fence who showed them Secret Service identification. "The man in a plaid/sports shirt," like "the suit man," would likely have had such Secret Service credentials as cover in case he was challenged.

270. CIA Memorandum from Sidney Gottlieb, Chief, TSD [Technical Services Division], to Carl E. Duckett, DDS&T [Director, Directorate of Science and Technology], May 8, 1973. CIA's "Family Jewels," pp. 215, 218. Available at http://www.gwu.edu/~nsarchiv/NSAEBB/NSAEBB222/family_jewels_full_ocr.pdf. I am grateful to Peter Dale Scott for alerting me to this item in the "Family Jewels."

271. Author's interview of Abraham Bolden, July 13, 2003.

272. For the preceding analysis, as well as this book as a whole, I am especially grateful for the work and inspiration of Vincent Salandria, who has long emphasized the importance of the government's ignoring the evidence of phony Secret Service agents in Dealey Plaza. In his landmark speech to the Coalition on Political Assassinations (COPA), given on November 20, 1998, Salandria stated: "We know from the evidence that at the time of and immediately after the assassination, there were persons in Dealey Plaza who were impersonating Secret Service agents. This was clear evidence of both the existence of a conspiracy and the commission of the crime of impersonating federal officers. But our government showed no interest in pursuing this compelling evidence of the existence of a conspiracy nor in prosecuting the criminals who were impersonating federal officers. In refusing to pursue the evidence of conspiracy and in failing to pursue the criminals who were impersonating federal officers, the Warren Commissioners, their staff, the Attorney General's Office, and the FBI became accessories after the fact and abetted the killers." Vincent J. Salandria, *False Mystery: An Anthology of Essays on the Assassination of JFK*, edited and published by John Kelin (1999), p. 114.

273. *Foreign Relations of the United States (FRUS), 1961–1963, Volume VI: Kennedy-Khrushchev Exchanges* (Washington: U.S. Government Printing Office, 1996), pp. 309–11.

274. Schlesinger, *Robert Kennedy,* p. 501.

275. Guthman and Shulman, *Robert Kennedy in His Own Words*, p. 338. JFK had even suggested to RFK that he, rather than Foy Kohler, should consider becoming ambassador to the Soviet Union—after first learning Russian. RFK said no, explaining later to an interviewer: "In the first place I couldn't possibly learn Russian, because I spent ten years learning second-year French. And secondly, for the first couple of months I might have done something; but after that I don't think it's my forte." Ibid., p. 339. The larger problem was that JFK needed RFK, the one person he could totally trust, almost everywhere in a government that was increasingly resistant to the president's policies.

276. Kohler to Secretary of State, from Moscow, October 10, 1963, 6:00 p.m. National Security Files, Box 184, JFK Library. USSR: Khrushchev Correspondence, Vol. IV-0, 6/7/63—12/9/63. I am grateful to Stephen Plotkin, Senior Archivist at the JFK Library, and his staff for finding, copying, and sending to me the entire file covering the paper trail of the State Department's ending of the Kennedy-Khrushchev correspondence.

277. *FRUS, 1961–1963,* vol. VI, p. 310.

278. Ibid.

279. Memorandum to Mr. Bundy from Mr. Klein. National Security Files, Box 184, JFK Library. USSR: Khrushchev Correspondence, Vol. IV-0, 6/7/63—12/9/63.

280. "Memo for Record," The White House, December 9, 1963, with the typed initials "BKS." National Security Files, Box 184, JFK Library. USSR: Khrushchev Correspondence, Vol. IV-0, 6/7/63—12/9/63.

281. Ibid.

282. Beschloss, *Crisis Years*, p. 663.

283. Aleksandr Fursenko and Timothy Naftali, *"One Hell of a Gamble": Khrushchev, Castro, and Kennedy, 1958–1964* (New York: W. W. Norton, 1997), p. 339.

284. Vladimir Semichastny to Nikita S. Khrushchev, October 2, 1963, SVR [Archive of the Russian Foreign Intelligence Service]. Cited by Fursenko and Naftali, *"One Hell of a Gamble,"* pp. 339, 401.

285. Fursenko and Naftali, *"One Hell of a Gamble,"* pp. 339, 401.

286. From their research in the Soviet archives for their book *"One Hell of a Gamble,"* Fursenko and Naftali reported no further messages after Kennedy initiated, and Khrushchev approved, the early fall 1963 reopening of their back channel. Are there perhaps more Kennedy–Khrushchev exchanges buried in the Soviet archives that would add still another chapter to this story?

287. Penn Jones, Jr., *Forgive My Grief III* (Midlothian, Tex.: Midlothian Mirror, 1969), p. 37.

288. Roger Craig, *When They Kill a President* (unpublished manuscript, 1971), p. 5 (emphasis in original).

289. Jones, *Forgive My Grief III*, p. 37.

290. Ibid.

291. William Manchester, *The Death of a President* (New York: Harper & Row, Popular Library, 1967), p. 37.

292. Jesse Curry, *JFK Assassination File* (Dallas: American Poster and Printing Company, 1969), p. 21. In spite of the Secret Service orders he had said he was following, Chief Jesse Curry still tried to explain away the lack of security in Dealey Plaza as "a freak of history": "Security was comparatively light along the short stretch of Elm Street where the President was shot. In the midst of comprehensive security it seems a freak of history that this short stretch of Elm Street would be the assassination site, and that the Texas Book Depository Building was virtually ignored in the security plans for the motorcade." Ibid.

293. *Appendix to Hearings before the HSCA*, vol. 11, p. 525.

294. Ibid., p. 527. *WCH*, vol. 7, p. 579.

295. "The Secret Service's alteration of the original Dallas Police Department motorcycle deployment plan prevented the use of maximum possible security precautions." *Appendix to Hearings before the HSCA*, vol. 11, p. 529.

296. Ibid. *WCH*, Vol. 7, pp. 580–81.

297. *WCH*, vol. 4, pp. 338–39. Winston G. Lawson stated a decade later, to the House Select Committee on Assassinations, that he had "no recall of changing plans" (for the motorcycles) at the November 21, 1963, meeting with the Dallas Police. *Appendix to Hearings before the HSCA*, vol. 11, p. 528.

298. Secret Service Final Survey Report for the November 21, 1963, visit by President Kennedy to Houston, cited in *Appendix to Hearings before the HSCA*, vol. 11, p. 529.

299. Ibid.

300. Vincent Michael Palamara, *The Third Alternative—Survivor's Guilt: The Secret Service and the JFK Murder* (self-published, 1993), 7. *WCH*, vol. 18, pp. 734–35, 749–50. Special Agent in Charge Roberts "attempted to defend his strange actions by noting the speed of the limousine, which was actually *decelerating* from an already slow speed of 11.2 miles per hour, and the distance between his car and the limousine, which was merely a scant five feet at the most, not the '20 to 25 feet' he noted in his report." *Third Alternative*, p. 7 (emphasis in original).

301. Ibid.

302. Secret Service agent Gerald A. Behn in *WCH*, vol. 18, p. 805. The Warren Commission documents claiming Kennedy wanted no agents on his limousine then became the source for books on JFK's death making the same claim. See, for example, Jim Bishop, *The Day Kennedy Was Shot* (New York: Bantam Books, 1975), pp. 34–35; drawing on *WCH*, vol. 18, pp. 804–5.

303. Palamara, *Third Alternative*, p. 7.

304. Vincent Palamara interview with Gerald A. Behn, September 27, 1992; cited in Palamara, *Third Alternative*, p. 4 (emphasis in original). Agent Behn "added that newsreel

footage from the period will bear him out on this point"—that President Kennedy did not bar Secret Service agents from riding on the back of the limousine. Ibid.

305. Palamara, *Third Alternative*, p. 8.

306. Ibid.

307. Ibid., p. 9. Besides the already cited Secret Service agents, Behn, Lilly, and Boring, those who told Palamara that JFK did not restrict agents from riding on the rear of the limousine included agents Rufus Youngblood, Robert Bouck, Abraham Bolden, Maurice Martineau, advance man Marty Underwood, and JFK aide Dave Powers. Ibid., pp. 7–8.

308. *WCH*, vol. 21, p. 547.

309. David T. Ratcliffe, *Understanding Special Operations and Their Impact on the Vietnam War Era: 1989 Interview with L. Fletcher Prouty Colonel USAF (Retired)* (Santa Cruz, Calif.: rat haus reality press, 1999), p. 205.

310. Ratcliffe, *Understanding Special Operations*, p. 206.

311. Craig, *When They Kill a President*, p. 6.

312. Ibid., p. 9. Roger Craig's testimony should be drawn from sources independent of his interview on April 1, 1964, by Warren Commission assistant counsel David W. Belin. Craig was disturbed by Belin's habit of turning off the tape recorder at key points in the questioning. He was even more disturbed when he read what the Warren Commission claimed he had said. *WCH*, vol. 6, pp. 260–73. Craig said his testimony had been changed in fourteen places, even apart from critical omissions. Several of the changes seemed designed especially to keep Craig's descriptions of the station wagon and its driver from serving as bases for their identification. *When They Kill a President*, pp. 14–16. Also Edgar F. Tatro, "Roger Craig and 1984," in unidentified issue of *The Continuing Inquiry*, p. 3. The best sources for Roger Craig's testimony on what he saw and heard in Dallas on November 22, 1963, are his own unpublished manuscript, *When They Kill a President*, and his filmed interview in April 1974 by Lincoln Carle that is contained in the video Carle made with Mark Lane, *Two Men in Dallas* (Alpa Productions 1976; developed by Lincoln Carle; written by Mark Lane).

313. Craig, *When They Kill a President*, p. 9.

314. Ibid.

315. Ibid., p. 12.

316. Ibid., pp. 12–13 (emphasis added). Roger Craig's description of the dialogue with Oswald in his interview in *Two Men in Dallas*. Marrs, *Crossfire*, p. 331.

317. Jones, *Forgive My Grief III*, p. 31.

318. After reading the anecdote about Sheriff Decker and Captain Fritz in an earlier draft of this chapter, researcher Steve Jones raised this pertinent question about why Fritz had to interrupt his early, critical questioning of Oswald and drive fifteen blocks across town rather than just talk with Decker on the phone. They apparently had to confer in absolute secrecy, with no possible danger of their being overheard on the phone.

319. Jones, *Forgive My Grief III*, p. 31.

320. Carolyn Walther said she saw the man with the rifle on the fourth or fifth floor. *WCH*, vol. 24, p. 522. She may have meant the fifth or sixth floor. As author Gary Shaw has pointed out, the fact that there were no windows on the first floor of the Texas School Book Depository made it easy for observers to overlook it and begin counting at the second floor. J. Gary Shaw with Larry Ray Harris, *Cover-Up: The Governmental Conspiracy to Conceal the Facts about the Public Execution of John Kennedy* (Austin: Thomas Publications, 1992), p. 12.

321. Commission Exhibit No. 2086, *WCH*, vol. 24, p. 522. The man in the window with the rifle passed up his best shot, when the president was driven directly toward and beneath him on Houston Street. That this man apparently did not open fire until the limousine, driving away from him, neared the grassy knoll, is itself evidence he was not meant to serve primarily as a shooter. His more important role was to draw attention to himself and thereby incriminate the scapegoat who worked in the Texas School Book Depository, Lee Harvey Oswald.

322. Ibid.

323. *WCH*, vol. 16, p. 959; vol. 2, pp. 193–94, 200.

324. Ibid., vol. 2, p. 195.

325. Ibid., vol. 16, p. 959; vol. 2, pp. 195–96. An FBI interview with James Worrell, Jr., claimed Worrell said he "had a profile view" of the running man and "felt" later it had been Lee Harvey Oswald. Robert P. Gemberling Report, November 30, 1963; cited in *WCH*, vol. 2, p. 201. However, Worrell stated flatly to the Warren Commission that he did *not* have a profile view of the running man, and that he "sure didn't" tell the FBI that he did. Ibid.

After reading Worrell's story of the running man in a Dallas newspaper, James Elbert Romack challenged it in his own testimony before a Warren Commission attorney. Romack claimed he watched the back of the Depository for four or five minutes after he heard shots fired and saw no one leave the building (*WCH*, vol. 6, p. 282). However, Romack also admitted he did "turn my back to the building" during that time to move a traffic barrier for a news crew parking its truck (ibid., p. 281)—precisely when he could have missed the man in the sport coat whom Worrell saw run out of the Depository.

The Warren Report tried to back up James Romack's testimony by that of his co-worker, George "Pop" Rackley, who also said he saw no one leave the back of the Depository. However, Rackley was a more distant witness, unaware of when the presidential motorcade passed, which he could not see. Unlike Worrell and Romack, Rackley did not even hear the shooting, making him a more questionable witness to its aftermath (*WCH*, vol. 6, pp. 275–77).

326. FBI interview of Richard Randolph Carr by Special Agent Paul L. Scott, February 4, 1964. Reproduced in CD-ROM for *Harvey & Lee*, Nov 22–45.

327. Ibid.

328. Ibid.

329. Ibid. Researcher William Weston has pointed out that Richard Carr gave a different story on the Nash Rambler at the Clay Shaw trial in New Orleans, and again to writer Gary Shaw for his book *Cover-Up* (p. 13). According to Carr's second version, "the Nash Rambler was not parked on Record Street, as stated in 1964, but rather it was parked on Houston, next to the TSBD, facing north. After the shooting, two or three men came out of the Depository and got into the Rambler. The car was last seen speeding north on Houston . . . Unfortunately for Carr's credibility, the second version contains one significant difficulty: it is impossible to see this part of Houston Street from the new courthouse building, as the old structure would have completely blocked the view." William Weston, "The Man in the Dark Sportcoat," *JFK/Deep Politics Quarterly* (July 1996), p. 17.

What made Carr change his story? An influential factor may have been the repeated threats and attempts on his life. One morning Carr found three sticks of dynamite wired to his car's ignition. Fifteen days before he testified in the Shaw trial, he was almost shot on the front porch of his home. *Cover-Up*, p. 13.

While recognizing that Carr's revised story has damaged his credibility, William Weston also makes the point: ". . . it is only fair to consider the severity of assassination-related persecution that he was suffering at the time of the trial . . . Given these circumstances, Carr's self-destructive credibility becomes more easily understandable as a matter of survival. When seen in this light, his early statements in 1964 actually gain in value—an account so important that the plotters of the assassination could not afford to leave it unsuppressed." Weston, "Man in the Dark Sportcoat," p. 17.

330. Helen Forrest interview by Michael L. Kurtz, May 17, 1974. Michael L. Kurtz, *Crime of the Century: The Kennedy Assassination from a Historian's Perspective* (Knoxville: University of Tennessee Press, 1993), p. 132.

331. Forrest cited in ibid.

332. Ibid., p. 189.

333. FBI interview of Marvin C. Robinson by Special Agents John V. Almon and

J. Calvin Rice, November 23, 1963. Reproduced in CD-ROM for *Harvey & Lee*, Nov 22–47.

334. FBI Memorandum by Special Agent Earle Haley on Interview of Roy Cooper, November 23, 1963. Reproduced in ibid., Nov 22–48.

335. *Warren Report*, pp. 161, 253.

336. Ibid., pp. 160–61. When questioned by the Warren Commission about Roger Craig, Captain Will Fritz said at first he had a hard time even remembering the deputy sheriff, in spite of Craig's having been chosen the Sheriff's Department Officer of the Year in 1960. With prompting, Fritz eventually acknowledged knowing Craig, but then denied that he ever brought him into his office with Oswald. *WCH*, vol. 4, p. 245.

337. FBI Report by Special Agents Bardwell D. Odum and James P. Hosty, Jr., March 2, 1964. Commission Exhibit 2125, *WCH*, vol. 24, p. 697.

338. In an incident that we will examine later in detail, FBI agent James P. Hosty, Jr., testified to Congress that he flushed down the toilet a note written to him by Lee Harvey Oswald. He said he did so in obedience to an order from the Special Agent in Charge of the Dallas FBI office, J. Gordon Shanklin, who in turn denied even knowing about the Oswald note. The House committee concluded the incident was "a serious impeachment of Shanklin's and Hosty's credibility." Hurt, *Reasonable Doubt*, p. 253. Filmed excerpts from Hosty's testimony are included in the video *Two Men in Dallas*. Because J. Edgar Hoover and the FBI were committed to covering up and even destroying vital evidence, as exemplified by Agent Hosty, it is impossible to determine from Hosty's report just what vehicles Ruth Paine owned and why Oswald would have been so defensive about her station wagon. Hoover and his agents, like Oswald, were protecting Ruth Paine. As we saw, Hoover recommended in a letter to head Warren Commission counsel J. Lee Rankin that he not release certain FBI "reports and memoranda dealing with Michael and Ruth Paine and George and Jeanne de Mohrenschildt." The consequences, Hoover warned Rankin, could jeopardize the Warren Commission: "Making the contents of such documents available to the public could cause serious repercussions to the Commission." J. Edgar Hoover Letter to J. Lee Rankin, October 23, 1964. FBI Record Number 124-10147-10006. Agency File Number 105-126128-1st NR 120.

339. Norman Cousins, *The Improbable Triumvirate: John F. Kennedy, Pope John, Nikita Khrushchev* (New York: W. W. Norton, 1972), p. 128.

340. Ibid.

341. Schlesinger, *A Thousand Days*, pp. 909–10.

342. Kenneth P. O'Donnell and David F. Powers, *"Johnny, We Hardly Knew Ye"* (Boston: Little, Brown, 1970), p. 285.

343. Robert F. Kennedy, *Thirteen Days*, p. 106.

344. O'Donnell and Powers, *"Johnny, We Hardly Knew Ye,"* p. 285.

345. *Public Papers of the Presidents: John F. Kennedy, 1963*, pp. 603, 605.

346. O'Donnell and Powers, *"Johnny, We Hardly Knew Ye,"* p. 375.

347. Norman Cousins's description of Kennedy's response to the note handed him by Evelyn Lincoln at the test ban meeting on August 7, 1963, and the president's abrupt departure, is found in Cousins's memorandum to himself, "August 7, 1963." It is preserved in Norman Cousins's home records in Beverly Hills. Cousins surmised in his memorandum that the note to the president was about the premature birth of his son. I am grateful to Professor Lawrence S. Wittner, professor of history at the State University of New York, for generously sharing this document with me from his own research records.

348. Sally Bedell Smith, *Grace and Power: The Private World of the Kennedy White House* (New York: Random House, 2004), p. 393.

349. Ibid., p. 394.

350. Sally Bedell Smith Interview of Dr. Judson Randolph; ibid., p. 395. Barbara Leaming, *Mrs. Kennedy: The Missing History of the Kennedy Years* (New York: Touchstone, 2001), p. 298.

351. O'Donnell and Powers, *"Johnny, We Hardly Knew Ye,"* p. 377.

352. Ibid.

353. Cousins, *Improbable Triumvirate*, pp. 138–44.

354. O'Donnell and Powers, *"Johnny, We Hardly Knew Ye,"* p. 378; Martin, *Hero for Our Time,* pp. 493, 497; Learning, *Grace and Power*, p. 399.

355. Learning, *Grace and Power*, p. 423.

356. O'Donnell and Powers, *"Johnny, We Hardly Knew Ye,"* p. 24. As a result of the media's special interests, what is best-known to a new generation about John F. Kennedy, apart from his having been a president who got killed, is that he was a philanderer. But if that was his most notable trait, why even bother asking why he was killed?

It is true that Kennedy was a philanderer. He was notoriously unfaithful to Jacqueline throughout their ten-year marriage. She would have been justified many times in ending it, but instead kept on seeking a genuine relationship with her husband.

It is also true, as their friends have observed, that in the wake of Patrick's death and in their last days together, especially in Texas, John and Jacqueline Kennedy were never more deeply together. Jacqueline had ample reason by then to be exhausted by her husband's behavior. Yet she seems to have seen a new future for them after their shared pain of Patrick's death. In his case, the death of their son seems to have finally broken him open to the depth of his wife's love and to his own capacity to return it. It was much too late, but in the last moments of their marriage and his life, John F. Kennedy seems to have been falling in love with his wife.

357. From Theodore H. White's notes of his November 29, 1963, interview with Jacqueline Kennedy; released by White on May 26, 1995. Cited by Vincent Michael Palamara, *JFK: The Medical Evidence Reference* (self-published, 1998), p. 50. Had Jacqueline Kennedy's words to White on her husband's death been made public when she said them, in addition to her reflections on the play *Camelot*, U.S. journalists and their readers would have had more cause to deal with JFK's assassination (and the reasons for it). Whether it was because of good taste, the cover-up, or both, the decades-long censorship of her immediate description of JFK's wounds discouraged critical questions about his murder.

358. *WCH*, vol. 2, pp. 138–39.

359. Ibid., p. 141.

360. Cited by Harold Weisberg in *Post Mortem: JFK Assassination Cover-up Smashed!* (published by Harold Weisberg, 1975), p. 380.

361. Ibid. Eight years after Jacqueline Kennedy gave her Warren Commission testimony, the government declassified her deleted words in belated response to a Freedom of Information Act (FOIA) request by Warren Commission critic Harold Weisberg. Ibid., p. 379. After the passage of twenty-nine more years, in response to filmmaker Mark Sobel's FOIA request, the government finally released in 2001 the court reporter's original stenographic tape of Mrs. Kennedy's interview. It was then discovered that even the "complete" Warren Commission transcript released to Weisberg had omitted two very specific descriptions by Jacqueline Kennedy of her husband's head wound: "I could see a piece of his skull sort of wedge shaped like that, and I remember it was flesh colored with little ridges at the top." Why had these details of the head wound been omitted from even the classified "complete" transcript? Unfortunately her interviewer, Chief Justice Earl Warren, asked no follow-up questions to the closest witness of the president's wounds. "Warren Commission Suppressed Jackie's Testimony on JFK's Head Wound," *Kennedy Assassination Chronicles,* vol. 7, Issue 2 (Summer 2001), pp. 18–19.

362. David S. Lifton, *Best Evidence: Disguise and Deception in the Assassination of John F. Kennedy* (New York: Carroll & Graf, 1980), p. 503. James H. Fetzer, editor, *Murder in Dealey Plaza: What We Know Now That We Didn't Know Then about the Death of JFK* (Chicago: Catfeet Press, 2000), p. 41.

363. In an interview with the House Select Committee on Assassinations, "Dr. Harper said the consensus of the doctors who viewed the skull fragment was that it was part of the occipital region." HSCA Memorandum on Interview Notes by Andy Purdy, August 17, 1977, p. 1. JFK Record Number 180-10093-10429.

364. Ibid., p. 2. Dr. Gerard Noteboom has reaffirmed the pathologists' conclusion from their firsthand examination that the Harper fragment's site of origin was the occiput, and "also recalled the lead deposit on the fragment." Dr. David W. Mantik's Interview of Dr. Gerard Noteboom, November 22, 1992, on Palm Springs radio show. Cited by Mantik in "Paradoxes of the JFK Assassination: The Medical Evidence Decoded," in Fetzer, *Murder in Dealey Plaza*, p. 279.

365. Lifton, *Best Evidence*, p. 504. The way a later researcher defined the significance of the contradiction described by David Lifton was: "if the [Harper] fragment is occipital bone, the autopsy X-rays of John Kennedy's skull cannot be authentic since the X-rays do not show sufficient bone loss in the occipital area." Dr. Joseph N. Riley, "Anatomy of the Harper Fragment," *JFK/Deep Politics Quarterly* (April 1996), p. 5. Dr. Riley's article goes on to dissent from the on-site pathologists' identification of the Harper fragment as occipital bone. Riley claims instead that the fragment's anatomical features show that it is parietal bone, "consistent with the X-rays being authentic." Ibid.

In a comprehensive essay on the JFK medical evidence, Dr. David W. Mantik counters Riley's argument in detail, stating that "Riley has overlooked much valuable evidence." Mantik concludes his analysis in favor of "the word of three Dallas pathologists who actually saw the real 3D bone. They all agreed that it was occipital, which is probably the best evidence we shall ever get on this question." Fetzer, *Murder in Dealey Plaza*, pp. 280, 282. That is especially true since, as Mantik notes, after the Harper fragment was turned over to the FBI, the FBI "lost" it. Fortunately, Dr. Gerard Noteboom had taken 35mm transparency slides of the Harper fragment, which have been preserved. Ibid., p. 279. Gerard Noteboom, August 25, 1998, letter to Vince Palamara. Cited in Vincent Michael Palamara, *JFK: The Medical Evidence Reference* (Self-published; updated 2005), p. 57.

366. Charles A. Crenshaw, M.D., *Trauma Room One: The JFK Medical Coverup Exposed* (New York: Paraview Press, 2001), Table 1, page 285.

367. FBI interview of Dr. A. B. Cairns, Chief Pathologist of Methodist Hospital, by Special Agent A. Raymond Switzer, July 10, 1964. Warren Commission Document 1395, p. 50.

368. Letter from David Lifton to Cyril Wecht, July 10, 1972; cited in Lifton, *Best Evidence*, p. 504 (emphasis in original).

369. David Mantik, "Optical Density Measurements of the JFK Autopsy X-Rays and A New Observation Based on the Chest X-Ray," November 18, 1993, p. 2. Cited by Harrison E. Livingstone, *Killing Kennedy and the Hoax of the Century* (New York: Carroll & Graf, 1995), p. 86.

370. When one examines the frames of Abraham Zapruder's twenty-seven-second home movie of the assassination, the film does not show what the twenty-one doctors, nurses, and Secret Service agents said they saw at Parkland Hospital in Dallas—a large exit wound in the right rear (occipital) area of JFK's head. Instead, as David Lifton observed, "the occipital area, where the Dallas doctors saw a wound, appears suspiciously dark, whereas a large wound appears on the foreword right-hand side of the head, where the Dallas doctors saw no wound at all." (*Best Evidence*, p. 557).

Lifton has suggested that the film was altered, partly to black out an exit wound in the rear of the head and to create the illusion of an exit wound in the front, thereby corresponding more to the Bethesda Naval Hospital's "best evidence" in the autopsy's body and the official X-rays and photographs. Another reason for altering the film (by removing frames and speeding up the car) may have been to eliminate evidence of the limousine stopping while the president was being shot, as Dallas witnesses claimed was the case. If the car-stop had not been removed, the film would have dramatically implicated the Secret Service in the assassination. (David Lifton, "Pig on a Leash: A Question of Authenticity," *The Great Zapruder Film Hoax: Deceit and Deception in the Death of JFK*, edited by James H. Fetzer [Chicago: Catfeet Press, 2004], pp. 404–5).

Those who argue that the film was not altered point especially to its depiction of the backward snap of JFK's head, providing evidence of a shot from the front. As David

Wrone writes, "Why would the government steal and alter the Zapruder film to hide a conspiracy only to have that alteration contain evidence that a conspiracy killed JFK?" (David Wrone, *The Zapruder Film: Reframing JFK's Assassination* [Lawrence: University Press of Kansas, 2003], p. 122).

However, if as we have seen the initial assassination scenario's purpose included scapegoating the Soviet Union and Cuba, evidence of a conspiracy was no problem, so long as it did not implicate the U.S. government per se—as would have been the case if the film revealed the Secret Service stopping the car to facilitate the shooting.

Those who reject the hypothesis of alteration see a chain of possession for the film from Abraham Zapruder to its purchaser, *Life* magazine, precluding that possibility (Wrone, *Zapruder Film*, pp. 123–24). A counterargument includes the documented fact that the Secret Service delivered such a film to the CIA's National Photographic Interpretation Center (NPIC) in Washington for analysis "1 or 2 days" after the assassination. Homer McMahon, then manager of the NPIC color lab, was asked to make color prints of "frames in which shots occurred." McMahon told the Assassinations Record and Review Board in 1997 that, in the process of selecting frames showing the wounding of Kennedy and Connally, "his opinion, which was that President Kennedy was shot 6 to 8 times from at least three directions, was ultimately ignored" (ARRB, June 12, 1997, call, and July 14, 1997, interview of Homer McMahon; Appendix C in Fetzer, *Great Zapruder Film Hoax*, pp. 457, 459).

The film's purchase by *Life* publisher C. D. Jackson, who as Lifton notes was "a close friend of former CIA Director Allen Dulles," may have provided a more flexible time frame for a possible alteration (Lifton, "Pig on a Leash," p. 405).

371. Author's Note on Change from Hardcover Text: I have removed here three pages of the text that go beyond the evidence as I now understand it—on the famous picture of the assassination taken by Dallas AP photographer James "Ike" Altgens that was wired around the world less than half an hour after President Kennedy was shot. Altgens's clear, black-and-white, head-on photograph of the approaching presidential limousine showed JFK through the windshield clutching at his throat, while spectators in the background lined the sidewalk in front of the Texas School Book Depository. This first pictorial evidence of the assassination also revealed the upper half of a man behind the limousine, standing in the doorway of the Book Depository. When the man's image in the picture was blown up, many people thought he looked like Lee Harvey Oswald. If it was in fact Oswald, how could he have been watching the motorcade from the doorway and at the same time shooting the president from a sixth-floor window in the same building?

In an appendix titled "Speculations and Rumors," the *Warren Report* identified the man in the doorway as Billy Lovelady, "an employee of the Texas School Book Depository, who somewhat resembles Oswald." *(Warren Report,* p. 644.)

The evidence I found most convincing over against the government's claim it was Lovelady, and Lovelady's own statement that he was the man in the doorway, was the unusual shirt worn by the man. It had a distinctive pattern, apparently with tears in it and several buttons missing—all of which seemed to match Oswald's shirt in photographs taken after his arrest.

Still prints drawn from a motion-picture film taken of Billy Lovelady immediately after the assassination seemed to show Lovelady had his outer shirt buttoned all the way up to the collar, covering his t-shirt. In contrast, Oswald (in his arrest photos) and the man in the doorway (in Altgens's photo) both had the upper halves of their outer shirts unbuttoned, exposing t-shirts with identical, pulled down collars.

I concluded: "Based on clothing alone, it was clear Lovelady could not have been the man in the Book Depository doorway when the presidential motorcade went by."

However, researchers such as Michael Green (letter to author, June 16, 2008), Robert Groden *(The Killing of a President,* pp. 186–87), and Richard E. Sprague (letter to Marguerite Oswald, May 19, 1970; Georgetown Univ. Library) have concluded from photographic analysis that the man in the doorway was in fact Billy Lovelady. In our correspondence, Green added the witness argument: "Since Lee Harvey Oswald puts himself in the lunchroom at the time of the shooting, and since numerous coworkers put Lovelady near the doorway *and do not put Oswald there,* that is very strong." (Michael Green email to John Kelin; shared by Green with Jim Douglass, June 17, 2008; emphasis in original.)

I agree. I tried unsuccessfully to find a witness to Oswald's being in the doorway. In the absence of such testimony, I think Green is right to argue that it is because Oswald was inside all the time.

On the other hand, photographic analyst Jack White has held for more than 30 years that the man in the doorway is not Lovelady, but neither is it Oswald or an Oswald double. (Jack White email to Jim Fetzer, November 16, 2009.)

In January 2010, having found no witness support for Oswald's presence in the doorway, I simply don't know who the man in Altgens's photo is. I have removed the claim in the text that I do.

372. *Warren Report,* p. 600. All of Oswald's police interviews are secondhand reports. For the twelve hours he was interrogated through three days by both local and federal investigators, the *Warren Report* stated incredibly: "There were no stenographic or tape recordings of these interviews." Ibid., p. 598. If we can believe that none of these officials tape-recorded the accused assassin's statements, we are then asked to accept their distillation of his words in only "the most important" of their "prepared memoranda setting forth their recollections of the questioning of Oswald and his responses." Ibid.

373. Ibid., p. 613.

374. Earl Golz, "Was Oswald in Window?" *Dallas Morning News* (November 26, 1978), p. 13A.

375. Ibid.

376. Summers, *Not In Your Lifetime,* p. 60.

377. "Was Oswald in Window?" p. 13A. Several of Carolyn Arnold's co-workers said they departed from the Texas School Book Depository at about the same time or a little before she did and stood with her outside the building to watch the motorcade. Betty Jean Dragoo said she left the Depository "about 12:20 P.M." with Carolyn Arnold, Bonnie Richey, Virgie Baker, and Judy Johnson. *WCH,* vol. 22, p. 645. Judy Johnson said she and two other friends left "about 12:15 P.M.," and were joined outside by Arnold, Richee, and Dragoo. Ibid., p. 656.

378. Summers, p. 60.

379. "Was Oswald in Window?" p. 13A.

380. A person planning to kill the president could have read a *Dallas Morning News* article on Wednesday, November 20, 1963, which stated that the presidential motorcade would arrive at 12:30 P.M. Friday at the Trade Mart. Warren Commission Exhibit No. 1364, *WCH,* vol. 22, p. 616. That schedule allowed for five minutes of driving time from Elm and Houston, where the Book Depository was located, to the Trade Mart. An assassin on the sixth floor of the Book Depository would have expected the motorcade to pass under the building's windows at 12:25 P.M.

381. To determine whether Oswald could have descended from the sixth floor by the time Patrolman Baker saw him in the lunchroom on the second, the Warren Commission timed a stand-in for a sixth-floor assassin, Secret Service agent John Howlett, enacting a quick transition to the second floor, and Baker reenacting his ascent to the second floor. Howlett "carried a rifle from the southeast corner of the sixth floor along the east aisle to the northeast corner. He placed the rifle on the floor near the site where Oswald's rifle was actually found after the shooting. Then Howlett walked down the stairway to the second-floor landing and entered the lunchroom. The first test, run at normal walking pace, required 1 minute, 18 seconds; the second test, at a 'fast walk' took 1 minute, 14 seconds." *Warren Report,* p. 152.

Because the minimum time required for Patrolman Baker's ascent to the second floor "was within 3 seconds of the time needed to walk from the southeast corner of the sixth floor," the *Warren Report* concluded Oswald had barely enough time to get downstairs for his encounter with Baker. Ibid.

However, the commission's own exhibits and testimony called the timing of its reen-actments into question. The photograph that is Commission Exhibit 723 *(WCH,* vol. 17, p. 504) shows a barricade of boxes stacked around the "sniper's nest" in the southeast corner of the sixth floor. As Warren Commission critic Howard Roffman pointed out, "the gunman would have had to squeeze through these stacks of boxes while carrying a 40-inch, 8-pound rifle. Considering these details, we must add at least six or seven seconds to the Commission's time to allow for the various necessary factors that would slow departure from the window." The escaping assassin then had an even more time-consuming task—hiding his rifle amid clusters of more piled-up boxes, where it would be found as shown in another photograph, Commission Exhibit 517 *(WCH,* vol. 17, p. 226). Even to discover the concealed rifle, Deputy Sheriff Eugene Boone said he had to squeeze through piles of boxes until he "caught a glimpse of the rifle, stuffed down between two rows of boxes with another box or so pulled over the top of it" *(WCH,* vol. 3, p. 293). The Warren Commission's trial runs for an assassin of a minute and a quarter, barely corresponding to Baker's time, had eliminated these original sixth-floor obstacles. It would have been impossible for an actual gunman at the time of the assassination to squeeze out of his box-barricaded corner, climb in and out of another cavern of boxes to hide his rifle under them, then still descend the four flights of stairs quickly enough to be calmly buying a Coca Cola by the time Baker saw Oswald in the second-floor lunchroom. Howard Roff-man, *Presumed Guilty* (Cranbury, N.J.: A. S. Barnes and Company, 1976), pp. 211, 216. I am grateful to Steve Jones for having brought Howard Roffman's work to my attention.

382. *WCH,* vol. 3, pp. 250–51, 255. *Warren Report,* pp. 151–52.

383. *Warren Report,* p. 151.

384. *WCH,* vol. 3, p. 251.

385. Ibid., p. 274. According to what Oswald told his interrogators, he was already drinking the Coca Cola when Patrolman Baker came into the lunchroom *(Warren Report,* p. 600)—which would have made even more implausible his transition from "the sniper's nest" in time to be seen by Baker. In a handwritten statement, Baker himself wrote, "I saw a man standing in the lunch room, drinking a Coke." However, he crossed out "drinking a Coke." Commission Exhibit No. 3076, *WCH,* vol. 26, p. 677.

386. *WCH,* vol. 3, p. 263.

387. *Warren Report,* p. 152.

388. Summers, p. 60.

389. "Was Oswald in Window?", p. 13A. FBI interview of Mrs. R. E. Arnold, November 26, 1963, by Special Agent Richard E. Harrison, File Number DL 89–43. RG 272, Records of the President's Commission on the Assassination of President Kennedy, Entry 10, Box 2.

390. "Was Oswald in Window?" Ibid.

391. David W. Belin, *November 22, 1963: You Are the Jury* (New York: Quadrangle/ New York Times Book Co., 1973), p. 466.

392. Ibid. Also David W. Belin, *Final Disclosure: The Full Truth about the Assassina-tion of President Kennedy* (New York: Charles Scribner's Sons, 1988), p. 204.

393. Weisberg, *Whitewash II,* p. 24.

394. *Warren Report,* p. 144.

395. Ibid.

396. Mark Lane, *Rush to Judgment* (New York: Thunder's Mouth Press, 1992), p. 83.

397. *WCH,* vol. 3, p. 144.

398. Commission Exhibit No. 1311, *WCH,* vol. 22, p. 484. Gerald D. McKnight, *Breach of Trust: How the Warren Commission Failed the Nation and Why* (Lawrence: University Press of Kansas, 2005), pp. 109–10. Given the sixth-floor window's physical facts, the Warren Commission conceded finally that its star witness, Howard Brennan, was wrong and that "most probably" the man in the window was "either sitting or kneel-

ing." *Warren Report*, p. 144. Nevertheless, the *Warren Report* asserted valiantly that Brennan, looking up at the sixth-floor window, could still have determined that a less visible shooter was 5'10" tall: "Brennan could have seen enough of the body of a kneeling or squatting person to estimate his height." Ibid., p. 145.

399. Ibid., pp. 19, 156.

400. Ibid., pp. 151, 154.

401. Ibid., p. 157.

402. Ibid., p. 157–63.

403. Ibid., p. 162.

404. Ibid., pp. 162–63. *WCH*, vol. 22, p. 86, Commission Exhibit 1119-A.

405. *Warren Report*, p. 162. *WCH*, vol. 22, p. 86.

406. *WCH*, vol. 6, p. 438.

407. *Warren Report*, pp. 163–65, 653–54.

408. Ibid., p. 165. *WCH*, vol. 7, p. 439; vol. 24, pp. 432–33, Commission Exhibit 2017.

409. *Warren Report*, p. 648.

410. Ibid., pp. 5–6.

411. Ibid., p. 6.

412. Ibid., pp. 176–79. *WCH*, vol. 22, p. 86.

413. *Warren Report*, pp. 159, 252.

414. Ibid., p. 604.

415. Ibid., pp. 157–59.

416. Craig interview, video *Two Men in Dallas*.

417. Kurtz, *Crime of the Century*, p. 132.

418. Craig, *When They Kill a President*, p. 9. What was the plotters' purpose in making "Lee Harvey Oswald" so visible at this point—by his departing from the front of the Texas School Book Depository minutes after the assassination in a vehicle driven by "a husky looking Latin"? We can recall that Oswald was set up as a Cuban-and-Soviet-connected assassin, by the introduction of false evidence to implicate him step by step, from Mexico City to Dallas, as a Communist conspirator. His being driven away from the Depository by a "husky looking Latin" was consistent with his having Cuban connections. After the new president Lyndon Johnson pulled back from exposing such a CIA-doctored Communist conspiracy, Oswald's faked Cuban and Soviet connections had to be suppressed or read innocently: his visits and phone calls to the Cuban and Soviet consulates in Mexico City, his letter received on November 18 by the Soviet Embassy in Washington, his accompanying two friends who tried to charter a plane from Wayne January for a November 22 flight toward Cuba, and his departure from the Depository with a "husky looking Latin" driving the car. As we shall see, even Jack Ruby's (now little-known) involvement in the 1950s as a gunrunner to Fidel Castro could be used, if necessary, to implicate the young man (a second Oswald?) who carried the gun case from Ruby's truck up the grassy knoll. Yet every such connection with a jettisoned Communist conspiracy scenario had to be covered up in the end for the sake of the Warren Commission's lone-assassin story. It all said too much about both the composite scapegoat and the domestic intelligence network that was writing his story.

419. *WCH*, vol. 6, p. 444.

420. Ibid., p. 443.

421. Ibid., p. 438.

422. An FBI agent walked the distance from Oswald's boarding house, 1026 North Beckley, to the point where Tippit was shot, near Tenth and Patton, in twelve minutes. *WCH*, vol. 24, p. 18, CE 1987. A Secret Service agent also did it in twelve minutes. Commission Document 87 in Dale Myers, *With Malice: Lee Harvey Oswald and the Murder of Officer J. D. Tippit* (Milford, Mich.: Oak Cliff Press, 1998), p. 514. The *Warren Report*, barely including the three or four minutes Oswald spent in his room, states: "If Oswald left his roominghouse shortly after 1 P.M. and walked at a brisk pace, he would have

reached 10th and Patton shortly after 1:15 P.M. [just in time to shoot Tippit]" (p. 165). If, as subsequent investigation would show, Oswald was spotted walking west on 10th just a minute before the shooting, an additional 1.5 minutes would have been needed to put him in position to do so, making the minimum walk time 13.5 minutes. Myers, p. 665. All these Warren-Commission-derived calculations assume, however, that there was only one Oswald involved in "Oswald's Oak Cliff movements." That this is a false assumption can be seen from the testimony of Butch Burroughs, Bernard Haire, Wes Wise, T. F. White, and Robert G. Vinson in the pages that follow.

423. Ibid., p. 444. When Earlene Roberts saw that the police car that stopped and honked was 107, instead of 170 (a car that she was familiar with), she was able to remember the number from its having the same digits as the car she knew. She said she confused the number in her retelling (CE 2781 in *WCH*, vol. 26, p. 165; vol. 6, p. 443), but was clear in the end (from its having the same digits in a different order) that the correct car number was 107.

424. *WCH*, vol. 24, p. 460, Commission Exhibit 2045. Norman Redlick of the Warren Commission staff followed up Earlene Roberts's identification of the police car as number 107 by phoning the Dallas Police Department with an inquiry "as to the location of police car number 107 on November 22, 1963." Ibid. In an August 4, 1964, letter in response, Charles Batchelor, Dallas Assistant Chief of Police, informed Redlick:

"Investigation reveals that the Dallas Police Department did not have a car with this number on the date in question. We had a 1962 model Ford carrying this number which was sold on April 17, 1963, to Mr. Elvis Blount, a used car dealer in Sulphur Springs, Texas. Before sale, all signs and numbers were removed from the car and the areas involved were repainted.

"We did not resume using this number (107) until February, 1964." Ibid.

425. *Warren Report*, p. 165.

426. Ibid., p. 166.

427. Ibid., p. 178.

428. Warren H. "Butch" Burroughs interview, *The Men Who Killed Kennedy, Part 5, "The Patsy,"* produced and directed by Nigel Turner. The History Channel.

429. *WCH*, vol. 7, p. 15.

430. Butch Burroughs tried to explain to the Warren Commission why Lee Harvey Oswald, on entering the theater, must have gone directly up the stairs to the balcony. If so, it was impossible for Burroughs to see his entry from the concession stand. Burroughs said he was in the process of counting stock candy and putting it in his candy case: "if he had came around in front of the concession out there, I would have seen him, even though I was bent down, I would have seen him, but otherwise—I think he sneaked up the [balcony] stairs real fast." Burroughs knew that, if he had not seen Oswald come in, he must have gone immediately up the balcony stairs on entering the theater. Ibid. Julia Postal, the ticket-seller for the Texas Theater, also tried to explain this logistical fact in her Warren Commission testimony: "You can go up in the balcony and right straight down, those steps come back down, and that would bring you into [the orchestra seating]. He wouldn't have to go by Butch at all." *WCH*, vol. 7, p. 13.

431. Author's interview of Warren H. "Butch" Burroughs, July 16, 2007.

432. *Warren Report*, pp. 6–7.

433. Jack Davis interview by Jim Marrs, fall 1988, *Crossfire*, p. 353. Author's interview of Jim Marrs, January 14, 2006.

434. Jack Davis interview by John Armstrong, *Harvey & Lee*, p. 841.

435. Warren H. "Butch" Burroughs interview by Jim Marrs, summer 1987, *Crossfire*, p. 353. Author's interview of Jim Marrs, January 14, 2006.

436. Burroughs interview by Marrs, *Crossfire*, p. 353. Author's interview of Burroughs, July 16, 2007.

437. Ibid. It is possible the pregnant woman gave Oswald the sign he seemed to need, confirming that she was the contact he was seeking. He apparently sat by her longer than

he did by anyone else. It was she, not he, who got up and left. Burroughs said of her, "I don't know what happened to that woman. I don't know how she got out of the theater. I never saw her again." Marrs, ibid.

438. Davis interview by Marrs, *Crossfire*, p. 353.

439. *WCH*, vol. 3, pp. 298–99.

440. Myers, *With Malice*, pp. 172–73.

441. *WCH*, vol. 3, p. 299.

442. Warren Commission member Senator John Sherman Cooper was especially puzzled by Officer McDonald's circuitous way of approaching the suspected murderer and questioned him closely about it. *WCH*, vol. 3, p. 303.

443. Ibid., p. 300. Also *WCH*, vol. 7, pp. 32, 39.

444. Author's interview of Burroughs, July 16, 2007. Butch Burroughs is a man of few words. When asked a question, he answers exactly what he is asked. Burroughs told me no one had ever asked him before about a second arrest in the Texas Theater. In response to my question, "Now you didn't see anybody else [besides Oswald] get arrested that day, did you?" he answered, "Yes, there was a lookalike—an Oswald lookalike." In response to further questions, he described the second arrest, that of the "Oswald lookalike." Ibid. Because Butch Burroughs saw neither Oswald nor his lookalike enter the Texas Theater, each must have gone directly up the balcony stairs on entering. Oswald crossed the balcony and came down the stairs on the far side of the lobby. There he entered the orchestra seats and began his seat-hopping, in apparent search of a contact. His lookalike sneaked into the theater at 1:45 p.m. and, like Oswald, went immediately up the balcony stairs. By the time Burroughs witnessed the Oswald double's arrest, he had also come down the balcony stairs on the far side of the lobby, either on his own or already accompanied by police who had been checking the balcony.

445. Ibid.

446. Ibid.

447. Ibid.

448. In the data base of the JFK Records Act at the National Archives, there is no record of Bernard Haire. Archivist Martin F. McGann to James Douglass, July 20, 2007.

449. In a photo taken about 1:50 p.m., November 22, 1963, that shows people gathering around the police cars in front of the Texas Theater, Bernard Haire can be seen at the edge of the crowd, leaning on a parking meter and trying to see. Photo by Stuart L. Reed; on p. 68, Myers, *With Malice*.

450. Bernard J. Haire interview by Jim Marrs, summer 1987. *Crossfire*, p. 354.

451. Ibid.

452. Dallas Police Department Homicide Report on J. D. Tippit, November 22, 1963. Reproduced in *With Malice*, p. 447 (emphasis added).

453. Letter from Detective L. D. Stringfellow to Captain W. P. Gannaway, November 23, 1963, Dallas City Archives. Cited in *Harvey & Lee*, p. 871 (emphasis added).

454. Reporter Seth Kantor jotted down in his notebook Oswald's November 22 remark, "I'm just a patsy," and the time he made it: 7:55 p.m. Kantor Exhibit 3, *WCH*, vol. 20, p. 366.

455. FBI Memorandum by Dallas Special Agent Charles T. Brown, December 14, 1963. Warren Commission Document 205. JFK Record Number 180-10108-10231.

456. Author's interviews with Wes Wise, October 31 and November 13, 2005.

457. Bill Pulte interviews with Mack Pate, October 1989. Notes and map from Bill Pulte/Gary Shaw interview with Mack Pate, October 10, 1989. I am grateful to Bill Pulte for alerting me to these interviews and to Gary Shaw for sharing with me his records of them.

458. Wes Wise citing mechanic T. F. White, "The Wise Allegation," in "Oswald-Tippit Associates," Staff Report of the House Select Committee on Assassinations (March 1979), *Appendix to Hearings*, p. 38.

459. Ibid. Mack Pate identified the vehicle T. F. White had spotted in the El Chico

parking lot as a 1961 red Falcon in his October 10, 1989, interview with Gary Shaw and Bill Pulte.

460. HSCA Memorandum from Andy Purdy to Bob Tanenbaum, February 19, 1977, p. 3. JFK Record Number 180-10108-10134.

461. Wise interviews, October 31 and November 13, 2005.

462. Wise interview, November 13, 2005.

463. Wes Wise retold the story of his encounter with Jack Ruby in a book he published in 2004, co-authored with three other Dallas newscasters who also covered the Kennedy assassination. Bob Huffaker, Bill Mercer, George Phenix, and Wes Wise, *When the News Went Live: Dallas 1963* (New York: Taylor Trade Publishing, 2004), pp. 125–26.

464. Ibid., p. 126.

465. Ibid.

466. Wise interviews, October 31 and November 13, 2005.

467. Wise interview, October 31, 2005.

468. Wise interviews.

469. Ibid.

470. Report by FBI Special Agent Charles T. Brown, Jr., December 14, 1963. JFK Record Number 180-10108-10237.

471. Report by FBI Special Agent Charles T. Brown, Jr., December 14, 1963. JFK Record Number 180-10108-10235.

472. "Castro Says C.I.A. Uses Raider Ship," *New York Times* (November 1, 1963), p. 1.

473. *Harvey & Lee*, p. 872.

474. "Rockwell Collins, Inc. Company Timeline," www.collinsclubs.com/history/timeline.html. At the Rockwell-Collins merger in 1971, Art Collins, the founder of Collins Radio, was named president and board chairman of Rockwell International. Ibid.

475. HSCA interview with Carl Amos Mather, March 20, 1978, p. 4. JFK Record Number 180-10087-10360.

476. Wise interview, October 31, 2005.

477. HSCA Memorandum from Purdy to Tanenbaum, February 19, 1977, p. 3.

478. In a May 31, 1978, letter to the HSCA chief counsel G. Robert Blakey, the U.S. Attorney General's Office extended a grant of immunity to Carl Amos Mather. Reproduced in CD-ROM for *Harvey & Lee*, Tippit-33.

479. Mather interview, p. 3.

480. "Wise Allegation," pp. 37–41. Given T. F. White's identification of the license plate and his and Mack Pate's identification of the red Falcon driven by the Oswald double, a question arises concerning the government's "counter evidence." The disassociation of license plate PP 4537 and the Falcon arose from the FBI's and the Dallas County Tax Office's "official verification" that PP 4537 was issued instead for a 1957 Plymouth owned by Carl Mather. However, we have reached a point in this story where the FBI, and other official sources subject to FBI pressures (such as a county tax office), cannot simply be assumed to be telling the truth in anything relating to President Kennedy's assassination. As we shall soon see, the FBI lied and even destroyed vital evidence, when it came to Oswald's note to FBI agent James Hosty. Given the FBI's consistent record in covering up, falsifying, and destroying evidence that might incriminate the government in the assassination, it is reasonable to ask if that may be going on again here. After the Oswald double's quick release following his Texas Theater arrest by the Dallas Police, he may have been given a Mather car to use that had a state-of-the-art Collins Radio for effective communications. The Oswald double keeping a low profile in the El Chico parking lot was apparently waiting to receive an order. Thanks to T. F. White's jotting down the license plate that was on the double's car, the government then had to disassociate that license as much as possible from Mather. But fortunately it was done clumsily, and White's documentation of the license plate provided a trail that led back to the CIA.

481. Huffaker, Mercer, Phenix, and Wise, *When the News Went Live*, pp. 129–30.

482. Wise interview, October 31, 2005.

483. Wise interview, November 15, 2005. Wes Wise showed the House Select Committee on Assassinations his luncheon invitation bearing his original notes, which the HSCA copied for its records. JFK Record Number 180-10108-10261.

484. Wise interview, November 15, 2005.

485. Retired Air Force sergeant Robert G. Vinson has told his story in a book co-authored by his lawyer, James P. Johnston, a fifty-two-page affidavit by Vinson to Johnston, a one-hour-and-fifteen-minute video, and a television interview whose substance was adapted into a chapter in a book: (1) James P. Johnston and Jon Roe, *Flight from Dallas: New Evidence of CIA Involvement in the Murder of President John F. Kennedy* (Bloomington, Ind.: 1stBooks, 2003). (2) Affidavit of Robert Griel Vinson to James P. Johnston, September 28, 1994. (3) Videotaped Statement of Robert G. Vinson (DVD-R), November 2, 1996. (4) Larry Hatteberg's interview of Robert Vinson, KAKE-TV Channel 10 News, November 23, 1993. (5) Larry Hatteberg, Suzanne Perez Tobias, and Vada Snider, "The Kennedy Connection," in *More Larry Hatteberg's Kansas People* (Wichita, Kans.: Wichita Eagle and Beacon Publishing Company, 1994), pp. 134–35. I am grateful to Robert Vinson for answering further questions during our phone conversations of November 26, 2005, and January 10, 2006.

486. Johnston and Roe, *Flight from Dallas*, p. 19; Vinson videotape, Nov. 2, 1996.

487. Johnston and Roe, *Flight from Dallas*, p. 19.

488. Vinson affidavit, p. 14.

489. Ibid.

490. Ibid., p. 17.

491. Ibid., p. 18. Johnston and Roe, *Flight from Dallas*, p. 23.

492. Johnston and Roe, *Flight from Dallas*, p. 24. Vinson affidavit, pp. 19–20.

493. Johnston and Roe, *Flight from Dallas*, p. 24. Vinson affidavit, pp. 21–22.

494. Johnston and Roe, *Flight from Dallas*, pp. 25, 28.

495. Ibid., p. 26.

496. Vinson affidavit, pp. 22–28, 44. Johnston and Roe, *Flight from Dallas*, pp. 25–26, 29.

497. *More Larry Hatteberg's Kansas People*, p. 134.

498. Johnston and Roe, *Flight from Dallas*, p. 27. Roswell Army Air Field, New Mexico, was redesignated Walker Air Force Base on January 13, 1948. Until the base was closed in 1967, it apparently was referred to commonly as "Roswell Air Force Base," although its official designation was Walker AFB. Topographic maps obtained by James P. Johnston, Robert Vinson's former attorney, show that Walker Air Force Base was located five to eight miles south of Roswell, New Mexico. Author's interview of James P. Johnston, February 4, 2008. *Joe McCusker's List of Air Force Bases*. See http://www.airforcebase .net/usaf/joeslist.html.

499. Ibid., pp. 27–28.

500. Ibid., p. 29.

501. Ibid., pp. 32–33.

502. Orders from Major Blake A. Smith, USAF, to R. G. Vinson, November 25, 1964: "For interview at Hq USAF in conjunction with a Special Project." Document reproduced in Johnston and Roe, *Flight from Dallas*, p. 52.

503. Ibid., pp. 33–36. Vinson affidavit, pp. 33–39.

504. Vinson affidavit, pp. 39, 41–43. Johnston and Roe, *Flight from Dallas*, pp. 37, 66–67.

505. *Area 51: The Real Story*, Discovery Channel. Cited in ibid., p. 68.

506. Johnston and Roe, *Flight from Dallas*, pp. 67–68.

507. Vinson affidavit, pp. 42–43.

508. Johnston and Roe, *Flight from Dallas*, p. 69.

509. Ibid., p. 68. Vinson affidavit, p. 43.

510. Technical Sergeant R. G. Vinson Air Force Retirement Order, June 1, 1966; effective October 1, 1966.

511. Johnston and Roe, *Flight from Dallas*, p. 69.

512. Ibid., p. 71.

513. Ibid., pp. 73–74.

514. Larry Hatteberg to the author; December 20, 2005, phone conversation.

515. Johnston and Roe, *Flight from Dallas*, p. 90.

516. Ibid., p. 91.

517. Ibid., p. 92.

518. Craig, *When They Kill a President*, p. 9.

519. Vinson Affidavit, p. 26. *Flight from Dallas*, p. 26.

520. Johnston and Roe, *Flight from Dallas*, p. 106.

521. I interviewed Malcolm Kilduff by phone on March 7, 2002. He died on March 3, 2003, at the age of seventy-five.

522. Author's interview of Malcolm Kilduff, March 7, 2002. Also Harrison Edward Livingstone's interview of Malcolm Kilduff, April 17, 1991; cited in Livingstone's *High Treason 2: The Great Cover-Up: The Assassination of President John F. Kennedy* (New York: Carroll & Graf, 1992), p. 503.

523. Livingstone's interview of Kilduff.

524. Martin, *Hero for Our Time*, p. 465.

525. Tom Wicker, *JFK and LBJ: The Influence of Personality upon Politics* (New York: William Morrow, 1968), p. 194.

526. Author's interview of Mrs. Zola Shoup, September 9, 1999.

527. Wayne Morse interview by David Nyhan, "We've Been a Police State a Long Time," *Boston Globe* (June 24, 1973), pp. A 1–2.

528. Thomas J. Hamilton, "Nations Get Thant Appeal To Hold Talks on Vietnam," *New York Times* (March 9, 1965), p. 4. I first came across this article, and the next four sources, through Peter Dale Scott's essay "The Death of Kennedy and the Vietnam War," in *Government by Gunplay: Assassination Conspiracy Theories from Dallas to Today,* edited by Sid Blumenthal and Harvey Yazijian (New York: Signet, 1976), pp. 157, 183.

529. Ibid.

530. Richard P. Stebbins, *The United States in World Affairs 1963* (New York: published for the Council on Foreign Relations by Harper & Row, 1964), pp. 193–94.

531. *Manchester Guardian* (August 9, 1965), cited by Franz Schurmann, Peter Dale Scott, and Reginald Zelnik in *The Politics of Escalation in Vietnam* (Boston: Beacon Press, 1966), p. 28.

532. National Liberation Front broadcast on November 8, 1963, cited by Jean Lacouture, *Vietnam: Between Two Truces* (New York: Random House, 1966), p. 170.

533. U Thant on February 24, 1965. Cited by Schurmann, Scott, and Zelnik, *Politics of Escalation*, p. 28.

534. Michael Charlton and Anthony Moncrieff, *Many Reasons Why* (New York: Hill & Wang, 1978), p. 84.

535. Crenshaw, *Trauma Room One*, pp. 61–62.

536. Ibid., p. 61.

537. Ibid., p. 62.

538. Ibid.

539. Ibid., p. 67.

540. Ibid., p. 285, table 1.

541. Ibid., p. 67.

542. "Mr. Kennedy was hit by a bullet in the throat, just below the Adam's apple, [Dr. Malcolm Perry and Dr. Kemp Clark] said. This wound had the appearance of a bullet's entry." "Kennedy Is Killed by Sniper as He Rides in Car in Dallas," *New York Times* (November 23, 1963), p. 2.

A United Press International report, datelined Dallas, November 22, 1963, stated: "Dr. Malcolm Perry, 34 years old, said 'there was an entrance wound below his Adam's apple.

543. Malcolm Perry's press conference statements from White House transcript 1327-C, November 22, 1963, 3:16 P.M. CST, Dallas, Texas, pp. 5–6. LBJ Library.

544. Jack Minnis and Staughton Lynd, "Seeds of Doubt: Some Questions about the Assassination," *New Republic* (December 21, 1963), p. 20.

545. Manchester, *Death of a President*, pp. 338–46.

546. *WCH*, vol. 6, p. 42 (emphasis added). Arlen Specter repeated his hypothetical question, which contradicted the doctors' own earliest testimony, as a way of putting on record their apparent retractions. See also *WCH*, vol. 3, pp. 362, 373; vol. 6, pp. 25–26.

547. Dr. Charles Crenshaw, "Let's Set the Record Straight" (unpublished manuscript), p. 22.

548. *WCH*, vol. 3, p. 376. In his testimony to the Warren Commission, Kemp Clark joined Malcolm Perry in backing away from newspaper reports of their first statements on the hole in the president's throat. Clark said, "I do not recall ever specifically stating that this was an entrance wound . . ." *WCH*, vol. 6, p. 28.

549. *WCH*, vol. 3, p. 379.

550. House Select Committee witness Jim Gochenaur to interviewer Bob Kelley on Gochenaur's conversations with Secret Service agent Elmer Moore. Notes by Bob Kelley on June 6, 1975; pp. 3–4. JFK Record Number 157-10005-10280.

551. From transcribed copy by House Select Committee on Assassinations of tape-recorded conversation with James Gochenaur, May 10, 1977, p. 22. JFK Record Number 180-10086-10438.

552. Author's interview with Jim Gochenaur, April 28, 2007.

553. Moore cited by Gochenaur. HSCA conversation with Gochenaur, May 10, 1977, p. 23. Also Jim Gochenaur's letter to the author, October 23, 2007.

554. Crenshaw, *Trauma Room One*, p. 109.

555. Crenshaw, *JFK: Conspiracy of Silence*, pp. 153–54.

556. *Dallas Morning News* interview on April 8, 1992, with Oliver "Buck" Revell, director of the Dallas FBI Office. Cited in Crenshaw, *Trauma Room One*, p. 151.

557. *Dallas Morning News* interview on May 17, 1992, with David W. Belin, counsel for the Warren Commission in 1964. Cited in Crenshaw, *Trauma Room One*, p. 152.

558. Dennis L. Breo, "JFK's death—the plain truth from the MDs who did the autopsy," pp. 2794–2803; Dennis L. Breo, "JFK's death, part II—Dallas MDs recall their memories," pp. 2804–2807; both in *Journal of the American Medical Association*, vol. 267, no. 20 (May 27, 1992).

559. Dr. Charles Rufus Baxter, *WCH*, vol. 6, p. 40. Dr. Robert Nelson McClelland, ibid., p. 32. Dr. Don Teel Curtis, ibid., p. 60. Nurse Margaret Hinchcliffe, ibid., p. 141. Dr. Kenneth Everett Salyer, ibid., pp. 80–81.

560. Crenshaw, "Let's Set the Record Straight," p. 3.

561. Charles A. Crenshaw, M.D., J. Gary Shaw, "Commentary on JFK Autopsy Articles," *JAMA*, vol. 273, no. 20 (May 24/31, 1995), p. 1632.

562. "Dennis L. Breo's Reply," ibid., p. 1633.

563. D. Bradley Kizzia, "On the Trial of the Character Assassins," in Crenshaw, *Trauma Room One*, p. 169. Kizzia adds: "It is also of note that in 1998, Dr. [George] Lundberg was fired as editor-in-chief of *JAMA*, allegedly due to a series of controversial publications. He was preceded in leaving *JAMA* by his writer, Breo, who was discharged not long after the Crenshaw litigation was settled. Also, the Chicago Headline Club determined in 1999 that its award for exemplary journalism probably should not have been given to Breo in 1992 for the articles in *JAMA* on the JFK assassination because fairly clear-cut "evidence now available proves that the journalist who wrote the award-winning story purposefully did not report it fairly at the time." Ibid.

564. Robert B. Livingston, M.D., "Statement of November 18, 1993," in James H.

Fetzer, *Assassination Science: Experts Speak Out on the Death of JFK* (Chicago: Catfeet Press, 1998), p. 162.

565. Ibid.

566. Ibid.

567. "Testimony of Dr. Pierre Finck," February 24, 1969, in the trial of Clay Shaw; Appendix A in James DiEugenio, *Destiny Betrayed: JFK, Cuba, and the Garrison Case* (New York: Sheridan Square Press, 1992), p. 291.

568. Ibid., pp. 291–92.

569. Ibid., pp. 301–302.

570. William Matson Law with Allan Eaglesham, *In the Eye of History* (Southlake, Tex.: JFK Lancer Productions & Publications, 2005), p. 45.

571. Ibid., p. 39. Paul O'Connor stated that, in addition to Admiral Galloway, head of the hospital command, Admiral George Burkley, the president's physician, also blocked the doctors from probing the neck wound and a back wound. Admiral Burkley claimed he was acting in the name of the Kennedy family, none of whom were present at the autopsy. Ibid., p. 43.

572. Ibid., pp. 75, 83.

573. Ibid., p. 106.

574. Ibid., p. 65.

575. Crenshaw, *JFK: Conspiracy of Silence*, pp. 153–54.

576. Kent Heiner, *Without Smoking Gun: Was the Death of Lt. Cmdr. William B. Pitzer Part of the JFK Assassination Cover-up Conspiracy?* (Watterville, Ore.: Trine Day, 2004), p. 68.

577. Ibid., p. 49.

578. Author's interview with Dennis David, June 30, 2006.

579. Law and Eaglesham, *In the Eye of History*, p. 16.

580. Ibid., pp. 16–17.

581. Letter from Dennis David to Joanne Braun, October 31, 1991 (emphasis in original). Cited by Harrison Edward Livingstone, *High Treason 2* (New York: Carroll & Graf, 1992), p. 558.

582. Law and Eaglesham, *In the Eye of History*, p. 23. How could Bill Pitzer have taken an autopsy film unobserved? "One of the more interesting recent developments in the Pitzer case is the revelation that a closed-circuit television (CCTV) camera existed in the NNMC morgue at the time of the Kennedy autopsy. A discreet CCTV recording made from a control room and later transferred to 16mm film is far more plausible than Pitzer's presence in the morgue with camera in hand, managing to go unnoticed." Heiner, *Without Smoking Gun*, p. 51. See also Law and Eaglesham, *In the Eye of History*, pp. 328–29.

Dennis David told me in an interview that Pitzer could have been in his office (in a separate building fifty to sixty yards away from the morgue's back entrance) monitoring a remotely-operated, closed-circuit filming of the autopsy, unseen by anyone there. The likelihood of such a process is increased by the camera's stationary nature in the movie film that David saw in Pitzer's office: "To me it had to have been a static [camera], because there was none of that movement or flutteryness you sometimes see with a hand-held [camera]." Author's interview of Dennis David, June 30, 2006.

Again from the film and slides David saw in Pitzer's office, he thought the filming must have been done before the autopsy actually began: "I would say the films which *I viewed* with Bill were prior to the commencement of the postmortem, as there was no evidence of a Y incision on the torso, nor was the scalp incised and peeled forward on the face as would be done during a postmortem." Letter from Dennis David to Joanne Braun, September 11, 1991. Cited by Harrison Edward Livingstone, *High Treason 2*, p. 557 (emphasis in original).

On November 22, Dennis David was a witness to the unloading of a "gray shipping casket" from a black civilian hearse at the back entrance of the Bethesda morgue around 6:30 P.M.—half an hour before the arrival at the hospital's front entrance, which he also witnessed, of the gray navy ambulance that was officially carrying the president's body in a bronze ceremonial casket. Law and Eaglesham, *In the Eye of History*, pp. 7–9.

In a brief conversation with David, the driver of the hearse that delivered the shipping casket "stated that he'd come up 16th Street, and then onto Jones Bridge Road, which would have brought him right by Walter Reed [Army Hospital]." Author's interview of Dennis David, June 30, 2006.

David's and other witnesses' testimony regarding the two caskets has been used to support the hypothesis that the president's body was altered before arriving at Bethesda, possibly at Walter Reed Army Hospital (on the route taken by the hearse that arrived at 6:30). Heiner, *Without Smoking Gun*, p. 62. If that were the case, Bill Pitzer's movie could have been taken at Walter Reed (to which he had ready access in his work), which would make its evidence even more explosive than a film taken at Bethesda. Ibid., p. 68.

583. FBI Report, Baltimore Field Office, January 31, 1967: "William Bruce Pitzer—Victim; Crime on a Government Reservation—Death by Gunshot Wound," Synopsis. Bureau File #70-44229.

584. FBI teletype, October 30, 1966, from Baltimore FBI Field Office to Director, FBI Headquarters, Washington, D.C. Copies: Tolson, DeLoach, and others. Bureau File #70-44229-3.

585. Letter of transmittal concerning the death of Lt. Commander William Bruce Pitzer, from Commander H. H. Rumble II, Naval Investigative Service, to J. Edgar Hoover, FBI Director, November 1, 1966. Cited in Heiner, *Without Smoking Gun*, p. 18.

586. LCDR T. G. Ferris and CDR J. W. Guinn, February 13, 1967, "Informal Board of Investigation to Inquire into the Circumstances Surrounding the Death of Lieutenant Commander William Bruce Pitzer, MSC USN, 416681/2301 on 29 October 1966," pp. 1–4; reproduced in Daniel Marvin and Jerry D. Rose, "The Pitzer File," *The Fourth Decade* (January 1998), pp. 19–22.

587. Ferris and Guinn, "Informal Board of Investigation," p. 3.

588. Heiner, *Without Smoking Gun*, pp. 46–47. When Bill Pitzer's nephew was a young man, he idolized his uncle. He tried to follow Bill's path, serving as an officer in Vietnam. Later, as the questions of the Navy's cover-up of his uncle's death deepened, he wondered what he had been doing in Vietnam, "if the country that I was serving could do this." Bruce Fernandez, nephew of Bill Pitzer, to Daniel Marvin in telephone conversation, October 12, 1995.

589. Law and Eaglesham, *In the Eye of History*, pp. 25–26. In the interview I did with Dennis David, he granted the possibility that Bill Pitzer's death could conceivably have been either murder or suicide. He suspected murder from the time he was informed of Pitzer's death, knowing of Pitzer's Kennedy pictures. As for the possibility of suicide, he said, "I have no idea why he would have committed suicide . . . I've heard the stories about his mistress—supposedly a mistress he had in Florida. But I don't think that would have prompted him to commit suicide." Author's interview with Dennis David, June 30, 2006.

590. Heiner, *Without Smoking Gun*, p. 36.

591. "The Navy has not made any original interview document available [on the alleged fatal affair], and reports that such material is routinely destroyed twenty-five years after the investigation." Ibid.

592. Ibid., p. 30.

593. Law and Eaglesham, *In the Eye of History*, p. 25.

594. Joyce Pitzer to Daniel Marvin in telephone conversation, January 31, 1995.

595. Interview with Dennis David on *The Men Who Killed Kennedy: Part Six: The Truth Shall Set You Free*, produced and directed by Nigel Turner. The History Channel.

596. Letter from Lieutenant Colonel Daniel Marvin to Jim Douglass, January 15, 2006. See also *Without Smoking Gun*, p. 119.

597. Joyce Pitzer to Daniel Marvin in telephone conversation, January 5, 1995. Cited in Heiner, *Without Smoking Gun*, p. 46. Joyce Pitzer made substantially the same com-

ment, about Naval Intelligence pressures on her to be silent, seven years earlier in a conversation with author Harrison Edward Livingstone. Livingstone wrote: "On January 21, 1988, I spoke at length with the widow of Bruce Pitzer . . . Mrs. Pitzer said that she was visited by Naval Intelligence who asked her never to talk to anyone about her husband's death. She was nervous to talk to me about it, but clearly remains concerned about what happened and evidently felt that it ought to be investigated." Harrison Edward Livingstone, "Lt. Cmdr. William Bruce Pitzer," *The Third Decade* (January 1988), p. 20.

598. Joyce Pitzer to Daniel Marvin, January 5, 1995.

599. Daniel Marvin to Joyce Pitzer, January 5, 1995.

600. Daniel Marvin, "Bits & Pieces: A Green Beret on the Periphery of the JFK Assassination," *The Fourth Decade* (May 1995), p. 14.

601. Ibid.

602. Interview with Daniel Marvin on *The Men Who Killed Kennedy: Part Six: The Truth Shall Set You Free*, produced and directed by Nigel Turner, 2002 DVD. The History Channel.

603. Ibid. This particular paragraph, as I have transcribed it from Marvin's interview, is taken from the 2002 DVD version of *The Men Who Killed Kennedy*. It was not in the original 1995 telecast.

604. Marvin, "Bits & Pieces," p. 16.

605. Ibid.

606. Ibid.

607. Ibid.

608. Ibid., p. 15.

609. Ibid., p. 16.

610. Ibid., pp. 16–17.

611. Heiner, *Without Smoking Gun*, p. 87.

612. Ibid., p. 88.

613. Marvin, "Bits & Pieces," p. 17.

614. Heiner, *Without Smoking Gun*, p. 88. Dan Marvin described to a friend "the real danger" for a member of the Special Forces: "We don't fear the enemy we are trained to defeat. We fear what may happen to us should those in power decide that our nation would be better served if we were no longer available for question or comment. Other volunteers, trained and dedicated as we were, would be asked to 'dispose' of us." Jacqueline K. Powers, citing Dan Marvin, introduction to *Expendable Elite: One Soldier's Journey into Covert Warfare* by Daniel Marvin (Walterville, Oregon: Trine Day, 2003), p. ix.

615. Telephone interview with Dr. David Vanek by Tim Wray/ARRB, November 4, 1996. Notes by Tim Wray and Chris Barger. Reproduced at the National Archives.

616. Ibid.

617. Ibid.

618. Ibid.

619. "David Vance Vanek: CURRICULUM VITAE; Military Employment." Reproduced at the National Archives.

620. Ibid.

621. Telephone interview with Dr. David Vanek by Tim Wray/ARRB.

622. Author's interview of Marcus Raskin, January 28, 2006.

623. Alsop, "Kennedy's Grand Strategy," p. 14 (Alsop's emphasis in original).

624. Reeves, *President Kennedy: Profile of Power,* pp. 230–31.

625. "Memorandum on World Order and Disarmament: Submitted to President John F. Kennedy by Representatives of the Friends Witness for World Order," May 1, 1962. Swarthmore College Peace Collection.

626. *Public Papers of the Presidents: John F. Kennedy, 1961*, "Address in New York City before the General Assembly of the United Nations," September 25, 1961 (Washington: U.S Government Printing Office, 1961), p. 620.

627. "The McCloy/Zorin Agreement," in Schotz, *History Will Not Absolve Us*, p. 257.

628. Kai Bird, *The Chairman: John J. McCloy; The Making of the American Establishment* (New York: Simon & Schuster, 1992), p. 515.

629. "Visit of Six Friends to President John F. Kennedy on behalf of Friends Witness for World Order, May 1, 1962," p. 1. The Quaker Collection, Haverford College.

630. Ibid.

631. Schlesinger, *Thousand Days*, p. 88.

632. Ibid.

633. "Visit of Six Friends," p. 2. Also Henry J. Cadbury, "Friends with Kennedy in the White House," *Friendly Heritage: Letters from the Quaker Past* (Norwalk, Conn.: Silvermine Publishers, 1972), p. 278.

634. E. Raymond Wilson, *Uphill for Peace: Quaker Impact on Congress* (Richmond, Ind.: Friends United Press, 1975), p. 79.

635. "Visit of Six Friends," p. 3.

636. Ibid.

637. Author's interview of David Hartsough, January 18, 2006.

638. Cadbury, "Friends with Kennedy," p. 278.

639. "Quakers Appeal to Kennedy," *Philadelphia Inquirer* (May 2, 1962). Swarthmore Peace Collection.

640. Sam and Miriam Levering, *Quaker Peacemakers* (self-published), p. 35. From the Papers and Writings of Samuel Levering, Guildford College, Greensboro, North Carolina. The Quakers' allotted fifteen minutes with the president had been scheduled for 10:15 A.M. When the meeting's beginning was delayed fifteen minutes, they wondered if it would simply be canceled. Instead, Kennedy extended their time with him to twenty minutes. "Visit of Six Friends," p. 1.

641. Margaret Hope Bacon, *Let This Life Speak: The Legacy of Henry Joel Cadbury* (Philadelphia: University of Pennsylvania Press, 1987), p. 192. George Willoughby and David Hartsough also remembered hearing this remark by John Kennedy to Henry Cadbury. April 25, 2006, conference call on the Friends' May 1, 1962, visit to Kennedy: interview by Jim Douglass of the three surviving members of the delegation, David Hartsough, Edward Snyder, and George Willoughby. Hartsough, Snyder, and Willoughby gave me permission to cite from their confidential report on their visit to President Kennedy, as preserved in the Quaker Collection, Haverford College.

642. Author's interview of David Hartsough, January 18, 2006.

643. Dorothy Hutchinson, as recorded on audiotaped report, "Visit of Six Quakers to President Kennedy, May 1, 1962: Dorothy Hutchinson, Edward Snyder, David Hartsough, George Willoughby, Henry Cadbury, Samuel Levering. Swarthmore College Peace Collection.

644. George Willoughby, as recorded on "Visit of Six Quakers."

645. Author's interview of Edward Snyder, January 24, 2006.

646. Author's interview of Marcus Raskin, January 28, 2006.

647. Marcus Raskin, "*JFK* and the Culture of Violence," *American Historical Review* (April 1992), p. 497.

648. Jerome B. Wiesner, Memorandum for the President, December 4, 1962. Papers of President Kennedy, National Security Files, JFK Library.

649. National Security Council, "Organization and Membership of the Committee of Principals," April 1963. National Security Files, Box 267, JFK Library.

650. "National Security Action Memorandum No. 239," May 6, 1963. *Foreign Relations of the United States, 1961–1963, Volume VII: Arms Control and Disarmament* (Washington: U.S. Government Printing Office, 1995), p. 692 (emphasis added).

651. Author's interview of Marcus Raskin, February 15, 2006.

652. *Public Papers of the Presidents: John F. Kennedy, 1963*, "Commencement Address at American University in Washington," June 10, 1963, p. 463.

653. Sorensen, *Kennedy*, p. 518.

654. O'Donnell and Powers, "*Johnny, We Hardly Knew Ye*," p. 381.

655. Ibid.

656. Sorensen, *Kennedy*, p. 742.

657. New Orleans Secret Service Report, "List of books obtained by Lee Harvey Oswald from New Orleans Public Library," Warren Commission Exhibit No. 2650. *WCH*, vol. 25, p. 930.

658. Ibid.

659. Ibid. Also Priscilla Johnson McMillan, *Marina and Lee* (New York: Bantam Books, 1977), p. 457.

660. McMillan, *Marina and Lee*, pp. 444–45. Marina Oswald had said, from the weekend of the assassination onward, that her husband had only a positive attitude toward President Kennedy. In an initial, tape-recorded interview by the Secret Service on Sunday evening, November 24, 1963, she was asked through an interpreter, Peter Paul Gregory, "what Lee's feelings were for President Kennedy." She answered: "This is the truth. Lee never spoke bad about President Kennedy."

It was for this reason that Marina Oswald was certain her husband "would not have been shooting at President Kennedy . . . Lee had nothing against President Kennedy."

She was asked again through the interpreter how she knew that. "She said this, that Lee expressed to her that Kennedy was a good President." Transcript of Marina Oswald interview, November 24, 1963, at Inn of the Six Flags, Arlington, Texas, pp. 41, 43. Warren Commission Document 344. David S. Lifton, *Document Addendum to the Warren Report* (El Segundo, Calif.: Sightext Publications, 1968), pp. 331, 333.

661. McMillan, *Marina and Lee*, p. 444.

662. *Public Papers of the Presidents: John F. Kennedy, 1963*, "Radio and Television Address to the American People on the Nuclear Test Ban Treaty," July 26, 1963, p. 603.

663. McMillan, *Marina and Lee*, p. 444.

664. Ibid., p. 445.

665. Letter from Eugene Murret to Lee Harvey Oswald, July 6, 1963, Warren Commission Exhibit No. 2648. *WCH*, vol. 25, p. 919.

666. As soon as Jesuit scholastic Robert J. Fitzpatrick of Spring Hill College heard that Oswald had been arrested as a suspect in President Kennedy's assassination, he obtained the written impressions of his fellow Jesuit seminarians who had attended Oswald's July 27 talk. He then typed up a five-page summary of Oswald's speech, as the seminarians recalled it.

Describing his three years living in Russia, Oswald had spoken about his work in a factory in Minsk, life in Russian villages, and the workers' attitudes toward him as an American. Oswald summed up his own position on the U.S. and Soviet systems by saying, "Capitalism doesn't work, communism doesn't work. In the middle is socialism and that doesn't work either." Warren Commission Exhibit No. 2649. *WCH*, vol. 25, p. 926.

In his handwritten speech notes, Oswald concluded with a similar skepticism toward both Communism and capitalism: "In returning to the U.S., I have done nothing more or less than select the lesser of two evils." Warren Commission Exhibit 102. *WCH*, vol. 16, p. 442.

667. "Notes for a speech by Lee Harvey Oswald," Warren Commission Exhibit 102. *WCH*, vol. 16, p. 441, where the Warren Commission's reproduction of Oswald's written text is too small to be legible. Using a blown-up version for double-checking, I have followed the spelling, punctuation, and capitalization as given "in the interests of clarity and legibility" on the Web site: mcadams.posc.mu.edu/speechnotes1.htm. I am grateful to Andy Winiarczyk and M. Steele Holt for bringing Oswald's speech notes to my attention.

668. Ibid.

669. Donald Janson and Bernard Eismann, *The Far Right* (New York: McGraw-Hill, 1963), pp. 174–76.

670. On the authority of Dallas Police detective Ira Van Cleave, the *New York Times* reported that the bullet fired into the wall behind General Edwin Walker on April 10, 1963, was "from a 30.06 rifle." "Walker Escapes Assassin's Bullet," *New York Times*

(April 12, 1963), p. 12. However, as in the case of much assassination-related evidence, the bullet was transformed while in the custody of the FBI. An FBI ballistics expert identified it instead as "a 6.5 millimeter bullet," thus making it compatible with Oswald's rifle, which the Warren Commission then ruled was its source. *Warren Report*, pp. 186–87. Under pressure from federal investigators, Marina Oswald gave a series of totally contradictory statements on her husband's involvement in the Walker incident, which the Warren Commission drew on selectively to accuse Oswald of shooting at Walker (used in turn as evidence of his capacity to kill Kennedy). After examining the same questionable testimony, the House Select Committee on Assassinations concluded: "we regretfully refuse to accept the judgment of the [Warren] Commission in regard to the Walker shooting." HSCA synopsis of Marina Oswald Porter testimony. Cited by Armstrong, *Harvey & Lee*, p. 520.

671. *WCH*, vol. 16, p. 441. mcadams.posc.mu.edu/speechnotes1.htm.

672. In what became known as "the Marine Corps incident of 1950," President Harry S. Truman sent a letter on August 29, 1950, to California Representative Gordon L. McDonough stating: "the Marine Corps is the Navy's police force and as long as I am President that is what it will remain." In reference to McDonough's and many others' requests that the Marine Corps be represented on the Joint Chiefs of Staff (contrary to Truman's position), the president added: "They have a propaganda machine almost the equal of Stalin's." When McDonough made Truman's letter public, the uproar was sufficient to ensure both the Marines' future in combat operations and their representation on the Joint Chiefs of Staff. Franklin D. Mitchell, "An Act of Presidential Indiscretion: Harry S. Truman, Congressman McDonough, and the Marine Corps Incident of 1950," *Presidential Studies Quarterly* 11 (Fall 1981), pp. 565–75.

673. Cited by Ray Marcus, "Truman's Warning," in Schotz, *History Will Not Absolve Us*, pp. 237–38.

674. Pioneer assassination critic Raymond Marcus has written of the lack of response to Truman's remarkable December 22, 1963, article: "According to my information, it was not carried in later editions that day, nor commented on editorially, nor picked up by any other major newspaper, or mentioned on any national radio or TV broadcast." Raymond Marcus, *Addendum B* (published by the author, 1995), p. 75.

675. Author's Note on Change from Hardcover Text: I have added here six paragraphs on Allen Dulles's attempt to get former president Harry Truman to retract his December 22, 1963, warning about the CIA. I am grateful to Raymond Marcus for bringing this incident to my attention, and for sharing his own thorough research into it.

676. April 21, 1964, Memorandum for Mr. Lawrence R. Houston, General Counsel [CIA], from A. W. Dulles. "Subject: Visit to The Honorable Harry S. Truman, Friday afternoon, April 17, 2 P.M." Truman Library Archives.

677. Ibid.

678. "From the Desk of Harry S. Truman," December 1, 1963. Document 94, Papers of David M. Noyes. Truman Library.

679. Letter from Harry S. Truman to William B. Arthur, June 10, 1964. *Off the Record: The Private Papers of Harry S. Truman*, edited by Robert H. Ferrell (New York: Harper & Row, 1980), p. 408. I am grateful to Tim Murphy for pointing out this letter to me.

680. Ibid. President Truman had either forgotten or was avoiding the fact that his National Security Council on June 18, 1948, approved top-secret directive NSC 10/2. U.S. intelligence agencies were thereby authorized to engage in "propaganda, economic warfare, preventive direct action including sabotage, anti-sabotage, demolition and evacuation measures; subversion against hostile states including assistance to underground resistance movements, guerrillas and refugee liberation groups." Peter Grose, *Gentleman Spy: The Life of Allen Dulles* (New York: Houghton Mifflin, 1994), p. 293. NSC 10/2 was the secret foundation for the enormous buildup of the CIA's "strange activities" that so alarmed Truman in December 1963.

681. *WCH*, vol. 4, p. 435.

682. *President's Commission on the Assassination of President Kennedy: Report of Proceedings Held at Washington, D.C., Monday, January 27, 1964*; published by Harold Weisberg as *Whitewash IV: Top Secret JFK Assassination Transcript* (Frederick, Md., 1974), p. 48; p. 139 of transcript.

683. Ibid., pp. 62–63; pp. 153–54 of transcript.

684. William Walter, February 27, 1978, interview by the House Select Committee on Assassinations, in the National Archives and Records Administration; cited by Joan Mellen, *A Farewell to Justice: Jim Garrison, JFK's Assassination, and the Case That Should Have Changed History* (Washington, D.C.: Potomac Books, 2005), p. 349.

685. Orest Pena interviewed on *CBS Reports*, November 26, 1975. Cited by Summers, *Conspiracy*, p. 282.

686. Summers, *Conspiracy*, p. 283.

687. After Mark Lane met with Marina Oswald, who told him of the pressures put upon her by the FBI, Lane wrote: "Marina was incredulous when FBI agents informed her that Lee had been in Mexico from September 26 to October 3, 1963. How could that be, she asked, without her having known about it? She said that Lee had never said he had visited Mexico, had never brought anything into the house suggesting he had been there. She said that during the period in question she had been in contact with Lee, and since she had not been in Mexico at all, how, she asked, could he have been there? The agents insisted that Marina was wrong, asked her if she wanted to be deported, and told her to be more cooperative." Mark Lane, *Plausible Denial: Was the CIA Involved in the Assassination of JFK?* (New York: Thunder's Mouth Press, 1991), p. 66.

688. Warren Commission Exhibit Number 2129; *WCH, Exhibits,* vol. 24, p. 704.

689. Earl Golz, "Salesman Insists FBI Discounted Facts on Oswald," *Dallas Morning News* (May 8, 1977), p. 12A. *Warren Report*, p. 321.

690. *WCH*, vol. 10, p. 380.

691. Smith, *JFK: The Second Plot*, pp. 269–70. Popkin, *Second Oswald*, p. 92.

692. Smith, *JFK: The Second Plot*, pp. 272–73.

693. Testimony of Nanny Lee Fenner, *FBI Oversight*, Hearings before the Subcommittee on Civil and Constitutional Rights, Committee on the Judiciary, House of Representatives, Ninety-Fourth Congress, December 11, 1975 (Washington: U.S. Government Printing Office, 1976), p. 37.

694. Ibid.

695. Ibid. FBI Special Agent James Hosty testified that the letter in the envelope handed to him by Nannie Lee Fenner was instead "an innocuous type of complaint": "the first part of it stated that I had been interviewing his wife without his permission and I should not do this; he was upset about this. And the second part at the end he said that if I did not stop talking to his wife, he would take action against the FBI." Testimony of James P. Hosty, Jr., December 12, 1975, ibid., pp. 129–30. The House committee that investigated the destruction of the letter found Nannie Lee Fenner's testimony more credible than James Hosty's—or his superior J. Gordon Shanklin's failure even to recall the existence of such a letter—and characterized the incident as "a serious impeachment of Shanklin's and Hosty's credibility." Cited in Hurt, *Reasonable Doubt*, p. 253.

696. Fenner testimony, p. 37.

697. Ibid., p. 38. Again in contrast to Nannie Lee Fenner's testimony, Special Agent Hosty thought the letter had been anonymous, not signed by Oswald: "I do not recall a signature on it." Hosty testimony, p. 129.

698. Hosty testimony, p. 125.

699. Ibid.

700. In the Congressional hearing that probed the FBI's destruction of the Oswald-Hosty letter, Representative Seiberling raised an obvious question to witness James Hosty: "Did you ever think that it was somewhat strange that Mr. Oswald, if he intended to

.assassinate the President in early November, would have come to the FBI and drawn attention to himself?"

Hosty answered: "It does seem strange, yes, sir." Ibid., p. 145.

The question was left unexplored by the investigating committee. To pursue it would have meant going dangerously beyond the government's lone-assassin story toward the source of a conspiracy in which Oswald was impersonated and set up as the scapegoat.

701. *WCH*, vol. 4, p. 437.

702. New Orleans bar owner Orest Pena, interviewed about seeing Oswald in the company of FBI agent Warren deBrueys. *CBS Reports*, November 26, 1975. Cited by Summers, *Conspiracy*, p. 282. Also Oswald's friend, New Orleans garage manager Adrian Alba, who saw Oswald meeting an FBI agent Alba knew and passing him a white envelope. *Conspiracy*, p. 283.

703. Col. Oleg Maximovich Nechiporenko, *Passport to Assassination: The Never-Before-Told Story of Lee Harvey Oswald by the KGB Colonel Who Knew Him* (New York: Birch Lane Press, 1993), p. 77.

704. *WCH*, vol. 16, p. 33.

705. Hosty testimony, p. 134.

706. Ibid.

707. Ibid., p. 137.

708. Martin Waldron, "F.B.I. Chiefs Linked to Oswald File Loss," *New York Times* (September 17, 1975), pp. 1, 21. The *Times* article noted: "The existence and destruction of the letter was first reported two weeks ago by *The Dallas Times-Herald*." Ibid., p. 21. In 1975 in the wake of Watergate revelations, the FBI Director took the step of acknowledging publicly the existence and destruction of the Oswald letter: "Clarence M. Kelley, who became F.B.I. Director in 1973 after Mr. Hoover's death, has said that there is evidence that the letter was received and destroyed." Ibid.

709. Ibid.

710. In terms of Cold War partners, Kennedy had one other important peacemaking ally, Prime Minister Harold MacMillan of the United Kingdom, who, as we saw, was pushing him toward a test ban treaty. Barbara Leaming, *Jack Kennedy: The Education of a Statesman* (New York: W. W. Norton & Company, 2006), pp. 421–27.

711. Norman Cousins, *The Improbable Triumvirate: John F. Kennedy, Pope John, Nikita Khrushchev* (New York: W. W. Norton & Company, 1972).

712. The meeting between U.S. and Soviet representatives at Phillips Academy, Andover, Massachusetts, in October 1962 was the third such "Dartmouth Conference"— named after the first, held at Dartmouth College, Hanover, New Hampshire, in October 1960. The second Dartmouth Conference took place in the Crimea in South Soviet Russia in June 1961. Cousins, *Improbable Triumvirate*, p. 13.

713. Ibid.

714. Ibid., p. 16.

715. Ibid., p. 11.

716. Ibid., p. 17.

717. Ibid.

718. Ibid., p. 18.

719. Cited by Hansjakob Stehle, *Eastern Politics of the Vatican 1917–1979* (Athens: Ohio University Press, 1981), p. 305.

720. Cousins, *Improbable Triumvirate*, p. 18.

721. Stehle, *Eastern Politics*, p. 305.

722. Thomas Cahill, *Pope John XXIII* (New York: Viking Penguin, 2002), p. 206; Stehle, *Eastern Politics*, p. 305.

723. Stehle, *Eastern Politics*, p. 305. Only two weeks before *Pravda* praised Pope John, the same Moscow paper had dismissed the Vatican as a "warm body that no magic formula can bring back to life." Ibid. Pope John's fervent appeal to both sides in the Cuban Missile Crisis was more effective than any "magic formula." Just as John Kenne-

dy's American University address would do the following June, the pope's message broke through doctrinaire barriers and made the author a voice for peace in the Soviet Union.

724. Cousins, *Improbable Triumvirate*, pp. 20–21.

725. I can testify personally to Norman Cousins's papal missions to Moscow. In 1964 I was an assistant to Father Felix Morlion at his Pro Deo University in Rome. There I met Norman Cousins during one of his consultations with Father Morlion and other Vatican representatives. On my return to the U.S. in 1965, I met with Cousins again at his *Saturday Review* office in New York. Through Morlion and Cousins I learned of "the improbable triumvirate" of John F. Kennedy, Pope John, and Nikita Khrushchev the year after it happened.

726. Cousins, *Improbable Triumvirate*, pp. 24–25.

727. Ibid., pp. 33–34.

728. Ibid., pp. 44–46.

729. Ibid., p. 49.

730. Ibid., p. 57.

731. Ibid., pp. 63–65.

732. Ibid., p. 68.

733. Ibid., p. 74.

734. Ibid., pp. 75–76.

735. Gaeton Fonzi, *The Last Investigation* (New York: Thunder's Mouth Press, 1994), p. 132. See also chapter 2 above.

736. "U.S. Curbs Miami Exiles to Prevent Raids on Cuba," *New York Times* (April 1, 1963), p. 1. See chapter 2 above.

737. Ellen J. Hammer, *A Death in November: America in Vietnam, 1963* (New York: E. P. Dutton, 1987), p. 116. See also chapter 3 above.

738. Michael Charlton and Anthony Moncrieff, *Many Reasons Why: The American Involvement in Vietnam* (New York: Hill & Wang, 1978), p. 84.

739. Cousins, *Improbable Triumvirate*, p. 91.

740. Pope John XXIII, *Pacem in Terris/Peace on Earth* (New York: America Press, 1963), p. 36.

741. Cousins, *Improbable Triumvirate*, pp. 92–101.

742. Memorandum by Norman Cousins, "April 22, 1963," p. 1. I am grateful to Professor Lawrence S. Wittner of the State University of New York and the Cousins Foundation in Beverly Hills for sharing with me, and allowing me to cite from, this Cousins memorandum.

743. Cousins, *Improbable Triumvirate*, pp.113–14.

744. Cousins, "April 22, 1963," p. 2; *Improbable Triumvirate*, pp. 116–17.

745. Lawrence S. Wittner, *Resisting the Bomb: A History of the World Nuclear Disarmament Movement, 1954-1970* (Stanford, Calif.: Stanford University Press, 1977), p. 375.

746. Norman Cousins to President John F. Kennedy, April 30, 1963, pp. 1–2. Nuclear Test Ban Folder, Box 36, Theodore Sorensen Papers, JFK Library.

747. Cousins, *Improbable Triumvirate*, pp. 122–23.

748. See chapter 2 above.

749. Fidel Castro, Address to the Tripartite Conference on the Cuban Missile Crisis, January 11, 1992; Laurence Chang and Peter Kornbluh, editors, *The Cuban Missile Crisis, 1962* (New York: New Press, 1992), p. 344.

750. Sergei Khrushchev, *Nikita Khrushchev and the Making of a Superpower* (University Park, Pa.: Pennsylvania State University Press, 2000), p. 659.

751. Richard Helms, Memorandum for the Director of Central Intelligence on "Reported Desire of the Cuban Government for Rapprochement with the United States," June 5, 1963; Peter Kornbluh, "Kennedy and Castro: The Secret Quest for Accommodation; An Electronic Briefing Book," at the National Security Archive's Web site: www .seas.gwu.edu/nsarchive.

752. Premier Nikita Khrushchev liked to call attention to Pope John's personal medal-

lion that was given to him through Norman Cousins. He told Cousins, "I keep it on my desk at all times. When [Communist] Party functionaries come to see me, I play with it rather ostentatiously. If they don't ask me what it is right away, I continue to let it get in the way of the conversation, even allowing it to slip through my fingers and to fall on the floor, so that they have to watch out for their toes. Inevitably, I am asked to explain this large engraved disc. 'Oh,' I say, 'it's only a medal from the Pope . . .

When Cousins told Kennedy this story, the president smiled at both the atheist premier's pride in papal recognition and the ironic contrast to his own situation. "You know," he said, "that's one advantage a Communist leader has over an American President, especially a Catholic. Khrushchev can go out of his way to boast about receiving a gift from the Pope. I've got to be careful about these things." Cousins, *Improbable Triumvirate*, pp. 108, 119.

753. *Pacem in Terris*, pp. 50–51.

754. Norman Cousins's hand is particularly evident in one turn of phrase found in this central paragraph of the American University address. On November 24, 1958, Cousins had written in a letter to a Presidium Member of the Soviet Cultural Relations Society in Moscow: "the overriding need of mankind today is to *make the world safe for diversity*" (emphasis added). Norman Cousins to Mrs. L. D. Kislova, November 24, 1958; p. 3. Lawrence S. Wittner identified this very specific contribution of Cousins to the text of the American University address in his *Resisting the Bomb*, p. 572, note 18. Cousins's letter to Mrs. Kislova, shared with me by Professor Wittner, is from Box 208 of the Cousins Papers at UCLA.

755. "Commencement Address at American University in Washington," June 10, 1963. *Public Papers of the Presidents: John F. Kennedy, 1963*, pp. 462–64.

756. Nikita Khrushchev to Averell Harriman. Cited by Schlesinger, *Thousand Days*, p. 904.

757. Associated Press dispatch from Vatican City that appeared in the New York *Herald Tribune* (European edition) on June 7, 1963.

758. S. Khrushchev, *Nikita Khrushchev and the Making of a Superpower*, p. 670. According to Sergei Khrushchev, his father refused to approve the mass production of tactical nuclear weapons because of their heightening the danger of war as well as their economic liability: "All these 'small things' struck Father as being very dangerous because of their down-to-earth quality, which lowered the threshold of fear. Moreover, such 'treats' could be extraordinarily expensive."

759. Ibid., p. 676.

760. Ibid., pp. 676, 719–20.

761. In addition to the transmission of the Soviet media, Soviet citizens heard the American University address from the U.S. government's Voice of America, broadcast from outside the U.S.S.R., which the Soviet government suddenly stopped jamming. Sorensen, *Kennedy*, p. 733. What U.S. citizens seem to have lacked for access to the president's peacemaking speech was a Voice of America in their own country.

762. Statement by Ralph Leon Yates to FBI special agent Ben S. Harrison, November 26, 1963, Dallas, Texas. Reproduced by John Armstrong on his CD-Rom for *Harvey and Lee*, "1963 November 1–21," image 22.

763. Ibid.

764. Ibid., image 23. In his first FBI interview, Ralph Yates said the man raised a question that (if seen later in retrospect) would suggest a connection between the hitchhiker and Jack Ruby: "Yates stated as they drove along, the man had asked him if he knew a certain party, whose name Yates cannot recall now, and he had indicated to this man he did not. He said the man then asked if he had ever been to the Carousel Club [owned by Jack Ruby] and Yates had replied that he had serviced refrigerators in the past in a number of clubs and that possibly he had been to this one, but he did not recall." Ibid., image 22.

In his second FBI interview, in which he made and signed a first-person statement, Yates remembered that the "certain party" mentioned by the hitchhiker was in fact Jack

Ruby: "The man then asked me if I knew a Jack Rubenstein, and I said, 'Who?' The man then said that Jack Rubenstein was more commonly known as Jack Ruby, and Ruby ran the Carousel Club. I then asked the man if Ruby ran Jack's Branch Office Lounge on Industrial, and the man said that he didn't. I told the man that I had serviced refrigerators in a number of clubs, in the past, and had possibly been to the Carousel Club, but did not remember it." Yates, December 10, 1963, image 24.

The hitchhiker's remarks pointing toward Ruby, whether implicitly or explicitly, were apparently part of the fallback, Mob-connected part of the scenario. The purpose, as we shall see, was to draw on Ruby's Mob involvements to implicate Organized Crime as a second-level (false) sponsor of the assassination. A Mob conspiracy to kill Kennedy was then used to replace the first-level, lone-assassin portrayal of Oswald when it inevitably fell to pieces. The "exposure" of a Mob plot, with Ruby and Oswald as its tools, would again leave the CIA and the Cold War system it represented safely in the shadows.

765. Ibid.

766. Statement by Dempsey Jones to FBI special agent Arthur E. Carter, November 27, 1963, Dallas, Texas. CD-Rom for *Harvey and Lee*, "1963 November 1–21," image 27. Dempsey Jones said Ralph Yates told him "the day before the President was shot" [November 21, 1963] about the hitchhiker "who discussed the fact with him that one could be in a building and shoot the President as he, the President, passed by." Yates stated in his first FBI interview that he picked up the hitchhiker "at approximately 10:30 AM on either November 20 or 21, 1963." Yates, November 26, 1963, image 22. In his second FBI interview, Yates said he picked up the man "on a date that I now believe was Wednesday, November 20, 1963." Yates, December 10, 1963, image 24. Yates and Jones agreed that their initial conversation about the hitchhiker took place at least one day before the president was shot.

767. Yates, November 26, 1963, image 22.

768. *Warren Report*, p. 130. WCH, vol. 2, pp. 222–23. Commission Exhibit 2003, p. 25. WCH, vol. 24, p. 209. Lee Harvey Oswald denied to Captain Will Fritz that he ever talked to Frazier about curtain rods. He also said that the only thing he carried with him in Frazier's car on Friday morning was his lunch. WCH, vol. 4, pp. 218–19.

769. Commission Exhibit 2003, p. 25. WCH, vol. 24, p. 209.

770. *Warren Report*, p. 133. WCH, vol. 2, p. 226. Buell Wesley Frazier's curtain rods story, supported in part by his sister, Linnie Mae Randle, who claimed she saw Oswald carrying a brown package Friday morning (WCH, vol. 2, pp. 248–51), was called into question by George O'Toole in *The Assassination Tapes: An Electronic Probe into the Murder of John F. Kennedy and the Dallas Coverup* (New York: Penthouse Press, 1975). Using a voice-measuring, lie-detection machine, the Psychological Stress Evaluator (PSE), O'Toole processed for his book the recorded statements of more than forty persons with direct knowledge of Kennedy's assassination. One of them was Buell Wesley Frazier relating his curtain rods story soon after Kennedy was killed. The stress in Frazier's voice was so great that one lie-detection analyst remarked, "On a scale of ten, this stress is somewhere near eleven." O'Toole, p. 172.

Buell Wesley Frazier was an early focus of investigation in the Kennedy assassination. The evening of November 22, he was arrested by Dallas Police. At the same time, the police confiscated his British 303 rifle. It was the same kind of rifle that the media first said had been found in the Book Depository. O'Toole, p. 205, citing Tom Webb of WBAP-TV, Fort Worth, Texas, *News Coverage of the Assassination of President Kennedy*, MR 74–52:1 (tape), JFK Library. If JFK was killed by more than one person, the most logical second suspect at the time, in addition to Lee Harvey Oswald, was his friend and fellow Book Depository worker, Buell Wesley Frazier.

Oswald witness Garland Slack, whose shooting target Oswald (or an impostor) had provocatively fired into on November 17 at the Sports Drome Rifle Range, said Oswald had been brought to the Sports Drome "by a man named 'Frazier' from Irving, Texas"— which Frazier denied doing in a statement to the FBI. Commission Exhibit No. 3077,

WCH, vol. 26, p. 681. In any case, from his undeniable situation as Oswald's driver to the Book Depository, the nineteen-year-old Frazier was in an unenviable position, where he was especially vulnerable to government pressures.

On the night of November 22 at Dallas Police headquarters, Buell Wesley Frazier was given a polygraph test. According to Detectives G. F. Rose and R. S. Stovall, who witnessed Detective R. D. Lewis conducting the polygraph, "the examination showed conclusively that Wesley Frazier was truthful." Commission Exhibit No. 2003, *WCH*, vol. 24, p. 293. However, O'Toole's PSE-measured interviews ten years later produced hard stress in Stovall when he denied being present at Frazier's polygraph test and in Frazier, Rose, and Lewis when they said the test showed Frazier was telling the truth. According to the PSE, all four men were lying. O'Toole, pp. 168–206.

771. *Warren Report*, pp. 130, 137.

772. Yates, November 26, 1963, image 26.

773. "To SAC [Special Agent in Charge] Dallas from Director, FBI (105-82555)," January 2, 1964. JFK Record Number 180-10033-10242.

774. "To Director, FBI (105-82555) from SAC, Dallas (100-10461)," January 4, 1964. JFK Record Number 180-10027-10351.

775. Author's interview of Dorothy Walker (formerly Dorothy Yates, widow of Ralph Leon Yates), August 12, 2006.

776. Author's interview of Dorothy Walker, October 16, 2006.

777. Author's interview of Dorothy Walker, October 6, 2006.

778. Walker, August 12, 2006; October 6 and 16, 2006.

779. Ibid.

780. Ibid.

781. Ibid. Dorothy Walker said the number of shock treatments Ralph Yates received was either forty-one or forty-two.

782. Ibid.

783. Ibid.

784. Author's interview of James Orvis Smith, uncle of Ralph Leon Yates, October 9, 2006. "J. O." Smith, as he was known, helped the poverty-stricken Yates family for years by bringing them groceries. Author's conversation with Ken Smith, cousin of Ralph Leon Yates, October 9, 2006.

785. Ken Smith, October 9, 2006.

786. Ibid.

787. Jones, November 27, 1963. In J. Edgar Hoover's January 2, 1964, teletype to J. Gordon Shanklin, the FBI director made a point of repeating Dempsey Jones's disclaimer. However, Hoover avoided citing Jones's corroboration in the same FBI report that Ralph Yates had told him before the president's assassination about the hitchhiker he dropped off at Elm and Houston, who talked about shooting the president from a building. Jones, November 27, 1963. Also JFK Record Number 180-10033-10242.

788. Interview of Larry Newman by Ralph G. Martin, cited in Martin's *Seeds of Destruction: Joe Kennedy and His Sons* (New York: G. P. Putnam's Sons, 1995), p. 449.

789. Ibid., pp. 448–49.

790. O'Donnell and Powers, *"Johnny, We Hardly Knew Ye,"* p. 378.

791. Ibid., p. 379. After the assassination, Dave Powers told Jacqueline Kennedy the story of her husband's visit to Patrick's grave, repeating his words, "He seems so alone here." Jacqueline said, "I'll bring them together now." She had Patrick's body reburied in Arlington National Cemetery alongside his father's grave. Ibid., p. 39.

792. Ibid. Rita Dallas, *The Kennedy Case* (Toronto: Popular Library, 1973), p. 10.

793. Interview of David Powers by Ralph G. Martin, cited in *Seeds*, p. 448.

794. Dallas, *Kennedy Case*, p. 11.

795. Ibid. O'Donnell and Powers, *"Johnny, We Hardly Knew Ye,"* p. 39. JFK's final visit with his father has been described in firsthand accounts by two witnesses: Joseph

Kennedy's nurse, Rita Dallas, in her book *The Kennedy Case*, pp. 9–11; David Powers in his and Kenneth O'Donnell's book, *"Johnny, We Hardly Knew Ye,"* p. 39. Dallas remembered the visit as occurring two weeks before the assassination, whereas Powers recalled it as October 20, 1963, a date confirmed from the White House Appointments Book at the JFK Library. Author's phone conversation with JFK Library archivist Stephen Plotkin, October 31, 2006.

796. O'Donnell and Powers, *"Johnny, We Hardly Knew Ye,"* p. 39.

797. *Harvey & Lee*, pp. 178, 193.

798. HSCA interview of Edward Browder by Mark Flanagan and Andy Purdy, January 12, 1978, p. 4. JFK Record Number 180-10077-10040.

799. "In it for the money" statement by Jack Ruby's poker-playing friend in Kemah, Texas, James E. Beaird. Interviewed and cited by Earl Golz, "Jack Ruby's Gunrunning to Castro Claimed," *Dallas Morning News* (August 18, 1978). I am grateful to Earl Golz for telling me of his interview with Beaird and sending me a copy of his article.

800. Ibid.

801. Seth Kantor, *The Ruby Cover-Up* (New York: Zebra Books, 1978), p. 44.

802. Ibid.

803. Ibid., p. 45.

804. Ibid. *CIA Assassination Plots: A Report from the Inspector General on Plots to Assassinate Fidel Castro* (Prevailing Winds Research, 1994), pp. 16–17. This 1967 report by the CIA Inspector General was also published by Ocean Press in Melbourne (1996) after the report's declassification. The QJ/WIN and ZRRIFLE references are on pp. 49 and 50 of the Ocean Press edition. After Davis's release in Algiers with the help of QJ/WIN, he was apparently arrested again soon after in Morocco, this time under suspicion of having a connection with the Kennedy assassination. J. Edgar Hoover noted in a December 20, 1963, FBI document that Thomas Eli Davis "was being held by the Moroccan National Security Police because of a letter in his handwriting which referred 'in passing to "Oswald"' and to Kennedy assassination." Memorandum from FBI Director John Edgar Hoover to Deputy Assistant Secretary for Security, Department of State, December 20, 1963. JFK Record Number 124-10011-10187.

805. While attending Jack Ruby's trial in Dallas, Dorothy Kilgallen became the first nationally known journalist to raise critical questions about the JFK assassination and the government cover-up. "She printed story after story of witnesses who had been threatened by the Dallas police or the FBI." Lee Israel, *Kilgallen* (New York: Dell, 1979), pp. 380–81.

In March 1964, Kilgallen got Jack Ruby's lawyer Joe Tonahill to convince Judge Joe B. Brown to allow her to see Ruby in private during a noon recess in the trial. Tonahill later confirmed the fact of this Kilgallen–Ruby meeting in correspondence with Kilgallen's biographer, Lee Israel. Letter from Joe H. Tonahill to Lee Israel, April 18, 1978. Cited by Israel, pp. 354–55. Kilgallen never revealed what Ruby said to her while they were alone together, harboring it for a future book that she would never have the chance to write. As Israel noted, "Dorothy would mention the fact of the interview to close friends, but *never* the substance." Israel, p. 355 (emphasis in original).

As Kilgallen's questions about Kennedy's murder deepened, she contacted Mark Lane and began "to bring to public attention, through her newspaper, the fruits of his investigation." She cautioned Lane, "Intelligence agencies will be watching us. We'll have to be very careful." Mark Lane citing Dorothy Kilgallen to Lee Israel, September 20, 1976; cited by Israel, p. 378. However, undeterred by the government surveillance, she pressed on in her own investigation, making research trips to New Orleans and back to Dallas. She told a friend repeatedly, "If it's the last thing I do, I'm going to break this case." Carmen Gibbia citing Dorothy Kilgallen to Lee Israel, p. 390.

Following Kilgallen's publication in her column of portions of Jack Ruby's then secret testimony before the Warren Commission, the FBI undertook a full-scale investigation to determine how she obtained the transcript. In an interview conducted by the FBI and reported to the Warren Commission, Dorothy Kilgallen was quoted as saying that she "would die" rather than reveal her source's identity. Kilgallen was direct and fearless in her refusal to cooperate with the FBI:

"She stated that she is the only person who knows the identity of her source and she will never reveal it . . . She stated that regardless of the consequences, she will never identify the source to anyone." FBI memorandum dated August 24, 1964, on interview with Dorothy Kilgallen on August 21, 1964. Included as attachment to letter from FBI director J. Edgar Hoover to J. Lee Rankin, general counsel, The President's Commission, August 26, 1964. JFK Record Number 180-10061-10186.

On September 30, 1964, an internal FBI memorandum that was circulated throughout the Bureau's hierarchy noted Kilgallen's comment in her column that same day on the *Warren Report*: "I'm inclined to believe that the FBI might have been more profitably employed in probing the facts of the case rather than how I got them which does seem a waste of time to me." FBI memorandum from A. Rosen to Mr. Belmont, September 30, 1964. JFK Record Number 180-10047-10339.

In the last column she would ever do on the Kennedy assassination, dated September 3, 1965, Kilgallen wrote: "This story isn't going to die as long as there's a real reporter alive—and there are a lot of them." Cited by Israel, p. 388.

Dorothy Kilgallen died on November 8, 1965, in her Manhattan bedroom. Her body was found in her bed. Her death certificate stated she died from "acute ethanol and barbiturate intoxication—circumstances undetermined"; in other words, from a toxic combination of drug pills and alcohol. Report of Death of Dorothy Kollmar (Killgallen) [*sic*], Office of Chief Medical Examiner of the City of New York, by James L. Luke, Case #9333, November 8, 1965. JFK Record Number 180-10071-10433. A chemist in the New York City Medical Examiner's Office told biographer Israel that he knew from a confirmative toxicological analysis that Dorothy Kilgallen died from a lethal dose of all three kinds of fast-acting barbiturates—secobarbital, amobarbital, and pentobarbital. Israel, pp. 424–25. A further important finding was that quinine, "which might have covered the bitterness of the secreted barbiturates" from Kilgallen's taste, was found in her "brain, bile, and liver." That fact, however, "was *not* reported in the official laboratory findings presented to the Department of Pathology." Ibid., p. 425 (emphasis in original).

Three days after Dorothy Kilgallen's death, friends asked her widower, Richard Kollmar, "What was all that stuff in the folder Dorothy carried around with her about the assassination?"

He replied, "I'm afraid that will have to go to the grave with me." Israel, p. 426.

Before her last Dallas trip, Dorothy had told Mark Lane that she expected "to learn something important" on a visit to New Orleans. Lane asked Richard Kollmar if he might look at Dorothy's folder because of its possibly containing information she had discovered "which could affect all of us in the future." Richard said he planned "to destroy all that. It's done enough damage already." Mark Lane citing Richard Kollmar to Lee Israel, September 20, 1976. Ibid., p. 427.

In 1975, four years after Richard's own death (an apparent suicide), the FBI was still calling on members of Dorothy's family to ferret out any assassination papers she might have stashed away somewhere. Ibid.

Israel wrote in conclusion: "Nothing of what Dorothy gathered, surmised, or wrote during her private interview with Jack Ruby or on her Texas or New Orleans sojourns has ever come to light." Ibid.

806. FBI interview of Jack Ruby, November 24, 1963. Hall (C. Ray) Exhibit No. 1. *WCH*, vol. 20, p. 39.

807. Kantor, *Ruby Cover-Up*, p. 333.

808. HSCA Testimony of Gordon Barton McLendon, May 24, 1978, p. 8. JFK Record Number 180-10076-10244.

809. Memorandum from Gordon McLendon and Fred Weintraub to Admiral Stansfield Turner, March 3, 1978. JFK Record Number 104-10105-10093.

810. McLendon testimony, pp. 56–57.

811. Ibid., p. 28.

812. Jim Garrison interview by Joe Manguno, "Was Jim Garrison Right After All?" *New Orleans Magazine* (June 1976), p. 29.

813. Kantor, *Ruby Cover-Up*, p. 89.

814. *Warren Report*, pp. 335–37.

815. Kantor Exhibit No. 7, *WCH*, vol. 20, pp. 429–32. The Warren Commission also dismissed Wilma Mae Tice's testimony that she, too, had seen Jack Ruby—"and if it wasn't him it was his twin brother" (*WCH*, vol. 15, p. 391)—at Parkland Hospital that afternoon. *Warren Report*, p. 336. *WCH*, vol. 15, pp. 388–96. Warren Commission Exhibits 2290 and 2293, *WCH*, vol. 25, pp. 216–18, 224–26.

816. Jack White, an art director with a Dallas advertising agency in 1963, had not been a supporter of President Kennedy. However, White happened to be a friend of Seth Kantor. When he read the *Warren Report* on Kantor and Ruby, he said to himself, "That can't be right. I know Seth. He wouldn't lie, and he wouldn't make anything up. He's a very diligent journalist." The Warren Commission's decision to believe Ruby rather than Kantor was the first factor that inspired White to dig into the case. He has continued doing so for the rest of his life, particularly as a photo analyst. In the 1970s he became a photographic consultant to the House Select Committee on Assassinations. Author's interview of Jack White, January 30, 1997.

817. Meagher, *Accessories after the Fact*, p. 397.

818. Ibid. *Warren Report*, p. 333.

819. *WCH*, vol. 7, p. 87.

820. Earl Golz, "Man Believes He Saw Ruby at Scene of Oswald's Arrest," *Dallas Morning News* (March 11, 1979), p. 32A.

821. Ibid.

822. *WCH*, vol. 7, p. 91.

823. "Man Believes He Saw Ruby," p. 32A. Since he gave his interview to Earl Golz in 1979, George Applin has, like Julia Ann Mercer, kept an extremely low profile.

In its argument against Kantor's story of seeing Ruby at Parkland Hospital, the *Warren Report* presented a chronology for Ruby that would also preclude his being present at Oswald's arrest in the Texas Theater between 1:45 and 1:50 P.M.:

"Upon arriving at the Carousel Club shortly after 1:45 P.M., Ruby instructed Andrew Armstrong, the Carousel's bartender, to notify employees that the club would be closed that night . . . At 1:51 P.M., Ruby telephoned Ralph Paul in Arlington, Tex., to say that he was going to close his clubs." *Warren Report*, p. 337.

However, as Earl Golz pointed out, "neither the time of Ruby's arrival nor a 1:51 P.M. call by Paul to Ruby is substantiated in Warren Commission testimony." "Man Believes He Saw Ruby," p. 32A. See Armstrong testimony, Ruby came in—"I don't recall what time it was"—about 5 minutes after Armstrong heard someone announce that Kennedy was dead (thus some time later than 1:30 P.M.), *WCH*, vol. 13, pp. 330–33; Larry Crafard testimony, Ruby came in "about 2 or 2:30, something like that," *WCH*, vol. 13, p. 452; Paul testimony, says he left work "a little after 2—and when I got home Jack called me and he said, 'Did you hear what happened? *WCH*, vol. 14, p. 151.

"Crafard said Ruby didn't tell Armstrong to notify performers that the club would be closed until 30 to 45 minutes after he arrived. When asked if Ruby made any phone calls, Crafard could recall only one call Ruby made to his sister." "Man Believes He Saw Ruby," p. 32A. *WCH*, vol. 13, pp. 453–54.

Golz repeatedly timed the trip from the hospital to the theater in heavy traffic, staying within the speed limit, and found it took no more than twelve minutes. "This would have permitted Ruby," he wrote, "to travel from the hospital at about 1:30 P.M. to the theater at about 1:45 P.M. without speeding.

"The 3.2-mile trip from the Texas Theatre, at 231 W. Jefferson, to the former site of the Carousel Club, at 1312½ Commerce took from 9 to 9½ minutes at an average speed of 30 mph. This would have given Ruby time to drive from the theater to his club in time to call his sister in Chicago at 2:05 P.M." Ibid.

824. Ronald L. Jenkins, KBOX Radio reporter, and police detectives A. M. Eberhardt and Roy E. Standifer all said they saw Ruby on the third floor of DPD headquarters early Friday evening. Both Eberhardt and Standifer, who had known Ruby for years, spoke with him at the time. WCH Exhibit 2254, WCH, vol. 25, pp. 178–79; vol. 13, pp. 187–88; vol. 15, pp. 616–18. Harvey & Lee, p. 896. However, Ruby himself denied being at police headquarters before late that night, and the Warren Commission once again accepted Ruby's word over that of the witnesses arrayed against him. Warren Report, p. 338. As John Armstrong observes, "The Commission's finding allowed them to conclude that Ruby's murder of Oswald was not premeditated." Harvey & Lee, p. 896.

825. From audiotape made by Vic Robertson, Dallas radio station WFAA, late December 1963; Robertson (Victor) Exhibit No. 2, WCH, vol. 21, p. 312.

826. FBI interview of UPI photographer Pete Fisher, WCH Exhibit 2253; WCH, vol. 25, p. 177.

827. Kantor, Ruby Cover-Up, p. 101. Jack Ruby's attorney, Tom Howard, also stated on November 24, 1963, to reporter Lonnie Hudkins of the Houston Post that Ruby had the gun with him on Friday night. Howard later confirmed this statement by phone to the Houston Post. Commission Exhibit No. 2003, WCH, vol. 24, pp. 364–65.

828. William Walter, February 27, 1978, HSCA interview; Mellen, Farewell to Justice, p. 349; Summers, Conspiracy, pp. 282–83.

829. WCH, vol. 4, p. 437.

830. Anthony Summers, Not in Your Lifetime (New York: Marlowe, 1998), p. 101. Lee Harvey Oswald's U-2 base was Camp Atsugi. Thomas Arthur Vallee's U-2 base was Camp Otsu. Both Camp Atsugi and Camp Otsu were parts of the CIA's Joint Technical Advisory Group (JTAG). Oswald's and Vallee's Marine units provided U-2 support. Ibid. Philip H. Melanson, Spy Saga: Lee Harvey Oswald and U.S. Intelligence (New York: Praeger, 1990), p. 8. Edwin Black, "The Plot to Kill JFK in Chicago Nov. 2, 1963," Chicago Independent (November 1975), p. 5.

831. Author's interview of Mary Vallee-Portillo, August 14, 2004.

832. Golz, "Was Oswald in Window?" p. 13A.

833. Craig, When They Kill a President, p. 9.

834. Ibid., p. 13 (emphasis added to both Fritz's and Oswald's statements).

835. Ibid.

836. Capt. J. W. Fritz, "Interrogation of Lee Harvey Oswald," Warren Report, pp. 608–9.

837. Seth Kantor's notebook cites Oswald saying, "I'm just a patsy," at 7:55 P.M., November 22, 1963. Kantor Exhibit 3, WCH, vol. 20, p. 366.

838. On Oswald's persistent efforts to reach lawyer John Abt, see Bishop, Day Kennedy Was Shot, pp. 259–60, 343, 393, 470, 523, 553, 569.

839. Ibid., p. 596. Also Manchester, Death of a President, p. 489. On Friday night, November 22, 1963, Gregory Lee Olds, president of the Dallas Civil Liberties Union, in a phone conversation with Captain Will Fritz, was told "that Oswald had been given the opportunity [of legal counsel] and declined." When Olds and three other ACLU representatives then went to Dallas Police headquarters, Captain King, assistant to the chief of police, "assured us that Oswald had not made any requests for counsel." WCH, vol. 7, p. 323.

H. Louis Nichols, president of the Dallas Bar Association, was allowed to meet with Oswald in his jail cell late Saturday afternoon. Oswald told Nichols that he wanted to be represented by John Abt or an ACLU member. Nichols said that he did not know any ACLU members. He asked if Oswald wanted him or the Dallas Bar Association to get him an attorney. Oswald said he would wait until he could see Abt, an ACLU attorney, or at least someone who believed in his innocence. He said that Nichols "might come back next week." Ibid., p. 329.

840. Pat Stith, "Oswald May Have Tried to Call Raleigh Man from Dallas Jail,"

Raleigh News and Observer (July 17, 1980), p. 11. Grover B. Proctor, Jr., "The Phone Call That Never Was," *Raleigh Spectator* (July 17, 1980), p. 6.

841. Alveeta A. Treon cited by Proctor, "Phone Call That Never Was," p. 6.

842. Proctor, "The Phone Call That Never Was," p. 6. Sherman H. Skolnick vs. National Archives and Records Service, U.S. District Court for the Northern District of Illinois Eastern Division, No. 701 790, April 6, 1970. I am grateful to Sherman Skolnick for sharing with me the complaint he filed and his documents.

Dallas City Hall switchboard operator Alveeta Treon moved to Springfield, Missouri, where she told her story about Oswald's attempted Raleigh call to Arnold Mickey Owen, the sheriff of Greene County, Missouri, in 1966. In a 1980 interview, Sheriff Owen said: "She gave me the impression she was scared to death. Absolutely afraid, period. In my opinion, she thought she was telling the truth." Stith, "Oswald May Have Tried," p. 11.

"The sheriff said Mrs. Treon told him that she and her daughter and another telephone operator were in the Dallas City Hall switchboard room on the evening of Nov. 23 when two lawmen came in [and said they wanted to listen to Oswald's call]." Ibid.

Raleigh News and Observer reporter Pat Stith wrote: "Mrs. Treon's daughter, who was working in November 1963 as a stenographer in the Dallas Police Department, corroborated her mother's story. The daughter asked not to be identified."

843. Proctor, "Phone Call That Never Was," p. 6.

844. Grover B. Proctor, Jr., "Oswald's Raleigh Call," *Raleigh Spectator* (July 24, 1980), p. 5.

845. Proctor, "Phone Call That Never Was," p. 6. After John David Hurt died in 1981, his widow told author Henry Hurt the following year that her husband "had admitted the truth before he died. Terribly upset on the day of the assassination, he got extremely drunk—a habitual problem with him—and telephoned the Dallas jail and asked to speak to Oswald. When denied access, he left his name and number." Henry Hurt interview with Mrs. John Hurt, March 1982. Cited in Hurt, *Reasonable Doubt*, pp. 244–45.

Besides conflicting with the description of the incident given by Alveeta Treon and her daughter, Mrs. Hurt's explanation leaves unresolved why there would have been phone numbers for both of the Raleigh John Hurts on the message slip, as if Oswald was trying to reach one of them but was uncertain of the correct number. If John David Hurt had initiated the call in the manner Mrs. Hurt claimed, why would he have left the phone numbers of both himself and John William Hurt? On the face of it, her story is implausible. Was Mrs. Hurt coerced into telling that story by government forces in a way similar to the pressures described by Joyce Pitzer, Lt. Cdr. William Bruce Pitzer's widow, after his death?

846. Summers, *Conspiracy*, p. 143.

847. Victor Marchetti and John D. Marks, *The CIA and the Cult of Intelligence* (New York: Dell, 1975).

848. Proctor, "Oswald's Raleigh Call," p. 9.

849. Interview with Victor Marchetti, "Marchetti: Call to Contact," *Raleigh Spectator* (July 24, 1980), p. 8.

850. Ibid.

851. HSCA Deposition of Ann Elizabeth Goldsborough Egerter, pp. 8–10. Cited by Lisa Pease, "James Angleton," in *The Assassinations*, edited by James DiEugenio and Lisa Pease (Los Angeles: Feral House, 2003), pp. 146–47. See also chapter 4 above.

852. James B. Wilcott's testimony before the House Select Committee on Assassinations, March 22, 1978, pp. 11, 47. Bob Loomis, "Ex-CIA Couple Tell of Disillusion," *Oakland Tribune* (September 18, 1978), p. B14. Warren Hinckle, "Couple Talks About Oswald and the CIA," *San Francisco Chronicle* (September 12, 1978).

853. Jim Wilcott, "The Assassination of John F. Kennedy: A C.I.A. Insider's View," *Stray Magazine* (February 1989), p. 38.

854. Billy Grammer interview on Central Independent British TV program; cited by Robert J. Groden and Harrison Edward Livingstone, *High Treason* (New York: Berkley Books, 1990), p. 461.

855. Ibid.

856. Report from Deputy Sheriff McCoy to Sheriff Decker, November 24, 1963. Decker Exhibit 5323, *WCH*, vol. 19, pp. 537–38.

857. *WCH*, vol. 24, p. 429.

858. Orders for Oswald's fatal transfer may have come down a chain of command through Dallas Mayor Earle Cabell to Police Chief Jesse Curry. The process puzzled members of the Sheriff's Department, who said it was odd that Oswald's transfer was even done by the Dallas Police Department.

Deputy Sheriff Bill Courson told researcher Larry Sneed, "Very seldom did the Dallas Police Department transfer any prisoner to the county jail." Larry Sneed, *No More Silence: An Oral History of the Assassination of President Kennedy* (Dallas: Three Forks Press, 1998), p. 488. Courson said, "I think it's a fact that [Police Chief] Jess Curry yielded to political pressure from Mayor Earle Cabell for the city to transfer Oswald. Normally that was a sheriff's department function." Ibid.

A second deputy sheriff, Jack Faulkner, agreed that for the police to carry out Oswald's transfer was unusual: "It was our normal procedure that we [the Sheriff's Department] transferred everyone after they filed on from the city hall." Ibid., p. 218.

When Police Chief Curry testified to the Warren Commission about a conversation between himself and Sheriff Decker concerning Oswald's transfer, he said the opposite of what the sheriffs knew was the normal practice: "I said [to Sheriff Decker], 'If you want us to bring him, we will bring him to you.' This is not an unusual procedure at all." *WCH*, vol. 15, p. 126.

Deputy Sheriff Faulkner commented: "I understand that the Warren Commission asked Jess Curry if it was the usual procedure for them to transfer prisoners to the county and he told them, yes, which was a lie!" Sneed, *No More Silence*, p. 218.

Why would Police Chief Curry lie about so simple a matter as the usual procedure for a prisoner's transfer? If Deputy Sheriff Courson was right that the order for the fatal transfer came from Mayor Earle Cabell—for what was, in effect, a police set-up for Ruby's murder of Oswald—then Chief Curry may have been covering for Mayor Cabell, who had an invisible link to the CIA. Earle Cabell, the mayor of Dallas when Kennedy and Oswald were killed, was the brother of Charles Cabell, Deputy Director of the CIA under Allen Dulles, whom JFK had fired along with Dulles after the Bay of Pigs. District Attorney Jim Garrison's discovery of the Cabell brothers' CIA connection was a milestone in his New Orleans investigation of the assassination. *On the Trail of the Assassins*, pp. 118–21.

I am grateful to John Armstrong in *Harvey & Lee*, p. 944, for leading me to Larry Sneed's interviews with the deputy sheriffs, and to Larry Sneed for sharing the texts of his interviews with me.

859. Martin, *Seeds*, p. 451.

860. Ecclesiastes 3:2. Sorensen, *Kennedy*, p. 751.

861. Martin, *Seeds*, p. 451.

862. William Manchester interviewed Ethel Kennedy on April 17, 1964, then drew on her description of JFK's preoccupation during his last night at the White House in *Death of a President*, p. 21.

863. William Manchester's interview with Supreme Court Chief Justice Earl Warren, May 18, 1964. *Death of a President*, p. 21.

864. Ethel Kennedy, ibid.

865. "*WELCOME MR. KENNEDY*," Commission Exhibit No. 1031, *Warren Report*, p. 294.

866. The "Chairman" of "The American Fact-Finding Committee," as identified in the ad, was Bernard Weissman. In fact, as Bernard Weissman told the Warren Commission, there was no such organization. The ad was conceived by Larrie H. Schmidt, William B. Burley III, and Weissman, three self-identified conservatives who had come together in the U.S. Army in Germany in 1962, and by Joseph P. Grinnan, an independent Dallas oil operator and local John Birch Society coordinator. The group decided to put Weissman's

name on the ad "in part to counter charges of anti-Semitism which had been leveled against conservative groups in Dallas" (*Warren Report*, p. 297), thereby in fact making Weissman, in the aftermath of the assassination, a focus of the Warren Commission's investigation into the genesis of the ad. *Warren Report*, pp. 293–97.

867. O'Donnell and Powers, *"Johnny, We Hardly Knew Ye,"* p. 25.

868. Manchester, *Death of a President*, pp. 137–38.

869. Matthew Smith, *Vendetta: The Kennedys* (Edinburgh: Mainstream, 1993), p. 119.

870. Faxed letter from Wayne January to Matthew Smith, December 27, 1992. I am grateful to Matthew Smith for sharing with me his faxed correspondence from Wayne January.

871. Ibid.

872. Ibid.

873. Working with Matthew Smith in 1993, Wayne January used his aircraft expertise to trace the DC-3 he and the pilot had worked on, whose FAA registration number he remembered. He had personally flown the plane over four thousand hours and readily recalled its number. January was dumbfounded when the Aircraft Owners and Pilots Association (AOPA) reported back to him that there was no such plane. He insisted that AOPA archivists double-check their files. They finally discovered that after the DC-3 had been bought at Red Bird Air Field, "the number had been changed and the original number given to a small aircraft." Faxed letter from Wayne January to Matthew Smith, February 3, 1993. Also Matthew Smith, *Say Goodbye to America: The Sensational and Untold Story behind the Assassination of John F. Kennedy* (Edinburgh: Mainstream Publishing, 2001), p. 167.

When Smith queried retired Air Force colonel Fletcher Prouty, former liaison between the Air Force and the CIA, on this development, Prouty said that aircraft numbers were never changed, except by the CIA. The CIA had apparently bought the plane.

January's partner had sold the plane to the Houston Air Center, which did not register the plane until 1965 when it was about to resell it. A Houston investigator, who had once worked for the CIA, identified the Houston Air Center as a CIA front, confirming Fletcher Prouty's analysis that the DC-3 had become a CIA aircraft upon its purchase at Red Bird Air Field. When the DC-3 flew out of Dallas the afternoon of November 22, 1963, with an undisclosed number of passengers, it was a CIA plane being flown by a CIA pilot. Ibid.

874. Research on the plane sold by Wayne January to the Houston Air Center was done by Larry Hancock and reported in his book *Someone Would Have Talked* (Southlake, Tex.: JFK Lancer, 2006), p. 256.

875. January to Smith, December 27, 1992.

876. Smith, *Vendetta*, p. 120.

877. Smith, *Say Goodbye*, p. 165.

878. Smith, *Vendetta*, p. 121.

879. Ibid.

880. Wayne January apparently made two exceptions to his otherwise total silence on the CIA pilot before he faxed the information to Matthew Smith in December 1992. He told Smith that on the day after JFK's assassination he briefly mentioned the incident to his business partner. January to Smith, December 27, 1992. He also revealed it to his wife, Sylvia January, as confirmed by her to both Smith and myself. See below.

881. January to Smith, February 3, 1993.

882. Smith, *Say Goodbye*, p. 166.

883. *Vendetta*, pp. 117–25; *Say Goodbye*, pp. 162–69.

884. Wayne January died from heart failure on November 29, 2002. In a phone conversation, his widow, Sylvia January, confirmed to me that her husband was in fact the same person whose story was told under the pseudonym "Hank Gordon" by Matthew Smith. Author's phone conversation with Sylvia January, October 1, 2006.

885. Matthew Smith presentation at JFK Lancer's 2003 "November in Dallas" confer-

ence. Matthew Smith, *Conspiracy—The Plot to Stop the Kennedys* (New York: Citadel Press, 2005), pp. 137–45.

886. Matthew Smith has suggested another reason beyond the working rapport between Wayne January and the CIA pilot for the latter's revelations. As noted in January's December 27, 1992, faxed letter to Smith, January and several friends ran a corporation from 1961 to 1963 comprised of a small fleet of planes filled with electronic equipment. The planes did top-secret radar mapping for the Defense Department. When the corporation was dismantled, the last plane sold was the DC-3 bought by "Houston Air Center." Because of January's top-secret clearance from his Defense Department work, he was on a list of approved CIA working contacts. For that reason, Smith thought, the CIA pilot may have felt a little freer to bond with January. Author's interview of Matthew Smith, January 3, 2007.

887. Guthman and Shulman, *Robert Kennedy in His Own Words*, p. 17.

888. Ibid., pp. 402–3.

889. Wicker, *JFK and LBJ*, p. 183. On his way back to Washington from his diplomatic post in Saigon, Lodge had stopped in Honolulu for a conference on the Vietnam War at CINCPAC (Commander in Chief Pacific) Headquarters, Camp Smith. National Security Adviser McGeorge Bundy, Secretary of State Dean Rusk, and Secretary of Defense Robert McNamara also attended the meeting.

890. Manchester, *Death of a President*, p. 33.

891. George W. Ball, *The Past Has Another Pattern: Memoirs* (New York: W. W. Norton, 1982), p. 366.

892. Ibid.

893. Wicker, *JFK and LBJ*, p. 185.

894. Ibid.

895. Ibid., p. 205.

896. Stanley Karnow, *Vietnam: A History* (New York: Viking Press, 1983), p. 326.

897. Gerard Colby with Charlotte Dennett, *Thy Will Be Done: The Conquest of the Amazon: Nelson Rockefeller and Evangelism in the Age of Oil* (New York: HarperCollins, 1995), pp. 364, 369.

898. Schlesinger, *Thousand Days*, p. 573.

899. Ibid.

900. *FRUS, 1961–1963*, vol. XXIII, p. 694. U.S. ambassador Howard Jones, citing President Sukarno, in telegram to the Department of State, November 4, 1963.

901. See, for example, the analysis of Kennedy's third world policies, as viewed in conflict with those of New York governor Nelson Rockefeller and his allies, in Colby and Dennett, *Thy Will Be Done*, pp. 391–92, 396–417, 665–66. Six days before JFK's assassination, Rockefeller gave a speech featured in the *New York Times* in which he expressed "deep concern" that President Kennedy "was undermining the nation's security and world peace." Donald Janson, "Rockefeller Says Kennedy's Policy Imperils Peace," *New York Times* (November 17, 1963), p. 1. Rockefeller's first example of Kennedy's undermining security was the president's support of Sukarno in Indonesia's conflict with its former colonial master, the Netherlands: "In New Guinea we sacrificed an old and valued ally, the Netherlands, to Indonesian aggression." "Excerpts from Rockefeller's Statement Attacking President on Foreign Policy," *Thy Will Be Done*, p. 43.

Rockefeller attacked Kennedy's support of neutralist policies in third world countries as a virtual surrender to Communism: "In Laos the Administration sacrificed a pro-Western government to one of those illusory coalitions which almost invariably have been a prelude to Communist takeover . . .

"Blinded by the illusion that a change of tone indicates a change of policy, the Administration has vacillated in the face of alternating Soviet aggressiveness and Soviet peace offensives. The result is that the West is bewildered and in many allied countries leftist tendencies with neutralist overtones are gaining ground." Ibid.

902. Hilsman, *To Move a Nation*, p. 407.

903. Ibid.

904. Ibid., p. 409.

905. Peter Dale Scott, "The United States and the Overthrow of Sukarno, 1965–1967," p. 7 of 19 at namebase.org/scott.html. Scott's article was originally published in *Pacific Affairs* 58 (Summer 1985), pp. 239–64.

906. Hilsman, *To Move a Nation*, p. 409.

907. Scott, "United States and the Overthrow," p. 7. In July 1965, the United States delivered two hundred Aero-Commander aircraft to its Indonesian Army allies. It also funded the completion of an army communications system. The additional light aircraft and improved communications aided Suharto on October 1, 1965, in implementing his swift purge of Sukarno loyalists and leftists.

908. Ibid., p. 9.

909. Ralph W. McGehee, *Deadly Deceits: My 25 Years in the CIA* (New York: Sheridan Square Publications, 1983), p. 57. One sentence cited from article by Ralph W. McGehee, "Foreign Policy By Forgery: The C.I.A. and the White Paper on El Salvador," *The Nation* (April 11, 1981), pp. 423–34 (with deletions by the CIA). McGehee also noted in his *Nation* article, as then cited in his book on pp. 57–58:

"Initially, the Indonesian Army left the P.K.I. [Communist Party of Indonesia] alone, since it had not been involved in the coup attempt. [Eight sentences deleted here by the CIA.] Subsequently, however, Indonesian military leaders [seven words deleted by the CIA] began a bloody extermination campaign. In mid-November 1965, General Suharto formally authorized the 'cleaning out' of the Indonesian Communist Party and established special teams to supervise the mass killings. Media fabrications played a key role in stirring up popular resentment against the P.K.I. Photographs of the bodies of the dead generals [who had been killed in the failed coup]—badly decomposed—were featured in all the newspapers and on television. Stories accompanying the pictures falsely claimed that the generals had been castrated and their eyes gouged out by Communist women. This cynically manufactured campaign was designed to foment public anger against the Communists and set the stage for a massacre . . . To conceal its role in the massacre of those innocent people the C.I.A., in 1968, concocted a false account of what happened (later published by the Agency as a book, *Indonesia—1965: The Coup that Backfired*) . . . At the same time that the Agency wrote the book, it also composed a secret study of what really happened. [One sentence deleted by the CIA.] The Agency was extremely proud of its successful [one word deleted by the CIA] and recommended it as a model for future operations [one-half sentence deleted by the CIA]."

910. Kahin and Kahin, *Subversion as Foreign Policy*, p. 230. Drawing on interviews and an article by Frederick Bunnell, "American 'Low Posture' Policy Toward Indonesia in the Months Leading to the 1965 'Coup, *Indonesia* 50 (October 1990), p. 60; n. 152, p. 59.

911. Kathy Kadane, "Ex-agents say CIA compiled death lists for Indonesians"; at namebase.org/kadane.html. Published in the *San Francisco Examiner* (May 20, 1990), pp. A1, A22. "Letter to the Editor from Kathy Kadane," *New York Review of Books* (April 10, 1997) at namebase.org/kadane.html. Michael Wines, "C.I.A. Tie Asserted in Indonesia Purge," *New York Times* (July 12, 1990), p. A13.

912. William Blum, *Killing Hope: U.S. Military and CIA Interventions since World War II* (Monroe, Me.: Common Courage Press, 1995), p. 194. The CIA's support of the massacre in Indonesia also included supplying communications systems from Collins Radio, its major contractor (whose employee Carl Mather, as we have seen, was linked through his automobile's license to a sighting of the second Oswald the afternoon of the assassination): "The supply of radios is perhaps the most telling detail [of U.S. logistical support to the bloodbath]. They served not only as field communications but also became an element of a broad, US intelligence-gathering operation constructed as the manhunt went forward. According to a former embassy official, the Central Intelligence Agency hastily provided the radios—state-of-the art Collins KWM-2s, high-frequency

single-sideband transceivers, the highest-powered mobile unit available at that time to the civilian and commercial market." Kadane, "Letter to the Editor."

913. Robert Martens cited by Kadane, "Ex-agents say CIA," pp. 1–2.

914. Kahin and Kahin, *Subversion as Foreign Policy,* p. 230; Howard Palfrey Jones, *Indonesia: The Possible Dream* (New York: Harcourt Brace Jovanovich, 1971), p. 401.

915. Urged by holdover Kennedy staff members, President Johnson had reluctantly asked Attorney General Robert Kennedy to be a presidential emissary to Sukarno to resolve another Southeast Asian political and military crisis—this one between Indonesia and Malaysia. Although Sukarno and Kennedy reached agreement on a ceasefire proposal, Johnson had no interest in doing any follow-up peacemaking with Indonesia, and the Indonesian–Malaysian agreement forged by RFK collapsed. Schlesinger, *Robert Kennedy and His Times,* pp. 634–35.

916. Cindy Adams, *My Friend the Dictator* (New York: Bobbs-Merrill, 1967), p. 78.

917. "Message from Chairman Khrushchev to President Kennedy," December 11, 1962. *FRUS, 1961–1963,* vol. VI, p. 228.

918. Ibid.

919. Ambassador David-Ormsby-Gore recounted his last conversation with President Kennedy to British journalist Henry Brandon. Cited in Henry Brandon, *Special Relationships: A Foreign Correspondent's Memoirs from Roosevelt to Reagan* (New York: Atheneum, 1988), p. 200.

920. Fursenko and Naftali, *"One Hell of a Gamble,"* p. 344.

921. Beschloss, *Crisis Years,* p. 706.

922. Salinger, *With Kennedy,* p. 335.

923. Ibid.

924. Sorensen, *Kennedy,* p. 135; Schlesinger, *Robert Kennedy and His Times,* p. 212.

925. William Walton oral history, March 30, 1993, p. 127 of transcript. JFK Library. Herbert S. Parmet, *JFK: The Presidency of John F. Kennedy* (New York: Dial Press, 1983), p. 35.

926. Parmet, *JFK: The Presidency,* p. 58.

927. Walton oral history, March 30, 1993, p. 34 of transcript. JFK Library. O'Donnell and Powers, *"Johnny, We Hardly Knew Ye,"* p. 244.

928. Fursenko and Naftali, *"One Hell of a Gamble,"* p. 344.

929. Ibid., pp. 344–46.

930. Ibid., pp. 109–29.

931. Ibid., pp. 344–45.

932. Ibid., p. 345. The anti-Johnson statements made by Walton to Bolshakov seem to have represented Robert Kennedy's and William Walton's views more than they did Jacqueline Kennedy's. Her more optimistic view of what Johnson's attitude toward Khrushchev would be was expressed in her December 1, 1963, letter to Khrushchev. See below.

933. Ibid.

934. Ibid.

935. Manchester, *Death of a President,* p. 706.

936. Ibid. When the interpreter had translated Jacqueline Kennedy's words to Anastas Mikoyan, the Soviet diplomat "blinked and covered his face with both hands." Six days later, on December 1, 1963, in a handwritten letter to Nikita Khrushchev, she repeated in an expanded form the message she had asked Mikoyan to give him:

"Dear Mr. Chairman President:

I would like to thank you for sending Mr. Mikoyan as your representative to my husband's funeral. He looked so upset when he came through the line—he was trembling—and I was very moved.

I tried to give him a message for you that day—but as it was such a terrible day for me, I do not know if my words came out as I meant them to.

So now, in one of the last nights I will spend in the White House, in one of the last letters I will write on this paper at the White House, I would like to write you my message. I send it only because I know how much my husband cared about peace, and how central the relation between you and him was in this concern. He used to quote your words in some of his speeches—'In the next war the survivors will envy the dead.'

You and he were adversaries, but you also were allied in a determination that the world should not be blown up. You respected each other and could deal with each other. I know that President Johnson will make every effort to establish the same relationship with you.

The danger which always troubled my husband was that war might be started not so much by the big men as by the little ones. So while big men know the needs for self-control and restraint, little men are sometimes moved more by fear and pride. I know that on our side President Johnson will continue the policy in which my husband so deeply believed, a policy of control and restraint, but he will need your help.

I send this letter entirely out of my personal sense of the importance of the understanding which existed between you and my husband, and also because of your kindness and that of Mrs. Khrushcheva in Vienna. I read that she had tears in her eyes when she left the American Embassy in Moscow, after signing the book of mourning. Please thank her for that.

Sincerely, Jacqueline Kennedy." Document #191, McGeorge Bundy Files, LBJ Library.

According to a State Department historian, Jacqueline Kennedy's original letter has never been located (FRUS, 1961–1963, vol. VI, p. 313). I have cited here the earliest typed version of her letter, preserved in McGeorge Bundy's files at the LBJ Library in Austin. The document shows Bundy's handwritten revisions of Mrs. Kennedy's original letter, prior to its transmission by the State Department to Khrushchev. Bundy's changes to the text are revealing. He crossed out the widow's poignant description of Anastas Mikoyan approaching her in the reception: "he was trembling." JFK's National Security Adviser also replaced Mrs. Kennedy's emphasis on mutual trust, conveyed by the phrase, "the understanding which existed between you and my husband," diluting it to read instead, "the relationship which existed between you and my husband."

937. Beschloss, *The Crisis Years*, p. 682.

After I finished writing this book, my friend Terry Taylor alerted me to one more account of what Jacqueline Kennedy said to Anastas Mikoyan. Viktor Sukhodrev, Mikoyan's interpreter, has described the encounter:

"She was standing there in that black dress, I think still with the veil. And as Mr. Mikoyan came abreast of her, she took his hand, outstretched hand, into both of her hands. And this I remember as if it were yesterday. I still have a tingling feeling even today, because I can see it as it happened.

"And she said, 'Mr. Mikoyan, thank you for coming. And would you tell Mr. Khrushchev for me that my husband and Mr. Khrushchev could have brought peace to this world by working together. Now Mr. Khrushchev will have to do it alone (from *JFK: A Presidency Revealed*, a History Channel DVD).

Afterword

1. Peter Grose, *Gentleman Spy: The Life of Allen Dulles* (New York: Houghton Mifflin, 1994), p. 293.

2. Cited by Grose, ibid.

3. Ibid.

4. Cited by Raymond Marcus, "Truman's Warning," in E. Martin Schotz, *History Will Not Absolve Us: Orwellian Control, Public Denial, and the Murder of President Kennedy* (Brookline, Mass.: Kurtz, Ulmer & DeLucia, 1996), pp. 237–38.

5. Thomas Merton, *Raids on the Unspeakable* (New York: New Directions, 1966), p. 4.

6. As we saw from Kennedy's secretly taped meeting with the Joint Chiefs of Staff

on October 19, 1962, the chiefs were pushing him to launch a pre-emptive strike on the Soviet missile sites in Cuba. They also tried to create a pretext for a nuclear strike on the Soviet Union by their independent, insubordinate orders. With both sides on hair-trigger alert, the U.S. Air Force sent its bombers beyond their customary turnaround points toward the Soviet Union and test-fired an intercontinental ballistic missile, trying to provoke the Soviets to react in a way that would counter-provoke superior U.S. forces to blanket the USSR with an all-out nuclear attack. Richard Rhodes, "The General and World War III," *New Yorker* (June 19, 1995), pp. 58–59. Scott D. Sagan, *The Limits of Safety* (Princeton, N.J.: Princeton University Press, 1993), p. 79.

7. Sergei N. Khrushchev, *Nikita Khrushchev and the Creation of a Superpower* (University Park, Pa.: Pennsylvania State University, 2000), p. 630.

8. Author's interview of Sergei N. Khrushchev, November 15, 2009.

9. *Nikita Khrushchev and the Creation of a Superpower*, p. 696.

10. National Security Action Memorandum Number 271: "Cooperation with the USSR on Outer Space Matters." Available at http://www.jfklibrary.org/Asset+Tree/Asset+Viewers/Image+Asset+Viewer.htm?guid={BFF5BEE . . .

11. Frank Sietzen, "Soviets Planned to Accept JFK's Joint Lunar Mission Offer," *SPACEWAR* (October 2, 1997), p. 3. Available at *http://www.spacewar.com/news/russia-97h.html* In my November 15, 2009, interview with him, Sergei Khrushchev said he thought that if Kennedy had lived, and if he and Nikita Khrushchev had stayed in power for another five-plus years, the two leaders would have ended the Cold War by 1969.

INDEX

Luce, Henry
  and coup against Diem, 164
  on JFK and big business, 140
  and Mary Bancroft, 427n209
Lumumba, Patrice (prime minister of
    Congo)
  CIA assassination plot against, xxi,
    211–13, 258–59, 436–37n213
Lundberg, George (doctor), 471n563
Lynd, Staughton (historian): on JFK
    wound, 307

MacArthur, Douglas (General)
  as military mind, 8
  warning against Asian land war, 102,
    182
Macdonald, Torbert (JFK friend)
  and coup against Diem, 167–68
  secret trip to Vietnam by, 211
Macedo, Joseph (Marine), 403n152
MacMillan, Harold (British prime
    minister)
  as peacemaking ally of JFK, 479n710
  and test ban treaty, 44
Mafia
  as CIA assassins, 318, 359
  and CIA attempts to kill Castro, 34
  and JFK assassination, x
Mahoney, Richard D. (author): on JFK
    and Africa, 8, 150–51, 212
Malcolm X: assassination of, xv, xvi, xvii
Manchester, William (author)
  on JFK's last event at White House, 368
  on security of motorcade, 271
Mankiewicz, Joseph: and film rights to
    Quiet American, 426n191
Mansfield, Mike (senator)
  cautioning JFK about Vietnam, xxiv–xxv,
    123–28
  and withdrawal from Vietnam, 150,
    180–81
Mantik, David (doctor): and Harper
    fragment, 284, 461n364
Manual, Mac (witness): and Rose
    Cheramie, 247–48, 446n138
Marchetti, Victor (CIA): on Oswald, 40,
    365–66
Marcus, Raymond (researcher): on
    Truman's CIA warning, 477nn674,
    675
Marrs, Jim (author)
  and Ed Hoffman's story, 266
  on Oswald in Texas Theater, 291,
    454n268
Marshall, George (Secretary of State):
    warning against national security
    state, 33

Martens, Robert (U.S. embassy official):
    on overthrow of Sukarno, 377
Martin, Ralph G. (JFK biographer): on
    JFK and death, 224
Martin, William R. (Garrison staff): and
    R. C. Nagell, 156, 423n121
Martineau, Maurice (Secret Service)
  and Abraham Bolden, 215
  and Chicago plot, 200–201, 203,
    214–15, 218
Marvin, Daniel (Special Forces)
  on danger of Special Forces, 474n614
  on training as assassin, 317–20
Mather, Barbara (friend of Tippit), 295
Mather, Carl Amos (CIA connection),
    295, 468n480
Matlack, Dorothe (CIA), 404–405n190
May, Ernest R. (author): and Cuban
    Missile Crisis tapes, 399–400n83
McCloy, John J. (JFK disarmament rep.),
    321, 399n60
McCone, John (CIA)
  and commodity aid cutoff, 432n91
  and coup against Diem, 425–26n183
  on JFK assassination, 80
  on Oswald, 231
McDonald, M. N. (Dallas P.D.): and
    arrest of Oswald at theater, 291
McGehee, Ralph W. (CIA): on Indonesia,
    376
McKnight, Gerald D. (author): on
    Oswald's "Crypto" clearance,
    404n160
McLendon, Gordon (CIA connection):
    and Ruby, 358
McMahon, Homer (photo lab): and
    Zapruder film, 461–62n370
McNamara, Robert (Defense Secretary)
  and Camp Smith conferences, xxiv,
    xxv, 121–23
  and Cuban Missile Crisis, 30
  and idea of first strike, 238–42
  and military buildup, 325–26
  and Operation Northwoods, 96–98
  and steel crisis, 138
  and Vietnam
    and coup against Diem, 426n191
    on Galbraith's proposal and JFK's
      plan to withdraw, 119–22,
      186–89
    recommending sending troops, 107
    Saigon conference in 1962, xxiii
    visit with Taylor, 106–7, 184–87,
      430n50, 431n78
Meagher, Sylvia (Warren Comm. critic)
  on Secret Service impostors, 452n235
  on Warren Comm., 38–39, 360

JFK and the UNSPEAKABLE

Why He Died and Why It Matters

JAMES W. DOUGLASS

Since John F. Kennedy's assassination in 1963, myriad authors have written works attempting to uncover the reasons behind the loss that changed the American landscape.

With meticulous research, compelling arguments, and an expert sense of narrative, James W. Douglass boldly supplies fully formed answers to the "why" of JFK's death. *JFK and the Unspeakable* offers a fresh perspective on one of America's greatest leaders, as well as insight into the political events that have shaped the America we currently inhabit. By the book's conclusion, we not only believe Douglass's depiction of the unspeakable forces that led to Kennedy's assassination; we yearn for the chance to advocate the vision of peace for which he gave his life.

1. In the book's introduction, Douglass asserts that because John F. Kennedy was turning toward peace he was in deadly conflict with what Thomas Merton called "the Unspeakable," a void of responsibility underlying systemic evil ranging from the Vietnam War to nuclear weapons proliferations and assassinations. Yet "the Unspeakable is not far away" (p. xvii). How does the government's doctrine of "plausible deniability" (pp. xvi, 33, 381) rely on a personal denial of responsibility for the Unspeakable? Douglass confesses that he "contributed to a national climate of denial" (p. xvi). How? Have we also done so?

2. *JFK and the Unspeakable* is rife with facts that are absent or glossed over in the mass media. Discovering and recognizing the significance of those facts, the author says, drawing on Gandhi, is "an experiment in truth . . . the most powerful force on earth" (pp. xviii–xix). Why is a Gandhian vision of truth seen as critical?

3. What elements in Kennedy's life formed him to become a president who could choose peace over against the dictates of the CIA, the Joint Chiefs of Staff, and the military-industrial complex? What were the signs and counter-signs of his breakthrough to a depth of humanity for which, as Merton prophesied, he would then be "marked out for assassination"?

4. At the climactic point in the Cuban Missile Crisis when Kennedy and Khrushchev join hands, Douglass writes: "Half a world apart, in radical ideological conflict, both Kennedy in his call for help and Khrushchev in his response had recognized their interdependence with each other and the world" (p. 175). What made it possible for Kennedy and Khrushchev to turn toward peace rather than nuclear war? How would you characterize their resolution of the crisis?

5. In his American University address, President Kennedy said, "What kind of peace do I mean? What kind of peace do we seek? Not a Pax Americana enforced on the world by American weapons of war" (p. 35–36). If JFK's rejection of a militarily imposed Pax Americana cost him his life, is it only up to his successors in the White House to resist the military-industrial complex? If peace is up to us, what steps can we take to choose peace in as courageous a way as he did?

6. Jean Daniel's back-to-back interviews with Kennedy and Castro allowed them to explore a possible bridge of understanding to normalize U.S.-Cuban relations. What previous steps by JFK and Khrushchev

opened Castro to that beginning dialogue? Why was this back channel dialogue for peace so threatening to others and so dangerous for Kennedy?

7. JFK's resistance to sending combat troops to Vietnam proved a huge factor in his eventual demise. When talking about Kennedy's decision, General Maxwell Taylor declared: "I don't recall anyone who was strongly against [sending ground troops], except one man and that was the President. The President just didn't want to be convinced that this was the right thing to do. . . . It was really the President's personal conviction that U.S. ground troops shouldn't go in" (p. 107). What do you make of Kennedy's solitary stand? Why didn't he just order an immediate withdrawal from Vietnam rather than prolong the struggle with his advisers over ground troops?

8. On page 202, Douglass observes: "If President Kennedy had been assassinated in Chicago on November 2 rather than Dallas on November 22, Lee Harvey Oswald would probably be unknown to us today. Instead Thomas Arthur Vallee would have likely become notorious as the president's presumed assassin." What were the similarities between Vallee and Oswald? What saved Vallee from becoming the ultimate scapegoat in the plot?

9. Why are the experiences of such witnesses as Abraham Bolden, Rose Cheramie, Julia Ann Mercer, Ed Hoffman, Roger Craig, Robert Vinson, Charles Crenshaw, Bill Pitzer, Daniel Marvin, Ralph Leon Yates, and Wayne January presented so fully? Are there any parallels between their stories and JFK's?

10. It would be easy for the reader to conclude that only the CIA's moves on its giant chessboard led to JFK's death, with Lee Harvey Oswald as the scapegoat. However, Douglass notes: "Understanding that the CIA coordinated the assassination does not mean that we can limit the responsibility to the CIA. To tell the truth at the heart of darkness in this story, one must see and accept a responsibility that goes deeper and far beyond the Central Intelligence Agency" (p. 307). How much deeper and how far beyond? What is "the truth at the heart of darkness in this story"?

11. Of what significance was Khrushchev's decision in November 1963 to accept Kennedy's proposal for a joint U.S.-Soviet lunar mission?

12. Is it possible, as the Afterword suggests, to find hope in the assassination of a peacemaking president?

1. In the dedication, acknowledgments, and an endnote (p. 449 n269), Douglass expresses his gratitude for the work and inspiration of pioneer JFK assassination researcher, Vincent Salandria. Have your book club read and discuss Salandria's essay, "The JFK Assassination: A False Mystery Concealing State Crimes" (http://home.comcast .net/~johnkelin/vs.html) together with the essay by E. Martin Schotz (to whom Douglass also dedicates his book), "The Waters of Knowledge versus the Waters of Uncertainty: Mass Denial in the Assassination of President Kennedy" (http://home.comcast.net/~johnkelin/schotz.html). Discuss as a group how Salandria's and Schotz's perspectives jar your own—where you agree with them, where you disagree, and if you see collective denial at work in this case on such a scale.

2. Two powerful films that cover the JFK assassination and the Cuban Missile Crisis are Oliver Stone's *JFK* (1991) and *Thirteen Days* (2000). Watch one (or both) of them as a group. Compare the movies with *JFK and the Unspeakable*.

3. Douglass writes: "John Kennedy's American University address was to his death in Dallas as Martin Luther King's Riverside Church address was to his death in Memphis" (p. 46). Read these two prophetic speeches, along with Douglass's article, "The Martin Luther King Conspiracy Exposed in Memphis" (http://home.comcast.net/~johnkelin/jwd.html). Discuss the implications of state murders that target not just visionaries, but the fulfillment of their visions as well.

4. At a crucial point in *JFK and the Unspeakable*'s storyline, five-year-old Caroline Kennedy recites JFK's favorite poem, *Rendezvous*, to him in the White House Rose Garden in front of the National Security Council. Have the members of your group, while picturing that setting and audience, read the poem in silence. Share your thoughts in a circle on what is going on here—in the father, the daughter, the members of the National Security Council, and in yourselves, as you reflect on this scene in the perspective of what is about to happen.

Questions for the Author

1. What was the most challenging aspect of writing this book? How did you meet and overcome that challenge?

    I was challenged, as I have been before, by the feeling that I couldn't write a book in the first place, much less one on this subject. But I knew that if I took the time and effort, I could at least write (by constant rewriting) a sentence, eventually a paragraph, and in the course of a few days and weeks, a series of paragraphs. I knew that if I kept on, I'd reach the end God wanted, whatever that turned out to be.

    So one prays every step of the way for patience and the Spirit. I understood it via Gandhi as an experiment in truth.

2. The book is so painstakingly researched. What difficulties did you face in finding your facts and sources?

    The main difficulty was my incompetence in so many areas that counted—computers, archival resources, access to witnesses . . . I couldn't find anything or anyone except through the help of generous, competent friends. They included friends in libraries, friends at the National Archives, friends at their computers searching the Web, friends praying—friends everywhere.

3. The structure of *JFK and the Unspeakable* is surprising, in that the events do not unfold chronologically, but rather in a fragmented manner, which increases the tension throughout. Why did you choose to arrange the story's narrative this way?

    The process was to see as far ahead as I could—never very far. Research and write through that image or question—for example, the image of Kennedy's turning, which became the first chapter. Then research and write through JFK's struggle with the CIA over Cuba, and Castro in particular. That led to the question (and story) of Vietnam. And so on. I wasn't arranging the story but following it.

4. What new or unexpected facts did you learn while writing *JFK and the Unspeakable*? Did anything surprise you in your research?

    I was surprised by John Kennedy. He was an extraordinary man. The twists and turns of the plotting around him were surprising, too, but the grace within his struggle was the big surprise. Most of all, I was surprised by the grace in the story as a whole. It saved us all.

5. Do you disagree with any of the choices Kennedy made during his presidency?

   I identify with the six Quakers who met with the president, pushing him toward general and complete disarmament. They thought he was wrong on the nuclear testing he began in the South Pacific, wrong in the nuclear weapons buildup he was engaged in, and wrong in not trying to share our surplus food with the Chinese. If you believe in nonviolence, many of Kennedy's foreign policy choices were wrong. But JFK had, in turn, a great question for demanding folks like us. He said, "You believe in redemption, don't you?"

6. It took you many years to write *JFK and the Unspeakable*. Was there ever a time when you were anxious about its completion? Did you feel any pressure to have the book finished by a certain time?

   Fortunately I had the most patient editor/publisher in the world, Robert Ellsberg. Given my limits, he has to be that. Years ago a friend gave me a T-shirt with the saying on it: "Patience is a revolutionary virtue." The T-shirt has long since disintegrated, but the mantra remains.

7. Do you think that JFK's story is inherently spiritual? Was it difficult to ignore your own religious leanings in the detailing of this story?

   I can hardly imagine a story more spiritual than the conversion of someone with that much power to peacemaking. In writing about it, I didn't ignore any of my own leanings. We can only write from where we are.

8. What do you hope readers take away from your book?

   Hope itself—from seeing what JFK, and all the supporting witnesses in the story, went through to live out the truth. Had he not turned from war, along with his enemy, Nikita Khrushchev, the world would now be a nuclear wasteland. Had these witnesses not been courageous enough to speak the truth, we would know far less of the liberating truth of the story. What I found remarkable was that the deeper the darkness, the greater the hope, because of his and their transforming witness to the truth.

   That leaves the question: Are we who hear their story prepared to carry on the peacemaking and truth-telling? Will we live out the truth as they did? It's a hopeful, inviting question.

9. Was it difficult to preserve a measure of neutrality during the writing of this book? Were there ever moments when you wanted to include your own personal opinions on the political and historical proceedings?

   Neutrality was not a goal, but telling the truth was—in as few words as possible, without getting in the way of a transforming story.

10. Is there anything else you uncovered about the JFK assassination conspiracy that you wish had been included in *JFK and the Unspeakable*, or were you able to fit all of your findings in the book?

I included only what I could back up with solid sources that the reader could check out. Hence all the endnotes. There is far more than this beneath the surface. Yet we know enough, and have known enough for a long time, to see the truth. I believe that what is written here about the assassination is only a tiny, visible piece of a systemic evil that continues to reach into the depths of our world. But grace also abounds. Peace is possible.